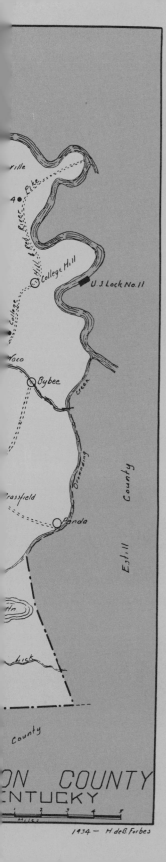

ville
4● Pike
College Hill
College Hill
U. S. Lock No. 11
Waco
Bybee
Crossfield
Canda
Estill   County
County
ON COUNTY
ENTUCKY

1934 — H.deB.Forbes

MADISON COUNTY: 200 Years in Retrospect

By
William E. Ellis
H.E. Everman
Richard D. Sears

Published by
The Madison County Historical Society

Library of Congress Cataloging-in-Publication Data

Ellis, William E. (William Elliott), 1940-
  Madison County: 200 years in retrospect.

  Bibliography: p.
  Includes index.
  1. Madison County (Ky.)—History. 2. Madison
County (Ky.)—Biography. I. Everman, H. E.,
1941-   . II. Sears, Richard D.,
1940-   .
III. Title.
F457.M17E44 1985   976.9'53   85-11618
ISBN 0-9615162-0-8

Dedication

To the people of Madison County: past, present, and future.

Table of Contents

Foreword

The celebration of the two hundredth anniversary of the establishment of Madison County is a significant milestone in our history. As we approach the bicentennial year of 1986, the Madison County Historical Society is pleased to have completed a very special publication—*Madison County: 200 Years in Retrospect.*

In 1934 our organization sponsored a publication entitled *A Glimpse at Historic Madison County and Richmond, Kentucky,* preparatory to the county sesquicentennial and the bicentennial of the birth of Daniel Boone.

For over two years Drs. William E. Ellis and H. E. Everman of Eastern Kentucky University and Dr. Richard D. Sears of Berea College have been researching and writing this first comprehensive and definitive history of Madison County. The authors have uncovered much new and rich primary source material and some unique historical photographs and illustrations that trace Madison County's fascinating past from the settlement of Fort Boonesborough in 1775 to the present.

This scholarly book is filled with significant events and vivid stories, such as the legendary exploits of Daniel Boone, Cassius M. Clay's antislavery crusades and conflicts with John G. Fee, the strong influence of the Burnam family, the establishment of Berea College and Eastern Kentucky University and their major impact on the development and culture of the county, the Civil War Battle of Richmond, and important economic advances in agriculture and industry are fully documented in this interpretive volume. Many other of the county's triumphs and tragedies are also chronicled in this remarkable publication.

Our deepest appreciation to the three authors, to Charles C. Hay, III, project Chairman, Donald R. Feltner and Donald Rist, all of Eastern Kentucky University, and the members of the county history committee, for making this book possible. We are also indebted to the Madison County Fiscal Court, the Richmond Tourism and Recreation Commission, and the many other patrons and underwriters for their financial support. Proceeds from the sale of this publication will be used by the Madison County Bicentennial Commission.

This book is intended to be thought-provoking to our readers, helping them to reflect on the past two hundred years of Madison County's rich and colorful history so that qualified collective leadership will plan ahead for the orderly growth of our county to insure the best quality of life for all of our citizens in the future.

James J. Shannon, Jr.
President, Madison County Historical Society

Acknowledgements

I wish to express my appreciation to several individuals who have given me encouragement, read portions of my manuscript, located materials for me, corrected factual errors, shared valuable information and primary sources, and prodded me through three years work on the manuscript. The final ante-bellum result was greatly aided by the late Mrs. Charles C. (Betty) Combs, Mrs. T. J. Curtis, Mrs. Sharon McConnell, Mrs. Tawanha Ray; by three of my colleagues, Dr. Ken Tunnell, Dr. Roy Barlow, and Mrs. Carol Roberts; by Dr. Gerald Roberts, Dr. Robert N. Grise, David Greene, Dr. Stanley Todd, Dr. James T. Coy, Mrs. Marie Beamon; and especially by Charles C. Hay and James J. Shannon, Jr. who have been most generous with their time, effort, and enthusiasm.

H. E. Everman

I would like to thank Gerald Roberts, director of the Berea College Archives, Charles Hay, director of the Eastern Kentucky University Archives, and Sharon Brown McConnell, director of the Townsend Room Collection in the Crabbe Library at Eastern for their cheerful and skilled assistance while I was doing research in Madison county history. Their staffs also deserve my appreciation. And the staff of the Berea College Computer Center rendered me invaluable assistance in this project.

Several people gave me advice, provided resources and encouragement, and—most importantly—saved me from publishing errors: David Greene, Robert Grise, James J. Shannon, Jr., and Warren Lambert. I should admit that the errors which remain in my portion of this history are solely my own.

Finally, my warmest thanks to my wife Grace and my sons Robert and Alden, who endured my periods of research and composition even when they resulted in books and papers all over the kitchen.

Richard Sears

The author of Part III expresses appreciation to those Madison Countians who shared their experiences with him. These oral history interviews are available in the Eastern Kentucky University Archives. In particular, the interviews with Woodard Adams, Nannie S. Lackey, Smith Park, and H.E. Richardson proved invaluable. To all those who read these four chapters in manuscript form, including James C. Klotter, Eugenia Scott, and my wife Charlotte, a special thank you is in order.

William E. Ellis

Publication project director, Charles Hay, would like to acknowledge assistance of the following people: Donald Feltner, vice president for university relations and development at Eastern Kentucky University for providing his sage advice in organizing and marketing the book. Don Rist, publications editor, Eastern Kentucky University for book layout and graphic art design. Professor William Adams of the Eastern Kentucky University geography department for assistance with historical maps. Larry Bailey and Paul Lambert of Eastern Kentucky University for photographic copying. Mrs. Joyce Hannan of Berea for investigating research collections. Dr. David Burg of Lexington for copy editing the entire manuscript. Dr. Melba Porter Hay, Ms. Anna B. Perry, and Ms. Mackelene G. Smith of the Henry Clay Papers Project for proofreading the entire text.

Charles Hay

List of Donors

Our deep appreciation to the special donors listed below who made this publication possible.

GUARANTORS

Madison County Historical Society

Madison Fiscal Court

Richmond Recreation and Tourism Commission

BENEFACTORS

Berea National Bank

Charles C. Combs and Betty C. Combs Memorial
by Clark C. Combs and Craig C. Combs

First Federal Savings and Loan Association of Richmond

Madison National Bank

State Bank and Trust Company

UNDERWRITERS

Earl B. and Ruth H. Baker
Jane L. Bradley
Jamie Caperton Burnam
Oren L. Collins
T.J. and Louise Curtis
Eastern Kentucky University Library
Donald E. Edwards
Tom Harper
Charles Cortlandt Hay, Jr.
Charles and Melba Hay
Brigadier General Merwyn L. Jackson
Mr. and Mrs. Raymond Kerns
D. Warren Lambert, Ph.D.
Robert E. Lanter
Senator and Mrs. Robert R. Martin

Minerich, Eidson and Wardlaw
   Charitable Foundation
Dr. and Mrs. James C. Murphy
Dr. and Mrs. Charles E. Parsons
Mr. and Mrs. John Patton
Joan and Jerry Perry
Margaret Greenleaf Pryor
Mary Frances McKinney Richards
   (Mrs. R. R.)
Rollin R. Richards
The Richmond Register
James J. Shannon, Jr.
Mr. and Mrs. Tom Snyder
Robert E. Spurlin
Robert L. Telford
Mrs. Wolfred K. White

PATRONS

Mr. and Mrs. Charles T. Adams
William G. Adams
Eunice Baker Allen
Bill and Betty Althauser
James Anderson and Son, Inc.
Mr. and Mrs. J.B. Arnett
Virginia Auvil
Dr. Robert E. Bagby
Mr. and Mrs. Bobby E. Baldwin
Joseph F. and Alice Tribble Ballew
Dr. and Mrs. Fred Ballou
Mr. and Mrs. G. G. Balog
Sarah Yancey Barker
Robert J. Begley
Esther S. Bennett
Dr. and Mrs. Richard E. Bernstrom
Jemima Boone N.S.D.A.R.
Boonesborough Chapter DAR
Harold K. Botner
A.R. Burnam
Caperton Burnam
Elizabeth Turley Burnam
Sara C. and A. Daniel Burns
Bybee Pottery
Mildred L. Calico
Betsy Igo Carr
Mr. and Mrs. Austin B. Carter
Mr. and Mrs. Douglas Walker
  Chenault
James S. Chenault
Hazel Lee Chrisman
Arch Clark
Dr. and Mrs. Bill Clouse
Cecil "Dude" Cochran
James E. Collins
John W. Collins, M.D.
Mrs. M. A. Collins

Oren L. Collins, Jr.
Clark, Cindy and Carolyn Combs
Craig C. Combs
Ruth M. Combs
Malcolm Miller Conlee, Jr.
Helen and Ervin Connelly
Continental Metal Specialty, Inc.
Drs. Ben and Rhonda Cormney
Mr. and Mrs. Billy Cosby
Betty P. Cox
Hallie Coy Cox
James T. Coy, III, M.D.
Verda Tudor Coy
Mr. and Mrs. Robert B. Davidson
Virginia B. Davison
Richard and Julia Drake
Dresser Industries
Cecil Dunn
Cecil F. Dunn
Mr. and Mrs. Joseph A. Dunn
Mr. and Mrs. Rondall Durham
Mr. and Mrs. Walter G. Ecton, Jr.
Geneva Ingram Edwards
Mr. and Mrs. Nelson W. Elder
Ellen Evans
Mildred B. Fassas
Blaine and Jessie Fennell
The Filson Club
Don Foster
Mr. and Mrs. Dean Gatwood
Ted and Jean George
Mary Jane and Ronald J. Ginter
William and Anne Ginter
Dr. and Mrs. J. Michael Gordon
David and Margaret Graham
Larry M. Greathouse
Barbara Tudor Griggs

Betsy Smith Toy Hall
Joyce M. Hannan
Dr. and Mrs. Charles R. Harris
Lt. Col. and Mrs. Alden E. Hatch
Col. and Mrs. Alden O. Hatch
Dr. and Mrs. Edward A. Hatch
Mr. and Mrs. Wayne O. Hatch
Mrs. Owen W. Hisle
Francis S. Hutchins
Dr. and Mrs. Jack Hutton
Irvin Industries, Inc.
Frances Ann Jennings
Charles K. Jett
Mr. and Mrs. Paul Jett
Neal O. Jett, Stephen W. Jett and
    Lucy Ann Jett in Memory of
    their mother, Margene Hatch Jett
Dr. and Mrs. John Moser Johnstone
Mr. and Mrs. David M. Jones
Delbert Reed Juett
Kenneth Sercey Juett
Alliegordon Park Kaylor
Kentucky Historical Society
    Library
Mr. and Mrs. W.C. Kindred
Harvey and DeEtte LaFuze
Connie Lawson
James K. and Joyce M. Libbey
Mrs. Jamie Bronston Long
Mr. and Mrs. Joe C. Lovell
Yvonne Lovern
Mr. and Mrs. Robert Luxon
Hugh Mahaffey, M.D.
Russell and Lucy Major
James T. Mason
Gladys Gilbert McCray
Alison Milby
William H. Mitchell, M.D.
Mr. and Mrs. Harry Moberly
Mr. and Mrs. Rhuben Moores
Anna B. Morgan

William J. Morgan
James J. Neale, Jr.
J. Walter and Delores H. Nelson
James Terry Noland
Robert Nunnery
Clark Kellogg and Margaret
    Orttenburger
Forniss R. and Maude Ella Park
Mr. and Mrs. James Cecil Park
Mr. and Mrs. K.S. Park, Jr.
Mr. and Mrs. Smith Park
Mrs. William Park
Alfred H. Perrin
Mrs. Mason G. Pope
Howard B. Powell
Elizabeth George Proctor
I. Max Reed
Nina Kanatzar Reed
Richmond Kiwanis Club
Richmond Rotary Club
Richard and Rita Rink
Mrs. George C. Robbins (Clara)
Mr. and Mrs. Roy W. Roberts, Jr.
Dale and Lorraine Robinson
Dr. and Mrs. George W. Robinson
Jack E. Robinson
The Sherwin-Williams Company,
    Richmond Coatings Plant
Sammye Million Shockley
Mrs. Thomas D. Shumate
Society of Boonesborough
Donald R. Snyder
Geraldine W. Spurlin, M.D.
Julia and Norbert Stammer
Diana L. Stapleton
Mary Ann C. Stokes
Mr. and Mrs. James E. Thompson
Eugene and Alpha Tipton
Dr. Stuart Tobin
James Caperton Todd
James Paul Todd and Daisy M. Todd

Dr. and Mrs. Stanley E. Todd, Sr.
Dorothy Tredennick
Mr. and Mrs. H. Thomas Tudor
William H. Tudor
University of Kentucky Library
Mr. and Mrs. Charles S. Wagers
Dr. and Mrs. Gordon Walker
Mr. and Mrs. Virgil R. Weddle, Sr.
WEKY Radio Station
Alice Walters West
Berea College Library
Dr. and Mrs. William W. H. Clay
Mrs. Larue Cocanougher
Walter C. and Martha Combs Brandenburgh Memorial
   by Mrs. Anna B. Morgan

Mr. and Mrs. Gary Westerfield
David J. Williams, III
Jimmy Dale and Marilyn Williams
R. T. Williams
Merle and Helen Winburn
Mr. and Mrs. Stanley Wylie
Mrs. Maudie H. Yater
David C. Greene
Margaret Mason Engelhardt

Introduction

For most Americans living in a predominately rural-agrarian region, the history of their county is most likely of greater personal significance than that of a state or the nation. Fundamentally the progressive stages of county development from frontier to modern age form an extended chronological history that is but a microcosm of the growth and maturing of a national people. Madison County, Kentucky, located astride the path of early western emigration in the latter part of the eighteenth century, fell under the whole gamut of pioneering experiences. Essentially it was one of the earliest points of destination of the human movement into virginal Kentucky by that great in-rush of emigrants from Virginia and the Carolinas. Its early history is inseparable from that of Cumberland Gap and the Wilderness Road.

The establishment of the early population anchorage at Boonesborough on the Kentucky River created a reasonably safe haven from which families could momentarily come to rest before fanning out into the fertile lands of central Kentucky to farmsteads and family bases. No rural Kentuckians made more immediate or intimate responses to the land than did those settlers who located themselves in Madison County. Geographical determinism was to work its magic from the outset within the county's ultimate political boundaries. Characteristic of emigrating people, from those of the Egyptian exodus to date, there have been those aggressive and farsighted individuals who laid claim to the most fertile and well-situated lands. Those Kentucky emigrants who halted just south of the Kentucky River numbered among them men who appropriated to themselves some of the choice tracts on that seductive sweep of rolling countryside which dropped off at the cliff line bordering the river, and which in the other direction shaded off into the mountainous western slope of the Kentucky Knobs. This pleasant pastoral littoral is penetrated by a series of creeks which follow the tilt of the river hills. These are lined with bottoms of varying widths, and, historically, they formed lines of inward penetration from the main plateau.

In these bottoms and across the sprawling Kentucky River anticline land hungry settlers found thrifty sites on which to generate family dynasties, to work slaves, and, in a phenomenally short time, to grow mountains of farm produce and pastures full of quality livestock. They, like the rural squires of Kent, Surrey, or Gloucester or those of the tidewater counties of colonial Virginia, formed a close-knit coterie of families and gathered unto themselves control of local government, commerce, and central institutions. They exerted powerful influences in the forming of public opinion, setting the general social tone of the county, and in preserving the continuity of conventional folk heritages and ways.

The rich lands of Madison County sustained a form of rural Kentucky aristocracy which stamped on the folk an indelible sense of public decorum and encouraged the establishment of norms of social, cultural, and economic values for the region. Fundamentally the long scope of history of the county has reflected the deeply embedded conservatism of the land-based slavocracy which in some measure felt continously threatened by the invasion of unsettling outside social forces. This fact comes crystal clear in the texts of several of the chapters of this book, expecially so in those relating to the founding of the town of Berea and its college.

In a more positive vein the landed gentry of Madison County planted firmly on the face of the land a loyalty to the family and generated a deep respect for standards of cultural refinements and sophistication. These things were generated within the context of a rural, and, sometimes, a closed community which created and lived by its own standards of provincial rural manners. If there is any one social and cultural characteristic which has been historically notable among Kentuckians generally it has been their ready and positive identification with a specific physical place in the universe, their home county. They have attached their loyalties and sense of geography not so much to an area with political boundaries as to a specific social background and provincial rurality. In this vein they have sometimes been vehement in their reactions to broader state public issues, in casting their votes at the polls, and in reacting to conditions of changing times.

By no means were all the emigrants who negotiated the Wilderness Road to settle in present-day Madison County discerning land claimants, ambitious yeoman farmers, power-hungry office seekers, or otherwise socially and economically aggressive. The lesser folk too reflected the ancient British pattern of countrymen who struggled constantly on the outer fringes of mere subsistence in East Anglia on the channel coast, or of the Welsh, the Irish, or the Scots highlanders. They built no imposing homes, opened no great farms, tended no prosperous village stores, owned few or no slaves, and wielded only limited political power.

In between the two extreme social groups was a basic yeoman class of modest farmers, businessmen, and craftsmen who played impressive roles in shaping the greater image of Madison County. They built comfortable country farm houses, many of chaste architectural design; raised community church buildings; and knotted their homes in social and economic clusters to form the rural roadside villages which have dotted the county. For the most part the yeomen were hard-working, God-fearing, and socially and politically reluctant to accept progressive changes. They have ever been conservative and provincial in expressions of their social and political views, as were their more affluent landed gentry neighbors.

From the outset there have been sharp physical and social contrasts in the history of Madison County. Geographically that part of the county which spreads eastward and southward to nestle itself in the picturesque curvature of the Kentucky Knobs or the Pottsville Escarpment has on its extreme edges sustained a human development closely akin to that of the more remote Appalachian highlands. Lands along Drowning, Muddy, Red Lick, and some of the other streams have tapered headlands which go into broken foothill terrain. The creek valleys have at once been social and economic entrapments and passageways inland and outward to the world. To date this geographical fact has given parts of Madison County more than a persistent image of being on a lingering contemporary frontier.

The varied land forms and qualities have played major parts in shaping county history. Whether one subscribes intellectually or not to the principles of economic determinism, the impact of the varying qualities of the land upon the composite patterns of social and economic organization can hardly be denied. On the outer rim of the inner Bluegrass region the patterns of life were often shaped in clear contrast to those prevailing in the less fertile areas. Outside contacts were more easily established, and farmers and slaveowners of this section related themselves more readily to the modes of life in the rest of the Kentucky Bluegrass region and even with that of the lower South. From the outset Richmond and Lexington bore a close social inter-relationship, shared common family connections, and enjoyed common economic goals. This was also true for the entire cluster of Bluegrass counties.

The authors of this thoughtful book, perhaps without intentionally doing so, have delineated eloquently the badly mixed social and political images of their county. They could hardly have avoided doing so. Madison County, like the Commonwealth of Kentucky, over two centuries has created for the historian a complex profile of its existence. No doubt the first recorded incidence of violence in the county was Felix Walker's account of the ambushing and murder of Captain Twetty's party on March 25, 1775. From that date forward the history of the county was to be stained by Indian fighting, rowdy frontier personal encounters, murders, mob actions, furious political disputes, Ku Klux Klan raiding, and racial incidents.

Some of this civil disorder most certainly stemmed from the intensive emotional struggle to wrest the land from Indians and nature. The pro and con arguments over the retention of slavery stirred both individuals and self-appointed regulators alike and provoked the commission of lawless acts. Political campaigns, and especially that of 1849 to select delegates to a constitutional convention, often resulted in senseless bloodshed.

Chapters of this book relating to the founding of Berea College detail a historical moment which now will appear to the modern reader to have been a social anachronism almost beyond human comprehension and common sense. Read outside the context of the disjointed times of the mid-nineteenth century, the violent occurrences in Madison County now seem almost a historical nightmare. Root causes of the Berea troubles no doubt were many, but basically the resistence to the Berea missionaries proved how sensitive was the slavocracy of the county to any outside threat to slavery, no matter how weak or modest. No doubt the mob reactions which disrupted efforts to establish Berea village and college were more reflective of the fact that by the 1850s the days of the existence of slavery were clearly numbered, not because of the labors of the Berea missionaries, but because of the intensification of antislavery sentiments nationwide.

On another front of social and moral irritation, Madison County has never really been totally free of its problems with the liquor trade—during the free-swinging frontier days, when making and selling grain and fruit-based spirits was virtually a common household industry, down through several subsequent stages of the county's more modern history. While there was a conservative early temperance movement in the county, and considerable public support of post-World War I prohibition, there was little chance of controlling the traffic in liquor. The rugged geographical nature of a part of the county mitigated against a strict enforcement of the liquor prohibition laws by state and federal revenuers. There are too many mountain defiles, fresh water streams, and thirsty nearby consumers to kill the industry by application of mere laws. Just as there currently is a glaring inconsistency in public attitude in Kentucky toward the open sale of liquor, Madison County has pursued its own ambivalent and inconsistent course in regulating liquor in the post-prohibition days. The county is dry, and the county seat city of Richmond is wet. A stranger approaching Richmond from the south along its Main Street would no doubt be impressed that he is entering a wide-open wild west boom town. There perhaps are few or no small city main streets east of the Mississippi which are so numerously lined with liquor stores on one end and churches on the other. It is on South Main that the thirsty horde from the large block of dry eastern mountain counties first reach sources of legal liquor supply. The chapters of this book dealing with the history of Madison County in the post 1870s years down to date give good accounts of its borderland position in the bizarre social and geographical pattern of the liquor industry and trade in Kentucky as a whole.

By no means has the history of Madison County been wholly one of violence or social indecorum. Few or no Kentucky counties reflect so sharply the contrasting cultural and social patterns of rural American life. The rolling bluegrass plateau which ends atop the towering limestone palisades of the Kentucky River has been a land of well-to-do and extremely conservative agrarian gentry who built solid, and sometimes, elegant homes where families have lived and multiplied, living for the most part comfortable self-contained lives. Here they nurtured hopes that no disruptive outside influences would disturb them or interrupt the tenor of their lives. Many of these homes still remain as monuments to an American rural-agrarian way of life which historically has borne a closer kinship to the older tidewater and lower southern plantation culture than to the neighboring Appalachian highlands.

Interspersed with the imposing country places are those remaining yeoman farmsteads with their modest but appealing houses of native architectural design which are surrounded by the universal nostalgic cluster of out-buildings. In kindred style, the Madison County village roadways are lined with homes of Kentucky country style which often reflected the well-being of their community. In their plain but substantial designs and solid seating upon the land the country homes of Madison County reflect the physical and economic mainsprings of more affluent everyday rural America. Wedding village, countryside, and county seat in a close bond is the spidery network of rural roads and lanes which fan out from Richmond and Berea to the outermost reaches of the county and on beyond as cultural and economic umbilical cords. Actually these roads act as centralizing conduits which draw most of the county into a community trading center about the courthouse, agricultural produce warehouses, main street stores, and schools and colleges.

Almost beyond the pale of the old and established homesteads is a third layer of rural and village life, bordering on the spartan mode of Appalachia, whose more pronounced regional folk mores have persisted historically. The authors of this history have demonstrated a keen awareness of the county's layered society, which has always existed, and have dealt with the social and cultural mix with discernment and objective discretion. Perhaps one of the most positive historical facts about Madison County is that its various social and economic groups, white and black, have lived together, with the exception of the Berea troubles, with little class conflict and rivalry.

Viewed from a much broader historical perspective, Madison County has evolved through various crysallis stages of development which, each in turn, have characterized so much of American local history. If there is in fact any broad practical application of the famous and intellectually well-worn Turner thesis of the significance of the frontier in American history, then surely Madison County's past is eloquently reflective of its progression from raw frontier beginnings to its expanding rural nonfarm-urban population and way of life. Every stage of its growth and degree of maturation has created its own physical and human landmarks of history. The pioneers who laid initial claims to the land, the farmers whose fields yielded mountains of prime farm products to be loaded aboard Kentucky River flatboats for transporation to downstream markets, the rise of the slavocracy on one side of the country and the unsettling activities of the tiny band of zealous Berea missionaries and abolitionists on the other, went far toward polarizing political and moral views and ill-conceived mob actions.

A civil war and at least four world-wide conflicts had enormous impacts on Madison County. The Civil War marked a sharp division of local allegiances and then was even more upsetting by direct military invasion, which resulted in the elongated Battle of Richmond that spread out from Kingston to the Clay's Ferry bridge on the Kentucky. Although this was by no means a decisive battle of the war, it did bring directly home to the local people the hard facts of a divided nation in travail. The world conflicts of later years drew the locality into the vortex of international changes. No mode of life or institution escaped their revolutionary impacts. World War I, especially, marked a distinct watershed between two historical eras in the United States, and Kentucky and Madison County were not to escape the changes which came in every aspect of life. What the war and its immediate reconstruction years failed to effect, the Great Depression and the New Deal of this century finished. The old rural ways and sentimental local attachments were forced to give way to waves of twentieth century modernization. More and more local businesses came under the management of chain stores, shopping malls appeared on the periphery of the towns, planned urban-rural subdivisions replaced the old casual streetside developments, residential housing reflected a national sameness and monotony of design of domestic housing, fast food stands largely replaced the traditional town restaurants, and tourist traps sought in every way to ensnare the bountiful tourist dollar.

Just as the ancient Wilderness Road had fed a stream of pioneers into central Kentucky and across Madison County, so did the improved federal Highway 25 bring in a rising tide of tourists. During the depression years of the 1930s the road was filled with an outward flow of impoverished rural emigrants who went north to the industrial cities in search of employment. More recently Interstate 75 has become a throbbing artery of commercial transportation and travel across the county. By the very circumstance of numbers this road has resulted in an enormous transitory influence on the course of life in Madison County. Although only a miniscule part of the traffic on this road stops to patronize local lodging and food establishments, filling stations, and merchants, the trade has been enough to create commercial rings of motels, restaurants, service stations, souvenir shops, and chain stores about the interchanges.

The authors of the chapters dealing with the history of the county since 1870 have described changing times in an almost rhythmic tempo. They have sensed the dynamics of change, which often time filtered downward from other sections of the nation to bring revision of the standards of life in even the remotest rural areas.

Madison County churches were to experience the effects of more modern theological thought. There sprang up about the county the church houses of the new evangelical faiths, these ministering to special social groups. The local educational system passed through evolutionary stages which resulted in the modernization necessary to meet the challenges of each new age. At the higher educational level old Central University in Richmond was merged in 1906 into Eastern Kentucky Normal School as a result of the whirlwind campaign in Kentucky in that year. In time this institution was to pass through the crysallis stage of being a college to become a university. This institution focused higher educational and cultural attention of the eastern part of Kentucky upon Richmond. On the southern end of the county Berea College grew out of its shaky beginnings to become one of the best of all the Appalachian educational institutions. It survived mob raids, racial antagonisms, discriminatory state legislation, and prejudices to gain a national reputation.

At ground level no single economic fact outweighed changes which came in the field of agriculture. As burley tobacco in the 1880s became more and more a main staple crop the landscape of the county was dotted with tobacco curing barns, and the crop became an economic mainstay for Madison County farmers. During the past century this industry has passed through years of prosperity and decline. Depressions, unpredictable weather conditions, and, currently, the health scare over cigarette smoking have all threatened this important rural economic source. The advent of the New Deal, with its complexity of laws and agencies, wrought deep changes in every aspect of farming and land management in Madison County. Never again was the land to be brought so heavily under the traditional mode of farming and product marketings. Restrictions on acreage of certain farm crops brought radical revisions of traditional landlord-tenant relationships, and greatly reduced the farm labor force. The authors of this history have demonstrated a keen awareness of the evolutionary processes which brought radical restructuring of much of the agrarian life in the county during these years. There were at work major historical forces which have borne upon the lives of the entire county population.

There is no doubt that history written at the local level must of necessity reflect the forces and contributions of individual personalities. This is the one area in American history where the greatest number of persons can expect to see mention of their accomplishments for the sake of posterity. Madison County has had a generous number of sons and daughters who have gained local, state, and national notice. They have participated in public affairs in the professions; as delegates to constitutional conventions, governors, legislators, judges, college presidents, professors, crusaders for civil rights and racial justice; and as successful farmers and businessmen. Behind them they have had generations of so-called common people who have comprised most of the population and have given stability to the local way of life and the institutions. Collectively, Madison County's people have generated the social dynamics which historically have characterized its rise from a frontier anchorage to emerge through successive stages to become a modern American county with distinctive characteristics and a generous measure of local pride.

This history takes a refreshing departure from the general format of the old-fashioned Kentucky county histories, which sometimes are poorly organized and are badly cluttered with the inclusion of so many personal names and local anecdotes that have often obscured the central facts of leadership and decision-making, if not the cardinal thread of the county's history. No historian should belittle the significance of genealogy. This is an area of meaningful personal concern which gives continuity to human and family involvement in a community, and gives to individuals a sense of direct relationship to the past as well as an attachment to the land itself. Genealogy, however, like leavening in bread, should be mixed discreetly with history. The authors in this book have done so with skill. There is reflected a discriminating sense of the human presence, but individual efforts have been blended into the broader aspects of the central county chronicle. In the history of an area of county proportions no individual has a monopolistic claim on being a central force within himself, no matter how important a contemporary role he or she may have played in public affairs. Ages merge into one another, and the perspectives of history constantly open new vistas of a region's past. Of necessity contemporary standards of historical scholarship must be applied to an interpretation of the past. Too, as time passes a fuller documentation of the past is made more available. Two strong virtues of this book are that the authors have gone to the basic sources and that they have amply documented their writings. They have not blundered into that historical never, never land of proclaiming "firsts" for Madison county—who knows for a historical certainty what was first?

Within the above context this is a highly competent county history written by authors who have made sound professional approaches to their subjects. They have been selective in presenting what they deem to be basic in the understanding of the rise and progress of a people congregated inside an officially prescribed piece of fairly diversified physio-political geography with a commercial and political center focused upon a county seat town. In no chapter have the authors allowed their emphases to become encyclopedic or burdened their narrative with irrelevant details, narrow genealogical data, anecdotes, or even inane vanities. The personalities who appear throughout this history, however, often seem almost too serious-minded. Surely there prevailed a sense of humor among the people of Madison County. As they appear in history they almost seem to have viewed life and local affairs as deadly serious business. There is no yearning in this book for the good old days, no romantic fantacising, and no set local biases or tunnel vision of the kind which have so often flawed far less competent Kentucky county histories. This book projects a dignified and objective profile of Madison County as a significant microcosm of local and provincial American life and struggles within the context of the broader national development. By this very fact the book promises to fullfill its proper mission of not only informing the present generation of Madison Countians of their historical roots, but, so far as a history can do so, lifting slightly a corner of the veil of the immediate future.

Thomas D. Clark
Lexington, Kentucky

Part 1

MADISON COUNTY: Pioneer Days, 1775-1850

By H. E. Everman

Chapter One
THE GARDEN OF EDEN

The frontier wilderness which became Madison county consisted of knobs, undulating plains, vast limestone and clay deposits, dense forests and undergrowth, and five large streams meandering northward to the Kentucky River. Paint Lick, Silver, Tate's, Muddy, and Drowning creeks emptied into the Kentucky River. Only Red Lick Creek ran eastward across the southern Madison perimeter. Indian mounds dotted the landscape. One near Boonesborough dated back to 1550. Long before white men migrated into the outer Bluegrass, the Madison frontier included twenty-one mounds, one rock shelter, one cemetery, one small fortification, and one large Indian fort.[1]

In that earlier time lush forests, abundant game, wild geese, wild turkeys, buffaloes, nut trees, and workable clay deposits attracted ancient Indians to the area. Early twentieth century geologists, anthropolists, and archaeologists unearthed prehistoric artifacts throughout present-day Madison County.

In the southeastern section of the county, Indian Fort Mountain offered an irresistible military advantage for prehistoric settlers, as did the surrounding knobs and hills. Thousands of years ago prehistoric Indians barricaded the steep slopes with rock walls, as high as three feet and as long as a thousand feet. A stockpile of stones, arrows, axes, and limestone clubs attested to the defense strategy of the mountain occupants. This largest fort covered almost 500 acres of land and was extremely elaborate. It had imposing barricades and a natural spring which provided an adequate water supply. It had numerous rockhouses, and Indians used the small caves of the area for graves. The occupants of

1

the Indian fort made a variety of artifacts, such as spearheads, axes, arrows, scrapers, and flint knives.[2]

Centuries later American Indians of the eighteenth century used more polished weapons and tools and renewed the barricaded mountain fort. They cluttered the knob area with a number of graves and material artifacts. One grave included copper armor plates and smaller copper articles. The Indians made a variety of tools from bone, shell, and horn, including awls, scrapers, fish hooks, flaking tools, hoes, whistles, handles, and arrowheads. Their ornaments included beads, pendants, combs, pipes, and animal teeth for jewelry. They used stone to fashion some drills, hammers, axes, knives, war clubs, and a variety of grinding tools, including pestles.[3]

The early mound builders constructed over twenty impressive mounds in modern Madison County. A conical mound near Kirksville was used as a burial ground. Many of the circular mounds of the Silver Creek area were well constructed. They served as military outposts or as burial sites. Many of the circular mounds were located near bodies of water, such as Hay's Fork, Taylor Fork, Muddy Creek, the Kentucky River, and especially Silver Creek.[4] The famous Moberly Mound was one of the most impressive burial mounds of the early period. It contained six remains, including the skeleton of a seven-foot man of unusual status, as evidenced by the elaborate burial preparations. A slate ornament lay near his head; a pendant of white stone, spearheads standing on end, and fine charcoal and ashes surrounded his body. He had a carved pipe near his right side, and it contained a black substance resembling nicotine. The site included scrapers, axes, whetstones, and vessels with red, pink, and white ochre for decoration. The body was covered with animal skins.[5]

Although the mound builders undoubtedly traversed Kentucky for centuries, they no longer inhabited the great hunting land on a permanent basis at the time the first Anglo-Saxons entered the wilderness. In the eighteenth century, Shawnees and Wyandotte warriors hunted throughout the Kentucky River basin area. Yet no Indians occupied the Bluegrass region, although several tribes utilized its hunting grounds. The first white men to see the area were also hunters from the western wilderness areas of Virginia and the Carolinas. By the late 1760s white hunters reported abundant game, lush forests, wild grass, and good land. Only the most adventurous or reckless scouts and surveyors braved the Indian danger. By 1769-70, Daniel Boone, John Findley, and four companions hunted and trapped the Kentucky River area. Alexander Neeley and Squire Boone, Daniel's brother, joined them the following year with new food and powder provisions. The Boones scoured the river valley, noting bountiful sycamore, ash, and walnut trees; lush cane, rye, clover; pea vines, berries, mosses, ferns; streams for fishing; salt and springs for buffaloes; and wild turkeys foraging along Otter and Silver creeks.[6]

In 1774 the white men made the first serious effort to establish a community in the new wilderness. Daniel Boone and Michael Stoner returned to Kentucky to survey land and to hunt. As the hunters crossed

Daniel Boone by Nicola Marschall, after Chester Harding's portrait. The Kentucky Historical Society.

the mountains at Cumberland Gap and advanced along the Rockcastle River into the old Madison wilderness, they met an array of wildlife and vegetation. It appeared to be a veritable "garden of Eden". Nothwithstanding, there were dangers. Indians killed Hancock Taylor, a deputy surveyor from Virginia, while he was exploring the bank of Taylor's Fork on Silver Creek.[7]

Once inside present Madison County, the settlers took several routes to the Kentucky River. In the eastern sector they passed near the Pilot Knob and traveled northward along the Wilderness Trace toward Otter Creek. As they approached the "Hollow" at Boonesborough they observed enormous sycamores and many elms bordering the various streams. Further to the east they followed Muddy Creek to the Kentucky River. The Muddy Creek area abounded in sugar trees, white oaks, hickory, blue ash, red oaks, mulberry, and black walnut.[8] On the western side of the county Silver Creek meandered northwestward into the Kentucky River. It was a picturesque area dotted with knobs, Indian mounds, and limestone (J. T. Dorris called it the Rhineland of Madison County). A buffalo run crossed Poosey Ridge and meandered down to the creek. The entire area included vast forests of walnut, oak, ash, coffeebean, buckeye, cherry, and poplar trees as well as thick clover and peavine. This area swarmed with buffalo, too.[9]

In 1774 Judge Richard Henderson opened negotiations with the Indians in hopes of acquiring the vast hinterland for his Transylvania Company. He instructed Boone to open a trail through the wilderness. Colonel John Snoddy, a Revolutionary War soldier, helped Boone clear that first road from Virginia. Boone's Trail from Clinch, Virginia, to Otter Creek was by way of the Cumberland Gap. Boone crossed the Cumberland River (near Pineville), advancing westward to Flat Lick, Hazel Patch, and finally the Rockcastle River. The road cutters approached Silver Creek via Boone's Gap, Brush Fork, and the "Big Hill," where they saw the plains through that wide gap in the last range of high knobs.[10]

Judge Richard Henderson, political father of Kentucky. *Kentucky Progress Magazine,* Vol. 8 (Summer, 1935), 362.

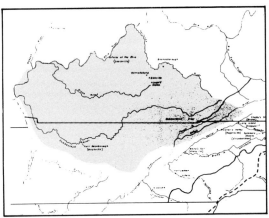

Transylvania Colony in 1775. Ralph W. Beiting, *Soldier of the Revolution,* vi.

On the night of March 25, some five miles south of Richmond, the road cutters pitched camp and erected a temporary construction of logs and dirt, a "little fort." Shawnee raiders attacked the party, killing Captain William Twetty and his Negro slave Sam. Despite the fatalities, Boone and the others buried the two dead men and continued their trek toward Otter Creek. The following morning they found a blue lick. They noticed the drainage from the creek as well as an abundance of cane. They decided to erect a fort near the mouth of Otter Creek.[11]

In early April, Richard Callaway, Nathaniel Hart, John Kennedy, Michael Stoner, and John Snoddy helped Boone erect the small fort on the south side of the Kentucky River. By the end of the month Judge Richard Henderson arrived with a party of forty men and ordered erection of a larger fort, closer to the river and on a flatter plain. The men completed the second fort by June, 1775. The Millions, Hoys, Snoddys, Millers, Woodses, and Callaways were among those settlers who planted beans, corn, and melons on plots near the fort.[12]

On May 23 to May 27, 1775, settlers from Boonesborough, Harrodsburg, Boiling Spring, and St. Asaph's gathered at Boonesborough for the formation of a government. Constituting themselves as the house of delegates of the colony of Transylvania, the men chose Thomas Slaughter as chairman, and Judge Henderson joined him on the platform as a speaker. Henderson urged the creation of a compact and assured the settlers of the title deed from the Indians. Although the land had other claimants, he avowed his purchase of a large tract of land inside the Cumberland, Kentucky, and Ohio rivers from the Cherokee Indians at Sycamore Shoals that year, for 10,000 pounds, was the legal and definitive title. Henderson urged the assembled settlers to seize the initiative. Accepting his ambitious advice, they quickly enacted nine laws for the new political entity.[13]

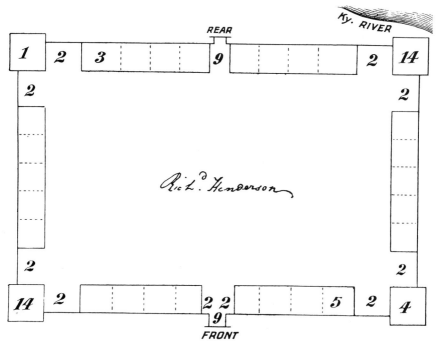

PLAN OF FORT BOONESBOROUGH.

From the Original in the Handwriting of Richard Henderson. Copied by James Hall. Henderson's Autograph from Original in possession of Wisconsin Historical Library.

1—Henderson's Cabin. 2—Stockades. 3—Henderson's Kitchen. 4—Luttrell's Cabin. 5—His Kitchen. 9—Gates. 14—Cabins for Hart and Williams. Unnumbered Spaces—Cabins.

Judge Henderson's plan for Fort Boonesborough, *Kentucky Pioneer,* **Vol. 4 (October, 1972), 19.**

The delegates provided for a judiciary and criminal punishment; forbade profanity and Sabbath breaking; issued writs of attachment; called for surveys; set sheriff and clerk fees; urged the preservation of wild game; promoted improved horsebreeding, conservation, and the regulation of a militia. The dictatorial policy failed at once. New settlers did not want a land company making decisions for them. Too, they recognized the significance of the power, land, and territorial controversies.[14]

Early pioneers readily understood the challenges they faced, and they maintained scouts and spies on the lookout for Indians. Judge Richard Henderson kept books and sold land to the settlers through his Transylvania Land Company. Despite their uneasiness, settlers sought tracts along the Silver, Otter, and Paint Lick creeks. Henderson assured farmers of 640 acres if they raised a crop of corn in 1775, and he urged them to acquire even larger amounts of land. Settlers quickly seized land near creeks and natural springs. Yet Indians swarmed the countryside in that decade and the fort became a symbol of security to the endangered settlers. The second Boonesborough fort had blockhouses on all four corners, with Henderson occupying the northeast corner. Squire Boone had a gunsmith shop, and Colonel Callaway resided within the walled fort as well.[15]

Colonel Richard Callaway, a veteran of the French and Indian War, was Judge Henderson's right arm in the Transylvania project. He joined the Boone expedition as a consultant and military escort. Callaway hauled supplies for Boone's trailblazers and served as a land agent at Boonesborough. At Henderson's designation, he and Boone laid out the lots in Boonesborough. It was Callaway who drafted the ideas concerning the judiciary for the early assembly at the fort. He received three large grants from Henderson and planted a crop of corn and watermelon in 1775.[16]

As white encroachments into their hunting grounds increased, Indians accelerated their attacks on the settlers. They killed several farmers and destroyed corn fields near Boonesborough. Indians even cut down apple trees. The most appalling incident occurred in July, 1776, when Elizabeth and Frances Callaway and Jemima Boone went canoeing just below the fort on a Sunday afternoon. Five Indians kidnapped the girls and forced them up the cliff-like hill on the north side of the river. The clever teen-age girls attempted to mark their trail, but the Indians soon recognized the ploy and threatened to scalp them if they did not cooperate. The following day they caught a pony near Winchester and attempted to speed up the escape, but the cunning girls kept falling off, thus slowing the retreat and leaving signals for their rescuers to find.[17]

Colonel Callaway and ten men proceeded on horseback to the Lower Blue Licks to cut off the retreating kidnappers, while Boone and five men followed the Indian trail on foot. William Bush and some cabin builders on the north side of the river joined the rescue party. Boone, discovering Indian chicanery in false trails, feared the murder of the girls, so his group decided to follow a direct line to the Scioto River. By

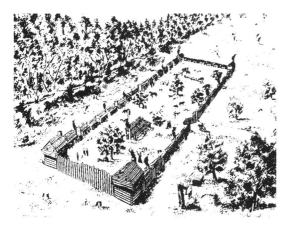

Sketch of Fort Boonesborough. George W. Ranck, *Boonesborough*, 72.

Sycamores at Fort Boonesborough. George W. Ranck, *Boonesborough*, 135.

Tuesday the Indians became less cautious and killed a buffalo, cooked part of the meat, and made camp. As the sentinel lit his pipe the rescuers opened fire from the thick cane. They killed two Indians and wounded a third who fled with his companions. Boone and his party returned home with the unharmed girls and the excitement abated.[18]

The fort resisted another Indian attack in September. Despite the danger, settlers continued to pour into the Kentucky River Valley that year. The Phelpses, Kennedys, Irvines, and Frenchs cleared land along Tate's and Muddy creeks. James French, a careful surveyor, was the brother-in-law of Captain Christopher "Kit" Irvine. The two men surveyed some of the richest land in the area. John Bush, a Boone companion in the marking of the Wilderness Road, crossed the river and established Bush's Station in present Clark County. Shortly he replaced the log station with the first brick house in the area.[19]

As the Indian danger deepened in 1777 fewer settlers ventured outside the fort, but David Crews did clear land near the Foxtown vicinity. Whites and Indians killed excessive numbers of elk, deer, and buffalo in the Silver Creek area, greatly depleting the abundance of game by the close of the decade. As late as the 1780s Higgarson Grubbs and other settlers hunted abundant buffaloes in the Drowning Creek area. Wild turkeys were so numerous that farmers made no effort to domesticate or raise them until well into the 1800s.[20]

Settlers cleared larger tracts of land, inciting new Indian assaults in 1778. Recognizing their vulnerability and anticipating an increasing Indian menace, the pioneers appealed to the capital in Richmond, Virginia, for aid. Colonel Callaway represented the Kentuckians in the Virginia legislature.[21] Indians, concerned over the depletion of hunting opportunities in the Kentucky River basin, launched vigorous offensives in the new year.

In many ways 1778 was the most crucial year in the struggle of Kentucky pioneers, as they suffered a series of disasters. The winter was exceptionally harsh, and the settlers at Boonesborough suffered many deprivations. The shortage of salt limited their ability to cure hides or preserve meat. Ultimately, the salt problem led Boone to decide on an expedition to the famed Blue Licks, some forty miles away on the Licking River. After establishing a camp, he hunted buffalo while his men collected salt. Indians soon took him prisoner. Black Fish, a Shawnee chief, led a war party of over a hundred braves. Boone bargained for the saltmakers' lives and exaggerated the number of defenders inside the fort so effectively that the Indians decided to return to Ohio with their thirty prisoners and wait until spring to attack the fort. Boone and all the saltmakers eventually had to run the gauntlet.[22]

By mid-March the Indians took Boone and ten of the prisoners on to Detroit to meet Governor Hamilton. Boone was able to further misrepresent the strength of the forces inside Boonesborough. When he returned to the Shawnee village, the Indian tribe adopted him. For months Boone pretended to accept Indian life while secretly preparing his escape. By June he returned to Kentucky in an epic four-day journey. Immediately he rallied the settlers and prepared a defense of the endangered fort. Boone resumed command and ordered the repairing of the fort, provisioning of it, and increasing of patrols. He led a reconnaisance party northward and discovered a war party of over four hundred Indians, under British command, enroute to Boonesborough. It was early September.[23]

Both sides attempted to avoid battle, and they held lengthy discussions concerning peace, surrender terms, and possible compromises. A truce ensued for a few days, but on September 9 the frontiersmen rejected a surrender order and promised to fight to the death. Surprisingly, Black Fish proposed a compromise peace treaty. At the peace talks which followed Boone and eight settlers met eighteen Indians at the lick spring. During the handshakes, by accident or design, fighting broke out. The frontiersmen retreated into the fort, and the battle began.[24]

Kentucky's most famous historian, Thomas D. Clark, called the survival of Boonesborough "one of the momentous incidents" in Kentucky history. The assault on Fort Boonesborough in that hot September of 1778 accelerated throughout the longest-lasting siege of frontier history. The Indians tried a variety of ruses, such as tricking the settlers with fake retreats, igniting flax and hurling it onto the cabin roofs, and finally beginning construction of an underground tunnel. This represented the greatest danger for the settlers. Siege warfare could have destroyed Boonesborough and lost the Kentucky frontier during the American Revolution. This in turn would have altered the outcome of General George Rogers Clark's expedition in the Northwest Territory, as the British-Indian force would have been in front and behind him at

Kaskaskia and Vincennes. A Clark failure would have eliminated the Americans' claim for western land at Versailles in 1783. As for Boonesborough itself, September heat and drought complicated the defense. Fire spread across the tops of the cabins. British artillery weakened the settlers' confidence. Miraculously, at the last moment rain began to fall. On the eighth day it poured. The following morning the Indian tunnel collapsed, and it was obvious they had withdrawn northward during the night. It was believed the Indians suffered a hundred casualties, whereas the fort had two dead and several wounded. The fort was saved.[25]

Following the near disaster at Boonesborough, Colonel Callaway and Captain Benjamin Logan brought treason charges against Boone. They complained of his surrender at Blue Licks salt springs, of his travels with the Indians, and of his weakening, if not outright betrayal, of the defenses at Fort Boonesborough. Boone deftly defended himself and explained how he outwitted the Indians by seeming to cooperate. His neighbors not only upheld him but even promoted him following his acquittal. Callaway and Boone never spoke again, and both refused to serve as trustees of the newly chartered Boonesborough in 1779 because of their mutual hostility. Callaway obtained a ferry license in 1780 and had begun work on the wooden structure when Indians killed him.[26]

The Indian problem was not the only challenge facing Kentuckians of the eighteenth century. The Virginia legislature declared Richard Henderson's purchase "null and void," thus undercutting the legitimacy of land claims by settlers as well as absentee land speculators. The Transylvania Company encouraged migration to the Kentucky River valley, accepted promissory notes, and sold land for low prices despite the Virginia legislature's authorization of a new Kentucky County as early as 1776. The Old Dominion recognized military warrants and established a land office. It encouraged 400-acre claims by settlers after one year's residence and the production of a crop of corn. It allowed pre-emption of an additional 1,000 adjacent acres and sold vacant land through treasury warrants whenever possible. The overlapping claims and counterclaims of Transylvania and Kentucky County pioneers led to tragic and long-lasting court litigation. The problem of land titles which surfaced in 1778 lasted for decades.[27]

Colonel Callaway was the Kentucky County representative in the Virginia Assembly of 1779 when it addressed the Kentuckians' Petition Number Nine requesting a grant for Boonesborough and the selection of town trustees. Virginia established Boonesborough in October, 1779, recognized a previous survey of twenty acres, called for the surveying of an additional fifty acres for town lots, and set the remainder aside as a commons for livestock. The legislature designated Callaway, Boone, Samuel Estill, and seven others as trustees.[28]

The Virginia assembly passed a new land law in 1779 which encouraged migration and provided for easier acquisition of land. Settlers could pre-empt 400 acres for $2.25 per acre and 100 adjoining acres for forty cents each. The Old Dominion gave Revolutionary War officers military grants varying in size according to rank. Settlers now obtained land via military warrants, treasury warrants, or outright purchase. Many new settlers came to Boonesborough in 1779-80. Among those destined to play a significant role in the development of the Madison frontier were Higgarson Grubbs, Joseph Kennedy, and Colonel Nathaniel Hart.[29]

Boonesborough settlers responded on April 15, 1779, by drawing up the "Articles of Association of Boonesborough." They asked all farmers to raise a crop of corn, to assemble at meetings, to forfeit corn crops for failure to attend assemblies, to serve on spy duty, to never hunt separately or leave the area without approval; and they appointed an overseer for the town. Nathaniel Hart and eighteen other men signed the rules of association.[30]

In Petition Number Ten, Richard Callaway requested the right to establish a ferry across the Kentucky River at Boonesborough. The Virginia assembly granted him the license as ferry operator and asked him to survey and mark potential improvements on the Wilderness Road. Despite his contributions to the development of Boonesborough, he and some of his friends refused to serve as trustees of the town due to differences with Daniel Boone. This complicated the organization of the new town. Consequently, the legislature named a second group of trustees, including Archibald Woods, David Crews, Higgarson Grubbs, William Irvine, and six other men. The following summer Callaway and a group of Negroes were building a water craft when a small Indian party attacked them. The Indians killed the entire group but scalped and mutilated the body of Callaway.[31]

With Colonel Callaway's murder the settlers continued to stress the security of the old fort, but Nathaniel Hart and a small group of Pennsylvanians erected a smaller fort at White Oak Spring about a mile above Boonesborough in 1780, and Captain James Estill established the largest station along the headwaters of Otter Creek that same year. Estill's Station included five or six cabins. Surveyors, travelers, scouts, and spies gathered here. John Miller, Adam Caperton, Green Clay, David Gass, and Archibald Woods resided at Estill's Station.[32]

Even before the Indian peril abated, pioneers began claiming land further from the fort. James Barnett, a Revolutionary War captain and participant in George Rogers Clark's expedition, settled on Silver Creek; John Kennedy pre-empted 1,400 acres along Silver Creek; Samuel Estill, Nathaniel Hart, and Christopher Irvine each claimed a 1,000 acre tract within a fifteen-mile radius of the fort and established stations. Joseph Kennedy settled along Paint Lick and Silver Creek. He was taken captive by the Indians in 1781 but escaped and continued to clear land. All these men constructed stations that provided security for additional settlers of the Madison area. The early station was nothing more than a well-fortified log house. In the early 1780s Madisonians took refuge in Hart's White Oak, Irvine's, Bell's (Paint Lick), Estill's Muddy Creek, Warren's Locust Thicket, Grubbs', Turner's (Clay's), Hoy's, and Crews' stations.[33]

Despite the development of these stations, Boonesborough remained in the Indian path and symbolized the forthcoming Anglo-

Saxon invasion. The Indians sent war parties into the Kentucky wilderness. On March 20, 1782, some twenty-five Wyandotte Indians approached Estill's Station and captured Monk, a Negro slave, who greatly exaggerated the number of defenders in the fort. Monk's craftiness saved the helpless women, children, and sick pioneers inside the fort. Already aware of the Indian presence and the accumulation of dead buffaloes in the area, Captain James Estill and seventeen men had left the fort in search of the Indian party. Due to Monk's fabrication the Indians retreated toward Little Mountain (Mount Sterling), with the Estill party close behind.[34]

Estill's force numbered thirty-five men by the time it overtook the Indians shortly before sunset on the twenty-second. Six of the Indians had stopped to divide up a buffalo. One pioneer impetuously opened fire too soon and the remainder of the Indian party returned. The Indians held the higher ground. Lieutenant William Miller and six of his men withdrew, allowing the Indians to attack a weakened flank. Fierce hand-to-hand combat ensued, with Captain Estill fighting the Wyandotte chief. After the chief stabbed Estill, James Proctor shot the chief. Nine of Estill's men laid dead on the battleground, while Monk, Estill's faithful slave, carried the wounded James Berry from the battlefield. James Proctor, founder of Proctor's Chapel, and William Irvine were among the few survivors. Although seventeen Indians were dead, it was a drawn battle and both sides withdrew. Significantly, it was the last major Indian raid into the county. As a result of Monk's heroism, Wallace Estill, his new owner, freed the slave. Monk continued to manufacture gun powder and to tan hides for the settlers. Kentuckians made three Indian campaigns into Ohio following the Battle of Little Mountain. The Indian peril abated, and pioneers claimed additional land further from the fort.[35]

By 1783 David Gass and Archibald Woods left Estill's Station and settled along Dreaming Creek. Woods claimed that Town Fork got its name because of an Old Indian town near the site of the first courthouse. Squire Boone established the first blacksmith shop on the lower Silver Creek. His neighbors built chimneys of slab stone, as there was no brick produced in the area. All the early farmers plowed in late February, planted corn in March, and harvested crops in July or August. Farmers complained that wild turkeys, foxes, rabbits, and ground hogs often destroyed their produce. Another early settler, William Hoy of Boonesborough and Hoy's Station, established a race track in 1783, indicative of Madisonian interest in horse racing.[36]

The economic activity of Madisonians was increasing. David Crews petitioned the Virginia Court for the right to establish a ferry at Jack's Creek where it emptied into the Kentucky River. Colonel John Miller, a Revolutionary War captain at Yorktown, bought land from William Hoy when he came to Kentucky in 1784. Miller settled along Otter Creek and then cleared the canebrake near the present site of the Richmond Courthouse, where he erected a house and barn. Miller paid Hoy $1,000 in Virginia money for the 1,000 acre pre-emption.[37]

By the 1780s Green Clay arrived at Estill's Station, where he joined Kit Irvine, James French, and John Crooke in their surveying expeditions. He purchased 1,400 acres of land from the Reverend John Tanner of Tate's Creek in 1785 and paid $233.31½for the tract. Within a short time he amassed over 40,000 acres of prime Bluegrass farmland.[38]

The original pioneers were struggling farmers, often failures in old Virginia or Carolina or Pennsylvania. They were hearty men, untutored, brave, and long-suffering, as they had to fight Indians and tame a wilderness. They relied on their flintlock rifles and hunting knives. Many of them fought in the Revolutionary War. As uneducated outdoorsmen they frequently made mistakes in filing their land claims at the court or land office. Conscious of the enormous acreage, many did not even bother to record deeds; thus the changing environment, clever land speculators, and scheming lawyers often deprived them of their vast holdings. The court record books reflected numerous survey problems, overlapping claims, inaccurate depositions, and faulty memories. Shrewd lawyers and land speculators openly defrauded many pioneers of their rightful farms. Landmarks often decayed or disappeared. The land litigation lasted for decades; some suits even remained undecided at the time of the Civil War.[39]

Although James French was the first official surveyor at Boone's Fort and completed surveys in the Silver Creek, Rockcastle, and Goose Creek area, the court named Major John Crooke official surveyor for the main period of adjustment. He and his sons surveyed the Wilderness Road, the township of Richmond, and most of the land claims of the Madison Court for fifty years. The court not only relied on Crook but also on his deputy surveyors; on depositions, or interviews with early settlers; on adjoining claims; on official filings, transfers, and record books. The court frequently held hearings. Nonetheless, there were problems.[40]

Two of the most famous and enduring land litigation suits were Higgarson Grubbs vs. William Lipscomb and Green Clay vs. Henry Banta. Each case dragged on for over a decade and in both, as so often happened, the original claimants, Grubbs and Banta, lost their land due to legal technicalities. The plight of these men was often repeated. Daniel Boone and Archibald Woods, two of the most important and well-known Madison County pioneers, lost all their land through technicalities. Boone migrated to Missouri and Woods to Tennessee. Woods, a defender of Estill's Station in 1782, magistrate from 1786 to 1798, and sheriff in 1801, did not return to Madison County until 1820. Due to his impoverished state he applied for a government pension at the age of eighty-four (1833), but he died three years later. Earlier, the penniless Boone fared no better on the Missouri frontier.[41]

By 1785 hundreds of settlers had migrated south of the Kentucky River and built scattered houses along the banks of Otter, Silver, and Tate's Creeks. These pioneers, especially those in the Boonesborough vicinity, circulated Petition Number Twenty-seven and sent it to the

Virginia assembly. It stated that they labored "under great inconveniences," especially in getting to court, and it requested the division of Lincoln County with the formation of a new county south of the Kentucky River that embraced the Paint Lick, Rockcastle, and Cumberland rivers. The assembly soon took up the matter.[42]

James Garrard, Benjamin Logan, and Christopher Greenup, three militia and legislative delegates from the Kentucky country, served on a Virginia house committee to consider further division of the three Kentucky counties with their burgeoning populations. These men were aware of the serious administrative and logistical problems of the pioneers. Consequently, they recommended the formation of three additional counties: Bourbon from Fayette, Mercer and Madison from Lincoln. Although the official organization took months, the path was cleared. Madison residents delayed longer than their counterparts and did not convene until the summer of 1786. Ironically, the House of Delegates approved an enabling act for Kentucky's separation from Virginia in 1785, with the conditions that Kentucky join the Confederation and validate existing Virginia land claims and land laws in the territory. Madisonians, and Kentuckians in general, failed to act.[43]

As to the formation of a new Virginia County, settlers gathered "at the House of George Adams in the County of Madison on Tuesday the twenty-second day of August in the year of our Lord, One Thousand and seven-hundred and eighty-six," and "a Commission of the peace and of ayer and terminer" formally organized Madison County, Virginia. "His excellency, the Governor, Patrick Henry" named "George Adams, John Snoddy, Christopher Irvine, David Gass, James Barnett, John Bowles, Jamie Thompson, Archibald Woods, Nicholas George, and Joseph Kennedy as Justices of the Peace." Joseph Kennedy produced his commission as high sheriff. The magistrates then elected William Irvine as the first clerk of the court and accepted the commissions of James Barnett and Thomas Kennedy as lieutenant and lieutenant-colonel of the Madison Militia respectively. Two farmers recorded the earmarks of their livestock on that first court day.[44]

The court continued to meet at the Adams house that summer. It devoted great attention to security provisions. It recommended Joseph Kennedy and Samuel Estill as captains for the Madison Militia, and drew up a list of potential officers and ensigns for the militia. In the months and years that followed, the court listed militia appointments and used the military districts as early precincts for tax lists. Militia service remained compulsory until Kentucky's third constitution in 1849.[45]

At the commencement of the Madison Court, James French and James Anderson applied for the office of surveyor. The magistrates, unable to reach a decision, referred the matter to the president of the college of William and Mary for an impartial judgment. Four months later the court designated James French as the county's first surveyor.[46]

The early court devoted increasing time to agrarian and economic problems. Due to the large numbers of livestock in the new county, farmers frequently disputed ownership, and the best means to avoid such controversies rested in recording earmarks at court. Green Clay showed great astuteness by recording a complex earmark of a crop and slit in the left ear and two slits in the right ear. Other farmers soon followed suit and also varied the marking in both ears.[47]

The early court met in the homes of prominent citizens. The October and December sessions convened at the residence of David Gass. The Madison Court decided that the most pressing problem was internal improvements. It found existing buffalo traces and paths inadequate for getting produce to markets and decided farmers needed to open new roads as well as to improve the existing routes. The court ordered frequent reviews of roads and appointed supervisors "to regulate the hands and assist in opening and repairing routes." During the Virginia years the Madison magistrates focused on a network of roads from Irvine's Lick to Tate's Creek, from Lincoln Court to Paint Lick, from Crab Orchard to Paint Lick, from Paint Lick to Silver Creek, from Jack's Creek to Boonesborough, and from Boonesborough to Paint Lick.[48]

An expanding populace and economy necessitated a tighter security system as well as the establishment of a permanent courthouse. Security was a primary concern because of the Indian threat as well as a rising tide of crime. Colonel James Barnett, lieutenant of the Madison Militia reported signs of Indians and recent mischief in the county in June, 1789. The Kennedy brothers, located on Silver Creek and Paint Lick, reported several thefts and robberies in the western end of the county. The court, in view of rising crime, designated "the south end of [David Gass'] house" as a public jail despite Sheriff Kennedy's protest over its "sufficiency."[49]

Joseph Kennedy, a big framed man and an expert marksman, had a dangerous job trying to maintain law over the large Madison County wilderness. The sheriff rode a hundred miles at times in order to make an arrest. He deputized some of his family. In the 1780s Kennedy noted that Natchez highwaymen sometimes attacked the Kentucky frontiersmen, travelers, or entrepreneurs, so he concocted a scheme to apprehend the most persistent felons. He spread a rumor that a large sum of money was deposited at the jail. The sheriff and his deputies shortly ambused a dozen badmen in the unsuccessful heist.[50]

At a session on February 27, 1787, the magistrates ordered the construction of a courthouse on the little ridge alongside Black's Branch of Taylor's Fork of Silver Creek. Despite the proximity of the great road, George Adams protested its location because of the "want of the necessary article: water." Nonetheless, the ridge was a compromise between the Boonesborough and Paint Lick communities and the court designated Adams, Barnett, Snoddy, and Archibald Woods, all magistrates of the court, to superintend the erection of the new public buildings. The following day the court appointed Woods and David Gass to "lay off the place for the new court." In April the magistrates authorized five pounds, ten shillings from the first county levies to be paid to Hugh and John Campbell for the *pro tempore* courthouse they would erect. The court also ordered the opening of a road from Silver Creek to the courthouse and the repairing of additional roads in the vicinity.[51]

The Milford area teemed with giant poplar, oak, walnut, and pine trees; cane, snakes, deer, and wild turkeys. A water shortage, the most serious problem, forced men to haul water from the creek in barrels and buckets. Women refused to carry water the quarter of a mile. Travel was by foot or horseback and difficult as well as dangerous. The town developed a dozen houses, including a blacksmith shop, Shackelford's Ordinary, and Oakley's Grog Shop in back of his carpenter's shop and oppostie the courthouse. Travelers sipped 100 percent corn juice, juniper berry tea, apple cider, potato beer, and rhubarb bounce in Milford. William Irvine's refusal to move the county court records to Milford was a serious handicap. Farmers had to travel the additional five miles to Irvine's estate along Tate's Creek in order to complete most of their court business.[52]

Despite the problems the magistrates faced in little Milford, the court attracted outstanding men in this early period. Some could be labeled Virginia aristocrats; others were agressive rising men of ambition. The court positions offered more than prestige. Magistrates held significant appointive powers often providing jobs for relatives. They had enormous economic powers by administering estates; appointing guardians; bonding apprentices; collecting taxes; regulating rates for ordinaries (taverns), ferries and turnpikes. They also designated the locations of potential roads, supervised the maintainence of the poor, determined salaries and fees, approved warehouse and mill construction, and awarded damages in a variety of suits.[53]

On the Madison Court magistrates rotated political offices. Annually or biannually the senior magistrate became eligible for the office of high sheriff. Here he possessed the power to collect taxes, nominate deputies, and receive a variety of incidental fees for transporting criminals, evicting paupers, or collecting delinquent taxes. Many of the justices held commissions in the militia; supervised the construction of roads; collected tithables; supervised elections; settled estates—a very profitable exercise; took in orphans or aged indigents for which they received compensation; approved liquor licenses; set liquor rates; approved mills, warehouses, and roads. The court appointed clerks, constables, jailers, surveyors, and attorneys. Few magistrates in old Madison County failed to achieve impressive wealth.[54]

The early justices did not have to have any legal training, and Archibald Woods, Junior, was one of the few lawyers on the early Madison County Court. Farmers dominated the court and made the most of their opportunities. Membership varied from seven to twenty members, but a quorum of three magistrates was necessary. Majority votes were also mandatory. The farmer-magistrates expressed keen interest in roads, mills, and warehouses for obvious economic reasons. The Madison County Court was unusually wealthy, and statistics show the magistrates owning eight times as much land, seven times as many slaves, and two and a half times as much other taxable property as their contempories. Green Clay, who joined the court in 1794, owned one-fourth of all land in the county and continued to be the largest landowner in the nineteenth century, with over 40,000 acres.[55]

On the local court all magistrates enjoyed political power, and the court always nominated or offered to nominate the two senior justices for high sheriff, with the governor making the final appointment. The sheriff's position was the most coveted, as he was commissioned to collect county and state taxes. Moreover, he sold deputyships to the highest bidders, often members of his own family. Well-to-do farmers could purchase a commission from the sheriff and, as constables, serve summonses and papers for the county, another profitible job.

County clerks enjoyed some prestige and could make a significant profit, but they lacked the political power of the magistrates. The court did insist on rotation of office due to the fear that age might deny someone seniority at the most opportune time. The Madison Court "shared the wealth" on a far wider scale than most of the other central Kentucky counties. As noted in the following table, the sheriff's office was particularly subject to rotation.

SHERIFFS OF MADISON COUNTY: 1786-1804[56]

1786-87	Joseph Kennedy
1788	George Adams
1789-90	John Snoddy
1790-91	David Gass
1792	John Gass
1793-94	John Pittman
1795-97	James Anderson
1798-99	James Barnett (The court records also refer to Joseph Barnett as sheriff)
1800-02	Archibald Woods
1803-04	Robert Caldwell

The eighteenth century Madison Court established a policy of nepotism which permeated the county's politial system for the remainder of the ante-bellum period. This heavy emphasis on "family" was in the Virginia tradition and resulted in an early political aristocracy. Of the original justices, Adams, Snoddy, Irvine, Gass, Barnett, Woods, and Kennedy, along with their families, dominated Madison County development well into the nineteenth century. Joseph Kennedy became the first sheriff, served as captain in the Militia, and supervised repairs on the jail and courthouse. He secured the appointment of his brother Thomas as lieutenant colonel of the militia and as a commissioner of the land tax, while Andrew Kennedy became a tax commissioner. Following his tenure as sheriff, Kennedy regained his seat on the court in 1789.[57]

Thomas Kennedy, like his brother, had been at Boonesborough; had secured large landholdings in the Paint Lick area; was an original member of the Madison Court and an officer in the militia. Thomas held higher political office by representing the county in the Virginia legislature in 1788 and 1791. He served at the Constitutional Convention in 1792 and was the first state senator from Madison County in the new Kentucky legislature of 1792. He later resisted removal of the county seat from Milford and, after losing the battle, secured formation of the new Garrard County in 1799. He served as its first representative in the state legislature.[58]

Sheriff George Adams was a magistrate on the original court and was supervisor of roads. He collected tithables, and he returned to the court in 1789 when he completed his term as sheriff. His son John was a constable, a commissioner of the tax revenue, and a deputy. Matthew Adams was captain of the militia. John Snoddy, a colonel of the militia, a road supervisor, and high sheriff in 1789-90, was an original magistrate as well as Auditor of public accounts. He returned to the court after his tenure as sheriff but resigned as magistrate in 1801 over a tiff with Archibald Woods concerning Woods' selection as sheriff. Perhaps to pacify Snoddy, Woods selected John Snoddy, Jr. as his deputy in 1802. Shortly thereafter the court recommended Samuel Snoddy for a magistrate's seat.[59]

James Barnett, an original magistrate, was lieutenant of the militia, high sheriff in 1798-99, a commissioner of the tax, superintendent of public buildings; and he was active in early politics. His brother (or son) Joseph became a magistrate in 1807. Schuyler Barnett was a deputy. Archibald Woods, an original jsutice, was auditor of public accounts, collected tithables, helped choose the court site, surveyed land, and served as sheriff in 1800 to 1802. His brother Samuel was the first coroner. Archibald Woods, Jr. was named commonwealth attorney for the court in 1809 and remained one of the most influential lawyers in the county. Young Woods eventually trained his nephew William H. Caperton in law.[60]

Although the Irvines, Clays, and Caldwells became even more important in the 1800s, they made their first impressions on county history at the eighteenth century court. Christopher Irvine was an original magistrate, while his son William was the first court clerk, an election officer, and captain of the militia. David, Christopher's grandson, followed his father into the office of court clerk. Thus William (1786-1819) and David (1819-1845) served as clerks throughout most of the ante-bellum period. David C. Irvine served intermittently on the court up to 1809 and returned in 1811. A year later he applied for a tavern license in Richmond. David also served as paymaster for the Seventh Regiment of the Kentucky Militia. Edmund Irvine served his uncle as deputy clerk, and the court authorized Benjamin Irvine to serve as a Presbyterian minister. The Irvines accumulated large tracts of land in the present Lexington Road area as well as in Richmond.[61]

Robert Caldwell, a son-in-law of William Irvine, was the most successful early merchant and taverner in Madison County. Caldwell served on the court by 1795 and became high sheriff in 1803-1804. He returned to the court in 1810 and shortly became manager of the Wilderness

Road. He became a trustee of Richmond in 1815. In 1828 he or his son
Robert Caldwell served as high sheriff of Madison County.[62]

Green Clay served as a commissioner of tax and as captain of the
militia by 1787. Although he represented Madisonians at the Virginia
Ratification Convention in 1788 and at the Virginia House of Burgesses
in 1789, he did not receive appointment to the local court until 1794. By
then he owned too much land to be ignored. Two years later his brother
Thomas became a magistrate and then lieutenant colonel of the militia.
Green Clay, however, was destined to become the dominant political
and economic figure in the county. Few men had greater impact on the
county's history.[63] The Clays, like the Irvines, Woodses, Snoddys, and
Kennedys, soon constituted a ruling political aristocracy for the new
county.

As Madisonians produced increasing surpluses in the 1780s, they
required more regulation and protection. Magistrates ordered the
"Fourth Tuesday in every month designated as a day for holding the
sales in the Clerk's Office." Court Day became a popular social and
economic event in the following years. The justices regulated ordinaries
through the liquor and provender rates, while the appearance of lawyers
in court requesting certification amply attested to the rising business as
well as crime cycle in the community. Thomas Hall, the future deputy
state attorney and Thomas Todd, the future Constitutional Convention
secretary and gubernatorial candidate, appeared before the court and
became the first attorneys authorized to practice law in Madison
County. John Allen, the famous Bourbon County politico, and Christopher Greenup, a future governor, soon followed suit.[64]

Madison county's economic growth is obvious from the types of
court cases these early lawyers prosecuted. Common felonies included
retailing spirits without a license, horse stealing, damage caused by mill
construction, and breach of peace (especially public drunkenness).
Adam Starnes was the first bootlegger tried and found guilty by the
Madison Court in 1787. The magistrates tried to regulate social behavior, as evidenced by trials for public drunkenness, profane swearing,
insulting the court, and buggering of mares. Nothing seemed to work.[65]

With the increasing use of the public gaol (jail), the court ordered
Thomas Crews to raise the chimney six inches higher than the house,
which might catch fire, and to plaster the walls with lime mortar and
remove earth from the floor. The court also appointed Samuel Estill to
repair the temporary courthouse and to construct a building for public
use on the Estill land. The court was equally concerned with the need
for a public warehouse.[66]

On June 24, 1788, the magistrates summoned John Collier, a farmer,
and asked him to construct a warehouse on his land. The court ordered a
survey of a roadway from Collier's to the main road connecting the
Tate's Creek area to the courthouse. It appointed a road surveyor and
ordered all hands to assist in opening the road. The court instructed
Collier to build a public warehouse "twenty-four feet long, eighteen feet
wide" at an appointed place encompassing an acre of land. It named

Aaron Lewis and Robert Rodes as building superintendents, and the Collier (Boonesborough) Warehouse prepared for business. When James French, the county surveyor, requested a leave of absence, the court named the popular Aaron Lewis as acting surveyor. It also ordered the examination of Daniel Boone as a capable deputy surveyor. The court further authorized payments to David Lynch and Harris Mays for construction work on the courthouse.[67]

The Virginia legsilature recognized the establishment of Milford Courthouse on the land of Samuel and John Estill in 1789. It designated George Adams, Archibald Woods, Green Clay, William Irvine, James Barnett, James French, and William Rodes as town trustees. Significantly, it named farmer John Miller as trustee. The court, accepting a degree of social responsibility, also laid off the county into three districts "for the purpose of electing overseers of the poor." These included the Paint Lick, Silver Creek, and Tate's Creek districts. James French reported surveying ten acres of appropriated land for public use including two acres for prison bounds in Milford. He also moved that the magistrates relinquish the court's right to a strip of public land extending to a spring to the trustees of "Millerford." The town was named Milford by Captain John Kincaid in honor of his favorite slave.[68]

By 1790 the court had recorded a plat of the town of Milford, and the following year it named John Miller as colonel and Samuel Estill as major of the Madison Militia. A year later Estill also became a magistrate on the court. As Kentucky approached statehood in 1792, a group of Madisonians followed the leadership of magistrate Green Clay and openly lobbied to secure Boonesborough as the new state capital. Clay and his brother signed a subscription list, with Clay offering $1,000 cash and 10,000 acres of land, while his borther Thomas offered 3,000 acres of land, if the delegates selected Boonesborough. Some thirty other Madisonians pledged $8,000 in money and a grand total of 18,500 acres. Frankfort's more generous bid and its location between Lexington and Louisville, two other competitors, made it the ultimate compromise choice.[69]

By 1790, Boonesborough, the first Kentucky town to be incorporated, had expanded to over one hundred houses. It boasted a town "commons" of over five hundred acres on which the frontiersmen could graze their livestock. It boasted a warehouse, a ferry, and a post office. Some farmers shipped produce from Boonnesborough to New Orleans. John Halley, a Boonesborough farmer, departed for the Crescent City on April 27, 1791, with a fleet of four boats laden with tobacco and farm produce. He kept a detailed journal of this voyage down river. The trip took six weeks by water and required an additional four weeks to return home with pack horses laden with sugar, cloth, and other necessities. Between Milford and Boonesborough, Madison countians enjoyed a unique frontier advantage-two bustling economic centers.[70]

During those last years as a Virginia county, Madisonians maintained an active concern for Indian invasions and greatly emphasized a strong militia. In 1791 the Madison Militia numbered 931 men with twenty-one officers. Of these 758 men were "fit for duty." Madisonians generally opposed the adoption of the federal Constitution of 1788, and Green Clay voted against its adoption at the Virginia Ratification Convention, while William Irvine abstained. Ten of Kentucky's fourteen delegates voted negatively. Farmer George Adams was greatly concerned over trade rights on the Mississippi River and possibly reflected some local opinion by becoming a part of the infamous Spanish Conspiracy masterminded by James Wilkinson in 1788, when frustrated Kentuckians flirted with the possibility of becoming a part of the Spanish empire. Adams' career did not suffer from his involvement.[71]

With one exception, the Madisonians who represented the county in the Virginia legislature continued to hold sway in the new Kentucky commonwealth. Richard Callaway, the Kentucky County representative of 1777 and 1779 was killed by Indians the following year. By 1788 Green Clay and Thomas Kennedy, prominent magistrates and landowners, traveled to the capital in Richmond. The following year Clay and John Miller served in the legislature. Higgarson Grubbs joined Miller in 1790, as Madisonians apparently worked out a rotation system for the Virginia assembly. Thomas Kennedy returned to Richmond in 1791 and was the last delegate, as Kentuckians prepared for their independence the following year.[72]

In the Kentucky Constitutional Convention of 1792, Madison County had three delegates: Kennedy, Grubbs, and Thomas Clay. Interestingly, Grubbs and Clay joined John Miller as Madison's three state representatives in Frankfort a few months later.[73] By the time the state of Kentucky emerged, Madisonians, as a result of their Virginia experience, wielded some influence in the politics of the new state. Yet their interest often remained parochial.

Madisonians felt the Virginia legislature had ignored them at times. Certainly their voice on taxation, their underrepresentation, and the Old Dominion's failure to assure them of their land claims aggravated the relationship between the settlers and the government back in Richmond. Although local interests varied considerably, most Madisonians recognized the economic opportunities and wanted to exploit these as quickly as possible. Agriculture was the key to success. Madisonians spent the remainder of the eighteenth century developing an agrarian economy.

Chapter Two

AN AGRARIAN ECONOMY

Even the long hunters entering the Madison wilderness in the 1760s immediately recognized the agricultural opportunities the rich soil in the Kentucky River basin offered. Water filtered through the limestone, characteristic of the entire Bluegrass region, adding minerals which enriched the soil and strengthened the bones of livestock, especially cattle and horses. Men claimed land by clearing acreage, erecting a house, and planting a crop of corn. For early settlers, corn was the staple crop for human and animal diets. Farmers mashed, fermented, and distilled it into a special liquor blend possible only in the Bluegrass, where the limestone water gave it a special flavor. In the Madison area, farmers easily raised rye, oats, and tobacco. Early court record books abounded in requests to construct mills, start distilleries, and open taverns.[1] The nature of the Madisonian economy took shape.

Farmers distilled corn because that was the best way of preserving it as well as transporting it down river or back east. Madisonian interest in the liquor industry permeated the old court records. As early as March 27, 1787, less than a year after its establishment by Virginia, the county court drew up a list of liquor and provender rates. The highest rates affected rum and whiskey but also covered meals, lodging, and even pasturage for the livestock. The following table was typical of the Virginia rates as adopted by the Madison magistrates in 1787.[2]

Rum by the gallon	1 pound, no shillings (rather high)
Whiskey by the gallon	10 shillings, no pence
Dinner	1 shilling, 3 pence
Breakfast	1 shilling, 10 pence
Lodging	6 pence
Pasturage, Hay or Fodder 24 hours	6 pence
Corn per gallon	4 pence

In subsequent years the court set new liquor rates almost annually, and required tavern or ordinary owners to renew their licenses each year. The court records showed an increasing variety of beverages, services, and charges by ordinary operators. Competition tended to lower rates for many liquors. By 1790 taverns added brandy and beer to their liquor lists, diversified their menus, distinguished between hot and cold meals and meals without beverages, and even listed rates for beds with or without clean sheets. By 1804 Madison County taverns offered any beverage available in the Bluegrass, including rum, wine, French brandy, old peach brandy, malt beer, cider, and whiskey.[3]

The profitability as well as the role of liquor in the early Madisonian economy was obvious to all. The court indicted and convicted farmers for retailing liquors without a license. One of the first offenders, Adam Starnes, carried the spirits in his leggings or high boots into little Milford and, like so many of his contemporaries, imparted the name bootlegger to us.[4] Most farmers opted for the court license and sold their liquor legally. The tavern business became a lucrative enterprise. On March 1, 1791, Samuel Shackelford, Jr. petitioned the court for the right to keep a tavern in Milford and entered bond at the clerk's office. His was the first license awarded by the Madison magistrates. John Phelps soon followed his example, opening a second tavern at the county seat. In 1793 Samuel Estill was awarded a tavern license, and Milford boasted three ordinaries. While the three men continued to renew their licenses, numerous additional taverns opened in the county during the remainder of the eighteenth century, adequately attesting to the popularity of the liquor business.[5]

In 1794 the court raised all liquor prices but especially discriminated against imported beverages in order to protect local producers and encourage consumption of domestic brews. The price of local rum was one pound, four shillings, while West Indies rum brought one pound, sixteen shillings; domestic wine was one pound, four shillings, while Madeira wine brought one pound, sixteen shillings. Higgarson Grubbs, sensing that a tavern might do well in the countryside, opened a popular establishment in the county, and three other farmers followed suit. The county soon had more taverns than little Milford. The court noted the increasing applications for liquor licenses.[6]

Significantly, in 1798, following the court's decision to move its operations to John Miller's farm, now Richmond, it awarded the opportunistic Miller the first ordinary license in the new county seat. Miller advanced his cause by donating two acres of public land for a courthouse as well as a log house near his residence which served as the public jail. Colonel Miller's Tavern, another log house, located on the corner of First and Main streets, served as the first hotel in the county by 1801 and was superceded by the brick building of 1812. By that time Groogat's Tavern also served as a hotel. 1812 was a significant year because the court finally set the liquor rates in dollars.[7] The new rates were:

Rum	$6.00 per gallon
Wine	$6.00 per gallon
French Brandy	$6.00 per gallon
Peach Brandy	$2.00 per gallon
Malt Beer	.50 per gallon
Cider	.06½ per quart
Whiskey	.25 by ½ pint

Taverns in Richmond often furnished rooms for travelers and hence developed into hotels. Tarlton Embry opened a hotel in 1815, and John B. Francis bought Miller's establishment and renamed it Francis House, which kept its doors opened up to 1860. Groogat's Richmond Hotel announced "Travellers and other visitants are respectfully solicited," while each ordinary posted its own symbol, such as a buffalo, a wooden Indian, or cross keys.[8]

The liquor business hit a snag after the War of 1812 and the court lowered its rates, which underlined the economic depression that carried over into the 1820s. Moreover, the cheaper liquors proved more popular, as Madisonians consumed increasing amounts of gin and Rumple, both of which sold for fifty cents a half pint. The following year Madisonians appeared before the court in record numbers requesting licenses to open or continue operating taverns. In the January, 1818, session, John Crooke, the long-time surveyor and math teacher, opened an ordinary at his home, while four other tavern keepers renewed their licenses. In April the court licensed a record nine ordinaries, bringing the spring total to fifteen.[9] One can only wonder if Madisonians were drowning their economic frustrations.

In the 1820s the *Richmond Republican* carried advertisements by local grocers who entered the liquor business by selling bottled spirits. By 1823, James W. Garrison may have been the first grocer to sell gin and whiskey in Madison County, but even the popular and conservative Howard Brothers sold wine. Despite the new competition, many of the same old families continued to dominate the liquor industry from the pioneer days into the 1830s. The Shackelford, Phelps, Miller, Francis, Newby, and Million families renewed their licenses as late as 1839, the year Sarah Reid became the first woman ever to receive a liquor license in Richmond. Although several members from these distilling families held political offices in the county, only Thomas Francis relinquished his license on becoming sheriff in 1843.[10]

By the 1840s the Madisonian economy had changed in its emphasis. Although it maintained an agrarian base and although corn production increased to 1,424,856 bushels, making Madison County fourth in the state, farmers no longer distilled their corn but used it to feed an expanding number of livestock. They used most corn to feed the largest livestock center collection in the Bluegrass state, producing the most cattle, the most sheep, the third largest number of swine, and the fifth largest number of mules. Insignificant amounts of the 1.5 million bushels of corn and almost 200,000 bushels of rye could be siphoned off for liquor.[11]

The development of the mill was an immediate result of corn and rye production. Farmers had to grind their grain into grist to use as flour and feed. Although a few mills, like that of Christopher Irvine, existed in the area prior to the organization of the county, the first reference to a mill in the Madison Court Records, occurred in June, 1787, when a farmer, Philip Williams, came to court and complained about damage to his property caused by neighbor William Hamm's mill. On June 24, 1788, John Carpenter and Archibald Woods petitioned the new court to allow them to build a watermill on Otter Creek. The court not only approved all petitions but also investigated all damage claims and sometimes forced millers to pay farmers in pounds or shillings.[12]

On July 2, 1793, Nicholas Hawkins of Silver Creek came before the court and requested the right to erect a water gristmill. As usual the court acted on his appeal by appointing the sheriff and a panel of twelve jurors to see if the "creek above and below will overflow the lands, houses, orchards, cottage, or office of any adjoining proprietor or endanger health" or "annoy neighbors" or prevent "the passage of fish." The panel reported approval in an *ad quod damun* decision, calling for the opening or improvement of a road to the mill site.[13] The presence of so many small streams in the area encouraged utilization of water power at the gristmills.

By the 1790s mill construction fever was rampant in Madison County. The court order books teemed with requests, panels, and approvals of new mill sites. In the late eighteenth century Elias Barnes operated a popular mill on Silver Creek; Richard and Samuel Haden had a gristmill at the mouth of Muddy Creek; Archibald Woods built a mill on Muddy Creek; Green Clay operated one on Tate's Creek. By 1809 Andrew Bogie operated a large mill on Silver Creek. He sold grain and wheat at his mill and opened a lumber business on the side. Bogie, at 480 pounds, was undoubtedly one of the most massive men residing on the Madison frontier.[14]

Although the tavern and the mill solved part of the farmer's problems, the warehouse was the third ingredient necessary to his economic success. Early Madison farmers planted significant amounts of tobacco as well as corn and rye. The early land laws required farmers to raise corn, but many, like Richard Callaway, planted tobacco prior to 1780 as a cash crop. The Virginia legislature provided for tobacco inspection at Boonesborough as early as 1787. The Madison court, like all its frontier contemporaries, used tobacco as a medium of exchange and paid all salaries and services in tobacco. The 1787 court set both the sheriff's and clerk's salaries at 1,500 pounds in tobacco, called for payment of prison and courthouse contractors in tobacco, and even paid court witnesses in tobacco. It ordered the sheriff to collect tithables and noted 20,000 pounds of tobacco would be necessary to meet bills.[15]

By April, 1789, the court recommended David Crews and William Jones as inspectors of tobacco for John Collier's warehouse in Boonesborough. The farmer's temporary construction proved inadequate and the following year the court ordered him to erect a building "forty feet long and twenty-four feet wide" and to complete construction by the fall. On September 6, 1790, Collier recorded the plat for his warehouse, and the tobacco inspectors gave a return on the hogsheads of tobacco they inspected.[16]

The Collier warehouse proved a problem for years. When the inspectors made their 1791 report, noting the inspection and shipment of 180 hogsheads of tobacco, they complained of the failure of the owner to enclose the house and noted the absence of any room for casks. Surprisingly, the court then named Collier himself as the new inspector of the Boonesborough Warehouse.[17]

The imbroglio over Collier's warehouse continued when the court ordered Aaron Lewis and Robert Rodes to try the weights, and make the necessary adjustments for the purpose of weighing tobacco at Collier's. The court instructed James French to make scales for the warehouse. In 1793 it designated a picker of tobacco and accepted a report on the warehouse as lacking "locks and hinges for the doors and weights" and as "unfit" for storing tobacco.[18] Three years later David Crews, the original inspector, reported Collier's as containing thirteen hogsheads and unfit for reception.[19]

Tobacco production accelerated at the close of the eighteenth century, and Governor James Garrard named John Goggin as Inspector of flour and hemp at Goggin's Warehouse in 1798, bringing the total number of tobacco warehouses in Madison County to three; Boonesborough, Biggerstaff's, and Goggin's. The new Goggin's Warehouse was forty-eight feet long and twenty-four feet wide, with a half-pitch cover of joint shingles and a large room capable of storing 150 hogsheads. By contrast the Boonesborough Warehouse reported sixty hogsheads inspected and shipped while Biggerstaff's Warehouse reported 123 hogsheads inspected and 122 shipped out.[20]

By 1800 Green Clay owned Jack's Creek Warehouse and planned the erection of a second one near Stone's Ferry on the Kentucky River. Clay's entry into the warehouse business evidenced the profitability and anticipated growth of local business. His Jack's Creek Warehouse handled a record 202 hogsheads and led to the request, approval, and completion of the Stone's Ferry project. The court ordered Clay and Goggin to enclose their new warehouses and appointed Clay and his friend Robert Tevis, another magistrate, to secure weights and scales for both of Clay's warehouses. Clay purchased the first London cast-iron weights and scales for his Jack's Creek enterprise and then requested the court to complete three roads on his land that would connect his warehouses to the main public roads.[21]

By 1800 Green Clay had emerged as a dominant economic leader in Madison County. Clay's diversified economic empire included 40,000 acres of Madison farmland, grist mills, distilleries, taverns, tobacco, slaves, surveying fees, toll roads, a resort, and two large warehouses. Clay and Robert Tevis, both magistrates, reported on the condition of

Clay's Jack's Creek Warehouse and secured the selection of Thomas Watts, a Clay ally, as tobacco inspector in 1802. Despite the accelerating competition, Groggin's Warehouse continued a brisk business.[22]

Green Clay portrait by Chester Harding. J. T. Dorris, *Glimpses of Historic Madison County, Kentucky,* **23.**

By 1807 a decidely independent inspector, Mitchell Overstreet, caused problems for the warehouse owners, especially Green Clay. Overstreet insisted on the discontinuance of inspections at Jack's Creek Warehouse until Clay made significant repairs. When Clay requested an additional investigation Overstreet returned, again complaining of the locks and bolts and stating that the warehouse did not meet the standards "requested by law." A fourth and fifth report to the court reaffirmed Clay's failure to meet legal requirements. In February, 1808, the frustrated Clay and his fellow justices requested that Robert Tevis accompany Overstreet on the next inspection. This time the return concluded Jack's Creek Warehouse was "sufficient for safe keeping of tobacco." When Overstreet resigned his post to accept a seat on the Madison Court, Clay's old friend Thomas Watts became the new inspector of tobacco, hemp, and flour at Jack's Creek Warehouse.[23] Everyone was happy!

Watts soon reported the record inspection of 234 hogsheads of tobacco at Jack's Creek Warehouse in 1808, although he noted "the falling in of the back wall." Goggin's Warehouse continued its activity, and the court approved weights and scales at the new Drowning Creek Warehouse. The following year Madison farmers raised a record crop of tobacco and all the warehouses were busy. Despite the deteriorating condition of Jack's Creek, it reported a record 378 hogsheads inspected and shipped. The Boonesborough Warehouse reported 230 hogsheads, Drowning Creek had seventy-one, and the reviving Goggin's reported 124 hogsheads inspected.[24]

In 1810 Watts finally declared Jack's Creek Warehouse "insufficient" and in need of considerable repair. At last Clay repaired it, and Watts reported the inspection of 372 hogsheads of tobacco. During the War of 1812 the other warehouses declined in activity, although Haden's Muddy Creek Warehouse struggled to remain competitive. By 1814, David Chenault was inspector for Haden's. Despite his promotion to the Madison Court in 1816, he continued to inspect tobacco, even weights and scales. In 1817 he reported a record 252 hogsheads at Haden's Warehouse and also announced their shipment to New Orleans. Jack's Creek maintained the lead with 260 hogsheads inspected, and the county shipped out some 700 hogsheads, signifying the largest tobacco crop since 1809, with its 803 inspected hogsheads.[25]

Tobacco was king. 1818 brought new records for tobacco production and warehouse activity. The old Boonesborough Warehouse reported a record 312 hogsheads inspected, Jack's Creek reported a record 438 hogsheads dispensed, while the other warehouses continued to compete for smaller business. On the death of his father, John, in 1819, Stephen Goggin became inspector at his own warehouse and announced its enlargement. A new Tate's Creek Warehouse opened in 1821. It was the largest in the county, 100 feet long and 30 feet wide, with a stone foundation, wooden pillars, board rafters, and proper enclosure. The court named Robert Million as inspector. All the old records fell in 1823 when Madisonians produced over 1,200 hogsheads of tobacco. Clay's Jack's Creek Warehouse reported a record 528 hogsheads. Tate's Creek shipped a record 515, and Goggin's Warehouse reported a record 151 hogsheads.[26]

By the close of the 1820s Captain Stephen Goggin recognized his survival in the warehouse competition with Jack's Creek and Tate's Creek depended upon major improvements in his building, so he weatherboarded the place and added a new shingle roof, a stone foundation, a special door, oak posts, and poplar planks to the floor. Immediately, he announced a revival of business, with 138 hogsheads, the third largest inspection in the warehouse's history. Although the court continued to supervise warehouse inspections and order repairs, the existing facilities served the public's need for the duration of the era. Tobacco remained one of the most important crops for Madison County farmers; however, it was only one facet of an increasingly diversified economy.[27]

Although early Madison County farmers relied on corn and tobacco as the staples, they raised other crops. The early tobacco inspectors were authorized to inspect hemp and flour as well. The Boonesborough Warehouse inlcuded a crop of hemp as early as 1797. Farmers who raised hemp frequently raised flax 'as well. By 1806 a Silver Creek Mill announced construction of a factory to spin hemp and flax on machinery powered by water. Two years later the state legislature authorized the Madison Hemp and Flax Spinning Company, with Henry Clay as an original proprietor, to sell 1,000 shares of stock at twenty-five dollars a share to the public. This company, having 160 spindles, encouraged the production of more hemp and flax. By 1813 Thomas C. Howard, a leading merchant, advertised for flax seed. A decade later Colonel William Rodes made rope and hemp bagging at his factory which sold significant quantities to southern planters for a decade. Hemp and flax production accelerated into the civil war period. In 1850 the county ranked fourth in the state, with 2,973 bushels of flax seed. By 1850 the county also raised enough beans and peas to rank first in the state. Madisonians also were in the top ten in production of potatoes, rye, and oats.[28]

Hemp stacks in Madison County. *Kentucky Progress Magazine,* **Vol. 8 (Summer, 1935), 378.**

Pioneers plodding along the Wilderness Road often brought livestock with them. Boonesborough settlers, like Richard Callaway, had a variety of livestock, including cattle, sheep, and hogs, as early as 1780.

George Phelps introduced the first jack stock into the area. As early settlers killed off the surplus of buffalo and turkey they became increasingly dependent on their livestock as meat for their tables. By 1789 John Halley sent barges to New Orleans laden with tobacco, flour, and notably, lard and bacon which attested to the increasing swine production in the county.[29]

By the 1790s Green Clay imported Merino sheep and continued to breed one of the county's finest flocks into the 1820s, when his son Cassius disposed of them and popularized Southdowns. Sheep production accelerated after the War of 1812 and led to the establishment of local carding factories and fulling mills. Lewis Francis had a treadmill with a thirty-foot wheel powered by horses, mules, and oxen. By 1812 William Brown and Joseph Lee had two treadmills in their Richmond carding factory. Surprisingly, the business even spun cotton and Lee continued operating the factory into the 1830s. Madisonians remained first in sheep production as late as 1850 with 28,915.[30]

As Madisonian production of fine livestock increased, farmers took horses, mules, cattle, and even hogs southward to the Carolinas. Spartanburg, Greenville, and Charleston, South Carolina were popular markets. As early as 1811, Benjamin Estill took twelve horses to Charleston. The following year he returned there with 100 horses, paid a fifteen dollar stable bill, and earned a nice profit. During the War of 1812 Estill drove hogs to South Carolina and to Virginia. By the 1820s Richmond newspapers carried advertisements from the New Orleans market requesting pork, bacon, and lard, among other agricultural commodities. Howard Williams and Company asked farmers to bring hog lard to the Richmond store. An ad in the Christmas edition, 1822, requested that farmers prevent their hogs from rooting along the turnpike. To aid farmers in disposing of their swine or beef, Charles Brooking frequently advertised his butchering business in the Richmond papers. Public barbecues were frequent on July 4, at militia musters, and at political rallies in the 1820s. For the duration of the ante-bellum period Madison County farmers produced the finest and greatest numbers of livestock in the state. In 1850 Madisonians remained first in cattle production with 18,456, third in swine production with 57,495, and fifth in mules with 8,635. Madison County was the livestock center not only of the Bluegrass, but of the entire state.[31]

Although cattle, sheep, and hogs determined the wealth of Madison farmers, many early settlers and nineteenth century aristocrats displayed an interest in horses. Madisonians never developed the fine horse breeding farms of their Bluegrass neighbors to the north, in Fayette and Bourbon counties, but they expressed an avid interest in horseflesh. Boonesborough settlers brought horses and other livestock to Kentucky in the 1770s. A decade later the Madison County tax lists reflected horse ownership by farmers like David Crews, Higgarson Grubbs, Green Clay, George Phelps, and Robert Rodes. In 1789 the Virginia legislature enacted a law preventing horseracing in Milford, the new county seat. Madison magistrates noted the first horse felony in May, 1787, and at that same session charged a farmer with "feloniously buggering a mare." By 1791 the court charged another man with "riding his horse through the different parts of the Courthouse."[32]

In 1795 the magistrates summoned Andrew Lackey to court for failing to list a stud horse for tax purposes, fining him six dollars for omitting the horse on the tax tables. Madisonians always were protective of their horses, and in 1806 the court erected a public gallows at the forks of Muddy Creek and Four Mile Road to be used for hanging horse theives. The court order books constantly referred to the maintainence and clearing of a stray pen at the courthouse and sometimes referred to the expenses of providing stabling or pasturage for stray horses as well as other animals.[33]

Richmond Republican, **April 16, 1823. EKU Archives.**

By 1812 Madisonians like Benjamin Estill were selling horses in the Deep South, especially in South Carolina. The following year the Richmond Jockey Club met at Irvine's Inn, which boasted the best liquors in town. Aside from hunting, card playing, and lodges, racing was one of the most popular pastimes in the county during the war era. Early advertisements in *the Luminary* showed saddles and wagons were available. By the 1820s the *Richmond Republican* carried a variety of news for the horse enthusiasts. It noted rewards for horses stolen and displayed their value, with twenty dollar rewards for regular horses and hundred dollar rewards for stud horses. Samuel Parrish, R. B. Williams, and Charles C. Porter competed for the saddling and harness market by frequently advertising their businesses. There is little doubt about the popularity of horseback riding in the era. Robert Caldwell's Blacksmith Shop reported an abundance of shoes, nails, and other livestock aids. Farmers advertised stud horses as standing on their respective farms and announced stud fees. In the 1820s Gallatin and Post Boy were popular stud horses of the area.[34]

Madisonians enjoyed horse racing and by 1823 the local newspaper announced "Sports of the Turf," stating that, on Wednesday, October 29, the Richmond Turf would open. The racetrack held sweepstake races for two-year-olds on a mile track, charging a twenty dollar entry fee. Five colts were immediately listed as entries. Thomas E. Stuart promised to serve refreshments. Despite the popularity of the fall races, difficulties surfaced publicly prior to the spring trials. Ebenezer Best assured the public that the fall races had not been fixed, as rumor had it, and that his horse had honestly beaten that of farmer J. H. Gentry. Furthermore, he stated the jockeys had done their best and he promised to run his same filly against the Gentry horse or any other horse for a $1,000 quarter-mile race. He denounced the falsehoods circulated by losers at the Richmond Turf. Apparently the possibility of fixing at the track deterred few Madisonians from attending the spring races the first Thursday through Saturday in May, 1824 (long before the first Derby Day!). The newspaper soon announced a purse for three-year-old colts and one and two-mile heats, and promised the public that everyone would enjoy a day at the Richmond Track in May.

The Richmond Track's success led to additional notices of other racing events in 1824. Fall races ran from Thursday, October 1, through Saturday, October 3. The course featured two-year-old colts and raised the entry fee to fifty dollars, ample testimony of the increasing popularity of horse racing in the area. The *Richmond Republican* announced additional races for "sportsmen" at the new Bowling Green Turf, four miles east of Lancaster.[36]

The accelerating interest in horses was evidenced in the tax lists and court order books as well as the newspaper. In 1841 Peter and Alexander Tribble paid taxes on twenty-seven horses, a large number for the area. Yet Madison County, which dominated so many statistical categories in livestock, made little imprint on the horse industry. However,

To Sportsmen.

IT is proposed to open a purse for three years old colts, to run on the Richmond track, the first Thursday, Friday and Saturday in May next, agreeably to the rule of turf racing. The first day two mil̄ heats, entrance two hundred dollars, to be run on Thursday; second day, one mile heats, entrance one hundred dollars; third day, one single mile, entrance fifty dollars. Each colt that is three years old carry eighty-six pounds, fillies excepted, which are to be allowed three pounds in riling. Three colts to make a race each day, The colt to be named and so designated, that no other is to run in the place thereof.

There are two colts entered; the subscription paper will remain open in the hands of Maj. Howard until the first of April, for the benefit of those who think they have fine colts.

March 19, 1824—22–3t.

To the Public.

HAVING recently understood, that some disappointed persons have stated, and endeavored to convince the public, that there was an understanding between James H. Gentry and myself, in relation to a race which was run last Fall between him and me, previous to the running of the race ; that it was to be a jockey race, or in other words, that his horse was to be held up, and that my mare was to beat, for the purpose of taking in certain individuals. I now avail myself of this opportunity of publishing to the world, that such statements are false and slanderous; and I challenge those men, who have fabricated and given currency to such statement, to produce any testimony, that will afford the least grounds of suspicion, that there was any trick or fraud in the matter. And to satisfy any reasonable mind, that there was no preconcerted arrangement, between Mr. Gentry and myself.

I now proffer to run my same filly against the very same horse, or any other horse or mare the world affords, for the sum of one thousand dollars in specie, the distance of one quarter of a mile, with a catch upon each. I confidently expect after this has reached those individuals who have been so active in circulating the above statements, for the purpose of casting infamy and disgrace upon my reputation, will promptly come forward and accept of this banter; or else desist from any further propagation of their foul and malicious calumny.

                     Ebenezer Best.
March 12, 1824.   21–tf

COMET

WILL stand at my stable in Richmond, where he stood last year. He is now in fine order, and will be let to mares at five dollars in specie, the season, or seven to ensure a mare to be with foal. For further particulars see hand-bills.

                    John Simpson.
February 27, 1824.   19–tf

The celebrated Diomed horse.
Sir Robert Wilson.

WILL stand the ensuing season at my stable one mile east of Lancaster, at the reduced price of ten dollars, in currency, the season—to commence the 10th inst. and end the 10th day of July. Further particulars will be given in hand-bills.

                    M V Grant.

NEW STORE.

THE SUBSCRIBERS have again commenced the
Mercantile Business
(IN RICHMOND KY.)
and have just received, and are now opening a very large and extensive assortment of

Merchandise:

Among which are the following articles
Superfine Black and Blue Cloths,
  do   do   do Casimeres,
Mersailles Quiltings,
Black Florentines,
Sattins and Figured Silks,
Crapes of various Colors,
  do   Robes,   do   do
  do   Shawls,   do   do
Bombazets   do   do
Calicoes and Chintz's,
4-4 & 6-4 plain Book Muslins,
4-4 & 6-4 Figured   do
4-4 & 6-4 Plain & Figured Jaconets do
4-4 & 6-4   do   do   Mull   do
4-4 & 6-4   do   do   Cambrick do
Ladies Elegant Jaconet Robes,
Bandannah and Madrass Handkerchiefs.
Ladies Cotton Shawls of various patterns,
Irish Linens, and Linen Cambrick,
Thread Lace of Superior Quality,
Black   do   do   do
Cotton and Silk   do   do
Black and White Silk and Worsted Hosery,
Silk Beaver and York Tanned Gloves,
Steam & Power Loom Shirtings,
English and Scotch Sateens,
Black and Brown Hollands,
Union Stripe and Mixtures,
New England Stripes and Plaid Cottons.
Ladies French Morocco, Kid and Prunella Shoes,
Misses   do   do   do
Childrens Leather and Morocco do
Morocco Hats,
Medicines and Shop Furniture,
Sithes and Sickles,
Millington Crawley ⎫
       and   ⎬ STEEL
Cast   ⎭
Wire Sifters of Various Sizes,
Shovels and Spades:
Together with a general assortment of
Hardware and Cutlery.
Queens, ⎫
China, & ⎬ WARES,
Glass   ⎭
Groceries, &c. &c. &c.
All of which we will sell extremely low for CASH—but to charge them is out of our power, owing principally to the unsettled state of our currency, and the very small profit at which we are determined to sell.

T. C. & G. Howard,
Richmond, May 23 1823—31—
P. S. We regret to be compelled to remind those (and particularly men of very desirable and elevated situations in point of wealth,) who have been indebted to us from four to seven years—of their entire failure to comply with their moral obligations in paying us for goods which they have purchased at those periods. *We can only say to them, in future such men can never have our funds to speculate upon—and as soon as we can have time, to list their bonds, we will try and make the money by law.*
                    T. C. & G. H.

REMOVAL.

JAMES HOLDER,
RESPECTFULLY informs the public and his customers in particular that he has removed his
BARBERS' SHOP,
to the house lately occupied by Samuel Parrish as a Sadler's Shop,
ON MAIN-STREET RICHMOND, (KY.)
Two doors below Thomas E. Stuart's Tavern.

He is well aware of the disadvantages he labours under with respect to his colour—he therefore, in justice to himself and for the satisfaction of those who should favour him by their calls informs the public that his house shall be kept orderly and genteely, *not admitting any but gentlemen.* He also hopes by his strict attention to his business to meet some encouragement. He informs the public that he will sharpen Razors and Surgical Instruments in the best manner and upon the shortest notice. He will call upon Ladies with pleasure who wish to have their hair cut or dressed, and binds himself to do in the neatest and most fashionable style.

In a short time he expects from Lexington a general assortment of RAZORS, HAIR-BRUSHES, COMBS, PERFUMERIES, and a variety of other articles in hi line, all of which he will sell very low fo CASH.

He will give a good price for LONG HUMAN HAIR.
April. 19 1823.

The Ladies

OF Madison and the adjoining counties, are respectfully informed that the subscriber has for sale,
Fine Soft well Heckled
HEMP,
That may be spun to any fineness, from a 600 to a 3000 at 25 cents per dozen. He has erected a HEMP MILL at the Hemp Factory, on Silver Creek, and
Mills Hemp
At the customary price of the customary fineness. He also continues to
Heckle Hemp,
At the following prices, viz: for a 400, 4 pence per pound of Heckled Hemp; for a 500, 5 pence; for a 600, 6 pence: and one pence per pound additional for each additional 100 in fineness.

He will receive in payment for Milling, Heckling, or for HEMP, Hemp from the field, from the Brake, or from the Mill, Wheat, Corn, Pork, Bacon or Beef, or any kind of country produce at a fair price.
                    JOHN GEO. BAXTER.
Dec. 5, 1823.   7–12m

Chair Making.

DAVID CHEVIS.
RESPECTFULLY informs the citizens of Richmond and its vicinity that he has opened his Shop in one of General Clay's houses on
Main-street, Richmond, (Ky.)
the second door below Mr. Reid's Silver Smith-shop, and nearly opposite Mr. Allison's Tavern, where he will shortly have
A HANDSOME ASSORTMENT OF
Fancy and Windsor

Madisonians continued gambling at the race track and lost significant amounts of money, even fortunes. John Speed Smith, a local attorney and son-in-law to Green Clay, lost his wife's estate and was forced to move in the 1820s. According to Cassius Clay, farmer James Estill lost $10,000 on a horse race in Louisville in 1840. Despite their interest in racing, Madisonians failed to develop the horsebreeding industry of other Bluegrass counties.[37]

As a result of their significant livestock and agricultural production, even early Madison farmers worried about ways to reach the markets. In 1788 the court recognized the existence of a ferry on the south side of the Kentucky River at Boonesborough (Stone's Ferry) and set the rates for consumers. A year later the court set rates for the ferry at the mouth of Paint Lick at six pence for a man and a horse, and proportionate rates for all other forms of transporation, as state law directed. In 1792 Madison magistrates ordered the establishment of a ferry across the Kentucky River opposite Boone's Creek and a second one at the mouth of Raven Creek where it crossed the Kentucky River. The court also ordered a survey of a potential ferry crossing below the mouth of Indian Creek.[38]

Interest in ferry crossings continued for decades. James Crews obtained the right to operate a ferry across the Kentucky River in 1794, while Robert Clark operated a ferry near the mouth of Four Mile Creek and the Kentucky River. A little later John Goggin and Alexander Black petitioned for the right to operate ferries across the Kentucky River. Most significantly, in 1801 the Kentucky River Company was chartered with $10,000 ($50 a share). Its purpose was to improve navigation on the river. The company removed obstructions on the river and prepared six locks. Madisonians subscribed twenty-two shares, with farmer John Patrick and magistrate James Barnett among the shareholders. Madison farmers, having used the river as a highway for sending produce to the New Orleans market since the 1780s, were excited about the project and pleased when the legislature authorized a lottery to raise money for it.[39]

Early farmers frequently urged the opening of roads to connect their mills, markets, and warehouses. At some of the first court sessions, magistrates ordered surveys of possible roads, heard complaints about the maintainence of existing pathways, and promised repairs. Farmers often served as overseers for the roads and provided tools and even labor for the road system. Under the early Kentucky laws all tithables were subject to the corvee or road tax and had to work or send someone else to work a certain period of time on roads in their neighborhood. The first Madison County roads ran from the mouth of Jack's Creek to Lewis's Mill, from Jack's Creek to Back Creek to Danville, from Four Mile Creek to Otter Creek, from James Lackey's to Boonesborough, from the mouth of Muddy Creek to Milford Courthouse, from Barnes' Mill to Milford Courthouse, from Archibald Wood's Grist Mill to the Kentucky River, and from Milford to Rockcastle Creek.[40]

Concerning transportation routes, the county court had to maintain that part of the Wilderness Road crossing Madison County. The court ordered John Crooke, its official surveyor, to view the state road and report any problems. Each county accepted responsibility for repairing its section of the state road, but most county repairs exceeded the tolls earned. Typically, in 1805 the Madison Court received a report from the commissioner of the Wilderness Road showing repair costs in each county and listing the turnpike keeper's salary. Madison County earned $511 of the $1,974.50 total, but the keeper was $100 short since the tolls did not match the expenditures.[41]

William Kerby, one of the managers of the Wilderness Turnpike, built a boat and ferry for crossing the Rockcastle River. He conveyed passengers as well as wagons and up to six horses at a time on the fifty-foot long water vehicle. He introduced cables for the ferry.[42] The various commissioners of the turnpike reported repairs, alterations, expenses, conditions, and balances to the Madison Court. They noted the purchases of equipment including axes, mattocks, hoes, crow bars, sledge hammers, ovens, frying pans, tents, bags, poles, wedges, bacon, rope, iron to mend the tools; oats for the pack horses; hundreds of bushels of corn meal and corn, and whiskey for the hands. Subsequent orders included sugar, chocolate; the usual necessaries; and more whiskey for the hands. A perusal of other court records shows that Madison County road workers were probably the happiest in the state or were uniquely honest in reporting their whiskey requests.[43]

Road construction often reflected the economic interests of the magistrates, and many of their names were given to the new roads. Green Clay used his political influence to promote his economic investments. He often requested the survey of roads through his lands. In the early 1800s he secured a new road from his blacksmith shop to the Stone Ferry Road, from the old Jack's Creek Road to his ferry on the Kentucky River, and onto Tate's Creek Road via his plantation. The court approved a new road from Stillwell's Tanyard to the mouth of Silver Creek via Clay's estate.[44]

During the War of 1812 the Madison County economy continued to expand and the court ordered the survey of a road from Colonel Irvine's plantation to Richmond to facilitate the clerk's work. It also ordered repairs on the Muddy Creek to Cane Springs road. In 1818, the court opened six new roads in the county and improved the old road from Barnes' Mill to Bogie's Mill. That same year the legislature chartered the Lexington to Boonesborough Turnpike, although it did not extend to Richmond until 1830.[45]

By the 1820s Madison County boasted a significant network of roads to aid farmers in their economic pursuits. Consequently, they asked for the construction of bridges. Some complained of ferry rates, while others noted the need for public bridges which would sustain heavier traffic. The court erected a bridge over Tate's Creek in 1819, two years later it provided the funds for construction of two new bridges on the Boonesborough Road—one across Muddy Creek, one to

Lexington—and ordered repairs on the State Road Bridge. The Muddy Creek Bridge, at $230, was the most expensive in the county.[46]

By 1824 the court paid William Rodes $150 to repair three public bridges, and in 1829 the magistrates authorized the erection of a stone bridge at Logan's Tanyard. During the bridge building era, the court constructed bridges at Main Street and at Second Street in Richmond, the latter one costing $500, easily the most expensive bridge in the county prior the 1830s.[47]

Farmers often supplied materials and extra labor for special road projects or repairs. George Million frequently supplied timber to repair the Madison highway, while many farmers supplied stone and loaned animals to haul the materials to the designated sites. Elias Barnes had the court designate all hands working in his backsmith and wagon-making shops to repair the road from his house to the far end of Goggin's Lane. The court also assumed responsibility for maintaining the famous Wilderness Turnpike. When William Kerby, the long-time manager of the Wilderness Turnpike from Big Hill to Crab Orchard, resigned, the court sought a new commissioner. By 1826 Richard Broaddus accepted the post, and the court ordered him to build a "first-rate" ferry for transporting wagons across Rockcastle River, promising to pay him with the money he collected as commissioner.[48]

In 1829 the court appropriated money for new signboards on the roads and laid off the county into 160 road precincts. It appointed several old-line farmers as road supervisors, including William Biggerstaff, Jeremiah and Napoleon Tevis, John Orchard, William Chenault, Josiah Phelps, John Miller, John and Squire Million, Andrew Bogie, Joseph Barnett, James Black, John Burnam, and Richard Cornelison. It instructed them on the use of "the hands" and noted the exact spots in the roads that needed repairing. The court also ordered additional timber for the signboards.[49]

In 1830 the court appointed Thompson Burnam and Howard Williams to recover the courthouse and tap out its chimneys. Too, it provided them with $500 to pave and "macadamize" one half of Main Street opposite the public square provided the businesses on the other side paid the expenses of the other half. Businessmen opposite the public square raised the remaining costs, and the paving of the two cross streets fronting the square proceeded. The court soon ordered new fences around the square.[50]

The court continued to allot money for road improvements and to replace timbers and even rock along the roads. It secured bridge repairs, requisitioned wagons for hauling the materials, and purchased new signboards for the local roads as well as the Wilderness Turnpike. It alloted $250 for construction of a bridge across Muddy Creek via the Richmond-Cane Springs Meeting House Road, and opened the state road from Richmond to London through the lands of Archibald Woods, Jr. When the court paid David Chenault for supervising the Muddy Creek

Bridge and Thompson Burnam for superintending the paving of the Cross Street fronting the public square, the total bridge, road, and street improvements for 1833 reached a record $1,271.50, by far the most lavish public works expenditures of the era. Moreover, this amounted to over one-third of the county levy in 1833.[51]

In deference to protesting farmers, the court approved the right of farmers to pass through the turnpike gate with their wagons and packages of grain to the other side of the Rockcastle River without paying pike fees. By 1836 Cassius Clay and a few farmers urged the court to take out stock in the new Lexington and Richmond Turnpike Company, but the court quickly declined the investment proposal. In 1837 the court began selling large tracts of vacant land in the county for fifty cents an acre. As a result of the increasing number of sales, the court appointed Edmund Shackelford as treasurer of Madison County and ordered him to keep and disburse "monies from the sale of vacant lands." The court apparently spent the proceeds on additional roads, as it opened a road from Moberly's Saw Mill to an intersection of the Richmond-Irvine Road, repaired Mitchell Million's Horse Mill Road, and by 1838 even subscribed fifty shares of stock in the Richmond and Lexington Turnpike Company to be paid in four annual county levies.[52]

Throughout the 1830s the court continued to repair old roads. It ordered hands to assemble and farmers to supply carts, beasts of burden, signposts, timber, rocks, and necessaries for the workers. The turnpike continued to prove a financial liability. Absalom Adams, the overseer, reported another deficit in 1837, as repair expenditures again exceeded gate receipts. Madison farmers often placed gates across the roads, partly to protect livestock but often to charge a toll they considered necessary since they had to maintain the roads.[53] State roads and turnpikes absorbed increasing amounts of traffic in the 1840s. The Madison Court subscribed another $1,250 in stock in the Lexington and Richmond Turnpike Company in 1840 and appropriated $350 for bridge repair and street macadamization. The network of county roads was virtually complete.

The court's concern for better transportation routes, although economically motivated, reflected advancements in technology, with the development of macadamization of streets in Richmond and parts of the county roads as well. By 1834 the court ordered the macadamization of both cross streets fronting the public square for $500. This process meant the finishing of a road by packing it with a layer of small broken stones on a well-drained earthen roadbed. It provided smoother movement of carts, wagons, and carriages. In 1837, the trustees of Richmond enlarged the town's limits, provided a new plat and survey of the town, and secured the court's order for completion of the macadamization of Main Street in Richmond from the courthouse to the city bridge.[54]

Although road construction in the ante-bellum period often resulted from expansion of Madison's agrarian economy, it also stimulated further growth, particularly in the villages or towns of the area. As early as the 1780s farmers gathered at mills and exchanged produce, tools, livestock, and gossip. The mill sites served as early marketplaces, although the court often encouraged marketing at the county seat, originally Milford and by 1798, Richmond.

With the development of the first courthouse, public square, stray pen, and blacksmith shop at Milford in 1788, Robert Caldwell, Samuel Estill, and John Phelps, nearby farmers and landowners, seized the economic opportunities and opened businesses to serve the public. Although Estill and Phelps provided lodging, food, and beverages for court visitors, Caldwell became the outstanding merchant of the little village. He often imported goods from Baltimore.[55] The time of the Madison merchant, however, had not yet arrived.

Robert Caldwell, son-in-law of Captain Christopher "Kit" Irvine, dissolved his drygoods store in Milford in 1795. Other merchants had a difficult time in the early period due to the shortage of cash as well as competition from courthouse market stalls. People attended court day for entertainment and for a social outing but also found it a golden opportunity to barter tools, weapons, livestock, and produce. Farmers required refreshments and sometimes lodging; thus the hotels and taverns flourished, although other businesses were less active. Colonel Samual Estill, an old Revolutionary War veteran, opened Estill's Station in 1781 and maintained a small hotel in Milford.[56] Many of the taverns mentioned earlier provided rooms for meetings and for overnight guests.

Citizens gathering at the courthouse used the public square as an informal marketplace from the outset, and the court, by 1812, officially recognized its importance by constructing, on Main Street, a forty-foot long, twenty-six-foot wide, roofed markethouse where anyone could sell vegetables, meat, flour, pottery, poultry, and other items.[57] The temporary public market house on Irvine and First streets continued to offer these items as well as leather goods, churns, crocks, and washboards for years. Farmers, townspeople, and tourists purchased a variety of articles at the public square, but individuals frequently peddled fresh meat, especially squirrel, rabbit, fish, and poultry as well as ham and mutton. Housewives could purchase molasses, butter, eggs, and cream. Business was brisk on Saturdays and court days. During the war era the outstanding vendor was a "big, fat dumpy, smiling mammy," the famed cook at Miller Tavern (later Irvine's) named Mammy Lou. The tavern operated a booth dispensing her hot corn sticks, spoon bread, and pies— a marvelous way of advertising Miller's Tavern. She often seasoned, mixed, and baked the items in front of the public. Surprisingly, she was allowed to keep part of her earnings and eventually saved enough money to purchase her own emancipation.[58]

Aside from Mammy Lou's corn meal products, pottery was the most exceptional article Madisonians purchased at the public market. Indians had made pottery centuries before the white man invaded the new world; and pioneer settlers soon recognized the value of the white and gray clay available in the "slashes" or "Sour Woods" enroute to Boonesborough and dug it up to produce churns, crocks, bowls, and jugs used in the pioneer forts. By 1812 artisans in southeastern Madison County, in the Bybee and Waco areas produced and sold earthenware at the county market as well as up and down the Kentucky River. In the 1840s Philip Huffman, an expert Swiss potter, resided on the Talton Embry farm, where he set up a pug-mill, brick oven, and shelter for drying racks. Bybee's domination of pottery production had begun and continues today.[59]

In 1810 the Richmond population totaled 366 residents and provided numerous business opportunities. Despite the competition of the public market, merchants surfaced once again. The Howard brothers, George and Thomas C., operated the most significant mercantile business, hardware, and grocery in Richmond from the war into the 1830s. The Howards sold clothing, hardware, cutlery, groceries, "ginseng," dye stuffs, and other items. The Howards and their competitors often advertised in the *Richmond Republican* (owned by the Howards) as well as in the *Farmer's Chronicle* of the 1830s.[60]

Newspaper advertising demonstrated the cyclical business expansion of the Richmond community in the 1820s. Although the Howard brothers dominated the scene from the war onward, they had competition. Howard Williams and Company as well as Field and McClanahan advertised "goods from Philadelphia." J. K. Dillingham Groceries and John Woods Groceries maintained an active role, while Thomas Huggins, providing gunpowder, coffee, spices, Queen's Ware, tin, and "mackerel" for consumers, presented the boldest challenge through large advertisements and varied articles.[61]

A variety of stores had appeared in Richmond by the 1820s, indicative of the wealth of the community as well as its diversified interests and tastes. Boswell Brown opened a new cabinet-making shop on Main and Cross streets, while William Burns operated a boot and shoe store on Main Street. Samuel Parrish maintained a saddling and harness shop, perhaps the most complete in the area, although R. G. Williams and Charles C. Porter operated additional saddleries. William H. Rayl reopened Caldwell's Black Smith Shop and announced he had shoes, nails, cast steel axes, and other farm items. These businesses continued to flourish for some time, as Madisonians depended on the horse for transportation throughout the ante-bellum era.[62]

Thomas Kennedy opened a rope walk near Main Street and promised to pay farmers cash for their best quality hemp for his rope-making business. Brown and Tevis Wool Carding Factory advertised for farmer's best wool and agreed to accept wool, feathers, and corn for their carding service. Charles Brooking advertised top quality beef and mutton at his butchering business. These enterprises underlined Madisonians' heavy dependence on agrarian produce.[63]

As agricultural wealth expanded in the 1820s, farmers increasingly sought material items. Jacob Miller's Hat Shop in Richmond was directly across from the Richmond Bank and vied with J. and B. Graves Hat Factory for fashion-conscious consumers. Several men opened tailoring shops to cater to the burgeoning middle class. Charles Gilkey and Henry Ready often advertised their tailoring trades. James Holder opened a barber shop in 1823, possibly the first in the county, selling razors, hairbrushes, combs, and perfumes. Too, he advertised the fact that he labored "under a disadvantage as to colour" although it was not clear whether he was white and the gentry wanted a black barber or he was a black and could not attract white patronage.[64]

By 1823 Richmondites welcomed the Ferguson Baking Business; William Dean's Fine Leather Goods, including calf skin and Indian Morrocco slippers; and Mrs. Saunder's Millinery, famed for its bonnets, ribbons, buckles, and artificial flowers. The following year, local citizens could purchase fine furniture at Chevis's Chair Making Business or at Brown's Cabinet Shop. David Chevis made fancy furniture and the ever popular Windsor chairs.[65]

Early newspapers not only attested to the business opportunities in Richmond and the Madison County area but also reflected professional growth and competition. Early doctors frequently took ads in the newspapers. Dr. Stout and Dr. William Baker advertised their availability. Several teachers advertised private lessons, while lawyers openly competed for business. J. Speed Smith advertised his law practice more than all other lawyers combined, although John White and three other attorneys frequently advertised in the *Richmond Republican*.[66]

Throughout the ante-bellum era the court certified new attorneys. The normal procedure included certifying an individual "as a man of honesty, probity, and good demeanor"; then administering the oath of practicing attorney. William H. Caperton, licensed in 1818, joined a distinguished elite cadre of Madisonian lawyers. For the remainder of the ante-bellum period, Caperton, Squire Turner, or Daniel Breck recommended most new attorneys for the county and attested to their character.[67]

Professional growth continued in the 1830s as the *Farmer's Chronicle* carried advertisements by lawyers, doctors, merchants, and a variety of other occupations. In 1835 four doctors, Venable, Moberly, Day, and Harris, advertised their fees and locations. Competition accelerated in other areas as six grocers and five tailors announced their services. In 1835 Richmond even acquired a branch of the Northern Bank, although the community had long boasted a Richmond branch of the old Bank of Kentucky located on north Third and Main.[68]

The county levy further underlined the prosperity of the 1830s. In 1819, the county levy was a record high of $2,109.06 and Madisonians marveled at a levy exceeding $2,000. But by 1836 the court established another record: $3,407.55. The total revenue of the county in 1839 and 1840 signified the new prosperity, although a slight decline occurred in 1840. The county boasted wealth of $8,272,000, with Richmond accounting for a record $300,000. By 1840 the city's revenue increased to $325,000, although the county wealth declined some $30,000. The tax rate in 1830 was twenty cents on each $100 worth of property, again the highest rate into the 1840s.[69]

Two of the most important aspects of the early Madisonian economy were slaves and land. The earliest trailblazers brought slaves into the area. In the spring of 1775 Captain Twetty and his slave Sam were killed on the Wilderness Trail at a temporary fortification, hence-forth known as Little Fort, a few miles south of present Richmond. Richard Callaway and some of his slaves were constructing a ferry when Indians attacked, scalped, and brutalized them in 1780. James Estill's slave Monk was a hero in the battles of Boonesborough, Fort Estill, and Little Mountain. Monk saved several lives. He also made gunpowder for the early settlers. Nathaniel Henderson requested that the Virginia legislature compensate him for the loss of one of his Negro slaves killed in the defense of Fort Boonesborough.[70]

Slaves were property, a source of labor, and a sign of wealth. Slavery, always an economic institution, was defended primarily with economic arguments. In 1790 the slave population of Madison County was 737, and there were no free colored residents in the original census. However, by 1800 the county had 1729 slaves and three free colored residents. The slave population counted for over 16 percent of the total. By 1850 the slave population rose to 5,393 out of a total 15,727, representing one-third, or over 34 percent, of the total.[71]

As late as 1850 there were only sixty-five free colored residents in Madison County, but the court constantly worried about orphans and freed Negro children and provided for their apprenticeship in one of the trades. In the early 1800s court order books abounded in cases of young mulatto boys or free Negroes learning the blacksmith, tanning, shoemaking, or stone mason trade, while young girls learned house work in order to support themselves. The court kept records on slaves who committed crimes and noted their offenses, particularly the "stealing of sundry goods." The court noted burglarizing of stables and corn cribs and the theft of saddles or clothes. It did supply "medical services for the Darkey, Venable, an object of charity."[72]

The value of slaves varied, but as early as 1814 Squire Boone owned a slave and a bond servant possessing a combined $1,200 value. George Pearson had four slaves, two under sixteen, valued at $1,800. Slaveowners distinguised between Negroes over and under sixteen years of age, as shown in the tax records. By 1816 Richard Broaddus owned fifteen slaves. Those over sixteen were valued at $600 each, while those under sixteen were valued at $300 each. A decade later slaves brought an average of $800. Because of the slave's economic value, the court frequently announced the need for more patrollers and purchased additional hand cuffs.[73]

Surprisingly, despite the fame of Cassius Clay and other antislavery advocates, Madison County actually had fewer emancipations than most Bluegrass counties. Thomas Watts provided a unique example in his will of 1820, by emancipating two male servants, "Tony, 33, and Spencer, 45, for faithful service." All emancipation documents described the physical appearances of the manumitted slaves. The records noted scars indicative of discipline or even mistreatment. Most slaves had scars above their eye or on their backs. Many were desbribed as "well made, "

$20 REWARD.

RANAWAY from the subscriber living in Winchester, Ky. on the 15th of April, a Negro Man named

DICK,

between thirty-five and forty years of age. He came away with him a Woolen Janes Coat, and also a Roundabout Cotton Coat. He is quick-spoken, and has a lump on the back part of his head, his beard was uncommonly long, and he is rather inclined to be hallow jaw'd. It is expected he will make ior Salisbury or Charlotte, North Carolina. I will give the above reward if taken out of the State or $10 if taken in the State.

WILLIAM HAMPTON
Winchester, April 23—27-3tp.

Entertainment.

THE subscriber has lately removed to Lexington, and taken the tavern formerly occupied by Mr. W.T. BANTON, on Short Street, nearly opposite the Public Square, where he is prepared to entertain *TRAVELLERS* and *BOARDERS.* Every arrangement for the comfort and accommodation of those who shall favor him with their custom, will be made. A good stable, conveniently situated, and well attended, has been attached to the Tavern. Prices will be reasonable.

WILLIAM CREWS.
Lexington, Oct. 7, 1822—1-4

DR. STOUT

INFORMS the public, that he has removed his MEDICAL OFFICE to the brick building lately occupied by Daniel & Cross, immediately oppo te the Branch Bank.

Grateful to his friends for past favors, he intends devoting himself assiduously to the discharge of his professional duties.

Richmond, Jan. 1, 1823—11-12m

GAZETTEER
Of the State of Kentucky.

THE subscribers are engaged in writing a Gazetteer of the State, accompanied with a brief historical account of its early settlement; which will be put to press as soon as the materials can be properly arranged.

In the mean time, they solicit the aid and assistance of those persons who are in possession of any information relating to the following subjects, by communicating it as soon as convenient.

Incidents of Indian hostility, and other interesting events connected with the early settlement of the country.

A description of the natural curiosities found in their neighbourhood.

The origin of the names of the different towns, settlements, rivers, creeks and salt licks in their vicinity.

Together with such information on the topography, agriculture, manufactures, population, &c. of the country, as it may be in their power to give.

JOHN BRADFORD.
JAMES W. PALMER.
Lexington, Jan. 29. 1823.

Richmond Republican, April 30, 1823. EKU Archives.

"mullatto", or "light color." A white mistress who freed Albert Mackey, a twenty-five-year-old lad, described him as 5'6, "well-made, copper colored . . . young and able, can care for himself."[74]

By 1820 even sheltered Madison Countians became aware of the fugitive slave problem, and the local court granted the jailer permission to receive "runaway Negroes with or without a certificate of a Justice." Throughout the 1830s vagrancy was an increasing problem for blacks and poor whites. Vagrancy trials accelerated with the court hiring out the "guilty," regardless of color, for months at a time, to the highest bidder. If an owner emancipated a Negro, he had to post bond to maintain the former slave. In 1824 the ever sharp Green Clay emancipated his slave Nanny for her loyal service but failed to free any of her ten children (the economic value was too great). Clay provided for her maintainance, however, as the court required.[75]

As time passed a few more slaveowners emancipated an occasional slave. John Bennett and William Chenault each freed a slave in 1830. The court continued to apprentice a "free boy of color . . . for three years . . . to learn the mysteries of shoe-making" and a girl "to learn the spinning and weaving business from Israel, a free man of color." In the most unusual case Jefferey Davis, a free man of color, emancipated his slave Nancy in 1836. She was fifty-four years old, dark colored, 5'6 in height, and weighed 150 pounds. Jefferey promised to provide for her so she would not become a "charge of the county."[76]

Because of their economic value slaves were rarely punished severely for crimes they committed. Whipping was normal for theft, improper attitudes, traveling without a pass, or even conducting business without a permit. The court records document slave crimes in detail. Typically the slave received mild punishment. Dick, a slave of Robert Miller, committed manslaughter against another slave, received the benefit of clergy, and was burned in the hand.[77]

As noted in early church record books, slaves worshipped with whites at Silver Creek Presbyterian, at Tate's Creek Baptist, and at Cane Springs Baptist. The church disciplined members of both races. Whites apparently held greater fear of miscegenation than any other activity. The great numbers of mulatto children explained the logic behind this fear. As early as 1804 the Tates Creek Baptist Church condemned white men for "whispering in ears of Negro servants" and for "accompanying mulatto women into the Cumberland area."[78]

During the ante-bellum period Judge Cabell Chenault noted the good relations between the races and spoke of the old-time "corn shuckings," when hordes of volunteers from neighboring farms would come and clean the corn fields for a good supper and a sharing of the whiskey supply. He noted that they sang, ate, drank, and made the labor a social outing. Moreover, the *Farmer's Chronicle* of 1835-1839 frequently advertised "Negroes for hire." Despite the apparent relaxation of racial tension in the rural areas the townspeople feared slave uprisings, and the Richmond trustees declared a strict ordinance in August, 1823, stating:

> No Negro, free or slave, can stroll in town after 8:00 curfew (ten lashes for slave violator, jail confinement for free Negro)
>
> No Negro to stroll in town, stand on sidewalk or sit on rail after 9:00 a. m.
>
> No merchants to sell or buy articles from slaves on the Sabbath (a five dollar fine)
>
> Slaves must bear legal permits to be in the market place
>
> Negroes in town must carry passes, clearly stating where they are going, returning, and their horses name if not on foot.[79]

Tension between the races finally led to separate religious services by 1847, as the Tate's Creek Baptists dismissed their colored members, thus terminating a sixty-year-old practice of integrated services. Blacks organized an African Baptist Church that same year.[80]

The economic value of slaves continued to grow throughout the 1820s as newspapers included advertised sales from time to time. Madisonians bought or sold slaves at public sales in the country, at farms along Muddy Creek, or in town at the public market on the Courtyard Square. On December 17, 1822, four Negroes were auctioned at a public sale. Runaways also proved an economic problem. A slave's value fluctuated, but one farmer offered a twenty dollar reward for the return of Dick, a thirty-five-year-old runaway, while a tradesman offered a one cent reward for a runaway apprentice. Richard Broaddus, a Muddy

Creek farmer, offered a ten dollar reward for Dave, a twenty-eight-year-old slave, dressed in "cotton jeans." It was amazing any runaways were ever identified or captured since newspaper ads were brief and vague, often describing runaways as "mean looking," "surly," "well-built," "dark or light-colored," "medium height," and "average weight."[81] Emancipated slaves, runaways, or family slaves often appropriated the names of their masters, thus leading to a variety of interesting social problems later in the century.

The most important economic goal of early pioneers was acquiring land. Madisonians throughout the eighteenth and nineteenth centuries made the ownership of land their great priority. Pioneers claimed land through squatter's rights, treasury warrants, and military warrants. Many took advantage of ambiguous or insufficient land laws. Early court records reflected the chaotic circumstances in which these land-hungry people made their overlapping, often illegal, claims to what seemed anyone's opportunity. In the 1790s the court surveyors returned and recorded mostly treasury warrants, although some other types of grants made the books. William Irvine's 1,950 acres acquired through treasury warrants proved the largest single Madison recording of the 1790s. However, a series of surveys resulted in the acquisition of 2,700 acres by Matthew Clay, 1,000 acres by James Barnett, and even 500 acres by Governor James Garrard, who owned 20,000 acres in Bourbon County. As early as 1792, when Kentucky became a state, the Madison County Tax List showed the largest landowners as Thomas Kennedy with 4,813 acres, Archibald Woods with 1,800 acres, Samuel Estill with 1,800 acres, and Joseph Kenndy with 1,300 acres. By the early 1800s Green Clay had become the wealthiest landowner, with some 40,000 acres, or one-fourth of Madison County.[82]

Colonel Samuel Estill (1755-1838), a Revolutionary War veteran, member of the early court, and Kentucky legislator, was a large land-owner in the Muddy Creek area. He had twenty tenant families on his estate and he ran a small hotel. Estill weighed 412 pounds and could not walk the last years of his life. (His portrait of 1830, painted by Chester Harding, hangs in the Richmond Courthouse.)[83] Green Clay, with his massive acreage, frequently advertised in local papers for overseers and tenants and offered to sell acreages of 5,000-6,000, including mill sites.[84]

The early court recorded numerous land disputes, depositions, resurveys, and land litigation. Land was the measure of a man. The amount, its location, and its state of clearance were important. Land brought power, wealth, influence. As noted in the Madison Court, as well as in other Bluegrass counties, magistrates were generally great landowners. In the 1790s the Kennedy brothers, Thomas and Joseph; the Clay brothers, Thomas and Green; Archibald Woods; George Adams; and David Gass and their associates owned large acreage and significant livestock. William Irvine, the county clerk, was the only political figure with less than 500 acres, and he soon acquired 1,950 acres through treasury warrants.[85]

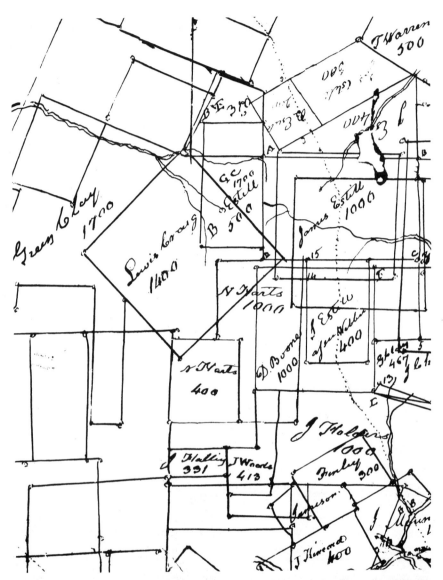

Overlapping land claim survey map in Madison County by John Crooke. EKU Dorris Museum.

Landowners enjoyed additional opportunities, as noted earlier, in constructing mills, operating ferries, determining the course of roads, opening warehouses, and engaging in trade at the public market. As they acquired wealth they often built impressive homes and adopted historic or majestic names for their estates. Examples in the early period included Woodstock, Castlewood, and Duncanon.

In many ways, elegant homes became the final symbol of the developing Madisonian wealth. The gentry erected frame, stone, or brick mansions in the countryside, while merchants, innkeepers, and lawyers constructed beautiful homes in town. Although the first homes were log, weather-boarded, simple structures frequently containing a "dog-trot" running between two square rooms, the pioneers soon enclosed them to make hallways. Windows had small panes of glass, and rough stone fireplaces were common. Many fireplaces had a small square window nearby for a "knitting light." If the structure had two stories there was a ladder stairway connecting the two floors.[86]

Although Nathaniel Hart's log home near Fort Boonesborough and Benjamin Howard's weather-boarded house near the Lexington Pike had been the first houses, by 1790 Madisonians were using stone as a building material for homes and even mills. Benjamin Hawkins of Silver Creek dressed stone. Samuel Phelps, an early pioneer, erected a stone office three miles north of Richmond on the Boonesborough Road. Phelps purchased the David C. Irvine home, a weather-boarded house with six rooms and large stone chimneys, and built separate slave quarters in the back. At the close of the century, Green Clay built Clermont, a brick home with three Greek porticos and impressive Doric and Corinthian columns. Clay fired the bricks on his own estate. Archibald Woods built Woodstock, an impressive brick residence a few miles south of Richmond. This house of the 1790s had two fronts, east and west, and exhibited several classical influences.[87]

Clermont, ca. 1975. *Kentucky Pioneer*, Vol. 3 (May, 1971), cover.

By the turn of the century, Madisonians, like their Bluegrass contemporaries, associated brick with affluence. Richmond and the larger
county area boasted several fine homes. John Duncan built most of his
elegant Duncanon on Duncan's Lane. The beautiful brick house had
exquisite wallpaper in the parlor, with vignettes of French scenes on a
pearl grey background. Most Madison County homes of the era had
hand-carved woodwork and tall Adams mantels. James Estill erected
Castlewood on Big Hill Pike in 1825. Colonel William Rodes erected
Woodlawn with its seventy-foot-long front hall, palladian windows,
stone portico, columns and handsome woodwork in 1822 near a natural
spring. And Colonel J. Speed Smith owned a brick mansion on North
Street in Richmond in 1820 which extended to Main Street and had a
brick wall and tall iron gates.[88]

Lawyers constructed or purchased many of these early brick homes.
Woods, Rodes, and Estill sat on the early courts and served as the first
lawyers of the area. Archibald Woods, Jr. of Woodstock was probably
the first trained lawyer, and he owned a library of lawbooks. In the
1820s his nephew Colonel William H. Caperton, Judge Daniel Breck,
Squire Turner, and J. Speed Smith dominated the legal profession and
owned the finest homes.[89]

By the 1830s William Chenault erected a brick home on the Lexington Pike, north of Richmond, formerly the old Irvine homestead. Edwin
Phelps constructed a large home on the Lexington Pike which contained
some of the most beautiful furniture, especially tables, chests of draw-
ers, and secretaries made by local cabinet maker, Boswell Brown. Bly-
thewood, at the intersection of Menelaus and Duncanon Road, rose in
the 1840s and included elegant grand parlors, a long ell, iron verandahs,
a springhouse of rough stone, and the most complete landscaping of the
ante-bellum era.[90]

In the 1850 Census, Madison County contained farm land and farm
implements valued at $4,785,130. By adding the slaves, homes, and
furnishings, as well as including the livestock and other property values,
Madison County clearly enjoyed an enviable position in the Kentucky
economy. It ranked among the top ten counties in amost every type of
agricultural wealth.[91]

Chapter Three

THE MADISON COUNTY COURT: KENTUCKY STYLE

The transition from Old Dominion status to that of a commonwealth county caused minimal disruption for the Madison Court. The same magistrates continued to preside over the court, and many of the same auxiliary officials remained in office. The Virginia nepotism and natural aristocratic domination continued. A local power struggle surfaced when a few of the newer landowners, who might not have made it in the old system, gained increasing influence via their landholdings in the new state. Two men gained enormous power during the 1790s. John Miller's political interests led to wealth, while Green Clay's economic goals led to political influence.

Miller, a revolutionary war veteran and relative newcomer to the county, purchased some strategically located farm acreage a few miles from little Milford. His farm, formerly William Hoy's Station, included a large natural spring and two small creeks. The land was flatter and afforded easier access to the greater Bluegrass region than "old Milford." Too, Miller became a key figure in the militia's frontier defense when Kentucky Governor Isaac Shelby named him lieutenant colonel of the Seventh Regiment in 1792, and he reported Indian incursions into Madison County to Shelby. Miller called fifteen men into service for patrolling the frontier. The following year an additional patrol was necessary, and he hired four spies to secure information on Indian activity in the area. By 1795, due to the county's extensive border, Governor Shelby called for the formation of a second Madison regiment: the nineteenth.[1] Miller was pleased with the expanding population, and he recognized future economic opportunities.

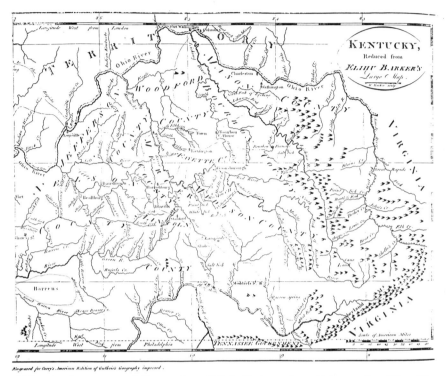

Elihu Barker map of Kentucky, 1794. University of Kentucky King Library Special Collections Department.

The Madison Court, in 1792, designated Green Clay as an official deputy surveyor. This was an important post, as Clay was actively acquiring enormous land acreage in the 1790s. Two years later he became a magistrate on the court, thus gaining an unlimited opportunity to acquire further wealth through the supervision and settling of estates; the power to approve locations and rights for roads, ware-houses, and gristmills; the appointment of inspectorships; and the establishment of rates for ferries, taverns, and turnpikes. By 1795 the court order books reflected Clay's diversified economic empire, including warehouses, ferries, distilleries, gristmills, livestock, tobacco, slaves, toll roads, surveying fees, taverns, and even a resort.[2]

Both Miller's and Clay's interests were outside the tiny, almost inaccessible, Milford area. As already noted, Milford lacked sufficient water, and the County Clerk, William Irvine, whose estate was only a few miles from Clay's "Clermont," refused to keep his records at Milford, insisting that farmers travel to his estate near Tate's Creek. Only a semicleared road connected Milford to the larger Boonesborough settlement. Some farmers, especially those outside the Milford or Paint Lick area, openly advocated moving the courthouse from Milford. Meanwhile the magistrates constantly ordered repairs on the old courthouse, and the sheriffs continued to complain of the "sufficiency of the gaol." The court appointed a five-man commission composed of Samuel and Wallace Estill, Nicholas Hawkins, Robert Caldwell, and William Irvine "to draw a plan for a new Courthouse to be built with stone or brick and to fix a situation for the said house." This committee was to superintend the construction and not allow the price to exceed "double the sum the present Courthouse [might] sell for."[3]

A month later the magistrates restated their intention to build a new courthouse "in a public or private manner as may be most convenient or most advantagous." Obviously public opposition was surfacing. Significantly the next court ordered the sheriff to clear the court and prevent anyone but judges or their guests from sitting on the benches. By 1796 Robert Caldwell and Joseph Kennedy were pushing for the construction of a new jail, but their motion was defeated by fellow magistrates under the leadership of Green Clay and Archibald Woods, who claimed there was no money levied for such a purpose and that a majority of the justices were not present. Clay probably favored moving the court itself and was minimizing expenses.[4]

Clay, assuming an increasingly important role at court, posted bond for John Crooke, the new official surveyor of the county. Clay's friend Robert Tevis became deputy surveyor, and the court named Clay and Aaron Lewis to inspect the records of the Surveyor's Office before they were turned over to Crooke. By now Clay, Woods, and Miller controlled the court, and in March, 1798, they declared "it expedient to move . . . to the center of population" on a ridge near John Miller's barn and brick kiln and fixed it as "the permanent seat of justice." The court did appoint a commission to ascertain "the losses that the citizens of the town of Milford may sustain by the removal of the seat of Justice therefrom." James French, the former surveyor, headed a damages commission.[5]

The following morning the court assembled "at 10 o'clock at the new seat of justice in John Miller's Barn" where it continued to meet until the completion of a new Richmond courthouse a year later. Significantly, Green Clay, his brother Thomas, Archibald Woods, and three associates made the decision to call for the establishment of a town on Miller's and Colonel James Barbour's land, containing fifty acres to "be laid off in lots and streets" and to include a two-acre plot for public buildings. Green Clay, John Miller, and two associates were "to superintend the building of a courthouse, gaol, whipping posts, a stock and stray pen." Too, this court approved Miller's request to establish an ordinary (tavern) in his home. Thus Richmond was born.[6]

Miller's original fifty acres in Richmond were dense with black walnut, ash, white oak, and cane thickets. The court condemned an old log house near his home and used it for the public "gaol" until a proper building was completed. The surveyor laid off prison grounds in the public square. The sheriff secured old locks, hinges, and irons from the Milford "gaol" and advertized the sale of the old courthouse and stray pen. Miller's barn was on the Courthouse Square, and he allowed the public to use his large spring (near Water Street).[7]

On July 4, 1798, the court formally established Richmond and reserved lots thirty-six through thirty-nine for Miller. It named ten town trustees, including Green Clay, William and Christopher Irvine, Archibald Woods, and Robert Rodes. The latter had followed Clay's leadership on all important matters, and the court named him a trustee as well as superintendent for the courthouse construction.[8]

The decision to move the court to Miller's farm was not universally acclaimed. Paint Lick residents, under the leadership of the Kennedy brothers, openly resisted the decision. Robert Caldwell, with his economic interests in the Milford area, formed a natural alliance to fight the Clay-Miller cabal; but water shortages, topography, population clusters, and economics worked against the Milfordites. Some Madison County historians have claimed that an epic four-hour fight between ruffian Dave Kennedy and William Kerly, in the Milford stray pen, was the decisive factor, with both sides agreeing that the winner of the fight would choose the court's location. It is a good story but totally misleading, as the state legislature had passed a law guaranteeing the change of a county seat by a simple majority vote of the magistrates as long as the former county seat received adequate compensation for improvements. The Madison Court had already decisively voted to move to Miller's farm, and it awarded Milfordites $1,600 compensation. The fight may well have occurred, but its outcome could not have altered the magistrates' action.

The court opened a road from Wood's farm to Richmond, from Milford to Richmond, and repaired other roads in the vicinity. The magistrates ordered stone work for the courthouse and its plastering inside, and they provided for repairs on the public jail. As the new town arose on Miller's farm, the court exempted Richmondites from working on roads but designated Samuel Logan, the tanner, to maintain streets of the town and superintend all repairs. By the spring of 1799, only one year after its removal to Richmond, the court ordered the discontinuance of the road from Milford to Barnes' Mill, clearly signaling the transfer of trade from the old centers to the new Richmond area.[9]

At the close of the eighteenth century, the correlation between economic and political power at the Madison Court is most informative. The Madison Court Tax List reinforced the assumption that a natural aristocracy ruled Madison County, Virginia, as well as Kentucky. Governor Isaac Shelby, married to Suzanna Hart at Fort Boonesborough, recognized this reality in his 1792 appointments. The following table reflects the correlation of economic and political power:

1792-1794 TAX LISTS[10]

Acreage	Horses & Mules	Cattle	Owner	Office
4,813	54	180	Thomas Kennedy, Jr.	J.P.
1,300	9	40	Joseph Kenedy	J.P.
1,800	17	73	Archibald Woods	J.P.
1,800	9	52	Samuel Estill	J.P.
950	8		George Adams	J.P.
850	18	100	David Gass	J.P. Sheriff
1,400	9	23	William Irvine	Clerk
40,000			Green Clay	J.P.

In the 1790s Madisonians ventured into state and even national issues at times. William Irvine, the county clerk, joined the Society for the Promotion of Useful Knowledge which met in Danville and promoted education, agricultural experimentation, and political rights. Kentucky's first three governors—Shelby, Garrard, and Greenup—were members. The group included a large number of the members of the more famous Political Club of Danville. This most famous of all early political clubs held regular Saturday night meetings and sponsored formal parliamentary style debates on suffrage, slavery, economics, constitutions, and basic political issues of the day. Surveyors, lawyers, magistrates, and planters enjoyed the hospitality and conviviality of meeting behind closed doors and keeping their disagreements from the public. They often sponsored subsequent debating societies in their local communities. Men traveled from various parts of the Bluegrass to participate in these discussions.[11]

William Irvine Sr., County Clerk, 1786-1818, portrait in Madison County Court House. Copied by Larry Bailey.

Although Madisonians normally poured their energies into local issues and the promotion of local power, they occasionally participated in larger statewide and even national issues. In 1792 dissident farmers met and complained about the General Assembly's June actions and petitioned the fall session for relief. They circulated a petition calling for the lowering of salaries, tax cuts, acceptance of taxes in farm produce, and regulation of licensing and practicing of lawyers.[12]

In the disputed gubernatorial election of 1796, Green Clay, a leader of the Kentucky senate, assisted a peaceful solution by questioning the constitutionality of the legislature to act and concluded that any power in its jurisdiction for settling the question was "unconstitutional." When the senate refused to act, Governor Garrard retained his executive office.[13]

The following year Madisonians provided the greatest margin for a constitutional convention by voting 975-to-0 in favor of reform or a new convention. When a second referendum became necessary in 1798, Madisonians reaffirmed their committment with a 907-to-1 endorsement. At the same time they opposed reform in representation or the organization of new counties. The opposition was especially evident when 827 voters appealed for creation of Garrard County (1797), which would have resulted in lost representation for Madison County in the General Assembly. When the Madison representatives unanimously blocked a change in the lower house, Garrard residents secured recognition via the state senate.[14]

In August, 1798, citizens of Madison County held a public meeting and openly protested the Alien and Sedition Acts of the federal government. Higgarson Grubbs led the denunciation and later endorsed the Kentucky Resolutions of the state legislature which declared the federal acts unconstitutional, "void and of no force" in Kentucky. Madisonians participated in the state constitutional conventions of 1792 and 1799. Higgarson Grubbs, Thomas Clay, and Joseph Kennedy, Jr. represented the county in the first convention but did not display much influence. In 1799, Green Clay and William Irvine joined Thomas Clay as Madison's delegation. Green Clay proved a more aggressive participant in the proceedings which followed.[15]

Green Clay—a planter-magnate, a power at the Madison Court, and a frequent state representative in the 1790s—wanted to maintain local power and assure legislative supremacy at the state level, recognizing that the assembly was more responsive to the local court parties than to the people. As Joan Wells Coward ably demonstrated in her study of *Kentucky in the New Republic*, Clay "perversely" delighted in outraging the 1799 delegates by applauding the Alien and Sedition Acts and asserting that the federal government exercised all significant power. He credited the states with the power to look after the poor and straighten roads![16]

The convention, despite Clay's sarcasm, named him chairman of the committee to draft the constitution. Clay and the court leaders worked for legislative supremacy and even advocated that the state legislature select the governor by joint ballot of the houses since the best-informed citizens of the state were found there. This antidemocratic move was defeated. Clay did propose judicial reform and pointed to the long trips and needless expenses the existing system entailed. Too, he wanted each county court to have its own circuit judge and two "associates" from the county. He thought untrained judges were more sensitive to local needs and threatened to introduce a motion excluding lawyers from the legislature. Although delegates defeated his circuit court proposal by a thirty to twenty-three margin, change appeared inevitable. Clay, despite political setbacks at the state level, continued to enjoy unlimited political and economic success at home.[17]

During the last decade of the eighteenth century, the Madison County population almost doubled from 5,772 to 10,490; the number of slaves jumped from 737 to 1,729; and little Richmond, founded in 1798 on Miller's Farm, boasted 110 citizens in 1800—this made it the fifteenth largest town in the entire state.[18] The court laid off the county into new districts for the purposes of appointing patrollers, collecting taxes, and maintaining the county roads. Although the number of districts varied from seven to thirteen over the next thirty-five years, the principal areas developed included Otter Creek to Jack's Creek; Richmond to Silver Creek to Jack's Creek; Silver Creek to Paint Lick to the Kentucky River; Estill's Old Station to Taylor's Fork to Silver Creek to Hayes' Fork; Muddy Creek to Estill's New Station; Muddy Creek area; Otter Creek to Crews' Saw Mill to Muddy Creek; Muddy Creek to Otter Creek to Quisenberry's; and Black's to Quisenberry's to Muddy Creek Districts.[19]

On April 2, 1804, the court recorded a plat of the town of Richmond. A year later it ordered the sinking of a public well on the court square and expressed the desire that the cost not exceed $100. The magistrates called for a cleaning of the jail and its improvement through the provision of "a pot or other vessel for the private use of prisoners." That same year the court ordered completion of the courthouse and enclosing of the public square.[20]

By 1806 economic activity on the public square reached alarming proportions and the court ordered that "no one be permitted to sell any article or things within the post and railing around the Courthouse . . . (or) hitch or confine a beast . . . to said post and railing." It instructed deputies to turn loose any beasts so confined and to prosecute offenders for contempt of court. The increasing livestock, especially horses, led to the courts decision to erect a public gallows at the forks of Muddy Creek and Four Mile Road for the purpose of hanging horse thieves. The first legal public hanging in the county followed this action.[21]

The early 1800s witnessed excessively cold weather and farmers had to increase their vigilance for wolves. In the late eighteenth and early nineteenth centuries the court paid farmers for killing wolves and bringing their heads to courts. The increasing numbers in the early 1800s not only underlined severe weather, but also hard times for some farmers who hoped to supplement their income by killing the scavengers. Although the 1801 record of thirty surpassed that of previous years, in 1804 farmers killed thirty-one wolves, and then in 1805 they set an all-time record by shooting forty-eight. In the cold winter of 1808, the magistrates constructed a new jail, and they purchased two tin-pipe-plate pipe stoves as well as window shelters for the courthouse.[22]

In the spirit of renovation and improvement, the magistrates secured new locks for the jail and ordered erection of a kitchen with chimney and also repair of the stray pen on the public square. Posts and railings soon surrounded the square. In 1810 the magistrates approved construction of a market house on the public square. They requisitioned a forty-foot long, twenty-six foot wide structure for the use of farmers and housewives to disperse produce in town. The court further ordered construction of a house for the jailor's family and enclosing of the jail grounds with a railing fence.[23]

The greatest political struggle of the era revolved around the establishment of a county clerk's office on the public square. Rhodes Garth, esquire, appeared in court and requested appropriation of money for the construction of a clerk's office as early as 1809, but the court rejected his proposal. By November, a citizens petition, with sixty-five signatures, surfaced at the court session complaining of the extra travel miles from the courthouse to the clerk's office on the Irvine estate. Green Clay, a virtual neighbor and a close friend of Irvine's, persuaded his associates to again reject the motion to move the clerk's office to town. Notwithstanding, court membership was changing, and public pressure accelerated for the pragmatic removal of the clerk's office from Irvine's home to the courthouse square. In 1810 the court finally approved construction of a separate clerk's office on the southwest corner of the public square. The building was twenty-by-thirty feet, contained fireplaces on the north and south ends, was one story high, contained a pitch wall, and was brick constructed.

By 1810 Richmond boasted a population of some 300 residents, and the consolidation of the clerical and magisterial activities at the public square assured its further economic and political development. The fledgling county seat offered opportunities for honest as well as questionable activities. The crime rate accelerated after 1810 but especially during the War of 1812.

The court utilized the public gallows in hopes of deterring murder, arson, and horse stealing. The court hanged Nelson, a Negro, for murder. It freed Dick, a slave, since he had murdered another slave in self-defense; indicted Joe for burning a barn of Green Clay's but found him "not guilty" and sent William, caught taking money from David C. Irvine's ordinary, to jail. Next William broke into Arch Woods's stable and corn crib and stole a saddle. Later he broke into a residence and took clothes. William was apparently an habitual offender. The court ordered the incarceration of at least one Negro woman, Mulitia, for burglary.[25]

As the War of 1812 approached, Madisonians demonstrated a strong patriotic emotion, and at the county's annual July 4 celebration in Richmond they openly condemned the British for violation of America's neutral rights, Madisonians claimed they favored peace, but only with honor. With the outbreak of war in 1812, 333 Madison soldiers from five companies enlisted for the war in the Northwest. Enthusiasm for the war waned with a series of military disasters in 1812-13. Notwithstanding, Richmond citizens collected several boxes of clothing for the Nineteenth Army and received notes of appreciation. As the war dragged on the General Assembly had to invoke a draft, especially after the River Raisin massacre checked the flow of volunteers. The new levies were substitutes and not good military men. General Green Clay had the unenviable task of commanding these reinforcements, and he led an expedition of some 3,000 soldiers up the River Raisin in the spring of 1813.[26]

Clay and his reinforcements fought their way to Fort Meigs by May 4, 1813, thus saving the entrenched garrison. Upon arrival at the besieged fort, Clay divided his troops. One advance section surprised the Birtish on the Maumee River but exceeded instructions and outran the rest of the army to the point that the British captured several hundred of them. The Indians executed the prisoners, but Clay's army managed to break the siege by May 9. Two months later when Harrison advanced northward he left Clay in command of Fort Meigs, and the Kentuckian repelled a second British attack. Clay came out of the war with a solid military reputation.[27]

Madison County produced several heroes in the war. Captain Christopher Irvine, son of the county clerk, William Irvine, was killed at Fort Meigs on May 5, 1813. J. Speed Smith, later distinguished as a Madison attorney, fought at the great Battle of Tippecanoe. Smith also married a daughter of Green Clay. As late as 1815, seventy-eight men from Madison County enlisted in the army. As the war ended, the Madison County Militia continued to include twenty-four companies as well as militia leaders like Captains George Shackleford, James Dejarnette, and Samuel Estill who reflected the influence of "older" settlers. After the war, the militia companies continued to collect taxes and maintain security.[28]

One of the great controversies of the period arose in 1815 over construction of a public road from Porter's Mill to Hawkins' Mill. Joseph Kennedy complained that the ridge route was nearly three miles long and not as good as alternative routes because of its rough, uneven terrain. He said it required too much labor to maintain and was not used by enough farmers to justify keeping it. Samuel Estill, William Stone, and George Alcorn agreed that farmers did not want a public road through their land and that travelers tore down fences. Yet John Harris said there was no shorter route, and he opposed the change. Finally, Nicholas Hawkins, who had lived there for thirty years, told the court the road was needed despite the labor involved and would help the hilly area residents. He said the entire area was rough and a wagon road to the mill must be maintained since Porter's served as a saw mill and ground the wheat and rye raised by farmers of that area.[29]

A variety of changes occurred in Madison County in the years immediately following the war. The original court clerk, William Irvine, died in 1818, and his son David succeeded him and served the next few decades. Only two senior magistrates, Green Clay and Robert Caldwell, had fifteen or more years' of experience. The other justices of the peace were newcomers although a few could claim family rights to power. Overton Harris. Archibald Woods, Jr., David Chenault, and James Dejarnette inherited land, wealth, and power. By 1820, three newcomers to the political scene who would be future powerbrokers surfaced at court. Thomas Francis, the tavernkeeper, would serve on the court and as high sheriff; Daniel Breck and Squire Turner would become outstanding lawyers, magistrates, and state legislators.[30]

Col. David Irvine. Sr.
Madison Circuit & Court, Clerk
For 40 years

David Irvine Sr., County Clerk, 1818-1845, portrait in Madison County Court House. Copied by Larry Bailey.

As a young man, Squire Turner served as commissioner of revenue in 1813. He then became deputy court clerk under William Irvine. After two years in the clerk's office, Turner resigned and appeared before the magistrates seeking certification to practice law. As usual the certificate stated "To all whom it may concern . . . [Squire Turner] is a person of honesty, probity, and good demeanor" and is authorized "to practice law in Madison County." After two years of law practice, Turner secured the enviable appointment as commonwealth attorney for the court and, as such, handled cases for the state.[31] Turner's rise to power was unusually swift.

Although court membership changed dramatically during the postwar era, traditional policies of deference and nepotism continued. The Harris family proved particularly active between 1809 and 1820. Robert and Christopher Harris served as constables, while the court named their brother Overton as a commissioner of revenue. Overton then became a magistrate in 1813, a position he held for four years. Upon his resignation, the court announced his brother Robert would take his seat at court. In the 1820s, John Harris served as paymaster for the Madison Militia's Nineteenth Regiment.[32]

The economy improved toward the close of the war, and the Madison Court in 1817 established its highest levy of the pre-1820 period at $1,878.50. It also ordered the opening or maintainence of new roads, another new stray pen, a stock and pillory at the courthouse square. Daniel Miller reported the difficulties of collecting taxes that year and complained of the "constant travelling, six to thirty miles per day," and "on my own horse," and at "my own expense." He concluded the expenses exceeded collections.[33] This was an obvious exaggeration, as men continued to seek the position.

In the early days the county court had to supervise many political decisions in the towns and villages. In 1817 the court approved the establishment of the Richmond Fire Company. The purpose of the company was to organize, discipline, and train men to extinguish fires. Based on citizen subscribers, all members were to assemble at the courthouse six times a year on the fourth Friday from January to November and any other times the captains or directors might require. Men were fined twenty-five cents for not attending. The company was to elect a captain and four directors, a clerk, a treasurer, and an inspector of firefighting utensils—including leather buckets, hooks, and ladders.[34]

Retail stores and shops were to furnish two buckets, and townspeople were to furnish one bucket per home for fighting fires. All buckets were kept in public view and there was a twenty-five cent fine for failing to do so. Men were fined one dollar for failing to fight a fire. An engine was purchased and men were required to train. There were nineteen articles of incorporation. Thompson Burnam, David Irvine, Daniel Breck, Squire Turner, and Sam Stone were among the original promoters of the fire company.[35]

In 1817 the court became embroiled in a great political and economic controversy. Oddly enough it was over the establishment of another ferry across the Kentucky River. Green Clay, the senior magistrate, secured permission from the court to send a ferry from his land to the opposite side of the Kentucky River to the old farm of William Bush. Clay apparently posed as attorney for heirs not in possession of the disputed land, and the real heirs charged him with a "fraudulent design" and of trying to "gain possession" of land belonging to the true Bush heirs. While Archibald Woods—the Bush attorney—was absent on public business, Clay found his opportunity and took advantage of Woods' absence. Clay and his colleagues ruled against the Bush heirs in this case. Although Clay seemed to have the upper hand politically and possibly legally, his ethics were questionable. By August, 1817, however, he established his new ferry at old Stone Mill on the Kentucky River. Once his ferry was operating, Clay asked the court for permission to erect another warehouse near the mouth of Drowning Creek.[36]

Although Green Clay's primary interest in the Madison Court rested in its economic decisions, he served on the court almost continually from 1794 until his death in 1828. Since the magistrates rotated offices and the senior justice normally became sheriff, Clay could have held this office much earlier in time, but he consistently turned it down. By the 1820s the magistrates probably assumed he would never serve as sheriff, and so they failed to nominate him in 1820, which led to his raising an objection—reminding them he was the "oldest judge in service." The court apologized and submitted his name to the governor, and this time he accepted the commission as high sheriff in January, 1821. Clay readily acquired the services of James E. Million as his deputy sheriff. He needed a younger man to assist in the more demanding physical labors of the office.[37]

Clay's return to the political arena was partly prompted by changing economic conditions in the countryside. The Panic of 1819 had finally reached into Madison County and there were numerous signs of serious economic problems. Farmers, especially the old revolutionary war veterans, checked their pride and sought pensions and economic assistance. The banks flooded the area with paper money. Politicians divided into relief and antirelief factions. Creditors were alarmed at the depreciation of their loans and insisted on hard money, while debtors, facing hopeless confusion, insisted they must pay their loans in paper if they were to pay them at all.

In 1821, a number of Revolutionary War veterans appealed to the Madison Court, affirming their participation in the war, revealing their desperate economic conditions, and petitioning for financial assistance. John Land, a veteran of the Brandywine and Germantown campaigns, noted his wife's disability, his age, and the uselessness of his limbs. He owned 156 acres of poor land at Paint Lick and listed one cow, seven hogs, eight sheep, and some poultry. Joseph Gowin, a sixty-three-old veteran, complained of a stiff knee, the cost of supporting four children, and property valued at less than $150. Christopher Coy, a three-year veteran, had a bad back, owned property valued at thirty-five dollars, and was indigent. William Chandler, a wheelright for three years during the Revolutionary War, was blind, infirm, seventy-five years old; and he had property valued at seventy dollars. Henry Lynch—a four-year veteran—claimed infirmities and recorded property valued at $19.25. Lynch was the poorest applicant to come to court. The magistrates could do little but validate the pension petitions and thank the old men for past services.[38]

Economic problems accelerated during this decade. Poor banking practices precipitated the greatest economic and political crisis of the era. A certain laxity characterized banks throughout the War of 1812, and many new state or local banks jeopardized their assets by overextending their loans as well as circulating too much paper money. Kentucky and Madison County banks were as guilty as some of the national institutions. In 1819 the Bank of the United States began foreclosing on creditors and demanding specie from the state banks. The Richmond Independent Bank, chartered in 1817, was one that had circulated excessive paper and consequently lost its charter in a repeal of 1820. Madison County's Thomas C. Howard, a state legislator, expressed his hope that half of Kentucky's currency be burned and inflationary policies crushed. He insisted that debts made in good money be repaid in kind. An Otter Creek farmer, writing to the local newspaper, also bemoaned the use of so much paper currency in the county. The state ultimately burned one million notes of the State Bank and the Commonwealth Bank, two of Kentucky's largest financial institutions. After May 1, 1823, all contracts had to be paid in hard specie.[39]

The public quickly divided into relief and antirelief factions. The same two groups later received the labels of new court and old court parties, as the economic argument resulted in a legislative and judicial struggle. The relief faction favored the acceptance of paper currency, time extensions and more generous loans to debtors, and legislative action to aid the debtor class. Ultimately, it supported the development of new courts to assist debtors in their judicial struggles with the conservative creditors and judges who dominated the old court system. The end result was the establishment of a new court which vied with the more legitimate old court for judicial cases involving the creditor-debtor controversy. Although the relief party carried the state by a two-to-one margin in 1820 (42,000 to 19,800), Madison County was antirelief in this election and in the 1823 and 1824 contests, when the relief faction reached its peak.[40]

During the early 1820s the relief faction implemented several changes, engulfing the state courts in the controversy. The legislature tried to enact laws to aid the debtors during the panic and banking collapse of 1820, including a replevin law which delayed payment of debts for up to two years. The legislators revoked banking charters and proposed various relief measures. The state abolished imprisonment for debt, established a Bank of the Commonwealth, made large loans, and printed additional paper money. As the antireliefers anticipated, the notes soon fell to a fraction of their face value.[41]

Thomas C. Howard, the prominent merchant, represented Madison County in the state senate, while Squire Turner was its most articulate representative in the state assembly. Both men tended to be antirelief conservatives, and they kept the public informed of legislative plans. Both opposed a constitutional convention and noted that a constitutional majority was lacking to remove the old judges. Senator Howard predicted the senate would fail to pass a constitutional convention bill, and an eighteen-to-eighteen vote soon followed, thus complicating the problem of reliefers in their legal approach to the problem. This failure of the reliefers to gain constitutional change or an elective judiciary forced them to focus on the gubernatorial election of 1824 as their last hope.[42]

In the meantime, the court of appeals endorsed the lower court's decision against the relief party. Howard's newspaper, to his credit, carried letters from farmers complaining about the new courts as well as the antirelief legislators. "An Otter Creek Farmer," a frequent newspaper correspondent, complained of taxes, of court clerks, and of judges.

He particularly noted that deputy clerks performed most official duties for overpaid clerks and condemned "judicial usurpation and power" that negated the legislative majority. He condemned the court's repealing of laws and the inability of the people to check court power. He contended that judicial usurpers were violating popular will.[43]

In 1823, as the relief party continued to inflate the currency and reduce the profits of creditors, Green Clay surprised Madisonians by announcing his candidacy for the state legislature. He wrote a long letter to the *Richmond Republican* reviewing his patriotic service to the community and describing himself as "a servant of the people" concerned for laborers and farmers. He promised to curb the paper circulation and restore hard specie. Anticipating attacks on his large land acquisitions, he defended his wealth. As candidates announced their willingness to serve in the legislature, the field became rather crowded. Clay's competitors were militia leaders or prominent local lawyers. Although all seven candidates were from "old families," only Clay represented the eighteenth century power brokers.[44]

The newspaper listed the Madison candidates for the three state legislative seats as Colonel James Dejarnett, Colonel William Black, Major William Kerley, General Green Clay, Daniel Breck, Esquire, Archibald Woods Junior, Esquire, and Major Squire Turner, Esquire. Turner enjoyed both militia and court support. At the close of the August election it was obvious that two lawyers, Woods and Turner, led the race, with Colonel Dejarnette running third. Clay was fourth and was elimintated. It was his last race and one of his few political defeats. The totals read:

ELECTION RESULTS[45]

Woods	1,213
Turner	1,140
Dejarnett	1,090
Clay	908
Breck	881
Black	298
Kerley	138

The legislative race of 1823 clearly reflected Madisonian support of antirelief forces, as Woods, Turner, Clay, and Breck were unequivocal in their opposition to relief or the new court discussion. In the months following, the *Richmond Republican*, ex-legislator Howard's paper, was equally predisposed. It carried a variety of articles, opinions, and news on the banking problems. By April, 1824, it stated that debtors to the Richmond Branch Bank could renew their notes and payments and make necessary arrangements on April 14, and that branch notes were insufficient for the Bank of Kentucky. That summer Squire Turner and Daniel Breck, prominent lawyers, announced their candidacies for the state assembly. Arch Woods, Jr. soon entered the race. The newspaper reaffirmed its antirelief position and condemned the new court, the inflationists, and reliefers. Howard's paper also questioned if "a creditor should acknowledge it a favor when a debtor pays a long over-due bill.'' The paper reaffirmed the sanctity of contracts and denounced the reliefers' efforts as unconstitutional and unethical. Senator Howard stated he had never favored replevin laws under any circumstances.[46]

In the August elections the antirelief candidates for the state assembly won all three seats by decisive margins. Breck polled 1,500 votes, Turner was second with 1,394, and Archibald Woods Jr. secured the third seat with 1,150. The most pronounced relief cnadidate, Simpson, won 398 votes. In the gubernatorial race Madison County gave Tompkins, the antirelief candidate, 1,278 votes to Deshea's 560, but the relief faction won the statewide campaign nonetheless. Deshea soon removed judges from the court of appeals and appointed new court justices under the reorganization bill of 1824. Madisonians began focusing on the national election as Arch Woods, chaired a Committee to Elect Henry Clay the next president.[47]

The presidential election was a mere interlude in the stormy relief battle. Madisonians frequently anticipated many of the arguments that followed in the old court-new court political struggle. The old court forces won the legislative races of 1826 and secured passage of a repeal bill eliminating the new court. Ultimately, by the close of the decade, the old court forces triumphed in the state as they had earlier done in Madison County. Senator Howard, through his newspaper, and Squire Turner, through the legislature, molded public opinion and emphasized the constitutional issues, the sanctity of contracts, and the conservative values of the era. They literally destroyed the credibility of the relief faction.[48]

The Madison Court tried an increasing number of vagrants during the mid-1820s. Squire Turner's son Archibald took the oath as a new attorney and counselor at law in 1824, while the senior representative continued to serve as commonwealth attorney before the Madison Court. Squire Turner, Daniel Breck, and Archibald Woods expressed similar political views on all the issues of the day, including property laws, court clerk powers, and relief. The concensus of the political elite was no accident, as ''gentlemen'' of the early nineteenth century often presented a united front.[49]

Social interaction often encouraged a cohesive community. In 1820 several political and professional leaders formed the Richmond Philosophical Society. Twenty-five gentlemen paid a dollar in dues that first year, and seventeen charter members attended the first meeting on December 12 at William Kerby's establishment. They adopted a constitution and elected officers, including Daniel Breck, an attorney and political figure, as president; Dr. John Stout, vice-president; and Abram J. Smith, secretary-treasurer. Joseph Turner became the secretary-treasurer one month later upon Smith's resignation. The society served as a social and intellectual exchange between men of similar interests and permitted political debate on numerous topics.[50]

The philosophical society was reminiscent of the famed Danville Political Club of the late eighteenth century. The list of members

Daniel Breck. Dorris Collection, EKU Townsend Room.

included the dominant lawyers, merchants, and farmers of the community. Breck, William Caperton, Squire Turner, and J. Speed Smith represented the legal system and joined Thomas Gentry and C. J. Walker as important political figures in Madison County. William Miller, Joseph Turner, and David Irvine were wealthy farmers, while James Bennett, Anthony W. Rollins, and John Stout represented the medical profession. William and Clifton Rodes were businessmen as well as farmers.[51]

The gentlemen discussed a variety of topics in the 1820s, debated many controversial political issues, and always voted on the presentations debated. The topics underlined their diversity of interests, which included political, economic, social, and educational subjects. In the initial debate, Caperton and Rollins presented persuasively the case for "Higher Duties on Articles of Foreign Manufacturers," and the group endorsed higher tariffs. The society split its decision on "Capital Punishment for Crimes" and on a proposal to "Increase the Navy." However, members debated and endorsed a proposal to "Repeal laws relating to Usury" and debated "Should all Laws for Imprisonment for Debt be abolished?"[52]

The gentlemen enjoyed their weekly meetings and did not object to the long hours, although several inn keepers discouraged them by raising prices for the meeting room, candles, and other provisions, which resulted in the society's relocating at least four different times in the early months. One proprietor, a Mr. Allison, actually "begged to be released" from providing a meeting room. Interestingly, the society overwhelmingly defeated a motion to limit speakers to three quarters of an hour on any subject.[53]

As time progressed the group turned to other, less politically charged issues, such as the "Progress of Medicine," "Are the Talents of the Sexes Equal?" "Is Love of Virtue and Hatred of Vice Instinctive in Man?" and "Should Females be Excluded from Suffrage?" The society had moved its bimonthly meetings to the courthouse by June, 1821.[54] In many ways the philosophical society represented power as well as intellectual curiosity, for all its members were men of influence. As it admitted new members it also continued to serve as a private means for settling issues before public debate divided the community.

Although a natural aristocracy continued to rule Madison County for the duration of the ante-bellum period, the old political powerbrokers were rapidly passing from the scene. Green Clay, one of the last of the eighteenth century politicos, came to court less frequently as he suffered increasingly from cancer of the throat. Clay, almost seventy years old, approached death with the same systematic businesslike attitude that characterized him in earlier days. He continued to complain to the court of the unnecessary expenses in repairing his warehouse at Jack's Creek and secured the court's revision of an earlier edict. Although he never shared the extreme antislavery sentiments of his son Cassius, he rewarded those slaves who served him faithfully through the years by emancipating them and providing for their maintainence. He freed ten of his favorite slaves—giving each money, a residence, and fifty acres of land below the Tennessee River. He divided his estate between his six surviving children—leaving each money in trust, slaves, and land. Cassius M. Clay received "Clermont and the surrounding land for his lifetime. On October 31, 1828, Madison County lost the dominant economic and political leader of it's early history.[55] In terms of economic and political impact on the county, Green Clay far surpassed his illustrious and controversial son Cassius.

By the late 1820s the old Jeffersonian Republican party had disintegrated, and the Henry Clay-Andrew Jackson split permeated all of the nation as the future Whigs and Democrats quarreled at the state and local levels. In Madison County the Jacksonians were the minority, and their plight deepened into the 1840s. The Jacksonians fielded only one electable candidate from 1824 to 1848, and that was J. Speed Smith, Green Clay's son-in-law, a military hero of the War of 1812 and a popular Richmond lawyer. Significantly, Smith's highest total of votes for twenty years occurred in 1823—prior to his alignment with the Jacksonians—when he polled 1,511 votes for the national congressional seat but lost the overall race outside Madison County to Robert Letcher.[56]

At the beginning of the partisan movement the Jacksonians appeared to be a strong minority, and although the Whigs consistently won the three house seats, Albert G. Daniel barely edged out Smith in

John Speed Smith. Dorris Collection, EKU Townsend Room.

1828 and again in 1829. Smith's showing in the last race probably assured him appointment as the U. S. district attorney for Kentucky in 1829 since President Jackson wanted to replace John J. Crittenden, an Adams administration appointee and Clay ally. Whatever the case, Smith entered the legislative race of 1830 and ran third, a hundred-odd votes ahead of the incumbent Daniel, thus allowing the Jacksonians to record their only election victory for over a decade in Madison County. Even Jackson himself had failed to carry the county in 1828, when Adams had won by an 866-653 total. The Jacksonians failed to secure over a third of the votes in any other state or national election for the remainder of the 1830s.[57]

Somewhat surprisingly, old Green Clay's death in 1828 did not mark a political watershed. The old politics continued, as nepotism dominated the local court into the 1830s. Following the death of Thomas Watts, a long-time ally of Green Clay, the court named his son William Watts as magistrate in 1825. It designated Joseph Miller as Colonel of the militia, and Joseph Turner and Thompson Burnam as trustees of Richmond. In 1830, Sheriff Nicholas Hocker appointed his sons George and James as deputies. The lone exception to this nepotic trend occurred in 1835 when magistrate John Broaddus resigned because his brother Richard was appointed Madison County sheriff.[58]

Throughout the 1820s and 1830s the old families dominated the court and even the state legislative races. From 1828 through 1835

William Harris, William Caperton, Clifton, Rodes, Squire Tuner, J. Speed Smith, Edmund Shackelford, Andrew Crews, and Cassius M. Clay won assembly seats with frequency, while Archibald Woods, Jr., and Robert Miller served in the state senate. At least one house seat went to the old aristocracy in every election, and in 1830 Squire Turner, Clifton Rodes, and J. Speed Smith made it a grand sweep of all three assembly seats.[59]

Interestingly, as early as 1824 all three victorious candidates for the state assembly—Breck, Turner, and Woods—were lawyers. The dominance of lawyers in Madison County was unsurpassed by any other Kentucky county. Although 12 of the 100 counties had more lawyers than Madison County in the 1850 census, none witnessed the political dominance of the Madison legal profession. Two decades after the lawyers' sweep of the 1824 election, the dominant court figures and state legislators of Madison County included Daniel Breck, senior and junior, Curtis F. Burnam, the three Capertons, William Chenault, the two Tuners, J. Speed Smith, and William Goodloe. All these men were lawyers. Chenault, Smith, and Breck even served in the state senate in the 1840s, and all three had served previous terms in the assembly. They won eleven elections in the 1840s. Only the Fields family, including Curtis F. and David J., failed to secure a legislative seat; however, the family did exert influence by intermarrying with the Burnams and the Smiths.[60]

The nepotism and economic manipulations of the local court also reflected Madisonians' provincialism, for most of the county's political leaders concentrated on local issues and rarely assumed state or national leadership. Madisonian politicos were predominantly Whigs during the Jacksonian era but avoided the more divisive political issues except relief and slavery well into the 1840s.

Lawyers replaced the old farmers and militia leaders who had dominated the political stage in the earlier period. Archibald Woods and Squire Turner frequently won elections, as Daniel Breck did. Despite his military connections, James DeJarnett lost as many election as he won. During the 1820s Madison County frequently elected three Whigs to the General Assembly and one to the Kentucky senate. Woods led the ticket with 1,213 votes in 1823, and Breck polled over 1,500 votes the next year.[61]

In 1834, William Miller defeated DeJarnette 1069 to 756 for the Kentucky senate while C. J. Walker (1,219) and Daniel Breck (1,091) were elected to the Kentucky General Assembly. A third Whig, Thomas J. Gentry, polled 884 votes. By 1835, Gentry did serve in the Kentucky house. Throughout the 1830s, the Whigs maintained a two-to-one margin. Madisonians helped elect and re-elect John White to the U. S. House of Representatives from 1835 to 1845. Unlike the other political figures, White frequently ran unopposed (in 1835 and 1839) and acquired national prominence. However, he was the exception, not the rule.[62]

In looking at the local representatives' contributions in the state legislature, it is easy to discern their local or provincial interests. J. Speed Smith (Green Clay's son-in-law) introduced a bill to reduce the price of unappropriated (vacant) land in Madison County, presented a petition of local citizens requesting another election precinct, sponsored a bill to prohibit the marketing and sale of ardent spirits by free Negroes, and on four occasions sought the establishment of county roads. Smith was actually one of the most active Madison legislators in Frankfort.[63]

At the local level, new names dotted the Madison county magistrate lists of the 1830s. Although some came from old-line farm families, such as the Chenaults and Millions, others such as the Lipscombs, Hockers, Newbys, and Francises were newcomers. The fact that politics surfaced in tavern discussions is evidenced by the number of tavernkeepers who became prominent on the political scene. By the 1830s the Shackelford, Newby, Million, and Francis families ran the most popular taverns. This was an old trend, as the Adamses, Phelpses, Millers, and Shackelfords had done likewise earlier.[64]

As noted earlier, in the decades immediately preceeding the Civil War, lawyers dominated the Madison County political scene. The state legislators as well as the powerbrokers who followed Green Clay were generally lawyers. Several of these men held significant offices and influenced local, state, and occasionally national policy. Squire Turner, one of the most significant constitutional framers of 1849, served as commonwealth attorney and as a state legislator throughout this era. Archibald Woods, Jr., a frequent legislative colleague and long-time Madison attorney, heavily influenced local politics. Woods introduced his nephew William H. Caperton to the Madison bar in 1818, and Caperton soon followed his uncle to the state legislature. He also headed political campaigns for three Whig presidential candidates in the 1840s. Daniel Breck, a magistrate, Richmond attorney, and state legislator, became chief justice of the court of appeals in 1843. John White, a dynamic, articulate, brilliant Richmond lawyer, became a U. S. congressean from the Bluegrass in 1835, served five successive terms in the House of Representatives, and presided as Speaker from 1843 to 1845. He accepted appointment to the federal circuit court in 1845 but served briefly since he committed suicide that same year. The domination of the Madison lawyers continued for the duration of the ante-bellum period.[65]

The court expressed increasingly great concern over public health in the 1830s as a result of cholera and small pox epidemics. In 1832 cholera resulted in several deaths in the county, and the court declared August 18, 1832, as a day of thanksgiving since the epidemic had passed. A year later cholera affected citizens of Richmond. Many fled the town until the epidemic subsided in the late summer. Again the court declared a day of thanksgiving on August 23. A small pox epidemic swept through the Bluegrass, including Madison County, in 1836. Once again the sheriff secured burial of the dead and the court appropriated $100 for the improvement of the public wells on the courthouse square.[66]

As the decade of the 1830s came to a close it was obvious that great changes had occurred in the Madison Court, its composition, its attitudes, and its concerns for public welfare. However, it was equally obvious that the court's power remained enormous, unchallenged, and all-encompassing. Politics remained nepotic, conservative, and economically motivated, although some reform efforts of the era were gaining momentum, and there was discussion of curbing the court's power in the immediate future.

Chapter Four

RELIGION AND CULTURE IN EARLY MADISON COUNTY

The Virginians, Carolinians, and Pennsylvanians who settled on the Madison frontier generally brought specific religious and cultural attitudes, traits, and patterns with them. However, they faced such serious challenges to survival that society and culture languished for years. Notwithstanding, there were significant efforts to establish churches, provide moral codes, encourage communal goals, punish crime, regulate behavior, assist the elderly and indigent, and educate the young. As the economy improved in the 1820s, the local court provided more social services and increased opportunities for citizens to improve their lifestyles. Religious, political, and social organizations disseminated more public information on a variety of topics. A community pride developed. Madison society proved increasingly complex.

In 1786 Madisonians established their first church, and by the close of the eighteenth century a dozen churches served as social and cultural centers for frontiersmen. The early Boonesborough attempts to organize enduring religious and cultural institutions failed, and a sparsely scattered population complicated the development of a cohesive cultured society throughout the Virginia period.

Early church and court record books reflected the community's desire to encourage an enlightened cultural viewpoint and to regulate social behavior. Education was a decided failure throughout the antebellum period. This in turn hampered the dissemination of information by any local newspaper or library. Social consciousness developed slowly, and social services were minimal. Madisonians preferred an active social life to intellectual development. They attended militia musters, political debates, barbecues, agricultural fairs, and public brawls. The churches, the most conservative socializing agent, were the primary enculturating promoter of "genteel" culture.

There were few ministers and fewer churches on the Kentucky frontier. Despite the difficulties and dangers pioneers faced on the new frontier, the Reverend John Lythe held the first [recorded] religious ceremony under the Great Elm at Fort Boonesborough on May 28, 1775. Early ministers like Squire Boone solemnized weddings but otherwise spent their time taming the wilderness, thus ignoring their religious calling.[1] Slowly, circuit riders entered Kentucky in the 1780s. After a brief appearance before the new county court to request permission "to solemnize marriages, agreeable to the rites and ceremonies" of their respective denominations, many disappeared forever. Few ministers had theological training or were supported by local congregations with their own meeting houses. Still, the arrival of any religious leader denoted a community's concern for its salvation.

On December 26, 1786, the Madison County Court authorized the Reverend James Haw, a Methodist, as the first minister who could "solemnize the rites of matrimony."[2] The Reverend Thomas Williamson, another Methodist, and Christopher Harris, an outstanding Baptist leader, produced credentials for their respective denominations in 1788.[3] The Reverend Fedregil Adams, one of the most active Baptist ministers in Madison County, appeared before the court in 1789. The Reverend Charles Kavanaugh, the longest serving and most active Methodist leader, took his oath in 1790.[4]

With Kentucky's admission to the Union in 1792, ministers returned to the court for new credentials. That year eight Madison clergymen took their oaths and gained authorization. Andrew Tribble, the famed Tates Creek separatist joined Adams and Harris as dominant Baptist spokesmen. Although Thomas Shelton and Thomas Chilton proved more active in Baptist congregations in neighboring counties, both also appeared before the Madison Court. Kavanaugh, the senior Methodist leader, renewed his license, while John Manier and Alexander McKay took the oath for the first time. The latter two did not renew their authorizations and apparently migrated westward.[5]

Six more trained clergymen entered the county during the 1790s. A Methodist, John Pace (1796), two Presbyterians, Samuel Findley (1796) and Matthew Houston (1797), and three Baptists—Peter Woods (1795), Dozier Thornton (1795), and Henry Brooks (1799)—appeared before the court.[6] Some churches organized without the benefit of trained clergymen, relying on elders who received the call. Other congregations shared ministers licensed in other counties. A Fayette minister, John Tanner of the Boone's Creek Church (Athens), founded the Tate's Creek Regular Baptist Church in 1793 but never sought proper credentials from the Madison Court.[7]

Until the turn of the century, the Baptist, Methodist, and Presbyterian sects alone claimed followers in Madison County. These three sects provided educated or semi-trained leaders and constructed meeting houses used primarily for worship services. Not all ministers in the county gained commissions to perform marriage ceremonies or religious sacraments, and some known lay leaders as well as clergymen are missing from court records. Despite the initial efforts of the other two sects, the Baptists dominated the religious scene throughout the early stage of Madison County history.

Madison Baptists, like their Virginia and Carolina antecedents, split into two distinctive groups in the eighteenth century. "Regulars" emphasized organization and formed many associations. They sought a trained and educated ministry; wanted authorized men to perform the ritual of baptism and other religious rituals; endorsed universalism, the doctrine that all men are eventually saved; endorsed the Philadelphia Confession, a popular creed of Baptists in the Northeast; frowned on the excessive emotionalism of frontier congregations; sometimes encouraged "open communion"; and frequently discontinued the laying on of hands and footwashing ceremonies. The Regular Baptists tended to settle in the upper Bluegrass, rarely moving southward across the Kentucky River.[8]

By contrast, "Separate" Baptists urged local control and reluctantly joined regional organizations. They permitted untrained men who possessed "the gift" to preach. Elders exercised significant powers and performed numerous rituals in the churches. Separatists rejected all creeds but the Bible, denounced universalism, urged exclusive communion, and stressed the laying on of hands and footwashing ceremonies. They were more emotional in worship and frequently shared religious experiences, confessions, and the "light," and trembled, wept, or screamed joyously. They saw religious experiences as crucial to salvation.[9] They settled south of the Kentucky River, especially in Madison County.

Baptist churches in Madison County reflected these theological divisions as well as the movement by moderates to unite the two groups. In Virginia, United Baptists emphasized the similarities of the groups and affected a union. In Kentucky, James Garrard, a three-time moderator of the Baptist Convention between 1790 and 1795, as well as future governor, tried to unite the two groups. At the local level, Andrew Tribble, the Tate's Creek Separate Baptist minister, helped organize the Tate's Creek Association of United Baptists in 1793 and sought reunion between the divided Baptists along the Virginia plan. Indians killed Thomas Shelton as he journeyed to Virginia with a religious petition for United Baptists.[10]

Tribble and the Madison churches offer special problems to the historian, as "Regular" and "Separate" labels changed. United Baptists sometimes included both groups, and control in local churches fluctuated. Too, the Tate's Creek Association admitted both groups after 1801. Tribble headed a Separate Baptist Church at Tate's Creek from 1786 until his death in 1822. However, he seems to have been inconsistent in doctrine and attended a variety of separatist and union meetings. He helped organize a dozen churches, some of which became Regular Baptist, eventually Campbellite denominations. He actively participated in the Elkhorn Association of Regular Baptists, the South Kentucky Association of Separate Baptists, and the Tate's Creek Association of United Baptists.[11]

Separate Baptists emphasized evangelism and organized several Madison churches in the eighteenth century. Although Tanner's Tates Creek Regular Baptist Church may have been the first, it did not survive the century. Nearby, Tribble's Tate's Creek Separate Baptist Church proved the most dynamic and claimed 175-200 members in the 1790s. Tribble helped organize a congregation at Otter Creek by 1795 (some records indicate 1786).Christopher Harris, an active Baptist missionary, helped establish Mt. Nebo at Dreaming Creek by 1796 and a United Baptist of Muddy Creek in 1797. The latter group changed its name to Viney Fork and boasted a membership of over 250 members by 1801. Along with the Tate's Creek separatists it claimed the largest Madison congregation for years. Baptists, generally separatists, also founded churches at White Oak (1790), Callaway's Creek (1801), Flatwoods (1801), Red Lick (1802), and Cane Springs (1803).[12] The White Oak and Flatwoods congregations erected buildings in 1801 and joined the Tate's Creek Association of United Baptists.[13]

The Tates Creek Baptists often reflected majority views on the Madison frontier. By 1805 the congregation insisted that transfers "be examined anew" and that members reject doctrinal impurities, membership in Masonic orders, and extreme emotionalism common at recent revivals, especially shaking and jerking.[14] Interestingly, the Richmond

Cane Springs Baptist Church. J. Winston Coleman Collection Transylvania University Library Special Collections Department.

Presbyterians, more tolerant of secret societies, shared a building with the Masonic order for years.

David Chenault, who helped organize Mt. Nebo, White Oak Pond, and Cane Springs, was a dominant leader during this period. His main church was at Cane Springs (1803). His congregation insisted on immersion and condemned any other form of baptism. New or transfer members had to undergo immersion for full membership.[15] Chenault joined Andrew Tribble, his father-in law, and Christopher Harris in organizing the Union Meeting House in 1812. They expressed grave concern "over the universal depravity" common in the community. They also recognized a sister as privileged "to exercise her gift in the church" contrary to more orthodox practices.[16]

Union Baptist Church set aside a day for fasting and prayer in 1823 and used "the practice of foot washing." Five years later it performed the foot washing practice at communion time rather than during traditional evening hours. Union Baptists also emphasized communion.[17] The Tate's Creek Separate Baptists emphasized personal experiences and admitted old Colonel Estill to membership only after he shared a revelation in 1832.[18]

Despite significant disagreements, Baptists continued to work in the vineyards. They founded new churches at Union Baptist (1812), Bethel (1813), Hays Fork (1819), Hine's Bent (1821), and Richmond (1828).[19] Following Alexander Campbell's visit to Richmond in 1824, Baptist record books express repeated concern over "the Campbell heresy."

Although Presbyterians and Methodists sometimes joined the Campbellite movement, it was the splintering Baptists who proved most vulnerable. Campbell encouraged localism, separatism, congregationalism, universalism, a New Testament emphasis, and liberal views on transubstantiation. In 1830 the Tate's Creek Association recognized the threat and excluded five of its Madison County ministers. During the furor, Viney Fork promoted a debate between Baptists and Campbellites.[20] Viney Fork excluded one brother for "imbibing the doctrine of universalism" and another for even allowing Campbellites to meet in the church building. Seven of the twelve churches in the association survived the bitter division. The Viney Fork congregation promised to continue its resistance to a philosophy "inconsistent with the Gospel" and never to "tolerate the heresy of Campbellism."[21]

Splintering Baptists particularly argued over Campbell's view of atonement or the doctrine of universalism. The Flatwoods, White Oak, and Mt. Nebo churches took on the Campbellite label, while dissident members joined older churches or formed new ones, notably in Richmond and Kirksville (1828 and 1838).[22]

During the pioneer period Methodists organized several congregations in Madison County. The Reverend James Haw, who preached at Estill's Fort, conducted the first great religious revival in the county in 1786.[23] The Reverend Haw converted Joseph Proctor, an Indian fighter and survivor of the Battle of Little Mountain. Proctor's conversion loomed important, as he later constructed a log chapel above Boonesborough.[24]

Viney Fork Baptist Church (Muddy Creek in 1797) had a 250 member congregation by 1801. J. Winston Coleman Collection, Transylvania University Library Special Collections Department.

Originally Flatwoods Baptist Church in 1801. Called Flatwoods Christian Church by the 1830s. J. Winston Coleman Collection, Transylvania University Library Special Collections Department.

Bishop Asbury visited the county in 1790 to encourage the Methodist leaders. During the 1790s the Methodists organized Proctor's Chapel (1790 or 1793), and a circuit including Muddy Creek, Green's Chapel, Concord, and Irvine by 1796.[25] In 1799, Methodists under William Burke charged Baptists with doing everything possible "to draw off our members and get them into the water."[26] Apparently the small numbers of members led to active proselyting.

Competition surfaced when the Cane Springs Baptists noted that Pheobe Hubbard had joined the Methodists and a committee appointed "to labor with the sister" and "show her her error" had failed.[27] Possibly recognizing the turmoil in the Baptist fold as a result of Campbellism, possibly motivated purely by missionary zeal, Methodists sought and gained seventy converts in Richmond in 1836, three years after the establishment of a church but almost a decade before they erected a building.[28] In an effort to underline their differences, the Reverend William Burke, a Methodist, and the Reverend Thomas Shelton, a Baptist, engaged in a four-hour debate on the topic of sprinkling versus immersion.[29]

Presbyterians were the third group to promote their denomination in Madison County. The Old Round Top (Silver Creek) Presbyterian Church was organized in 1790. The Reverend James Crawford was its minister.[30] By 1797 it shared a minister with the Paint Lick Presbyterians. Eight years later the Paint Lick people purchased land for a building.[31] The two churches cooperated in holding a joint revival in 1802 in an effort to attract new members. Revivalists were emotional and engaged in falling, rolling, barking, and the "jerks." The Presbyterian revivalists promoted the Arian Doctrine, which denied the trinity and traditional atonement. Shortly, the Reverend Houston and several of his followers joined the Shaker movement. Although the Presbytery dismissed Houston and reorganized the Silver Creek Church in 1807, the damage was done. Silver Creek Presbyterians denounced "absence from communion."[32] Some later joined the Campbellites. Paint Lick Presbyterians repaired their brick building in 1814 and lost their minister three years later because of "insufficient pay," a problem in many early churches.[33]

First Presbyterian Church of Richmond, 1828. W. R. Shackelford, *Annals of the First Presbyterian Church,* **inside cover.**

Mt. Pleasant Christian Church. J. Winston Coleman Collection, Transylvania University Library Special Collections Department.

As the 1820s drew to a close the three pioneer sects continued to dominate the county's religious attitudes. However, theological differences, numerous revivals, dissent within existing churches, and the development of the Campbellite movement led to alterations in religious patterns during the 1830s. As noted earlier, five of the old "Separatist" Baptist churches broke their ties with the Tate's Creek Association and soon took the name of Christian Church. These included Flatwoods, White Oak, and Mt. Nebo. Additional Disciples or Christian churches were organized in Richmond and the county after 1840.

Early church record books reflect community mores and behavioral modes far more than theological differences. Pioneer denominations often promoted similar ideas. Madison Baptists reflected a conservative position and proved less tolerant of non-Baptists particularly, and they condemned membership in Masonic orders, while Richmond Presbyterians shared a building with the Masonic Lodge. Baptists insisted on baptism by immersion, even for transfers, while Methodists and Presbyterians accepted sprinkling as sufficient. Baptists required testimonials or religious experiences by new members and were suspicious of transfers. Yet Baptists and Methodists proselytized to such a degree that each denounced the other for aggressive tactics.

Madison Baptists, at least the Tate's Creek variety, excluded a member for "selling cake or candy on Meeting days"—the forerunner to modern Blue Laws.[34] Cane Springs Baptists denounced a brother for "hunting on the Sabbath."[35] Most early churches took a dim view of profanity. Presbyterians and Baptists frowned on it. The Cane Springs Baptists excluded a brother for "swearing" in 1813, while the Silver Creek Presbyterians suspended Doctor Alex Miller for "using profane language, viz. dang it, dern, and damit."[36] Tate's Creek, in 1818, excluded a sister for using "saucy language."[37]

Baptists and Presbyterians condemned music. The Tate's Creek Church excluded a brother for dancing in 1826, while Cane Springs Baptists reprimanded one brother for "fiddling" in 1821 and another for "playing the violin." The Richmond Presbyterians excluded a sister for "permitting balls and a dancing school in her home."[38] Churches sometimes promoted temperance. The Tate's Creek Baptists excluded a member for "selling liquor on Sunday." Cane Springs reprimanded old Sister Tincyer for "drinking too much." The normally tolerant Presbyterians of Richmond excluded a sister for "dispensing spirits."[39] Since it is the only instance in which Presbyterians promoted temperance, it was probably the issue of a sister selling spirits, not the liquor itself.

Sexual behavior was a common concern, and illicit sex was universally condemned by frontier churches. The Tate's Creek Baptists excluded a sister "for having a child without a legal husband." It condemned a brother for "visiting a house of ill fame," although no reference to its location is given.[40] The Union Baptists excluded a brother with "the disease." He claimed "he doesn't know how he caught it." They excluded another brother for being "familiar with a married woman."[41]

Sexual trespasses had no racial bounds. Cane Springs Baptists excluded two black sisters for "raising a [scandalous] report on a White male. . .a false report at that." It excluded a sister "caught by her husband with another man in unchaste conduct."[42] Tate's Creek Baptists excluded "Tilly for having a child" and another sister for "showing her pantaloons."[43] The Cane Springs Baptists excluded "Brother George, a black man, for getting drunk and going after women," and Moses for improper conduct toward a young woman.[44]

Baptists maintained a close surveillance on economic activities in the community. The Tates Creek Church frowned on business transactions of any kind on the Sabbath. It excluded one member "for not paying debts" in 1804 and another for "purchasing lottery tickets" in 1816.[45] Cane Springs condemned a brother for "weighing bacon" improperly, and another for "taking U. S. money and refusing to bear arms" in 1813. It also condemned "temporal business on the Sabbath."[46]

Fighting also ran counter to Baptist codes. The Cane Springs Church reprimanded Brother William Harris and his wife, as they had "fell out and fit" in 1808. It excluded a member in 1821 for his continuous involvement in fights. The Tate's Creek Baptists excluded a brother for fighting, too.[47]

Although the early churches accepted slavery as legal, several of them scrutinized owner-slave relations and openly condemned mistreatment of those in servitude. The Methodist Episcopal Church officially discouraged members from buying slaves after 1813. It justified the purchase of slaves only "for mercy and humanity" and urged buyers to state how long a slave must work for compensation.[48]

Richmond Presbyterians condemned a brother for "dealing in Negroes as merchandise." Cane Springs Baptists investigated rumors of white-black sexual relations. Tates Creek Baptists excluded Harry "for running away" and noted good slaves remained faithful. The Tates Creek Church, however, voted to allow "Black people to hold meetings in the house" when it was not otherwise occupied.[49]

Although religion was the most important enculturating effort of the early pioneers, it was not the only evidence of social coercion. The court records also reflect an effort by the community to mold acceptable behavioral patterns. Once again, Madisonians recorded deviations and corrections in their court records. There were frequent petty crimes as well as more serious offenses. In the eighteenth century the most common crimes were retailing liquor without a license, engaging in profanity, public drunkenness, gambling, robbery, horse felony, disorderly behavior, fighting, failing to pay debts, playing cards, and failing to list one's property for tax purposes.[50] In 1789 the court ordered erection of a public whipping post, stocks, and a pillory.[51]

Concern over robbery was great. The court found Hugh Ross guilty of "robbing or breaking open the storehouse of Samuel Estill" and immediately sentenced him to a term in the public jail. Petty crime was common in Madison society in the early 1800s. The court often described crime as "feloniously stealing and carrying away" items of a specific value. Horse stealing, which accelerated in the early 1800s, was a more serious theft. As a result of this attitude, the court erected a public gallows near the intersection of Four Mile Road and Muddy Creek. The 1805 burglary conviction of Archibald Woods, a blacksmith and son of the late magistrate Archibald Woods, was especially alarming.[52] Crime seemed to be spreading.

Fights were a frequent problem near the courthouse and John Caperton, an early pioneer and road overseer, appeared in court in 1797 to show that "part of his right ear was bit off in an affray with William Young." Peter Bonner came to court and charged James Bates with "voluntarily, feloniously, maliciously, pulling out his right eye." In the early period the court discussed at least one sensational murder, that of Baptist Clark in 1789, but it failed to solved the crime.[53]

The most common crime in Madison County, aside from theft, appears to have been fathering illegitimate children. All the court order books are filled with examples of the court ordering a man to "maintain the bastard child begotten on the body of . . ." a specific woman. The court always maintained a strict attitude concerning the economic well-being of illegitimate children. Typically, it charged "David Chinault Junior with bastarding a child on Peggy Smith" and required him to maintain the child by "paying $30 in six annual payments as well as providing a second rate cow with her first calf."[54]

Madison Countians had a great fear of having to maintain bastard children, vagrants, the aged, or the indigent poor. Their attitude was often appalling compared to the policies of neighboring counties. The court swiftly apprenticed orphans or children of freed Negroes in order for them to learn a trade and not become a burden to the court. These apprentices learned the tanning, weaving, fulling, shoe-making, cabinet-making, wheelright, saddling, stone mason, wagon-making, printing, blacksmith, hatting, or farming business, while young girls learned to spin, weave, sew, or housekeep.[55]

The court recognized the problems of the aged or infirm by exempting them from the county levies in the 1780s. The court sometimes asked a magistrate like Thomas Kennedy to keep an older poor person, such as Charity King, in his home. The court expressed its typical opinion in 1802 by ordering the sheriff to pay "old Mrs. Bradley four dollars on the condition she will promise to leave this county and not return." The following year it reluctantly provided expenses for maintaining a blind man and expressed concern over the "increase of vagrants and other idle and disorderly persons" in the county. By 1804 the court hired out vagrants and indigents for months at a time. They earned $2.34 to $10.00 for their services. This provided cheap labor and also alleviated part of the court expense for maintaining them. By 1810 the court provided for the care of orphans, the aged, and the blind. It even supplied them with some medical services.[56]

Although Madisonians neglected indigents for years, the court at last, in 1823, alloted $1,500 to construct a poorhouse. It also designated any surplus from the county levy of that year to be used for the poor. The sudden generosity may have been due to the largest levy in county history: $4,713,75. The following year the court ordered construction of a poorhouse and named two farmers, Higgarson Grubbs and Asenith Gentry, as superintendents at an annual salary of $100 each. Grubbs soon emerged as the lone keeper of the poorhouse at $150 and held the position until his death. William Black, a magistrate, also assisted in supervising the public project.[57]

During his tenure Higgarson Grubbs built several log houses near the old Union Meeting House to accommodate the increasing number of county wards. In 1826 the court announced Grubbs had accepted four more charges for the poorhouse. Upon his death in the fall of 1830, the court named his widow Lucy to complete his term, and then designated John Hawkins as the next agent, beginning in January, 1831. Concern over the indigent fluctuated, and court policy proved inconsistent in the ante-bellum period. After Grubbs' death the court had difficulty maintaining a keeper, as William Parish, Robert Crews, and John Hawkins took turns in the job in the following few years. The poorhouse accepted the "old and infirm who were willing to pay for their own maintainence" [sic] in addition to the indigent. The court requested that Crews furnish "his own Negro woman to render services at the Poor-house" while he "managed the farm."[58] The court continued appointing new keepers of the poor and hoping for minimal expenses in public welfare. Keepers furnished a work animal for the farm, an attendant, and a cook, and paid all expenses from county proceeds.

The court proved as reluctant in its maintenance of a public jail as of a poorhouse. From 1786 into the 1820s every sheriff protested "the sufficiency" of the jail. The court made repairs only as a last resort and normally after some criminal had escaped. The court paid patrollers but normally hired special guards to convey prisoners from one jail to another only when necessary.[59]

The court made infrequent repairs on public buildings during the eighteenth century. It ordered repairs on the jail, with new stone for the chimney and reconstruction of the door. It ordered the erection of a stray pound and improvement of the courthouse grounds in Milford. It also ordered Sheriff Pitman to remove "the ball alley and other incumbrances from the public grounds" in 1794. Later the court, now removed to Richmond, purchased a railing for the public spring, a pump, and steps leading down to it. In 1822 the court ordered the purchasing of four blankets for the jail and paid Dr. Venable Turner for treatment of the prisoners.[60]

Madisonians' lack of interest in public information and public education was truly appalling in the ante-bellum era. They founded thirteen newspapers between 1804 and 1848, and each of them failed, most lasting about a year. Although few copies of any of these early newspaper efforts are extant today, the following chart provides the apparent years of publication.[61]

> *The Enquirer,* 1804-1806.
> *The Globe,* 1809-1810
> *The Luminary,* 1811-1813
> *The Richmond Republican* 1822-1825
> *The Farmer's Chronicle,* 1822-1839
> *The Statesman,* 1827
> *People's Press,* 1828
> *The Western Observer,* 1831
> *The Kentucky Register,* 1844
> *The Ploughboy,* 1847
> *The Richmond-Whig Chronicle,* 1848-1850
> *The Madison Banner,* 1848

Madisonians long dragged their feet on providing educational opportunities for children. Although Joseph Doniphan tutored youngsters at Boonesborough as early as 1779, only a few children benefited from such private instruction. The Kentucky legislature, on December 22, 1798, passed an act providing public land in the underdeveloped Green River area which each county could sell in order to establish a local academy. Madison County, like the others, received 6,000 acres of vacant land. The legislature empowered trustees to raise a lottery and sell subscriptions not exceeding $1,000 to facilitate erection of a building, purchasing of books, etc. The act required each academy to offer English, math, and writing for no less than twelve students by 1808. Any county failing to develop an academy was to forfeit its public land.[62]

Predictably, Madisonians failed to act, and the General Assembly passed a second act on February 24, 1808, giving the trustees an additional ten years. Despite this extension, Madisonians continued to drag their feet, and the state appóinted a special commission, February 1, 1814, consisting of Archibald Woods, Jr., John Patrick, Curtis Field, Anthony W. Rollins, and Moses Rice to sell the public land and to purchase land in Richmond. These trustees purchased stock in the Bank of Kentucky in 1815 and received 6 percent commissions for the transaction.[63]

On June 15, 1816, Robert Caldwell, a merchant, former sheriff, and long-time magistrate of the Madison Court, recorded a deed in which he gave Madison Academy an acre and a half of land on north Third Street in Richmond for the sum of one dollar. The transaction provided for the erection of a schoolhouse as well as a church or Masonic building. Despite Caldwell's philantrophy, Madison Academy remained a dream. Not until February, 1818, did the General Assembly approve the trustees' purchasing of bank stock. Shortly it mandated all fines and forfeitures of the county court to go to the Academy too.[64]

On December 18, 1821, the legislature again addressed the education problem in the state and set aside one-half the net profits of stock held by the state in the Bank of the Commonwealth as a permanent public school fund. It established a committee to study the common school plans and return a report.[65]

By 1821 Madison Seminary (not Academy) was a reality. *The Richmond Republican* carried the announcement of the seminary's third session to commence in January. Students were to pay six dollars for elementary courses and ten dollars for the English, grammar, and science sequence. Subsequent issues called on subscribers to meet at the courthouse to promote education and to reform the seminary. Thomas C. Howard, a state senator, prosperous merchant, and newspaper owner, served as chariman of the board of trustees. The list of trustees included Madison's best-known political and business leaders. Thompson Burnam, Squire Turner, Green Clay, Daniel Breck, William H. Caperton, Dr. Anthony W. Rollins, and David Irvine served on the board. These men supervised the funding of the school, requested additional teachers, and called for the enclosing of the seminary grounds.[66]

By spring, 1823, Squire Turner, treasurer for the seminary trustees, announced that $1,200 was available for building a house on the seminary lot. The trustees requested the building of a thirty-eight by twenty-two foot one-room structure with a chimney. They called for additional subscription increases, the hiring of a teacher, at a $300 salary, and an increase in tuition fees. They also named construction superintendents, and Squire Turner posted a $4,000 bond.[67]

By this time there were a few private schools in the county, although little is known about them. The Silver Creek Grammar School advertised its commencement in February, 1823, and new sessions in 1824. Major John Crooke announced the opening of his math school in his home and offered instruction in surveying. He also maintained student boarders at "reasonable terms." Philip P. Denham announced the opening of his private elementary school with a fee of nine dollars per scholar, and other private tutors at Boonesborough and across the county offered a variety of math, woodcrafting, sewing, and handicraft courses during the 1820s.[68] None of the private educational efforts, however, proved enduring or enrolled significant numbers of students.

Madison Seminary remained the primary educational opportunity in the county, and it served a small number of students who could afford the tuition fees. John Patrick emerged as chairman of the trustees in the summer of 1823. He announced construction of a new building and assured the public it would be completed by the opening of the January, 1824, session. The school offered the three Rs, Latin, Greek, and science. The Reverand I. G. Cooper was its principle teacher. By the summer of 1824 it was an acclaimed success. The newspaper reported the public examination of all pupils and their impressive display of knowledge from the ancient classics, philosophy, history, and geometry, to logic. The paper urged continued public support of the seminary.[69]

In 1830 the General Assembly passed another education act "to encourage the general diffusion of education . . . by the establishment of a uniform system of public schools." This act proved meaningless. Seven years later the General Assembly set aside $1 million of its $1,400,000 federal subsidy for public education. This time Madisonians did move in a positive direction. Daniel Breck, one of Richmond's most prominent lawyers, and three other commissioners called for the division of the county into school districts in compliance with the February 11, 1838, Legislative Act. In the immediate years that followed, the Madison Court failed to follow up the state effort. The Reverand R. T. Dillard, the state superintendent of public instruction, made speeches throughout the Bluegrass denouncing the apathy of the public toward education. Eleven different Madison county commissions failed to act.[70]

In 1840 the Madison Court began a serious discussion of education and noted the state superintendent's report, which cited only 100 Madison County scholars entitled to part of the common or public school fund. The low figure was due to the fact that most children did not attend any school, while the wealthier ones attended private academies. The court ordered the school commissioners to take the roll in the school districts pursuant to the new law and to ascertain which districts might adopt the system of "common" schools. The court soon accepted a report on school houses near John Parker's and one at the meeting house in Clover Bottom. The word "common" reflected the magistrates view of public education as well as the shared prejudice of many of their contemporaries.[71]

By 1839, young ladies had an opportunity to receive limited educational experiences at the new Richmond Female Academy. The *Farmer's Chronicle* advertised the school's opening session in Spetember, with James Madison Putney as principal. Young ladies would be able to study French, painting, drawing, chemistry, and geography. By 1845 the General Assembly approved the charter of a Richmond Female Institute and empowered six local trustees to supervise the school. Madison Female School eclipsed the older institute in the following decade. Another private educational effort was begun in 1844, when the Silver Creek Academy opened on Stone Lick, a branch of Silver Creek. The academy included a two-acre plot and a small schoolhouse, but it failed after a couple of years.[72]

In 1849 the General Assembly imposed a two cent tax for education, and voters endorsed it by a two-to-one margin. It was turned over to the counties in proportion to the number of school children aged five to sixteen. Under the new incentives Madison County began to make some progress, and in 1850 the county reported a population of 15,727, with 1,762 children attending school, and 195 pupils attending college. If one recalls that only 100 children attended school a decade earlier, this was great progress. Yet, the largest number of students Madison County had ever boasted remained a small percentage. The total was somewhat tarnished when the census admitted there were 1,268 illiterate whites in the county.[73]

Madisonians who lagged behind their neighbors in supporting newspapers and schools, proved even more derelict in supporting a public library. Madisonians, however, had never been readers of books. Dr. Thomas W. Ruble, one of the most creative and inventive Madison County minds of the early 1800s published *the American Medical Guide: For the Use Of Families* (Richmond, Kentucky, 1810). This superb guide explained the common diseases and their cures for children and adults in a layman's terms. It included an excellent section on anatomy. Although Ruble influenced local physicians, he did not reach the desired public. When his newspaper, *The Globe*, failed he migrated on to Louisville, where he introduced a one-cylinder steam engine in his *Firefly* as well as a unique cotton gin. Madisonians failed to support writers or newspapers. Not until 1830 did the county seek and obtain a charter from the General Assembly to establish a library company. The one-room library, with its few books, was demolished in 1849 to make room for a new courthouse. Madisonians finally held a lottery to benefit the library in 1852. Thus, somewhat sadly, the county's failure to support a public library in the 1980s has historical precedence.[74]

Although Madisonians shirked newspapers, schools, and books, they maintained an active social life and enjoyed a variety of cultural activities. By 1812 the town of Richmond, the county's largest, boasted a population of some 300 residents, and the principal forms of entertainment included hunting, racing, and card playing. As early as 1813 Richmondites formed a Jockey Club which met at Irvine's Inn (formerly Miller's Tavern). The inn boasted a bar with the finest liquors available and had a wooden sign above the entranceway depicting James Madison. The Jockey Club encouraged local horse races in 1813-14. Several citizens, anxious for more socializing, formed a fraternal lodge: the Masonic Lodge of Richmond. In 1812, Dr. Anthony W. Rollins served as first master, while Thomas C. Howard, the prominent merchant, and David C. Irvine, the court clerk, were wardens. The following year, Howard became grand master. Membership expanded continuously up to 1824, with nineteen members joining by 1820. The lodge met in the Presbyterian church building after 1827.[75]

By 1821, the Richmond lodge split, and Colonel William Rodes, as grand master, and eleven other men, formed Irvine Lodge Number Sixtynine. The strong anti-Masonic attitude of the 1830s affected both groups. The Campbellite movement also reduced membership in the Masonic orders. General John Tribble returned to the Richmond lodge in 1830, and some forty-eight men joined it in the next decade. The Masons actively aided the public in the cholera epidemic of 1840 and buried the dead. At the close of the decade Curtis F. Burnam, the grand master, led twenty-three active Masons, the largest group of the era.[76]

During the 1820s Madisonians participated in an increasingly diversified society. Garnett Lane opened a dancing school at Stuart's Public House. The Richmond Turf held its fall races of 1823 with competition between two-year olds. The track offered a mile race with a twenty dollar entry fee and a significant sweepstakes award, and it included additional "entertainment from a distance" according to the announcer Thomas E. Stuart. These Richmond Turf races were held in the spring and fall, May and October, for several years in the 1820s. In this early period Madison County also boasted the "Holy Trinity," more popularly dubbed "Hell's Trinity." Three young farmers, John Crooke, John White, and John Patrick, all famed for later political involvement, gained a notorious reputation because of their tobacco chewing, big yarns, and heavy drinking. The more genteel elements, including "a Lady of Madison," bemoaned the immorality of the community and the failure of "Richmond citizens to build a church" by 1823.[77]

Madisonians frequently celebrated July 4 with a public barbeque in Richmond. Mrs. Irvine's spring, near Water Street, was the popular gathering place, as it was one of the largest natural springs in the area. William H. Caperton or some other lawyer normally read the Declaration of Independence. The public then heard a speech by a guest orator, and then made toasts that saluted Henry Clay, the Madison Fair, Transylvania University, the farmer, and other important subjects. A sumptuous meal followed. From time to time a circus or theatrical group passed through the county and provided popular entertainment. On July 15, 17, and 19, 1823, the Lexington Company put on two farce comedies: "No Song, No Supper" and "Lying Valet." The newspaper proclaimed both plays great hits. That same month, a traveling musician, Mr. Lewis, and his five children performed three concerts utilizing the piano, harp, violin, and cello.[78]

That Madisonians maintained interest in their horses is evidenced by newspaper advertisements for breeding stud horses like "Comet" and "Post Boy." As the spring races approached Ebenezer Best announced the fall races had not been "fixed by jockeys, or owners." Moreover, he offered to run his filly against the same horse or any other horses for a $1,000 purse in a quarter mile race. He denounced those who circulated such rumors as "poor losers."[79]

THE CELEBRTED AND NOTED
HORSE

COMET,

WILL stand at my stable in Richmond, and let to mares for six dollars in specie, or ten dollars in Commonwealth paper for the season, or eight dollars in specie, or fourteen dollars in Commonwealth's paper to insure a mare with foal, either of which must be paid on or before the 25th of December next, unless what may be paid in *Corn, Rye, Oats* and *Hay,* all of which articles I would prefer to money.

COMET was formerly the property of the late Samuel Brooking of Woodford county, and is now owned by myself; he is a dark Chesnut Sorrel, full fifteen hands three inches high, with such beauty, action and muscular strength as are seldom to be found connected in any horse.—He was got by the noted horse Decius, his dam by the imported horse Comet, his grand dam by the imported Apollo; Decius was got by the noted horse Celar: Celar by the imported Janus; Decius was out of the noted mare Kellester, got by Col. Baylor's imported Fearnaught.

For the information of those who have not a thorough knowledge of this celebrated horse (Comet) suffice it to say that Comet's Colts excel any others upon the continent of America; and more fine Stud-Horses have been produced by him than any other in Kentucky, which may be seen, in various parts, and particularly near his former stands viz: Slasham, Farmers Glory, Vance's Comet, Ratler, Defiance, Carol's Comet, Hill's Forester, Mad Anthony, Jones's Comet, Gaines's Comet, Harrison's Janus, with many others too tedious to mention, which studs are now selling highter than any other Horses colts in Kentucky from five to fifteen hundred dollars each; as to his geldings and mares they are surpassed by none, for swiftness, beauty and activity, viz: Col. Matsons gelding which took the premium from a number of other geldings last fall at the Bourbon agricultural society show; Col. Arbuckells gelding, Palmers mare &c. one of Comets colts a gelding, was lataly run at Charleston South Carolina, by John Atckinson and James Gentry, for three thousand dollars, and won the race with great ease. A number of his mares and geldings are now selling from one hundred and fifty to five hundred dollars each.

Any gentleman wishing to breed from Comet, and not being entirely satisfied of him being one among the finest foal getters in the state, I will refer them to the different counties where he has stood since he was brought out from Virginia, and I am persuaded that his colts, will say more for him than can be said on paper.

Pasture gratis for mares brought from a distance.

JOHN SIMPSON.

April 2, 1823.---23--tf

Richmond Republican, April 9, 1823. EKU Archives.

Militia musters proved to be social outings, as families often accompanied their soldiers to the drill practice and shared picnic lunches. The newspaper even announced dinners to be served by various militias at Big Bald Hill and other areas. Ignatious Mattingly supplied additional refreshments on the Richmond-Boonesborough Road. Not to be outdone, Captain James hosted a dinner at the militia muster on his Silver Creek Farm. The most unusual entertainment passing through the county in this early era, however, was the Bates' Museum of Wax Figures, exhibited at James E. Miller's in August, 1824, in Richmond.[80]

In June, 1823, Madisonians formed a Bible society, named Ezekiel Field as treasurer, and promoted the dissemination of Bibles in the community. The Madison County Bible Society held periodic meetings and worked dilligently in the 1820s. In 1827, a group of citizens met at the White Oak Pond Church and organized the county's first temperence society. Although Madisonians held fairs in the 1820s, they apparently did not organize an agricultural society until 1837.[81]

The 1830s represented a time of social turbulence, as small pox and cholera reached epidemic proportions in the Bluegrass. The court, alarmed at the spread of small pox, actually hired guards, urged vaccinations, and evacuated everyone within a three-mile radius of the pox locations in an effort to contain the epidemic. The court asked Jacob White to assume command and ordered the sheriff to cooperate fully. When the 1833 cholera epidemic resulted in several fatalities, the court determined to minimize future threats. The 1849 epidemic, nonetheless, proved costly in lives and was especially devastating in Richmond, where Irishmen had been laying the foundation of a new courthouse. The disease swept through their temporary quarters on the edge of town. Acute diarrhea, vomiting, muscle cramps, dehydration, and high temperatures characterized the disease. Churches closed and volunteers buried the dead, without ceremony, sometimes without a casket, and even without a prayer. Three-fifths of the population fled town.[82]

In 1840 Madisonians decided to hold a great celebration commemorating the pioneer settling of Boonesborough. The Celebration of May 23-24, 1840, was unprecedented, and several thousand people attended, including veterans of the American Revolution and the War of 1812, eleven militia companies, numerous settlers and descendants of settlers. Ex-governor James T. Morehead gave the principal address following a military review. Mrs. French, the last of the Boone girls, and her servant Dolly, joined John Hart and other original residents of the fort and recalled the trails and tribulations of the pioneers, including weather, Indians, and the British.[83]

Madisonians took pride in their courthouse in the early period and improved the edifices and grounds from time to time. In 1815 the magistrates purchased new seats and tables for the court. Two years later they organized the Madison Fire Department and required citizens to own a two-gallon leather bucket, while the town furnished hooks, ladders, and an engine. All males sixteen and over were to serve during emergencies and pay a twenty-five cent fine for refusal to aid in the fire fighting.[84]

In 1836 the court appropriated $300 for Squire Turner and Thomas C. Howard to purchase a piece of land for the public jail. The court required a new log jail with two safe rooms to be erected and ordered the removal of the existing one from the public square. It was hoped public bids for the old one would help pay for construction of the new one, and the magistrates insisted the new jail not be built in front of any private dwelling houses. The court further ordered gutters and piping repaired on the courthouse building.[85]

Madisonians became increasingly conscious of their public buildings and the importance of landscaping them. During the 1840s, the court appropriated money "to repair the fence around the Court land and to set out trees in the Courtyard." Further, it empowered Jacob Hinkle "to prevent the boys from abusing grass and trees" on the courtyard or "maring public buildings." The culmination of this activity was the construction of a new courthouse. In 1848 Colonel Thomas Lewinski, an architect, received $260 for his plans and specifications. Colonel William Rodes supervised the erection of the new classic structure with its impressive Doric portico and clock tower. The new courthouse with its beautiful iron fence cost $40,000 by the time of its completion the following year.[86]

The composition of Madison County society did not change significantly during the ante-bellum period. The main alterations were in total numbers and in percentage of slaves. In 1790, the population was 5,772, with 737 slaves. By 1800 the total population was 10,490 with 1,729 slaves. Because of the loss of territory Madison's total population declined in 1840 and again in 1850. The percentage of slaves remained significant, however. The following chart shows some relevant totals:

U.S. Census, Madison County

Date	Total Population	Slaves	%	Free Negroes
1790	5,772	737	12%	0
1800	10,729	1,729	16%	3
1810	15,540			
1820	15,594			
1830	18,751			
1840	16,355	5,413	33%	82
1850	15,727	5,393	34%	65

By 1850 Madison County had the largest percentage of slaves in its ante-bellum history. Undoubtedly the presence of so many slaves explained many of the ordinances concerning their movement and activities. Even their religious services required the attendance of a white overseer. Many social customs of the era resulted from the fear of slave uprisings.

Violence in Madison society was nothing new. Even in the eighteenth century there were frequent fights. Churches attempted to regulate such behavior, and the courts incarcerated and fined pugilists. Early court records attested to the violent, even bitter political and social disagreements. As noted earlier, men had their ears cut off, their eyes extracted from sockets, knife wounds, cuts, and scrapes. Murders occurred. Two exceptionally violent episodes in Madison social history during this period included the Stone-Munsey confrontation of 1830 and the epic Clay-Turner brawl of 1849.

Munsey, a teacher, whipped student William Stone for misbehavior at school. Munsey, allegedly, exceeded the boundary of propriety in his enthusiasm, and Thomas M. Stone, the pupil's father avenged the incident by cowhiding the teacher, who then left town only to return with a friend. The two men stopped at White's Tavern and when Stone arrived in town he and Munsey both drew pistols. Stone fired three times but missed while Munsey mortally wounded Stone. The teacher and his friend escaped in a buggy and were never seen again.[87]

In 1849, Cassius Clay, campaigning on behalf of Thompson Burnam, a candidate for the State Constitutional Convention, castigated Squire Turner, a Burnam opponent. Clay was a staunch anti-slavery figure, while Turner defended the peculiar institution. In the hot and bitter July campaign an epic struggle ensued at Foxtown near Clay's home. During a confusing, partially misunderstood rhetorical exchange Squire Turner's son Cyrus acused Clay of being a "damned liar" and attacked the orator. During the brawl Clay received numerous blows from a cane, and fists and a treacherous knifing. Clay wrested his own knife from the hand of an assailant but cut three of his own fingers to the bone. As his vision cleared, the orator struck young Turner "a mighty blow in the abdomen and cut out his intestines." Although a dozen men were wounded in the melee, Clay and Turner were almost dead. Surprisingly Clay survived, while Turner died. Although the community continued to dissent from Clay's political opinions, it did not condemn his violent behavior or that of his belligerent opponents.[88]

As the 1840s came to a close it was obvious that Madison County society remained complex, even paradoxical. The old pioneers, with their crude clothing, coarse manners, and oral contracts, gave way to backwater lawyers in fine clothes, a rising gentry living in fine homes and having significant land acquisitions, polished manners, and limited private educational experiences. According to the 1850 Census the churches of Madison County could accommodate over 20,000 worshippers, considerably more than the total population of the county. The more democratic frontier Protestantism dominated the county, and the Campbellites and Baptists easily outnumbered all other sects combined. The churches often disciplined members for failure to confirm to expected moral behavior and openly complained about immorality. The crime rate was high for a county its size, and Madisonians' acceptance of violence was puzzling to say the least. Despite their affluence Madisonians were especially derelict in supporting public education, libraries, or newspapers. There was little in the ante-bellum era to indicate they would ever change the apathetic attitude toward cultural improvement. Paradoxically, the county boasted antislavery spokesmen and significant emancipations at times, yet increased the total percentage of slaves steadily during the ante-bellum period. Madison County remained one of the most complex of all Bluegrass societies.

Chapter Five

THE FRACTIOUS FORTIES

In many ways life continued as usual in Madison County during the 1840s. The Madison Court's primary concern remained the development of roads, including one from Foxtown to Marshall's Factory. The court ordered new signboards, and carts and teams for road repairs. It provided money for the expenditures on timber, crushed rock, and shovels, and reimbursed farmers who supplied carts, wagons, oxen, or mules for the roadwork. The court decided upon alterations in existing roads and surveyed or approved any new roads. Too, it ordered the repair of roads damaged by winter weather. It maintained bridges and macadamized the streets of Richmond. In a similar action, it approved the erection of gates across existing roads—a sign of more livestock as well as an economic opportunity for the road overseers.[1]

The court continued to sponsor a varety of improvements. It paid Cassius and Brutus Clay for furnishing planks to build a fence around the jailhouse. It ordered a bridge built on the Richmond to Old Town Road and opened a road from Round Hill to Paint Lick. The court purchased additional crushed rock for the county roads and ordered an abundant supply of coffee for the workers.[2]

Although the court spent most of its time designating road overseers, hands, and locations, and altering and maintaining specific roads, it expressed concern over other transportation needs for Madisonians in the decade. By 1843 the magistrates noted the existence of fifteen ferries operating throughout the county. Magistrates, concerned over the lack of uniformity in rates, decided to establish "regular rates." They notified all ferry operators to show cause why the court should not subject them to "standard modified rates." Cassius M. Clay, Winfield Cosby,

Jonathon and Squire Bush, and William Harris represented older families of the county who owned and operated a local ferry.[3]

At its October 7, 1844, session the court established twenty-two separate rates for the proprietors of the different ferries. The lowest rate was one cent for a barrel of salt, while the highest rate was fifty cents for a wagon and six oxen or horses. Rates varied according to the number of passengers, livestock, hogsheads of tobacco, carriages, wheels on the vehicles, horses, or pounds weight loaded on the ferry. Drivers were exempted from charges. The court required ferry operators to keep records and maintain "substantial ferry boats . . . free of leaks."[4]

The court continued to devote great attention to the maintenance, alteration, or opening of roads throughout the period. As road costs rose, the court ordered that "all claims presented for work done on roads . . . state the work done was on the regular working days . . . and was certified by the Surveyors." Apparently some abuses were occurring in several areas of the county by this time. The court continued to designate surveyors for the roads, including Samuel Kirkendall for the Round Hill Road to Gentry Farm (near Kirksville). The court empowered Kirkendall to name the hands to help maintain the road. It further authorized several farmers to erect gates across the road to protect livestock and discourage trespassers.[5]

As the economy expanded and the court record books became filled, the court, in November, 1844, noted its deposits in "the Bank" and authorized the county clerk to use part of them for binding new record books at the courthouse. The court continued to influence the local economy by setting tavern rates and by licensing new tavernkeepers, including one woman Patsy Thurman, in 1846. Forever concerend over the county's expense in maintaining "poor children of color," the court apprenticed orphans and indigent children of whatever color to farmers, blacksmiths, tanners, and shoemakers.[6]

In the 1840s slaveowners continued to issue deeds of emancipation for favored slaves, always listing age, special marks of identification, and experience or training, and assured the court the freed Negroes would not become a charge of the county due to their acquisition of a trade or because of bond posted by the master. The value of slaves continued to average $300 throughout the early 1840s. John F. Burnam emanciapted his slave Stephan, leaving $500 for the old man's maintenance so he would "not become a burden to the county." The court normally supervised young apprentices of "free color" until they reached the age of twenty-one.[7]

The court reappointed David Irvine as clerk of the court in 1840 and stated he was to serve for "good behavior," which meant indefinitely. It named James M. Shackelford his deputy assistant. The following year Thomas H. Irvine and John Newby presented their commissions as new magistrates of the court. Their appointments followed the traditional pattern of older families and tavern owners exercising enormous political influence.[8]

As a carry-over from the olden times, Thomas Francis, John Newby, and John Miller maintained their taverns while serving as magistrates on the county court. William Parrish and Burrell Million, who maintained two of the most popular rural taverns during the decade, joined the court. Once in power they looked out for their relatives' welfare. Parrish had his brother Wesley named county agent of the poorhouse, while Million perusaded his fellow magistrates to name his brother Squire to the court itself. Thomas Francis, the most popular Richmond tavernkeeper, became sheriff in 1843 and appointed his son John as deputy. William Parrish gained the sheriff's office in 1847. Two years later Samuel Estill, a representative of a pioneer family, vacated his seat on the court to serve as sheriff.[9]

Madisonians continued to select either members of the old aristocracy or lawyers as their political spokesmen throughout the decade. The tavernkeepers were the lone exceptions to the traditional rule. These three groups not only dominated the local court but also represented the county in the Frankfort legislature. William Chenault won assembly seats in 1840, 1848, and 1849. He was elected to the state senate in 1842. J. Speed Smith served in the house between 1841 and 1846, then won the senate seat in 1847. Daniel Breck followed him in the state senate two years later. Nicholas Hocker (1842), David Irvine (1846), and Cyrus Turner (1847-50) maintained legislative seats for the "old families." In 1848 Madisonians cast 1,562 votes for Chenault, 1,503 votes for Turner, and 1,035 votes for Breck as their three Whig assemblymen in an unusually high voter turnout. Chenault's total broke Squire Turner's old record of 1,526 votes in 1830.[10]

Lawyers dominated Madison County politics from the 1820s up to the Civil War. In his "Reminiscences" Judge Curtis F. Burnam drew vignettes of the early leaders. He viewed J. Speed Smith, Colonel William H. Caperton, and Squire Turner as three of the ablest lawyers of the era. Smith, one of the greatest Jacksonian attorneys, had a keen wit, a sarcastic approach, and an eloquent voice. Caperton, the best rounded of the three, loved to hunt and fish. The greatest criminal lawyer with his penetrating mind, Caperton even bested Henry Clay in the famed Shelby murder case—it was a duel of eloquent orators. Squire Turner was a taciturn, workaholic with few hobbies or pleasures. Turner was the most durable and practiced law for over fifty years, including the last week of his life at the age of seventy-eight. These men and their antebellum contemporaries gravitated into the Whig party.[11]

Madison County remained predominantly Whig in its national, state, and local political expressions. It supported Henry Clay and his party's nominees throughout the decade. Madisonians organized a Tippecanoe Club which met at the courthouse during the presidential canvass of 1840. Henry B. Hawkins served as clerk of the electors at a public rally in Richmond that November. Four years later Madisonians held demonstrations throughout the county on behalf of their great hero, Henry Clay. At a rally at Poosey, in 1844, Governor Thomas

William H. Caperton portrait in Madison County Court House. Copied by Larry Bailey.

Metcalfe spoke to citizens from five counties, and some partisans estimated the crowd attending was two thousand strong. At the least it was one of the most enthusiastic political demonstrations of the era. General John Tribble soon organized a Democratic Association to respond to the Whig onslaught, and Democrats canvassed the county.[12]

Although Madison County supported every Whig presidential candidate from 1824 through 1852, the elections of the 1840s proved a high tide for the Whigs. Except for John Quincy Adams, every National Republican or Whig candidate carried the county with over 60 percent of the vote. In 1840 General William Henry Harrison gained the greatest landslide in local history by polling 77 percent of the vote in a 1,318 to 391 margin. His total was the highest individual figure of the antebellum era. General Zachary Taylor did almost as well in 1848, when he defeated Lewis Cass, the Democratic presidential nominee, by a 1,313 to 564 vote. The Madison vote was in line with the state turnout, as Harrison and Taylor swept the bluegrass state by equally large majorities.[13]

Madison Whigs carried each gubernatorial race in the 1840s and elected state legislators in all but one instance. The lone exception was 1842, when Samuel M. Fox, an antirelief Democrat headed the ticket with 1,144 votes by promising to vote for a Whig as U. S. Senator. Nicholas Hocker, an antirelief Whig, ran second with 964 votes, but Thomas J. Gentry, a former representative in the 1830s, and an avowed relief Whig, polled 932 votes and failed to regain his legislative seat. Signficantly, J. Speed Smith, a one-time Jacksonian who had not served in the legislature since 1830, switched party labels and recaptured the second house seat in 1841. Following another victory in 1845, Smith gained Madison County's lone senate seat in 1847, but again as a Whig.

Thus Fox was the only Democrat to represent Madison County in the state legislature during the entire decade.[14]

Despite the obvious Whig successes there were problems beneath the surface. Changes were occurring which would have a long-range affect on the local, state, and national party. In 1845, John White, the most popular of all Madison County Whigs and the most successful in national leadership, accepted appointment to the appellate court. White, a five-term congressman and outgoing Speaker of the House of Representatives (1841-1845), suddenly and inexplicably committed suicide. Madison County citizens bemoaned his death, and Curtis F. Burnam, a prominent lawyer and eloquent orator appeared before the bar of the Madison Circuit Court on Spetember 23, 1845, and introduced a resolution expressing the legal community's grief over the judge's death. Burnam praised White's independence, generosity, and intellect. He said, "We shall long cherish with the fondest regard and admiration, the memory of those high personal virtues which ever characterized the deceased." The court enthusiastically adopted the resolution and sent it to Mrs. White.[15]

The year 1845 brought changes on the Madison Court. David Irvine, the long-time clerk, resigned. His deputy clerk, James M. Shackelford resigned as commissioner of accounts and took the oath as the new clerk, vowing to support the constitutions of the United States and the Commonwealth of Kentucky, and promising to abide by the state Dueling Act and to perform his duties as clerk. Shackelford registered a $10,000 bond. He named Thomas H. Barnes as his deputy. The court noted the many years of faithful service of Colonel Irvine and expressed its "extreme gratitude" for his leaderhsip. A year later Shackelford had to resume duties as commissioner of accounts due to the extended absence of Barnes, who was participating in the Mexican War.[16]

Madison County acquired a new sheriff in 1845 and the local court continued to accept new members. Although the older families continued to occupy seats on the court, the Turners, Irvines, Harrises, Estills, and Millers were now a minority. More disturbing news circulated through the county in 1847, when John Crooke, the long-time surveyor, resigned. His forty years' service as the official county surveyor had made him the symbol of continuity and security for many Madison landowners. Despite the magistrates' recommendation of his son Kiah as one of the nominees, the governor selected John H. Parrish as the new surveyor. Parrish's brother William continued as a magistrate and a popular tavernkeeper.[17]

Economic opportunities accelerated with political contacts, as evidenced by the Parrish family. William, the long-time magistrate, secured the surveyor's job for John and the position of county poorhouse agent for Wesley. When magistrate Burrell Million secured the appointment of his brother Squire to the court in 1846, the Million brothers became the first to serve on the court simultaneously since Green and Thomas Clay in the 1790s. Upon becoming sheriff in 1847, Joseph Turner appointed

Horace and Edward Turner his deputies. Nepotism remained a way of life and assured continuity in Madisonian political behavior.[18]

The economy remained basically agricultural throughout the decade. Cattle, sheep, hogs, and mules dominated the livestock picture, while farmers produced corn, flax, rye, and oats in significant quantities. Agricultural production led to a diversity of businesses in Richmond, including Brown and Lee's Wool Carding Factory; Rodes' Rope Walk and Bagging Factory; Rodes' Manufacturing Company, which sold horseshoes, nails, axes, and agricultural implements; Chevis's Furniture Store; Kirtz Furniture Company, several tanneries, blacksmith shops, and three tailoring businesses. Several Richmond businesses promised greater varieties of consumer goods at lower prices. Goodloe's Dry Goods, David I. Rowland Boots and Shoes, Miller and Harris Bootery and Mrs. McMillan's Millinery competed for customers. The millinery even announced the availability of artificial flowers for bonnet repairs. On the surface, the Madison economy implied stability.[19]

In that early era merchants went to Maysville, thence to Pittsburgh, and on to the eastern seaboard, where they purchased goods. They sold articles on a twelve-month credit basis. Thompson Burnam, the Howard Brothers, the Walker Brothers, William Miller, Solomon Smith, and Howard Williams ran the biggest mercantile houses in Richmond. Thompson Burnam was the most active merchant until his retirement in 1844, when he turned to farming near Kirksville.[20]

During the 1840s lawyers and physicians continued to advertise in the local newspapers. The county boasted its share of physicians, and Richmond had a dozen or more with Dr. Anthony W. Rollins the preeminent doctor of the community. Each village, even Foxtown, boasted its own physician. Kirksville had three resident doctors. Advertisements noted location of offices and cited degrees earned.[21]

Despite its outward appearances, the Madison political and economic scene was encountering turbulence. The slavery issue created tension throughout the community. Politicians often fanned the flames rather than easing the problem. As early as 1840 Cassius M. Clay, Green Clay's famous, often controversial son, and an outspoken critic of the peculiar institution, conducted a bitter, vitriolic campaign against Lexington Robert Wickliffe, Jr. for the state legislature. At a meeting near Russell Cave Springs in Fayette County, Samuel M. Brown, a New Orleans thug, attacked Clay, and a violent melee ensued.Clay used his knife to open Brown's skull to the brain, dug out an eye, and cut off an ear. Although Clay was exonerated at court, he lost the election.[22] The violence and bitterness of the campaign underlined the growing uneasiness over race relations.

The economic aspects of slavery remained a matter of great concern, even to an antislavery spokesman like Clay. As he liberated his slaves in the 1840s he noticed the increasing difficulty of obtaining agricultural labor for White Hall. He wrote his brother Brutus, of Bourbon County, asking for assistance and advice. He particularly requested help in cleaning his pastures. Despite his economic headaches, Cassius M. Clay edited and published an antislavery newspaper, *the True American,* in Lexington during the following year. In it he warned of mob rule, and an end to freedom of speech in Kentucky, and he anticipated the destruction of his and all antislavery publications.[23]

Although political confrontations over the slavery issue were increasing in the 1840s, slave life remained much the way it had been for decades. Some slaveowners proved more lenient and concerned about the life of their slaves than others. Both blacks and whites enjoyed and recalled good relations between the races, particularly in the Cane Springs and Pilot Knob areas. Corn shuckings, tobacco cutting, sugar making, weddings, and church services served as opportunities for the two races to mix.[24]

Madison Campbell, a famous slave and long-time minister in the county, recalled only one instance in his lifetime in which an overseer whipped a slave, and that was following an altercation between the owner and the slave. He noted that slave children spent great amounts of time with their masters' children, playing together, chopping wood, carrying water, hunting, and fishing. By the age of ten black children hoed corn and only white boys attended school.[25]

Education and family life made slaves recognize their limits. Campbell was more fortunate than most of his race, since his master's son, David Campbell, taught him to read. The young slave also learned to make excellent baskets and chair bottoms and this allowed him to accumulate some money for the purchase of his liberation. Madison Campbell received his reading lessons at night after he completed his tasks.[26]

Family life for slaves remained difficult at best. Slaves always took the last names of their masters. If they were sold they adopted new names. Campbell's parents and grandparents all had different last names and lived apart, since they had different owners. They were allowed to visit each other from time to time. Even white owners bemoaned the disruption of slave families, and Lucia Burnam's mother (Mrs. Curtis F. Burnam) thought the breakup of families the most distressing aspect of slavery.[27]

Despite their constant labor, Campbell and other slaves found time for hunting, fishing, dancing, and singing. Campbell viewed himself as a "very wild" teenager and a definite "sinner" when he had a religious experience in 1841. He attended Baptist revival some nine miles from home but could not join the church, since slaves had to belong to the churches of their masters or present a certificate from their masters allowing their independent conversion. After much prayer and soul-searching Campbell joined his master's Methodist denomination and was baptized the following year. Despite his testifying to other black Methodists he frequently attended revivals at the Bethel Baptist Meeting House. After his master's death a decade later, his new owner allowed Campbell to join the Baptists. In the 1850s he became an active Baptist minister, ordained by the Tate's Creek Association and examined by a council of white ministers.[28]

Slaves enjoyed little religious freedom in the ante-bellum period. However, they gained full membership in their masters' churches, attended, worshipped, and even "spoke out" if they had received "the light." The Tate's Creek and Cane Springs Baptist Church record books note the active participation of slaves. They received the same reprimands as white members and were equally subject to exclusion for misbehavior.[29]

Since slaves were not allowed to own even church land, if they or "free coloreds" saved enough to buy church land, it was purchased by a white trustee such as Thompson Burnam, Sr. The first black church in Madison County, a log structure, was constructed in Richmond in 1846. All other black denominations could use it, as long as they helped maintain it. Madison Campbell was a missionary for the church, whereas Edmond Martin was its first minister. A decade later a brick structure replaced the old log meeting house.[30]

The blacks of Madison County, sometimes encouraged for whatever reasons by whites, moved toward religious separation or independence in the 1840s. They held segregated evening services or shared alternate Sundays at older rural churches like Tate's Creek and Cane Springs Baptist. Slaves in town worshipped at the new Richmond Baptist Church under the leadership of Brothers Martin and Campbell. In his autobiography Madison Campbell claimed his greater appeal to other slaves was a result of his ability to communicate on their level, whereas the educated ministers confused the typical slave. The Methodist Conference continued licensing black leaders like Fielding Jones, "a man of color . . . to exhort."[31]

The 1840s proved a time of religious fermentation. By 1840 the Tate's Creek Association claimed nineteen churches in the area with a membership exceeding 1,100. The Methodist Conference, in 1841, claimed eighteen churches in the Madison circuit. In Richmond itself, Methodists were finally constructing a church building. At their quarterly conferences Methodists discussed the need for parsonages, more trained ministers, financial difficulties, camp meetings, and friction concerning baptismal ceremonies. The expense of traveling ministers far exceeded the support members gave them. The conference, without exception, accepted reports by local churches concerning the reprimanding, even exclusion, of members engaging in immoral conduct.[32]

On December 7, 1844, a group of Campbellites assembled at Mr. Brown's Cabinet Shop on Main Street in Richmond and organized the First Christian Church. Thomas S. Bronston, Jr. served as clerk for the church. Fifty-one members joined and pledged support for the construction of a frame building.[33] Although the Baptists and Presbyterians had formed congregations by the close of the 1820s, the addition of the

Methodists and Christians in the 1840s led to accelerated religious activities in Richmond.

The Campbellites organized one other church in the 1840s: Kirksville Christian. It proved to be an active congregation and boasted a membership of a hundred within a decade. The Arbuckles, Bogies, Cornelisons, Covingtons, Longs, Morans, Walkers, and Whitlocks dominated its roll for decades. Slaves were included in the early membership. Although several families met in homes in the early 1840s, the formal organization of the church occurred in 1849.[34]

Kirksville Christian Church. Dorris Collection, EKU Townsend Room.

The Kirksville community became a viable township during the 1840s. Although Samuel Kirkendall had a general store and a carding factory there in the early 1830s, the community went by the name Baghdad until 1843, when it changed its name to Centerville because of its equidistant location between Silver and Paint Lick creeks. It was also almost equidistant between Richmond and Lancaster. Residents of the town wanted to honor its distinguished merchant, so they renamed it Kirksville in the late 1840s. Besides a church and carding factory, it boasted a blacksmith shop, a harness shop, a small school, and Kirkendall's General Store. The Kirksville area included many slaves and had the second largest black population in the county until the close of the nineteenth century.[35]

Race relations were tense during the 1840s. Although a few sla-veowners continued to emancipate slaves, especially those who could support themselves, the number of emancipations dwindled throughout the decade. Many citizens seemed afraid to speak out for emancipation for fear "their businesses would suffer." Almeron Dowd confirmed Madisonians' reluctance to discuss controversial issues.[36]

In 1845 the number of black tithes surpassed the white tithes in the county for the first time by a 2,499 to 2,350 total. The following year the black tithes increased to a 2,510 to 2,434 margin. Racial tension increased. The average price of field hands in mid-decade rose to $800. A few slaves brought even higher prices. Some slaveowners regretted the division of slave families but found the costs of keeping them together impossible to meet. Equally deplorable, many young slave girls had children without marriage. Given human nature, as one slave girl remarked, she would "have pleasure with or without marriage."[37]

The problem of "free Negroes" complicated the slavery issue. Many slaveowners worried about the presence of the emancipated blacks and some did not permit "free Negroes" on their farms. By 1845 J. Speed Smith introduced a bill into the state legislature which would have prohibited the manufacturing and selling of ardent spirits by free Negroes.[38] As noted earlier, the local court passed several ordinances limiting the activities of free Negores at the courthouse market, and resticting jobs, movement, and rights of the free Negroes.

During the decade the number of free Negroes reached sixty-five; the total slave population was 5,393—that is, 36 percent of the total Madison County population of 15,727. Although most slaves served as field hands on the various farms, a few developed skills which allowed them to earn some money and even to buy their emanicpation.[39]

By the close of the 1840s Madisonians openly discussed the spiral-ing crime rates and their fears resulting from racial tensions. They pressed the magistrates for greater restrictions on "free Negroes" and slaves in the community. The court designated two new patrollers for the county and specified that militiamen must "serve without charge." Ten months later the court provided an additional $100 for paying special patrollers in Richmond.[40]

Despite local problems and worries, several hundred Madisonians voluntarily enlisted for service in the Mexican War of 1845, and General James C. Stone commanded the Madison Company. Local interest in the war is evidenced by the few newspaper clippings extant from the period. All Kentucky newspapers of the era devoted a great deal of attention to the heroism and progress of the American forces in Texas and later in Mexico. Even Cassius M. Clay polished his reputation by his military activities in the war. Critics increasingly labeled him eccentric rather than radical.[41]

Clay saw the war as "an opportunity" to gain greater influence politically and to promote his antislavery views. The men who served under Captain Clay attested to his patriotism, heroism, unselfishness,

Cassius M. Clay in Mexican War soldier uniform. University of Kentucky King Library Special Collecitons Department.

and leaderhsip abilities. Despite his capture at Encarnacion, he counseled his seventy men sagaciously and helped them survive the eight months of imprisonment. He even saved their lives when a scout escaped and linguistic problems led the Mexicans to suspect a conspiracy. Clay sent several letters home describing Texas as a worthless, "miserable country." The more he saw of the war, the more he hated it "in all its consequences." Clay questioned the "expenditure of blood and money," and condemned military appointments based on political influence. It was a happy soldier who returned home following an exchange of prisoners in December, 1847.[42]

During the Mexican War many Madisonians enlisted and made the journey south of the border. Captain James Stone's First Regiment included numerous mounted volunteers from the county. They were to serve a twelve-month period. In addition to the many officers and privates from the county there were three specialists, a blacksmith, a musician, and one surgeon, William J. Chenault. Several pioneer Madison County families were represented in the company, including Barnes, Broaddus, Chenault, DeJarnette, Field, Harris, and Tudor descendants.[43]

During and after the Mexican War, Madisonians continued gathering at the courthouse or at taverns to discuss the political and economic issues of the day. Richmond boasted a variety of taverns but also witnessed the development of a more diversified mercantile business during the era, as furniture stores, millineries, shoe stores, market houses, jewelry stores, and groceries competed. Richmond, essentially a wooden village at the turn of the century, included an increasing number of brick buildings. However, brick remained a luxury, and was used primarily in the finer homes.

Although Green Clay's Clermont as well as the Shanks' house in Richmond were completed near the turn of the century and David Crews' Homelands opened its doors in 1812, three of the great mansions of the county emerged during the 1820s. Two of Green Clay's sons-in-law, J. Speed Smith, the attorney, and Colonel William Rodes, the hemp manufacturer, constructed Castle Union and Woodlawn, respectively, near Muddy Creek and Big Hill Pike. Both houses were noted for their architecture, spacious rooms, and wood carving. Dr. Anthony W. Rollins purchased Irvineton at about the same time.[44]

In 1837 Daniel Breck built a new home, the palatial Brighton, one of the most impressive homes in ante-bellum Richmond. General Samuel Estill completed another fine brick edifice on the Barnes Mill Pike at the close of the 1840s (presently the Turley Noland home). Both two-story structures boasted spacious rooms, although Brighton was more ornate.[45]

Madisonian society developed a variety of popular pastimes in the ante-bellum era. By the 1830s there was a local Thespian Society which staged plays with some frequency. The community was supportive of traveling circuses and sustained a two-to-three day visit by the entertainers. Many Madisonians loved horse racing and attended local turfs as early as the 1820s. Gambling was not restricted to horses, as chicken fights were popular entertainment for all classes and races. Card playing was socially acceptable for those outside the gambling circuit as well as more serious poker players. Stakes could be high, and some farmers lost substantial sums of money. Curtis F. Burnam recalled his family's enjoyment of foxhunting. The Burnams shared this sport with only a few Madison families like the Gentrys, the Maupins, the Whites, and the Walkers. Fishing was a popular sport for some of the gentry, especially old Colonel Caperton, but also a marvelous escape for slaves and a necessity for some poor families.[46]

Despite their increasing social activities and wealth, Madisonians continued to neglect public education. Although the Kentucky General Assembly passed a law creating a common school system in 1838 and urged the development of a board of eduation, the division of the county into school districts proceeded slowly. Even after the county court acted to create the divisions, nothing happened at the local level. Ryland Dillard, the superintendent of schools, 1842-47, campaigned across the state but failed to ignite public action. When the state legislature passed a school tax on property in 1848 Madisonians remained passive.[47]

During the 1840s the Madison Court continued to fret over the opening and maintainence of roads and bridges. It apprenticed orphans and indigent youths who might become wards of the court. It appointed guardians, settled estates, provided a poorhouse, and required men found guilty of fathering bastard children to maintain the children during infancy. Politically, the court was less active than in past years. Clerks even delegated increasing authority to deputies, and the public often complained of the inefficiency or expense of the court.[48]

By November, 1847, the court recorded that a fund of $5,430.91 on hand and drawing interest was to be used by a courthouse commission for construction of a new court building. The magistrates ordered Squire Turner, William Goodloe, William Rodes, and James W. Shackelford to select the cite and to submit plans at court. The following April the commission submitted a written report on plans for a courthouse, and John Newby cast the only dissenting vote on the proposal. The court ordered the commissioners to advertise for bids on brick, stonework, and carpentry in the Lexington, Frankfort, and Richmond newspapers. All interested parties were to report at the June session of the court. By a thirteen-to-three vote the magistrates approved the new plan on July 4, 1848. William Parrish, Palestine Ballard, and Christopher Harris voted in the negative.[49]

Madison County Court House. French Tipton Collection, EKU Townsend Room.

Bids submitted at the July session included $245 for cleaning the lumber and brick as well as doing the actual stonework, $725 for the bricklaying, and $9,350 for the carpentry work. Although the commission filed a report, maintaining a balance of $2,526.27 in the bank account, magistrates allotted another $5,000 for additional construction expenses anticipated by November.[50]

A year later, on November 6, 1849, the court provided an additional $4,150 to the commission for construction costs and authorized the payment of $350 to Richard Runyon for the destruction and removal of the old public library from the courthouse square. The court also called for payment of the painters and plasterers. The total cost of the new courthouse was $40,000. It was one of the most elegant ante-bellum courthouses in Kentucky. An excellent example of classic architecture, it included a Doric portico and columns, a clock tower, brick vaults , the finest timber, and natural plaster. Colonel William Rodes, nephew of the builder of the first courthouse, served as the principal superintendent of the new one.[51]

The year 1849 was remarkable for reasons other than the completion of a new courthouse. It was the year a great cholera epidemic swept through Madison County, forcing 60 percent of the Richmond population to flee town. According to Curtis F. Burnam, in his "Reminiscences," seventy-two people died. The Odd Fellows and other philanthropic groups hurriedly buried the dead without elaborate funeral ceremonies. Shops, markets, and even churches remained closed throughout the scare.[52]

The most important event of the year was the third Kentucky Constitutional Convention. As noted earlier, Cassius M. Clay actively campaigned on behalf of Thompson Burnam as a delegate to the proposed convention. Squire Turner and William Chenault were proslavery candidates, and the Clay-Turner animosity erupted at a Foxtown rally on June 14, 1848, when Clay's vicious sarcasm provoked an assault by Squire's two sons, Thomas and Cyrus. In the ensuing brawl Clay was seriously wounded but killed young Cyrus. Despite Clay's physical triumph his reputation suffered, and Chenault and Turner decisively defeated the antislavery forces.[53]

At the Constitutional Convention which followed, Turner, a recognized spokesman for the proslavery majority, introduced the resolution making it unconstitutional for the state legislature to emancipate slaves without the consent of their owners. An additional resolution gave the existing slaveowners a monopoly in supplying the state with slaves by limiting movement of slaves into Kentucky from outside areas. Turner's motion led to acrimonious debates. His motive was pecuniary, as he was protecting existing slaveowners and minimizing competition. As a conservative he saw his approach as traditional and less disruptive. William Chenault agreed with Turner's position and voted with him. Back in Madison County, Clay predictably denounced both delegates and their votes.[54]

Madisonians in general were pleased with the new constitution as many of their grievances abated. They had long urged reform and criticized the corruption which permeated state and local government. They had bemoaned election abuses and noted the costliness of annual ballots which drained the economy. Richmond's refusal to hold elections forced the county court to appoint city trustees during the 1840s. The new constitution called for biennial elections and legislative sessions. Moreover, voters had to go to the polls one day instead of having the traditional three-day exercise, which had encouraged fraudulent voting during the first fifty years. All legislators, but more importantly, all county judges, sheriffs, and magistrates, and most urban officials were to be elected. The number of appointive positions was greatly reduced.[55]

The 1849 constitutional delegates finally discussed the long-neglected topic of public education. They even provided for a school fund which evoked activities at the local level. A Madison legislator, William Harris, presented a petition to the General Assembly signed by the newly elected school commissioners representing the Kirksville School District and asking for "their portion of the school fund for 1849-1850." Other districts soon followed suit.[56]

As the decade came to an end it was clear that many ties to the past were unbroken, especially the role of the local court over internal improvements, estates, apprenticeships, and licensing. Nepotism remained a part of the political pattern. Provincial interests continued to be paramount. The court continued to register deeds of emancipation, and the number of free blacks rose. The economy rallied from the depression of the late 1830s. Yet, beneath the surface frictions increased.

The Whig party lost several of its most skillful leaders. Whereas Henry Clay's death affected the national and state party, John White's suicide undercut Madisonian unity. For ten years White had dominated the Madisonian Whigs, often running without opposition. The local scene also changed because of the retirement of Colonel David Irvine as county clerk. From 1786 to 1845 he and his father were the only men to occupy that crucial political post in Madison County. After forty years service, John Crooke resigned as county surveyor, further undercutting stability and continuity on the Madison political front.

In addition to changes in political leadership, Madisonians witnessed divisions and tensions. Squire Turner, a prominent political force in the Whig party since the War of 1812 openly broke with the traditional powerbrokers like James D. Caperton, the long-time county attorney, and Cassius M. Clay, the outspoken antislavery leader. The Whig party was dying, and Turner was moving toward an allignment with his old rivals in the Democratic states-rights camp, while Clay and Caperton would join the Burnams in the new Republican party. Significantly, the first crack in Whig solidarity occurred in the legislative election of August, 1850. William Terrill, a Democrat, won the second assembly seat in the Frankfort legislature. Although Terrill benefited from Whig divisions and the fact that five Whigs contested the two house seats, the trend toward Democratic victories had begun.[57]

Mt. Pleasant, headquarters of the Madison County Historical Society, was donated by Betsy Smith Toy Hall of Indianapolis in 1977. Mrs. Hall is a descendant of Solomon Smith and George Brown, original owner. Russell Todd, *This Is Boone Country,* **42.**

In addition to the frictions in the political arena, Madisonian society divided over the slavery question. Emanicipations dwindled in the late ante-bellum era. Restrictions on slaves and free blacks increased. Tensions between slaveowners and antislavery proponnents quickened. The Clay-Turner confrontations underlined the animosities and the depth of feeling between the two extremes. Racial tension resulted in religious segregation. Blacks held separate meetings or formed their own churches for the first time. This reflected the loss of the church as mediator or the end of its willingness to speak out on the racial or slavery issues. The church had been one of the few institutions to encourage a degree of mixing between the races in the early nineteenth century. Opposition to the education of blacks, free or slave, increased. Madisonians expressed concern over Negroes' use of liquor and over the rising crime rate, and fretted over the increasing numbers of "free Negroes" in the community. An era of bad feelings had begun, and eventually it would lead to armed conflict.

Part II

MADISON COUNTY: The Middle Period, 1850-1900

By Richard D. Sears

Chapter Six

COLONISTS IN
SOUTHERN MADISON
COUNTY

The founding of the town of Berea was in part political, in part religious, with Cassius Marcellus Clay providing the politics, Reverend John Gregg Fee the faith. In 1853 Clay invited his friend to establish residence in the Glade in southern Madison County, where a small antislavery group, supporters of Clay's political ambitions, had formed a church. Fee was to serve as one of the ministers there, and in three or four other tiny congregations nearby, along with Wiley B. Fisk, who had been working in Madison County since 1849. As an inducement, Clay offered Fee a tract of land—part of some 600 acres Clay owned in the Glade—as a homestead. Fee could have it if he would live on it; the exact site and even the amount of land was to be at Fee's discretion.[1]

At Clay's urging Fee visited Madison and Rockcastle counties and, beginning in the spring of 1853, held a series of protracted meetings, helping to organize congregations as free churches along new abolitionist lines. In his mind he was only paying the region a ministerial visit—his work was established in Bracken and Lewis counties on the Ohio River. But in June, 1853, Fee wrote, "I have received quite a number of letters from Madison and Rockcastle Counties, urging me to come back and settle there." In August he wrote, "[Clay] & the people were favorably impressed with what they suppose I can do. . . . He & they are importunate that I go to Madison."[2]

By the spring of 1854, Fee had decided, very reluctantly, to accept Clay's proposal. Fee wrote that he "decided to come [to Berea] without any reference to salary or spot for a home." When the surveyor came to mark off his land Fee was speaking at a revival meeting which he had

Reverend John G. Fee about the
time of his arrival in Madison
County. Berea College Archives.

Cassius M. Clay. Berea College Archives. (An original oil portrait of
Clay, now in the drawing room at
White Hall, was donated by the
Madison County Historical Society
along with two other Clay por-
traits and a bust of C. M. Clay.)

initiated almost instantly upon his arrival. He refused to leave his preaching to accompany the surveyor, but asked a couple of local men, Hamilton Rawlings and William B. Wright, to choose a spot for him. Wright
wanted Fee to live near him, and on that basis Fee's surrogates picked
"the extreme corner of Mr. Clay's tract . . . the corner least valuable;
and there marked off . . . ten acres. Mr. Clay," Fee stated, "would have
been quite as well pleased if they had marked off ten times as much land
and in the best part. . . ." He described his own reaction: "At the close of
the meeting I took my horse and rode up, a mile distant, to see the spot
which, in the providence of God, had been chosen for me. When I came I
could not 'see the end from the beginning,' and saw not then either
desirableness or wisdom in the choice." "About one acre of hillside was
half-cleared and the rest of the land covered with a dense undergrowth of
'blackjacks' and a frog pond in the midst."[3]

Fee, long accustomed to self-sacrifice for his work, would come
virtually penniless to his new missionary endeavor. Later, he was to see
the homesite—soon to determine the placement of church, town, and
school—as providentially chosen, not in man's ignorance, although there
was plenty of that to go around, but in God's wisdom. Even though the
work in Madison county might appear trivial and unpromising, Fee
wrote to the American Missionary Association to urge its importance:
"Brethren, let us be united and step into this wide and effectual door
which God is opening. . . . Let us not despise the day of small things." Fee
advised, "God can take the weak things of this world and confound the
wise."[4]

Still, his removal to Madison County was delayed. In June, 1854, Fee wrote to Clay to explain that he had not yet started for his new home because of "biliousness arising from anxiety and labor." But his enthusiasm for the new project and his new patron had not waned: "You have done much for Madison," he wrote to Clay. "[You] feel deeply interested in the success of free principles there—so do I. . . ." "Slavery must die," Fee said, assured of Clay's agreement, "or we must be slaves. Despots know not color." Fee proposed to move to Madison County in August, and duly departed from his old home on the second of that month.[5]

"I gathered our household goods into a two-horse wagon. . ." he wrote,

> and I, wife and two children, in a one-horse carriage, started for the new home, one hundred and forty miles in the interior. . . .
>
> In the evening of the third day we camped in the new house, then without a chimney, or glass in the windows, or a fence around the yard.
>
> Believing as we did, that we were exactly where *the Lord mine* would have us, we lay down and slept calmly, sweetly.[6]

For many years Cassius M. Clay had been working to build a community for himself in southern Madison County. He had supported Wiley B. Fisk in his ministry, offering to build a church for him. In a letter to the American Missionary Association (written January 5, 1853), Fisk reported, "My friend C.M. Clay is doing all he can in every way for the cause." Clay had given Hamilton Rawlings a tract near the Glade worth about a thousand dollars; Rawlings, Clay wrote, "had been my ardent and intelligent friend for years, and had at once adopted my liberal views. Clay sold several lots of land "at nominal prices to our most courageous friends for self-protection." So, in 1854 the Glade (which was never a town but simply a designated region, sometimes referred to as the Big Glade, later Glade Precinct) was populated mostly with citizens sympthetic to emancipation, nonslaveholders, potentially Republican (some Free-Soilers actually), economically and perhaps morally indebted to Cassius M. Clay. Clay wanted the Glade to be the beginning of his political success with the mountainous regions of the state, his doorway into the Appalachian stronghold. He had a vision of the mountains of Kentucky, "where there were but few slaves, and people courageous; so that, if they were once committed to liberation of the slaves, we could have a permanent nucleus of political and physical force. . . ." The establishment of Berea, Clay stated, "served a great purpose in my political career."[7]

Later Clay would refer to the Bereans as his "boys" and imagine himself leading them in guerilla warfare against the slaveholding establishment, and he did, upon occasion, call them to arms in his own defense or in defense of Fee. Clearly, the Glade was to him a political powerbase—it represented votes and even, as he said, "physical force," his potential army.[8]

Nothing could be further from Fee's view of the same people. Since Clay wanted to retain control of the Glade and its inhabitants, he made a singular error when he invited Fee to minister there. No man in Kentucky, perhaps in the whole country, was less likely to yield to the ambitions of Cassius Clay. Fee was, in his own estimation and in the opinion of many who knew him, God's man, his mission based on "a covenant, made with God to preach in [his] native state, the gospel of impartial love." For him that gospel implied a stance of radical abolitionism. He called for immediate, uncompensated emancipation of all slaves; he demanded that Christians refuse to commune with slaveholders because slavery itself was sinful—in fact, it was, in John Wesley's words, "the sum of all villainies." Clay's political base was to John G. Fee a mission field.[9]

In 1854 anyone looking at the Glade itself would have required a gifted, perhaps fevered, imagination to see evidence for the possible realization of either Clay's or Fee's vision. Clay imagined a constitutional overturning of the slave power from the political base that would begin in the Glade and filter throughout the mountain region; Fee envisioned a religious revival spreading by "moral suasion" throughout the South. Both men were looking at a sparsely populated wilderness when they conceived these dreams.

Cassius Clay himself spoke of the Glade before Fee's coming:

> I knew the community in and around Berea when I was a boy, and I say that they were of the most vicious people that ever I did know; a drunken, tobacco-chewing, whiskey-drinking people; debauching and fighting could there be seen as plainly as the noon day sun . . . The inhabitants dwelt in huts without windows and with mud floors; the children [indulged] in idleness and dissipation.[10]

Old water mill near Berea. Courtesy David Greene.

The Glade was known (for the distance of a few miles, that is) for only two things in 1854—its tiny abolitionist church, utterly powerless in its social and geographical context and scarcely more than irritating to slaveholders in the neighborhood—and for its racetrack. In 1916 a former Madison County slave who lived to be over a hundred recalled taking part in "horse racing on the Glade Course" before Berea existed. Although one would hardly expect there to be any connection between the race course and the church, it seems that Wiley Fisk, minister of Glade Church, was "a victorious jockey."[11]

A few families were established in the Glade and its immediate neighborhood. John Burnam, Sr., William Stapp, and Thomas Jefferson Renfro, charter members of the church, later to be among the first trustees of Berea College, were among the oldest, most respected members of the community—prosperous, nonslaveholding farmers, belonging to prominent families in Madison county. Teman Thompson and John Hamilton Rawlings (usually called "Ham") were also communtiy leaders, although their roots were in Paint Lick. On the ridge where Berea College now stands only two families resided: William B. Wright (Berea's first postmaster and son-in-law of William Stapp) with his house in Stapp's woods near the site of the present post office; and James Maupin, a widower with many children, located at what is now known as Van Winkle Grove. Some families in the neighborhood were small-scale slaveholders—Moores, Ruckers, Todds, Harrison Burnams, Elders, Ballards, and others.[12]

Most of the communities around the Glade were slaveholding. Even the Rockcastle County neighborhoods in the mountainous regions had slaves, while slavery was very common in Paint Lick and Silver Creek and not unknown even in Big Hill. So on the east, the west, and the south there was slavery, not to the extent that it existed in the Bluegrass, but still powerfully entrenched.

North of the Glade stretched the Bluegrass, all slavery. Lexington was the biggest slave market in Kentucky and by 1849 Fayette was the largest slaveholding county in Kentucky. Nothing could have seemed more ill-advised than locating Fee's abolitionist ministry deep in central Kentucky. Fee's enemies described Berea's position as being "in the heart of as strong a pro-slavery community as can be found in the South."[13]

At Berea slaveholders, slaves, and nonslaveholders met. The efforts of Clay and Fee would add yet another element to the already volatile brew: abolitionists. Berea was always a place of potential conflict, and, for that very reason, a region ripe with possibilities. Both Clay and Fee looked at the Glade and saw possibilities. Their visions drew them together long enough to give an incredible undertaking its start—an undertaking that would result in a town, churches, schools, a college, and, most importantly, a daring and unique social, economic, educational, and religious experiment.

In January of 1851 Fee's church at Cabin Creek, Kentucky, in Lewis County had been visited by Elder E. Mathews, an abolitionist missionary from the Free Mission Baptists. Mathews conducted a series of "interesting and profitable meetings—especially," Fee said "on the subject of the fugitive slave bill." Sometime in February or March Mathews traveled from Cabin Creek to Madison County, where interesting and profitable meetings proved to be impossible, as he was seized near Richmond and "most unjustly and brutally treated by four men, plunging him many times in a pond of water. He was required to leave the state, with a solemn pledge never to return; which pledge he gave. . . ."[14]

Probably Mathews undertook his journey to Madison County because Cassius Clay had written Fee a year earlier (by February 25, 1850) saying he believed that Fee's colporteur could travel in Madison County unmolested. Clay was wrong, of course, for a lone abolitionist traveling into Madison County in the 1850s was obviously in grave danger.[15]

Clay's overconfidence may have resulted from his knowledge of one radical abolitionist who had been operating in Madison County all alone since 1849. This brave man was Wiley Bennington Fisk, the first abolitionist minister of Glade Church, whose roots were in Puritan New England as much as in slaveholding Kentucky. He himself had been a slaveholder, but he had freed his slaves sometime before 1853. In his own description of himself, written for the American Missionary Association in January, 1853, Fisk said, "For some four years I have stood by myself as a minister upon the broad grounds of fellowship with all names and parties who will not tolerate human slavery. . . ." And again he said, "I stand alone in several counties around, on this subject of all the ministers in the field."[16]

He was pastoring the Glade Church and another church, as yet unnamed, in the neighborhood of Clay's White Hall. As early as 1851, Cassius Clay had noticed the ministry of Wiley Fisk and approved it. In a letter dated July 28, 1851, Fee stated, "Clay says there is material in his county—Madison Co. for an antislavery church and a minister there of fair talents. . . ." In the same letter, Fee, on Clay's recommendation, requested an American Missionary Association commission for Fisk. By October of 1852 Clay himself was trying to procure AMA sponsorship for Fisk's ministry.[17]

Fisk was indeed commissioned by the American Missionary Association, an organization which never allowed any man in the field without keeping a careful check on his activities. Wiley Fisk had to be scrutinized. The study of his life and habits, his character, began as soon as he started to work for the AMA with Fee acting as chief informant to the mission board. This examination of Fisk, his past and present, proved fatal to his career in Madison County. In a very long, detailed letter to George Whipple, corresponding secretary of the AMA, Fee laid his colleague bare. Fee believed that Fisk held the right principles and that he had many virtues, such as frankness, generosity, and hospitality; but he was also, according to Fee, excitable, "ready for fight as an Irishman," rash and violent, a horsetrader, and a Mason.[18]

Fisk's career in Madison County was basically at an end as soon as John G. Fee appeared. By March of 1855 Fee had discovered Fisk claiming payment from the American Missionary Association for services he apparently had *not* conducted in Jessamine County. "He is not truthful," Fee wrote, "yet I suppose God has brought good out of an evil man—he has opened ways which otherwise would not have been opened." Fisk's preaching in Madison County had begun drawing the people of the Glade into a community of abolitionists; moreover, his activities there had attracted Cassius Clay's attention to the region.[19] As an abolitionist Fisk had all the right principles, but not the right piety. His deficiency as a minister was a key factor in Fee's decision to come to Madison County. "It is important that the work there succeed," Fee wrote, "I do not believe it will with Bro. Fisk."[20]

Wiley B. Fisk's congregation had been but loosely established before Fee's first visit; membership had not been confined to nonslaveholders. Fee organized a free church along the same lines as his earlier churches in northern Kentucky. His was to be a thoroughgoing abolitionist and reforming church, refusing fellowship to slaveholders; recognizing slavery as a sin in itself; opposing castes, sectarianism, rum, and secret societies. (One might add it was antitobacco and antipapist, which would be true, although these last two features seldom appear on the official lists.) The church was free in the sense that it was under the jurisdiction of none of the recognized denominations, because all the established churches in the South condoned slavery in one degree or another. It was also free in that pews cost nothing; no ranking by wealth would be permitted. It was not free in internal discipline, for Fee's churches were extremely strict and demanding upon their members. Many of Fisk's former congregation, also calling themselves Glade Church, remained as a rival church in the neighborhood, unwilling to submit to Fee's doctrines.[21]

In the records of still another rival church, Scaffold Cane Baptist, appears evidence of Fee's impact on the religious community of the region. In the entry for June 3, 1853, we read that a charge was brought "against bro. John Dobbs and Samuel Williford junr [sic] for abruptly leaving the church declaring a non-fellowship with all slave holders and joining another society." Both Dobbs and Williford were excluded from the church's meeting on August 3, 1853, and at the same time "a charge was. . .laid in against Bro Elisha Dobbs for the same offence and after a few remarks he was Excluded." These three men may have joined Union Church in Rockcastle County (also one of Fee's new free churches) rather than the Glade church but, in any case, the entries concerning them cast light on the origins of all Fee's churches. When Fee entered a neighborhood, he was not asked to join the ministerial association, not welcomed by established pastors. His avowed intention was to draw people out of those churches where slavery was not viewed as a sin, and he succeeded in doing just that. Fisk claimed the 1853 revival drew converts from Baptists, Methodists, and Presbyterians.[22] Certainly Scaffold Cane Baptist Church was not the place to protest slavery. One of its deacons, holding the office, it is said, for fifty years, was John Todd, owner of thirteen slaves in 1850. Many of the members added to Fee's Glade Church represented growing enmity in the surrounding community.[23]

Fee's church began with external conflict virtually inevitable and internal dissension highly likely. One of the deponents in a Madison County court case, *Burnam vs. Burnam*, mentions that the church had been sharply divided, adding specifically that Sarah Kennedy Burnam had been on one side of the issue and her husband, although not a church member, on the other. In any case, the doctrine of nonfellowship with slaveholders was as divisive as anything could be. For example, John Burnam, Sr., charter member of Fee's abolitionist congregation, had wealthy Richmond relatives, particularly Thompson and Curtis F. Burnam, who owned many slaves; and his son Harrison Burnam was a slaveholder, while his daughter-in-law was both a slaveholder and a member of the rival church. Other members of Fee's Glade Church, such as Thomas Jefferson Renfro, William Stapp, and George West, had many slaveholding relatives.[24]

The establishment of Glade Church under Fee's leadership was also to have an immediate practical effect upon the region. About this time Cassius Clay was subdividing his 600 acres in the Glade, "and several persons then expressing a desire to be in the new church movement, with its protest against slave-holding and for a gospel with justice and mercy in it, Mr. Clay directed the surveyor to lay off, in the Glade, a village plot." Turning to Fee, Clay said, "Mr. Fee, you name it."

"We were then," Fee said,

> maintaining that the scriptures of the Old and New Testaments taught the doctrine of love to *all* men; the duty of justice and mercy, and that they were specific against man-stealing, slave-holding—oppression in all of its forms; and what we then asked was that the people imitating the example of the ancient Bereans, "inquire whether these things be so," and, as suggestive of this duty, called the place Berea. But, after a time, finding that the place for the church and co-operation with working friends was not down in the valley, but up on the ridge—the little plateau—we transferred the name, with its purposed work, up to the present site on the ridge; and now, as then, propose to inquire, in the light of God's word, what is truth—in reference to all things—in church and state.[24]

So Berea, a town named for biblical principle, was on the ridge, not in the Glade; even Fee's Glade Church was no longer in the Glade. Location on the ridge also represented a degree of freedom from Cassius Clay's influence, as he did not own all the land there.[25]

In many Southern churches blacks attended with whites, because whites were determined that their chattel should absorb exactly the right doctrines in church, not what they might hear in an unsupervised black church. Many prominent white Madison Countians felt "that separate Negro preachings and ignorant negro preachers should be suppressed by law."[26]

Fee described the practices of a typical Southern church in an account of the Sharon Presbyterian Church, where his parents and other relatives were members:

> Here, slaves, though members with their masters, were not allowed to sit in the same part of the church house nor at the same time partake of the Lord's Supper with their white fellow Christians. The slaves at this time sat in a gallery at the end of the church house, and when white Christians had been served, one of the elders would say: "Now you black ones, if you wish to commune, come down." This they did by an outside, uncovered rough stairway, and then around outside the house came on to the doors of entrance, and facing the congregation came to the seats vacated for them, and thus ate the Lord's Supper. Thus did slaves indeed "strive to enter into the kingdom of heaven."[27]

In the Glade Church in Madison County, blacks and whites communed together. Although slaves generally were not permitted to attend antislavery churches, two black women, both slaves, had joined Fee's congregation sometime between 1854 and 1858. In a letter published in the *American Missionary*, Fee described a service at the Glade:

> The next Sabbath was Communion season. [One of the slave women] was present. When I was preaching, I saw her lips, like Hannah of old, move in prayer whilst tears of love stole down her sable cheeks. We make no distinction at our Communion, because of the color or condition of members: we know our Savior would not: and when the invitation was made for communicants to come to the Lord's table, she came with others, as a sister. At the closing hymn she extended her hand, in token of fellowship, and it was cordially received by brethren and sisters. As I turned, I saw the good brother at whose house she lives (he is not a slaveholder, nor is this woman hired to him) literally bathed in tears.[28]

The emancipationist movement had some effect in Madison County before John G. Fee took residence. In 1850, the year after the defeat of emancipationist hopes by the new Kentucky constitution, dozens of slaves were legally freed in Madison County. On April 1, 1850, for example, Edmund Baxter emancipated fifteen of his slaves; and on the same date John D. Harris freed his Negro woman Eliza; Shadrach Williams, his slaves Claibourn Fox and Edmund Williams; and Alfred Pettiford emancipated two slaves, whom he also acknowledged as his children. Two of the groups of slaves freed in 1850 belonged to men who were themselves men "of color." William Shackelford of Richmond freed his slavewife Caroline (formerly a slave of Thompson

Burnam) and five slavechildren (one of whom was also purchased from Burnam) on January 5, 1850. George White, "a free man of color," set free his "children & servants," George, Spicey, Mitchell, Sophia and Miriam White, on February 25, 1850. Throughout the 1850s emancipation of slaves, while never at the peak level of 1850, was not uncommon. Edmund Baxter freed four more of his chattel in 1851. But by 1852 freed men and women had to swear their willingness "to be removed out of this state" in order for their new status to become legal. On September 6, 1852 Hardin M. Greene and William S. Collins were appointed trustees "to take charge and hire out such slaves as may be emancipated in this county for whom no provision is made for sending them out of the state." In November, 1852 three freed slaves appeared in Madison County Court to announce their willingness to be removed, the first of dozens. One of Edmund Baxter's former slaves, Milton, "a very bright mulatto," received his freedom on the condition that "he will not become chargeable upon any county in this commonwealth." Milton was "entirely blind."[29]

One method of removal was widely publicized but seldom used. In February, 1853, half a dozen slaves freed by the will of Brook Butler, deceased, agreed to be removed from Madison County to Liberia. Those who could not be removed were frequently placed in the poorhouse— such a case was Jupiter, "a free Negro," who was to be confined "until further order of the Court." And, in some instances, freedom itself was not easily achieved. The fifteen slaves of Sarah Robinson, emancipated by her will, were not granted their freedom for years while her heirs contested the estate.[30]

Many freed men and women remained in Madison County for many years without obtaining their certificates of freeedom, the reason presumably being that cetification required a promise to remove from Kentucky before a given date. So Albert Mackey, for example, freed in 1841, did not seek (and receive) his certificate until December 7, 1857. Many freed slaves brought their children, born in freedom, into court to obtain certificates for them. For example, Mary Johnson, freed by her master in 1844, applied for certificates for her seven minor children twenty years later.[31]

When asked directly about slavery in Madison County, citizens of the region tended (and tend), as most Southerners did (and do), to relate some anecdote of "happy, lighthearted" blacks singing, eating banquet-style, and expressing undying love and loyalty for their masters and delight in their bondage. Such accounts appear repeatedly in John Cabell Chenault's original *Old Cane Springs* (the thesis of which "was to reveal the very favorable condition of slavery in a prosperous part of Madison County"), in which old Aunt Millie is quoted as saying, "I tells you, honey-chile, a free nigger ain't no good. . . ." A slave preacher, obedient to a fault, is also cited: "I know that neither master nor servant in this community wants any change in the present state of affairs." In a recent interview, a descendant of one Madison County slaveholding family stated that "slavery was never bad here."[32]

PUBLIC SALE!!

THE undersigned Administrator's of Robt. Cochran, dec'd., with the consent of his Heirs, will sell at Public Auction to the highest bidder, on the premises,

On TUESDAY, 6th day of October next,

The tract of land on Silver Creek, in Madison County, Ky., on which said Robe t Cochran lived at his death, containing

ABOUT 400 ACRES.

This land adjoins the lands of Wm. H. White, Edward Elmore, and Jane Moss, on the road from Irvine to Lancaster. It is in fertility, equal to any land in the county, and has substantial improvements of all kinds. Also,

About 20 Head of Horses,

10 or 15 head of Cattle; about 90 head of drove Hogs, 100 Shoats; Corn, Oats, Wheat, Rye; Farming Tools, Household and Kitchen Furniture of all kinds. We will also sell 12 likely and

VALUABLE SLAVES,

3 men, 2 women, 3 boys, and 4 girls, at the same time and place, to the highest bidder, but negro dealers for the trade are not permitted to buy them, as the heirs do not wish the negroes to be taken out of the county. Possession of the Slaves and personalty will be given immediately, and of the land on or before the 1st day of January 1858. Terms made known on the day of sale.   GEO. W. BALLEW,

August 21, 1857.   JAS. S. COCHRAN, Adm'rs.

Courtesy of Mr. A. C. Rucker of Richmond.

Ample evidence to the contrary exists, however. During a trip to Richmond (1859), Elizabeth Rogers witnessed a black man, recently sold, being taken away on the Lexington stage, with his wife, groaning and entreating, running behind the vehicle trying to say goodbye or reach him before he disappeared forever. "Far up the street the woman pursued her hopeless journey, and not one hand was lifted to help. . . . One of the men at my side remarked carelessly, "She takes it hard, don't she?" The testimony of Elizabeth Rogers, a Yankee, an abolitionist and a Berean, might be discounted as mere prejudice. No such disavowal could be made for Lucia F. Burnam (native of Richmond, member of a prominent slaveholding family), who wrote that in Richmond "a strong negro man was literally whipped to death by his master and his sons, because he had taken a horse out of the stable and ridden him one night." Nothing was done to punish these particular slaveholders, although the entire community felt "great indignation." Miss Burnam also quotes Dr. Charles J. Walker, who told her "that in the course of a long Medical practice [in Madison County], he had never known a year, when he was not called upon to minister to some slave who died from the effects of cruelty or neglect."[33]

Inadvertent revelations concerning the peculiar institution abound in Madison County records. An excellent example is a civil court case, *Burnam vs. Burnam,* tried in 1859-60, involving a divorce suit by Sarah Kennedy Burnam against her husband Harrison Burnam. The case contains some twenty depositions written by ordinary people of Madison County. None of them is attempting to analyze conditions of daily life, although all of them contribute to a portrait of society in Madison County in the years immediately preceding the war.[34]

Sarah Kennedy was a member of a very distinguished Kentucky family. Her grandfather, John Kennedy, Sr., had come to Kentucky as early as 1775; two of her uncles had been at Fort Boonesborough with Daniel Boone, and a third, General Thomas Kennedy, was one of the largest plantation owners and slaveholders in the state (Harriet Beecher Stowe visited his plantation near Paint Lick and supposedly referred to it in *Uncle Tom's Cabin.* By marriage the Kennedys were allied with the Irvines, Estills, and Millers—among the very oldest and most prominent of Madison County clans. Her father, like her uncles, had served in the American Revolution; he had prospered as a planter in Garrard County near Paint Lick. From him Sarah Kennedy inherited a slave at his death in 1850.[35]

In 1822, when she was twenty years old, Sarah married James Best, another prosperous slaveholding planter, by whom she had four sons and one daughter. When he died Sarah received money, livestock (including a valuable and well-known racehorse), dower land (thirty-seven acres on Walnut Meadow Fork of Paint Lick Creek), and four dower slaves from his estate. She had been a widow for a very brief time when she married (February 25, 1840) a much younger man with little or no property, Harrison Burnam, twenty-six-year-old son of John

Burnam, Sr. (the Berea College trustee, himself a first cousin of Thompson Burnam, Sr., of Richmond). Sarah was in her late thirties. To Burnam she bore three children, a son James and daughters Eliza Jane and Sarah Martha.[36]

In September, 1859, she sued her husband for divorce. By that time her children by her first husband were grown and many of them had children of their own; she was an old woman married to a man in his prime. Burnam had managed her property well, and, after almost twenty years of marriage, was prospering.

Sarah had moved out of her husband's house to live with her daughter-in-law, Nancy Harris Best, widow of James Best; but she had no means of support, since Harrison Burnam was receiving all the proceeds from renting her land and hiring out her slaves. She said Harrison Burnam had combined with one William B. Wright to defraud her of lawful rent due her for use of her dower land.

In her suit for divorce, Sarah K. Burnam testified that her husband had taken control of all her property, including her dower land and slaves. She seems to have expressed a good deal of resentment at the fact that Harrison Burnam had traded off her noted racehorse Jane; by 1859 she had no horse of her own to ride to church or anywhere else. (She was a slaveholding member in good standing of Wiley B. Fisk's Glade Church.) She accused her husband of cruel and inhuman treatment calculated to destroy her health and happiness; his behavior, she said, revealed a settled aversion to her—because of his "outrageous & ungovernable temper" she feared "great bodily injury" and "probably danger to her life."

In addition, Harrison's "intercourse" with her female slaves had been, she alleged, for a long time "so disgusting and obscene as to render him totally unfit to be the guardian or controller of her young son & infant daughters." ("Infant " is being used here as legal terminology—the girls were fourteen and fifteen, their brother nineteen.) She asked for custody of her children and various economic redresses, including control over her own slaves.

The three children were not given into Sarah Burnam's custody. One of her daughters married while the divorce case was in process; the other, who was nearly blind, lived with her uncle Henry S. Burnam in Paint Lick, where she remained; the son James, apparently by choice stayed with his father. The disposition of the slaves in the affair receives a great deal more attention in the legal documents than the custody of the children.

Harrison Burnam, with Thompson Burnam, Sr. as his surety and Curtis F. Burnam his attorney, launched a defense. Harrison denied all his wife's charges and countered with accusations that she was not industrious, neither a good manager nor a good mother. She was extravagant, he said, careless of her household duties, possessed of a violent temper, lacking in good sense, and obviously—since she had leveled so many false charges against her innocent husband—deranged.

This, basically, was the case for which the Burnams' relatives, friends and neighbors were asked to supply evidence. The twenty depositions taken over a period of several months show a surprising amount of agreement among the people, especially about financial matters. Most of the witnesses were asked to estimate a fair hiring price per annum for each of the Burnam slaves; on this question the deponents achieved virtual agreement. They also knew each slave by name and agreed perfectly concerning the physical condition, age, and work potential of each black. In reference to Mrs. Burnam's dower land no conflicting details were reported.

Virtually all the deponents had lived in Madison County near the Burnams for many years; some had known both Harrison and Sarah all their lives. Both men and women, slaveholders and nonslaveholders, served as witnesses. Their uniform knowledge of the slaves involved in the case is some measure of how all-pervasive the system had become, how intimately entwined with all aspects of daily life.

From her father Sarah Burnam had inherited one slave, a woman first called Lucy, then known as Cinda (both nicknames for Lucinda, of course). Cinda had a little daughter named Susan, about five years old in 1859. These two slaves accompanied Sarah Burnam when she moved out of her husband's house into her daughter-in-law's. There the older slave died, leaving the child Susan as the only slave in Mrs. Burnam's possession. The others, five in number, were hired out by Harrison Burnam to various people. The original dower slaves were Arch, Jack, Agnes, and her daughter Ann; but Agnes had another daughter, Clara, born after Sarah Burnam's second marriage.

It was common practice in Kentucky for slaveowners to hire their slaves out, usually on a yearly basis. Frequently, January 1 was the traditional day for "hiring out," with large crowds gathering at the courthouse to select their workers.[37]

In 1860 Harrison Burnam had hired out all his wife's dower slaves but one—Ann was far advanced in pregnancy and so considered worthless until after her delivery. The others were all hired to different people—the small girl Clara to Samuel Kincaid, her mother Agnes to Emanuel Mitchell. Much has been written about permanent separation of slave families by sale, little about short-term separation by hire. Even when one family of slaves belonged to the same individual there was no guarantee that the blacks could live together or even close to one another. At any rate, the hiring of slaves was a common and acceptable practice in Madison County, where nonslaveholders rented workers by the year, even when they disapproved of the institution of slavery. John Burnam, Sr., for example, whose affiliation with Fee's church and Berea College bespeaks his abolitionist sympathies, hired the slave Jack for the year 1860.

Arch, "a very able bodied boy & very stout," was hired out for $130 to $135 for the year; Jack, who had suffered from a "fever" which crippled him for life, brought $77.50—even though he was lame, unable to walk without a stick, and could not plow, John Burnam, Sr., found him a "good, obedient slave." Agnes, an old woman, was considered worth very little more than her food and clothing, but she was a good cook and washerwoman—estimated value about $20 to $30 a year. Ann, pregnant at hiring time, could not be placed, as she would be an expense; apparently she remained on Harrison Burman's farm. When she was not pregnant, she was hired out for $40 to $50. Clara, young and small, was worth only some $10 or $15 a year. For that trifling sum the child was separated from her mother for a year!—a routine injustice, mentioned by several deponents without emphasis.

Several witnesses expressed themselves on the subject of slavery— all speaking in a very specific way, not theoretically, but practically. John Burnam, Sr. remarked, "I have not been in the habit of hiring slaves or meddling with them." His hiring the slave Jack for the year was apparently an unusual action, which he did not bother to explain. One witness, James Blackburn, said, "I have but little knowledge how Negroes hire having never owned any or hired any myself." But he said he knew the blacks belonging to the Burnams. One deponent [Mary] Jane Karr [wife of Harrison Karr, daughter of William Stapp], being asked what she would give for the hire of the slave girl Susan (some four or five years old), replied, "The little girl presant [sic], I would not take her at presant [sic] for her victuals & clothes—I think she would at this time be an expense if there were any Doctor bills to pay. I would not be willing to take her and pay anything for her under ten years old. . ." Asked about another slave, she stated. "The old negro woman Aggy would not be worth anything to me. I never hired or owned any negroes. I would not take her for life & give anything for her—I do not know what she would be worth to other people." Harrison Karr, deposing at a different time, simply agreed with his wife.

The problem of blacks who were too old or too young was obvious to everyone. Slaves could be simply an expense. In fact, slaves might belong to people who were themselves poverty-stricken and unable to live well themselves, much less provide adequately for their unprofitable property. For some Madison County slaves their condition meant sharing the deprivations of a family which could not make ends meet. Even when their owners were relatively prosperous, slaves might incur hardships automatically as a result of white peoples' problems. A white man died and the slaves in his estate were up for sale, or at least liable to removal to another plantation. A white woman sought a divorce and slaves might have to suffer in all innocence. What was to be done with a five-year-old black girl whose mother had recently died and who was unwanted by her white mistress, could not live with her white master, and was unhirable? This question is raised in *Burnam vs. Burnam* only incidentally. Even though the slaves in the case were personally known to many of the witnesses, no one mentioned any of them with sympathy—each slave was an item of property and a financial problem.

Harrison Burnam and Sarah Kennedy Burnam, the two principals in the case, were, of course, the primary subjects of all the depositions in their divorce proceedings. For the most part, their friends and neighbors were very cautious about criticizing either of them, although several depositions mention his violence toward his wife in striking and cursing her. Nevertheless, he emerged as a man of good reputation, sound business sense, and an active life outside the home (for many years he was a constable and away from his house a great deal). One deposition directly denied that Harrison had a reputation as a rake with women. The usual reports about Sarah depicted her as hard-working, sensible, and thrifty. Although some neighbors characterized her as a gadabout, since she wanted to have a horse to ride to church and go visiting, and others felt she was extravagant in dress, she emerged generally as a woman who lived a life of incredible drudgery. One witness said she had never visited Sarah Burnam without finding her at work, weaving, working in the garden, canning, or carrying washing to a nearby stream with her slave women in attendance.

When John G. Fee attempted to convince his congregation that slavery was a sin, he had the enormously difficult task of dealing with a perfectly ordinary aspect of perfectly ordinary daily life. Slavery was invisible to people who lived with it day-in and day-out. The deponents in *Burnam vs. Burnam* had all seen slaves, all known slaves personally; but the witnesses saw dollars and cents, business deals, possibilities of profit and loss—not human beings. Finally, the evidence in *Burnam vs.Burnam* reveals clearly that one of the cruelest aspects of slavery was not some hidden violence or sadism, but simply the way it tied the lives of slaves inextricably to the accidents, hardships, and disasters incurred by white owners.[38]

*   *   *

Cassius M. Clay was a large, handsome man with an impressive voice; John G. Fee was small and homely, with a "piping" voice. In some important respects, however, the friends were well matched; for a decade their relationship was marked by a sense of mutuality and growing affection. Each man read, praised, encouraged and distributed the other's writing. Fee's *Anti-Slavery Manual* appeared in separate numbers in Clay's ill-fated antislavery newspaper, the *True American*, and Clay "personally distributed . . . many copies of the Manual . . . and many copies of [Fee's] tract on 'Nonfellowship' " in Madison County. Fee had, likewise, worked to distribute Clay's writings; he wrote Clay in 1849 requesting copies to sell.[39] Their mutual support extended into their respective realms of politics and religion. Clay gave his approval to Fee's ministry, and Fee supported Clay's political career for years. Fee was Clay's preacher, and Clay was Fee's politician.

As early as 1846 Fee invited Clay to Lewis County to speak to the citizens there on slavery and emancipation. "C.M. Clay approved the [abolitionist] movement here [in Cabin Creek]," Fee wrote, "from the first . . . attending our meeting . . . last fall in Bracken, Clay said to one

The first page of John G. Fee's first letter to Cassius M. Clay. Berea College Archives.

of the members, 'if he had a free church in Madison to go to he should attend church every Sabbath.' " (When he had a free church in Madison County, Clay did *not* attend it every Sunday!) In 1849 when Clay campaigned on behalf of emancipation candidates, Fee supported him, also serving as corresponding secretary of Clay's Republican Club.[40]

As delegate from Lewis County, Fee met with such eminent Kentuckians as Senator Joseph R. Underwood, Henry Clay (delegate from Bourbon County), Robert J. Breckenridge (Fayette County) and Cassius Clay (Madison) at the State Emancipation Convention held in Frankfort in April, 1849, as preparation for the Constitutional Convention in October. After some disagreement about a method of emancipation, the delegates adopted a resolution that slavery ought not to be perpetuated in Kentucky, and recommended that importation of slaves be outlawed and gradual emancipation authorized. The emancipation convention had no noticeable effect on the new Kentucky constitution, ratified in May, 1850—which stated that no slave could be emancipated in Kentucky without being sent out of the state, while no free Negroes might emigrate into Kentucky at all. The 1850 constitution established the right of property as "before and higher than any other," and clearly identified slaves as property. Slavery was, thus, much stronger under the new constitution. This early failure in political action did not discourage Fee from later involvement, although his ultimate antislavery goals for Kentucky were even farther away in 1850 than they had been earlier. Ten years later (December 12, 1859), Fee was still writing to Clay to emphasize his (Fee's) support of the Republican party, particularly if Clay should be on the ticket.[41]

In most respects the Fee-Clay relationship up to 1854 seems to have been well balanced—neither man was actually dominant, in spite of Clay's edge in physique and finances. After Fee accepted Clay's invitation to Madison County, their friendship underwent a great change. It had always been more than a personal relationship. But the new deal made their bond inescapably a public matter—now Clay was Fee's patron-protector, a role that was to become a two-edged sword.

Fee had suffered persecution before he ever came to central Kentucky; he had been "waylaid, shot at, clubbed, stoned," frequently harassed. But what he was to endure after coming to Berea made his earlier encounters seem tame.[42] In the spring of 1855, Fee was mobbed at Dripping Springs near Crab Orchard, where he had a regular appointment for preaching. He was dragged from the church and forced to leave the neighborhood.[43] Fee's congregations at the Glade in Madison County and at Boone's Fork and Green's Schoolhouse in Rockcastle County adopted and published resolutions in his defense, and Fee made an appeal to the Garrard Civil Court, which refused to bring any suit against the mob. He always sought legal redress in civil courts, believing it to be "not only wise policy, but religious duty." In central Kentucky, his appeals to magistrates never resulted in anything; local authorities simply would not protect him or see justice done on his behalf.[44]

But Cassius Clay, returning from an antislavery speaking tour of the East, took more direct action. "If we were not allowed to speak freely according to our constitutional rights," he said, "our whole scheme for emancipation failed." Clay was convinced that the attack on Fee had really been directed toward himself. After making an appointment to lecture in Crab Orchard himself, Clay appeared there "surrounded with armed followers" and exercised his freedom of speech. In fact, his army probably consisted of his followers from the Glade, armed "with rifles, shotguns, revolvers and kitchen knives." He followed that up by speaking at Stanford, seat of Lincoln County. His appearance there has become a legend (the details of which he disclaimed). He is supposed to have carried up the aisle a carpetbag containing a Bible, a copy of the Constitution, a bowie knife, and two pistols, and to have challenged anyone who did not recognize the authority of the printed words to deny the authority of his weapons.[45]

In May, Clay organized a meeting in Jessamine County, far from the scene of the mobbing. There he spoke for three hours, encouraging the citizens to adopt resolutions supporting freedom of speech, press, religious opinion, and worship. On June 29 Clay spoke at Brush Creek. The next day he was at Scaffold Cane in Rockcastle, reading the Jessamine Resolutions and asking for support in his proposed return to Dripping Springs with Fee, so that the minister could have another chance to speak there.[46]

In Clay's friendship and presence there was safety. At Fee's suggestion Fee and Clay organized a Fourth of July meeting in 1855 to speak together "in behalf of human freedom." The meeting was a great success. "A large audience gathered was collected of orderly, quiet citizens. C.M. Clay in an address, eloquent and pertinent, enchained the audience for two hours," on the subject of the evils of slavery; this was followed by Fee's short address on "the relation of the church of Christ to the subject of liberty."[47]

In reaction to these events a Rockcastle County meeting of antislavery opponents convened at Mount Vernon to forbid antislavery speaking in the county. The demands of the committee were presented to Clay, who refused to abide by them, but immediately began publicizing the issue of free speech in Kentucky throughout the state and the nation. In addition, he announced that he and Fee would both speak at Scaffold Cane on July 21.

Opposition began to organize, with representatives from five counties coordinating resistance to antislavery. Orators tried to incite the slaveholders. Some antislavery families fled from their homes, and blacks were thrown in jail in Mount Vernon and Crab Orchard. The day before the meeting Clay wrote the *Cincinnati Gazette*: "Tomorrow I go to the field of contest to determine whether liberty of speech and religious freedom is longer possible in a slave state!" On July 21, Clay and Fee kept their appointment and spoke before an attentive audience made up mostly of sympathizers. Clay had offered to escort Fee to the county with a hundred armed men, but Fee refused the offer. The opponents of the meeting "feebly rallied in the neighborhood," but gave up without a fight. "Clay's victory was complete. He had vindicated freedom of speech in a slave state and had given the 'Slave Power' their first check in a slave state." In addition, he had enhanced his political prestige in the state, and elevated himself to a commanding position in the Republican party.[48]

Now Clay had the stature of a hero in John G. Fee's eyes. In Fee's defence Clay had spared neither trouble nor expense—he had exposed himself to danger and had publicly won for them both the right to speak. For Fee July 21, 1855, must have marked the zenith of his relationship to a great patron. Their Fourth of July meeting and the later assembly had been so successful that the pair decided to repeat it the next year at Slate Lick Springs in Madison County.

Neither Clay nor Fee expressed any opinion at Slate Lick Springs to surprise the other. Both men were well aware of their differences—they had passed a decade in close communion with one another's views. Yet their public disagreement on July 4, 1856, brought about a painful breach between them and resulted finally in the dissolution of their relationship as fellow workers.

They had been in disagreement already that year. Clay, in proposing a Republican ticket for Kentucky, had said, "The National Government has nothing more to do with slavery than with concubinage in Turkey." Fee had replied, "The National Government is responsible for the strength and perpetuity of slavery, by the enactment of the Fugitive Slave Law." This little exchange laid the groundwork for their more well-known disagreement.[49]

The Republican Association of Madison and Rockcastle counties had agreed to sponsor the meeting, to which all parties were invited. "At [an] early hour many persons were on the ground. The people continued to come male and female, from all directions until a large and orderly assembly was convened." Fee later estimated the crowd as "hundreds of people." The Declaration of Independence was read, followed by the platform of the National Republican Association. Preliminaries over, the two principal speakers approached the podium.

Fee describes how the debate began:

> Mr. Clay insisted that I should speak first. I declined. He insisted. The people, slaveholders and nonslaveholders, were waiting. I decided in my own mind, to meet the issue squarely, and rising, with a copy of the Declaration of Independence in my hand, I repeated the words, All men are created free and equal, and endowed by their Creator with certain inalienable rights. I said, "If inalienable, then such are man's relations to God and to himself and family, that he cannot alienate; society cannot, governments cannot alienate. 'Endowed by their Creator,' if so, then it is impious in us to attempt to take away."[50]

What is more, he said, "This invasion of human rights [slavery]" is condemned by the word of God. "That which outrages natural right and Divine teaching is mere usurpation, and, correctly speaking, is incapable of legalization." In other words, there can be no law for slavery. He concluded his presentation by saying, "A law confessedly contrary to the law of God ought not by human courts to be enforced," and, referring to the Fugitive Slave Law, he said he would refuse to obey it and then suffer the penalty.[51]

Afterward Cassius Clay spoke, first expressing "high personal regard" for Fee, then saying, "As my political friends, I warn you; Mr. Fee's position is revolutionary, insurrectionary. As long as a law is on the statute book, it is to be respected and obeyed until repealed by the Republican majority." Speaking of the Fugitive Slave Law, he said, "As far as this is concerned, I would not obey it; it is contrary to natural right, and I would not degrade my nature by obeying it." Fee wrote, "I seized the concession and in my reply said, 'My friend, Mr. Clay has conceded the whole point at issue—that there is a *Higher Law*.' He, now seated in the midst of the congregation, cried out. 'The Fugitive Slave Law is unconstitutional.' " Significantly, Fee adds, "There was manifest confusion in the crowd."[52]

Fee and Clay did not cause much of a disturbance at Slate Lick Springs; James Scott Davis, another of the speakers on the platform that day, wrote, "On the 4th the gathering was much larger than last year. Bro. Fee, Clay and I made speeches. Bro. Fee took strong radical ground, Clay replied, before his main speech. Quite an animated discussion followed." That is all Davis had to say, writing only two weeks after the event. Pressed for more details, he wrote a few days later, "I believe that in my last I told you of our meeting on the Fourth. There was not the least sign of disturbance."[53] There had, indeed, been a disturbance, but it was not primarily an observable event. In spite of Fee's entreaties Clay refused to visit his friend for thirteen months after the Slate Lick Springs incident. Their debate was to continue in newspapers in both Ohio and Kentucky for four years.[54]

Before he was done Fee had published virtually every nuance of the Slate Lick Springs argument and systematically refuted Clay's embattled position. What made this all so trying for Clay was not just the stubbornness of the little man who opposed him—Clay had learned to tolerate that, and even perhaps to admire it. But Fee opposed him in public, right down the road from Berea, in front of Clay's 'boys,' and on one level at least, it was winning opposition. Once Fee began an argument he would not let up. It was his conviction that people were so constituted that they could be convinced of truth. When Clay did not respond to truth on the Fourth of July, Fee's assumption was that his friend would certainly come about if he (Fee) would simply sharpen his argument. The effect was to put Clay into a position of self-defense.

Cornered, Clay always fought—no, not always, for how could he fight with a man so much smaller than himself, a minister, a pacifist? Nothing that Clay was accustomed to use would work; to perform his usual ritual in the face of insult would simply make him look ridiculous. He could not challenge Reverend John G. Fee to a duel. So he withdrew his support.

In 1857 he explained his decision in this way:

> In the first place . . . I did not withdraw my influence from [Fee], but he his from me. We acted together, from before 1848, upon the basis of *constitutional* opposition to slavery. On the 4th of July 1856, against my urgent advice and solemn protest, he publicly, from the stump, not in the capacity of a minister of the Gospel, but as a politician, made avowal in substance of the doctrines of the *Radical Abolitionists*. That is, as I understand him, slavery being contrary to the higher law—the law of nature and of God—is "no law," unconstitutional and void.
>
> [The same letter ends with what Clay must have felt was the last word in his relationship with John G. Fee]: With regard to Mr. Fee, personally, I entertain towards him the most friendly feelings. I consider him honest and "godly". . . . He is a man of ability and mature mind. In the wide verge of life, destiny separates us; he, and those who act with him, must reap the good and evil of their deeds.[55]

The letter just cited was published in a newspaper. Clay's abandonment of Fee was blantantly public—a tacit withdrawal of protection which Fee's enemies were all too ready to understand.

In his role as patron-protector Clay stressed the patron aspect, with a feudal emphasis on what was due him as the provider of money, land, and favor. In the political arena he wanted only what he considered as political views to be presented, and certainly he wanted his companion-in-arms to be a political asset. Ironically, Clay seems to have been as eager and willing to suppress Fee's freedom of speech as any other aristocratic Southerner might have been. Fee stressed the idea of the protector: Clay was to insure for Fee his civil liberties. Fee had never promised to agree with Clay or anyone else, but both men had agreed on the importance of freedom of speech—and Clay had taken steps in the past to give Fee a public forum and to defend him. Both men felt betrayed and deeply wounded.

In June, 1857, the new church which Fee's congregation had built in Rockcastle County was burned by arsonists. The next month, after many threats, Fee was mobbed again. He was preaching in an unoccupied dwelling house, when some local men "entered with threats of death, and with hands on their weapons." Once again Fee was forcibly removed from the pulpit and marched almost ten miles (from Rockcastle County to Crab Orchard) by a threatening, jeering mob. Friends of Fee's sent for Clay while Fee was still believed to be in the hands of this particular mob, but Clay refused to come on grounds that Fee was a radical with whom Clay could not be identified.[56]

Once again Fee wrote to Clay:

> I think your standing aloof is an injury to the cause here—the enemy construes it in various ways, but all, as much as to say, 'he (Fee) ought not to be protected.' Protection is the duty of *man to his fellow*—when the officer cannot or will not then the people exercise the right belonging to them. This the friends here are determined to do. They have invited me here and they intend to see me protected [Fee is referring to Berea, which is the return address on this letter] whilst guilty of no crime—no violation of law. You ought to. It will be an injury to you not to. When you were mobbed in Lexington Henry Clay stood aloof because he could not 'identify himself with your principles.' You are doing the same now. My position is a solemn conviction of my duty to God. I care not for party or names. You refuse protection to one guilty only of an expressed opinion different from your own—but no crime. . . . The Quakers say the military law ought not to be enforced—yea even refuse to obey, yet they are protected. I know I ought to be. . . . I do not want you to do anything for friendship's [sake] merely, but I suggest what I think is duty and for your good as well as that of the cause of freedom & righteousness. I have been routed again—you will hear from the bearer particulars. John G. Fee.
>
> P. S. Copernicus when threatened with death and required to say 'the earth does not turn'—still said, 'it does turn'—so Fee still says 'a wicked and impious law ought not be enforced'. . . . When Herod said destroy all the men children under two years *ought that law to have been enforced?*[57]

Clay's withdrawal of support had one result that he surely did not foresee. If he would not provide protection, then other people would. In August, 1857, two of Fee's churchmembers came to meeting armed. A mob threatened Fee at church, but, Fee wrote, "one of these friends placed his hands upon his revolvers and stepped between them & me." And Fee found another mode of protection by organizing a band of men who worked for him as distributors of tracts, colporteurs—leaders of the antislavery friends, one of them a magistrate of some influence—to organize meetings, pass resolutions to send to civil authorities for protection, and distribute Fee's own "Address," an appeal for civil liberties in Madison County. All this Fee accomplished before Clay "had time to pour cold water." With some satisfaction Fee wrote, "almost every antislavery man had committed himself and gone through the fire with me."[58]

Now Clay not only refused to protect Fee himself, but also urged Fee's friends—some of them Clay's followers—not to do so either, on the grounds that defending Fee would identify them with Fee's cause. And those who defended Fee anyway were liable to Clay's censure. Clay told the people that Fee had been "ungrateful."[59]

However, Fee's friends were willing to go to great lengths. "At one time," Fee wrote, "it was expected that the mob was on their way to my house to take me out. Friends offered to guard my house during the night. I said no—it is not necessary. They insisted. I consented. In space of one hour about 30 armed men were around my house to defend it." Clay's opposition to Fee was now fed by a dawning realization that Clay's 'boys' were no longer simply *his* followers. A certain defiance of Cassius Clay was growing up in the Glade. When Clay perceived that the man he had brought to central Kentucky to consolidate his (Clay's) position among the Bereans might become their leader himself, his determination to "stand aloof" became absolute.[60]

By this time the rift between Clay and Fee was fostering still another change in allegiances. In December, 1857, Fee wrote to Lewis Tappan, "C.M. Clay stands off and cries 'Revolution & insurrection.' At such a time words of consolation from those who are known friends are most timely—a cordial to a wearied spirit. . . To know that I have *friends* even in distant places who sympathize with me & pray for me is a most sustaining thought." More and more it seemed to Fee his friends were in the East and North—Christians, not politicians. The eventual plan for Berea would be shaped by a preference for "outside" people and ideas, a preference that Clay had virtually forced upon Fee. The Berea that began to spring up in 1858 had little or no resemblance to any plan of Cassius Clay's.[61]

Chapter Seven

RELIGIOUS MISSIONARIES AND ABOLITIONISTS

Before Berea College was founded, Berea was primarily the center of a Christian mission field. From the tiny village on the ridge, Fee supervised a band of colporteurs, teachers, and fellow preachers, three of whom besides himself (John A. R. Rogers, George Candee, James S. Davis) were considered to be "missionaries," ministers with relatively permanent assignments to found new free churches in Kentucky and maintain established ones.

The founding of Berea College resulted directly from the religious fervor of Fee and his coworkers, most of whom were from Oberlin College in Ohio, where such piety was common, or at least expected. Oberlin was built by intensely religious people who believed they could do something to improve the world. A virtual embodiment of all the Christian reform movements which sprang up in the United States in the first half of the nineteenth century, Oberlin promoted temperance, manual labor, antislavery, the peace movement, moral reform, feminism and experimental education. From the beginning Oberlin doctrine included the goal of spreading itself all over the world, beginning in the valley of the Mississippi. The Oberlin portfolio of reform was probably the most radical version of the gospel the United States had yet seen.[1]

Fee, like his Oberlin helpers, believed his task was to convince the citizens of a slaveholding state that they must as Christians refuse to hold slaves themselves and oppose the whole institution of slavery as practiced by others. Fee had no other brand of Christianity to offer, no accommodation to make the doctrines easier for anyone—and his evangelical abolitionism was unattractive and utterly "foreign" to most of Madison County.

One of Fee's first attempts to disseminate antislavery information involved the use of workers called colporteurs. As the word was used by Fee and others, a colporteur was a person hired to distribute and sell books and tracts, especially antislavery writings. Generally colporteurs worked under the supervision of a missionary, moving out from some central location into relatively inaccessible districts. Fee's workers almost always rode horseback, carrying their literature in specially made saddlebags. All Fee's colporteurs were commissioned workers of the American Missionary Association. They gave Bibles and testaments free to slaves who could read and to white people too poor to buy them; they distributed tracts, sometimes temperance or antitobacco tracts, usually antislavery writings, including Fee's "Nonfellowship" and *Anti-Slavery Manual*. Sometimes colporteurs were expected to lecture or exhort. Always they undertook the labor of riding from house to house and—even if a sale were impossible—engaging each household in conversation about slavery. In an area where many people were proslavery such activities did not insure a welcome for colporteurs at every home. In the course of their work they inevitably "spied out the land"—learned, at first hand, who was friendly and who was not, which neighborhoods safe and which dangerous.[2]

Even before settling permanently in Berea, Fee was already supervising colportage in Madison County and the surrounding regions: as early as 1853, when he was still based in Lewis County, Fee was trying to find the right workers for central Kentucky. In 1854, forty-two men from Madison and Rockcastle counties sent a petition to the American Missionary Association enunciating abolitionist sympathies and asking for tracts to distribute. The signatures on that document constituted the list of possible candidates for colporteur work around Berea. Three of the signers actually became colporteurs (Peter H. West, S. M. Shearer and A. G. W. Parker).[3]

Fee found his workers lacking in common sense, too outspoken, indiscreet, full of rivalries and jealousies, contentious, belligerent, greedy, and, most of all, lazy. Fee discovered from West's reports that the colporteur was claiming virtually every move he made as work for the cause. West persisted in claiming a day's labor for attending church services. Peter H. West, Fee maintained, "charges for all he does." In addition some of his claimed days were short on both ends. Fee reported,

> He loves to sleep late of mornings—loves to stop too soon of evenings—spend his time going to meetings and then sit & talk with the company rather than talk to sinners or visit— loves a fine horse to ride and will neglect the cause to save his horse—He loves to get money easy. . . . He talks right and [he] sings well but that is not enough.

Faithfulness to the cause was rare. A. G. W. Parker, who was inclined to be faithful in spite of his occasional drunkenness, was repeatedly thrown into prison in Rockcastle County for his abolitionist activities. When he was released from jail (partly through the efforts of Cassius Clay), his enemies burned his house down to drive him from the mission field.[4]

Parker's last report, composed for him by John A. R. Rogers (since Parker himself was semiliterate) gives an insight into a little-known aspect of Madison County life before the Civil War:

> A. G. W. Parker to the Am. Miss. Assoc. for *Services in Distributing Bibles to Slaves.* I have spent eleven days in visiting slaveholding families for the purpose of giving Bibles to such slaves as could read. In 52 of such families I found 507 slaves and of that number 21 read a little. To 18 of the 21 slaves I have given Bibles. Twelve of these were men & 6 women. All of the men but one were professed Christians & most of them preachers & I think good men. One of the 6 women who received Bibles was a professor [of Christianity].
>
> In prosecuting my work I receive many looks from the slaveholders who not infrequently put on very long faces when I announce to them my errand.
>
> The number of slaves in the families visited range from 2 to 83. In two of these families there are two slaves in each who can read, in none of the others but one who can read at all and in many of them not a slave who can spell out a word of the story of Jesus.
>
> June 11, 1859   A G W Parker[5]

At this stage of his career Fee was less troubled by the illiteracy of slaves than by the ignorance of his coworkers. Fee's idea that education was essential to overcome slavery in Kentucky owed a great deal to his experiences with ill-educated colporteurs during the period from 1846 to 1859. The colporteur trouble also moved him to look north and east for help. Natives of Madison and Rockcastle counties would not do. What he needed was enterprising, efficient, go-getting New England Puritans in the field.

In his efforts to recruit Northern abolitionists for Kentucky, Fee appealed to his sponsors at the American Missionary Association in New York, who arranged a number of speaking/fund-raising tours for Fee, giving him exposure to many influential figures in the abolition movement, sending him to abolition centers like Oberlin in Ohio and Syracuse and Peterboro in New York in the summer of 1854. At Oberlin College, President Charles Grandison Finney gave Fee the opportunity to address the whole student body, pressing the claims of the mission field in Kentucky—and there many of Berea's future workers heard him speak for the first time, including John A. R. Rogers, Elizabeth E. Rogers, George Candee and his future wife, William E. Lincoln, and Otis B. Waters.[6]

The American Missionary Association put Fee and his work in contact with the whole realm of evangelical abolitionism, powerful in Ohio,

New York, and all of New England. Money—eventually lots of money—clothes, advice, good will, encouragement, and workers would come to Berea from rather unlikely corners of the nation. Funds for rebuilding a burned schoolhouse in Kentucky might (and did) come from a church in Union City, Michigan, or from the Ladies' Antislavery Society of Dover, New Hampshire.[7]

The journal of the American Missionary Association, the *American Missionary*, promoted the cause of abolition in Kentucky well for many years. Fee's letters from Madison County emerged year after year, and much of his more formal writing also appeared first in the pages of this periodical. The *American Missionary* built up a sizable number of readers, many of them wealthy and concerned, who were aware of Fee's ministry and especially his work at Berea. In the East and North in abolitionist circles, a tiny village in Madison County, Kentucky, became a very well-known place, a fact that made obscure Berea no easier for the traveler to locate.

In the fall of 1854 George Candee, a young Oberlin student who had been inspired by hearing Fee speak, found himself in Kentucky trying to find Berea. He knew that Berea was in Madison County and that the county seat was Richmond and that Richmond might be reached from Lexington, but that was the extent of his information. "So," Candee wrote,

> I must . . . go on my hunt for Bro. Fee. I found when I paid my fare to Lexington I had just 23 cts. left. Yet on I went, praying the Lord to provide for me. When I got to Lexington I found I was 25 miles from Richmond, but that there were two stages running there. I hastened to one of the stage offices and inquired the fare to Richmond, was answered "25 cts., cheap enough." I told the agent I had only 23 cts. "That will do," he said and gave me a ticket. I rode on hungry and lonesome enough.[8]

Arriving at Richmond almost overcome by anxiety, he took supper and lodgings at the Francis House, where he had to leave his overcoat and satchel for security until he could find Fee and "then send and pay the bill and get my things." By this time he had only the clothes on his back. And when he asked at his hotel where Berea was, no one had ever heard of it!

At the post office he had better luck, being informed that there was a post office called Berea "somewhere" in the neighborhood of Big Hill. He started toward Big Hill, asking for more directions along the way. He was told that "Cash Clay had started a town out at 'the Glade' and had named it Berea. It was somewhere at the right from Gay's store [present Bobtown]." On he went, found Gay's store, asked directions again—on the final leg of his journey he "met an old man on an old horse," who told Candee to his great relief that Berea did indeed exist and Fee was at home. "If ever a wanderer was made happy," Candee wrote, "I was the boy." Although it must have been something of a surprise when the young man arrived without coat or bag or money—or prior notice for that matter—Fee made him welcome and immediately put him to work.[9]

Sometime in the fall of 1855, Candee and Fee, while chopping wood together, began talking about a school, perhaps a college, "in which to educate youth of the land—educate not merely to a knowledge of the sciences, so called, but also to the principle of love in religion, and liberty and justice in government." Fresh from his own Oberlin experience, Candee spoke enthusiastically of that school's merits. This conversation is said to have been germinal in the eventual founding of Berea College.[10]

On January 4, 1856, Fee wrote to Gerrit Smith, giving a most succinct, emphatic version of his plan: "We have for months been talking about starting an academy and eventually look to a college—giving an education to all colors, classes, cheap and thorough."[11] Fee believed that a good school would help solve two continuing problems with the churches in Kentucky. The first was their loss of membership by people moving to free states. Once Southerners were convinced that slavery was wrong they tended to become dissatisfied with slave territory and to move away. Connected with that problem was a second—the incidence of young people who had to seek education in the North. Six young men from Fee's free churches in Kentucky went off to Oberlin College and Knox College before 1855; none would necessarily return. Fee wrote:

> We ought to have a good school here in central Kentucky, which would be to Kentucky what Oberlin is to Ohio, Anti-slavery, Anti-caste, Anti-rum, Anti-secret societies, Anti-sin. We have here a very healthful country, far more than Oberlin ever was. Why can we not have such a school here?
>
> Could we have even a good Academy, and offer facilities for an education to the young men and women, in the mountainous and non-Slaveholding districts, we could do much, and that too most effectively for the overthrow of slavery.[12]

Several major aspects of this scheme should be emphasized—antislavery and anticaste are mentioned first, very appropriately, as the Christian battle against bondage and for equality stood foremost in Fee's own mind. A second major emphasis is education for Appalachians, an education that would lead to the overthrow of slavery. Another distinctive feature of Fee's first plan was coeducation, still rare at this time, Oberlin being exceptional in that respect. Since Oberlin was a manual labor school, any school modeled on it would naturally incorporate a work program for its students.

Fee was thinking of locating the college, if the charter could be obtained, in Rockcastle County, about fifteen miles from his house. The drawbacks he saw: Rockcastle was "not so level, sightly or fertile" as Madison, "nor so favorable for roads." But he was convinced that Rockcastle could be "brought under a righteous influence" sooner because it had fewer slaveholders, only about seventy-two, whereas

Madison in the fertile portions was solid slavery. Postal routes were about equal in either place. Rockcastle, Fee thought, would be a good place, with cheaper land—"good location, soil, timber, water, altitude." Fee was also interested in Rockcastle County because integrated education had already taken place there, and he counted on the support of free black families in the region. "It is all important," Fee pointed out, "that we be able to demonstrate to the world that true Abolitionists can gather and teach successfully, schools at the south and schools in which *caste* shall be *lived* down."[13]

After the publication in the *American Missionary* of an article called "A College in Kentucky—needed," Fee was much encouraged by the response. People wrote him letters about the prospects of colonizing and even more letters about the proposed college. Delia A. Webster, an abolitionist from Vermont who had achieved immense notoriety in Kentucky by being imprisoned in Lexington for helping a runaway slave, wrote Fee offering grounds for a college on her farm across the river from Madison, Indiana, on the Kentucky side, just below the mouth of the Kentucky River. This prospect tempted Fee—the site was extremely pleasant, with easy access to the East, West, and North. Fee believed that a flourishing college could be built up there very rapidly and Ms. Webster was promising $2,000 in addition to the land. Fee was also invited to Newport, Kentucky, a place he found most attractive and considered the best possibility for his family's sake. Still he believed the interior location would be most beneficial for Kentucky, as location on the border would encourage students to seek employment in the free states instead of laboring in slave territory, where they were most needed.[14]

By June, 1857, however, Fee was beginning to incline toward a location near his own home on the ridge in Berea, partly because more problems were materializing elsewhere. The recently completed meeting house in Rockcastle County was burned down, just as "the prospects for a good church were daily increasing." Then Fee was mobbed in Rockcastle County and A. G. W. Parker's house was burned down. "During his absence from home—hour of night—the family (wife & four small children) escaped narrowly saving but little," Fee wrote. "Quite a number of men last week at court swore publickly that they would take my life." The prospects for a school in Rockcastle were cut off.[15]

The people of the Glade met and passed resolutions against mob law and in favor of liberty of speech and press. Fee wrote that he thought "most of the friends [at the Glade] would stand firm" and that they would avoid violence themselves.[16] Still the mob spirit grew and threats of violence multiplied. But the work continued. As the Bereans moved forward with their schemes, external conditions worsened almost daily. Fee's congregation, for a while, was composed almost entirely of women. "Some men who were friends stood around in the forest, some with guns near by."[17]

Fee wrote in December, 1857, "I am here a sojourner, a stranger, a pilgrim—the endearments of relatives & scenes of youth I crucified to come here. In times of mob violence & popular fury even friends here look upon me with suspicion or distrust." The plan had become by now Fee's ultimate goal: "If I can see a good school started in Ky I shall feel that I have accomplished the greatest work of my feeble life. I intend to struggle on for this object."[18]

The mobs continued. In January, 1858, Fee and colporteur Robert Jones were mobbed, Jones was whipped, and both were threatened with death. "For weeks there was a reign of terror." People were so fearful during this period that no men, except Berea's teacher Otis Waters and Hamilton Rawlings, would go into Fee's house for fear of being identified as abolitionist sympathizers. George Candee was driven out of Pulaski County; his schoolhouse was burned. Cassius Clay remained aloof. "We may be crushed out," Fee wrote.[19]

Meanwhile, the school was, amazingly enough, succeeding very well. Fee described their activities: "The pupils speak and write freely upon the subjects of slavery and freedom." A new facet had been added to the whole educational scheme, for three slaveholders were sending their children to the school. No one had anticipated the possibility of an abolitionist institution attended by both slaveholders and nonslaveholders. (When John Rogers and his wife Elizabeth became the teachers later in 1858 that was the distinctive feature of the pre-Civil War institution.)[20]

Fee found some encouragement in 1858, for Candee located in Jackson County that year with renewed hope; and the Rogers family, John, Lizzie, and their little son Raphael, arrived at the end of March. The work of the two Rogers impressed Fee and constituted an enormous step toward the realization of his dream. By September, 1858, John G. Hanson and his new wife Ellen were settled in Berea, both of them teaching in the new school. The coming of these cousins of the Fees must have been cheering indeed. In addition, John Hansel, a deacon in the church at Oberlin, arrived in Berea in the summer to look over the field "with the view of emigrating thither"—it was hoped that he represented the beginning of such a movement by many.[21]

In November, 1858, the Berea project received a distinguished endorsement from world-famous novelist Harriet Beecher Stowe, who praised John G. Fee's achievements in Kentucky very highly. Her opinion altered nothing in Kentucky, but toward the end of 1858 something happened which changed the whole picture, finally deciding the question of where the community and school should be permanently located.[22]

Fee had for some time made it a practice to invite black people home to eat with his family whenever the opportunity presented itself. In December "a colored man regarded in the community as a good man & who held religious meetings in different places" attended the sabbath afternoon prayer meetings at Glade Church. Fee twice asked him to pray and then invited him home—and, Fee wrote, "sat him down to my table with my family and other friends." John A.R. Rogers and John Hanson likewise entertained the black man in their own homes. "Against this many of the people & some of the church members rebelled. The question arose about colored persons coming into the school." (Otis Waters' first teaching assignment had been in Rockcastle County, where children from a family of free blacks had been among the students.) Trustees of the prospective school met, although a full board was not present, and decided that it was unwise to purchase land at Berea "until the people should test or settle the point—Shall we have a school upon gospel principles—treat man as man—if not we go hence."[23]

"I think nothing short of the power of the Holy Ghost will give the victory," Fee said, "We are now holding daily prayer meetings & shall probably pray ten days longer." At the meeting of the trustees it was discovered that some were "tenderfooted," as Fee put it, on the subject of race; some of the friends around Berea were not strong on the issue either.[24] But on April 3, 1859, Fee wrote an historic report to the American Missionary Association. The Glade district had held an election with two sets of trustees in the running, one group supporting Fee's policy of integration in the school, the other opposing it. "The anti-caste question carried in our school district," Fee exulted, "23 to 7."[25] The church, the colony, the school would be at Berea.

On March 31, 1858, a young couple from Ohio arrived in Berea. Their journey had taken them by stagecoach through the Bluegrass region, past "the great homes, with their slave quarters close by, the beautiful pasture lands, the thrift of wealth and the shiftlessness of poverty . . . . " In any case, as Elizabeth Rogers remarked, "Nothing could have been much drearier than Berea was."[26] In a livery carriage they traveled the last stage of their journey. Mrs. Rogers felt wholly unprepared for the last six miles before reaching Berea, on a road so terrible that it was hard to see how any carriage could make the trip without breaking down. "I must have held on to my baby with a clutch like grim death," she wrote, "and my husband with that never-say-die look on his face, no doubt stiffened my backbone."[27]

And what did they discover when they arrived?

> The smallest imaginable speck on the map of Kentucky would have been out of all proportion to mark the town, and to a traveler in search of it, it was a place hard to find. A crooked, narrow dirt road that wound up and down the ridge bordered on either side by tall trees and underbrush.

There were a few houses, some homes in the low lands round about, many more out toward the Bluegrass, and even on the ridge a few cabins at either end, but all too far at that period to be called part of Berea. Like the schoolhouse they were to see the next day, Berea was almost nothing: Fee's house, three cabins, and the district schoolhouse. (Later, Elizabeth Rogers wrote that Berea "was all in the brush & full of possibilities.")[28] On April 12, 1858, John Rogers recorded in his journal "Commenced teaching. All favorable." Fee had "drummed up fifteen pupils, and his three children among the number." Later, Lizzie Rogers viewed that opening day as an historic occasion: "On Monday morning," she wrote, "we found ourselves duly installed over the beginning of *Berea College*."[29]

Elizabeth Embree Rogers; one of the first teachers at Berea. Berea College Archives.

The school immediately antecedent to the foundation of Berea College was taught by John A.R. Rogers and Elizabeth (Embree) Rogers, both former Oberlin students, in 1858 and 1859. For a short time John G. Hanson, his wife Ellen (Shoals) Hanson, and Mrs. Anna Shailer assisted in teaching. This school was simply the district school taught in a building provided by the local citizens and under the trusteeship of three men in the neighborhood: William B. Wright, James M. Elder, and Joseph Williams. It differed from most district schools in Kentucky by having imported teachers who were acknowledged abolitionists, students in attendance from neighboring districts, and an anticaste rule making it theoretically possible for black students to attend. The last factor was most important, even though no blacks applied to the school in 1858 or 1859. The family of free blacks in Rockcastle whose children had attended Waters' school apparently never approached Berea. Nevertheless in 1858 and 1859 the relationship of the American Missionary Association missionaries to local education was basically a planned infiltration, entering the Kentucky school system at the lowest level and in the simplest way.[30]

The pre-Civil War school was conducted for four terms from April,1858, until July, 1859. For the last six months of their first period in Berea (from July to December, 1859) none of the Berea colonists were teaching at all. Their energies were devoted to establishing their colony, maintaining their churches (with Silver Creek an important new obligation), and getting a new school ready to open. But even the legal necessities for a college charter were never completed prior to the Civil War. Thus, Berea College had no formal existence before 1866.[31]

Pre-Civil War Madison County as it appeared to a well-bred, eighteen year-old, Oberlin-educated Quaker girl from Philadelphia: "The whole Southern problem," Elizabeth Rogers wrote, apparently assuming that Madison County could represent the problem,

> was a new one to us. The habits of the people were so different from what we had known . . . . At the time of which I write (1858-9) there was a most deplorable state of lawlessness all through the South. Morality among the men was at a low ebb, but low as it was, a true Southerner was always chivalrous toward one whom he considered a lady. The men were too ready, doubtless, to take offense at imaginary insults, and just as ready to settle every difficulty at the point of a pistol. Work, only as far as it was a necessity, was tabooed among the wealthier Southerners, and their poorer neighbors imitated their superiors, so that people of the poorer sort went without many a comfort that a little industry and hard work might have given them . . . . Drinking was all too common, and fire arms were worn openly and considered a necessary part of their daily outfit. The best of the men (I think the women were even more illiterate) possessed little more than the simplest rudiments of an education, while some could neither read nor write their names.[32]

She was shocked that "severe justice" was so seldom "meted out to the fiery young fellows whose quarrels so often ended in the taking of another's life." Whores formed a class by themselves—Mrs. Rogers remarked that "there were far too many of them."[33]

As teachers Lizzie and John Rogers found themselves recipients of a flood of invitations to visit the families of their pupils; usually they were asked to spend the night and always they were entertained with the best each household could offer. "What a variety of homes we entered," Lizzie said, "now at the home of the planter, and again in lowlier cabins."[34] The Rogers were entertained by "the Bests, the Burnams, the Moores, the Ruckers, the Denhams, the Todds, the Prestons, the Williams, the Wrights, the Elders, the Thompsons," and many others. "I remember so well in some of the homes we entered," Rogers wrote, "we were waited on by obsequious slaves, and in others the mothers prepared our bounteous meals," sometimes in a log cabin with a single room where the frying of the chicken was directly before the guests' eyes.[35]

When John and Lizzie began teaching in 1858 they had 15 pupils. The school increased rapidly to 50. When school opened the next year attendance had doubled to 100 students. Children came to the school from all directions; even though Berea began as a district school, from the first it engaged the interest of people outside the Glade. Many families from Fee's Rockcastle and Jackson county churches sent their children to Berea, and students came also from Paint Lick and Big Hill, although, of course, families from the Glade and its immediate vicinity provided most of the students.[36]

Even from its inception the Berea school could not be homogeneous. The mountains and the Bluegrass were represented, and a variety of communities, some of them very different from one another in spite of their geographical proximity. Paint Lick and Big Hill were more than miles apart. Berea's location at the seam of two different cultures shaped its existence from the first. The Bereans were surprised that slaveholders sent their children to the new school. "We had in that school," Lizzie Rogers wrote, "planter's daughters, pretty Southern girls, and little maidens who wore most bewitching little print dresses, and white aprons, while close by them sat children clothed in plainest garb, children gathered from the neighboring hillsides."[37]

In the total number of students one-third belonged to slaveholding families—some 38 students out of 104 had parents who actually owned one or more slaves. Many more students had uncles, aunts, grandparents or cousins who were slaveholders; if such connections were taken into account more than half of the original students at Berea would be included. Although none of the students with slaveholding connections themselves belonged to the elite families of Madison County, some of them were allied to large-scale slaveholders with a great deal of power and money. Ballards, Maupins, Moores, Todds, Bests, Cornelisons, Denhams—to name a few—were closely akin to Madison County citizens owning fifteen slaves or more in 1860. Some of the Berea students were closely related to the few families who owned *most* of the slaves in the whole county, a group that has been called the slaveocracy.

In 1860 there were 881 slaveholding families in Madison County; 110 of those families, representing 12 percent of the slaveholding population, owned 2,337 slaves out of the county's total of 6,118—12 percent owned 38 percent of the slaves. These 110 families, the elite of Madison County, constituted a ruling class in a population of approximately 11,000 whites.[38]

The two Best girls, Ann Eliza and Mary, were related through their mother Nancy Harris to four families of Harrises in Madison whose total number of slaves came to 118 in 1860; through their grandmother they were descended from the Kennedys who were very prominent in Kentucky before the nineteenth century began. The Denham students had an uncle, George Dejarnette, who owned 24 slaves; the Maupin children were related to George W. Maupin (15 slaves) and Leland D. Maupin (23 slaves). Many more examples could be cited if relatives with different surnames were also considered. Many Berea students at the school's inception came from families with strong connections to the wealthiest and most prominent slaveholders in the county. No wonder Berea's abolitionist founders and teachers were surprised![39]

At the same time, of course, the school attracted many of the poverty-stricken mountain students who had been expected; some of them were, indeed, grindingly poor, some far too poor to pay the tuition, although Elizabeth Rogers said no one was turned away on that account.[40]

John A.R. Rogers' account book, 1857-68, provides many details concerning the financial and labor arrangements of pre-Civil War Berea. Some students worked for the school or for their teachers; but at this period Rogers' accounts list little student labor—parents of students worked for the school more frequently than their children did, trading labor for books and tuition. Mary Jane Moore's tuition for July, 1858, was paid by her father Fergusson Moore's pasturing, salting, and providing corn for Rogers' horse.[41] The barter system was used extensively, with books being traded for a turkey (from Hamilton Rawlings) and tuition being paid with meat (by James Maupin). Mrs. Elder obtained books for her children by sewing a pair of pants for the teacher.

The school and the new settlement at Berea provided some small jobs for many people in the region. Many students, such as David Preston and Valentine Williams, worked for Fee, Rogers, or Hanson for cash, which they had to hand right back for fees, in the time-honored system of student labor. The entire neighborhood became financially involved with the Berea project—hundreds of individual entries in Rogers' account book attest that fact. Most of the people who traded with the Bereans or who worked for them were parents or siblings of students at the school. They did hauling, horseshoeing, woodchopping; built the daily fire in the schoolhouse during the winter months; repaired the building; cleared forestland; sewed clothing; babysat; ran errands; and they were duly paid by Rogers for their work. They provided soap, eggs, hay, wheat, molasses, and other staples.

A few students received their tuition free, and John G. Fee personally paid the school expenses of a few, including Elizabeth Rawlings (daughter of Hamilton), who had ambitions to be a schoolteacher. John and Lizzie Rogers paid for some poor students' books.[42]

What emerges from the pages of Rogers' account book for 1858-59 is a sense of the immediate interaction of the Berea school and the Berea community. Hundreds of tiny exchanges of goods and services may be translated into growing friendships, trust, interdependence—a web of relationships which incorporated the work of the American Missionary Association missionaries into the day-to-day fabric of life in the Glade. In a way, the people of southern Madison County had chosen Berea, by inviting Fee, by supporting him and his church (not always with great enthusiasm), by voting to maintain a district school with no racial discrimination, by sending their children to that school.

Three prominent citizens of the Glade District became charter members of Fee's Glade Church and later trustees of Berea College: William

Stapp, Thomas Jefferson Renfro, and John Burnam, Sr. In addition, two local men who did not serve Berea College in any formal capacity became known as sturdy supporters of Fee's ministry in church and school: John Hamilton Rawlings and Teman Thompson. These men and their families, particularly Rawlings and Burnam, represented the complexities of family, social class, and political affiliation in Madison County.[43]

John Burnam, Sr., "one of Kentucky's noblemen," according to John Rogers, was the oldest of Berea's local trustees. Burnam was born 1787 in North Carolina. His father, Henry Burnam, Sr., with his brother John, who through his son Thompson, Sr. became ancestral to most of the Burnams of Richmond, settled in Madison County in 1790. John Burnam, Sr. located northwest of Berea on Walnut Meadow Fork of Paint Lick Creek, having purchased over 200 acres there by 1836.[44]

One of the original members of Fee's Glade Church, Burnam led the local citizens in proposing to Fee that he found a school, and Burnam himself offered to pay for the building if William E. Lincoln would agree to teach in it for six months free of charge. In his *Memoirs* Lincoln frequently identified John Burnam, Sr. as a slaveholder, although the evidence shows clearly that he was not. He is not listed in the slave censuses of 1850 and 1860, and the Madison County tax list for 1854 says he owned no slaves. The confusion in Lincoln's memory probably resulted naturally from an identification of Burnam with others of the same surname in Madison County.[45]

The Burnam family in all its ramifications presents an excellent example of the diverse connections of the Glade community. Three Burnams served as trustees of Berea College. John Burnam, Sr. was followed by his cousin Curtis Field Burnam (trustee from 1896 to 1909), and Curtis's son Thompson Burnam (trustee from 1909 to 1923). The latter, a wealthy distiller, may have had some uneasy moments on the abstinent board of Berea College.[46]

Before and during the Civil War the Burnams represented such a diversity of interests that it is almost impossible to untangle the strands. While John Burnam, Sr. was a nonslaveholding abolitionist, his son Henry S. Burnam of Paint Lick owned slaves but listened to John G. Fee's doctrines with eagerness in 1854 (Fee described him as "a warm friend"). Another son, Harrison Burnam, owned slaves by dint of having married Sarah Kennedy Best, a member of one of the largest slaveholding families in Kentucky, the Kennedys of Paint Lick (legendary models for the slaveholding family depicted in the opening chapter of *Uncle Tom's Cabin*).[47]

Thompson Burnam (grandfather of the Thompson already mentioned), first cousin of John Burnam, Sr., was a large slaveholder who advocated emancipation. In fact, Burnam was Emancipationist candidate for a seat in the Constitutional Convention in 1849, with Cassius Clay working as his campaign manager. At Foxtown, Clay was in the midst of trying to introduce Curtis F. Burnam to speak (Squire Turner, the proslavery candidate would not yield the floor) when violence erupted—the occasion when Clay killed Cyrus Turner with a bowie knive.[48] One of Thompson's sons, Edmund Hall Burnam, became a slaveholding minister of the Regular Baptist church, while Curtis Field Burnam, like his father and brother, owned slaves until after the Civil War.[49]

The Burnams of Richmond, all descendants of Thompson Sr., were wealthy, prominent, influential people. By marriage they allied themselves with other powerful families: Field, Rollins, Caperton, Shackelford, Hume. All belonged to the upper echelons of Madison County society along with the Clays, who moved in the same circles and formed marital alliances with the same families.

A brother of Thompson Burnam, Sr., John Burnam of Bowling Green, Kentucky, served as representative in the Kentucky assembly and city judge, and became treasurer of Kentucky (appointed by the provisional government) in the Confederate States of America. At the time of the retreat of the rebels from Kentucky to Tennessee, he went with the army to Corinth, Mississippi, in that capacity.[50]

So Burnams were abolitionists, emancipationists, confirmed slaveholders, Union men, Confederate men, wealthy and powerful, or only moderately well-off. Martha ("Patsy") Burnam, a daughter of John Burnam, Sr., married Jesse Kirby, member of a distinctively Appalachian family, while one of Burnam's sons married a Kennedy. In Madison County dividing lines between slaveholding and nonslaveholding people, between rich and poor, between abolitionists and secessionists, were never as clear as some accounts make them seem. All these categories of economics or allegiance could occur in one family living mostly in the same county within a decade.

As the first term of the Berea school came to its successful conclusion the teachers planned their final show performance for the term (they had been conducting such exercises every Friday afternoon to increasing community attendance). Rogers' journal entries concerning the last ten days of the term show something of the school's progress and reveal how the work of the school was entwined with other interests and events:

> 31st [June] Worked on an arbor for holding our Exhibition.
>
> July 1st Bro Fee thought one thing & I another about the arbor.
>
> 2d Col Clay made an address on Education.
>
> 3d A long talk with C. M. Clay & Bro Fee. Regret I did not more fully push the claims of God to perfect obedience regardless of consequences. C.M.C. made a political speech at the Glade.
>
> 4th Preached at the arbor in the morning. Had not made a sufficient preparation.
>
> 5th A quiet & pleasant day. Greatly interested in Botany.
>
> 6th Spoke to the school about their souls as kindly as possible. Bro [John] Hansel here from Oberlin.

7th Wed. Commenced preparing a stage in the arbor.
8th Thurs. Prepared for the morrow.[51]

The exhibition of July, 9, 1858, Berea's first "graduation exercise," was encouraging and memorable—the most heartening occasion Fee had enjoyed since his arrival in Madison County. For the young teachers it was simply wonderful. The whole community, not just parents and scholars, prepared for the occasion. "A leafy bower, with towering oaks for pillars, was prepared to seat a larger number than had ever come into the vicinity. . . . Stirring music had been prepared and the community arranged for a free dinner spread on long tables in an adjoining grove." The weather was perfect.[52]

Rogers wrote of the occasion: ". . . the closing exercises were captivating. At one time the people made the grove ring with their cheers, at another they were bathed in tears." Elizabeth Rogers recalled it: "our first term of school finished," she stated, "with a great blaze of trumpets, so to speak." People had come from miles around, from adjoining counties, everyone was there, even former mobs were in attendance, attracted by excitement and free food. "The school became at once popular, the flags were flying and banners waving . . . and the Yankee teachers were apparently not so bad after all."[53]

The exercises began with singing and a prayer. The students gave their presentations in a varied program, with older boys orating, followed by little girls reciting, music, and so on—"orations and debates, essays and recitations."[54] The valedictory was delivered by Green Renfro, who was completely overcome by emotion and moved his audience to tears. The grand finale of the student program was the goodbye speech by Minerva Denham. "This young girl," Lizzie said, "starting out with great ease and gusto, suddenly as the goodbye words were to be uttered, broke down in tears and left the stage."[55]

After an interlude of social chat the people returned to the arbor for six short addresses. The first speaker, Dr. Chase (a relative of Salmon P. Chase, later secretary of the United States Treasury), a native of New Hampshire and then practicing medicine in Madison County, was interrupted by "Old Bill Wood," who insisted on being allowed to speak immediately on grounds that he could not tarry until the exercises were over. (William Woods, of Garrard County, was an ex-member of the state legislature.) Fee described Woods' impromptu utterance for the amusement of Cassius Clay:

> The old fellow stormed away about God's designs in our improving our talents and man making living by the sweat of *his* brow—then to morality and men doing as they would be done by—Liberty our country &c. He expressed his surprise at the large & respectful audience and interesting school instead of a little handful in the bush.

As he was leaving the platform Woods confirmed to James Blackburn, "Jimmy, the Niggers will be free yet but damn it I intend to hold on to mine as long as I can."[56] Chase spoke again, or rather resumed. Then

Fee addressed the assembled multitude. His topic was classes which should be educated. In his letter to Clay, Fee sketched his categories in very few words: "Females & mountain boys—poor. . . ."[57]

Fee wrote up the occasion, as an official report for the *American Missionary* magazine, on the day of the exhibition, using it as evidence that the time was now ripe for a new kind of school to begin: the Berea College of his plan, anticaste, antisectarian, open to the poor, encouraging manual labor. Known and committed abolitionists could teach in Kentucky; and Rogers and his wife had demonstrated "how prosperous and efficient" such a school could be. Fee saw the wonderfully successful exhibition as the opening of the final door in central Kentucky. Some five or six hundred people had attended the closing exercises.[58] "If there are any who think of [this exhibition day] as an ordinary closing day to an ordinary school," Lizzie Rogers protested, "I think they miss its touch of glory."[59] Fee summed it up: "The outlook on that day, was good for Berea."[60]

Chapter Eight

EXILES

New settlers for the colony of Berea did not begin to arrive in appreciable numbers until the fall of 1859, when some twelve people moved into Madison County within three months. Although colonists were not numerous, they were very promising, with practical and spiritual qualifications, including two new ministers to aid Fee and Rogers, and three carpenters, who immediately began to use the building materials amply supplied by John G. Hanson's new sawmill. Of the men who had settled at Berea by the fall of 1859 only three were family men, but one of them never had time to bring his family. The four remaining were single, although one of them married after he arrived. Most of them were from Oberlin.[1]

This tiny group of emigrants motivated the slaveocracy of Madison County to strike at last. For five years Fee had been roughly tolerated. With the noticeable arrival of Yankees all toleration ceased. Small as the colonizing movement was, it struck the elite slaveholders as exactly analogous to the settlement of Kansas by abolitionists and other Northerners determined to have the state enter the Union free. A civil war had already been fought in "Bleeding Kansas," which provided also the terrifying example of John Brown, the antislavery fanatic who, with a little band of followers, had massacred five proslavery colonists in Kansas in 1856. During October 16-18, 1859, John Brown, financially supported by a number of New England and New York abolitionists (including Fee's friend Gerrit Smith), led a raid against Harper's Ferry, Virginia, designed to foment a slave uprising and to establish a free state in the southern Appalachians. Brown's raid, even as it failed, spread terror throughout the South, which blamed the abolitionists and the

'Black Republicans' for the incident. To some abolitionists Brown was a hero and eventually a martyr. To some citizens of Madison County, he was frighteningly similar to their own local abolitionist "fanatic," John G. Fee. What was Fee preparing in the Glade? Why were the Northerners settling there? When would he strike and how?[2]

The terror of a slave uprising, which had haunted the South since Nat Turner's rebellion, was roused to a fever pitch. Berea, in all innocence, was suddenly more important to everyone in Kentucky than it had ever been before. For years the place had been too insignificant to notice. But now it became a region of nightmares, a hot-bed of wild-eyed murderers, aiming to wake all those blacks, thousands of them, to violence. In this apocalyptic vision the slaves who had not been allowed to escape became themselves the inescapable danger—they were everywhere.

If the slaveholders of Kentucky feared and hated people who wanted slaves to be freed through peaceful means, imagine their reaction to people they thought were encouraging slaves to revolt, as they came to believe the Bereans were doing. The proslavery Kentucky press made sure that its readership was fully misinformed about the Berea project. On some level, a few people must have known they were printing exaggerations, distortions, and outright lies; a very few probably knew there was nothing to fear. Most, however, simply believed what they read and feared accordingly. Eventually only the obliteration of Berea from the map of Kentucky could ease the fears which grew in the fall of 1859.

In October, 1859, John G. Fee began a fund-raising/recruiting tour for the new colony and the prospective college. After several weeks of encouraging success in New England, Fee came to the wealthy and influential church of Henry Ward Beecher, Plymouth Congregational Church in Brooklyn. Beecher himself was one of "the princes of the pulpit," son of Lyman Beecher, brother of Harriet Beecher Stowe, an enormously successful minister who preached on most of the current issues of the day, including slavery, and edited two widely read journals. His name a household word, he was a religious "star" of the first magnitude, the Billy Graham of his day. For a relatively obscure country preacher from Kentucky the opportunity to address Beecher's congregation was the chance of a lifetime.[3]

Fee's address was delivered in the evening service on Sunday, November 13. Beecher introduced Fee as a man who had suffered persecution for his belief "that slave-holding disqualified a man for church-membership." Fee spoke for an hour and a half to a large, attentive audience, detailing for them his entire missionary career in Kentucky and appealing for money and workers. He ended by saying the Bereans "wanted men like John Brown—of his boldness and honesty—of his self-sacrificing spirit—not to carry the sword, but the Gospel of Love."[4] After Fee's sermon Beecher displayed a draft for $15 that he had received from Switzerland, "with a request that he would give it where it would do the most good in the cause of Emancipation." Beecher made a contribution of his own, and the congregation responded, too, giving $217.50 that evening.

The meeting was a definite success. No one was shocked that Fee had mentioned John Brown. That name was appearing in every newspaper in the United States at the time; Brown had been tried, but not yet convicted. Fee would have been asked his opinion of Brown, even if he had not volunteered it. No abolitionist could speak at this period of America's history and say *nothing* about John Brown.[5] The *New York Tribune* printed what were purported to be Fee's exact words:

> We need more John Browns—not in the *manner of his action, but in* his spirit of consecration—men who would go not to entice away a few slaves, for that would not remove the difficulty—men who would go out, not with carnal weapons, but with the 'Sword of the Spirit,' the Bible: and who in love, would appeal to slaveholders and non-slaveholders, if needs be, to give up property and life.

Fee's notes for this sermon, scribbled in pencil, provide evidence that the *Tribune*'s version of his words was perfectly accurate.[6]

In Lexington, Kentucky, the story about Fee's sermon in Beecher's church appeared with the headline "JOHN BROWNS FOR KENTUCKY." The *Kentucky Statesman*, November 18, 1859, story stated:

> The Louisville Courier of yesterday says, "Rev. John G. Fee, a fanatical abolitionist, who is a native of this State, and a resident of some one of the mountain counties, is now in the east collecting founds [sic] for his nefarious work. Last Sunday night he preached in Henry Ward Beecher's church in Brooklyn and said that more John Brown's were wanted, especially for Kentucky. He also gave a detailed account of his operations here, which partakes somewhat of the Munchausen style of story-telling [fairy tales]."

The article from that point followed a portion of Fee's sermon almost exactly, sometimes word for word, including such details as the donation from Switzerland. The story concluded in this way: "Well, let brother Beecher and brother Fee come along to Kentucky with their John Browns. The mountaineers know how to welcome such traitors with bloody hands to hospitable graves."[7] One fact emerges clearly from the *Louisville Courier's* account: whoever wrote the story had an accurate and substantial version in front of him, from which he deleted all details which might clarify Fee's real position.

Ironically, a speech of Cassius Clay's also touching on John Brown (no politician could speak at this time without mentioning Brown either), was unfavorably reported in the same issue of the *Kentucky Statesman*:

> C. M. CLAY AT COVINGTON—Col. C. M. Clay addressed the people of Covington on Wednesday last. Sub-

ject (of course) *antislavery* . . . . He is reported to have frequently referred to the Harper's ferry affair, and although he admitted that Brown and his confederates had committed a fearful crime, he warned "some of his Fellow Kentuckians, that if they did not mend their manners they would make a few more Ossawattomies." . . . . His speech was only applauded by the colored "element" of the opposition.[8]

On November 20, at a prayer meeting at Berea, John Rogers spoke of "the privilege of self-denial and not shrinking from death." The next day he read the newspaper. "Did not feel very happy in so doing," he wrote. On the twenty-second he went to Richmond and found there "much excitement against Bro. Fee." He recorded a prayer in his journal, "Lord, dwell in me so richly as to deliver from fear of sinning & dying."

A Richmond newspaper, the *Kentucky Messenger*, carried the following story at about this time:

JOHN G. FEE

This man has been at Brooklyn, New York, and addressing the people in the church of Beecher, on the subject of slavery in the South generally, and in Kentucky particularly . . . . The only thing that induces us to notice him is the fact that he lives in the county and is surrounded by a gang of his followers, at a little village called Berea, some sixteen miles south of this town. That he is a fanatic we have no doubt; that he is a bad man, we doubt still less . . . . As to his opinions, and those of his followers, they amount to nothing, but if ever he is found interfering with the slaves of his neighbors, teaching them disobedience, or in any overt act stimulating them to revolt, we hope he will on a proper case made out, be brought to trial, and we do not doubt that a Madison jury will send him to the penitentiary.

The Louisville *Courier* containing an epitome of his remarks at Brooklyn, has been very mysteriously taken from our office, and we therefore cannot publish them; but they are *inflammatory* and *incendiary* in character, and the people of the county owe it to themselves to hold a meeting, at least by next County court day, to consider whether or not the carrying out of the principles of Fee, requires THAT THEY SHALL BE MURDERED IN COLD BLOOD![9]

The threats against Fee, still absent in the East, and against the whole Berea settlement, were becoming more and more frequent and frightening. A few members of the Berea community reacted with a martial spirit. A. G. W. Parker, for example, "was loud in his denunciations against slaveholders & declared they should never interfere with him." He was, it seems, "one of the ball & rifle men," accustomed to arming in defense of Cassius Clay.[10]

On November 29, 1859, Matilda Fee wrote to Simeon Jocelyn, a leader of the American Missionary Association; her letter conveys the state of affairs at Berea very directly and poignantly. "The religious part of our community who stand as our friends," she wrote,

> are now coming to me daily and almost hourly to tell me to warn my husband not to attempt to return to Ky now so much excitement prevails at Lexington & Richmond. I was urged two weeks since to go to meet him at Cin. [Cincinnati] & warn him of his danger. Since that time the excitement is much greater, owing to many false statements in the southern newspapers. What the result of this great commotion will be & how it may affect the efforts put forth here time only will reveal. For months past the cause here has been prospering beyond our most sanguine expectations & we are by no means cast down in spirit. All appear calm & full of hope & trust in god. If you know of my Dear husband's whereabouts please forward this to him. If the Lord has work for him in the north he will retain him if not his arm will be sufficient to protect him. If Mr Fee thinks it best I will meet him in Richmond, Lexington or Cin. My anxiety is sometimes so great that one would think my faith small. I often think the purest & best will be the most fit sacrifice to offer on the altar of liberty. May the Lord direct us all.[11]

Matilda Fee did go to Cincinnati to warn her husband, leaving her children behind in Berea.

The *Kentucky Statesman*, a Lexington paper, of November 29, 1859, quoted a long story from the *Richmond Democrat* of the week before. Under the headline "Excitement in Madison County" the article commented first upon the fact that "the two leading men of the Black Republican party" in Madison, Clay and Fee, had both made public addresses within the last two weeks alluding "in almost similar terms to the inhumane outrage at Harper's Ferry." The connection Clay wanted to erase was still present in the minds of central Kentuckians.

The *Richmond Democrat* continued:

> The Glade precinct of this county is the head-quarters of Black Republicanism in this section. The village of Berea, the home of this man Fee, is in the precinct . . . . For several weeks past there has been an almost constant stream of Northern immigrants passing through this place for that point. Besides this, numerous heavy boxes have been forwarded to Berea through this place, and each party going there have been heavily loaded with baggage, even the ladies' trunks being so heavy to require the united strength of several men to transfer them from place to place. In addition, the leading men of this faction openly boast that they intend to

revolutionize the sentiment of this portion of the State, and to
hereafter hold the controlling influence in political affairs.

Much excitement has been created in this county by these
facts, and it seems constantly on the increase.

While the Bereans were a very insignificant portion of Madison County's
population, their intention seemed to be to augment their numbers and
importance and thus draw the support of Black Republicans of the
North.

Their position, in the heart of as strong a pro-slavery community as can be found in the South, is being urged by this man
Fee as an inducement to collect money from his political
brethren of the North, with the implied and expressed purpose of making converts among his neighbors; when he well
knows, and any honest Northern man who will spend a few
weeks with us will be convinced that so far from this little
faction gaining recruits from their neighbors, their numbers
are insignificant, and their principles looked upon with loath-
ing and utter contempt by almost every citizen of our glorious
old county. Madison will never be revolutionized by such
patriots as these, and the sooner they are convinced of this
fact, the better it will be for their well-being and happiness.[12]

On December 5, 1859, the citizens of Madison County held a preliminary meeting at the courthouse in Richmond. John D. Harris called the
meeting to order. Colonel Reuben J. Munday was elected chairman; John
C. Terrill, appointed secretary. A committee was named to report to the
next meeting on "the proper course to be pursued"; it consisted of
twenty-eight men from the most prominent, wealthy, influential families
in Madison County.[13] The committee resolved:

WHEREAS. The present attitude of the Abolition party,
and their open and avowed assaults upon the constitutional
rights of the South; and the strong reasons which we have to
believe that they have sent their agents and emissaries into
our midst, whose sole and only purpose and design is to
propagate their political heresies, and thereby to disturb our
vested constitutional rights and our public peace and quiet,
therefore.

Five resolutions followed. The first one enunciated the committee's
opposition to and repudiation of abolitionism and announced the pledge
"to put a stop to it by all fair and proper means and measures." The
second resolution stated that the committee would circulate a copy of
the resolutions for their fellow citizens to sign. The other resolutions
dealt with revising the resolutions themselves, called for Richmond's
two newspapers to announce another public meeting on the seven-
teenth of December, and directed the same papers to publish the proceedings of the meeting. The committee also "Resolved, in the opinion

of this meeting, the association of J. G. Fee and others is a combination of an incendiary character, not only at war with the best interest of this community, but destructive of all organized society.[14]

The movement against abolitionists in Kentucky was statewide. On October 28 and 29 a mob had destroyed the office of an abolitionist newspaper, the *True South* published by William Shreve Bailey at Newport, Kentucky. Candee had been threatened in Jackson County. In Bracken County, where James S. Davis was minister, it was rumored that abolitionists were going to set fire to Germantown, and a military company had been organized to patrol at night. On December 10 Davis arrived in Berea with his wife, John Rogers' sister Amelia, and his mother-in-law, who had been visiting them. "The coming of our brother Mr. Davis and family," Lizzie wrote, "escaping from danger [in Lewis County] did not particularly add to our feeling of safety." The night before the Davises arrived, John Rogers had received a message that thirty-six men were coming to tell the Bereans to leave or take the consequences.[15]

The slaveholders around Berea said little. "While they with their Richmond neighbors disliked Berea's sentiments," Elizabeth Rogers said, "they loved *us*." But they were too cowed to speak up—although one old man did plead for the Bereans, he was silenced at a public meeting and told that only his age prevented him from sharing the fate of the Feeites. Hamilton Rawlings remained loyal—"our traveling newspaper," Lizzie called him, "bringing us news that we could not get outside. His advent in our home was a signal of hope or despair, and in those days he brought no cheerful news."[16]

Still the Bereans intended to stay. On December 12, with fifteen scholars in attendance, Rogers opened the Berea School, Davis and Reverend John F. Boughton, a new colonist, assisting him. This session of the school lasted only a few days; nevertheless, its opening reveals the determination of the Bereans to remain and continue in the face of mounting opposition.[17]

On December 14, John G. Fee, then in Pittsburgh, completed a pamphlet entitled "To the citizens of Madison Co., Ky." in an attempt to explain his position. It was already too late, but communication was so slow that on December 27 Fee composed another installment, "Circular No. 2," also addressed to the citizens of Madison County, who by that time had already taken decisive, indeed irreversible action. Prophetically Fee wrote:

> Freedom will come to the slave. God and humanity are against slavery. The world is moving for its overthrow. If moral means can be used, it will pass away peaceably, as in the West Indies . . . . If not then God will let loose his judgments. [I] feel at this time that I would be willing to bleed at every pore if by so doing I could induce Southern men to come to a fair investigation of the truth . . . .[18]

On December 16, as Richmond seethed with preparations for the public meeting to be held the next day, Rogers rode to the county seat to attempt to drum up some support there. "In many things greatly failed," he wrote in his journal, "Assume an apologetic attitude too much. Was too anxious to be thought well of . . . Coming home looked death in the face & was at peace."

On December 17, while the Bereans kept a day of fasting and prayer, the people of Madison County held their public meeting as scheduled. The Bereans prayed God to "so move those in authority that we might lead quiet lives." In Richmond the courthouse was filled.

> although it was a cold, wet, disagreeable day . . . the oldest, most respectable, and law-abiding citizens were in attendance. The tone of the meeting was firm and dignified, the whole county being united . . . . The meeting . . . proved that the *whole* people are in favor of first principles—self-preservation.[19]

Chairman Reuben J. Munday called the public meeting to order. The resolutions of the previous meeting had received 773 signatures, none of which were obtained from the slaveholders in the immediate vicinity of Berea, and during the meeting a great many other Madison County citizens signed. R. R. Stone reported to the meeting the following address, and resolutions which were adopted:

> We, the citizens of Madison County, believing that there exists in communities, as in individuals a right of self-preservation, of which no law can deprive them, and justly amenable to God and enlightened public opinion for all our acts—having in our own bosoms a living reason for what we do—make this our justification.
>
> That notwithstanding every plan of emancipation which ingenuity could devise, was fully discussed during the canvass which preceded the formation of our present Constitution, and all rejected by almost universal consent, as working injury to both the black race and the white, and the future policy of the State settled for long time to come, if not forever, there has been a continual agitation for the question of slavery, and particularly by very small numbers of (factious) men, abolitionists, and others getting together, and calling themselves a meeting or convention of the Republican party, when it is perfectly notorious that no such political party has any existence here, or even in the State, so far as we know, and that such agitation does and must excite in our slaves a spirit of rebellious insubordination, causing large numbers to be sold into a severer bondage than any amongst us, to the disruption of family ties, laceration of feelings, of both white and black, without any accompanying good; that such agitation, when followed by such effects is a crime,

which is not, but should be suppressed by Law. More especially when following upon, and in consequence of this there has come amongst us a set of men, not citizens of this country, and with the exception of one, not of the State, agents and emissaries of Northern Abolition societies, from which they receive remittances, among which they take up collections, and from which they derive their support—That these societies are our enemies, if indeed they are not the enemies of all mankind, teaching a new religion, to be propagated by the pike, with a baptism of fire and blood, worshipping a new God—not the God of our revolutionary fathers, from whom we derive all our blessings and whose wise and beneficient will is the peace and happiness of the whole family of man. Having a higher Law than any known to the Constitution under which we live, justifying plunder, treason, and survile insurrection.[20]

The forces of repression in Kentucky society at this time must not be underestimated. During the early months of 1860 Kentucky passed laws repealing the prohibition against importing slaves into Kentucky; subjecting all gipsies to arrest and fine or imprisonment, and making the writing, printing, or circulating of incendiary documents punishable by confinement in the penitentiary. In addition, a bill was passed (in March, 1860) with the following provisions: "No slave hereafter to be emancipated except on condition of immediately leaving the state. Free Negroes non-resident not allowed to come into the state, upon penalty of confinement in the penitentiary."[21] Commenting on these enactments, while they were still in debate, Curtis F. Burnam said (in the hall of the house of representatives in Frankfort),

> We are now in the midst of a discussion on one of those *damnable* atrocious bills to sell into slavery and make felons of the free Negroes of *this commonwealth*. I have just made an earnest and impassioned speech against, but it will all be of no avail. [We are] doomed to a long night of political darkness— *Demagogues rule the house. Mad men are listened to as sages.*[22]

During the December 17 meeting charges brought against the Bereans included their open avowal of abolitionist doctrines and their intention to propagate them; their leader's public proclamation of his "sympathy for and approbation of" John Brown and his asking for funds to revolutionize Kentucky; their establishment of a school "free for all colors" and a church "excluding all who uphold slavery"; their having "erected machinery (and) built a town, the location of which, in a strategic point of view, either for stampede or servile insurrection is faultless." Furthermore, the Bereans were charged with having an "Abolition Post Master" and a regular mail "Loaded . . . with incendiary documents." The Bereans even "boast[ed] of their intention to establish an Abolition College." Berea was steadily increasing "by accessions of

Northern men, all avowing the same doctrine; thus evincing a systematic and well-laid plan, not only to destroy (the slaveholders of Madison County), but in accordance with the declaration of their leader, to revolutionize the whole state."[23]

The meeting affirmed that the people of Madison had always been peaceable and law-abiding. "Loyal to the Commonwealth, loyal to the Constitution, and the Union," but now they stood "wholly unprotected by law." "We would be untrue to ourselves," R. R. Stone said, conveying the committee's address, "and utterly unworthy of the immunities and heritage bequeathed us if the town of Berea were permitted to remain, 'a standing menace' to the peace and security of our firesides."

For their security, then, the meeting adopted five resolutions which the preliminary committee had drafted. The first recommended that "a committee of 38 discreet sensible men such as the whole community may confide in be appointed to remove from amongst us J. G. Fee. J. A. R. Rogers and so many of their associates as in their best judgement the peace and safety of society may require and to this end all good men in this community will lend them support and assistance to the *utmost.*" The second resolution directed that in discharging their duty the appointed committee should be instructed "to act deliberately, humanely . . . but most firmly and *most effectually*"; meanwhile the present legislature should be petitioned to enact laws effecting the complete security of the citizens of Madison County. The third resolution defined "the true policy of Kentucky" as an effort "to bind together the domestic tie between slaves and their owners . . . . To this end they should not only worship the same God but at the same altars . . . . Separate negro preachings and ignorant negro preachers should be suppressed by law." The fourth resolution stated that laws "for the expulsions of free negros should be gradual, prospective and humane." The fifth resolution called upon senators and representatives for their "best energies" in support of the Madison County resolutions of December 17.

The committee was appointed, a roll call of prominent citizens once again: Thomas S. Bronston, Jr., Thomas Willis, Reuben J. Munday, Alfred Stone, Durritt White, A. J. Dudley, J. P. Estill, Benjamin Moberly, Squire Million, John D. Harris, Coleman Covington, Thomas J. Maupin, Samuel Shearer, Solon Harris, Capt. C. A. Hawkins, Henry Dillingham, Alexander Tribble, G. B. Broaddus, William Mitchel, John W. Browning, E. W. Turner, Stephan D. Walker, Thomas W. Miller, John W. Francis, Charles Oldham, Humphrey Kavanaugh, James W. Caperton, Martin Gentry, John C. Terrill, R. J. White, Peter T. Gentry, Thomas S. Ellis, John Hagan, Willis Shumate, George Dejarnette, A. J. Tribble, Green B. Million, Thomas J. Gordon, J. R. Gilbert, William K. Hocker, R. R. Stone.

John G. Fee's first circular addressed to the citizens of Madison County was read, as was a letter Rogers had written to the editors of the *Messenger* and *Mountain Democrat* (both Richmond papers). The appointed committee was instructed within ten days to "wait upon" Fee, Rogers, and all others "that the said committee may think inimical and dangerous to our institutions, our interests, and our public safety and tranquility.'' The Bereans were to be informed that they had to leave the county and the state, being outside the limits of the county within ten days of receiving ''said notice.'' If they should be found within the county after the ten-day limit, the committee was directed by the meeting ''to take such steps as they deem right and proper in removing the said Fee, Rogers &c. from the county.'' With these instructions set, Major Squire Turner, Colonel William H. Caperton, Thomas Bronston, and other prominent citizens addressed the meeting until its conclusion.[24]

Meanwhile, in Berea praying continued. On December 18, a Sabbath, James Davis preached ''upon not fearing him that can only kill the body & fearing Him who can destroy both soul & body in hell.'' Rogers also spoke that day. ''The Lord enabled me,'' he wrote, ''to fearlessly & faithfully exhort the brethren.'' That afternoon the community held a prayer meeting at Fee's house and that night another one. ''The Holy Spirit sweetly and solemnly present at the prayer meeting,'' Rogers stated, ''Myself & others expressed a solemn purpose to labor personally for the salvation of some soul on the morrow.''

In a final attack, the slaveholders of Madison County set the following story loose in the Kentucky press: ''Sharpe's Rifles—We hear that a box, directed to Jno. G. Fee, was landed at Cogar's landing on the Kentucky river, a few days since; and suspicions being aroused by its great weight, it was opened and found to contain Sharpe's Rifles.'' The story was, of course, utter nonsense—the Sharpe's rifles were in reality Rev. John F. Boughton's crate of candlemolds.[25]

On December 22, John A. R. Rogers spent the night in prayer. Lizzie Rogers wrote:

> They were terrible days. I remember one night hearing the merry voices of young people shouting as they coasted down a hill nearby, taking advantage of the little snow squall which so seldom came to Kentucky, and I wondered how any one could be merry; and I wondered too . . . if life and property were safe, was there anything else that could cause great anxiety?[26]

Christmas was coming; ''nearer and nearer grew the threats,''Lizzie wrote, ''I thought I had known danger before; I had lain awake nights trembling at every noise, and I had stood terror stricken before the drunken crowd who used to swagger up and down our streets, but there was a more savage element than ever before in the threats toward us.'' She added, ''We almost forgot it was Christmas [time]. How could we hear the 'Peace on Earth, goodwill to men' when the nearer voices were so loud in their hatred.[27]

December 23, 1859, a Friday, was bright and cold. ''A light snow had fallen and the men came up so quietly that their approach was not noticed.'' Some sixty men on horseback drew up ''in a wedge shaped array, the point of the wedge at the front of the (Roger's) house." The family, including the Davises and Rogers' mother, had just sat down to eat their noon meal. Someone said, "They have come."[28]

In his journal for December 23, 1859, John Rogers wrote one sentence: "Sixty three men from various parts of Madison Co. called on me & 10 others & warned us to leave the state in 10 days on pain of expulsion." John and Lizzie and their little son Raphael, then three years old, stood in the doorway of their house to receive the committee. In his report to the American Missionary Association, Rogers emphasized that the committee members had behaved well, using "no harsh or personally disrespectful language." Many years later Rogers wrote of the event much as if it had been a social call, testifying to the courtesy of the visitors and their gentlemanly manners.[29] Elizabeth Rogers' accounts give a very different picture. "Sixty armed men full of whiskey look like so many fiends," she wrote; ". . . it seemed as if all the powers of Hell were let loose. Slowly I scanned those faces, and found among 'Kentucky's best sons' not one I could trust or look up to for protection."[30]

The leader of the group, Reuben Munday, gave Rogers a letter which ordered him to promise to leave the state within ten days.

"Gentlemen, let me speak a word," Rogers said. "If I have failed to keep your laws, I am willing to be tried by law; for what am I called in question?"

"We consider you a gentleman, but you are from the north and you must go," Munday answered.

Lizzie said, "Judging from appearances, gentlemen in Kentucky are scarce; you had better let him stay."

Munday again demanded that Rogers promise to leave. "I have but one Master to serve,"Rogers replied. "I cannot promise."

Some angry men rushed foward, but Munday wheeled in front of them and said, "Not now, boys, come back in ten days and do your worst." According to Lizzie's account the committee fell into a drunken fight among themselves on the way back to Richmond—several being killed or wounded, although their numbers were quickly replenished.

The committee paid a call that day on ten other people—some of them representing families, some single men. Included were Matilda Fee, John G. Hanson, John Smith, Rev. John F. Boughton, Charles E. Griffin, A. G. W. Parker, Swinglehurst Life, E. T. Hays, J. D. Reed and W. H. Torry. (James S. Davis, who was included in this exile, was staying with Rogers and so was not counted.) The committee's official visits were over in about two hours.

The Bereans agreed to meet that evening to pray and consult about what to do. At the meeting John Hanson read Psalm 37: "Fret not thyself because of evildoers . . .," a rather ferocious psalm of comfort for the oppressed, promising retribution for the wicked. Rogers, at first, was in favor of staying in Madison County to put the burden of removing the Bereans upon those who wished to get rid of them. Others were convinced that to stay would mean certain death. Rumor had it that Rogers was destined to be hanged to the tree nearest to his house, and the town was to be burned.[31]

On December 24, the people who had been warned to leave met and arrived at a consensus to comply with the committee's order, but the group decided they should first appeal to the governor of Kentucky for protection. Rogers composed a petition which eleven men signed. J. D. Reed and Swinglehurst Life, two of Berea's recent colonists, rode to Frankfort and personally presented the document to Gov. Beriah Magoffin, who said it was impossible to do anything for their protection, although he received the bearers of the petition "courteously." He advised them for the sake of preserving the peace of the state to leave it, saying that "the public mind was deeply moved by the events in Virginia, and that until the excitement subsided, their presence in the State "would be dangerous." He did promise that they would be safe while they were departing and that their property would be protected.[32]

Fee wrote to Jocelyn on December 24 concerning his intention of starting for Berea on Christmas Day. He thought there would still be time—that he might go "and improve . . . (the) time and then come away peacefully—not stubbornly . . . I suppose," he wrote, "it is best to come away." Fee's friends in Cincinnati prevented him from going into Kentucky even for a short time. Hamilton Rawlings had written Fee that he would certainly be killed if he returned to Berea.[33]

On Christmas Day, 1859, the Bereans heard farewell addresses from those warned to leave Kentucky. The next day Rogers began to settle his debts. On the twenty-seventh George Candee arrived from McKee and advised the Bereans to go. The people who were to remain behind were full of grief at the prospect of losing their leaders and the school on which they had set their hopes. William B. Wright gave a farewell dinner for the exiles on December 28, with 150 people attending. "It was more like a funeral than a feast." Lizzie Rogers wrote, "yet it was a beautiful thing to do." Rogers was less receptive: "Did not enjoy the occasion," he stated, characteristically taciturn.[34]

Rogers, in his official report to the AMA, suggested that if the exiles had chosen to stay civil war might have resulted, but if the governor had provided protection the group would certainly have remained. The little band proposed to spend a few days in Cincinnati "counseling for the future." Rogers urged the association not to give up on Kentucky. "My sympathies," Rogers stated, "are strongly toward every class—the slaveholder with his fine bearing and more generous impulses—the slave in his degradation and the nonslaveholder great . . . with his underdeveloped powers." A slaveholder, with his "more generous impulses," was represented in an article in the *Daily Commonwealth* of Frankfort (December 28, 1859), which stated: "Rev. John G. Fee and other noisy and incendiary abolitionists in this county should be driven from it."[35]

Thirty-six people in all prepared to leave Berea. With the Rogers family some twenty people planned to travel together to Cincinnati. The others, perhaps a dozen, dispersed to various places.[36] On December 29 the exodus began. All the people met in front of Roger's house. "A drizzling rain was falling, the snow had melted and everything," Lizzie said, "was as dreary without as our hearts were within. [John Smith] sat in an open wagon with his arm around his aged wife, Olive. Mrs. Fee drove her own carriage full of children; the newlyweds, Charles and Anna Griffin, sat in another carriage; a few of the men were on horseback. There was "a great white covered wagon which carried . . . trunks"; a lady or two sat in that vehicle waiting for Lizzie and her

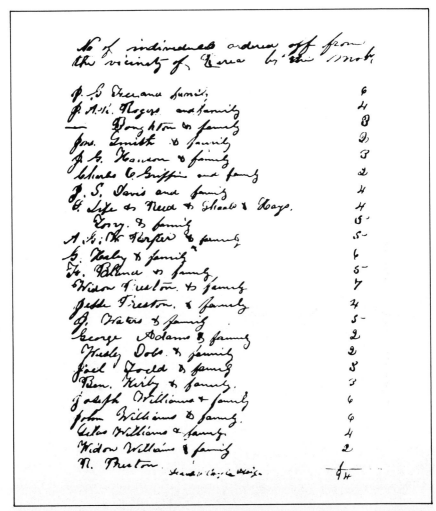

Cassius M. Clay's list of exiles showing Yankees and natives of Madison County who were driven from Kentucky by Richmond's slaveholders. Berea College Archives.

babies. Neighbors and friends, many weeping openly, were gathered about to say goodbye. George Candee led the assembly in prayer, committing the travelers to the guidance of God.[37]

At Silver Creek the procession found that an ordinarily small babbling brook had been transformed into a roaring torrent by heavy rains and melting snow. The covered wagon in which Lizzie rode was chosen to cross the stream first since it was the heaviest vehicle. The driver, although fortified with Kentucky bourbon, noticed that the women in his vehicle were visibly frightened. "With a roguish wink," he said, 'Now, Ladies, you do the praying and I'll do the driving.' " All the wagons crossed safely.[38]

The little group spent the first night in Richmond, although they felt some anxiety about how they would be received in the county seat of Madison. One of the hotels opened to them, and the Kentuckians kept their word—since the ten-day limit was not up, the Bereans went unmolested. A local merchant, Colonel William Holloway (source has misprint "Hathaway"), granted Rogers a few weeks' grace on paying his bill and even offered to lend him money. Not all the citizens of Richmond had participated in the committee work, or condoned it.[39] On the day of the exodus Fee was writing: "The possibility of being shut out from a work so dear to my heart almost crushes me. We may not be able to go on with our school, but we will try to pay for our Land—that will not run off."[40]

The Holloway House where some Berea exiles spent their night in Richmond. Dorris Collection, EKU Townsend Room.

The next day the Bereans reached Lexington, where they dined in one of the best hotels without any trouble, although everyone knew who the travelers were. "I doubt if Barnum's circus could have produced among the older folk, greater curiosity," Lizzie wrote. In Lexington the exiles boarded the train to Cincinnati. "I was glad of every mile behind me," Lizzie recalled, "rejoicing that every hour was carrying us toward the North Land, the old feeling of safety came back and when at last we reached the Ohio side, I could have knelt and kissed the dust of her streets."[41]

The next morning the Berea exiles woke to find themselves famous. Front page headlines in major newspapers blazoned the news of Kentucky's injustice to the citizens of Berea. For the next few days, in a clamor of publicity, the Bereans were much in demand to speak at churches and lecture halls in Cincinnati. Prominent Ohioans denounced the exile from Berea as "an unparalleled outrage."[42]

Fee met the exiles who had traveled to Cincinnati. There the little group divided again—some remaining in Cincinnati, some moving on. Of the exiles only members of three families ever returned to Berea: the Fees, the Hansons, and the Rogers. The rest of the colonists—ministers, carpenters, two trustees—went their separate ways.

The distinction drawn between mobs and committees accosting the abolitionists seemed to be one of class. Local roughnecks coming together for this purpose were a mob; Kentucky gentlemen joined for the same purpose—and much more effective in realizing it—were a committee. Actually, most of the bands of Kentuckians who had molested Fee or his helpers had been committees, at least in the sense that they had planned their action together beforehand. Frequently these groups signed petitions or other documents to constitute themselves as committees. In this way a committee had been formed in Rockcastle County in 1853 to denounce Fee and Clay. This group had tried to drive A. G. W. Parker out of the county within ten days and to prevent Peter H. West from distributing tracts, and so on.

The mob which whipped Fee's colporteur Robert Jones in 1858 had a military organization, under the leadership of Coleman Covington and with officers in charge—the usual committee arrangement, as many of the men had been soldiers, frequently having served together in the Mexican War or the militia. Officers in the regular army became officers in committees, since an important aspect of "committee work" was the deployment of troops. Fee described the retreat of the whipping mob as "ludicrously orderly. The Captain ordered all to march away in double file. The column was quite long and imposing." Some committee members had been "Patrollers" in the 1850s, small bands of militia directed to patrol specific districts of the county for runaway slaves and other dangers. (Jeptha Rice Gilbert was captain of such a group in 1850, with Humphrey Kavanaugh one of his assistants.) Committees resembled vigilante bands, and a few years later some committee members may have moved quite naturally into the ranks of the Ku Klux Klan.[43]

The Madison County committee of 1859 had both kinds of structure. The planning committee members were bound together by signing a petition; the committee for executing plans—mostly the same people as the earlier committee—signed a document and also maintained a quasi-military organization under the leadership of Colonel Reuben Munday. The members of the vigilance committee that tried to destroy Berea were men of property, social standing, wealth, prominence, education—respectable men, well-known and, in some cases, popular in the community. As Fee remarked, "So much the greater peril to society when men of property and standing will consent to disregard law and order."[44]

In 1860 slightly over 100 individuals in Madison County owned as many as fifteen slaves or more; 24 of those slaveholders were themselves committee members. At least 26 more were people closely related to committee members, so that the committee of 1859 represented the prominent Madison county slaveholders very directly. Probably more than half of the total number of slaves in Madison County was owned by the committee men and their relatives. The same people—a relatively small group out of the total white population of Madison County—also possessed most of the political power in the region, although nonslaveholders outnumbered slaveholders in the county.[45]

A small sampling of the committee members reveals a great deal about their positions in Madison County: Samuel Bennett, a prosperous farmer (his son married Cassius Clay's daughter); Green B. Broaddus, high sheriff of the county, 1st lieutenant in Humphrey Marshall's regiment in the Mexican War; Colonel James W. Caperton, attorney, president of Richmond National Bank, one of the county's wealthiest citizens; Coleman Covington, representative of the county in the Kentucky legislature in 1855-57; Curtis Field, Jr., lawyer, member of the Kentucky house, 1857-59; Major William Harris, common school commissioner for the county for twenty years, member of Kentucky house, 1851-53, wealthy farmer; Humphrey Kavanaugh, soldier in the Mexican War; Thomas Woods Miller, colonel in the Kentucky militia; William Malcolm Miller, member of Kentucky house, 1855-57; Green B. Million, wealthy citizen and justice of the peace; Colonel Reuben Munday, member of Kentucky senate, 1851-55; Charles Oldham, sheriff of the county; Robert R. Stone, lawyer and banker; John C. Terrill, attorney at the Richmond bar, later officer in the confederate army; William T. Terrill, member Kentucky house, 1850; Edward W. Turner, member of the Kentucky senate; Squire Turner, member of the Kentucky house 1824-26, 1830, 1831, 1839, lawyer and farmer ("amassed the largest fortune from his practice of all lawyers ever at the Richmond bar"); William Jason Walker, wealthy merchant, banker, and farmer.[46]

Most committee members were descended from one of a few founding families of Madison County—Harris, Miller, Woods, Kavanaugh, Gentry, Maupin, families which in some cases had been interrelated and allied to one another for almost a hundred years by 1859; they had originally been settlers of Albemarle County, Virginia, and virtually all of them had come to Madison County between 1786 and 1795.[47]

For example, at least ten committee members are known to have been direct descendants of one founding family—the Harris clan. In addition to the men bearing the name (William, Solon, and John D.), Harris descendants on the committee included James W. Caperton, Robert R. Stone (who delivered the address on December 17), Samuel Bennett, Durret and Richard J. White, Clifton Rodes Estill, and Ambrose J. Dudley. And William Jason Walker married a Harris descendant.[48] Many other committee members were related to one another and were descendants of the Madison County founders from Albemarle County. Virtually all of them were connected in some way to the Virginians who had fought in the Revolution.[49] In the near future many of the members of the committee would be fighting in another war. Ironically, they would be fighting each other; some of them became soldiers for the Confederacy, others fought for the Union. As much as they had in common, the prominent citizens who banded together to oust the Bereans did not constitute a monolithic group. Their common enmity toward abolitionists held them together only briefly.

Throughout the ordeal of the exiles Cassius M. Clay attempted through various public disclaimers to divorce himself from the proceedings. Clay redoubled his efforts to "stand aloof." He could not keep silent on the matter: that form of aloofness was never part of his approach. The week before the first exile an article had appeared in the *Mountain Democrat* of Richmond representing Clay as opposed to the Bereans, and "as saying they *ought* to be driven off." On December 26, 1859, George Candee wrote to Clay to warn him that the report of his remarks about the Bereans would do him (Clay) great harm with the Jackson County constituency, for all the citizens of Jackson were in sympathy with the Madison County exiles.[50] Immediately after the exile was effected, Clay made a speech in defense of the Bereans on the capitol steps in Frankfort; he said that driving Fee out was "lawless and unjustifiable." He also claimed that he had written to the Madison County papers before the exile stating that Fee had no Sharpe's rifles, that Fee had never approved of John Brown's actions, and so on. Unfortunately, his defense of Fee had been delayed—it "had not been allowed to reach (its) destination in time to disabuse the public mind." Indeed, finding that his article had not been published before the exile actually took place, Clay went to the *Messenger* office and "took it away, as the occasion for its publication had passed." In his own defense Clay had written that his "whole connection with the Radicals at Berea" had consisted of being "all the time against their doctrines; all the time for the peace and safety of the community."[51]

His self-defense continued in an explanation of his abandonment of Fee, based, of course, on the Fourth of July disagreement at Slate Lick Springs. "Well," Clay added, "I am no Don Quixote to go forward and fight the battle of every man who may venture an opinion on the subject of slavery. . . . ." In spite of his unwillingness to "stand" with Fee, Clay said of Fee ". . . he is as pure a man as ever I knew. . . ." Clay's actual defense of Fee was eloquent and forceful. The real loss with the exile of Fee and his friends, Clay stated, would be not to Fee but to the Commonwealth of Kentucky, especially to those ill-educated citizens of the mountains. Then he spoke of Fee's actual invasion of Kentucky: not "with Sharpe's rifles, pistols and bowie knives . . . but with the New Testament, the school-house, the church and the saw mill."[52]

Clay was caught in a very dangerous position. He was not only afraid that the Madison County slave power would turn on him next and drive him out of Kentucky simply because he had once supported Fee, but also that he would lose all his political support in the mountain region if he sided with the slaveowners. Those people who still counted as followers of Cassius Clay had a tendency to sympathize with John G. Fee.

John G. Fee, writing to Clay from Cincinnati in February, 1860, still regarded him as a friend. "I have just rec'd your kind and frank letter of 21 inst.," Fee wrote,

> I love you for it. I love principle so do you. I have a desire to
> be faithful spoken. If I had not you could not have respected
> my fidelity or felt that I was faithful. We do not need to
> part—I do not part with a man because he differs when I feel
> he is honest. Moreover you have uttered sentiments as radical
> as I and I am glad of it . . . .

Fee reproached Clay only very briefly: "You had power to protect me," Fee said; "if I violate no law I ought to be protected." With that single sentence Fee concluded his personal recriminations against the friend who had done most to endanger Fee's life and ministry. "I wish I could see you as you return," Fee wrote, "I would love to see you. I have the kindest of feelings toward you. Shall rejoice in your welfare."[53]

Nevertheless, Fee had repudiated Clay's leadership forever. And, although Fee apparently forgave his friend on a personal basis, his estimation of Clay's character was henceforth low, indeed. Clay "is sceptical and wicked," Fee wrote, "& it may be God will not in the work in Ky have his help." From now on, Fee indicated, he would no longer follow the leadership or ambitions of Cassius Clay; instead he would "follow Christ."[54]

Chapter Nine
TROUBLED TIMES AND WAR

In March,1860, when John G. Hanson returned to Madison County in defiance of the Vigilance Committee, Cassius Clay found himself once again in a completely untenable position. John G. Hanson was an integral part of the Berea project. Although he taught only one term, he soon became a member of Berea's first board of trustees, serving as secretary and as one of the Prudential Committee. By July, 1859, his circular sawmill was in operation—his contribution to "the cause of Christ." His first mill was located at the mouth of Log Lick Hollow Branch on Old Slate Lick Road, in a small settlement he called Glendale, about a mile south of the district schoolhouse. Before the December exile Hanson's mill had been in full operation. Fee wrote of Hanson as one of the most hard-working of all the Bereans during this period and said his cousin could have paid for his sawmill "nicely if he had not been driven out." Hanson did not want to sell his precious mill to the slavepower, whatever happened.[1]

About March 3, 1860, (he left Cincinnati on the first) Hanson returned to Berea "to saw out some 300 logs left at the mill" and to try to sell the mill itself unless he saw some chance of coming back permanently. He arrived on a Saturday. The following Monday was a county court day at Richmond.[2]

Hanson, unfortunately, had not been the only exile to return. A. G. W. Parker, Fee's former colporteur, ordered to leave at the same time, had gone away. But some of his northern friends had given him money, and apparently in sheer bravado, he had come back and commenced drinking and carousing. The day after Hanson's arrival Parker had used "rough" and threatening language to one Mr. White. Parker, unlike

Hanson, had attracted a great deal of public attention to himself. On the Monday court day a call was issued for the committee to assemble at Glade Church a week later and to take steps to expel Parker and Hanson.[3]

Friends warned Hanson to be gone by Saturday. "It left me but 4 days to hunt up buyers," he wrote,

> sell my mill & arrange my business. I set about the work with as much haste as my wounded spirit could summon & what I felt the loss of most seemed to be wisdom to know what to do. One thing after another had come up to intervene in my selling out so that by Friday noon I had not sold & we were told that a company of 150 would be out next day . . . .

In haste he boxed his goods for shipment, said goodbye to his friends and started as if he were bound for Cincinnati. Actually he stopped and spent the night with a friend in the mountains; but his friend's cabin was not a suitable hiding place, as it was too near the road that committee members would be taking to reach the Glade Church.[4]

The committee of some thirty or forty men met on schedule, stayed together about twenty-four hours, and drank—it is reported—a great deal of whiskey. The group spent some time talking about the American eagle, a cast-iron ornament which Hanson had placed on top of one of his mill buildings. Two committee members volunteered to take the eagle down. Since the eagle was replaced the next day, one may assume that sobriety revealed its removal as basically pointless.

Forty armed men—or the rumor of forty armed men—pursued Hanson, who fled to Rockcastle County and composed an "Appeal to the People of Madison Co.," appearing under the date March 13. Meanwhile, the committee reported Hanson had left the region, although many people knew that was not true. Eventually Hanson returned to Berea, where his friends were very surprised to see him. On the Sabbath he preached there twice, and he decided to stay on. "I am here," he wrote, "& still own property & want to do what God directs." Meanwhile, some of his Richmond enemies were planning "to pounce on him unawares and hang him. . . ."[5]

On March 24, Cassius Clay went to Berea accompanied by his friend John Hamilton Rawlings, and there "used all [his] influence" to persuade his Republican friends not to identify themselves "at all in any manner with Hanson." Clay told his friends to ask Hanson to sell his mill and move from the state "as his presence would be a continual source of discontent and might possibly involve the Republicans in conflict, when innocent men might be killed." Clay spent the night at William Stapp's, where he expressed the same views to general agreement. On his way home through Berea the next day Clay was stopped by Hanson, who "hallooed" at Clay as he was leaving. Rawlings introduced the two men; then Hanson asked Clay about the public attitude toward him. Clay told Hanson "that the feeling of bitterness against him was greater than ever on account of his return," and advised him to leave the state for his own sake and also "to avoid the possible fight between [Clay's] friends and the committee." Hanson replied "that every one must stand on his own convictions; and that 'every dog has his day,' " or words to that effect. (Clay reported at the time that Hanson had said "every tub must stand upon its own bottom.")[6]

His interview with Clay frightened Hanson, as it was intended to do. "Under an apprehension of danger [he] left [his] boarding place and travelled around some three miles, so that no one at Berea should know where [he] was." He spent a night of anxiety with a friend near Berea. He planned to finish sawing his logs, leave someone to run the mill, and get out the next day. On Monday morning, however, Hanson found his plans drastically altered. "I had just put on my hat and coat, after breakfast," he wrote, "to go to the mill, when a neighbor [Benjamin Kirby] ran in, and told me, the mob, some 25 in number, were then at Berea." They had already searched his boarding place, and had announced they intended to hang him. Hanson fled to the woods in Jackson County, hiding "up in high cliffs and caves" in the mountains during the day and staying in a friend's house at night. A reward of $100 was offered for him on published handbills. Nevertheless, many citizens of Jackson county invited Hanson to stay with them and pledged their protection.[7] The committee's renewed action was, according to Clay, a direct result of his visit to Berea over the weekend. In fact, he said, the mob had come to Berea expecting to take Clay there by surprise. Whoever they were looking for, the men found neither Clay nor Hanson.[8]

What happened next became a matter of such controversy that reports of it vary on almost every point. The only matter of agreement is simply stated. The committee men, returning to Berea from their unsuccessful search for Hanson, were met by a small group of Fee's supporters, also armed, under the leadership of Green Haley. Both words and shots were exchanged. Contemporary reports of this skirmish present it from many different points of view. Hanson's account, which appeared in the *American Missionary*, is most circumstantial—some of his narrative is necessarily hearsay (as are most of the contemporary accounts).

> The mob, after searching my boarding place . . . proceeded to my mill. They abused Mr. Walters, who lives near the mill, and tried to make him tell where I was, threatening to shoot him. They then went to the house of Geo. West, a mile south, where, as I learn from Mr. Clay, they jumped their horses over the yard fence, and were coming toward his cabin, when his eldest daughter, a young woman, shut the front door, and was closing the back one, when they broke it down upon her, and entered the house, over the door, she being under it. They rushed up to Mr. West, (who sat propped up in his bed with pillows, being low with consumption,) and

putting their pistols to his breast, demanded where Hanson was. In the meantime, the daughter (who is a motherless orphan) freed herself from the door, when one of them put his pistol against her breast, and pressing her back against the cupboard, told her she ought not to have shut the door against them. Indecent language was also used to a younger sister. They then went into Rockcastle Co., to the house of Mr. Burdett, Mrs. B. and five of her daughters, being alone at the time. Before they reached the house, one of the mob fired a pistol, as Mrs. Burdett states, and then rushed up to the house, calling out "who shot at us?" She replied, "no one shot at you," and closed the door. They burst in the door, and putting their pistols to Mrs. Burdett's and her daughter's breasts, told them they would shoot them if they did not tell where I was. Two or three of the mob, cocked their guns, and went up stairs, and tore off the beds. They also tore a part of the underpinning from the house, and afterwards searched for me, for quite a distance round, in the woods and mountains. As I could nowhere be found, they returned. They reported that I had been seen to escape from Mrs. Burdett's in woman's garb. This story arose from the following incident. One of the elder daughters ran down to a little thicket below the house, to bring up her two little sisters, who had gone there to hide, and were crying bitterly. As she passed a drunken wretch cried out, "there he goes in woman's clothes."[9]

An account appearing in a Cincinnati paper was written by J. B. Mallett from the testimony of one purporting to be an eyewitness, one of the people who was later exiled. According to this story, twenty-four armed men from Richmond came to Berea on March 26 and "commenced scouring the country and searching houses for Mr. Hanson." The mob went first to the residences of Preston, Bland and Haley, where they insulted "the wives of these gentlemen." They then visited William B. Wright and "threatened to take him out and paint him," presumably with tar. Proceeding to the Waters' house, they cuffed James Waters, "pulled his hair, drew pistols, talked indecently to his wife, and in various ways attempted to provoke him to a fight." Thence to the house of George West, who was in the last stages of consumption. (West lived in a log house on Silver Creek out toward the Pinnacle and near the Baptist church.) West saw the mob coming and told his daughter to shut the door. The visitors broke the door down, searched the house, insulted West's wife, and said they would "bring out a buck nigger for the benefit of his daughter." Finally, the committee called on Josiah Burdett, "six miles from Berea, drew pistols on his wife & daughters— threw beds on the floor—said they 'held the women as much accountable as the men.' "[10]

The Richmond band returned to Berea, but the Bereans, in the meantime, had "rallied and sought to defend their wives and families from further violence." Fifteen Bereans on the way to George West's met the mob, which called out to them, "What in hell are you doing with your guns!" The Bereans replied, "We are going to defend our families from violence." The mob "bore down on them in full gallop," yelling, "Shoot, shoot!" The leader of the Bereans told them to hold their fire. Part of the mob dismounted, made "a breast work of their horses and commenced the attack by firing some fifteen or twenty shots." The Bereans made ready a second time but, obeying orders, did not fire. Seeing that a fight was inevitable, twelve of the Bereans now moved a short distance to a high point of woodland and determined to resist to the last. Three remained, and as the mob came up, two fired and then went to their comrades on the hill. The mob fired several shots at the three as they retreated.

The mob returned to Richmond for reinforcements, after threatening to return the next day and "hang the Bereans and burn their houses." Two hundred and nineteen armed men came on Tuesday, "tore the roof off and logs out of a dwelling house [Waters]," and the roof off a meathouse. Then they went to Hanson's mill, "disposed of the roof, smashed up the [castings?], chopped the wood work, injured the boiler, leveled the furnace and chimney." Then they opened his tool chest & scattered the tools about . . . . [The end of the newspaper clipping is badly frayed.]"[11]

Hanson's description of the destruction at his mill is most detailed: "They went to my mill," he wrote, "tore off the roofing, pulled down a smoke stack, broke all the wheels of the mill, and cut a hole in the top of the boiler, leaving all a complete wreck." In addition to their other work at Waters' house, the committee shot many of his chickens, "for sport."[12]

Other extant accounts of the Madison County trouble were written by David Preston (one of the Berea leaders), Cassius Clay, Franklin Bland, Green Haley, some anonymous Richmond observers and a Lexington reporter. From these letters and newspaper articles one may gather that the skirmish in Madison County was fought to defend the insulted wives and daughters of various Bereans, or over John G. Hanson, or over George West or Bland and Haley, or possibly Cassius Clay; that the vigilance committee behaved bravely and wounded several Bereans; that the Bereans behaved bravely and wounded several committee members; that someone was killed; that no one was killed; that very little happened, although the committee returned to Richmond in such an hysterical state that everyone in Richmond became hysterical, too. In addition, one may choose among a wide variety of estimated numbers of people on both sides.[13] Certainly the Richmond committee ordered a cannon from Lexington, with a p.s.: "If you can, send us two or three of your boys who know how to load and shoot, and are competent to direct the piece, etc. . . . We have no one who has been accustomed to loading or shooting a cannon and would like for some one to come who is convenient."[14]

On March 27, Clay gave a speech in Richmond at the courthouse, disclaiming any connection with Hanson or his doctrine and maintaining that he (Clay) had told Hanson that "any man advocating the doctrines he held, could not live peaceably in this community." On the same day Clay had written to New York papers:

> The mob increases in violence; I lie upon my arms awaiting an attack; my family absolutely refuses to retire, saying they will run bullets and aid as in 1776. If driven into the woods, I shall attempt to hold my position as long as possible, standing on the Constitution, the Laws and my right. I will defend them or die. The cannon at Lexington is sent for, and the Governor aids. Is this my cause only, or that of the American People? Is it to be vindicated in this way and now? Shall I stand or fall alone? May God defend the right![15]

The *Kentucky Whig* at this time published a story claiming that the vigilante committee had turned their attention to Clay. The *Whig* editor remarked, "They are on the right track now," and went on to maintain that the committee in Madison County should either invite Fee and his men to return or else exile Cassius Clay along with them, since it was pointless to get rid of Fee and allow Clay to remain.[16]

On March 29, Clay wrote the *Louisville Journal*, attempting once again to disclaim all connection with Fee and his doctrines. But he said he knew he was himself included in the violent intentions of the Madison County Committee. He considered any action against him unjust because he had cut himself away "from the revolutionary doctrines of the 'Radical Abolitionists,' " — as he put it — "in good faith."[17]

Once again Clay wrote to a New York paper (the *Tribune*). The committee was to go to Berea that day to see if their orders had been carried out. "If some are killed," Clay said,

> God only knows the end! We will at once take to the woods and the mountains and defend ourselves to the last.
> If we had fifty or one hundred Sharpe's rifles, it would give us immense power in the mountain recesses where cannon could not touch us . . . . God knows we don't want the scenes of Kansas again re-engaged—*first disarming us and setting our foes upon us!*[18]

On March 31, Clay wrote his "Appeal to the People of Madison County," which was published in newspapers and distributed also as a handbill. In this appeal Clay spoke of himself as a free citizen of a constitutional commonwealth, and as such he "solemnly" protested "against any power on earth but the legal and regularly constituted authorities of [his] country to decide in any manner upon [his] "life, liberty or property." He reiterated his repudiation of Fee and Hanson and his refusal to defend them. "My reasons for this," he wrote, "are these: I regarded the radical doctrine that 'there is no law for slavery' as revolutionary." Even as he announced his unwillingness to protect or defend John G. Fee, Clay proclaimed his ardent desire to defend the people who fought against the committee. "You may drive these men into the mountains," Clay said,

> you may burn their houses; you may hunt them down like wild beasts; till the last one falls by superior force; but their cause is the cause of American liberty, and of the noblest instincts of human nature. Their martyrdom will light up the fires of civil war, which will pervade the Union, and be extinguished only by the downfall of one or the other of those great powers, Liberty and Slavery, forever! Men of Madison, *I stand by those men!*[19]

Simultaneously, Clay was making other provisions. He "anticipated violence and prepared for it." He sent for Hamilton Rawlings and dispatched him "posthaste" to Jackson and Rockcastle counties "to gather together enough loyal friends to protect him in his home in case of armed attack." He placed the two cannons from the office of the *True American* at "advantageous points" and set his wife and children to work molding lead balls for the cannons and bullets for rifles. "Rollins [sic] returned from the mountains with a horde of stout-hearted men of the hills." They established a camp in tents and in the outbuildings of White Hall, completely surrounding Clay's house. Men stood picket duty every night. Meanwhile, Clay fed the men, some 100 "expert riflemen," but the committee did not appear. On April 4, escorted by his men, Clay gave another speech in Richmond. From that point on he heard no more of expulsion and "in a few days disbanded his armed guard and bid [sic] them Godspeed with an eloquently expressed gratitude for their loyal support and friendship."[20]

Hanson, who had been hiding in Jackson County, left on April 3 and walked all night, going past his mill and his home, "now desolate and ruined." Near Kirksville (in Madison County) some of the original committee pursued him, caught him, and searched him for weapons. They found none, since he never carried any. They had expected him to be loaded down with guns and knives, like the incendiary he was supposed to be. Nevertheless, they headed toward the county seat with Hanson, assuring him, "You must now go to Richmond and pull rope."

> We then began to move slowly towards Richmond; they riding, and I walking in front of them. We had gone but a short distance when the man with the revolver proposed that they let me go, as he did not think I wanted to hurt any one, and was then going out of the State. The others did not consent. I still walked on in front of them, till the man who proposed to let me go, got off of his horse and told me to get up and ride. Thus we went on a quarter of a mile further,

when the man who had searched me for "fighting tools," said let us get down and talk it all over. We did so. They wanted to know what was the difference between Fee and myself, and asked if I had seen Clay's appeal, and when I said no, gave me one, saying, "He denounces you," &c. They told me I was in their power, and that they were in honor bound to deliver me up; and if they did, I would never leave Richmond alive. (I saw they felt it to be so.) They said, they did not want to see a hair of my head hurt; they had been deceived in me, and had expected to find me loaded down with weapons. I asked them if they ever heard of any threats I had made. They answered no; and then told me I was in great danger, and that $100 reward had been offered to any one who would deliver me in Richmond. They told me where the chief danger was, and thus we parted without their asking or I making any pledges.

Still enemies pursued him—"three times during one night they passed so near him, while he lay concealed, that he could hear them talking about him, and the reward offered for him." Traveling by night, he made his way through "plowed fields, and along the line of a rail road." One day he walked fifty miles and rode fifty more, hiding in box cars. Finally, he made his way to Cincinnati, arriving on the night of April 12, "in tolerable health," although "for three previous nights he had not slept in a house." He had traveled 125 miles on foot, "part of the time without food."[21]

The final report of the Madison County committee, submitted April 3, 1860, summarized all the actions the committee had been involved in since its initial proceedings in Dec 1859. "No violence of any kind was perpetrated," the committee reported, "except to break Hanson's mill . . . . The whole proceeding of this committee have been characterized by the greatest moderation, patience and forebearance, under circumstances of the greatest and most trying provocation."[22] The document was signed by Reuben Munday, T. J. Maupin, J. W. Caperton, Thomas S. Bronston, Jr., and Robert Rodes Stone.[23]

In a speech at the Republican State Convention of Kentucky, Clay defended his desertion of Fee, this time on purely political grounds. They had been "political comrades up to such time as he [Feel], in his wisdom and what he conceived to be his duty to his God and his country, felt in conscience bound to separate himself from the Republican Party." In the conclusion of his defense Clay asked if Fee had "any more right to my physical and personal sacrifice of limb or of life than the Democratic party or the Union party in this Commonwealth? I say he has not."[24]

Clay suffered a great deal of criticism for his stand against Fee during the exile. His political image in the North was certainly not enhanced by it. A Cincinnati paper wrote that before Reverend John G. Fee became an exile from Madison, Cassius Clay had been asked "if he would not use his influence to prevent the expulsion of Mr. Fee . . . . Mr. Clay, on this occasion, showed a bitterness towards Mr. Fee rivaling that of the mob itself. He refused assistance in any shape or manner, adding that *Mr. Fee ought to have left Kentucky long before."* Clay later boasted that he had advised John G. Hanson to leave the state.

> Had Mr. Clay, instead of notifying the public that he had *advised* Fee and Hanson to leave, proclaimed in ringing words that these men had violated no law, and that, therefore, they had the same right to live in Kentucky that he or any other man had, his position would have been far better, and he would have stood infinitely higher in the estimation of all true Republicans.[25]

The *Chicago Press and Tribune* also protested Clay's stance:

> We do not like Cassius M. Clay's Appeal. It is not what we expected—not what we had a right to expect, from that courageous and self-sacrificing friend of human rights. By implication, if not directly, it sanctions the lawlessness of the mob that despoiled the peaceful church at Berea, and drove John G. Fee and his brethren out of the state. As we understand it Mr. Fee was punished for his opinions—not his acts.
> He believed that human slavery has no foundation in law; and that theoretical conviction was the offense. For it he was driven off. Mr. Clay says he could not defend him. We ask why not? He had a right to his opinions and opinions have never been punishable in this country. . . .[26]

The Radical Abolitionist Convention at Syracuse, New York (August 29-30, 1860) framed a resolution which pronounced Clay's actions "in perfect keeping with his baseness."[27]

Such criticisms from abroad may have been easier for Clay to face than some he received from much closer to home. Reverend George Candee wrote to Clay on April 24, 1860, from McKee in Jackson County, pulling no punches. He asserted that Fee's work had secured many friends for Clay and had made him no enemies. "Your recent acts toward him, however," Candee said,

> have made you enemies. The poor have regarded the Berea exiles and their work as friendly to their interests, and when you take so much pains to separate from them, many look upon you as an enemy to their interests . . . . Is it fair for you to encourage Fee to come here, as you did, giving him land and money to build with, then cause him to be exiled and degraded before the world, as I consider that you have done, for fear of personal harm?

In a final stinging rebuke, Candee wrote that he believed Clay had "an overly anxious desire for self-preservation."[28]

In the public controversy over Clay which raged in the press during the spring of 1860 even some careful readers may have overlooked the fact that Madison County had expelled a second group of exiles much larger than the first group. After the battle of Hanson's return fourteen families were ordered out of Kentucky by the committee.[29]

The headline in Cincinnati read: "Fifty more Bereans Expelled from Kentucky," but the article said only, "Several families numbering about fifty persons have just left the Berean settlement and gone to the free States, having been ordered out of the State by the pro-slavery mob-ites." One article in the *Kentucky Statesman* reported that "the whole of the attacking party" was ordered to leave with the exception of one "penitent" old man. At that time two people, Green Haley and Franklin Bland, had already left Kentucky for Indiana. In a joint letter to John G. Fee, written April 20, 1860, Thomas J. Renfro and William B. Wright mentioned some of the men who had been forced to leave, including "Uncle" Joel Todd and James Waters. "In the midst of the confusion," Wright said, "the Prestons [had] to leave together with others."[30]

Actually the number of people exiled early in April of 1860 was at least sixty, a sizable group to be put out of their homes and their state on a week's notice. Virtually no protest was heard in their favor because for the most part they were poor mountain people, defenceless in relation-ship to the wealthy men who wished to expel them. They could not speak publicly for themselves; and their chief defenders, Fee and his people, were already gone. Clay had been expected to defend them—in fact, had promised he would. But somehow he did not appear. J. B. Mallett asked, "Where is he? 13 families have been driven this week . . . . Clay attempts to defend himself by *not* defending others."[31]

The most nearly complete record of the exiles from Madison County is a list (dated 1860), in the handwriting of Cassius Clay, which gives the name of each exile who was head of a household and the number of persons in his or her family. Clay's list is headed "No. of individuals ordered off from the Vicinity of *Berea* by the mob." The first ten lines give names of the people who were exiled in December, 1859; the next fourteen, although no distinction is made in the document itself, identify the exiles of April, 1860.[32]

Many of the Madison County exiles traveled to Cincinnati to ask John G. Fee what to do and where to go, numbers of them staying with his family while they searched for lodging and work. On April 5, 1860, William Kendrick met some of them as they arrived in Ohio, having fled a mob "who threatened death." Joel Todd was among these travelers. He had been "in the affray" and stated that none had been killed "as he knows of." Todd reported that John Hanson was "hunted with greatest anxiety to put him to death," and that he (Todd) was "quite certain that Bro Candee [would] be killed or kidnaped & moved out of the state." At this point, Fee, burdened now with a new responsibility for numbers of poor Kentucky exiles, was suffering from such bad health that some of his friends thought he was going to die.[33]

But more exiles kept coming. By April 9 the Preston family, Jerusha and her children, had arrived in Cincinnati. "They were poor before, still more so now," Fee stated.

> The families last driven are poor & some of them are now in want . . . Sister Preston with her six promising children . . . had not more means than would barely take them out of the state. They were three days on the roadside without house or home. After crossing the River David the eldest son went to work for bread.[34]

Somewhat later, Fee reported that James Walters and his family, who had settled in Macoupin County, Illinois, were suffering and needed aid. The Walters family's plight grew so much worse that in August, Fee suggested that $30.00, which had been donated for Benjamin Kirby, should be divided with the Walters. "James Walters," Fee wrote, "is in much distress. All sick with chills, life not expected to one child. They are *suffering*. Kerby is poor but not sick."[35]

In any case, the Kirbys had not been having an easy time either. On July 13, 1860, Benjamin and Nancy Kirby wrote a joint letter to John G. Fee, sharing the trouble that exile had caused them. Their notes are written in almost illegible scrawls:

> Der frendes I take my pen in hand to in forme you that I am well at present time and family friende I am come back to Madson Ct. Ky. the mob is dis banded and says that all them may come back to ther homes if they chuse. Some has come back. Haly and Blan and son have come and Tine [Valentine] Willames has come and Shady Robbers [Shadrach Roberts] is come back to his home.
>
> My frinde I in forme you that I am in trubble I loste all my plunder on the roade when I wente oute and I hant hearde from them I hante gote no bede and and [word missing] withe us to goe to house keapings on, & I would be glad if you can see your friends and you and send me some money John G. Fee I be sure that you will helpe me now trye you frendes and see what tha will do fore me & fambly
>
> I los all my things on the road to Indiana and i cant hear of them i was sick alls the time when I was there but too weeks and then I cum back to Ky and i am well. Now I hope you will help me sum if you can you form Benjamin Kearby to John G Hanson and John G. Fee yor frend benjamin Kearby John G fee and hanson god bee withe all you Willam Wright he has joined the mob party which i think he has lost all his frends on both sids

Miss Nancy L. Kerby
To my Dear Frens I take my pen in [hand] to inform you all we are well at present and hopeing at the same [time] that these few lines may find you all enjoying blessing of health we

walk to indiana and Sent our boxs on the cars and never got
them and walked back to ky Madison couty I send my best
Love and Respects to you all.[36]

From Madison County to any point in Indiana is well over 100 miles.
Benjamin Kirby was twenty-two in April, 1860; Nancy Kirby was seventeen. Their first child was not yet two years old. Nancy had another
baby sometime in 1860; the chances are good that she was pregnant when
she walked from Madison County to Indiana and back.

Little is known of these people, but they occupy an important
position in the history of Madison County. Many of the families involved
in this incident later became some of the staunchest supporters of Berea
College. In fact, few events in the history of Madison County made more
friends for Berea than the 1860 exile. This exile represented the oppression of poor people by rich people, of mountain whites by Bluegrass
planters. These exiles were put out of their homes—no one could call
them interlopers, as they were not Yankees but Kentuckians—and a
great many of them, although they were poor, belonged to families that
had been in the state for generations, just as long as the "founding"
families. Many of them had supported the Berea school by sending their
children; some were members of Fee's church; some had done construction work for Rogers; some were employed at John Hanson's sawmill.
Virtually all of them returned to central Kentucky because their roots
were there. When Fee returned, these people were prepared to support
his school and his church again, more strongly than ever. A great number of them were even willing to cooperate in his incredible scheme for
interracial education. Ironically, the Madison County committee had
insured that Berea would be supported, in the future, by citizens of
Madison County.

In the meantime, the citizens of Madison County were experiencing
troublous times. Some were delighted with the nomination of Abraham
Lincoln (Curtis F. Burnam, for example), but many more were not.
Cassius M. Clay created excitement by "haranguing the Republicans in
the Court House," while speeches for candidates Bell and Everett also
gathered crowds.[37]

As the election grew nearer, "Southern proclivities" were growing.
Curtis F. Burnam described one influential proponent of the southern
cause in Madison County:

Old Squire Turner made today (October 18. 1860) in our
Court House, a detestable speech—his vile slang I can not
bear—his vulgar commonplaces are natural to him—but
beneath all there was a slime which bespoke the presence of
the snake in our Eden. Into the ears of honest farmers from
Tate's Creek he was whispering words of guile and poison.[38]

In November, 1860, Lincoln was elected president; South Carolina
seceded from the Union about a month later. Early in January, 1861,
Mississippi, Florida, and Alabama followed suit. The citizens of Madison
County were, like all Americans, distressed about the "State of the

Union." On January 12 a Union meeting was called at the courthouse. With a large crowd in attendance, Martin Gentry was elected chairman; James B. McCreary, secretary. Some prominent Madison countians, Elbridge J. Broaddus, for example, favored secession, while Curtis F. Burnam and Judge Daniel Breck, among others, opposed. Many of the leading figures at this meeting had also been members of the vigilance committee which exiled the Bereans.[39]

In a second meeting on January 19 a committee which had been "appointed to draft resolutions on the positions of the citizens of Madison County in respect to the national difficulties" (W. F. Holloway, E. J. Broaddus, and T. S. Bronston) reported to one of the largest assemblies in the history of the county. Their report was "decidedly Southern in sentiment," but resulted in no action because some of the leaders of the community still advocated secession, while others demanded three cheers for the Union, which were duly given. The resolutions were tabled.[40]

Still the unionists feared that Kentucky would become a Confederate state. Curtis F. Burnam wrote, "I cannot see how we are to save Kentucky from following that ruinous example [of secession] . . . Still we will struggle on for the old Flag of the United States—not for the new flag of the Confederate South."[41]

On April 12, 1861, the War between the states began with the firing on Fort Sumter. Some of the citizens of Madison County readied themselves for war almost immediately. Before Kentucky had declared itself on the question of allegiance in the war, James M. Shackelford of Richmond requested 100 Enfield or Sharpe's rifles for one of the "Companies of everlasting Union men" which were organizing from Richmond and Madison County: a company in Richmond, a company in Doylesville, and one at Bear's Wallow near Big Hill (the latter company under the command of Captain Boston Dillion). By May 18, Madison County had received the 100 muskets and bayonets delivered from Washington, D. C., for $1.00 apiece.[42]

Curtis F. Burnam described the general reaction in Madison County:

> The terrible news from Baltimore & Harper's Ferry reached us on Saturday night . . . . general gloom and apprehension overhang the county, intermingled with general military ardor. Every town and precinct in Kentucky is beginning to organize military companies.—If the war is general between the two sections I presume more havoc will be made in this State than anywhere else.[43]

By May 20, Kentucky—the entire Commonwealth as divided as Madison County—declared its neutrality in the conflict. Madison County's Curtis F. Burnam served on the Committee on Federal Relations which presented a report (May 16, 1861) recommending neutrality, a recommendation which the house of representatives adopted. Kentucky's position never exempted the state from war, however, as both Union and rebel troops moved into and through the neutral zone, and both Abraham Lincoln and Jefferson Davis asked for volunteer regiments from Kentucky. Although Governor Beriah Magoffin denied the request of both presidents, the citizens of Kentucky became soldiers for both causes. Confederate recruiting stations in the state were provided for by the Confederate Congress in August, 1861. Ultimately 75,000 Kentuckians served with the Union army, but hundreds of men left Kentucky to go south and join the Confederates, and on November 18, 1861, a convention in Russellville established the provisional government of Kentucky, formed a constitution, and set up an election for the new Confederate state. (Madison county was in the Confederate state of Kentucky's 11th District, even though the county was unrepresented at the convention.) Every political and military position of Kentucky as a whole was represented in Madison county, which frequently mirrored the shifting fortunes of the entire war. If Kentucky as a whole was, in Ross Webb's phrase, "a microcosm of conflict: a civil war within a civil war," Madison County was equally a microcosm of Kentucky.[44]

The first regiment from Kentucky was a Confederate one formed at Harper's Ferry, Virginia, May 15, 1861; and soon large numbers of the State Guard resigned and left the state to enter Confederate service. However, the federal government planted its army within Kentucky simply by opening military camps there in direct violation of Kentucky's neutrality. Camp Dick Robinson in Garrard County was established in August, 1861, and served as a camp for many troops from all over Kentucky, as well as from east Tennessee. (The next month in retaliation the Confederates occupied Columbus, in western Kentucky.) Within Madison County itself, Camp Moody near Big Hill was a center for local Union companies.[45]

In some cases, shooting in Madison County had begun before the war. "Bitterness between the two parties" led James Shackleford, superintendent of the Presbyterian sunday school in Richmond, to shoot James Breck, who "never fully recovered from the effects of the wound." Friends and neighbors in Madison County were certainly divided by the Civil War ("The Bennetts were Union people, but all the Chenaults were rebels"), but families also split on the issues. In the Burnam family, Thompson, Sr. and his sons Curtis F. and Thompson were strong Union men; but Thompson, Sr.'s sons John and Edmund and his daughters Mary Ann Wilson and Eugenia were "*violent* rebels," while his brother John of Bowling Green was a member of the Confederate government of Kentucky, and his sister Nancy Hall was "a strong *Union* woman," with a son in the Union Army. Curtis F. Burnam's wife, Sarah Rollins Burnam, was a "southern sympathizer," and her uncle by marriage, Samuel Stone, was "a great Rebel" (so great he had to flee to Canada once Yankees took possession of Richmond), with one son, Robert H., in accord with him, and the other, James C. Stone, a Union man. At least seven men of the Maupin family were Confederate soldiers, while J. D. and Waller Maupin fought for the Union at the Battle of Richmond. Judge Daniel Breck of the Richmond bar was a strong union man (understandably, since the old man was from New England), but all his children were rebels. One Reuben Munday was a Confederate soldier in Company H, 11th Kentucky Cavalry (mustered in September 10, 1862), while the other, his cousin Colonel Reuben Munday, commanded a regiment of federal troops fighting in the Battle of Richmond. The situation was so entangled as to be almost ludicrous at times. One day in the summer of 1862, Lucia F. Burnam and her sister Sallie and their cousin Lou Wilson were stopped on the Barnes Mill Pike by a Union sentry. Cousin Lou told the soldier they were all good Union People, an obvious untruth, since she herself was "a great rebel."[46]

"Families," Lucia F. Burnam wrote "were terribly divided." Even children were caught up in the great controversy. In 1861 the little boys in the Burnam neighborhood of Richmond formed a company of rebels. Captain James T. Shackleford furnishing them with uniforms, "black velvet jacket and trousers and *red* sash with gay cocked hats with plumes." Curtis F. Burnam, returning home from the legislature, found his nine-year-old son Thompson ("Tomp") a member of this group and sternly forbade such an allegiance; even though he offered to buy the child a uniform for the rival company of Union boys, "Tomp could not be moved and though he left the rebel company he never joined the Union forces."[47]

In the fall of 1861, many Confederate sympathizers were arrested by federal troops. In Madison County, for example, James B. Clay of Lexington (son of the famous Henry) was arrested on September 26 as he was attempting to make his way south; the man he had hired to guide him had betrayed him into the hands of the enemy. Another indication of federal power in the state was the closing of newspapers with rebel views. Richmond's *Mountain Democrat* among them (suspended September 27).[48]

On October 21, 1861, one of the first skirmishes of any consequence in Kentucky occurred on Madison County's doorstep—at Camp Wildcat (one of the new federal military locations), or Rockcastle Hills, where the roads leading to Mt. Vernon, London, and Richmond all met. The area was densely timbered with ridges and gorges easily defended. The 7th Kentucky Infantry under Colonel Theodore T. Garrard was attacked by Brigadier General Zollicoffer with 7,000 Confederates. Garrard, reinforced by some Indiana, Ohio, and Tennessee regiments and the 1st Kentucky Cavalry, repulsed the Confederates, who suffered 30 killed and about 100 wounded and retreated the next day. Union forces lost 4 killed, only 18 wounded. This early battle confirmed many in their belief that Kentucky could be firmly held by the Union.[49]

At this point many more Madison County men, frightened because of their own reputations as southern sympathizers, began to flee south to join the Confederate army. Robert Chenault, for example, left his plantation in the Old Cane Springs region, because "it was not safe for him to remain at home." Others, such as Othniel Oldham and his sons, quickly followed his lead. Men from Clark, Bourbon, and Harrison counties passed through Madison County at night, trying to make their way to the Confederacy. But the Home Guards were on special watch, "arresting every man they found going towards the South." In addition, it was rumored that the Home Guards (all, it seems, northern in their sympathies) "made almost nightly visits" to slave quarters in the neighborhood (Old Cane Springs) in order to make slaves "dissatisfied with their masters." The blacks, it is reported, perceived the Home Guards as "po' white trash" and disregarded their opinions. For awhile the prosouthern citizens of Madison County, especially in Old Cane Springs, practiced "dangerous hospitality" to men on their way south. But soon Richmond was declared under martial law and a provost judge, Captain Palestine P. Ballard, was appointed, with orders to arrest any citizen giving aid or comfort to "anyone who desired to become connected with the rebellion." So enlistment in the Confederate army became, if not impossible, exceedingly difficult. In spite of these hardships, a whole company under the command of Captain Ambrose Dudley "made up exclusively of Madison County boys and especially those who had gone South from Old Cane Springs" eventually joined the Confederate army.[50]

One of the most violent indications of federal power was the murder of prominent citizens, "southern sympathizers," by the Home Guards. One such incident involved the death of William Reed Wallace, who lived near Elliston and was murdered June 18, 1861, "for his political convictions being a southern sympathizer." More specifically, a member of the guards knifed Wallace for speaking in "a derogatory manner about President Lincoln."[51]

Another instance which became a noted scandal in Madison County was the murder of Durrett White. The events leading up to this crime involved some Union soldiers perpetrating a number of infringements against the rights of local citizenry before the actual murder. It all began on the afternoon of October 26 at a house of ill repute which two women were running in an abandoned schoolhouse on the road near Menelaos. The whores, sisters-in-law, both married to soldiers stationed elsewhere (one in the Union army, the other a Confederate), had set up their business on a military route from Madison County's Camp Moody to Camp Dick Robinson. Cavalry frequently traveled by and apparently stopped almost as frequently. On this particular occasion, four Union soldiers, drinking, encountered some of the other clientele, which, according to later testimony, were creating a surprising amount of traffic on the small county road—many men on horseback, drinking, riding and "tomcatting around." The four Union men—Thomas and Ham Cliff, Mr. Shocklesy, and Cornelius Kelly—had fought at the battle of Camp Wildcat a few days earlier, killing many "Secesh." They said they were authorized by their officers to "take all Secesh dead or alive," and claimed a party of cavalry was due to arrive at any minute. Their first victims were three men riding along together; Larkin Mullins, a Mr. Smith, and H. G. Reese. Kelly ordered them to halt and dismount, carried them back to the schoolhouse, and arrested two more men, Madison Todd and Eli Nichols. All these men were threatened with death, and Nichols, an old man, was badly beaten. Throughout this incident the four soldiers kept repeating that they were authorized to bring in all Secesh, dead or alive; but they especially mentioned Durrett White, a wealthy slaveowner (he owned twenty-four slaves in 1860), whose "scalp" they intended to take. One of the ladies of the house managed to get the guns away from the soldiers, who were apparently too drunk to notice for awhile, although one of them later threatened to kill her as well. Eventually the Union soldiers tried their captives, some of whom were quite drunk too, by making them kneel at gunpoint and swear allegiance to the United States. One of the soldiers, Kelly, kept repeating (according to many witnesses) that "he intended to have Durrett White's scalp before daylight."[52]

Even though some friends of White's ran through the fields to warn him, he was not particularly frightened, but he did leave his house. Quitting the schoolhouse-brothel, the soldiers, with a prisoner, Charles Keenon, proceeded on horseback to the White plantation. There they brutally struck Keenon, bloodying his face, ripped up a bed with their bayonets, and, finding food on the table where White had abandoned his meal, sat down to dine. Shocklesy was so far gone that one more drink of whisky caused him to lose consciousness, and he spent the rest of the time lying on the floor in a drunken stupor, observed by many witnesses. (Some slaves eventually dragged him outdoors.) Kelly, an east Tennessee man and the leader of the little pack of Union soldiers, "sat at the table [in White's dining room] eating with his musket between his legs." Later, Durrett White, misled by a friend who told him it was safe to go home, was shot down by Kelly at his own back door. Some family slaves then shot at Kelly and the others as they were fleeing the premises. White died of the wound in his thigh two days later. The trial of his murderers, held before Union magistrates, resulted in Kelly's being released on bail of $1,000 for a charge of manslaughter, while Shocklesy, who had been too drunk to participate in killing White, was discharged as guilty of "no offense."[53]

In the course of the conflict, conditions in Kentucky changed repeatedly, as armies and power bases shifted in the state, but late in 1861 the Union seemed to have central Kentucky fully under control. By December John G. Fee was able to visit Lexington in safety. On the twenty-first of that month, Fee reported that he had spent three consecutive Sundays in Berea, which he found quiet and relatively safe—people were able to assemble with some security and many more were willing to listen to him than before. He conducted an antislavery meeting near the Jackson County border, although he thought Jackson County rather insignificant, with its 13 slaves to Madison's 5,000 (Fee's own figures). Slaves were still being bought and sold in Richmond, where on May 5, 1862, eleven blacks were auctioned at an average price of $296 apiece. And, ironically, Kentucky, by act of the Provisional Congress, had been admitted as a member of the Confederate States of America on December 10, 1861.[54]

Chapter Ten

THE BATTLE OF RICHMOND

On July 20, 1862, John Hunt Morgan and his rebels, in the midst of Morgan's first Kentucky raid, which made him famous, spent some sixteen hours (from midnight to 4:00 P.M.) in Richmond, where they acquired fifty new recruits. Morgan had determined to make a stand at Richmond, "as the whole people," he said, "appeared ready to rise and join [him]." He altered his plans upon hearing that large bodies of cavalry, under General Green Clay Smith, Colonel Reuben Munday, and others, were trying to surround him in Richmond. While Morgan was in town, Curtis F. Burnam, at his wife's entreaty, spent the day hiding in the woods near his house, in the company of two other strong Union men, John Bennett and Colonel James W. Caperton. All three were later reported to have had "a happy day together enjoying the beauties of nature and feasting on blackberries."

Soldiers called at Burnamwood to arrest Curtis Burnam and, finding him gone, ordered food to be cooked for themselves. Mrs. Burnam had a ham prepared and "bushels of . . . beaten biscuits made," then dressed in her best to sit in the doorway awaiting Morgan. When the general arrived Sarah R. Burnam, although a "southern sympathizer" herself, greeted him by asking, "Is *this* the great General Morgan who makes war upon women and children?" Later in the day, Morgan's raiders, assembled in front of Burnam's house while they waited for an order to march, were served "great trays full of biscuits and beautiful dishes of sliced ham." Among these men was James B. McCreary (later to be governor of Kentucky).[1] Some two days later General Green Clay Smith and his men arrived in Richmond in pursuit of Morgan, and this group was also fed at Burnamwood, which apparently had an endless supply of ham and beaten biscuits.[2]

One result of Morgan's successful raid into Kentucky in July, 1862, was the encouragement it gave to Major General E. Kirby Smith, commander of the independent Department of East Tennessee. On July 4 Kirby Smith had sent John Hunt Morgan on his first raid into Kentucky, in the course of which Morgan took Tompkinsville, Glasgow, Springfield, and Harrodsburg. By July 14, Morgan and his men were only fourteen miles away from Frankfort. Morgan was struck by the possibility of arousing Kentuckians to support the Confederacy. From Georgetown he telegraphed Kirby Smith to urge an invasion: "The whole country can be secured," he stated, "and 25,000 or 30,000 men will join you at once." Morgan lost the country outside Lexington and Frankfort the day after he sent this message—and only 300 Kentuckians had volunteered to join him during July, some few from Madison County. But Kirby Smith was greatly stimulated by the possibility of taking Kentucky. On August 9 he notified Major General Braxton Bragg that he intended to invade Kentucky, by-passing the Cumberland Gap and striking directly for Lexington. His determination to push rapidly into the Bluegrass was partly based on his knowledge that his troops could be amply provisioned in that rich and fertile part of the state. An invasion of Kentucky would promote the cause of the Confederacy in six important ways. It would (1) relieve heavy Union pressure on Tennessee, north Georgia, and north Alabama; (2) achieve enlistment of large numbers of Kentuckians in the Confederate army; (3) bring about the establishment of a Confederate government in Kentucky and the state's secession from the Union; (4) bolster Confederate morale by winning battles for the South; (5) result in the collection of much needed supplies and equipment; and, most importantly, (6) with full success, it would force the Union to ask for terms.[3]

On August 14, Smith moved out of Knoxville, his departmental headquarters, with two divisions; Brigadier General Patrick R. Cleburne's, consisting of the brigades of Colonel Preston Smith and Colonel B.M. Hill; and Brigadier General Thomas J. Churchill's, consisting of the brigades of Colonel T.H. McCray and Colonel Evander McNair. The army, some 6,000 to 7,000 strong, passed through Roger's Gap, west of Cumberland Gap, on August 18, arriving at "a dilapidated village" known as Barbourville. Major General Henry Heth, commanding nearly 4,000 men, arrived in Barbourville on August 22, having followed Smith by way of Big Creek Gap. At the forefront of Smith's army was Colonel John S. Scott's cavalry of approximately 1,000 troopers.[4]

E. Kirby Smith was in command of a "magnificent veteran army, perfectly trained, inured and disciplined," many of them veterans of Belmont, Shiloh, Elkhorn, and Springfield. Their journey from Tennessee into Kentucky was dangerous and very difficult; they had marched day and night over rough mountainous roads, dragging wagons and artillery, carrying their meager rations on their backs. They were ragged and footsore, "some wearing out their shoes entirely, and marking their bare tracks with blood.'' Kirby Smith later boasted that ''the accomplishment of his men was 'a feat rivaling [Hannibal's] passage of the Alps.' ''⁵

When Smith's army began arriving in Madison County, fighting commenced at once. The Battle of Big Hill, on August 23, resulted in the ignominious defeat of Colonel Leander Metcalfe's 400 dismounted Union Cavalry (7th Kentucky) by the 1st Louisiana Cavalry, under the command of Colonel John S. Scott. Metcalfe's men, who had only been in uniform for a week, ''at the first cannon shot, turned tail and fled like a pack of cowards,'' while 10 were killed, 40 wounded, and more than 150 taken prisoner. The conduct of Metcalfe's men was so disgraceful that he refused to command them any longer. Dispersed over half a dozen counties, these deserters were arrested as they arrived in Lexington and other population centers, and some who returned were later hanged. A battalion of the 3rd Tennessee Infantry under Lieutenant Colonel John C. Chiles comported themselves better than Metcalfe's men, meeting the enemy bravely, checking the Confederate advance, and even rescuing Colonel Metcalfe, who had been abandoned by his own regiment. The Confederate Army lost 4 men killed, 12 wounded, and 21 horses in this engagement.⁶

On August 24 ''great excitement'' was reported in Fayette and Madison counties, where slaveholders had been served with a military notice to furnish on a stated day a specified number of able-bodied male slaves ''for the use of the U.S. government as laborers.'' The Union army needed to repair the road between Mt. Vernon and the Cumberland Gap. General Jeremiah T. Boyle wanted to build a railroad between Lexington and the gap, saying he could accomplish the task in two months with enough impressed Negroes. (Eventually, he would call for some 6,000 slaves to extend the railways from Lexington to Danville.) Masters who failed to deliver slaves were theatened with arrest and imprisonment, and all their slaves between the ages of eighteen and forty-five were seized. Payment for slave labor was promised to ''loyal owners,'' while the disloyal were guaranteed trouble. The blacks furnished for this work were ''the first contingent of slaves impressed into United States military service'' in Kentucky.⁷

Meanwhile, Colonel John S. Scott, with Kirby Smith's brigade at Big Hill, reported that forty or fifty local men had come into his camp in one evening to join up. These new recruits claimed that ''large numbers [were] anxious to enlist in the Confederate service, but [had] no means of escape,'' being hemmed in by Home Guards and federal troops.⁸

On August 25, 1862—two days after the Battle of Big Hill (but, of course, news traveled slowly in those days)—Matilda Fee started across country in a carriage, from Augusta, Kentucky, accompanied by John A.R. Rogers, who was planning his own return to Berea, and her children Laura and Burritt. On the twenty-seventh they met the Union army at Richmond, and with some difficulty persuaded the Union pickets, who suspected them of being rebel spies, to allow them to go on to Berea. They reached Berea only with great difficulty, since the area was full of both Union and rebel soldiers, "each scrutinizing closely every person, horse and carriage."[9]

Fee himself had to go to Cincinnati to get a tract published before he made his way to Berea. His son Howard, then the youngest of Fee's children, accompanied him. Arriving in Richmond on August 29, Fee managed to rent a single horse, which he and his son rode double. That same morning Lieutenant Colonel Reuben Munday, commanding a small detachment of cavalry near Kingston, about five miles south of Richmond, had reported to General Mahlon Manson that the Confederate army was advancing in considerable force. Manson immediately ordered the 1st Brigade to stand to arms in readiness to move at a moment's notice. In addition, he sent four additional companies forward to strengthen the picket near Kingston, which was under the command of Lieutenant Colonel Joel Wolfe of the 16th Indiana. By two o'clock in the afternoon the cavalry led by Metcalfe and Munday and the infantry under Wolfe were retreating with the enemy "pressing hard upon them." About halfway home, near Kingston, Fee and his son met these Union forces retreating before the Confederate invasion. Finding it impossible to reach Berea that day, because rebel lines now lay between Richmond and Berea, Fee returned to Richmond to await another opportunity. It would be a long time coming.[10]

Major General William Nelson, commander of the Union army of Kentucky, knew that Smith's army was approaching, as did Major General H.G. Wright, commander of the Department of the Ohio, of which the Department of Kentucky was a part. Wright had determined not to risk a battle at Richmond unless the Union could be certain of victory, so the Union strategy was to fall back to the Kentucky River line. Brig. General Mahlon D. Manson, however, in command of a federal force in and near Richmond, was apparently not aware of his superior's plans. In the morning he had sent a courier to Lexington to inform Nelson of the enemy's advance, but he had received no orders from his commander by the same afternoon.[11]

Manson's 1st Brigade consisted of four exceedingly new Indiana regiments—the 16th, 55th, 69th, and 71st, and a battery of artillery under Lieutenant Edwin O. Lanphere—some 3,415 troops. A part of Manson's command near Richmond was the 2nd Brigade under General Charles Cruft, including the 18th Kentucky, 95th Ohio, 12th Indiana, 66th Indiana, a battalion of the 3rd Tennessee, and Andrews' Michigan Battery—3,085 men. Cruft's almost totally inexperienced recruits had not arrived until August 26, only four days before the Battle of Richmond. Manson had, therefore, an army of approximately 6,500 raw troops to face a seasoned army of nearly 12,000 Confederates.[12]

Manson commanded the 1st Brigade to move forward against the Confederate advance. Apparently, he never considered retreating, since it seemed to him better to go forward than to be attacked in his camp by the Confederates, who could easily occupy the hills which completely commanded Manson's camp. About four o'clock in the afternoon, at an engagement near Rogersville lasting about an hour, the Union army drove the Confederates "in some confusion from the field, capturing some prisoners, horses and one cannon." For miles around soldiers heard roaring of artillery in the direction of Rogersville, and, although it lasted only a few minutes, they knew the contest had begun. "Colonel Scott's cavalry brigade, sick men, baggage wagons, servants leading horses, came flying in [to the Confederate camp], in the utmost consternation, closely pursued by. . .United States cavalry, who were firing on them and yelling as though they were all excited by liquor." A Confederate line stopped the advance, but Union soldiers fired repeatedly at the enemy's campfires (it was now pitch dark), before retreating amidst "curses and threats" in the darkness. Manson's success in the late afternoon and evening, however, was no preparation for the next day's events.[132]

That night, the Union soldiers slept on their arms, those who slept at all. Some of the troops assembled for this battle had been in service less than a month, some a little over a week. "Some of the regiments never had had a battalion drill and knew not what a line of battle was. They were undisciplined, inexperienced, and had never been taught in the manual of arms." Many of the official reports of the Battle of Richmond emphasize the rawness of the Yankee recruits. "The men knew nothing of the duties or habits of soldiers. Most of them had been less than a fortnight away from their homes," reported Cruft. To add to the problem, the men were ill-equipped, with no "ordinary camp equipage or conveniencies. They were lying exposed to the hot sun by day and heavy dews by night." In addition, the Union army had insufficient ammunition, as events of the day would demonstrate. According to Manson, reporting after the battle, some pieces of artillery had run out of ammunition during the first engagement in the morning, while all ammunition had been exhausted by the end of the last battle in the evening. His army was, Cruft stated, "a mere collection of citizens, hastily assembled, armed and thrown together. . . ."[14]

In the Confederate camp, the troops may have been seasoned, but they had every reason to be fatigued. They had been, E. Kirby Smith reported, on "a forced march, almost day & night, for three days, over a mountainous wilderness, destitute alike of food and water." He stated that his men had undergone "without murmur the fatigues and privations of one of the most difficult marches of this war. For several days and parts of nights . . . over stony roads, with their almost bare feet, and with green corn and beef without salt as their only food . . ." Some of them slept in the "line of battle without any supper" the night before the Battle of Richmond.[15]

The Battle of Richmond on Saturday, August 30, 1862, was fought in three engagements: the first at Mt. Zion Church near Rogersville, about six miles from Richmond; the second at White's Farm, some two miles closer to Richmond; and the third in and around Richmond itself. At all three of these engagements the pattern of battle was the same—an overwhelming Confederate victory. John G. Fee, watching from a hill-top, described his distant, but all-too-accurate, view:

> Early that morning an engagement came off between the Union and Confederate forces. I obtained another horse and went to the scene of the conflict. To me it was a sad sight. The Union forces were small and badly managed. Soon they were outflanked on both sides. Overpowered and continually deci-mated, they were compelled to retreat, again and again.[16]

On the morning of the thirtieth Manson had caused his men to stand at arms at four o'clock, and they were ready to march by six o'clock, when Manson ascertained that the rebels were advancing upon him. Manson himself commanded the Union advance, riding with the 55th Indiana. They met the Confederates (General Patrick R. Cleburne and his two brigades were in the advance) half a mile beyond Rogersville at Mt. Zion Church and there drove them back long enough to take possession of some woods and high ground on the left side of the road. The line of battle was formed with the 55th Regiment on the left of the road behind a fence, 69th on the right side, artillery on the left of the 55th on high ground, and the 71st 300 yards to the rear. The 55th opened the battle "in gallant style." When the 16th came up, Manson ordered it into position to the left of the 55th in the woods. There the 16th maintained its position, in spite of a heavy attack, for more than an hour. Cleburne and Preston Smith attempted to turn its flank with fire of infantry and artillery, and the 71st was ordered to its support, exposed to heavy fire as it moved into position. Scores of men were wounded or killed, and the Confederates continued to advance. From the right Manson trans-ferred seven companies of the 69th, but Cleburne countered this move with one regiment of Preston Smith's brigade.[17]

Just then Cruft, with two sections of artillery and the 95th Ohio, arrived and took up the position the 69th had occupied. (As Cruft was approaching the battlefield with his reenforcements, he had met the artillery wagons driving back to Richmond for ammunition, which had already been exhausted.) Cruft's men had been in line of battle since three o'clock in the morning—they had heard firing at the front about 7:15 A.M., but Cruft had waited for a dispatch to give him orders before making his own decision to approach the battlefield, commencing to move the troops at 11:00 A.M. He met his own messenger on the way, but the courier had been unable to communicate with General Manson, who was already in the heat of battle. Although the column was already tired from heat and thirst, it was pressed on rapidly. Near Rogersville Cruft finally received a message from Manson, urging immediate reen-forcements. "The artillery," Cruft reported, "was sent forward on a trot and the infantry hurried up."[18]

In the meantime, Kirby Smith himself had arrived on the battlefield with two brigades (McCray's and McNair's) forming General Churchill's division. Churchill was immediately dispatched with one brigade to turn the Union's right. Ordered to charge a battery a short distance in front and on the right, the "green" 69th Indiana was subjected to a "severe and raking fire," which threw the men into a panic. Meanwhile, the Union right was being charged by the Confederates under Churchill, "where," according to Kirby Smith, "by a bold charge [Churchill's] men completed a victory already partially gained by the gallantry of [the] troops on the right."[19]

Kirby Smith's strategy was for his right under Cleburne and Preston Smith to attack the Union left, convincing Manson that the main attack was there. Manson responded just as Smith desired by transfering the 69th from the right to the left. Smith also planned to hold the Union center, while the real major attack would be executed on the Union right by Colonel T. H. McCray's Texans and Arkansans, who made "a well-timed and dashing charge," putting "to flight the hosts of the enemy."[20]

Churchill's account of the Arkansas and Texas troops in McCray's brigade praises their heroism. Executing a flank movement on the enemy's right, they "proceeded cautiously through a corn field and a ravine," while the Union forces formed in a skirt of timber. The Confederates charged, the Federals retreated, with many killed and taken prisoner. Moving on farther to the right, McCray's brigade approached the entire force of the enemy in a strong position on the left of the road, concealed by a cornfield and a wooded area. McCray ordered his command to lie down (they were under "terrific fire" from artillery and musketry) protected by a fence and a ditch. For a full five minutes they did not fire, waiting for the enemy to advance. "When they arrived," Churchill reported, "within less than 50 yards of my lines the order was given to rise, fire and charge." The Union troops could not withstand "the desperate courage" of Churchill's men,

> but still for a while they contested every inch of ground as they were driven from it, until finally, finding it impossible to check this gallant charge, they gave way in every direction. The victory was complete. The field was covered with the dead and wounded of the enemy, and some (though comparatively few) of the gallant sons of Arkansas and Texas fell martyrs to the cause of liberty.

According to Churchill, this was the "most severely-contested fight of the day."[21]

By this time, General Cleburne, one of the Confederates' most skillful leaders in this contest, had been seriously wounded in the face, but his division, under the command of Colonel Preston Smith, continued to attack. The Union center and right broke about the same time, although the left, held by the 18th Kentucky under Col. William A. Warner's command, made a show of resistance. They "contended singlehanded and alone" for twenty minutes in a costly attempt—they suffered severe losses before being overwhelmed by superior numbers—to halt Kirby Smith's advance. By this point (at 10:30 A.M.), however, "the panic was well-nigh universal. . . . The whole thing," Cruft reported, "was fast becoming shameful."[22]

A soldier eyewitness at this engagement reported his impressions for a Cincinnati newspaper (September 5). He found the noise almost overwhelming.

> The musketry was sharp, quick, rattling, crashing, almost deafening, surpassing any thing I had ever conceived in the way of infantry firing. To add to the horror of the scene, the wounded were now pouring in rapidly, covering the floor of Mr. Rogers's dwelling [being used as a hospital] and the smooth lawn in its front. One poor fellow had been shot through the head, and was just breathing his last. Another was most shockingly disfigured in the face. Another had lost his good right hand, and was nursing the bloody stump. . . .[23]

Manson managed to control and rally his men after a short retreat—approximately two miles north of the first battle. The 12th and 66th Indiana regiments, which had not arrived in time to take part in the first battle, served as the nucleus of Manson's new line, about a mile in the rear of the first battlefield, on elevated ground. As soon as he surveyed it, however, Manson saw that this position was untenable. He deployed the cavalry of Metcalfe and Munday on high ground in front of the infantry and placed one piece of artillery in the road. Then he moved the infantry to the rear about three-quarters of a mile—at the point which he had occupied in the skirmish the evening before. Manson ordered Cruft to take his brigade to the right, putting two regiments in the woods and two behind the fence fronting a cornfield; the 1st Brigade was formed behind fences on the left side of the road, artillery on the right and left, "on the same ground occupied the previous afternoon." The cavalry and artillery which had been left in front then retired rapidly to the new line. With his men in place, while he was awaiting the Confederate attack, as the rebels were "advancing in great force through the open fields," Manson received his orders from Nelson to retreat without risking an engagement. It was 12:30 P.M. Manson now had no choice; the battle began five minutes later.[24]

The second engagement—at White's Farm—fought at the hottest time of day (the temperature reached 96 degrees in the shade), resulted in the same disordered retreat, the battle raging "with great fierceness along [the] whole line," through woodlands and a cornfield for an hour. During this period a portion of the 3rd Kentucky Infantry joined Manson's ranks and "did excellent service." But to no avail. The Confederate's right gave way under fire from the Union artillery on the left, but turned immediately to attack Manson's right, rebel infantry advancing through woods and open fields. Cruft's brigade met the attack "in the most gallant manner," although some of the cavalry to Cruft's rear simply refused to obey his commands and were described by their own commander as "a pack of cowards." The 12th Indiana and 18th Kentucky regiments in the woods managed to repulse the rebels several different times, against "fearful odds," and the 66th Indiana and 95th Ohio even drove the enemy back a short distance. But the Confederates soon rallied, attacked the right wing again, and, "after a terrific engagement," forced the Union troops to retreat in confusion. Cruft and Manson rode forward "endeavoring to stay the flight and panic," but it was a "hopeless task."[25]

Manson tried to rally his troops at his old camp two miles south of Richmond, but at this point General William Nelson arrived from his headquarters in Lexington and took over the command, informing Manson that a stand would be made near Richmond. Nelson had received Manson's August 29 communique about the Confederate advance at 2:30 on the morning of August 30, and immediately sent couriers to order Manson not to fight. But Nelson was so anxious about the danger in Madison County that he started himself "to see that the troops at Richmond moved in the proper direction and in order." Arriving in Lancaster, he heard artillery firing in the distance, immediately procured fresh horses, and set off for Richmond accompanied by a single member of his staff. Nelson was delayed, however, forced to take by-paths because enemy cavalry was on the road. When he finally arrived on the field (at 2:00 P.M.) he "found the command in a disorganized retreat or rather a rout."[26]

Under Nelson's command the Union army (now some 2,200 men) fell back again to the Richmond Cemetery, where Confederates were "posted behind the fence [a stone wall] and the tombstones," and finally to Richmond itself (the first rebels came down Fourth Street, now Lancaster Avenue) in the last engagement, "the bloodiest of the day." It was shortly before five o'clock when Benjamin F. Hill's brigade stalked into the cemetery full of Union soldiers. After "a few moments" of battle (Kirby Smith reported "fifteen minutes"), including hand-to-hand fighting among the tombstones, the whole Union line "broke in wild confusion and a general stampede ensued. Both officers and men became reckless of all restraint or command, and rushed pell-mell to the rear, amidst a mingled mass of horses, wagons, artillery, &c. in an utter rout." By now it was just before sunset. "For the third and last time," Churchill wrote, "the enemy fled in great confusion through the streets of Richmond as night closed upon our victorious arms." Only nightfall stopped the Confederate pursuit of the totally demoralized, absolutely beaten Union forces. At one point, the Union retreat was hampered by a large number of killed and crippled horses, entirely blocking the road from Richmond to Lexington.[27]

Nelson, infuriated by the defeat, had attempted to force his terrified men to stand and fight, "shouting at the top of his stentorian voice," according to one eyewitness. Even though he had himself received a painful wound in the hip during the first fire, he slashed and cut with his sabre at panic stricken men who only wanted to flee, "using the most profane, vulgar and abusive epithets." Nelson and his officers were left alone as the Union army, now a totally demoralized mob, deserted the battlefield. Nelson reported: "the enemy attacked in front and on both flanks simultaneously with vigor. Our troops stood about three rounds, when struck by a panic, they fled in utter disorder . . . the panic [was] at such height that it was a sheer impossibility to do anything.''[28]

The 66th Indiana Infantry seems to have been typical of Union forces in its participation in the Battle of Richmond. Arriving at the site of the morning engagement, the 66th found Manson's brigade already falling back in some disorder. Eventually the 66th formed a line of battle on the left and opened fire on the enemy in the cornfield until they exhausted their ammunition. They fought very effectively up to that point, when they were ordered to retreat toward Richmond. Some three miles to the rear they formed in line of battle in the graveyard, from which they were quickly driven. (Cruft's horse was shot in the jaw. He "dismounted when the enemy's bullets were falling thick around him and examined the wound with that coolness that belong to none but the brave." Then the general remounted and "called on the Sixty-sixth to remember Indiana.") Captain John F. Baird was ordered by Cruft to rally his men in the streets of Richmond. Baird described the ensuing events:

> The Sixty-sixth retired in order through the streets, firing as they went. The Sixty-sixth then followed the pike toward Lexington for 3 miles, the enemy shelling us in the rear. We soon discovered the enemy's cavalry directly in our front and on our right and left, supported by a heavy body of infantry. They commenced firing on us from every direction, men and horses falling. We soon discovered that we were bagged and completely surrounded and our retreat cut off. We were ordered to lay down our arms and that we would not be hurt. Then our brave Sixty-sixth surrendered and not till then.

A less restrained reporter, J.N. Rodman, captain of Company B, 66th Indiana, stated that when capture seemed imminent "the wildest confusion . . . prevailed, and each one tried to save himself . . . the whole force [was] scattered in all directions.''[29]

Throughout these engagements prisoners were being taken by the rebels. Colonel John S. Scott's brigade, which, at the time of the second battle, had been sent around Richmond by another route, lay in wait on the road to Lexington to capture the stampeding enemy. "About 4 o'clock [in the afternoon]," Scott reported, "stragglers from the battlefield commenced passing into my lines and gradually increased in number until 6 o'clock, when the main body of the enemy, apparently about 5,000 strong, with nine pieces of artillery, came upon us." After Scott's men commenced firing "the entire force [of federal troops] immediately surrendered." Scott had only 850 men in his force, so a large number of these prisoners escaped in the ensuing darkness. Manson himself and about a hundred of his men, who had passed through Richmond, were stopped by Scott's cavalry about four miles beyond the town. In attempting to drive through them, Manson's little band was cut to pieces by the Confederates: seventeen killed and twenty-five wounded. Wolfe was killed by a stray bullet while he was in the act of delivering his sword to a rebel officer; other staff were severely wounded. As Manson attempted to excape, his horse was killed and fell on him, crushing his chest. He and all his surviving men were captured. Later, Nelson was also apprehended, but he fought his way clear, ran into a cornfield, and escaped to Lexington. Only a remnant of the 55th Indiana, by fighting their way from Richmond east to the Kentucky River, reached Lexington, where the men, whose terms of enlistment had expired, turned in their guns. They returned to Indiana; no doubt they had had enough of war. Some Madison County soldiers (Union) enlisted in Captain John Taylor's company in August, 1862, were captured by Kirby Smith before they were armed or mounted. Many of these men were from southern Madison County, including Jeff Lamb, John Lakes, Howard Ogg, and David Preston, who had been a leader of the Bereans in the skirmish of Hanson's return.[30]

That evening Kirby Smith began his report on the Battle of Richmond, writing jubilantly: "It is my great pleasure to announce to you that God has thrice blessed our arms today." In another report—to Major General John P. McCown, commander of the Department of East Tennessee—Smith wrote, tersely summarizing:

> We had three fights on the 30th near this place; enemy completely routed; General Nelson wounded in the thigh; General Miller killed; 3,000 prisoners captured, including General Manson and staff, together with all their artillery, small-arms, wagons, &c.; our loss small.[31]

An adjutant in the 16th Indiana, Jim R.S. Cox, wrote a dramatic account (dated September 8) of the Battle of Richmond, which appeared in the *Indianapolis Journal*. His summary of the battle differs significantly from the military reports:

> The moving forward and sleeping on arms in readiness the night before, the picket-firing during the darkness, and when the sun rose and the gray dawn was lost in the gorgeous day, the hurrying of dark columns forward to where the cannon's blazing throats were sending shell and shot upon the foe, where the distant flashes of smoke as well as the screaming shells, crashing through trees and bursting around, told that their batteries were answering back. Crackling shots increasing to one tremendous roar, till shouted commands were scarcely heard, men falling on all sides dead and wounded, throwing up their hands, as struck, blinded with a shriek of hopeless agony, they fell. A battle where seven thousand undisciplined men fought sixteen thousand a whole day, overwhelmed, surrounded, slaughtered. Still they fought desperately for twelve miles, through woods, corn-fields, and meadows; hand to hand they met in lonely glens; like huge waves breaking on rocks came the shock of regiments. Still backward swept the tide of battle, through gardens, among trimmed yards filled with beautiful flowers, around houses,

through streets and cemeteries, places the most holy and the
most profane were alike strewn with bleeding corpses. Such
forms the dark reality of the battle of Richmond.[32]

Lucia F. Burnam, narrating her childhood impressions, recalled that
everyone in the Burnam household "ran down the walk bordered by
honeysuckle on trellises, beds of pansies, . . . columbines, moss roses and
many other flowers, to listen [to] to great *guns* in the distance." Federal
soldiers were fleeing through town, "huge army wagons drawn by four
mules, cracking of bullets." Mrs. Curtis Burnam, like her neighbors, ordered her carriage, so she and her family could also flee from Richmond.
Accompanied by the mother of Samuel F. Miller, the Burnam family, with
a slave at the reins, galloped down the pike toward Lexington.[33]

By evening, with Confederates surrounding Richmond, Fee and his
child accompanied the Union forces as they fell back to the Kentucky
River, crossing by the bridge at Clay's Ferry, and then to Lexington. "I
saw flocks of slaves escaping in the direction our army was retreating
when the retreat began," Fee wrote, "I suppose they were surrounded
by the rebel forces & delivered up. I do not think we will begin to
succeed until we begin to free the slave & obey God." By the evening of
the next day the Union army was vacating Lexington.[34]

The flight from Richmond, according to one account, beggared all
description. "Driverless teams of maddened horses hitched to heavily
laden supply wagons, running in aimless terror, spread still further
dismay and confusion in the roads that were already blocked with
fleeing throngs of panic-stricken men." The main retreat was along the
Lexington Pike; nearly 900 men took this route, reaching Lexington in
safety. About the same number fled by the Boonesborough Road from
Foxtown to Winchester and on to Paris, where they boarded trains to
Cincinnati. Hundreds of men left the roads and wandered through the
woods and fields.[35]

One of the fleeing Union soldiers wrote graphically of his experiences in the retreat:

> We were surrounded—the enemy in our rear—we were
> overwhelmed—surrounded—lost! Still from behind came
> their shots. A shell passed over my head, killing a man just
> before me. His horse leaped high in air, and the blood-spout-
> ing corpse fell to be trampled with cannon-wheels and ruth-
> less horses' hoofs. Soon we came upon the rebel cavalry
> drawn up in line, cutting off all retreat. Gen. Manson tore
> down the fence, thinking [he] could get to the enemy's rear.
> Myself with others followed. It was a ride for life. Rider-
> less horses went plunging by. Away we went through woods
> and fields, up hill and down. Catching sight of their cavalry to
> our right, we wheeled to the left, but the chase was soon
> ended. Coming through a corn-field into a ravine, a squadron

of rebel cavalry drawn up poured in a volley. All turned; my horse threw me. As I fell I heard some one scream. My foot caught in the stirrup. As my frantic horse dragged me along, a horrible death seemed before me. I wished I had fallen in the heat of battle; but my foot got loose. The rest swept by; and I was left with the rebels upon me—a prisoner. . . .[36]

Grave in the Richmond Cemetery, far left, of a soldier who died in the Battle of Richmond. Dorris Collection, EKU Townsend Room.

The memorial for the slain, left, in the Battle of Richmond. Dorris Collection, EKU Townsend Room.

In the Battle of Richmond the Confederate army, under the command of General E. Kirby Smith, lost 450 killed and wounded from his original force of 6,850 (Heth's 4,000 men had not been used in the battle); but Union forces, commanded by General William Nelson, lost 1,050 killed or wounded and 4,303 taken prisoner from their original force of 6,500. In addition, the confederates captured nine pieces of artillery, 375 wagonloads of supplies, 10,000 small arms, approximately 300,000 Minie balls, and a variety of stores of supplies. The evacuation of all Kentucky east of Louisville and south of Cincinnati was brought about at one stroke. With incredible suddenness a "neutral" state had come under Confederate rule. Lexington and Richmond, at this point, had become Confederate recruiting stations.[37]

The Battle of Richmond was a disaster for the Union cause. Major General H.G. Wright, commander of the Department of the Ohio, visited Lexington on August 31 to assess the situation. Only 800 of those federal soldiers who had fought in the battle had managed to reach safety. All the rest were "killed, captured or scattered over the country," leaving much of Kentucky defenseless against the rebels. Madison County was now, of course, a Confederate stronghold, where the local citizens were faced with the task of burying the dead and caring for the wounded.[38]

On Monday 1st day September 1862 there was no County Court held for the County of Madison the State having been invaded by the rebels, and the town of Richmond having been invested by a portion of their forces under the rebel General E. Kirby Smith after having defeated the Union forces under Gen. Wm. Nelson on the preceding Saturday in the Great battle of Richmond.[39]

Thus the clerk of Madison County recorded the event, while the court-house itself was transformed into a hospital for wounded and a jail for prisoners.

During the battle the Mt. Zion Church on Big Hill Pike, although struck by cannon fire, housed many wounded, and the Madison Female Institute in Richmond was converted into a federal hospital. In that makeshift facility one visitor saw crowds of disabled soldiers, suffering in the extreme heat, wounded "whose groans rent the air as their limbs were being amputated, and whose cries for water were pitiful to hear." Hundreds of arms and legs had to be amputated. Private homes all along the Big Hill Pike offered assistance to the wounded and dying, both Union and Confederate. General John Miller, a member of Richmond's founding family, died six days after the battle; he had been trying to rally a disordered column of Union soldiers near Mt. Zion Church when he was wounded. Forty or more soldiers were buried in one grave near the church, and eventually hundreds of bodies had to be buried at various sites near Richmond.[40]

Mt. Zion Christian Church which served as a hospital during the Battle of Richmond. Dorris Collection, EKU Townsend Room.

Farmers of Madison County loaded their wagons and brought in "huge supplies—eggs, flour, meat, meal, cream and butter" to the vari-ous improvised hospitals. Some citizens, like Thompson Burnam, Cur-

tis's father, refused to give their food to the rebels. Others fed only
rebels; while still others, James Moran, for example, "brought . . . supplies to both parties." The Burnam household carried cooked food to
the Union hospital every day. One of Curtis Burnam's daughters, Sallie
Rodes Burnam, then about fourteen, had "her soldier," a young man
from Indiana whom she provided with a meal every day.[41]

Judge J.M. Robb of Williamsport, Indiana, a private in the 71st
Indiana Regiment which was engaged in the Battle of Richmond, wrote
to French Tipton years later to state:

> . . . a great many more [soldiers] would have died from the
> same cause [wounds received in the battle] had it not been for
> the humane and generous action of the noble-hearted people
> of Richmond and Madison County, who took our sick and
> wounded boys into their houses, and nursed many of them
> back to life and health.[42]

With Confederates in power, many pronounced Union men had to
flee from their homes after the battle, "like the partridges in the mountains," John A.R. Rogers said. "Some grey-haired men in our vicinity,"
he wrote, "to keep out of the way of the rebels, left their homes and
spent their time in thickets and mountain fastnesses for weeks, sleeping
in the open air, in caves, and getting food as they could from friends."
Rogers himself, trapped in Berea, was threatened with hanging by some
former residents of Madison County who had enlisted in the rebel army,
but he managed to escape and eventually reached safety in Ohio.[43]

The Battle of Perryville (October 8, 1862) changed Kentucky again,
from a Confederate state to a Union stronghold. Later on in October
there were skirmishes near Paint Lick and Big Hill. By early November
nine Confederate soldiers were hanged in Rockcastle County in retaliation for the hanging of sixteen Union men by some pickets of General
Kirby Smith's army.[44]

Meanwhile, Fee had been separated from his wife and children for
almost ten weeks. Although he had made repeated attempts to reach
them, violence against him had made travel in Kentucky impossible. Still
another Madison County citizen had been separated from his family
during the time of battle: Curtis F. Burnam, who had left home on
August 14, for his duties in the Kentucky legislature, had not seen his
family by October 1, when he reported:

> The disastrous battle at Richmond has given up all Central
> Kentucky to the Rebels, and we have no communication with
> that region—I have word indirectly from my wife—she and
> the family are well. . . . She has been devoting [portion miss-
> ing] nursing our wounded soldiers in the hospital. She sends
> me word not to go there, *that a price is laid on my head.*
> The devils have destroyed my grain fields, burnt up my
> fences, stolen my horses and I regard myself pretty much a
> ruined man. In living I shall abhor them, and in death I shall

curse them. [On a more positive note, Curtis stated proudly], my boy Rollins was in the Richmond fight and fought like a tiger.[45]

During this legislative session, convened on September 3, driven to Louisville by the threatening Confederate advance on Frankfort, Curtis reported that the vote for Kentucky's staying in the Union and opposing the rebel invasion was carried by only four votes.[46]

Curtis Field Burnam. *In Memoriam, Curtis Field Burnam,* inside cover, EKU Townsend Room.

Shortly after writing this letter (October 1) and before the Battle of Perryville, Burnam attempted to get back to Richmond to his family. But a detachment of General John Hunt Morgan's cavalry captured him in the Phoenix Hotel in Lexington. Burnam was held as a prisoner of war because of his prominence as a leader of the Union party in Kentucky. Morgan was willing to free Burnam if he would take the oath of allegiance to the Confederacy. When Burnam refused, Morgan offered to trade his prisoner for Morgan's younger brother Calvin, and Burnam immediately went to Washington to arrange the exchange, giving his word of honor to return to Morgan's custody if his (Burnam's) mission could not be accomplished. Burnam had no difficulty, however, in arranging Calvin Morgan's release from Camp Chase.[47]

When Kirby Smith marched into Lexington on September 2, the occupied city gave him a very enthusiastic welcome, with Confederate flags displayed, bells ringing, crowds waving flags and handkerchiefs. The region received the conquering hero, the *Kentucky Statesman* reported,

with such demonstrations of delight and gratitude as astonished the gallant veteran and his glorious followers. The whole constituting one of the happiest scenes that mortal eyes ever beheld. The ladies—God bless them—poured out their whole hearts in gratitude.

"It would be impossible for me to exaggerate," Kirby Smith wrote, "the enthusiasm of the people here on the entry of our troops. They evidently regarded us as their deliverers from oppression and have continued in every way to prove to us that the heart of Kentucky is with the South in this struggle." An explosion of joy met John Hunt Morgan and his cavalry when they rode into town on the morning of September 4: "the most enthusiastic shouts, plaudits, and congratulations."[48] An article in the *Kentucky Statesman* expressed the sense of liberation many citizens of Richmond and Lexington felt after the Battle of Richmond:

> After passing many weary months under the oppressions of the ruthless military despotism of Mr. Lincoln's administration, the people of this portion of Kentucky have at last been liberated by the conquering army of heroes under the command of Major-Gen. Kirby Smith.[49]

In Richmond many Confederate sympathizers were equally enthusiastic. On August 31, in response to Kirby Smith's call for a regiment of cavalry to be recruited from Madison and surrounding counties, a movement began to form the 11th Kentucky Cavalry, C.S.A., to be part of Morgan's men. By September 10, some 800 men, mostly from Richmond and the surrounding countryside, had volunteered. (At the death of Colonel Chenault, who was killed at Green River Bridge, Kentucky, July 4, 1863, the regiment numbered 500 "effective men"—in the extant military rosters some 300 of these men are designated Richmond recruits). Among the officers were Colonel David Waller Chenault (a farmer from near Foxtown), Lieutenant Colonel Joseph T. Tucker, and Major James B. McCreary. Several of the recruits were, not surprisingly, former Vigilance Committee members (C.H. Covington, G.W. Maupin, A.H. Tribble, for example), ready at last to do battle with others of the same group who had joined Union forces. As far as Confederate Generals Bragg and Kirby Smith were concerned, the response to their call for Confederate recruits from the Kentucky Bluegrass was simply disappointing. Smith had expected 25,000 Kentucky troops to be added to his command within a few days of the Battle of Richmond, a number which certainly did not materialize. (Smith had reported optimistically, "The country is rising in arms. . . . If I am supported and can be supplied with arms 25,000 Kentucky troops in a few days would be added to my command.") Bragg and Smith agreed that "the hearts of Kentuckians may have been with the Confederacy, but their heads kept them at home with their horses," a remark that was certainly unfair to the willing rebels of Madison County who flocked into Morgan's cavalry.[50]

Basil W. Duke, John H. Morgan's brother-in-law and second in command, wrote that all the Kentuckians who joined the Confederate army at this time "wanted to ride." Not a single infantry regiment could be raised, because "if [Kentuckians] went to war at all, they thought it a too great tax upon them to make them walk." In addition, many companies and regiments already had "their men bespoken and ready to enlist with them as soon as a favorable opportunity should occur." Many had made up their minds beforehand to join Morgan when he next came through the county. Naturally, all these prospective soldiers expected to enter cavalry regiments.[51]

A reunion of Morgan's Raiders from Madison County. Courtesy David Greene.

Madison County men had begun serving as Morgan's Raiders before the Battle of Richmond. William King Maupin, for example "piloted Gen. E. Kirby Smith's army through the Kentucky mountains into Madison County." The first cannon of the Battle of Richmond was "planted on the farm of William King Maupin's uncle, George Washington Maupin, known as the Hart Land, on Hay's Fork." Like many of the men who joined later, William King Maupin was captured during Morgan's raid on Indiana and Ohio in July, 1863, and imprisoned at Camp Douglas near Chicago. Hezekiah Oldham (son of Othniel Rice Oldham) and John Miller Wallace Harris (son of Judge Christopher Harris), scions of several noted Madison County families, were also Morgan's men before the massive recruitment at Richmond on September 10, 1862. Both were wounded in a fight at Pine Mountain on September 8.[52]

Colonel David Waller Chenault had been authorized to recruit a regiment for Morgan's cavalry, and the vast majority of volunteers from Madison County joined various companies of Morgan's raiders on the same day, September 10, 1862, probably one of the most exciting days in the history of Richmond. Hundreds of local men signed up "at a sort of barbecue and picnic in a grove on the Big Hill Pike," and rode out to serve under the leadership of the magnificent, notorious John Hunt Morgan.[53]

Some of these men were quickly disillusioned, and desertions became common. Two soldiers, Tine Tillett and William Farris, deserted on the same day they signed up. William Jones deserted at Big Hill in October and John Shearer and Tilman Shanks in November, having never left Kentucky. Later, in Tennessee, many more deserted, probably dozens in all, especially near Columbia and Smithville (James and John Turner, for example), while desertions near Albany, Kentucky, at the beginning of 1863 were numerous. The men tended to disappear when their ranks moved through the mountainous regions of Kentucky and Tennessee. Such familiar Madison County names as Bronston and Broaddus appear in the ranks of deserters. Many of them simply disappeared; others sought out federal lines and took an oath of allegiance to the United States.[54]

Morgan's Madison County men, killed and wounded in battle, fell all along the lines of his marches: Pine Mountain, Springfield, Monticello, Mt. Sterling, Bacon Creek Bridge, Greasy Creek. The first time the Madison County recruits of September 10, 1862, saw action as a group was at Hartsville, Tennessee, December 7, 1862, where Chenault's regiment gave a good account of itself. There Craven Peyton, who had been one of Morgan's orderlies, was wounded and captured, dying a few days later. (One of the most important "captures" of this action, according to Duke, were boots and shoes, since the men of Chenault's regiment "had no other covering for their feet than old rags.") Thomas Baker died of camp fever in Kentucky exactly a month after his enlistment. Every month had its list of casualties: Alexander Woods (private, Company B, 11th Kentucky Cavalry) died November 13, 1862, near Knoxville; John Doyle (Company A), November 25; Joseph Hampton (Co. A), November

30. Madison County's best families continued to be represented: Colonel David Waller Chenault was himself slain at Green River Bridge, where Alex Tribble, Henry Goodloe, John and A.S. Cosby, and many others also died. Lieutenant Robert Christopher Harris Covington died March 22, 1863, of brain fever at Monticello, Kentucky, where Cabell Chenault was killed. Captain Joseph Chenault of Company B was killed May 8, 1863. Lieutenant Seth W. Maupin died as a result of a wound received at the Battle of Mt. Sterling (June, 1865).[55]

But most of the troops from Madison County accompanied Morgan on his Ohio and Indiana raids in July, 1863, only to be captured with him. In Camp Douglas during their long internment many more died. Captain Jack May was shot while in prison; Samuel Turpin died (November 26, 1864) of smallpox; John Asbill (November 25, 1864), of consumption; John ("Pap") Hill (February 18, 1864), of smallpox; Joel Watts (February 25, 1864), of pneumonia—to name only four of dozens. They perished with smallpox (raging in the camp all through 1864), dysentery, pneumonia, and consumption. Some managed to escape. Joel W. McPherson and Robert D. Miller jumped from a transport train on the way to Camp Douglas. Two of the Chenault brothers, David and Anderson, after escaping from Camp Douglas, were recaptured and tried in Louisville as spies but found not guilty. Eventually, all who survived were released, and most of them returned home to Madison county, where their terrible experiences as Morgan's raiders became part of the great romance of the Lost Cause.[56]

One of the men who had helped to recruit Confederate soldiers from his county, Thomas Bronston Collins, was captain of Company F, 7th (afterwards 11th) Kentucky Cavalry, February 10, 1862 (months before his twentieth birthday). Collins' company became one of the most popular for the rebels racing to the standards of Morgan and Colonel David Waller Chenault on September 10, 1862. Collins was wounded in the thigh at the battle of Greasy Creek; and later at the battle of Cynthiana, Kentucky, he became separated from Morgan's command, eluded the Yankees, and was imprisoned in Montreal, Canada, after the St. Alban's raid. Escaping from Canadian authorities, he went to Novia Scotia, from there to Germany, and thence to Paris, where he died in exile, April 12, 1869, while he was engaged in studying medicine. In a statement taken in Montreal on November 14, 1864, Collins said: "I owe no allegiance to the so-called United States, but am a foreigner, and a public enemy to the Yankee government." Yankees, he said, had "stolen negroes and forced them into their armies, leaving their women and children to starve and die. They have pillaged and burned private dwellings, banks, villages and depopulated whole districts, boasting of their inhuman acts as deeds of heroism. . . ."[57]

The war made many exiles, and Madison County was never home again for many of the men who left it in September, 1862. For those who did return, their experiences had left an indelible impression which years of peace would never eradicate. They would become chief among those people who determined to fight the Civil War for decades after it was officially over.

The bloodiest battle ever fought on Kentucky soil, at Perryville, October 8, 1862, resulted in the defeat of the Confederates, who virtually abandoned the state, after failing in their aim of arousing Kentuckians to support the South. The Confederacy made no further major attempt to invade the state, but conditions in Kentucky and in Madison County remained dangerous. On February 20, 1863, Colonel Roy S. Cluke's regiment of Morgan's cavalry captured some federal troops at Mt. Vernon in Rockcastle County and fought another skirmish ten miles south of Richmond, with twenty-four Union soldiers being captured. On February 21 the same troops pursued a force of 250 Federals from Richmond to Lexington, "skirmishing briskly at Comb's Ferry."[58]

It was probably this pursuit which Lucia F. Burnam described in her childhood recollections:

> Another vivid memory is of soldiers fleeing at breakneck speed down the street pursued by other soldiers, of the crack of bullets, and seeing a man fall from his horse directly in front of the Peter Smith gate by the telegraph post. . . . The saddle of the dead soldier fell off with him . . . Later, the man was laid on the grass under the aspen trees in the Stone Avenue and we children were taken to see him.[59]

The author's younger brother, Robert, then no more than four years old, rushed across the street and got the saddle as soon as the dead man was moved, and the Burnam brothers used it for years thereafter.

"You must realize," Miss Burnam cautions,

> that Richmond was a little village and that as soon as this skirmish occurred, it was over in a few moments and everything was once more quiet, with only a little boy flying across the street for *loot* and a group of children taken by their nurse to see a *dead* man lying on the grass under the trees—this man was a *Union* soldier."[60]

In July, 1863, a small action was fought at Richmond (on the twenty-eighth), and martial law was imposed on Kentucky, which had the effect of quashing the prosouthern faction. Eventually, orders were given for confiscation of "rebel" property and the requirement of a "loyalty" oath was instituted. In the fall of 1863, Lincoln called on states not in rebellion for troops; if sufficient volunteers were not forthcoming a draft would be instituted. Eventually, federal authorities announced that able-bodied Negroes might be enlisted to substitute for white draftees, white substitutes of proper age being very difficult to find. In Madison County the black population was indignant, although numbers of slaves were sent to the Union army in substitution. Those who had been forced into service helped bring about a change in the attitude of Negroes toward joining the Union army. Very soon, blacks would be enlisting for themselves, not as substitutes, and the Union army would profit from the service of thousands of Kentucky slaves.[61]

During this period (1863 and early 1864), numbers of blacks were leaving Madison County. Some, like three former slaves of Matthew Johnson, were claiming certificates for the freedom they had received twenty years earlier; many others were seeking freedom certificates for their children born out of slavery—all promising to leave the state. All seventeen of the slaves emancipated by the will of Durrett White (murdered in 1861) were freed in February, 1864, upon their expression of willingness to be removed from Kentucky. At the same time runaways from other places were appearing in Madison County in unusual numbers. Those who were caught were jailed and, if unclaimed by their owners, sold at public auction. One such fugitive, Henry, runaway slave of James Williams, was sold for $265 after a period in the Richmond jail.[62]

Fee was visiting in Berea again by December, 1863, finding there more friends than at any previous time. He was able, he said, to visit thousands with freedom. He requested Bibles for slaves at work on the roads and boxes of tracts for the local citizens and soldiers. He wrote, "The people are very destitute—both armies have passed through here again & again—many will suffer this coming winter—provisions are very high & very scarce."[63]

In February, 1864, Fee convened an "immediate emancipation" meeting at Berea, where he delivered two lectures. The audience, large and orderly, provided a "bountiful basket-dinner" and elected six delegates to attend the Border-State Emancipation Convention at Louisville (February 22). Some slaveholders were present, but "past dissensions and persecutions were forgotten," at least according to the too-hopeful Fee. Later, Fee preached at a camp of soldiers six miles away from Berea. He was so well-received, both at home and at the camp, that he became convinced the door in central Kentucky was wide open again.[64]

In March, 1864, Fee was preparing to return to Berea. The school there was reopened, with Matilda Fee and Fee's son Burritt in charge, on April 28, 1864, although Fee also taught one class himself. "Nothing but an experience where there has been the desolution [sic] of war and that carelessness which slavery & war engender," Fee wrote, "could enable you to comprehend the difficulties. House, garden, well, fencing, stables everything to repair." Rebel raids were still expected; Fee was afraid to import female teachers from abroad to take a subscription school because of the uncertainty of the war. Asked why he had returned to Berea, Fee answered it was because of the principles and policies that had been enunciated there. "The immediate locality," he said, "is poor in soil but rich in moral principles."[65]

Along the road near Berea, which led through the Cumberland Gap, passed the fighters and the victims of the war—soldiers and guerilla bands, and "flocks of women and children in most destitute condition on their way to some other part of the state or to free states." But the school at Berea was started, and people there had regular preaching from Fee again. In addition, he continued to address soldiers in their camps. In spite of the war, or perhaps because of it, Fee's work in Berea prospered. Congregations were increasing, as were the number of students at the school. "There are some good men in Jackson county," Fee reported, "who now purpose to purchase lots and go to Berea."[66]

On May 25, 1864, an "Unconditional Union" State Convention was held at Louisville, with Richmond lawyer Curtis F. Burnam addressing the delegates, unanimous in their desire for the reelection of Lincoln. Such unanimity was not apparent in Richmond itself, where one respected citizen, Colonel James M. Shackelford, a strong Union man, shot and dangerously wounded another, Squire Turner, then aged seventy-two, whose sympathies lay with the rebels. While white men fought among themselves, more and more black men simply fled.[67]

The slaves, Fee wrote on June 4, were leaving Madison County "without let or hindrance," although slaves were still being sold in the Lexington slave market as late as the summer of 1864. The experience of Madison County citizen William Malcolm Miller may have been fairly typical. Only one of his thirty slaves (Moses) remained with him till freedom, the rest having left their master, "a number of them enlisted in Federal service." On June 6, 1864, Fee reported from Richmond, where he had been talking to black men anxious to enlist if they could have freedom and pay. "Hundreds of these colored men know me," Fee wrote, "& would have confidence in what I would say to them." Unlike most of his fellow Kentuckians, Fee was encouraged by the sight of black men in uniform, and he urged them to seek liberty through military service. With the increasing enlistment of slaves in the Union army, Fee dedicated almost all his time to working with black soldiers and contrabands at Camp Nelson in nearby Jessamine County. This work virtually replaced Fee's Berea mission for a while, delaying his official return to Madison County.[68]

In January, 1865, the citizens of Madison County fell under the 'hog order" of General S.G. Burbridge, which required them to sell "all the hogs" in the county to a government-appointed agent. Some 60,000 hogs from eleven counties were sold at an average loss to the farmer of $5 per head. This swindle by military authorities—and possibly private individuals as well—caused great indignation throughout the state, and did nothing to increase Kentucky's loyalty to the Union.[69]

On March 3, 1865, Congress passed the Freedmen's Bureau Bill, legislation which would prove, for years to come, disastrous to Kentucky's relationship with the federal government. The institution of slavery remained legal in Kentucky, the Emancipation Proclamation not being applicable to "loyal" states; Kentucky had not ratified the Thirteenth Amendment nor repealed her own slave code. Madison County's taxable property list for January, 1865, still itemized slaves, while the estate of one John Todd had a record of division of slaves as late as October 2, 1865. By January, 1866, the tax list, for the first time, showed no slaves. Since Kentucky refused to grant freed men and women their rights, the Freedmen's Bureau, created for secessionist states, was extended into Kentucky as well—to massive protest. While most Madison Countians were hostile to the operations of the bureau (French Tipton's papers contain dozens of instances of protests and complaints against the bureau), one group were to find this aspect of Reconstruction very helpful—the returning Bereans almost immediately and very successfully claimed the support and protection of the new federal agency.[70]

In April, 1865, a few days after Lee's surrender at Appomatox, Rogers visited Berea, where the prudential Committee planned to open the school within the year; a school building was to be built and the town laid out. Reporting this visit, Rogers wrote as if the war had never happened:

> The church [at Berea] is receiving new life and is hopeful. The Trustees of the Lit. Inst. at Berea, have arranged to erect a desirable building for the growing wants of the school. A town planned before the rebellion has been more fully laid out, machinery is being introduced, and new desires are being enkindled in the minds of the people. With God's blessing it will not be many years before mighty streams of influence for good will go forth from Berea in every direction. The seed sown will yet bear fruit an hundred fold.[71]

A Note Concerning Civil War Soldiers in Madison County

A large proportion of Confederate soldiers from Madison County belong to those families which owned the most slaves (at least fifteen in 1860). Indeed, some of these families were represented in the rebel forces by numbers of individual soldiers: Joseph, Waller, Cabell, David, and Anderson Chenault; Archibald, Joel W., Caldwell C., Joseph, Robert, Seth, Sidney, George W. and William King, and Calvin Maupin (a list including George W. Maupin and *five* of his sons); Othniel, James F., Charles K., Joseph, Richard, Presley, Abner, James, William, Hezekiah, and Thomas Oldham; Squire, William T., Robert, and James Tevis. Almost all the foregoing were in Morgan's raiders. Among Union troops, the one Madison County family which provided the most soldiers was the Gabbards, at least six of whom served, four of them in the 8th Kentucky Infantry.

Madison County may have provided many more white soldiers for the Confederate army than for the Union. When the war was almost over (December 31, 1864), the county had supplied 539 soldiers for the federal army, but some 800 men (not *all* from Madison County, but probably more than half) had enrolled in the 11th Cavalry, C.S.A., alone—after the Battle of Richmond. In 1890 the veterans who had served as Morgan's raiders were by far the most numerous of those mentioned (inadvertently) on the census of Union soldiers: out of 55 Confederate veterans listed, 28 were former raiders. Madison County's Confederate soldiers tended to be from richer, more prominent families (with some notable exceptions, like the Clays, Millers, Burnams, and

Capertons among Union men). So many well-known men of the county were Confederate soldiers any listing would be pointless. James B. McCreary (later governor of Kentucky), Squire Turner, David Waller Chenault, Nathan Deatherage and George W. Maupin might serve as examples. Confederate veterans in 1890 were most numerous, presumably, in Richmond, although the census lists only one for the whole town; those listed in outlying areas were most numerous in Union City (10), Red House (8), Waco (8), and White Hall (7).

Union soldiers from Madison served in many different regiments: 1st Kentucky Cavalry, 6th Kentucky Cavalry (Reuben Munday headed the 1st Battalion of this regiment, which was organized in Lexington), 7th Kentucky Cavalry (under Colonel John K. Faulkner of Madison County), 8th Kentucky Infantry, 11th Kentucky Cavalry, 14th Kentucky Cavalry, 21st Kentucky Infantry, 47th Kentucky Infantry, and many others, none of which were manned solely by Madison Countians. In some instances, whole neighborhoods appear to have enlisted together. In 1890, twenty-two veterans living in the neighborhood of Perkins all listed the 1st Kentucky, and twenty of them had been in Company K together, many enlisting on the same day.

Of the veterans living in Madison County in 1890, the largest number (thirty-two) had served in the 1st Kentucky Cavalry, the vast majority of them having enlisted in the first few months of the war. The 8th Kentucky Infantry was the regiment of thirty-one veterans in 1890 (four of them Gabbards associated with Berea); the 14th Kentucky Cavalry had thirteen veterans (seven of them from Waco); the 7th Kentucky Cavalry, twelve; the 47th Kentucky Infantry, eleven men, mostly from the neighborhood of Jackson County. Company D of the 21st Kentucky Infantry consisted of fifty-eight Madison County men. But Madison County Union veterans altogether represented almost all the Kentucky regiments.

Madison County men had been officers primarily in the 1st Cavalry and the 8th Infantry. Among officers in the 1st Kentucky Cavalry were William A. Coffee, major; Boston Dillion, captain; F.W. Dillion, captain; William T. Ballard, 2nd lieutenant; J.F.N. Hill, first lieutenant; Thomas Rowland, captain and major; Philip Roberts, captain; and N.B. Burrus, captain. In the 8th Infantry officers included Green B. Broaddus, major; Thompson Burnam, quartermaster; J.M. Kindred, chaplain and quartermaster; G.W. Lewis, second lieutenant; and Bart S. Dixon, captain. Some officers who were not necessarily commanding Madison County men in significant numbers were Green Clay, a major in the 3rd Cavalry; George T. Shackelford, colonel in the 6th Infantry; C.J. Walker, a colonel in the 10th; Cassius M. Clay, major general; and Reuben Munday, lieutenant colonel.

In the 1890 Census of Union Soldiers (also listing Confederate veterans), the men, most of whom had been Madison County citizens before and after the war, gave their regiments and dates of enlistment (at least, those who *remembered* did so): a sampling of some 365 Union veterans in Madison County (probably more than half of the total men who served in the Union army from Madison County) and 55 Confederate veterans. In 1861, the first year of the war, 114 of the veterans had enlisted, by far the largest number for any given year: 12 of them had been Confederates, 102 Federals. In 1862, 73 had enlisted: 41 Union and 32 Confederates, most of whom enrolled in Morgan's cavalry shortly after the Battle of Richmond. In 1863 only 21 had enlisted, with no Confederates among them. In 1864 no Confederates are listed, but 61 Union soldiers, 10 white and 51 black, most of the latter enlisting in June, 1864. In 1865 there were 19 enlistments: all Union, 6 white and 13 black. The county's waning enthusiasm for service in the Union army is amply illustrated by a comparison of two figures: by July 28, 1863, the county had supplied 477 Union soldiers, while by December 31, 1864, more than a year later only 62 men had been added to that number.

The 1890 census suggests that all the neighborhoods of Madison county contributed soldiers: the largest number from Richmond (ninety-five), followed by Berea (forty-six, three Confederate, forty-three Union), Perkins (forty-one, none of them Confederates), Waco (thirty-eight), and Speedwell (thirty-one). Other neighborhoods included Harris, Combs, Terrill, Silver Creek, Edenton, Red House, White Hall, Ford, Million, Union City, Doylesville, College Hill, Wallaceton, White's Station, Kingston, Big Hill, and Yates Precinct. In 1890, veterans from both armies were living in close proximity in virtually all the regions of the county, even Berea having some citizens who had been rebels. Most neighborhoods contained both white and black veterans of the Union army and veterans of the Confederate army as well. Union veterans (black and white) were most numerous in Richmond (ninety-four), Berea (forty-three), and the Perkins neighborhood (forty-one, with no Confederates).

The men in Madison County in 1860 who might have been eligible to be soldiers (between the ages of fifteen and forty) numbered 2,231 whites, 1,114 blacks (16 of whom were free). Approximately 600 white men became Union soldiers; about 800 may have been rebels. No iron-clad estimate of black soldiers can be made, as they enlisted to serve in various regiments, including many outside Kentucky. If approximately *half* the eligible blacks from Madison County actually served, their number would be about 500. Madison County may have supplied 1,900 soldiers in all—out of slightly over 3,000 adult men.

Of the Union veterans living in Madison County in 1890, seventy-six were black; their surnames, most of which are common Madison County family names, indicate that they had probably been slaves in the county before the war. The most common regiment for these soldiers was the 114th U.S.C.T. (United States Colored Troops) with twenty-eight men (eight of whom lived in Richmond in 1890; ten of whom gave Speedwell as their mailing address). Ironically, the names in this regiment could be mistaken for a roster from Morgan's cavalry, including Maupin, Collins, Chenault, Shackelford, Phelps, Broaddus, Embry, Miller, Ellis, Dillingham, Munday, and Parkes. Clearly the 114th enrolled slaves of some of Madison County's largest slaveholders. The commonest period of enlistment for these black veterans had been from May to July, 1864, but a few (nine) were enrolled before 1864, probably among those who were forced to substitute for white draftees. Eleven veterans were members of the 119th; nine of the 122nd. Heavy artillery units accounted for the service of twelve black soldiers. These Union veterans were most numerous in 1890 in the Richmond neighborhood, where twenty-five were living, and in Speedwell, where seventeen resided. Eight veterans lived near White Hall, while five gave Berea as their address.

The Madison County white families which supplied the most soldiers to Confederate forces also supplied many former slaves to the Union army—at least four black soldiers from Madison County were named Chenault (maybe ten, since at least that many Chenaults fought on the Union side and all whose regiments are known were black), three Maupin, and one Tevis.

Sources: French Tipton Papers 1: 206-07, 210B-E; 9: 211 ff.; Chenault & Dorris, *Old Cane Springs*, 199; Copeland, "Where Were . . .?" 34463; Captain Thomas Speed, *The Union Regiments of Kentucky* (Louisville, 1897), 22 167; *Military History of Kentucky*, 198; *Eleventh Census of the United States, 1890*, "Schedules Enumerating Union Veterans and Widows of Union Veterans of the Civil War: Kentucky, Bundles 56 and 57, Microfilm—FM123, Roll 3 (Washington, 1948); see *Kentucky Documents 1863-1864*, no. 26, 11-15, for numbers of Union soldiers from individual counties.

Regiments Which Fought in the Battle of Richmond

Regiments of the Confederate army commanded by General E. Kirby Smith in the Battle of Richmond were mostly from Tennessee and Arkansas. The infantry included 4th Arkansas Regiment; 4th Arkansas Battalion; 13th Arkansas; 15th Arkansas; 1st Arkansas Mounted Riflemen; 2nd Arkansas Mounted Riflemen; 2nd Tennessee; 5th Tennessee; 12th Tennessee; 13th Tennessee; 47th Tennessee; 48th Tennessee; 154th Tennessee, and a company of sharpshooters. The cavalry regiments were 1st Louisiana, 1st Georgia, 3rd Tennessee. Artillery comprised the Texas Battery, Douglas' Battery, and Martin's Battery.

Federal troops in the Battle of Richmond included soldiers from Indiana, Michigan, Ohio, and Tennessee, as well as Kentucky. Infantry regiments from Indiana were the 12th, 16th, 55th, 66th, 69th, and 71st. From Ohio came the 95th Infantry; from Tennessee one battalion of the 3rd Infantry. Michigan supplied Batteries "F" and "G" of the 1st Light Artillery. The four regiments from Kentucky were the 6th and 7th Cavalries and the 3rd and 18th Infantries.

Only one of the Indiana regiments had been in existence as long as two weeks. The men of the 12th had been mustered in August 17 at Indianapolis; the 16th two days later in the same place; the 66th on the same day in New Albany; 69th on the same in Richmond, Indiana; the

71st on the 13th in Terre Haute. The 55th Indiana had been organized (for a period of three months) on June 6, 1862, but the men of this regiment had spent most of their time guarding prisoners at Camp Morton, Indiana, although they had participated in some operations against Morgan's raiders in July.

The men of 95th Ohio, like those of the Indiana regiments, had been mustered in August, 1862 (on the nineteenth at Camp Chase in Columbus, Ohio).

The Michigan batteries had been organized for a few months (both since January of 1862; Battery F from Detroit and Coldwater, and Battery G from Kalamazoo).

The battalion of Tennessee's 3rd Infantry had actually been organized from December 1861 to February 1862, earlier than any of the other non-Kentucky regiments. It had been formed at Flat Lick, Kentucky, and the men had seen action at Somerset, London, and Big Hill, where they had fought well, before the Battle of Richmond.

The four Kentucky regiments which fought at Richmond were the most experienced ones among Union troops, but they were not totally seasoned either. The 6th Cavalry was organized in central Kentucky from July to October, 1862, but Reuben Munday's 1st Battalion Cavalry, organized earlier, was assigned to the 6th as Companies A, B, C, D, and E. The 7th Kentucky Cavalry was organized at large and mustered in at Paris on August 16, 1862; but before the muster it had participated in operations against Morgan, July 4-28, 1862, and a week afterwards it became one of the disgraced regiments at the Battle of Big Hill. The 3rd Kentucky Infantry, organized at Camp Dick Robinson on October 8, 1861, had been in existence longer than any other Union regiment in the Battle of Richmond, while the 18th Kentucky had been formed on February 8, 1862.

Virtually all of the following regiments were captured at the Battle of Richmond (some regiments were apparently captured to the last man, while others were "mostly" captured): all the Indiana regiments, the 95th Ohio, and the 18th Kentucky. The Indiana regiments were all paroled and sent—in most cases—to Indianapolis. The 16th Indiana and 95th Ohio were exchanged in November, 1862. The guns of Battery F of Michigan's 1st Light Artillery were captured in Richmond. The 3rd Tennessee, 3rd Kentucky Infantry, and 6th and 7th Kentucky Cavalry were not captured, it seems, in significant numbers.

The Battle of Richmond was primarily fought between Tennesseans and Arkansans on one side and Hoosiers on the other. Madison County provided the setting but few of the actors in the drama of August 30, 1862.

Sources: A.C Quisenberry, "The Battle of Richmond, September, 1862," xeroxed pamphlet in Townsend Room, Crabbe Library, EKU; Frederick H. Dyer, *A Compendium of the War of the Rebellion* (1909; rpt. Dayton, Ohio, 1978), I, 731, 1122, 1125, 1140, 1143-45, 1192, 1193, 1198, 1205, 1277, 1278, 1538, 1644.

Chapter Eleven
POSTWAR RECONSTRUCTION

When the War between the States ended, vast social changes had altered the village of Berea, the town of Richmond, the county of Madison, the state of Kentucky and the whole nation. But one thing had not changed: the most dedicated workers of pre-Civil War Berea—Rogers, Fee, and Hanson. A teacher, a preacher, and a lumberman determined to resume their work in Madison County.

On November 30, 1865, Rogers and all his family arrived at Berea to take up residence again, almost six years after they had been driven out. John G. Hanson, also one of the first settlers to return, rebuilt his sawmill, with the help of his younger brothers, Arthur J. and Samuel, who visited Berea in February, 1866, and decided to join him in his work. "This mill," Rogers remarked, "and the money brought by students and newcomers added to the wealth of that part of the county and interest in the growing school." The lumber mill immediately began supplying building material for new homes for colonists and new buildings for the college, the first of which were constructed in the summer of 1866.[1]

By January 6, 1866, Fee himself was settled permanently in Berea for the first time in many years; and Berea Literary Institute, under the supervision of the college board of trustees, reopened in the same month, with Rogers as principal and Willard W. Wheeler, an Oberlin graduate, and Eliza Snedaker as assistant teachers. Fee had procured the services of Wheeler, his fellow worker from Camp Nelson, as district teacher for the term, with the understanding that the next session of the school would provide "impartial education"—for black students as well as white. Wheeler agreed to Fee's proposal, and his wife Ellen P. T.

Wheeler also assented. In addition to his district school teaching Wheeler undertook to tutor some black students in preparation for their entrance to Berea later on, while Mrs. Wheeler taught a small class of primary students in their home, only eight or nine children, but all black—probably the first organized teaching of free Negroes in Madison County. Thus, before Berea College reopened, its purpose was clear: the school was to be integrated. The idea for such an institution had been formed years earlier, but in 1865 Fee's first positive action as a trustee was taken to insure that the college he was founding be anticaste.[2]

Some other educators in the South of this period—Lyman Abbott, for example—considered attempting to bring blacks and poor whites into schools together. When Abbott asked Clinton Fisk, Freedmen's Bureau commissioner for Kentucky and Tennessee, about the possibility, Fisk replied "that it could not be done," because both classes opposed it. Separate schools under the same organization might work but "he knew of no successful experiment in mixing the races." "In practice, white children, with few exceptions, refused to attend institutions run by northern societies. They were determined not to associate with blacks in this way, they disliked the idea of charity schools, and they hated "Yankee Schoolmarms." Fisk's pronouncements on the impossibility of an interracial school were issued in April, 1866, only a month after Berea's educational experiment began to contradict his conventional wisdom.[3]

Negro and white students at Berea, 1887. Berea College Archives.

In the spring of 1866 Berea College (or Literary Institution, as it was then known) produced a promotional leaflet asking for donations. The

school was "open to *all* of good moral character." Thus Berea's proclamation appeared before the "benevolent" world—the new school
would be for black and white, for female and male, for the poor instead
of the rich. The principles of Berea, by the time this advertisement
appeared, had been dramatically expressed in action.

On March 6, 1866—a red-letter day in Madison County's history—
the school at Berea became interracial in practice. Rogers wrote in his
journal, "Four colored children entered the school. Eighteen of the
students left. There was no little excitement. Twenty-five remained. The
Lord was with us to bless and cheer." Fee's report of the incident to the
American Missionary Association: "Yesterday the colored children
entered our school here—quite a number of white children left, more
than half. . . . This is our time of trial." Willard W. Wheeler reported on
the incident to the board of trustees (March 31,1866) and later described
(November 22, 1866) consequences of the events in March. In his report
he stated that twenty-seven members of the school had "unceremoni-
ously and in a very disrespectful manner left the school." But their
absence had been compensated by the addition of eighteen black students within the month. According to his November summary, after the
walkout, the district trustees refused the use of their house to the
Bereans for a while, even though they had known beforehand about the
admission of black children. About two-thirds of the white students left,
Wheeler said, and "most [people] prophesied another mob and the total
annihilation of the school." The faculty and students went on and had
an exhibition at the end of term anyway.[4]

Although no contemporary account mentions the names of the
black students whose attendance made Berea an interracial school, it is
still possible to determine who they were. Ellen P. (Topping) Wheeler
recalled the students, who had been part of her earlier class of blacks in
1865: "Two of the 'three,' " she wrote, "were Mr. Miller's children and I
think the 3rd *was* a Dudley." Willard W. Wheeler's class lists for 1866-
67 confirm his wife's identification.[5]

The Miller girls, young children in 1866, were three in number.
Rogers' journal, which states that four black students came to school on
March 6, may have been accurate. Margaret Ann, Sarah, and Viney Miller
were almost certainly all daughters of Madison Miller and his wife Mary,
early black settlers.[6]

The Dudley girl was named Laura Belle, a daughter of Oliver and
Esther Dudley, settlers in Berea by 1866. Laura was between eight and
ten years old when she entered Berea—she spent 10 years as a Berea
student. Her father, Oliver Dudley, is mentioned in Roger's account
book by June, 1866. In 1867, Rogers noted several payments to Dudley
for grubbing and credited some of his labor toward tuition for Dudley's
children, six of whom attended Berea. Oliver Dudley bought land on
Brushy Fork from John G. Hanson.[7]

One of Dudley's children, Napoleon Bonaparte ("Bony"), student
from 1870-86, attracted the attention of an American Missionary Association district superintendent, Reverend G. D. Pike, when he visited

Berea in 1870. According to Pike's report, Napoleon's father had been murdered by the Ku Klux Klan. Pike does not give the date of this crime—it can be fixed only between September, 1867, when Dudley paid tuition, and sometime in 1870, when Pike conducted his Berea interviews.[8]

On April 12, 1866, the Prudential Committee meeting reconstituted the Berea board of trustees with new members, who then incorporated the college. One of the new trustees, a friend of Fee's from Camp Nelson, was former slave and former soldier Reverend Gabriel Burdett, the first black to serve on Berea's board and surely one of the first Negroes—if not the first—to hold such a position in the South.

Financially, Berea's second term as an integrated school was altogether hopeful, with supporters from the North and East pledging funds. The teaching staff still consisted only of Rogers, Wheeler, and Snedaker. Several black children were added to the ranks of the students early in the second term, which began with a total enrollment of seventy. White students and the surrounding community had evidently accepted the presence of black children in the Primary Department.[9]

But when black soldiers began to arrive, controversy was briefly renewed. In late April or early May, 1866, the first of these soldiers, Angus Augustus Burleigh, age eighteen, a mulatto, entered the school as a grammar school student, still in uniform. He had been a sergeant in Company G 12th U. S. Colored Artillery (Heavy), mustered in at Camp Nelson August 22, 1864. There Fee had found him and invited him to become a student at Berea. When he arrived he was the first black adult to enroll in the institution; he was to become one of the first black men to be graduated from Berea College—class of 1875.[10] Burleigh recalled his first day of school: "There was a holding of breath and look of surprise around the room when I went in." Wheeler reported "another exodus of white students" after Burleigh's entrance.[11]

The school was first located near the old district schoolhouse, where a couple of "neat cottages" were constructed for increasing numbers of students. What is now the main campus, some half mile distant from the district building, was being cleared. Students, mostly blacks, were hired to cut down underbrush and superfluous trees and grub out stumps. This was "no small task," Rogers remarks, "but was gradually accomplished in the course of two or three years." The work was done by students who were enabled in this way to pay part of their school expenses. "The Hanson's saw and planing mills gave employment for many persons, and mechanics were needed for the new buildings, both of the college and the citizens."[12] Many temporary buildings were thrown together in haste, dormitories and a rude chapel, "very rough and barn-like," which also served as school rooms with swinging partitions.

In the fall of 1867 the Prudential Committee concerned itself with purchasing land, planning buildings, buying livestock, a clock, etc. On

September 28, 1867, the Prudential Committee voted to sell bricks from the college brickworks to the citizens of Berea and to ask Cassius M. Clay to give the Glade tract to Berea College.[13] In October and November the Committee hired carpenters (John Irvine and Mathias J. Gabbard) and dealt with John G. Hanson as supplier of lumber. On October 31 the committee ordered a carpenter shop built, and on the first of November they turned their attention to the rock quarry.

After a respite from town and college building in 1868, the ferment of activity continued in 1869. On July 2 a committee was appointed to make a topographical report of the grounds of Berea College in reference to laying off the town, and on November 16, 1869 the committee voted that Prospect Street should run from a marked tree, a black oak with a hickory pointer in front, northeast "along the ridge." They decided the street should be seventy-five feet wide.

In 1870 the board met late in June (28 through 30) and decided to name one of the new dormitories Howard Hall. The board then voted that the new Ladies' Hall (present Fairchild Hall) should be located near Wheeler's house, provided the land could be purchased from Teman Thompson. The board ended its transactions of 1870 by affirming

> that the Prud. Com. be recommended to offer one half of unappropriated land lying off the main avenue beyond the second cross streets, on such terms and such sized lots as shall be best calculated to secure the actual settlement among us of families who desire to patronize the College.

The board was in control, during this era, of a college growing by leaps and bounds and of a small town which was likewise burgeoning. Berea's board was, in effect, the city council as well, deciding questions of zoning (who was allowed to live where), pricing land, laying out streets. In addition, for better or worse, virtually all the resident trustees were also officers in the only church in town—Union (once Fee's Glade Church), the official college and colony church. Everyone who came to Berea to teach joined it; for many years almost all students joined it, and almost all townspeople, who for many years were either workers at Berea College or were related to students or both.

Berea at this time was a place of great excitement. An enormous social upheaval was taking place. Rogers described a movement that was to transform Berea for decades to come: "The coming of black people to Berea," Rogers wrote,

> for a time was phenomenal. Black Valley, a mile away from the college, swarmed with them . . . Berea was the land of promise, and to reach it, with all they had on their backs, or at best in a rickety old cart, was the fulfillment of their hopes.[14]

Mountain people were also settling in Berea. In August, 1866, Fee traveled to Jackson County and found that it was fully prepared because of George Candee's ministry there. "Now there is a generation of men & women," Fee wrote,

> educated to the principles of justice & mercy of righteous-
> ness, who now stand firm against the tendencies of conserva-
> tism & Rebelism.
>   Four heads of families . . . with large families are arrang-
> ing to move to Berea—more than that number of single young
> white men—of much promise, are ready to come soon as our
> term of school that opens.[15]

Fee announced that his Jackson County tour was to be followed up by a trip to Camp Nelson to recruit blacks, and he detailed the school's plans for use of the Avery fund (some $10,000) to buy several hundred acres, "then sell out every other lot to good men—thus enhance the value of the remaining lots in which we propose to erect houses with proceeds of previous sales, thus secure population & patronage & enhanced value of the capital invested."[16]

"The third term of the school is now in session,"Fee wrote,

> about half the school are colored. The issue of educating the
> two classes together has been fairly met and the people of the
> community have made up their minds. A majority of the
> white voters decided to give us trustees who were in favor of
> our using the district house for our mixed school, until we
> could erect buildings of our own. . . . Threats have been
> made against us. This also has intimidated many. This very
> malice in men is giving the place quite an advertisement.

Still the school and the community continued to grow. "We have access now to large congregations of these colored people in this and adjoining counties," Fee wrote, "The congregations of white people in Jackson co. are very encouraging. There is an open door here that no man can shut."[17]

Regional students from the immediate vicinity of Berea included some who had been Rogers' students before the exile. But most of those people did not return as students because they had grown up in the meantime—many of them were married and raising families of their own by the time Berea reopened. The students who came from Jackson County were very numerous. In most cases, whole families moved from Jackson County to settle near the new school (Gabbards, Van Winkles, Coyles, Durhams, Lakes, Bakers, Powells, Gays, and many others). At Fee's urging, Elisha Harrison with his wife and ten children moved to Berea from Jackson County in 1865, and he owned land in Berea by 1866.[18]

Some Rockcastle County families, notably the Brannamans and the Roberts, became "regulars" at Berea, a few moving north to settle in Berea. Morgan Burdett bought land in Madison County in 1860, in what is now Berea, and was living in Berea with his large family by 1866, when he became a college trustee. (One of his sons, Josiah, became trustee at his father's retirement, and when Berea was incorporated in 1890, he was elected first chairman of the Village Board.) An Estill County family (from Station Camp), the Richardsons, settled in Berea in the fall of 1865.[19]

Some Ohio families, like the Robes, settled permanently in Berea and intermarried with families of the region (Burdetts and Van Winkles). Others, such as Dr. Samuel John Mills Marshall, trustee and first resident physician at Berea, maintained family connections with Oberlin throughout their Berea sojourn.[20]

But the black migration to Berea was most striking. Many families came from Camp Nelson—it is impossible now to determine how many. Fee invited numbers of black families and individual black soldiers to the Berea settlement, and many accepted his invitation. The Ballards and Walkers, for example, originally Madison County slave families, were taken to Camp Nelson and returned to settle near Berea. Sampson [Simpson] Gentry (father of many Berea black students), a native of Madison County, born the slave of Richard Gentry near Richmond, served in the Union army (Company K 13 U.S. Colored Artillery [Heavy]) and was hospitalized for eight weeks at Camp Nelson; when his army service ended he moved to Big Hill, and then in 1872 to Berea. Like Gentry, Alexander Miller and Anderson White were members of Company K 13 U.S. Colored Artillery (Heavy) and were certainly stationed at Camp Nelson. Many of the fathers of the black families settling in Berea had been soldiers: Horace Yates, Gordon Glascoe, Henry Adams, Alexander Chenault, Larkin Farris, John Moss, Stephen Willis, and others. Virtually all of them may be assumed to have formed their connection with Berea by meeting Fee at Camp Nelson.[21]

Fee wanted to expend money directly on black young men and women, keeping them constantly in school until they were fitted for positions as teachers. Desiring to keep tuition and board low as an inducement, Fee suggested using the income from the endowment in direct aid to blacks. As a matter of fact, Berea's black students were encouraged to teach while they were themselves attending school (much as Oberlin students had been a few years earlier). So some blacks from Berea, along with a few black students from Oberlin, taught in freedmen's schools in Kentucky during this early period (1866-70). Angus Burleigh, for example, conducted a school in Garrard County in 1869; John H. Jackson instructed a class in Madison County in 1868, and Cornelius C. Vaughan taught a day school and a night school for his people in Cynthiana in 1869 and in Richmond in 1870. Another Berea student, Belle Mitchell, taught in the Howard School for colored students in Richmond from February to April, 1867.[22]

Some of Berea's black citizens, former slaves who arrived in town virtually destitute, became prosperous enough to write wills. Ned Blythe, for example, made specific bequests to his many children, as did Anderson Crawford and others—from slaves to men of property in a few short years.[23]

Probably most of Berea's black citizens had been slaves in Madison County. The fifty prominent slaveholding families represented on the committee which drove the Bereans into exile may have owned many of them. Of the fifty surnames of committee members, thirty-seven were borne by black students at Berea from 1866 to 1904. In the census of 1870, the first to list freed slaves, Madison County black families (not the Bereans) frequently bore the same names as Berea's black settlers. In fact, many black founders belonged to families with the commonest surnames for blacks in the county (Chenault, Ballard, Gentry, White, Blythe, for example).

In one instance, which may represent similar cases, a wealthy and prominent white Madison County planter sent several of his mulatto children, offspring of his slave mistress, to study at Berea College. He came to support the institution in the postwar years because it gave him a place to educate his own children. (Since I have this story in confidence, but on very good authority, his name must remain undisclosed.)

From the beginning a great many of Berea's "black" students were mulattoes and quadroons. At one commencement an observer noted that of the fifteen student speakers, eight were white and seven colored, "though to determine this other than ocular proof was necessary, for almost if not quite the fairest of them all was born a slave." When James H. Fairchild visited the Berea commencement exercises in 1868, he reported, "It required a keener discrimination than mine, notwithstanding my long experience, to divide [the students] properly [according to race]." We can only speculate about the white families of most of these people, but there is a great deal of evidence that many blacks of Madison County, including those who attended Berea, were descendants of very distinguished white families.[24]

Perhaps representative of blacks in Madison County, Burnams who had been slaves abounded in the county after the Civil War around Berea and in Richmond. Of the Burnams who attended Berea, most had been possessions of Curtis F. Burnam. Curtis advanced money to Jackson Burnam (black) to buy land on Silver Creek after the war. Jackson was the son of Solomon ("Sol") and Dolly Burnam of Richmond, who had at least one child in attendance at Berea when they themselves were quite elderly (Solomon was born in 1794, Dolly in 1809); their son Frank, born in 1851, was in Berea's Primary Department by 1870-71.[25]

Several of the children of Jackson Burnam and his wife Nancy were early students: Alexander (1867-71), Mary (in 1868), and Maria Burnam. The latter studied in the Ladies' Department, 1866-67, but soon married Joel Elder, born the slave of another well-known local family. Their marriage bond, executed March 21, 1867, was witnessed by W. W. Wheeler, William H. Robe, and J. D. Roberts, with Elijah Best acting as bondsman. The actual ceremony on March 23 was performed by John Rogers in the presence of witnesses, Elzy McCollum and William N. Embree—both white and black citizens attended this event. This marriage is only one of many which illustrate the social equality practiced at public events in Berea. The Burnams of Berea were part of the community and school there for many years.[26]

By 1900 more black Burnams lived in and near Berea than in Richmond. Those in Richmond were all illiterate by that date, and only one of them, Narsis, owned her own home. Their occupations were the usual ones in their hometown: cook, laundress, hotel waiter, for example. Those black Burnams who had moved to Berea were not all literate (many of them were), but most of them lived on farms they owned themselves, and only one was listed as a servant. In Richmond, Troy Burnam (formerly Curtis F. Burnam's slave) was shot to death (May 27, 1877) by the marshall of Richmond while resisting arrest.[27]

In 1860, Curtis F. Burnam had owned eleven slaves, five of whom were mulatto, and several more were born into his possession in the war years—a group of blacks which he valued at $20,000 by the time they were freed. Before these slaves were emancipated one of them, a lively young man named Manch, disappeared on the day of the Battle of Richmond. Of those that remained, all departed with the coming of freedom, although two, Louis and Martha, stayed at Burnamwood for about a year after they were free. (Both were living in Richmond in 1870; Louis was a common laborer with four children who were probably born in slavery, while Martha had one daughter who was an infant when emancipation came). Another of Curtis's slaves, Jackson, chose to buy a farm, and his former master, as we have seen, helped him to do so. Another Burnam slave, Ann, returned to Missouri, where she had been born. Curtis Burnam's slaves chose the various options open to Madison County's freed men and women: life much as usual in Richmond, a new beginning in a new county or state, or a chance for learning and autonomy at Berea. As late as 1955 some Madison county blacks lived in a segregated village called Burnamtown, a little ghetto.[28]

One of the most prevalent solutions to the social problems involving freed blacks in Madison County was a simple, legal expedient, which restored former slaves to slavery under another name. As soon as the institution of slavery was over, the citizens of Richmond and its environs began apprenticing young blacks in great numbers. Apprenticing—until age twenty-one for males, until age eighteen for females—was not unknown in Madison County; both whites and blacks had been employed as bond servants since the settlement of Kentucky, but not as they were from 1866 on. Beginning in the latter part of 1866, until late in the 1870s, all black orphans became bond servants, whereas apprenticeship of whites became almost nonexistent (white orphans were given court-appointed guardians; black ones received masters). In most instances, these black apprentices were already "in the possession of" the white men who became their apprentice-masters, some of whom were designated former owners. Most of the former slaves were bound "to learn the arts & Mysteries of farming" or "the art & Mystery of Housekeeping." Frequently the black "orphan" was accompanied by his mother or father, or indeed both parents, who consented to the apprenticeship. Many were as young as ten—over a decade of bondage would be involved in a male child's life if he were apprenticed at that age. One mother, Patsy Turner, protested the binding out of her fifteen year-old son and her daughter. The daughter was not bound, but the boy's father prevailed in apprenticing young Jordan Turner. The mother "finally consented upon condition that said Jordan be taught to read and write instead of paying him $100 at the end of his apprenticeship." Dozens of indentures appear in Madison County court order books from 1866 to 1870. The apprentice system and tenant farming would soon restore something like the status quo for Madison County's proslavery element.[29]

In Berea something quite different was happening. Fee's scheme for interracial education required, from the beginning, a total social context—the relationship of school to church and community was integral to his conception of a practical recognition of equality. During the 60s and 70s, social events like weddings in Berea were attended by both races. The student body, board of trustees, and faculty were integrated. The first black person to give instruction at Berea, perhaps the first person of black descent to teach white students in Kentucky, was Julia A. Britton, teacher of instrumental music 1870-72. A musical child prodigy, Julia Britton began playing the piano in public performances at the age of five; she supplied music for several Berea commencements. Born May 4, 1852, in Frankfort, Kentucky, Julia was only eighteen years old when she began teaching at Berea, only twenty when she left the school (she was a junior in college herself at the time), but her work at Berea was an historical landmark for the county and for the entire state. By 1872 Berea College's board of trustees had passed a rule permitting interracial dating on campus and making it permissible for students of different races to contract engagements to marry.[30]

It was never enough, in Fee's view, to teach equality without having the means to practice it; and he would have considered it pointless to speak of a person possessing a right, if that right could not be enjoyed. Even though his plans began at a very specific, local level, he envisioned a school which would contribute to "national well being" by its active demonstration of principles. Berea was designed as a sign for the entire United States.

Part of the reason for Berea's early success—and those forty years of actual interracial education must be construed a success—sprang directly from one of Fee's most daring and effective ideas. He had determined that Berea would be the place where black people could own property of their own. He did not wish to promote a system of racially segregated ownership, however, but insisted on a kind of "interspersion," with blacks and whites being interspersed about the countryside and in the town. In the 1860s and 70s Fee's "interspersion" policy became successful in action.[31]

Fee's ideas about the new project, ideas clarified and strengthened by his experiences of two unique racial situations (Berea and Camp Nelson) were both humane and practical. "They [the blacks]," he wrote, "to [attain?] highest development must not remain a nation of boot blacks or mere stevedores. They must become owners of land and producers of valuable commodities. Then they will be esteemed in their own eyes and in the eyes of others."

"[Unfortunately]" Fee wrote,

> most white men here [in Kentucky] who have two to four hundred acres will not sell a scrap to a "nigger."
>
> But friends of the colored man will & then so arrange sale of lots as to have them in community so as to have for them schools & churches.
>
> Someone may say "let the colored man alone—let him find his own way"—why not then dispense with educational efforts for him. I do not propose to feed him but put an axe & land within his reach & let him work out his salvation—help him to a home.[32]

Fee's proposal, while it received no particular attention in the country at large, was fully enacted in Berea. The flood of black settlers arrived in part because land *was* available to them in Berea, farms and town lots, with many white neighbors sworn to help them.

Berea's early achievements were made in the face of much external hostility. The activities of the Ku Klux Klan in Madison County during the period 1866-70 seem to have been extensive. With a characteristic minimizing touch, Rogers reported "The Ku Klux Klan or the coarse jeers of drunken, hostile men and the careless firing of their pistols through the streets and the whizzing of bullets sometimes dangerously near did not often produce any permanent fear." Actually, the Bereans came to believe that their opponents were afraid of them, fearful of doing them harm, holding them in "superstitious regard." Fee's enemies had a disconcerting way of dying violently and the Berea abolitionists seemed always to reappear stronger than ever.[33]

Edward Henry Fairchild, Berea's first president, wrote that the Ku Klux Klan never paid Berea a visit. But he also described a number of violent incidents, usually involving murder, in the neighborhood of Berea—evidently Fairchild was defining Berea as a small village on the ridge when he said it had not been visited. In any case, the Klan's activities must have been a source of fear and anxiety for the Berera community for years. "Many rumors of their hostile intentions reached us," Fairchild wrote, "and rumors that our College buildings and some of our private houses had been burned, spread through the country; but, from what we knew of their operations near us, we did not apprehend any disturbance from them." If Fairchild's account stopped there, one might assume an incredible lack of concern among Bereans, but he continued, "For a year or two, about 1870 and later, the country was completely under their control. There was no protection for anybody against whom their violence was directed." (Incidentally, William N. Embree's college store and his house, which was nearby, both burned to

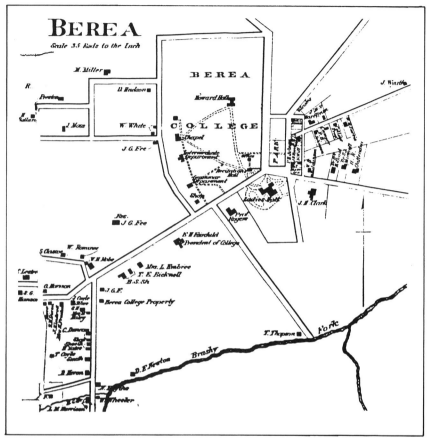

Berea in 1876. A. G. Beers map of Madison County, EKU Archives.

the ground the night of May 21, 1871, the same night Ladies' Hall also caught fire but was saved by the students. Strangely, Embree's store was apparently located more than a city block away from the hall. Deliberate arson? The contemporary accounts say no.)[34]

Some Bereans took necessary precautions for self-defense. George Candee recalled that when William Robe and Josiah Burdett were building Candee's house on Center Street the Ku Klux Klan was threatening, so the carperters were "armed with revolvers as well as saws and hammers."[35]

"In Ku Klux times" (apparently 1871), Willard W. Wheeler, in Lexington on Berea College business, dined with a black family and, after leaving a prayer meeting at a Negro church, was ambushed by five men who shot at him seven times and left him for dead. The would-be murderers had missed, however. Wheeler, "returned to his hotel where at 3 A. M. 30 masked men dragged him from his bed, took him to the woods and gave him 61 lashes with a hickory whip.'' Rogers, a particular friend of Wheeler's, later wrote:

> His back was so lacerated that he carried the scarred ridges to the day of his death. His faithful wife, who was with him, tried to follow him, but before she could dress, the lawless mob had got her husband way far in the darkness. Her sufferings as she thought they might be hanging her husband were greater than his. Mr. Wheeler's conduct during this scourging and his replies to the cowards who were threatening his life were worthy of the martyrs of early days.[36]

Elizabeth Rogers, writing of the threats to Berea, conveyed more sense of danger than do the men, so determined to be brave. "Perhaps we were in greater danger after the war than before, " she said. "The school had opened its doors to the colored people and we were threatened constantly by Ku-Klux bands, or in danger from the reckless shooting of half-drunken southerners who rode up and down our streets at all hours.'' Her son Raphael, recalling the days of his youth, wrote:

> For four years (1867-71) the lives of Mr. Fee and my Father were in more or less danger. On several occassions [sic] to prevent the school buildings being fired armed pickets patrolled around them all night. For years when my Father was away at night my mother had us all sleep on the first floor on cots rather than in our bedrooms upstairs so that if the house were fired in the night we could be gotten out quickly. The anxiety was more intense at times than at others, but it was there for years. I have heard the bullets sing into our yard to strike the trees several times fired by drunken men at the house.

These dangers were incurred simply because of the school's anticaste principle for which Fee and Rogers were willing, Raphael wrote, "to imperil a great school, and their own lives & the lives of their families. . .'' In Raphael Rogers' eyes—from his early teenage years, and then forever after—his father and Fee were "heroes defending at all risks a noble, righteous principle." The perils of attending Berea College may have given an incalculable depth to the education of Berea students in the early years. Raphael Rogers wrote, "Some things were burned into my soul from the age of ten to fourteen which I am not likely to forget. . .''[37]

Education for blacks, whether integrated or not, was met with determined and violent opposition in Kentucky and throughout the South in the late 1860s. Reverend Abisha Scofield was mobbed and driven out of Camp Nelson, where he superintended a black school. In March, 1868 John Rogers reported, "A house near Kirksville (a town in Madison County quite near Berea) which the colored people rented for school purposes and where they intended starting a school, was a few days ago burned." Some teachers at Freedmen's Bureau schools were 'insulted, threatened, ostracized, and even flogged or forcibly exiled,''

during this period. Schools which involved white teachers and black
students were most violently opposed. "Of the 165 teachers (of blacks)
remaining in Kentucky in August 1868, only twenty-one were white and
they were located in towns where they might be protected. The report
of the Kentucky Superintendent of Education for 1868 contains a two
page enumeration of outrages, threats, beatings and burnings." On January 1, 1869, John Watson Alvord reported to the Freedmen's Bureau,
saying ". . . old prejudices remain, equility of rights is, more or less,
resisted and the education of the freedmen, throughout most of the
southern states receives as yet too little practical encouragement."[38]

The Ku Klux Klan was active in central Kentucky throughout this
period. Blacks living in Kentucky convened in Frankfort in 1871, having
drawn up a list of 116 outrages by organized bands in Kentucky from
November, 1867, to February, 1871.[39]

The "first mention" of the Ku Klux Klan in Richmond, according to
French Tipton, was on April 1, 1868. Later in the same year (November
1) the Klan appeared in town and hanged a man on Tate's Creek. Exactly
a year later, the Klan struck again. This time a black man awaiting his
trial for murder, Frank Searcy, was taken from the jail one Sunday night
and "hanged [from a] locust limb" in front of the courthouse; the victim
had a card pinned to his back reading, "This man must not be taken
down until 7 o'clock Monday evening." In December, 1869, two black
men were taken from the jail, one seriously whipped, the other taken to
a point beyond Foxtown and hanged. On January 5, 1870, Jim Sims was
hanged in White's Hill; the corpse bore the characteristic note of instruction: "not to be took down until 9 o'clock P. M. KKK." Later, in January
of 1870, another victim, identified as a rebel and a Klansman, was
hanged on "Searcy's limb" in the courthouse yard by a counterband.
This man had a ten dollar bill pinned to him "for funeral expenses. Let
him be buried as soon as possible," the note directed.[40]

By 1870 Berea College possessed property valued at $45,000,
employed eleven teachers to teach 250 pupils, with boarding accommo-
dations for 100. Fee's church at Berea had a membership of 151, with
232 attending Sunday school.[41]

Berea's achievement from 1866 to 1870, which must be measured
in more than numbers, should be seen in its context of the opposition,
prejudice, and violence of that time—in Kentucky and the entire southern United States. Perhaps the total effect of organized lawlessness in
and around Berea was more positive than negative, however, making
the Berea community more closely knit than it would otherwise have
been.[42]

Another factor binding the Bereans together was their united oppos-
tion to alcohol. Rogers had founded a temperance society in Berea in
May, 1859, which had disappeared during the exile, but it was inevitably
revived as Berea began anew. One of the favorite reforms of this period,
of course, was temperance. All Oberlinites promoted it, and Fee had
carried antirum sentiments with him everywhere, founding temperance

unions himself in Lewis and Bracken counties. In addition, the neighbor-hood had a history of temperance, having organized the Glade temper-ance Society as early as 1840. Berea's newly organized temperance society had its preliminary meeting in January, 1867—a committee consisting of William N. Embree and W. W. Wheeler was appointed to draw up a constitution, and temporary officers were elected. In June, spurred on by news that J. P. Moody was attempting to get a liquor license to open a tavern near Johnson's Shop, Berea's temperance organ-ization went into action, electing John G. Fee president and selecting three vice-presidents (W. E. Lincoln, Burritt Fee, and Morgan Burdett), with Josiah Burdett, treasurer, and W. W. Wheeler, secretary. (Inciden-tally, Moody was granted a tavern permit but denied a liquor license.)[43]

By October 10, 1867, the new reforming group was in full swing—by that time some fifty persons had taken the pledge "not to use intoxicating liquors as a beverage nor to trafic [sic] in them, nor to provide them as an article or entertainment, nor for persons in our employ and to discontinue their use in all suitable ways." Administra-tors, faculty, trustees, students and townspeople, old and young, white and black, male and female were represented among the signers: an integrated crosssection of Berea. In 1867, Richmond also saw the organ-ization of a temperance society; one need hardly add, it was not inte-grated.[44]

Some citizens were so determined to keep Berea "dry" that they inserted liquor clauses into their deed agreements, specifying that the real estate would revert to the seller if alcoholic beverages were ever bought or sold within its boundaries. It may be that some property in and near Berea still lies under this legal stricture. At any rate, the town of Berea and all the southern portion of Madison County have been dry territory from the late 1860s to the present day—something of an accomplishment, no doubt, in the state where bourbon and bluegrass, moonshine and mountains are so intimately linked.[45]

In 1868 Fee reported that Berea Literary Institution had over 300 students, almost two-thirds of them black. "The School," he wrote, "is harmonious in an eminent degree." All who attended, he said, knew that they must conform to the anticaste rule or leave. "We seek to make this a matter of Christian *privilege* rather than a legal duty," Fee explained. "We teach that when Christ Jesus took upon him human nature, he dignified the nature of every man." That year every room at the Berea school was full, and many were "so desirous . . . for knowledge that they [were] willing to crawl up into low attics and there endure cold and privation."[46]

In a report for 1869 Colonel Benjamin P. Runkle, assistant commis-sioner of the Freedmen's Bureau for Kentcuky, described Berea College for General Oliver Otis Howard, chief commissioner for the Freedmen's Bureau—this "outside" view of Berea provides crucial insights into the institution as it existed then. To Berea, Runkle said, come "the sons and daughters upon whom the curse of slavery weighed more heavily than on any other class, the White Mountaineers of Kentucky." For this class, he maintained, neither the state and national governments, nor the benevolent societies of the United States had made provision. He also thought Berea would "be of great importance to the colored people of Kentucky," although that seems to have been a lesser concern to him.[47] At Berea the commissioner saw "managers" who were "honest and trustworthy," who believed in God and loved their fellow men. "I never saw men working under such difficulties," he wrote, "and I never saw men with such faith. . . ."

Runkle had attended a gathering of students in the chapel which he called "one of the most singular sights I ever witnessed . . . all shades and colors, all ages and conditions and all intent on one object, to escape from the bonds of ignorance." Accomodations for the scholars were crowded and uncomfortable; students lived "in little rooms or dens, called attics." They were poor, "living upon nearly nothing, and working between time to pay for it." Runkle had observed "two bright, intelligent white boys," waiting on a table where both white and black students were seated. "And this they did cheerfully," he exclaimed, "for six cents an hour in order to get money to pay their board." He had heard one of the same white students read Latin and had found the young man "had opinions of his own." Runkle had seen "white girls sitting in the same class with black ones." It seemed to him that "it must have cost these young people a terrible struggle to come to this." He interviewed three black men, former soldiers, who had been at Berea for two years, and "intended to remain there six more."

He met Elizabeth Rogers and found her "a lady . . . fit to adorn any place in society." There she was: "living by no means surrounded by luxury, far out in that wild, mountain country, taking care of her family, providing for her boarders (for everybody [in Berea] takes in boarders) and teaching a number of these poor people besides." He was evidently struck with wonder: 'I have not seen many such people."

In fact, he said he had never seen anything like Berea before and never expected to see anything like it again. He concluded by advising General Howard to give Berea all the money the institution needed.

On March 30, 1870, upon the announcement of the adoption of the Fifteenth Amendment guaranteeing their right to vote, Negroes in Richmond celebrated by firing of cannon on Burnam's Hill.[48]

In August, 1866, white and black citizens had voted together in Madison County for the first time. Madison County, like Kentucky as a whole, went overwhelmingly Democratic. There was much disorder; it was rumored that as many as twenty men were killed in the state on election day, and Madison County had its own disorders, although no deaths resulted on that particular day. At Hickory Corner, for example, where the Bereans did their voting, "a band of forty men (supposed to be Ku Klux) armed with shotguns, paraded around the voting place all day, supposedly to frighten colored and white abolitionists away from the polls." After most of the Bereans had departed, one of the few who remained was surrounded by the mob, threatening him with shotguns, clubs, and bowie knives. The man was saved by young Josiah Burdett, who leaped into the middle of the angry band, and distracted them until their proposed victim escaped. George Candee, a witness to this scene, later called Josiah Burdett's action, "the most heroic deed [he] ever witnessed."[49]

At an earlier election Richmond witnessed a much more violent encounter in the courthouse itself on January 15, 1866, during the second balloting in a contested election between A. J. Mershon, Democrat, and George Ballew, Sr., Republican. One group consisted of C. K. Doty, Boyle Doty, Azariah ("Az") Doty, Archibald ("Arch") Kavanaugh, Humphrey ("Humph") Kavanaugh, and Warren Harris; the other, of Henry and Ed Parrish, Amos Worlds, John Shifflet, and John Jones. The Kavanaugh party had been in the Confederate army; the Parrish party in the Union army. It was the first time Humphrey Kavanaugh and Henry Parrish had met since the war. A "deadly encounter" followed upon their greeting, with both men shot and seriously wounded. Immediately, indiscriminate firing followed, and "the court room filled with smoke." Seventy-five or a hundred shots were fired. "Arch Kavanaugh, wounded and stretched on the floor, rolled over and over until he reached the prostrate form of Henry Parrish in whose head he buried the hammer of his pistol, after which Parrish died. Worlds and Harris engaged, with Worlds being killed. C. K. Doty shot Ed Parrish, who fell. Stepping over him, Doty then shot John Jones, who also fell.[50]

Ed Parrish got up and killed Azariah Doty and wounded Arch Kavanaugh. Arch Maupin was killed accidentally by Azariah Doty. C. K. Doty shot Ed Parrish a second time outside the house. Humphrey Kavanaugh was taken to the house of James Shaw, east of town on the Irvine Pike. There, a week later, he was killed by a shot through a window at night.

A year or so later, Ed Parrish was killed in Garrard County by Ebenezer ("Neze") Best, the trouble stemming from the earlier courthouse fight. The encounter in the courthouse may have had roots in the past, as well as repercussions in the future. Both the Dotys and the Kavanaughs believed that the courthouse "trouble" had been instigated by William Haley, Green Haley, and Frank Bland. Humphrey Kavanaugh had been one of the Vigilance Committee which drove the Haleys and the Blands, supporters of Fee's Berea, out of Madison in 1860. Apparently the exile from Berea was not simply over and forgotten when the exiles returned.

When Green Haley's family removed to Illinois, one of the Parrish women went with them; she later made a deathbed confession to the murder of Humphrey Kavanaugh. Green Haley and his son were killed while committing a burglary, and his wife returned to Madison County with news of the Parrish woman's confession.

Throughout the Reconstruction period, election disturbances continued, as Kentucky was in continual political upheaval during those years. Berea, during this era, is scarcely mentioned in Richmond newspapers, except in references like the two following. The first instance is a political cartoon (after a Democratic victory at the polls) published August 7, 1874, in the *Kentucky Register*. The crude drawing depicts a black hobo, his clothes in a bundle tied on the end of a stick, walking barefooted under the caption "The colored Radical orator on his way back to Berea after the Election! He proved to be the Democrats' Best Card!"; the other (on July 30, 1875) briefly dismisses a speech by John G. Fee under the headline, *Ad nauseum*. In 1875, Cassius Clay reported two deaths in Madison County—one white man, one black—in connection with the election. He and his kin routinely armed themselves to go to the polls, and, at one point, he marched "the blacks from [his] camp in columns of two with all the arms [he] could obtain from them and all [he] had in [his] rockaway." He guided his men through "an open field which reached the polls . . . so that they could not be easily jostled and their ranks broken." This martial spirit was not confined to Cassius Clay. Many prominent citizens approached public life in the postwar years as if warfare had never ceased.[51]

"No county in Kentucky, and perhaps not one in the United States . . . is so productive of crime and casualties as Madison," wrote native-born French Tipton, analyzing his home county for the *New York Herald* on December 16, 1878. He was writing at the end of a two-year period of incredible violence. The end of Reconstruction in Kentucky came to a climax with a great surge of murder in Madison County. In two years forty-two people were killed, forty-three wounded. The calendar of violence through 1877-78 is staggering. Fist fights, knifings, and actual duels on the streets of Richmond seemed routine. A small selection of the crimes listed for one year follows. Toward the end of January, 1877, "unknown men went to the house of a Negro, Henry Royston, near . . . College Hill, shot him in the shoulder, maltreated his wife and children, robbed him of $250 . . . and burned his house."[52]

On February 6, "near the town of Berea, at a party at Pal Coats' house," three Harrises on one side, two Farises and Tom Lackey on the other, "engaged in a desperate and indiscriminate shooting." Shots were fired by all; "Rote" Harris was killed; William Harris and George Faris were wounded. The parties were all acquitted. On February 9, Sam R. Parks shot at Bland Ballard but missed. On the night of February 10, Jordan Turner, at a party in Richmond, was stabbed "in a general row." Everyone involved in this melee was black; three arrests were made. On the night of February 24, at a party given by a black man in Richmond, Dave Briscoe shot and killed Arch Rodes.

On March 13, on Tate's Creek at Stringtown, "the noted Billy Patterson" and Joel Hill grappled hand to hand, cut one another's throats from ear to ear "at the first dash," but fought on "for near a minute, and their faces, heads (ears, noses), arms, breasts, sides and abdomens were fearfully gashed." Both finally recovered. On March 15, Seth Maupin, at the town of Kingston, severely cut John O. Sullivan, an East Tennesseean.

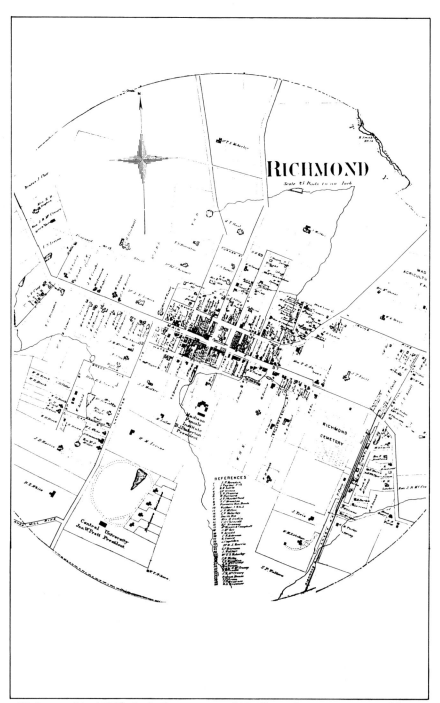

Richmond in 1876. A. G. Beers map of Madison County, EKU Archives.

On April 16, near the village of Waco, one 16-year-old boy shot and killed another about the same age. On May 27, A. J. Edwards, Richmond's marshall, attempting to arrest Troy Burnam, former slave of Curtis F. Burnam, shot and killed him. On July 2, at Kingston George Moody shot and killed Thomas M. Stivers. On August 27, Walter Saunders and J. T. Ballard were killed and others wounded in the Garnett house in Richmond in "general firing," with twenty or possibly thirty shots fired.

On September 20, 1877, "Richmond was the scene of the most deadly fight" since the Kavanaugh-Doty incident. John Burnam and Jasper Maupin, "both desperate men," came to town, each "backed up by a number of friends," to attend their trial for an earlier difficulty between them. Everyone expected violence, but the whole day passed without an altercation.

> All was about to end quietly, when Burnam, accompanied by Kit Ballard and W. A. Cornelison was going to Turley's Stable to get their horses, came upon Maupin standing where his friends had gotten on their horses to go home. Without a word Burnam drew his pistol and almost simultaneously Maupin's was drawn, both fired, and the Maupin party followed in rapid succession, firing deadly shots, and even dismounting and shooting men after they had fallen. . . . The scene was one of terror. Soon the officers came . . . and found Maupin, Burnam, Ballard and Cornelison dead on the street. . . .No indictments followed this incident.[53]

Even this brief selection from Tipton's list of incidents becomes horrifying in its repetition. The complete account presents the same kinds of crimes over and over. Every level of society in Madison County is represented, from the "best" families to the "trashiest," both black and white, including crimes of blacks against blacks, whites against blacks, and the other way around, scarcely a week going by without its incident. Public shooting sprees involving large groups of people were quite common, suicides prevalent, cold-blooded revenge a matter of course. Many men, especially those from prominent and influential families, surrounded themselves with armed bands which accompanied them in every public appearance—so Humphrey Kavanaugh, Henry Parrish, John Burnam, and Jasper Maupin were all backed up by their own small "armies." The enmities of the war extended far into the postwar period, and some of the skirmishes of the 1870s far exceeded in bloodshed the pre-Civil War encounters. Even some of the incidents which have entered Kentucky history books as skirmishes in the Civil War did not result in as many deaths as the worst Reconstruction battles.

Madison County's troubles were so well publicized Curtis F. Burnam expected that his brother-in-law, James S. Rollins, in faraway Missouri, would have read about them. "This county," Burnam wrote, "as you no doubt have seen from the papers, has been of late the theatre of much crime, a homicidal mania seeming to have broken loose. There are eight or nine murderers in our jail who ought to be hung or imprisoned for life." With the court docket backed up, and suspects awaiting trial,

> a most determined spirit prevails that these [indecipherable] must cease, even if the deadly remedy of appeal to Lynch justice has to be invoked. The idea of a proud historic old County filled with many people of the highest culture, civilization and wealth, to say nothing of Christian virtue, should be disgraced by the barbarism of those who have never yet learned that Civil War has ended, is absolutely unendurable. They blacken our fame—they shame us all. Still we must not be judged by them. They are but clouds on the surface of the sky. Behind them stretches the serene and everlasting heavens.[54]

Chapter Twelve
PROGRESS AND CONFLICT, 1850-1900

In the half century from 1850 to 1900 Madison County progressed, at least in most of the ways progress is ordinarily measured: general increase in population and prosperity, technological advances, diversification of religion and education. The number of choices available to Madison Countians grew enormously in the period, with a variety of new options in such institutions as banks, schools, and churches.

The total population of Madison County grew from 15,727 in 1850 to 25,607 in 1900, with an increase of approximately 2,000 people each decade. Throughout the period blacks numbered about one-third of the total population. Richmond's growth rate was far greater than that of the county as a whole: 411 people in 1850, more than twice as many (845) a decade later, more than ten times as many (5,073) by 1890. The proportion of blacks and whites in Richmond also differed greatly from the county at large. In 1860 almost half (400) of Richmond's population was black: 12 of these Afro-Americans were free. In 1890 the proportion remained the same with 2,638 white to 2,432 black. Berea, Madison's next largest population center, remained very small throughout this era, with a population in the village of 580 in 1880. In 1898 Berea, by that time an incorporated town, possessed a population of only 771 (567 white, 204 black).[1]

Foreign-born people remained very rare in Madison County from 1850 to 1900; in 1850 only 886 people in the county had been born out of state, 51 in foreign countries. In 1890 the foreign-born numbered 189 for the whole county, 90 of whom lived in Richmond. Madison County was no one's idea of a cosmopolitan region. In the 1860 census, in which the census taker frequently recorded the *county* of birth for each individual, it is clear that most Madison Countians were born in Madison County.[2]

Throughout this fifty-year period new centers of population or business, all rural and tiny, sprang up in Madison County. Newly named villages and newly established post offices proliferated in the 1880s and 1890s especially. In 1883, for example, post offices were established at Red House, Terrill, Wallaceton, and Shearer; in 1885, at White's Station. Million Station, Valley View, and Newby were named in 1890 and a new post office was opened at Baldwin. The most important change in the map, however, was the incorporation of Berea as a town on April 3, 1890.[3]

McKinley Day in Valley View, November 7, 1896. Courtesy David Greene.

On May 9, 1890, "in the office of the Treasurer of Berea College" (an indication of the college's continued "ownership" of the town) five city trustees were elected, including Josiah Burdett, member of the board of trustees of Berea College, chairman. A. W. Titus, a black citizen, made Berea's first board interracial, and James S. Hathaway, a black faculty member at the college, served as town clerk (elected May 6, 1893). The board remained interracial at least until the turn of the century.[4]

Berea was not much of a town in 1890, or even a decade later. One of the first actions of the board was to appoint committees on (1) streets and sidewalks, (2) stock and sanitation, and (3) law and order. The only one of these items that Berea actually possessed in any quantity was stock. After June 10, the council ruled, "all hogs shall be taken off the streets," and they imposed a fine of fifty cents for every pig still on the loose. The council was looking into the fine points of hog control for years, adopting a new hog law on April 4, 1898. "Shooting promisculy [sic] about the streets" was also an activity apt to be fined in 1890, while galloping "horse, mule or ass" in Berea became illegal in 1896. By 1898 the pace of life in Berea had slowed even more, with fines for bicycle speeding and regulations forbidding playing marbles or rolling hoops in the streets.[5]

Main Street of Berea before 1900. Berea College Archives.

Main Street of Richmond before 1900. EKU Archives.

Richmond continued to change and expand during this fifty-year period. The new courthouse (commissioned by April 3, 1848; William Rodes, Joseph Turner, and J. W. Shackelford were appointed as the building committee on January 7, 1850) was completed by November 1852, at a cost of $34,462. The markethouse was removed from the public square by order of the County Court, after the trustees of the town "peremptorily" refused to tear it down to make room for the new jail. A motion to allow room in the courthouse for the Library Company was dismissed (February 3, 1851), although Masons and Sons of Temperance had free rooms in the structure for years on end. By 1855 the courthouse was surrounded by a wooden fence. The new jail, by 1857, had several outbuildings, including an icehouse built from materials of the old jail, a privy, and a smokehouse. In 1866 Richmond's area was increased by the Estill addition, and the limits of Richmond were extended to three-fourths of a mile in 1868 with the Ellis addition. The first three-story business structure built in the county was Gormley's in Richmond in 1871. Richmond expanded again with the Crow addition in 1887, and extended her limits to one mile from the courthouse in 1890 with the Dillingham addition.[6]

Richmond suffered the consequences of its size, with the common trials of the nineteenth century city—fires and epidemics. Richmond's large fires occurred in 1854, 1871, 1874, 1884, 1887, 1891, and 1892. Many of these were great disasters; the one in 1854 (February 6) burned eighteen houses, a whole square of Richmond on Main Street between Second and Third. The fire of 1871 was nearly as bad, destroying almost a square of buildings, including two hotels, the post office, and several "fine stores," at a total loss of $150,000. The third great fire (1874) raged along Main, First and Irvine streets. The fire of 1884 was so extensive that "country people for miles perceived Richmond was burning." For a while it seemed that Richmond might be totally destroyed: a young man named Dick McKee fended off firemen, who needed to raze his shack adjoining the Second Presbyterian Church. If McKee's shack ignited, the church and next to it the mammoth livery stable full of hay and the McKee coal office would quickly follow. Brutus J. Clay galloped up in best heroic fashion, seized McKee, threw him out of the way, grabbed an axe and destroyed the "tinder box" shack, thus saving Richmond. The fifth great fire destroyed Richmond's opera houses. Four years later (1891) Hotel Glyndon burned.[7]

Cholera ranged the county in 1852. In February, 1864 smallpox was "prevailing in the town of Richmond" and a petition was presented praying the County Court to establish "a pest house or hospital for the reception of those afflicted with said disease." In October and November of 1872, fourteen people died of smallpox in Richmond. The smallpox epidemic in Richmond in 1898 frightened Bereans so much that they quarantined their town against Richmond, guarding all approaches to the town and meeting all trains to turn away travelers from the county seat.[8]

The typical head of household in Madison County through this entire fifty-year span was not a town dweller, however, but a farmer. Agriculture had remained the biggest business in Madison County from the very beginning—at times it was virtually the only business. The number of farms increased from 1,185 in 1850 to 2,741 in 1900, but that is no indication that farms were growing smaller, since the number of acres improved also increased from 149,164 in 1850 to 229,185 in 1900, with cash value of farms (with improvements and implements) growing from $4,785,130 to $8,998,560.[9]

Madison County was almost literally "a land flowing with milk and honey." It produced 28,393 pounds of bee's wax and honey in 1850, even more in 1860. Madison County was second only to Bourbon County in the production of cattle in 1870 (with 14,970 head) and produced 13,811 gallons of milk in 1880, and 179,694 pounds of butter and 4,796 pounds of cheese (ranking second in the state in cheese production). In 1899 the county produced 578,000 dozen eggs (only three Kentucky counties produced more) and was fifth in number of beehives. Virtually every major crop in the county shows an increase in production from 1850 to 1900. And Madison County was among the top seven counties of the state in cattle-, hog-, and corn-production in 1870 (second in cattle, outranked only by Bourbon). In 1879 some 1800 hogs were shipped from Madison County in special trains. Local accounts of Madison County abound with stories of extraordinary numbers of live-stock sold and gargantuan crops produced.[10]

Some farm production did not grow steadily in this period, how-ever. Horses, for example, were much more numerous in 1860 (9,454) than in 1870 (6,957), a drop in equine population which may reflect the fact that every mounted soldier in the Civil War also endangered the life of a horse. The number of mules and asses also decreased in that decade; so did hogs, sheep, and "working oxen." In addition, production of corn, oats, and wheat was all substantially lower in 1870 than a decade earlier. Too many factors (weather, land fertility, economic conditions) enter into farm production for us to conclude that the war "caused" this decline. But it does seem rather likely that war-torn Madison had a hard time recovering. Still, in 1870, by one measurement—number of large farms—Madison County was the leading farming county in the state. In 1870 only one county (Taylor) had more farms of 1,000 acres and over than Madison, while Madison led the state in numbers of farms in the 500 and under 1,000 acres category and in farms of 100 acres and under 500.[11]

Bybee Pottery. Dorris Collection, EKU Townsend Room.

By 1900 the most distinctive feature of Madison County agriculture was perhaps a matter of social relations rather than of productivity. Who owned these fertile tracts of Kentucky land? In 1900 Madison County's

2,741 farms were farmed primarily by whites (2,389), while 352 black farmers were operating. But more farms were actually fully owned by black citizens in Madison County (243) than in any other county in the state (next highest was Logan with 182 black owners). To see the significance of this figure, compare Madison County with two of its neighbors: in Garrard County 81 farms were owned by blacks; in Fayette only 48. In Madison County 12.8 percent of the farms were owned by blacks, as compared to 4.8 percent in the state as a whole. The five counties with a higher percentage of black ownership than Madison were also regions where black sharecroppers were very numerous. In Henderson County, for example, where 84 farms were owned by blacks (27 percent of the farm ownership), the ratio of owners to sharecroppers was 84 to 752. Madion County's ratio was 243 owners to 51 sharecroppers. The commonest social system in Kentucky agriculture had blacks farming on the shares for whites. For the whole state 58.6 percent of all farms were operated by owners; 25.7 percent by share tenants (other arrangements account for the missing percentage points). Compare 4,240 black farm owners in the state of Kentucky to 4,984 share tenants. This arrangement did not prevail in Madison County; for whatever reason, blacks in the county may have had more opportunity in the total economic scheme of their region than in any other part of Kentucky.[12]

Certainly, opportunities in Madison County did not lie in the realm of industry. In 1850, only 133 people were employed in manufacturing of any sort, and more than one-third of the manufactured goods were produced by families at home. By 1860 Madison County had fifty-four establishments for manufactures, including the following (an exhaustive list): agricultural implements (1), blacksmithing (4), boots & shoes (3), carriages (2), cooperage (1), flour & meal (8), leather (3), liquors, distilled (9), lumber, sawed (11), printing, newspaper & job (2), provisions, pork, etc. (1), pottery ware (2), saddlery & horses (3), tin, copper & sheet iron ware (1), wool carding (2), woollen goods (1). The largest of these industries (in annual value of products) was provisions, with the production of distilled liquor second. Many of the industries on this list are obviously obsolete, but one, pottery, remains one of Madison County's flourishing trades. The longevity of potmaking in the region is amazing; in fact, pottery is the oldest known industry in Madison County, beginning with J. P. Grinstead, a Virginian, who worked at Waco around 1840. As early as 1845 the Bybee establishment was opened in the same neighborhood by the Cornelison family. In factories of 1860 only six women were employed, all in the woollen goods industry. The same number (probably the same women) was employed in 1870, but by 1880 no woman worked in any Madison industry, although six male children did.[13]

In 1870 and 1880 the varieties of industrial establishments remained virtually unchanged, although most of them were decreasing in productivity, with the exception of distilled liquor, which grew from 118,624 gallons in 1870 to 319,398 in 1880. Richmond's dairy production progressed in 1869 with the opening of a cheese factory, and in

1885 with a new creamery. Throughout these years it seems that virtually nothing was made in Madison County to be consumed elsewhere.[14]

While manufacturing scarcely changed life in Madison County for fifty years, other technological advances made major alterations, chief among these being the railroad and turnpikes. Richmond began to agitate for the Cincinnati and Knoxville Railroad as early as 1852, and a big railroad convention was held in town the next year. In 1854 a subscription was proposed to the Kentucky Union Railroad Company to build a railroad from Lexington through Richmond, or near it, to the Cumberland Gap. The county's biggest official movement to obtain a railroad began March 30, 1867, with a

> petition requesting that the court of Madison County cause a poll to be opened at the various districts or precincts of said county on the 20th of April 1867 to take the sense of the voters of Madison County on the propriety of subscribing for and in behalf of said county, stock in the Branch Railroad from Stanford to Richmond, to the amount of $350,000, it being a proposed branch of the Louisville and Nashville Railroad.

On March 26, 1869, the full $350,000 was paid to the railroad, but the arrangement became a matter of controversy since "some of the moneyed men of the county, especially Squire Turner and Daniel Breck" opposed it. On June 25, 1881, Madison County voted to take $200,000 stock in the Central Kentucky Railroad from Paris through Winchester and Richmond on south; and in the spring of 1883 Madison County approved the Richmond-Irvine Three Forks Railroad, entering the county at Valley View and extending on through Richmond to Irvine.[15]

The roads in Madison County had been improving from 1850 on (when the Richmond-Lancaster Turnpike was rechartered), and certainly increasing in number, with dozens of new roads appearing in the 1850s and 60s. Literally hundreds of entries in the order books of the Madison County Court from 1850 to 1860 deal with roads, surveying, maintenance, rerouting; and dozens of men served to view the "nearest & best" way for various new roads. The road between Richmond and Irvine was built in 1851. On July 18, 1854, the citizens of Madison County voted on a tax for a "McAdamized, grave, plank or other artificial road" from Richmond to Big Hill, from Richmond to Irvine, from Richmond to Paint Lick Creek, from Richmond to the Kentucky River between Paint Lick and Tate's Creek, from Richmond to the Kentucky River near the mouth of Muddy Creek or the mouth of Red River, and from Richmond to near Boonesborough. In 1854 the Richmond-Big Hill-Muddy Creek and Richmond-Kentucky River-Tate's Creek turnpikes were chartered, while in 1856 the Kirksville-Kentucky River Turnpike was rechartered. Two new bridges—one across Paint Lick Creek between Madison and Garrard counties, and one over Silver Creek—were constructed in 1857. The justices of the peace of Madison County inspected the completed Richmond-Lancaster Turnpike in February, 1857, and approved it; the Richmond-Big Hill Turnpike passed inspection in June, 1858; while the Richmond-Boonesborough Road was almost completed in August, 1859. On May 15, 1860, Madison County was subscribing shares of stock in the Richmond, Otter Creek and Boonesborough Turnpike Road Company, the Mill Grove and Kirksville Turnpike Road Company, and at least seven other local road construction projects. By May 7, 1861, 5¾ miles of the Richmond, Otter Creek, Boonesborough Turnpike were completed, and other roads were slowly but surely growing. A stageline from Richmond to Irvine was established in 1865 (remaining open until 1891), and the Richmond-Lexington Turnpike Road Company bought ferry rights at Clay's Ferry from Brutus J. Clay and R. C. Rogers; but a new bridge to span the Kentucky River at Clay's Ferry was begun in 1868. Stock of Silver Creek Turnpike Company was on sale by June 18, 1868, and a Richmond-Union-Doylesville Turnpike was chartered in 1869, the same year the Richmond-Barnes Mill Turnpike was completed. By 1870 the Paint Lick-High Point Turnpike was chartered (rechartered in 1872), the Jack's Creek Turnpike as well, and the Clay's Ferry Bridge was opened for traffic. The last turnpike chartered in this period was probably the Speedwell-Kingston-Menelaos Turnpike in 1887 or 1888.[16]

Mule drawn trolley in downtown Richmond, 1895. Courtesy David Greene.

Telegraph had joined Richmond to Lexington in 1863, but it was torn down in 1865. By 1875 the railroad telegraph from Richmond to Stanford was in operation. In 1878 Professor T. W. Tobin of Central

University constructed telephones modeled after a description of Bell's recent invention, and by 1878 Richmond had its own internal telephone party-line (the only one in the state outside Louisville). By 1893 Richmond was connected to Lexington by telephone. Two years later the U.S. Express Office opened. Gas was turned on in the city May 14, 1874 (French Tipton says the night of February 16, 1871). By 1888 a waterworks corporation was chartered (in 1881 Richmond had been served by twelve public wells and cisterns). Richmond had a street railway in operation by 1890, and the Richmond Ice Factory by 1891. The electric company received its charter in 1898; the electricity was tested on the night of Thursday, August 3, and regular service began on August 4. By the next month the company was in "receivership" because two of the organizers were charged with fraud, but the electricity stayed on. Tagging along behind, Berea installed the Berea Telephone Company in 1895 (a small system had been in use by September, 1894), but Berea's waterworks was the town pump, the sanitation of which was discussed at many town board meetings. After it was reported (July 11, 1895) that Berea's "town pump was useless," the council duly appointed a Committee on the Town Pump.[17]

Some of Madison County's biggest internal changes from 1850 to 1900 were in its multiplying institutions: banks, presses, hospitals, churches, and schools. In 1859 the Madison County Mutual Insurance Company was chartered; Farmer's National Bank, in 1865. The Madison National Bank was organized January 24, 1870, under the directorship of Thomas S. Moberly, John A. Duncan, Thomas D. Chenault, Alexander Tribble, and James B. McCreary. Moberly was the bank's first president. The Irvine and Walker Bank (reorganized in 1897 as the State Bank and Trust Company) was approved by the National Banking Association June 22, 1874; William M. Irvine, J. Stone Walker, and June Walker, all members of prominent Richmond families, were the organizers. The bank opened January 13, 1875, in a building located across the street from the courthouse, with William M. Irvine as president. The bank was renamed the Second National Bank (January 1878), but Walkers and Irvines continued prominent in its management. The board of directors in 1878 was composed of J. Stone Walker, June Walker, William M. Irvine, R. B. Terrill, R. E. Little, W. T. Tevis, David W. Irvine, and Dudley Tribble, Jr. The Building and Loan Company was formed in 1887.[18]

Newspapers in Richmond multiplied during the war, with the short-lived *Kentucky Rebel*, its appearance due to the Confederate victory in the Battle of Richmond, beginning publication in September, 1862, and folding shortly thereafter. The *Mountain Boomer* and the *Mountain Democrat* also appeared and disappeared during the course of the war; but the *Kentucky Register*, a Democratic paper, continued from 1866 to 1879, when it was replaced by the *Herald*. The latter paper after 1887 was called the *Climax* and was mostly operated by French Tipton until his tragic death in 1900. In the 1890s Richmond had three papers, the

Kentucky Register and the *Climax*, both Democratic, and the *Semi-weekly Pantographic*, a Republican paper which began in 1894. (The *Register* and *Climax* were among the first Richmond industries to install gasoline engines, both in 1896.) The press in Berea was first represented by the short-lived *Reporter*, which was replaced by the *Berea Citizen*, published continuously, almost without competition, from June 21, 1899, to the present day.[19]

In 1885 the Faith Cure Hospital opened in Richmond, but not until 1892 did the county establish a medical facility that was destined to last—Pattie A. Clay Infirmary, endowed by Brutus J. Clay in honor of his wife. Another public institution, Madison County's poorhouse, continued to be necessary (the first one had been in 1823). A commission was appointed by the court in 1857 to buy land for a poorhouse, and the next year the commission was ordered to erect a house not to exceed $5,000 in cost. After it was completed no more appropriations were to be made to paupers living outside its confines.[20]

Religious life in Madison County was very undiversified in pre-Civil War days—all Protestant; almost all Baptist, Methodist, Disciples of Christ, and Presbyterian. In 1860 the county had fourteen Baptist churches, nine Christian, eight Methodist, and five Presbyterians. Lutherans, Roman Catholics, and Episcopalians were virtually nonexistent in the region. By 1890 the majority of Madison Countians were Baptists, the three denominations of which counted a membership of 3,729. The largest single church in memberships was the Colored Regular Baptist (with 1,929), while the African Methodist Episcopal Church also accounted for a relatively large group of church members (439). Of white churchs the Regular Baptist was the largest with 1,685 members, followed by the Disciples of Christ with 1,036 members, and the Methodist Episcopal Church, South, with 493. The divided Presbyterian Church had only 23 members in its Northern version; 314 Southern. The Protestant Episcopal Church had established itself in Richmond with 75 members. The Roman Catholics had three separate congregations (only one church), some 198 members; and a very small cultish group, the Church Triumphant (Schweinfurth), claimed 25 members. In spite of their very small memberships, the Presbyterian Church in the United States of America (Northern) and the Protestant Episcopal Church had the most valuable church buildings in the county ($10,000 apiece), while some small church identifying itself as Christian (Christian Connection) met in a building valued at $20, which was probably little different from assembling outdoors.[21]

A new Presbyterian Church was dedicated in Richmond in March, 1859, and in the country the Silver Creek Chapel (now White's Memorial) was begun in 1876. The Second Presbyterian Church (Northern) was built in 1884 near the intersection of East Main and B streets. The Kirksville Presbyterian Church was organized in 1878 by some members of the Richmond-Silver Creek Church, and it dedicated a new building in 1880. The Disciples of Christ, long active in Madison County, built Mt.

Zion in 1852, later to figure in the Battle of Richmond; and they established a new church in Richmond on Big Hill Avenue (second Christian
Church) in 1895. In the same year in Berea, John G. Fee, splitting with
his own Union Church on the issue of immersion, established the First
Christian Church of Berea.[22]

Catholic communicants in Madison County were first served by
priests from Bardstown, and by 1853 by priests from Lexington and Mt.
Sterling. In 1858 the church had three mission stations, Richmond,
Boonesborough, and Rogersville, with 150 communicants. A small
frame church was built in Richmond in 1865, a more substantial building
in 1867. The Episcopalian church in Richmond, a large church for the
region at that time, was consecrated June 19, 1887, by Bishop Dudley.[23]

A church known later as the "Republican" Baptist Church was erected
and dedicated in 1852, and a Baptist church at Waco was constructed in
1858. New Baptist churches included the First Baptist (or Missionary
Baptist) Church of Richmond, organized in 1867. Silver Creek Baptist
Church constructed a new building in 1869, while the Baptist church in
Berea was organized in 1896. Middletown Baptist (a black church in the
outskirts of Berea) had its origins in the 1880s.[24]

Baptism in Silver Creek, 1894. Dorris Collection, EKU Townsend Room.

Methodists were already so firmly established in Madison County by
1850 that many congregations were organized long before that time. A
second Methodist church appeared in Richmond in 1882. About the
same time the Doylesville Church was established. The African Methodist Episcopal Church of Richmond began with nine members in 1872.
Their first meeting was held in a boxcar on the Louisville and Nashville

Railroad by Malinda McClannihan Cobb, former slave of William Holloway. The first pastor of this church was C. T. Shaffer of Cincinnati, a
student at Berea, who walked between his college and his parish each
Sunday.[25]

Education in Madison County witnessed epoch-making developments in the nineteenth century. The founding of Berea College, already
detailed, was one of the most significant breakthroughs in the history of
the country, much less the state or county. But Madison County had
other significant advances as well, particularly with the founding of
Central University.

The Madison Female Institute, located in Richmond, was incorporated January 26, 1858, with trustees Thomas H. Barnes, Thomas S.
Bronston, William Chenault, John A. Duncan, Clifton R. Estill, William
Harris, William Holloway, Thomas S. Moberly, Robert R. Stone, Samuel
Stone, William J. Walker, and William H. White. During this period the
school flourished, becoming famous as "a southern finishing school"
which attracted students from all over the South and eventually
included a college department. (The school went out of existence in
1919.) This institution's most historic occasion was not a graduation,
but a battle. Following the battle of Richmond, the Madison Female
Institute was used as a hospital for several months, with teachers and
students caring for the wounded. In February, 1863, the trustees filed a
claim against the United States for damage done the property while it
was used as a hospital but did not receive payment ($5,200) until 1915.[26]

Madison Female Institute. EKU Archives.

Around Foxtown (c. 1850) several wealthy families in the community established private schools for their children, hiring college students, usually from Yale, to tutor for ten months out of the year. This system, basically college preparatory, produced some students who duly entered the freshman class at Yale and other colleges after completing their course.[27]

Shortly after the Civil War, Texas Seminary, under the auspices of the Methodist Episcopal Church, was founded. The then Texas neighborhood of the county was renamed College Hill, and before 1890 the seminary, which in its heyday attracted boarding students from eastern and central Kentucky, became "a rural school in the county common school system because the Church ceased to support it." Elliot Institute, an academy, was founded in 1882 with three departments, primary, preparatory, and collegiate; it once counted as many as 127 students. This school eventually became part of the Kirksville Public School about 1900. Kingston School, founded 1886, operated as a high school until around 1904.[28]

Co-educational and interracial classes at Berea College before 1900. Berea College Archives.

Much of the lower grade instruction in Madison County was in private schools, exclusive and by subscription, run by people like W. Rodes Shackelford and Mrs. French Tipton. Children who attended these schools were generally spared the experience of ordinary children in Madison County, who studied in schoolhouses "almost totally inadequate to the requirement made of them, generally poorly lighted and ventilated . . . almost totally unfit to be used in cold weather" (commissioner's report in 1871). In 1884, the commissioner found only seven or eight schoolhouses in the entire count "fit for the purpose and many of them unfit for horse stables." Colored schools were worst of all, most of them being located in colored churches or rented houses. Before 1884 there were only two or three schoolhouses for black children in the county. "Conditions were not much better in 1900."[29]

The popularity of Berea in this period is certainly understandable, since the school there had some of the best educational facilities in the state and a growing endowment (from $75,000 in 1875 to $106,000 in 1890, for example). Berea College, with its adjunct primary and preparatory departments, was the most desirable school for blacks in the whole state, and one of the most attractive for whites as well.[30]

Richmond tried to build a school of equal attraction, but not for Negroes. In 1874, after the citizens of Richmond had spent years of effort to obtain the institution, Central University, with a charter providing for a liberal arts college, a college of law and a university high school (all located in Richmond), opened in Richmond. It was under the jurisdiction of the Southern Presbyterians, and its founding was a direct result of the split in the Presbyterian Church during the Civil War. Central represented what had been the proslavery element in the controversy, so that its origin was in direct contrast to the founding of Berea College.[31]

Certainly, the two schools were seen as rival institutions. For example, John G. Fee's estranged sister, Sarah (they split on the question of slavery), left bequests to sponsor young men attending Central University, particularly her own cousins and nephews, some of whom had already been "ruined" by attending her brother's interracial institution fifteen miles down the road. Even if the opposite was not official, it was clear to everyone who knew about the two schools: Berea and Central represented educational developments of opposing sides of the Civil War.[32]

Central also represented possible progress and some excitement. Curtis F. Burnam expressed it this way:

> Our little town moves on in the same groove as of old, we have the community, however, occasionally stirred up, by some local or foreign excitement. Just now two influences are at work to break the ordinary monotony. One an effort to secure the location here of the *University* which the Southern Presbyterians think of establishing some where in Kentucky, and the other the location, soon to be made, of the route of the Cincinnati and Chattanooga Railroad, and which it is hoped will go through Madison.

Burnam's own hopes for the University were related to his desire for the whole community's betterment: "We greatly need all the refining influences of education and internal improvements to lift the State out of the slough of [indecipherable] and crime, which for years back it seems to have been . . . in."[33]

After Central University's brief existence of twenty-seven years, its eight buildings and campus became the property of Eastern Kentucky State Normal School (now Eastern Kentucky Univeristy) and its other assets were merged with Centre College in Danville. Nevertheless, Central produced some distinguished alumni—French Tipton, for example, the college's first and only graduate in 1875. And some very prominent families provided faculty and students—for example, William Chenault, president of the law school at Richmond, professor of equity, jurisprudence, constitutional and common law; and William Shackelford, adjunct professor of ancient languages. Such familiar Richmond names as Burnam, McCreary, Clay, Irvine, Shackelford, Cornelison, Stone, and Bennett appear on lists of graduates, in many instances numerous times.[54]

University Building on the Central University campus, EKU Archives.

In 1892 Central University distinguished itself by recruiting the first college football team in Madison County. Actually, the university's emphasis on athlctics, fraternities, and military science rendered it indistinguishable from hundreds of other American colleges and universities; indeed, from its inception the university was intended to be a *standard* institution of higher learning for central Kentucky, "ranked with other Southern institutions of learning." Unlike Berea College, Central University was not unique, although its contribution to the region was, no doubt, substantial.[35]

1899 Central University football team. *Cream and Crimson* (Central University yearbook), 121. EKU Archives.

Central University's first chancellor was Reverend Robert L. Breck, pastor of the Southern Presbyterian Church in Richmond, who had led the movement in Madison County to procure subscriptions for establishing the school in Richmond. Breck was in charge until 1880, when a former Confederate chaplain, Reverend Lindsay H. Blanton, took office, holding it until the university's demise in 1901 from financial weakness. The total amount collected for Central University from every source from 1895 to 1901 was only $104,076; much of the money subscribed to the institution—even the fund to establish it—was never collected. By contrast, in January of 1899, Berea College was celebrating its new $200,000 endowment with public meetings of prayer and thanksgiving.[36]

One mark of the importance of agriculture in Madison County life was its inclusion in the largest recreational institution of the county—the annual fair to advertise, display, and sell local produce in a carnival atmosphere, which eventually included horseracing (and unofficially a great deal more). The first was held in Richmond in 1833, with Cassuis M. Clay as its president. Richmond fairs continued to be held in the Civil War period—in 1860 and 1861 in Bogg's Woods, in 1866 (with R. S. Martin and D. A. Chenault presiding), and in 1868 (with J. D. Harris in charge). The 1868 festivities included a tournament with a $50 silver crown as a prize. By 1867 a permanent fair ampitheatre had been partially completed for Richmond's annual celebration, and General E.

Kirby Smith, an honored celebrity, attended that year. In 1868 Kirksville held its own fair, and Berea initiated still another in 1872. (The first Colored Fair in Madison County was in 1866, while the first to be staged in the new ampitheatre was in 1876; Berea's Colored Fair began in 1887.) By 1889 a racetrack had been constructed on the county fairgrounds, and by 1899 fairs had become so popular that two were opened in Richmond in the same season.[37]

Baseball appeared in Madison County in 1867. Apparently a club had been organized in Richmond by 1868, with James Tevis as president. Horseracing had been a favored sport for decades, and it continued to flourish with races at Embry Race Track in Richmond (some particularly notable ones in 1869), and the fighting of roosters also continued "in suburbs of Richmond." A notable fox chase was held in April, 1866, at Red House. [38]

More formal entertainments were offered by Green's Operahouse, which opened in 1872, and a new opera house appeared in 1885 (only to be burned in the fire of 1887). Nothing daunted, the Richmond Operahouse Company began operations in 1890. But the most important innovation in entertainment or amusement for Richmond citizens was, undoubtedly, the ability to leave Richmond—the first round trip on the railroad from Richmond to Cincinnati in a day was a big event in 1879.[39]

An important aspect of social life for many men of Madison was lodge membership. Masonry continually expanded in the county during the 1850s, with new lodges opening at Menelaos in 1852 (disbanded about 1870), at Kingston in 1855, and at Waco in 1856. In 1867 the Daniel Boone Lodge at Boonesborough was chartered. Waco's masonic celebration in 1872 was an "event." Richmond's Commanding Masonic Lodge was established in 1875, and in 1876 Union City established its branch. Berea's Masonic Lodge was late in its establishment (not until 1882) because the Berea Church had been founded on anti-Masonic principles.[40]

The social order of Madison County was altering in small ways as well. Two examples may serve to remind us of the diversity of changes which shaped the county during the post-Civil War era. In 1873 roller skating struck Richmond; in 1896 the Daughters of the Confederacy organized. Perhaps the latter example is actually a sign of something larger.[41]

It has been said that Kentucky only became a Confederate state after the war. Perhaps the election of native Madison Countian James B. McCreary—to the state legislature in 1869, '71, and '73 (speaker the latter two terms); governorship of the state (in 1875 and again in 1911); Congress in 1886, '88, and '90; and the Senate, 1902-08—might be taken as symptomatic of the determined southern sympathies of postwar Madison County. McCreary had begun a law practice in Richmond in his youth, but abandoned it in August, 1862, to become a major (later lieutenant colonel) in the Chenault regiment of Morgan's raiders, a position guaranteed to stamp him forever as a proponent of the heroic Lost Cause. [42]

Many of the Madison Countians who had been Morgan's raiders enjoyed careers in local politics after the war. Their Confederate sympathies, proven by their service in Chenault's regiment, insured their later success. Nathan B. Deatherage (who enlisted in Company B, Collins' Company of Chenault's regiment on September 10, 1862) became sheriff of Madison County in 1876 and again in 1878; once more in 1884 and again in 1866. Abner Oldham (also mustered in on September 10, 1862) was deputy sheriff, while his brother Charles was high sheriff of Madison County from 1870 to 1874; afterwards Abner served as chief of police and marshall of Richmond. His brother Charles Kavanaugh Oldham, Lieutenant in Company F, 11th Kentucky Cavalry, was sheriff of Madison County in 1870 and was reelected in 1872, afterward serving as marshall of Richmond. Another Oldham, James William, likewise a soldier in Collin's company, Chenault's regiment, served as deputy sheriff under his brother-in-law, Nathan Deatherage, from 1878 to 1882. James Tevis, who became second Lieutenant in Collins' Company, was elected clerk of Madison county for two four-year terms, and afterwards became judge of Richmond Police Court. All these men were mustered in on the same day, saw action in the same battles, were captured on Morgan's raid into Ohio and Indiana, were imprisoned in Camp Douglas. Other Confederate soldiers held political office in Madison County. Captain Robert Bruce Terrill of Company E, 11th Kentucky Cavalry, was badly wounded at the Battle of Mt. Sterling, but returned to Madison County to be elected clerk of Madison Circuit Court, serving from 1868 to 1874. George Daniel Shackelford, the only Confederate soldier in this listing who was not one of Morgan's raiders, was a dry goods merchant in Richmond after the war and was elected clerk of the county court, dying in office June 28, 1874. Another Confederate, Thomas Thorpe (whose regiment is not known) served two times as county assessor and two terms as county clerk.[43]

These examples illustrate how strongly Confederate Madison County had become at war's end, with Morgan's raiders dominating local politics until well into the 1880s. It is easy to believe Clarence E. Woods' unsympathetic account of a near massacre in the county courthouse which occurred (probably in the fall of 1886) when W. O. Bradley (later governor and senator of Kentucky) accused his opponent in a campaign for Congress, James B. McCreary, of having "wobbled and delayed his decision whether to join the Confederates or the Union Army." Knives and pistols were drawn when McCreary yelled, "That is a LIE!" and open warfare between two factions was narrowly averted.[44]

In spite of the bucolic appearance of statistics about enormous farm productivity, virtual nonexistence of factories, burgeoning comforts and increasing culture, Madison County was far from being a peaceful place in the years after the war. The violence of Reconstruction times has already been recounted, but it did not suddenly cease in 1877. Social

problems of all sorts, including crimes, persisted in the county throughout this era. In the 1880s Richmond was billed in newspaper headlines
as "The Most Burglarized Town in the State"(this article follows several
pages of clippings about burglaries in French Tipton's scrapbook).[45]

James Bennett McCreary: Ken-
tucky governor from Madison
County. University of Kentucky
King Library Special Collections
Department.

Less dramatic, but much more compelling, is evidence from the
1900 census of Madison County, which demonstrates that, while slavery
no longer existed, a social caste system very much like slavery flourished.
In the city of Richmond in 1900, the majority of adult black women
listed occupations outside their own homes: 286 cooks, 141 laundresses,
71 house servants, 26 nurses (25 for children, 1 "sick" nurse), 10 seam-
stresses—a total of 534 black women working, almost all for white
families. (The total number of families, black and white, in Richmond
was 708, at least one-third of them black.) In the same census, virtually
no white woman lists an occupation of any sort; many of them apparently did no work whatsoever since cooking, cleaning, washing, and
other domestic duties were performed, as always, by numerous black
servants. The majority of black men listed "Day Laborer" as their
occupation, an indication that they simply sought jobs of work from a
series of employers. Those mentioning specific jobs listed porter (26),
houseboy (many houseboys and cooks were married couples working
for the same white family) (26), railroad laborer (23), hotel waiter (15),
barber (14); virtually all the rest were employed in strictly menial labor
(bootblacks, hod carriers, quarry workers, gardeners, janitors, horse
rubbers). Almost no white men listed *any* of these occupations. A few
blacks worked in "professions": teaching (22 females, 7 males), preaching (6), practicing medicine (1). One black woman, Sallie Chenault,
unable to read or write, called herself an "actress." It is possible that the
one black grocer and the two restaurant keepers operated their own

businesses, the only ones in Richmond; and the woman who called herself a "cake baker" may have had a degree of independence. One black man was a mail carrier.[46]

These figures indicate, beyond any doubt the southern caste system was virtually intact in Madison County by the turn of the century. Blacks had a very small range of choices in their daily lives. Serving white people was, in a sense, still the only occupational option, as it had been in 1850.

However, by contrast, one area of Madison County was not maintaining the old system. In the town of Berea in 1900, black citizens provided not one cook, no nurses, no laundresses. Only nine servants were listed, and two of them were white. Black men in Berea, as in Richmond, usually called themselves day laborers, but black women most frequently listed no occupation for themselves at all. Much progress remained to be made, but in Berea, where dedicated people had sworn to break the caste system of the South, it was indeed broken. Figures for the entire Glade Precinct showed fewer than twenty black women working as servants of any kind, while black men were frequently farm owners in their own right.[47]

The period from 1850 to 1900 in Madison County might be characterized, on the whole, as a permanent conflict, on every level: Fee vs. Clay, abolitionists vs. slaveholders, mountaineers vs. Bluegrass planters, Richmond vs. Berea, Yankees vs. Confederates, former federal soldiers vs. former rebel soldiers, one family vs. another in years of blood-feuding, Central University vs. Berea College. In the midst of this half century of antagonism, one reconciling figure emerged who was involved in virtually every aspect of Madison County's divided history. From 1850 to 1900 Curtis F. Burnam did more than any other single individual to draw oppositions together, and, as he worked for reconciliation, he himself emerged as the best product of Madison County's nurture: humane, informed, eloquent, generous, honorable, deeply and practically concerned for his county, his state and his nation—a fully civilized man. On March 24, 1909, Kentucky's former Governor James B. McCreary, himself a Madison Countian, in a posthumous tribute to Curtis F. Burnam called him "one of the greatest and best men ever born in Kentucky." McCreary and Burnam had fought on opposite sides of the Civil War.[48]

Born in Richmond on May 24, 1820, the son of Thompson Burnam, Sr. and Lucinda Field, Curtis Field Burnam was allied with most of the wealthiest and most influential families of Madison County. His mother's family intermarried with Clays, Irvines, Millers, Moberlys, Embrys, Holloways. Through blood and marriage, Curtis was an unquestioned member of Madison County's elite; through tradition also the Burnams "qualified" as quality. Curtis's grandfather, John Burnam, native of Cecil County, Maryland, a soldier in the American Revolution, had settled in Madison County as early as 1790 (the family "pitched their tents at the Village of Milford" in that year). He had bought land by September 9, 1809, in the city of Richmond, where the family was living by 1802. Curtis's father was one of the county's most prosperous slave-owners, usually owning about twenty slaves (valued at $800 each) at any one time, with an estate worth $58,700 in 1854, including four town lots in Richmond, over 500 acres on Silver Creek, 26 acres on Otter Creek, a stable of horses, 135 head of cattle, ninety hogs, $200 worth of carriages and "pleasure buggies," and a piano worth $300. He was elected to the Kentucky legislature in 1844 and 1849.[49]

Curtis F. Burnam attended Madison Male Seminary, and in January, 1837, he left home for college, remaining in New Haven until his graduation from Yale in June, 1840. Upon his return to his hometown, Curtis studied law in the office of Judge Daniel Breck. He was soon graduated from the Law Department of Transylvania University. Sworn into the Richmond bar in March, 1842, he entered his own practice (briefly in partnership with William C. Goodloe) in Richmond in 1842. In 1846 he was appointed commonwealth's attorney.[50]

Politically, he had become an emancipationist. His father was a candidate for the office of delegate to the Constitutional Convention of 1849 as an emancipationist, supported by and supporting Cassius M. Clay, running against Squire Turner, Mr. Willis, and Mr. Chenault. But Curtis Burnam did not approve of all Clay's actions or all his associates, as the following passage, written August 9, 1855, reveals: "I am against all mobs whether in Louisville, Kansas or *Scaffold Cane*," Burnam stated. "As much as I abhor the principles of John G. Fee, C. M. Clay and the other men who are crusading against Negro slavery in our midst, I wish no injustice done them." Curtis was chosen a presidential elector in 1852 and again in 1864, for the state at large, supporting Lincoln. He was elected to represent his county in the state legislature in 1851, 1859, and 1861, winning the latter seat by a large vote of 1,383 against his opponents, David Waller Chenault (with 551) and John M. Hume (95). Between 1850 and 1860 Burnam was twice a candidate for Congress, losing by a narrow margin. ("Madison County," he wrote, "was almost a unity for me" in the election of 1853.) In 1860 he was delegate to the Baltimore Convention which nominated John Bell of Tennessee and Edward Everett of Massachusetts (for vice-president), but he "rejoiced" in the election of Abraham Lincoln. In fact, he became a personal friend and ardent supporter of Lincoln, whose reelection he had strongly advocated in 1864.[51]

He stood unilaterally for the preservation of the Union. As a member of the Kentucky Legislature from 1860 to 1864, he was chairman of the Committee on Federal Relations which promoted Kentucky's neutrality in the War Between the States. As a recognized leader of the Union party, Burnam opposed all efforts to drag Kentucky out of the Union. He was his party's candidate for United States Senator in 1863, but was defeated in spite of "the unbroken vote of [his] party." His fame and prominence as Union leader resulted in his capture by General John H. Morgan in October, 1862, when he was pro tem. Speaker of the state house of representatives, but he was soon exchanged for one of Morgan's younger brothers.[52]

In spite of his Union allegiance, Burnam and his law partner James W. Caperton worked hard to secure the release of rebel soldiers from federal prisons. In January and February, 1865, for example, Burnam and Caperton were "engaged by a number of persons in and near Madison County to secure the release of their Confederate kinsmen from Camp Douglas." (These men were mostly members of the 11th Cavalry which had joined Morgan's raiders, only to be captured with him on his Ohio raid.) In all, Burnam's firm secured the release of seventeen prisoners from Camp Douglas near Chicago, Illinois, and three from other prison camps. Burnam himself labored successfully for the pardon of Othniel and Thomas Oldham, two Madison County citizens who were found guilty of spying for the rebels and sentenced to be hanged.[53]

After the war Kentucky was intensely Democratic, and Burnam's refusal to give up his Union party allegiance, cost him his political career during what might have been his most productive years. (He was nominated to run for Congress from Madison in 1865 and almost became the candidate.) Both former rebels and former Union soldiers continued to employ him as a lawyer, in spite of his political losses.[54]

In 1875 he accepted the position of assistant secretary of the United States Treasury in Grant's administration. He was a member of nearly all the state conventions of his party and a delegate to a number of national conventions. In 1883, while he was vacationing in Europe, he was elected president of the Kentucky Bar Association. In 1890 he was chosen delegate to the constitutional convention by an overwhelming majority from his county. (His opponent, Brutus J. Clay, had 89 votes to Curtis's 2,711.) His formal political career resumed, even though he was now an aged man; he was elected to the state senate in 1899, at the age of 79, and again in 1903.[55]

Throughout his incredibly active life, Curtis F. Burnam supported religious, educational, and social institutions of his own region. In spite of his involvement in statewide and even national issues, his contributions to Madison County's development are unequalled by any other citizen of the period. In 1868, when the Baptist Church was incorporated, C. F. Burnam was one of the incorporators. An "Old Baptist" in religion, Burnam "clung to an old church when hundreds and even thousands passed from its fold to others." In fact, *loyalty* was the keynote of Burnam's character. When others of his class, his own friends and associates, abandoned the Union, he remained steadfast. In his work for Madison County his loyalty and generosity are clearly expressed. He was interested in everything pertaining to the progress of the community—banks, schools, and public improvements.[56]

He was a supporter of the Pattie A. Clay Infirmary, working tirelessly for that early hospital. In 1863 he became a member of the board of the Richmond Cemetary (dedicated in 1856); he was president of the Board in 1884. He was a member of the committee appointed by the Madison County Court (in April term, 1891) to form a Madison County Historical Society. As a legislator he was author of the bill establishing the Confederate Home at Peewee Valley.[57]

By 1880 he was a trustee of the Madison Female Institute, which he had helped to plan in 1857. A supporter of the movement to locate Central University in Richmond, Burnam was chosen president of the College of Law and professor of equity jurisprudence in 1874, although he served only a few months in that capacity, because his duties in Grant's cabinet called him to Washington in 1875. (William Chenault replaced him.) Burnam continued to support Central University, donating some thirteen volumes to the university library. His sons, Robert Rodes and Edmund Tutt Burnam; his nephew, John Miller Burnam; and his grandsons, Curtis F. and George S. Burnam, were all graduates of Central University.[58]

In June, 1896, at their annual meeting, the Berea College board elected Curtis F. Burnam trustee. Reelected in June 1902, Burnam tried to resign on June 3, 1903, but he withdrew his resignation upon request and accepted an honorary degree from Berea the same year. Even though he was far advanced in age by now, Burnam continued as a Berea trustee until his death. In fact, one of the most active periods of his public life involved his defense of Berea College in the great Day Law controversy and lawsuit before the Kentucky Court of Appeals. (The Day Law made it illegal for blacks and whites in Kentucky to attend school together, even in private institutions like Berea, which the law was designed to destroy.) His last speeches, the final productions of his dedicated life, were in behalf of Berea. At the annual meeting of the board (June, 1909), Thompson S. Burnam was elected to fill the vacancy caused by the death of his father. (Thompson served until 1923).[59]

It is symbolic of the character of his life that at Curtis F. Burnam's death (March 19, 1909), memorial tributes were conferred by the Citizen's National Bank of Richmond, the Madison County Bar, Morgan's men in their annual reunion, and the board of trustees of Berea College. He had worked with or befriended virtually every significant public figure in Madison County during his lifetime. When the bust of Samuel F. Miller, perhaps Madison County's most nationally prominent native, was unveiled, Curtis F. Burnam delivered the presentation speech, since he and Miller had been friends from their youth.[60]

During the second half of the nineteenth century, three men whose lives and careers were variously intertwined became Madison County's most well-known (sometimes notorious) citizens. Living and working mostly in Madison County, this triumvirate became nationally known, influencing events and opinions far beyond the borders of their home county. All three of them effected changes in their world which continue to influence our own lives. If we could remove any one of these three from its history, Madison County in its present incarnation would be simply inconceivable. These three men were, of course, John G. Fee, Cassius M. Clay, and Curtis F. Burnam. As the nineteenth century drew to a close, these three men, all aged, all near the end of their own careers, represented many of the achievements and problems of Madison County. The region entered the twentieth century with a legacy of progress and conflict which Fee, Clay, and Burnam had done much to shape.

On October 16, 1895, Cassius M Clay, at the invitation of President William G. Frost, delivered an oration at Berea College on the annexation of Alaska. By this time Clay's adventures in Washington, D. C. (with the Home Guard) and in Russia (with hypothetical ballerinas) were long past, and he was living as a local legend in his mansion at White Hall. In his speech at Berea, Clay described himself twice, repeating the same phrase at the beginning and end of his address, as "The Projector, Donor and Defender of Berea College." He also claimed, in a very controversial passage, full credit for the annexation of Alaska. He stated: "I think when what I have done as liberator, what I have done for education, what I have done as dictator in defense of Washington in 1861—and what I have done for the most liberal constitution in the world—the Kentucky Constitution—are all forgotten, I shall be remembered as the author of the annexation of Alaska."[61]

White Hall in 1894 with Cassius M. Clay standing in front. J. Winston Coleman Collection, Transylvania University Library Special Collections Department.

Whether Clay was responsible for Alaska is not a matter of Madison County history, but this late reminder of the egotistical colorfulness of his character certainly is. Whatever else he was, Cassius M. Clay in his heyday was the most flamboyant citizen Madison County ever produced, and one of the most outrageous. His achievements may never have been what he thought they were, but no man did more to stir the fires of controversy in pre-Civil War Kentucky. As representative of Madison County's own internal conflict, Clay is supreme: an embattled figure through his long life, violent and immoderate, a unique symbol of his native county. He was never *alien* to Madison—even the opposition he found in his own hometown is simply representative of the deepest divisions in Madison County life.

It is quite possible that John G. Fee, founder of Berea College, sat in the audience to hear his old friend claim the laurels that belonged to Fee himself. Fee, late in his life, had grown disillusioned with Berea College, which, under the leadership of President William G. Frost had drawn back from the totally radical vision of Berea which Fee had promoted. More and more white students were being recruited from the mountain regions, fewer and fewer blacks from the Bluegrass; the abolition school was rapidly becoming the Appalachian school. Fee had already withdrawn from the church he had founded in Berea, and before his death he would withdraw from his school, too. In one of his last public addresses to the Berea student body, he urged the college to halt its movement toward Appalachian commitment. He wanted to maintain the ratio of white and black students at half and half, claiming that the enrollment of more and more white students would make Berea "a mere white school" like any other in the South. Later, he was minded to repudiate Berea College altogether. At his death in 1900, Fee's final vision, radical as ever, seemed to be unfulfilled by the actual institution he had founded. In a way, he simply stood, throughout his long career, for the purest interpretation of the New Testament faith: absolute love to God and absolutely impartial love to fellow men and women. He had always demanded total social equality as a sign of faith; in his latter years he did not change this ultimate standard. Like Cassius Clay, John G. Fee also symbolized an important aspect of Madison County history. Berea was never simply an alien presence in the region—it was, as surely as Richmond was, an achievement of the county's own citizens. They had supported, defended, settled Berea, attended its college, joined its church, and *followed* John G. Fee. They had, with their own children, kept alive a unique experiment in interracial education for almost fifty years. Fee had adopted Madison County as his mission field; in the end, Madison County adopted him.[62]

Curtis F. Burnam, first citizen of Richmond, in 1903 delivered his great speech on the Berea Bill (the Day Law) before the house committee of the Kentucky legislature. "Its eloquence, rhetoric and logic" were reminiscent of the greatest days of Kentucky oratory; one listener recalled Henry Clay and John J. Crittenden as Burnam's only equals.[63]

Shortly before his retirement in 1906, Burnam would speak for Berea again—as the case was tried by the court of appeals after the passage of the Day Law in 1904. "We [felt] warranted," he said,

> in testing the constitutionality of this act before our local
> court. There was rendered a decision which seemed to us to

be colored by prejudice and passion. And so we have appealed from the judgment of the lower court to this tribunal: where [here he paused] passion and prejudice are, of course, unknown.

The appeal was denied. The Day Law brought about an almost total change in the character of Berea College. Frost's great Appalachian school, rather than Fee's interracial experiment, would develop through the next fifty years.[64]

Nevertheless, the character of Curtis F. Burnam, in his defense of Berea, was symbolic of yet another aspect of Madison County. He was a man who, throughout his life, opposed the actions and reactions of passion and prejudice. His region supplied too much of both, but it also formed him. And he sought to reconcile the divisions of spirit which he knew so well from his own experiences as a citizen of Madison County.

In the year 1900 "a motorized buggy" was driven into Richmond by a Lexington traveling salesman of patent medicines. It was, probably, the first automobile in the county, and it was the beginning of a quite different story.[65]

Part III

MADISON COUNTY: Growth and Maturity, 1900-1985

By William E. Ellis

Chapter Thirteen

CONTINUITY AND CHANGE IN A NEW CENTURY, 1900-1919

January 1, 1900, did not immediately thrust Madison County and its inhabitants into a new era. The heralded new century had little initial impact on the lives of most Madison Countians. Many people believed themselves isolated from most of the world's events. Moreover, geography, land ownership, culture, and economics insulated them from the rapid technological, social, and economic changes taking place in much of the rest of the country.[1]

Life went on much as it had a half century earlier. A few people had read about new inventions like the automobile, and some of the wealthier folk had traveled beyond the confines of the county; but most lived, worked, and died much like their nineteenth century ancestors.

And yet, in 1900 the first stirrings of changes—many of which would revolutionize American life—could be seen on the horizon. What did Madison Countians give up when they crossed the threshold from the old to the new—from the unhurried, hard-working, somewhat circumscribed world of the horse and buggy to the frenetic, harried life of the 1980s? They remembered living with unlocked doors, but actually lived in a violent world. Life was tenuous, as the age-old scourges of smallpox, diphtheria, polio, and tuberculosis stalked young and old alike. Many tradeoffs were made in the intervening years. The history of Madison County from the turn-of-the-century to the mid-1980s offers many illustrations of continuity and change that have affected the nation. That history, in microcosm, is the history of the United States in the twentieth century.

The old way of life of the early twentieth century is now almost forgotten, except by the remaining older citizens. They can still remember what it was like to carry water from wells and can recall the stooped shoulders of mothers or grandmothers caused by hauling water and doing a thousand other necessities over the years. These same women often had hard, leathery complexions from cooking over hot iron stoves in winter and summer and from working outdoors. Also remembered are the hard, calloused hands of fathers or grandfathers who labored from daylight to sundown for their entire lifetimes, working mules and horses, perhaps oxen, in the chill of Kentucky winters or on steamy summer days.

Gone too are the days of stirring clothes in boiling water, of scrubbing them on a washboard with lye soap, of starching and bluing, and of heating irons to just the right temperature on a stove. If there was much drudgery, there were also the offsetting joys of picking blackberries in the first flush of summer, swimming in a nearby stream, anticipating a full smokehouse with the fall hog-killing, or sleighing on the first snow of winter. All these activities flowed naturally in a time when life came at the slower, measured pace dictated by climate and the seasons.

Life continued to revolve around the family, the school, the church, the community. Lack of transportation and communication kept most residents of the county closely tied to their communities. Even in the most isolated rural areas, people identified with a village, which often consisted of a post office, a school, and a store or two. The individual identity of most of these men, women, and children, of course, is rarely if ever recorded in history books; but in composite form their lives give a deeper understanding of the county as it entered the twentieth century.

Census data from the late nineteenth century give a clear profile of Madison County. Moreover, many of these demographic features illustrate developments in the state of Kentucky and the South. The total population of the county grew slowly in the last two decades of the nineteenth century—from 22,052 inhabitants in 1880 to 25,607 in 1900. White population grew more rapidly than black. In 1880 Negroes numbered nearly one-third of the county population, but by 1900 that proportion had dropped to slightly over one-quarter of the population. The reasons for this rapid change in composition of the county's population corresponded with major trends taking place in the state and the South. First, the white and black "death rates" varied widely. As late as 1915 the death rate of blacks of 22.9 per 1,000 was twice that of whites in the state. Negroes were particularly hard hit by tuberculosis and pneumonia in this era. This appalling statistic, along with the beginning of black migration, led to the declining Negro population in Madison County.[2]

The influence of geography and the choices of individuals also reinforced the demographic changes in the county. Three physiographic regions slash diagonally across the county, with the hills of the inner Bluegrass occupying the northwestern part of the county, the outer Bluegrass taking the middle third, and the Knobs beginning at Berea and extending north and east to the boundary with Estill County. Soil types, fertility, and friability vary immensely from one region to another, determining the forms of agriculture to be followed by farmers over a long period of time. Much of the land of the county has always been too steep for other than grassland-cattle farming. Erosion in many of these regions led to economic decline for those living there.[3]

As one of the earliest settled areas of Kentucky, Madison County has been dominated by agriculture well into the twentieth century. Slavery became a common institution in the northern and central areas of the county before the Civil War. Being on the periphery of the Bluegrass that region took on the tone of central Kentucky land tenure and agriculture with a decidedly "southern" flavor. The large landowners of the northern and central sections of the county, including the Clays, Bennetts, Burnams, Irvines, Chenaults, and Arnolds emulated a culture and lifestyle corresponding with that of the quasi-southernness of the central Bluegrass area. Their plantation-sized holdings before the Civil War served as the dominant force in Madison County politics. During the Reconstruction era and well into the present century, much of Madison County history, culture, and politics continued this adopted southern attitude. The southern end of the county, ironically, in most respects represented a different way of life, that of the antislavery advocates who founded Berea College in the midnineteenth century. The influence of John G. Fee and Cassius M. Clay gave a much different bearing to the Berea (Glades) area than that of the northern section of the county. Long after Fee was forced to flee and crusty old Clay gave up on reforming his fellow Kentuckians, Berea College's activities made it a separate community within the county. Too, the foothills of the Cumberlands begin in the southern end of the county. For this reason alone many Madison Countians there have identified with the attitudes, lifestyle, and culture of eastern Kentucky. Madison County has always been a border county, with one foot in the Bluegrass and the other in the mountains. Moreover, many eastern Kentuckians moved to Madison County, looking for economic and educational opportunities and bringing with them their distinctive heritage.[4]

Before the Civil War, agriculture production in the county concentrated primarily on hemp, cattle, and corn. Swine and sheep took on a larger share of production after the war, and by 1880 Madison County could be credited as one of the leading livestock producing counties of the state. All farms, regardless of size, were really subsistence agricultural units, producing the bulk of food consumed by the people living there. Cash crops became more important on the largest farms, where the acreages produced bigger yields.[5]

In the post-Civil War years began one of the most important agricultural revolutions in the history of the Commonwealth: the introduction of burley tobacco into central Kentucky. By 1880 Kentucky had become the leading tobacco producing state. The western region dark-fired varieties still dominated, with over 12,000 acres raised in Henderson County alone. "White Burley" production rapidly increased in the 1870s in the Knobs region, particularly in Owen and Grant counties. In 1880 the agricultural census reported only two acres of burley raised in Fayette and eighty-two acres cultivated in Madison. The demand for burley increased as blended smoking brands, such as "Bull Durham," combined several varieties for taste. By the end of the century Fayette County had increased burley production to over 5,000 acres, and Madison Countians, reacting somewhat more slowly, raised their total yield to over 1,600 acres. The move to tobacco production drastically changed central Kentucky agriculture. Hemp production immediately plummeted, as all economic levels of farmers found a more readily marketable product in tobacco. Cattle and corn production remained at high levels, but hog and sheep numbers dropped. More and more, tobacco became the primary cash producer for Madison County farmers.[6]

The shift to increasing tobacco production encouraged the development of sharecropping and hastened the move of black families away from the farms of Madison County. Sharecropping and other varieties of tenant farming fit the raising of tobacco. While Kentucky did not follow this trend as severely as states in the deep South, by 1900 one-third of Kentucky farmers were tenants. Madison did not match this number, but over 25 percent of Madison farmers were tenants or "croppers." The number of farms increased and the average size decreased as the proportion of sharecroppers increased. To be more precise, in 1880 Madison had 2,048 farm units, whereas by 1900 that total had increased to 2,741. The number of farms operated by owners decreased in that twenty-year span. Racial composition also changed. Over a period of years Madison blacks' influence on agriculture began to be eroded by white tenant farmers. Most blacks continued to be concentrated in small communities like Peytontown, Farristown, Middletown, and Brassfield well into this century. As whites took over as farm tenants, many blacks shifted to working on farms as day laborers, or working at distilleries and railroads near their communities. As these jobs dried up, they drifted to towns like Richmond or after the turn-of-the-century moved on to larger urban areas.[7]

A further look at statistical data for 1900 reveals other changing features. The population of Richmond dropped from 5,073 in 1890 to 4,653 citizens, primarily due to a decline in the black population living within the city limits. Berea, beginning as an outpost of Oberlin College and eastern missionaries, slowly increased in population but still remained a village. After incorporation as a sixth-class city with over 500 population, this southern Madison County community rose to 762 souls in 1900.[8]

In sum, the surface statistical data indicate that Madison County had not changed drastically since the Civil War. Agriculture continued to dominate the lives of most inhabitants, as tobacco took on increasing importance. Everyone from the local banker to the section hand on the railroad depended on the prosperity of the farmer for a livelihood.

In a "do-it-yourself-or-do-without" age Madison Countians depended upon each other for a variety of services. Many black women and children in Richmond were employed as servants. Day labor was relatively cheap, even for these hard times, and a white or black "hand" could earn between thirteen and eighteen dollars a month plus board. Rural blacks and whites with little or no land worked for farmers as day laborers or servants. Their earnings were far below the sum considered necessary for an adequate standard of living for a family at the turn-of-the-century.[9]

A traveler, like one of the steady stream of "drummers" who frequented the hotels of Richmond, would have noticed little change in the community in the late nineteenth century. This salesman probably would not have entered the county by road. Although a bridge connected Madison with Fayette County at Clay's Ferry, ferries were still in use at Valley View, near College Hill, at Boonesborough, and at other points along the Kentucky River, a waterway that provides most of the northern boundary of the county. Roads, "turnpikes," or "pikes" in the county were simple dirt paths that turned to seas of mud during heavy rains. However, toll roads no longer existed. Travel was free if uncomfortable and hazardous. A stage coach operated between Richmond and Irvine, but only those who had to make the journey braved the jolting ride. In the best weather one might encounter a flock of turkeys or herd of cattle being driven on a roadway to Richmond for sale on Court Day or to the railroad. Generally, only locals or a peddler with a pack or cart penetrated onto the backroads of Madison County.[10]

Valley View ferry, ca. 1930. EKU Archives.

Northern access to Madison County at Clay's Ferry on the Kentucky River, ca. 1935. EKU Archives.

Southern access to Madison County. University of Louisville Photo Archives.

The railroad provided the best and fastest means of traveling to many points in the country in 1900 and for many years afterward. Our fictitious drummer had a choice of trains depending on his point of embarkation. In 1900 two railroads intersected in Richmond, the Richmond, Irvine, Nicholasville, and Beattyville Railway, or "Riney-B," connected those cities with Versailles and Middlesboro. It entered at Valley View, maintained a station in Richmond, and exited at Panola. In 1899 the road reorganized, becoming the Louisville and Atlantic line. Another railway, the Louisville and Nashville Railroad, connected Richmond with central Kentucky through Winchester and points south to Knoxville and beyond. A locomotive on the Fort Estill branch of the L. and N. became known as "Old Henry" after a long-time engineer who worked on the line. Many small communities had their surest contact with the outside world by use of either of these lines. The lack of a direct route to Lexington by railroad or comfortable travel by road helped isolate Richmond and Madison County, making Richmond a trade center not only for its own citizens but also for inhabitants of the nearby mountain counties.[11]

If our drummer friend alighted from the L. and A. at its depot on North Third Street or the L. and N. on East Main, he would have been carried to his hotel by one of several local entrepreneurs with buggies or wagons looking for a small income by meeting the trains. Unfortunately, in 1900 he would have missed riding on Devore's mule-drawn streetcar, that ill-fated venture having failed in 1898.[12]

With a choice of several hotels the salesman might have chosen either the St. Charles, opposite the courthouse on North Second Street, or the Glyndon, on West Main. The latter would have offered more plush surroundings, having been rebuilt after a fire in 1892. A side porch ran along Third Street by the entrance most often used by "Ladies." Many of the younger set enjoyed "promenading" along the balcony, both to see and to be seen. Leather upholstered chairs in the lobby offered a fine place for relaxing. To local inhabitants the lobby served as the most convenient meeting place in town. Not to be outdone by any similar establishment, the Glyndon installed 150 "incandescent" lights in 1901, removing the old gas lights. The Glyndon had a plush dining room, where, for only seventy-five cents, one could purchase a full-course meal on Sunday, including everything from turtle soup to dessert. Or a hungry individual could wander over to the restaurant of A. Dinelli, next door to the post office, for more simple fare.[13]

Main Street in downtown Richmond, ca. 1908. EKU Archives.

Madison County Court House, ca. 1906. EKU Archives.

Federal Building in Richmond shortly after completion of construction, 1897. EKU Archives.

The post office, with Federal District Court meeting on the second floor, gave the city of Richmond a second impressive public building, one ranking with the antebellum county courthouse. Built of Rockcastle County "Freestone" and completed in 1897 at a cost of $100,000, the "Federal Building" came about because of the influence of local Congressman, former Governor, and later Senator James B. McCreary. The quarterly meetings of the district court brought crowds in from surrounding counties and added to the business coffers of Richmond for many years.[14]

If our drummer happened to be a door-to-door salesman he might have visited such homes of the well-to-do as Irvinton or Brighton on Lancaster Avenue still unpaved at the time, or the Bennett or McCreary homes on Main Street. A short walk up Lancaster would have taken our visitor to the old campus of Central University, a school founded by the southern wing of the Presbyterian Church after the Civil War to counter the northern influence of Centre College in Danville. The Madison Female Institute operated on a nearby hill overlooking the downtown area of Richmond and offered a classical education for young ladies with a decided southern flavor. A lilac hedge that surrounded the campus hid a genteel world that recalled another era, one soon to disappear in the twentieth century.[15]

Richmond offered citizens and visitors alike some of the amenities of urban life not found in rural Madison County. The Richmond Water and Light Company, Jere A. Sullivan, president, provided its patrons water from Lake Reba via a 135-foot tall standpipe and maintained a "gas plant" for producing coal gas for lighting. Only a few customers used that fuel for cooking. Competition came from the Hume Cooperage and Electric Company which had run wires to several homes. On any but moonlit nights streetlights burned on Main at First and Second streets. As the largest industry in the county, the Hume workers, numbering nearly two hundred, turned out 1,000 barrels daily. Telephone service was available from the Richmond Telephone Company, operated in connection with the East Tennessee Telephone Company. Over a half-dozen operators were on call throughout the day. One could have clothes cleaned at the steam laundry operated by the Tevis brothers, who maintained branches at Irvine, Berea, Millers Creek, Panola, and "other points." The Richmond Cold Storage and Ice Company provided ice for "ice chests" that for the first time made it possible for Madison Countians to store fresh food for extended periods. The proprietor promised only the purest product made from distilled water.[16]

Almost anything one needed could be purchased "downtown." Our drummer could have supplied the paint sold at Willging's store for $1.25 a gallon. A gentleman could purchase a tailormade suit at Stouffer's for ten dollars or buy "gents' furnishings" at the James P. Tribble store. The ladies had a bit more choice and could buy a Butterick pattern at Owen McKee Dry Goods and Notions and a hat next door at the Richmond Millinery Company. The two white mortuaries in town also offered furniture as well as funeral services. W. S. Oldham promised, "If not right, I will make it right."[17]

Zaring Mill on Main Street in downtown Richmond, 1904. Courtesy David Greene.

Of course, much of the town's business revolved around the trade with farmers, including those of surrounding counties. On most Saturdays farm families swelled the population of Richmond. Our drummer might have called at J. W. Zaring Grain and Mill Company on East Main Street, established in 1892, the largest mill in the county, having the capacity to turn out 150 barrels of flour, 600 bushels of meal, and six tons of feed daily. "Zaring's Patent Flour" could be purchased either at the mill or at retail outlets in the county. Other important ancillaries to the farming community included Douglas and Simmons Hardware on Second Street, where a farmer could purchase a Syracuse chilled plow; the Kentucky Carriage Works, which housed rubber-tiring facilities for fancy buggies; and C. E. Douglas and Company Hardware and Farming Implements, which handled stoves and numerous other metal products. Richmond also provided another service as a market town and transportation center. Although much trading of cattle, horses, mules, and other farm commodities took place on an individual basis throughout the year, on Court Day, the first Monday of each month when the circuit court convened, trading took on a special fervor. Hundreds and sometimes thousands of people, in good weather, flocked to Richmond for trading, selling, visiting, and sometimes a bit of carousing. Cattle were generally sold at either the old county fairgrounds site on East Irvine Street or at Norris Brothers and Embry's. On one occasion soon after the turn-of-the-century, over 1,500 head of cattle sold in one day for an average of three-quarter cents per pound. On the First Street side of the courthouse hundreds of mules and horses would be congregated for more informal trading. Often livestock would spill over onto the back streets, and trading would go on into the evening hours. Peddlers of various wares from patent medicines to vegetables would parade the streets or set up shop along the side streets. In an era when entertainment was limited and when most people worked long hours on isolated farms, Court Day offered a chance for economic gain and a much needed change of pace to life.[18]

Other forms of recreation were available to Madison Countians. Whether enjoying the summertime Friday evening concerts at the courthouse bandstand or the simple pleasures of visiting on the front porch with friends, entertainment could be found. Holidays like the Fourth of July, had a special double role in public entertainment as a time for display of patriotism and a good bit of fun. Political campaigns gave all the opportunity to hear a "public speaking." With Kentucky's annual election schedule political "barbecues" were never in short supply. County fairs offered entertainment as well as prizes for many categories of contestants. As Kentucky society became more segregated in the late nineteenth century, a separate Colored Fair was usually held a week or so after the fair for whites only. In addition, Berea College sponsored similar activities for southern Madison County, and service organizations like the Elks held special events.[19]

Organized sports eventually found their way to the county, after having already swept the nation, as Central University joined in intercollegiate competition at the turn-of-the-century. Local football buffs took heart in 1900 when Central hired a former Columbia University halfback as coach. He soon rewarded their hopes by leading their underdog team to a tie with the vaunted Centre team, 5-5. Baseball also became a popular pastime and Richmond eventually fielded a team in the Bluegrass League. Rural communities often organized baseball teams for regular play in the summer.[20]

Bluegrass baseball league game on Eastern Kentucky State Normal School campus, 1909. EKU Archives.

Most of the older forms of entertainment were still popular, church "socials" and dances taking up the energies of the young folk. If not opposed to a bit of travel, Madison Countians could make the trek to Boonesborough, which offered dancing at an outdoor pavilion, swimming, a beach area, and a hotel and cabins for vacationers. Outside the county, the more affluent could enjoy the "waters" at the Estill Springs Hotel at Irvine or Crab Orchard Springs in Garrard County. The latter boasted of its three kinds of "iron water" and southern cuisine.[21]

Traveling shows like "Old John Robinson's Ten Enormous Shows Combined," featuring circuses, menageries, and hippodromes, made their yearly rounds, as did the old faithful medicine show with its cures of snake oil and life-giving elixirs. But Richmond offered something that could not be found in most other towns of its size, the Grand Opera House, a theatre that booked everything from vaudeville acts to comic opera, minstrel shows to serious drama like *Faust* and *Romeo and Juliet*. Eventually, about 1910, this theatre began showing the newest form of mass entertainment, the moving picture, on an irregular schedule.[22]

In an age when life was harsh and often brutal, the church offered comfort to a majority of Madison Countians. Churches like the Baptists, Disciples of Christ, Episcopalians, Methodists, and Presbyterians maintained large sanctuaries in Richmond, and smaller churches were scattered throughout the county. Many people took their religion seriously, enough so that Baptists and Disciples of Christ still wrangled over church doctrine, accusing each other of apostasy. Not long after the turn-of-the-century Catholics built a new church on Main Street. Blacks and whites maintained separate facilities, with the church offering Negroes one of their few avenues for self-expression and leadership. Interdenominational meetings drew large crowds, with as many as one thousand people attending a countywide Sunday school convention in Berea in 1901.[23]

While many local parishioners followed their religious beliefs as they saw them, perhaps none worked harder at it than did Isabel Harris Bennett, known as Belle Bennett. In a busy lifetime she worked in missionary fields at home and abroad, organized Sue Bennett College in London to honor a sister, and helped black Methodists in the county.[24]

The religious community of the time reacted somewhat more quickly to changing technology than one might expect. For example, the Richmond First Christian Church added a telephone transmitter to its auditorium in 1900 so that parishioners could listen to the weekly Sunday morning service at home. Ministers came and went with regularity, though sometimes with the slightest hint of controversy. For example, the First Presbyterian Church "virtually starved out" Reverend Dr. W. H. Dodge in 1905 when he did not resign after a period of internal strife.[25]

If the religious institutions provided for the spiritual needs of the county, the banking institutions also served a vital function. These banks provided for the financial needs of Richmond and the surrounding area, being the lifeblood of the business and agricultural communities. The largest, the State Bank and Trust Company, was controlled by the

Hanger family, whose mansion at Arlington dominated the scene just outside Richmond on Lexington Pike. Other old and wealthy Madison County families controlled the two remaining banks. The Bennetts and the Burnams governed the Madison National Bank, and the Caperton family managed the Richmond National Bank.[26]

Our drummer could have visited other areas of Madison County. The majority of residents of the county lived in rural areas or clusters of houses that blended into communities like Panola, Union City, Valley View, Kirksville, and others too numerous to mention here. Almost every crossroads formed such a community. Along the Kentucky River lumber mills like the Southern Lumber Mills still thrived at communities such as Valley View, where a weekly newspaper, the *Argent*, a bank, and several stores served a population of over one thousand. At Panola, located on the Riney-B, two mills turned out crossties and other lumber products, providing employment and economic stability for the village. Country stores provided many services for their communities, including being most often the local post office, "if your politics were right." They dispensed everything from lace to horse collars, from farm machinery to needles. In Panola or other villages in eastern and southern Madison County, mountain men would make an annual appearance in the spring in the process of "going below" to work on the farms of central Kentucky. They would purchase a pair of shoes, a shirt or two and a pair of overalls in which to work during the summer before winding their way back into the upcountry before the first snow.[27]

Southern Lumber Company at Valley View. Courtesy David Greene.

Communities on railroad lines grew more important than those at intersections of dirt roads. For example, turn-of-the-century Waco, in the eastern part of the county on the Louisville and Atlantic line, served as the focal point of much activity. Crockery clay deposits in that region supported two active pottery plants, including one that sent tile to be used on the Kentucky Building at the 1904 St. Louis World's Fair. A large grist mill, a bank, three stores, a school, two churches, and dozens of houses gave this small village a sense of community. Other businesses like the distilleries at Foxtown or on Silver Creek offered rural folk a job and contributed to the growth of small villages.[28]

In southern Madison County the town of Berea functioned as an entity, mostly serving the college. R. J. Engle's store on Chestnut Street took care of most of the community's needs. On the edge of the college campus Boone Tavern, completed near the end of the decade, provided lodging and meals for the weary traveler on the Dixie Highway at a modest cost of two dollars per day. Already Berea had developed a reputation as a center for the production and distribution of mountain crafts. The slow growth of the town also depended on the usage of the L. and N. facilities by the population of southern Madison and northern Rockcastle counties. The college provided most of the jobs in the town, encouraging migration from surrounding counties, and operating the utilities, a hospital, schools, and a newspaper, the *Citizen*, that served the entire community. Lincoln Hall housed most of the academic activities of the school. Moreover, Berea reached into outlying areas with

Boone Tavern in Berea, ca. 1920. University of Louisville Photo Archives.

various programs, including operating the Berea College Extension Library. For many an area resident the mule-drawn sleds of this service were their only source of books.[29]

Perhaps Berea, Richmond, Kirksville, Cottonburg, and the dozens of other communities and isolated farms in Madison County would not have seemed much different than other Kentucky counties to our visiting drummer. He might have traveled on to another sales area with little reflection on what he had seen in Madison County. The material culture and the place names of Madison County would not have differed much from similar counties of the time. The foregoing description provides some important reference points, but individuals are the bone and sinew of history. And certain people, for better or worse, influenced the life of Madison County in the first decades of the twentieth century.

Madison Countians have never been isolated from the major events that have shaken the history of Kentucky. The state's annual elections kept the political pot aboiling; and local, state, and national politics and issues became entangled in controversies that sometimes led to violence.[30]

The presidential election of 1896 pitted William Jennings Bryan, the fusion candidate of the Democratic and Populist parties, against William McKinley, the choice of the Republican party. This campaign caused an irrevocable split in the Democratic party over the free silver issue. French Tipton, a Richmond lawyer, former judge, and amateur historian, became the central figure in a local conflict during this campaign. A hard money man, Tipton gave up the editorship of the *Climax*, a local Democratic paper, went over to the Republicans, and became editor of their organ, the *Pantagraph*. Judge John C. Chenault bought the *Climax* from Tipton and touted the candidacy of Bryan and the merits of free silver. The other Richmond paper, the *Kentucky Register*, owned by Charles F. White and edited by Clarence E. Woods, also represented the Democratic side and supported Bryan. Tempers flared during the campaign, and all three papers allowed the local battle to degenerate into personal conflict.[31]

After Bryan lost the election, narrowly in Kentucky but by a landslide throughout the nation, Woods left the *Kentucky Register* after having been connected with that paper for ten years. He immediately joined the newly renamed *Richmond Climax*, claiming that the *Register* did not fully support the silver issue. Woods maintained his sole interest to be "the cause of the poor people."[32]

The bitter battle between the Bryan and McKinley forces in the state did not end with the election of 1896. Another political figure closer to home, William Goebel, stirred up even more passion in the hearts of Kentuckians just at the turn-of-the-century. In the 1899 gubernatorial election Goebel faced Republican W. S. Taylor. Woods took over full-time editorship of the *Climax* and molded that paper into the strongest local advocate of the Goebel candidacy. Tipton in the *Pantagraph* just as adamantly supported Taylor. Both sides wisely saw Madison County as crucial to carrying the state, because the county was evenly split in most elections. Goebel made at least two appearances in the county, with supporting speeches made by former Missouri Governor W. J. Stone, a Madison County native, and by none other than William Jennings Bryan. The latter, famous for his booming speaking voice, had to apologize for a somewhat milder intonation because of a busy schedule; but he turned on the old Bryan charm before an audience at the courthouse. Woods pressed hard for the Madison County vote, claiming that Goebel's enemies slandered his hero. "Those who are deluded into believing him a creature of horns and hoofs," Woods implored, "will be treated to the spectacle of one of the most genteel of gentlemen, as polished as he is patriotic, and as brainy as he is brave."[33]

Taylor narrowly carried Madison County by ninety-one votes in the November election, enabling a Republican to win the county judgeship. In the following weeks the entire state fell into near anarchy as both Goebel and Taylor claimed victory. The *Climax* did not give up easily, noting that the vote of Kentucky blacks for Taylor accounted for his apparent plurality. With the General Assembly in turmoil, Frankfort became an armed camp and the *Climax* ominously reported sighting "four extra coaches with armed men" from the mountains traveling through Richmond on the L. and N.[34]

Within days an assassin's bullet felled William Goebel, throwing the entire state into a frenzy. Democrats cried for Taylor's blood, and Republicans refused to admit any guilt. The *Pantagraph*, under the leadership of Tipton, continued its endorsement of Taylor long after Lieutenant Governor J. C. W. Beckham assumed the mantle of Goebel. The local Democratic papers, the *Richmond Climax* and the newly renamed *Semi-Weekly Register*, as well as other Democrats throughout the state fully intended to capitalize on the death of Goebel. United States Representative McCreary kept alive the issue by chairing a Goebel Memorial Committee. The temper of the moment was perhaps best illustrated in a letter from one bellicose young girl who donated a dollar to the cause with the admonition: "Won't you please kill the man that killed Mr. Goebel?"[35]

Within weeks another incident brought violence to the streets of Richmond. In mid-1900 a battle developed over ownership of the Richmond Water and Light Company. Editor Woods of the *Climax* took a typical Progressive stance, advocating public ownership of utilities. He claimed that the *Register* served as the "Water and Light organ." Judge Chenault believed the attack too strong and asked for Woods' resignation. The editor complied in late August.[36]

In a few days tragedy struck when two prominent citizens met "in a fatal encounter" on Main Street. Tipton and Woods had been feuding for years on everything from the free silver issue to finally the question of public ownership of utilities. Late in the afternoon of Saturday, September 1, 1900, the conflict moved from words to action. Tipton confronted Woods on the street while the latter talked with some other men. Witnesses swore that Tipton struck Woods on the face without warning from the side, so that the ex-editor did not see the blow coming. Momentarily stunned, Woods fell to his knees; but he arose with a pistol in hand and fired one shot into Tipton's abdomen. The bullet struck vital organs before exiting Tipton's back. Tipton slumped to the brick sidewalk calling for mercy. The men nearby immediately took him to his home and several doctors came to his aid. County Judge Million placed a $5,000 bond on Woods. The mortally wounded Tipton lingered on into Monday and, only hours before his death, exonerated Woods by corroborating his story and that of witnesses. Tipton's testimony on his deathbed ended the threat of an indictment against Woods, who soon resumed his editorial career.[37]

The death of French Tipton has deeper meaning than simply the killing of one man by another. Tipton and Woods represented the best of Kentucky society. If men of this stature and breeding took part in such violence, then is it any wonder that a stigma of bloodiness is attached to Kentucky to this day? The violent legacy of the Civil War and Reconstruction, the blood feuds of the Kentucky mountains, the era of lynchings, the murder of Goebel (the only governor ever assassinated in the United States), and incidents like the Tipton killing rightfully identified the Commonwealth as a state with little respect for human life.[38]

Madison County politics slowed not a beat with the Tipton-Woods incident, if anything, intensifying with the fall election of 1900. Bryan again went down to defeat at the hands of McKinley, this time losing Madison County by a close margin of forty-one votes. In a special gubernatorial election Democrat Beckham lost the county by forty-four votes but carried the state. Most other local and state races in Madison County continued to be just as closely contested. Voting patterns normally found Richmond narrowly voting Democratic, with Berea and southern Madison County following the Republican banner. Precincts with a heavy black vote always went into the column of the Grand Old Party. The areas of the county that identified with the South, particularly the northern end and white citizens of Richmond, voted Democratic. Most city and county races continued to be very competitive.[39]

County politics centered upon the election of a county judge, fiscal court, jailer, and school superintendent. The fiscal court took up most of its time caring for the pitiful road system while keeping down taxes. Richmond, on the other hand, demonstrated some of the same patterns that altered American urban areas in the early twentieth century. Historians have identified the time span from the turn-of-the-century through World War I as the Progressive Era, a period of reform on a massive scale never before seen in the county. Richmond became one of the few towns in Kentucky influenced by this movement, led by Clarence E. Woods.[40]

By 1900 Richmond had grown to the size of a fourth-class city, using the mayor-council system of government. Many of the town's problems mirrored those of even larger cities. Sewage created a more pressing dilemma as the population grew. Cesspools often overran during rainstorms, and trash disposal was haphazard at best. Keeping the peace posed serious problems, and already some citizens recognized a drug problem, practiced by those with "ways that are dark." One street had even been given the name "Dope Alley." Brick sidewalks extended throughout most of the town, the dirt streets forever dusting the weekly wash or stubbornly clinging to one's best pair of shoes. Animal wastes piled up on the streets, adding to pollution and creating an aesthetic eyesore as well.[41]

The city fathers reacted to these difficulties, and by 1901 Richmond had a rather specific code of ordinances addressing most of the problems of the era. Richmond collected fees for most any type of activity carried on in the city limits including a charge of ten dollars per day for operating a "ball-and-baby game." Wholesale and retail merchants as well as peddlers paid a standard fee of twenty-five dollars a year. Animals created problems, and an ordinance strictly prohibited "all standing teams" from being tied to trees, hydrants, and fences. Privies were inspected twice a year and large fines could be meted out for "introducing smallpox, diphtheria, yellow fever, etc." into the city. Keeping a "bawdy house, house of ill-fame, disorderly house, or house at which lewd or obscene acts are permitted" was strictly forbidden. Moreover, the city fathers expressed concern about the city's image and forbade bathing in any pond without a bathing suit.[42]

Woods' bloody confrontation with Tipton did not slow his career, and he became the leader of Progressivism in Richmond. One of the most fascinating and energetic leaders in Madison County history, Woods, a Central University graduate, returned to Richmond in the early nineties after founding the *Lebanon Enterprise* in 1887. After the tragedy of early September, 1900, he expended his energies working for Sigma Nu Fraternity as editor of its paper. It was not long, however, until J. C. Chenault and A. D. Miller patched up their differences with Woods, and they initiated a campaign to nominate Woods for mayor of Richmond in 1901. After several weeks of editorials and letters to the editor pushing his candidacy, Woods consented to enter the May Democratic primary. He lamented the problems of the city in paying its bills, promising with typical Progressive rhetoric, "If elected I shall try with all strength to do right—that is all." The *Climax* editorially compared Woods with the famous Progressive mayor of Cleveland, Tom Johnson, and published endorsements of Woods from papers in surrounding counties. However, on election day David R. Tevis won in a four-man race, defeating Woods by forty-eight votes. Tevis went on to win the fall election, doing little during his tenure as mayor to bring about needed change in Richmond.[43]

During this period Woods continued his fraternity work, wrote occasional articles for the *Climax*, and served briefly as an aide to Senator McCreary. The *Climax* never relented in its pro-Bryan, antigold, anti-Wall Street brand of Progressivism. Editor Miller often fell back on moralistic arguments, a stance typical of Progressives. On occasion he took after local Republicans, associating them with "King" William McKinley. Prominent Republican families like the Bennetts and Burnams he usually characterized as leaders of a local political machine.[44]

As time neared for the next mayoral election, Woods wasted no time, declaring his candidacy in late December, 1904. He received the nomination against token opposition in the Democratic primary and won unopposed in the general election. In many respects his four years in office exemplified an archetypal Progressive administration. Old Richmond was to see changes of a reform nature that were to shake its very foundations.[45]

Other citizens of Richmond associated themselves with the Progressive cause, including Reverend Hugh McLellan, pastor of the First Christian Church. Just prior to Woods' inauguration, McLellan delivered a clean government sermon to his congregation in which he lashed out at political bossism, pleading for liquor and drug control. "I call upon you," the minister urged, "to wake to an interest in Richmond."[46]

Woods' four years as mayor typified much that Progressives desired, including control, if not prohibition, of liquor, applying business practices to government, abolition of gambling, and support of crime control. The mayor's stringent code of morals immediately ran afoul of Richmond's prominent reputation as a wide-open town. He went after the saloon owners and forced them to follow state law and not sell their wares on Sunday. The city also prosecuted gambling violations with more regularity than previously. Like his counterpart in Louisville, Mayor Robert Worth Bingham, Woods enforced previously ignored statutes. He immediately put forward other reform ideas before the council.[47]

The new mayor stressed fiscal responsibility and he initiated a uniform system of public accounting, one of the primary Progressive thrusts of the era. He maintained a strict code of ethics for himself and others, declaring that no city official could sell to the city or violate any other conflict of interest dictum. Woods qualified as a "business Progressive" in other ways. For example, he believed that Richmond and Madison County had fallen behind their neighbors in economic development. To move forward he proposed improvements in municipal facilities. During his term the fire department improved its capabilities "to the standards of Winchester," more street lights were added, the city began improvements on Lancaster Avenue, more streets were oiled on a regular basis, and work began on a sewerage system.[48]

However, Woods best exemplified the Progressive ideals of morality. This concern led away from a laissez-faire attitude toward government to an assurance that the state should be used to directly control society "for the better." On the state level, Woods helped organize the Kentucky State Law and Order League, a group that expressed concern about liquor and gambling and their connection with politics. As mayor of Richmond, Woods worked hard to control the flow of liquor during his first year in office. In early 1907 he led dry forces in a local option election. At five A.M. on March 12 church bells pealed, awakening the town. Temperance forces organized a parade of students from Caldwell High School, Madison Female Institute, and Richmond Colored School complete with the singing of hymns and chanting of slogans. Many ladies of the community opposed to the liquor trade worked throughout the day, sometimes in a pouring rain, to get men to the polls. Expecting a close vote, the owners of Richmond's twelve saloons allegedly paid as much as twenty dollars for a vote in their favor. At the end of the ballot count early in the evening, from the courthouse bandstand, Mayor Woods announced victory for the antisaloon side by 148 votes.[49]

Woods continued to work for the prohibition cause when he left office. He and other Progressives did not look kindly toward the unemployed and vagrants. In a middle-class moral tone Woods vowed that "the creature who neither toils or spins is a menace to our community." And, also exemplifying the conservative racial views of most Progressives, he proposed that "the laws against such diseased germs should be put into rigorous effect, which will greatly minimize the vexations of the servant question," referring to the difficulty of keeping blacks at work as servants.[50]

On a loftier plane Woods stood for more liberal Progressive ideals. He completely supported the right to vote for women and cooperated with Laura Clay, a Madison County native and president of the Kentucky Equal Rights Association. Local state Representative R. W. Miller also received Woods' approval of an antilobbying bill the Richmond native introduced in the General Assembly. One final example of Woods' Progressive zeal will end description of this period in Madison County history. When the L. and N. railway first attempted to take over the L. and A. line, he protested by taking a petition to Frankfort. True to form Woods argued that this union violated the Progressive ideal of free competition, giving the Louisville-based railroad a monopoly of rail transportation in the county.[51]

This Progressive episode in Madison County history ended with the election of the next mayor, Samuel Rice. Woods and his supporters for a brief moment joined the national Progressive trend in government and public service. Only a few communities in Kentucky shared this experience in the first decade of the twentieth century. After serving as mayor, Woods soon began to sever his connection with Richmond, moving to Florida to edit several newspapers in the next decade. His time in Richmond had been one of the most exciting and "progressive" in this century.[52]

The first twenty years of the twentieth century in Madison County were years of struggle. With each step forward, progress appeared slowed by tradition, economic stagnation, and poor educational opportunities. Moreover, Kentucky lost ground in the early twentieth century as its southern neighbors bypassed the Commonwealth in economic development. The traditions of the nineteenth century proved formidable obstacles to needed change in Madison County.[53]

Perhaps nothing better illustrated the crossroads at which Madison County found itself than the advent of the first automobile in the county and the celebration of the Kentucky Homecoming festivities in 1906.

Many Kentucky communities planned activities for mid-June of that year. The Madison County celebration lasted for several days, but most of the formal activities took place on June 18. That day Storms' Military Band led a parade up Main Street in Richmond witnessed by a crowd estimated at ten thousand. In the evening Senator McCreary presided as toastmaster at a large banquet at the Glyndon. Former Governor David R. Francis of Missouri, a native of Madison County, announced that he would give the county a stone monument-fountain in commemoration of the area's pioneers. The inscription read: "In memory of the pioneers who with energy born of conviction, wrested from the earth and gave an empire to untold generations to come, this memorial is dedicated by one of Kentucky's sons, 1775-1906." When placed at the northwest corner of First and Main by the courthouse, one side of the fountain served human passersby and the street side slaked the thrist of animals. Local tradition has it that a local "sport" in an immaculate carriage pulled by a high-stepping horse flashed up to the fountain upon its completion, watered his steed, and then dashed off. More often in the first decade of this century workhorses, mules, and oxen drank there. Shortly before this celebration of Madison County's rich heritage a Richmond merchant, Ben Banks, became the first resident to own an automobile. This inaugural event did not draw anywhere near the crowd of the homecoming, but a group estimated at about two hundred witnessed the wave of the future as Banks sped off down Main Street. The fact that the engine soon sputtered and died and the auto had to be ignominiously returned by a team of horses, notwithstanding, Madison Countians were impressed by this newfangled "machine."[54]

The second decade of the century opened with the automobile no longer being an oddity on Richmond streets while still raising a few eyebrows at Poosey Ridge or Speedwell. The *Richmond Climax* claimed that forty-three autos puttered around the county in 1910. Other outward signs of change became evident. Men wore fewer beards and mustaches, and the clothing styles of both sexes lost that "Gay Nineties" look. After the passage of the first Pure Food and Drug Act in 1906 patent medicines no longer played as prominent a role in the health care of Madison Countians. However, one could still purchase "Electric Bitters" for indigestion at Perry and Thomas Drug Store or rely on "Dr. Pierce's Pleasant Pellets" for other ailments. Gone from Richmond was William G. White, a druggist whose remedies gained such a large following that he moved on to the greener pastures of Louisville to continue his patent medicine business.[55]

As the Civil War receded in time the generation that had lived and fought in that titanic struggle began to die out. The "Lion of Whitehall" Cassius Marcellus Clay; Judge William Chenault, one of the founders of the Louisville-based Filson Club historical society; Colonel James W. Caperton; and Major Curtis F. Burnam, a temporary member of Grant's cabinet whose "politics were ever Republican," all died in the first decade of this century.[56]

William Jennings Bryan and Governor James B. McCreary on steps of Eastern Kentucky State Normal School Sullivan Hall dormitory, 1911. EKU Archives.

Another member of that generation, James Bennett McCreary, proved to be one of the most durable politicians in Kentucky history. After serving as governor in the midseventies, McCreary went on to terms as United States representative and senator. In 1911 "Gentleman Jim" became the gubernatorial nominee of the Democratic party with the full support of the state's wealthiest entrepreneur, John C. C. Mayo of Paintsville. On election day, McCreary carried his home county by only 112 votes, but he swept into office against Republican Judge E. C. O'Rear. Kentucky historians Thomas D. Clark and Harry Caudill give no credit to the McCreary administration, citing the "Old Roman's" proclivity of straddling issues as earning him the nickname of "Bothsides." Moreover, McCreary is charged with being a pawn of the millionaire Mayo and eastern business interests. Another historian, Nicholas Burckel is a bit more charitable, finding some evidence of Progressivism during the second McCreary administration. Burckel cites a state legislature that had enacted laws governing direct primaries, a uniform system of accounting, workmen's compensation, life insurance, and public school textbooks. Clarence E. Woods' close contact with McCreary over the years left the former Progressive mayor with only contempt for "Bothsides." Moreover, he maintained that the two-time governor only served for self-seeking purposes and enjoyed retelling the old adage that "McCreary is all high heels, hairdye, and hypocrisy." If nothing else, McCreary typified the consummate Kentucky politician who existed solely to win election and perpetuate his party. His political longevity proved again that politics is "the damnedest in Kentucky."[57]

The roles of women and blacks in the first decades of the twentieth century further illustrated the clash of continuity and change. The "southernness" and belief in the Lost Cause of the Confederacy that dominated the minds and folkways of most Madison Countians allowed little room for social advancement for women and none at all for Negroes.

Opportunities for women came primarily in education and public service. As mentioned above, Belle Bennett broke new ground for women with her efforts in behalf of education and religion. A band of ladies continued to lead the development of the Pattie A. Clay Infirmary, one of the few public hospitals in the region. Mary E. Letcher, a Richmond native, graduated from the Cincinnati College of Medicine in 1900, but her place of practice is not known. Miss S. M. Templeman practiced law in the county. Anna D. Lilly, the wife of Judge Grant E. Lilly, took over the editorship of the *Kentucky Register* for a brief period. For many women, the right to vote became their greatest cause at the turn-of-the-century. Madison County native Laura Clay, the daughter of Cassius M. Clay, served valiantly in the national effort to win the right to vote. Like her illustrious father, she did not easily hew the line adopted by others. For example, while fully supporting the suffrage right, she opposed the passage of an amendment to the United States Constitution, preferring instead to work through state statutes. With the passage of the Nineteenth Amendment Madison County women entered a new era.[58]

Laura Clay. University of Kentucky King Library Special Collections Department.

The lot of blacks in Madison County was less sanguine. White Madison Countians for the most part did not approve of the influence of blacks in politics. Negroes generally voted Republican out of tradition. Apparently blacks voted in substantial numbers, and the pro-Democratic *Richmond Climax* often accused local Republicans of manipulating the Negro ballot. The *Climax* itself occasionally used the "bloody shirt" of racial politics during an election. One must remember that the so-called Progressive Era witnessed a time of literal terror for many black people as lynchings, burnings, and segregation swept the nation. When *Climax* editor Miller complained about the administration of Theodore Roosevelt treating Booker T. Washington as an equal while praising the Democratic party as the "white man's party," he was only following the accepted mores of white southern society.[59]

Just after the turn-of-the-century Madison County played a key role in the growth of segregation in the state during the passage of the Day Law. Berea College and its preparatory school provided blacks with their greatest educational opportunities in Kentucky in the late nineteenth century. Almost any hope for higher education for Negroes rested at the school in southern Madison County. Berea turned out numerous black graduates who went into the service of education for their race by becoming teachers. These instructors fanned out across the state and contributed their skills in the successful battle against black illiteracy.[60]

By 1904 the white racial consensus determined to put a stop to racially integrated classrooms in Kentucky, a nearly completed movement in the old Confederate states. Berea President W. G. Frost has been accused of abandoning the cause of racial justice, one of the primary goals at the founding of Berea in the 1850s, in his quest to provide more opportunity for mountain whites. Whether guilty or not, it is difficult to see how Frost or any other educational leader at the time could have forestalled the segregationist trend. With a public school segregation law already on the books and the number of blacks in attendance at Berea declining, the passage of the Day Law simply concluded the segregationist onslaught.[61]

In early January, 1904, Representative Carl Day of Breathitt County, a graduate of southern-oriented Central University, introduced a bill providing for penalties for maintaining public or private racially mixed classrooms. He had plenty of support from Madison Countians. The *Richmond Climax* bitterly complained about "The Berea Nuisance," claiming that it would be "better by far to let them [whites] go back to the mountains—and let Berea go to hell" than continue integrated education there. The white consensus held firm, as even old "uncompromising Union man" state Senator Curtis F. Burnam endorsed the Day Law. The Day Law passed both houses and Kentucky joined its sister states to the South in their bent for strict segregation in education and most other public activities. Not surprisingly, the same General Assembly that passed the Day Law also appropriated $57,000 to build a cottage at the Confederate Home at Pee Wee Valley. The trustees of Berea College carried their fight to remain integrated all the way to the United

States Supreme Court, where, on November 9, 1908, that court upheld the previous decision by the Kentucky Court of Appeals. Berea responded by organizing a campaign that led to the formation of Lincoln Institute in Shelby County. That school was incorporated in 1910. Appropriately, the first building constructed was named Berea Hall.[62]

The passage of the Day Law, however, was only symptomatic of far deeper problems facing Negroes in Madison County and the state at large. These difficulties are reflected in census data, particularly for the decade after 1910. Black population in Madison County declined by over 26 percent from 1900 to 1920, with the bulk of that decline coming in the latter decade. With a death rate twice that of the white population, blacks were dying out and moving out, particularly in rural areas. Their economic plight is mirrored in the published notices of impending sheriff's delinquent tax sales. For example, in one such announcement in 1915 one-half of the land listed, mostly small lots and farms, belonged to "colored" residents, clear evidence of their declining ownership of land. Madison County did escape one of the worst blemishes in American history: lynching. There are no recorded incidents in the first two decades of this century, a time when not a few Kentucky communities were wracked by the tyranny of mob rule.[63]

However, there were some signs of hope, albeit limited, which gave promise of change in later decades. Education offered both whites and blacks their best chance for improvement in their lives. A short-lived black newspaper, the *Rambler*, edited by teacher Emmett Embry, stressed the Booker T. Washington teachings of work, saving money, and education as the surest way out of the dilemma facing Negroes. George Albert Miller, another teacher, wrote poetry. Perhaps no Negro leader, however, had more impact than did Henry Allen Laine.[64]

Born in the Old Cane Springs community and educated at Berea College, Laine taught school briefly in Clark County before returning to his native county. For the next three decades he devoted his life to the welfare of the area's black population. Teaching school for over twenty years, he became interested in extension work. In 1915 he organized a farmers' group for blacks. The next year, with the aid of Belle Bennett and other white church leaders, he initiated a black Chautauqua. For a few years Laine served as an unofficial county extension agent for Madison Negroes, with the title of "County Demonstrator for the Colored People." The fiscal court briefly funded this role. Laine founded farmers and homemakers clubs in the county and organized community fairs and exhibits. These acivities soon tapered off, as funding dried up and racial tensions increased in the county in the 1920s.[65]

Something of a poet, Laine published at least one book of verse, *Foot Prints* in 1914. A devotee of Booker T. Washington's school of racial uplift, Laine maintained in "My Solution of the Race Problem":

> Here's the plan I would adopt,
>   And success would surely follow,
> So much talking I would stop—
>   Educate and save the dollar!

Henry Allen Laine. J. T. Dorris, *Glimpses of Historic Madison Country, Kentucky,* 163.

In "Saloons Must Go" he identified many of the problems of his race with the evils of strong drink. A deeply religious sense permeated almost every poem, and he sometimes wrote in black dialect. Only in "I'm a White Man" did bitterness and frustration at being denied equality seep into his generally optimistic verse. After censoring the white race for its bigotry, Laine prophesied:

> But its coming yet! Yes a better day.
> When the false by the true, shall be swept away.
> When the standard of justice is lifted high,
> Yea, the standard the world shall be measured by,
> In the clearer view of enlightened man,
> When he falls in line with his Maker's plan.
> If I, then, measure in heart and mind,
> To manhood's stature I'm the right man.
> Altho my skin be as black as ink,
>   I'm a White Man!

Perhaps no more meaningful summation of the aspirations of the black race was ever penned.[66]

For all Madison Countians, white and black alike, education offered the best hope for the future. In the late nineteenth century the schools of Louisville and other larger urban areas improved as those of rural Kentucky declined. Educational progress in Madison County came slowly. At the turn-of-the-century Madison County contained more variety of educational opportunities than most Kentucky counties. Central University and Berea College, as well as Madison Female Institute and Caldwell High School, made Richmond a regional education mecca. Opportunities for blacks and county residents, however, were far behind those of Richmond.[67]

Caldwell High School in Richmond, 1910. Courtesy David Greene.

The fate of Madison Female Institute illustrated the changing nature of Kentucky education. Always a small school, the institute provided a "southern finishing school" education popular until the turn-of-the-century. The school struggled for existence after 1900 and could not develop an endowment fund which would tide it over the problems of declining enrollment and increasing debt. As more opportunities for girls and women developed in public education, the pull of weaker schools like Madison Female Institute faded even after the admission of male students. The development of a normal school in Richmond aided this process. Not long after World War I the trustees of the institute gave up the battle, sold some property, and leased the site of the school to the Richmond Board of Education.[68]

Public education advanced slowly in the period from 1900 through World War I. As the twentieth century opened Kentucky law required only eight weeks of continuous school for ages seven to fourteen. A 1908 statute forced county school districts to authorize at least one high school. Moreover, the General Assembly also passed a child labor law aimed at ending the worst abuses of keeping children out of school to work. Two years later another law lengthened the school year to 120 days, also requiring a five-day teacher training period each year. Teachers took examinations, with certificates divided into two classifications. In 1909 only one teacher in the entire county system had a normal school certificate. Accountability also extended to students who could only enter high school after passing a "common school" examination at the end of the eighth grade.[69]

The city school system offered greater opportunities than did the county. In the nineties the city board purchased the Madison Male Academy, building a new school, Caldwell High School, at the site on North Second Street. After 1907 the eleventh and twelfth grades were added to the curriculum, thereby offering a full high school course. In 1909 the city board contracted to allow county students to attend Caldwell, as the county did not have a single high school at the time. As the elementary and secondary classes become more crowded city Superintendent T. J. Coates pleaded for more tax money and buildings. Just prior to the outbreak of World War I Caldwell graduated twenty-three, its largest class ever. The leasing of Madison Female Institute in 1919 eased the overcrowding of white students. Before 1898 all black education took place in black churches. Shortly afterward a $12,000 facility built on Irvine Road housed the new "Richmond Colored School." An addition was made to the school at the end of World War I. School attendance for black students fluctuated more than that of white pupils, but it generally increased during this time.[70]

County students faced the problem of distance, and getting to school often took a walk of several miles across fields or on muddy roads. The county system had a larger number of sudents to educate well. One-and two-room schools predominated, with over 100 of the former in 1910. In 1912 new schools were constructed at Waco, Union City and Kirksville to accommodate high school classes. Seven years later new schools with high school facilities were built at Newby, Speedwell, Red House and Whitehall. Negro schools in the county only extended through the eighth grade, but their graduates could attend the Richmond black high school under the same agreement as that used for county white students. Like their counterparts in Richmond, county teachers attended institutes at the beginning of the school year, listening to such speeches as "How do you use the blackboard and chart?" Berea did not initiate its own separate school system until 1915 after an extensive subscription campaign. With the founding of the new Eastern Kentucky Normal School, "The Model School" opened for primary through high school grades.[71]

What kind of education did Madison Countians receive at the turn-of-the-century? How good were the schools? John Grant Crabbe, a former state superintendent and president of Eastern Kentucky Normal School, in a 1911 Louisville address argued that Kentucky schools were generally in deplorable condition because of poorly trained teachers. He stressed that the citizens of the Commonwealth should be told the real state of their public educational system "and then must be told the truth again." Organizations such as the Madison County School Improvement League sought ways and means to advance the cause of education.[72]

The quality of education varied as much as the qualifications of the teachers, the work of the students, and the interest of the community. Undoubtedly some pupils had more opportunities than others. Two examples from the county system in 1911 illustrate the efforts being made, however halting, to improve educational facilities. Marian Noland's school at Speedwell received special notice because of improvements in the physical appearance of the school. A "nicely polished" stove, flowers in a fenced yard, and croquet and tennis courts gave a sense of pride to the students. Moreover, the boys engaged in a woodworking manual training class while the girls had sewing projects. At Brookstown Nannie Boudenot raised funds to install a heating and ventilating system in her school, adding to the physical comfort of the students. A few students supplemented the six months of public education with work in "subscription schoools" during the spring months. Nevertheless, Crabbe was undoubtedly correct in his general indictment of Kentucky education, as the state and Madison County lagged far behind the rest of the nation in educating their young people.[73]

The role of higher education in Madison County expanded in the early part of this century. Berea College grew and reached deeper into the Appalachian chain, developing a complex labor, academic, and vocational program. The school practiced what it preached about self-sufficiency and the rewards of hard work and diligent study. All students worked, and the school produced nearly everything consumed by the small community from the water supply to food. Labor Day became a celebration of the work ethic and the hope of economic uplift for mountain people. Extension efforts with mountain farmers expanded in the nearby region with the hiring of one of the first county agents in the state with responsibilities for southern Madison County and Rockcastle County.[74]

Greater changes took place in the form of public higher education. Central University, founded by southern leaning Presbyterians in the mid-1870s, struggled for survival at the turn-of-the-century. Fundng of the school created serious problems for the Southern Presbyterian Synod as Central competed with the better-financed and endowed Centre College. The difficulties of funding the school came to a head in early 1901, when "consolidationists" proposed merger of Central with Centre. Local alumni of Central in Richmond quickly organized under the leadership of R. W. Miller, W. R. Shackelford, and J. A. Sullivan. In early April in a petition they expressed their "indignation" at the suggestion of consolidating the two schools. Richmond businessmen claimed that they would lose money, grumbling about the fact that they had put up money to help found Central nearly three decades earlier. The old antagonisms between southern and northern Presbyterians in the state immediately came to the fore in the debate. Judge Charles H. Breck called the merger plan "abject surrender," while H. B. Smith echoed the same sentiments with the question: "But shall 26,000 Southern Presbyterians surrender to 5,000 Northern brethren?'' In late April both Kentucky Presbyterian synods passed the same resolution calling for the merger of Central and Centre after "heated discussion" by the anticonsolidationists.[75]

The latter still hoped to quash the consolidation by carrying the vote before the Central University alumni group, which had to ratify the merger before it became final. In early June both factions sought support from all available alumni. Local anticonsolidationists led by Miller, Shackelford, and Sullivan maneuvered to get enough votes to win. At one meeting of alumni Shackelford spoke for four hours on a point of order, filibustering the session in hope that "re-enforcements" would arrive at dawn. Word of the death of the wife of Central Chancellor Harvey Blanton finally broke up the meeting without a decision. Two weeks later the Central alumni voted fifty-nine to forty-one to consolidate with Centre. As part of the agreement, Walters Collegiate Institute, a preparatory academy for young men, took over the old Central campus. Anticonsolidationists promised to go to court to halt the merger, but they soon gave up, allowing Central University to fade into memory.[76]

In less than five years Richmond had another college to replace old Central. Many leaders in the state understood the need for better-trained teachers. The normal school movement was growing in the Midwest, and Kentucky followed the lead of her northern neighbors. That reason alone, however, was not enough for the establishment of normal schools, colleges dedicated primarily to the education of teachers.[77]

Only by passing through the gauntlet of special interests in the General Assembly could the ambition of creating a public college in Richmond become a reality. Representative R. W. Miller introduced a normal school bill at the opening of the 1906 Kentucky General Assembly. Senator A. R. Burnam pushed the bill through the upper house. Mayor Woods, J. A. Sullivan, and other Richmond citizens supported passage of the bill, intending that one of the first schools be located at the Central University campus. The intact school plant made a good argument for placing a public normal school in Richmond. The citizens of the city owned the campus, valued at $150,000, and promised to deed the property to the state if the site were chosen. With pressure exerted by both Richmond and Bowling Green, the bills passed in early March and Governor J. C. W. Beckham signed them into law March 21, 1906. The General Assembly granted both schools $10,000 for buildings and $40,000 for teachers' salaries for the first year. Ruric Nevel Roark, former head of the normal department at the University of Kentucky, soon took his place as the first president of Eastern State Normal School. At first the school offered only a two-year teacher certification program, not adding the fourth year until the early twenties. When Roark became ill, his wife, Mary C. Roark became acting president and continued in that capacity after his death for a brief period of time. Eastern's next president, John Grant Crabbe, served until 1916, giving way to the administration of Thomas Jackson Coates.[78]

Richmond Secures Normal School by Unanimous Vote.

(Special to The Climax)

Louisville, Ky., May 7th. Richmond wins and so does Bowling Green. Vote unanimous' Shout the glad tidings along. One of the many advantages in Richmond's favor was the Pattie A Clay Infirmary supported by the city and county where sick students could be properly treated and cared for. Their argument had great weight and it now becomes the sacred duty of the Council and Fiscal Court to liberally provide for the support of this noble institution.

The above telegram Monday afternoon stated that Richmond had secured the State Normal School by a unanimous vote. The Commissioners met in Louisville Monday for the purpose of deciding this question, which has been before the public for quite a while. Although it was almost a certainty that our city would be favorably considered we are glad to know for sure that such an institution will be in our midst. Last Tuesday the commissioners visited Richmond and were greatly impressed with the place, her beautiful homes, well equipped business houses and other public necessities, and most of all with the famous and imposing Old Central University buildings and grounds, which was offered to the state for the location of this school. No town in the state has ever offered such inducements, and so liberal an offer could not well be refused. The Commercial Club, of which Mr B L Banks is President, has been untiring in its efforts to place before the state and her different committees the many benefits and the liberal offers made by our town. Richmond should feel greatly indebted to this Club for the interest shown and the efforts made, and to their repeated efforts is largely due the decision reached Monday. No town in the state the size of Richmond can boast of more business thrift and progress. Our citizen at large are on the alert to make this even a more beautiful city than at present. All lines of business, professional and otherwise, are flourishing and all about with one accord, hurrah for the Normal School. But few, perhaps, fully realize what such an institution will mean to this community It will bring yearly into our midst a great body of students, which fact alone means an increase in all lines of business. Hons J. A, Sullivan, R. W Miller, W. R. Shackelford, R. E. Turley and Mayor Woods were the gentlemen from here who went to Louisville Monday to attend the Commissioner's meeting. The other school went to Bowling Green, which offered a $125,000 site. Hon. R. W. Miller of this city, introduced the bill into the Legislature. He submitted a deed to the Central University property which showed that the original tract of land was purchased by his great-great-grandfather for 1,000 pounds.

Richmond Climax, May 9, 1906.

With two colleges in the immediate area young men and women in Madison County had more opportunity to attend college than did the residents of most counties. Some families moved to Madison from other counties so their children could attend Berea or Eastern. Both schools were financial assets to their communities, as they provided jobs for maintenance and support workers. Over the years many a Richmond widow supported herself and her family by renting rooms to students.[79]

Beginning in 1912, another eduational opportunity annually came to the county. That year the Redpath Chautauqua circuit made a week's stopover. For the next two decades Chautauqua offered entertainment, serious drama and music, light opera, lectures, and a variety of other programs. Sometimes important political speakers addressed the audiences not long after a juggler had entertained. In 1914 a Madison Countian could attend all sessions for the entire week for only $8.20. Young men like John Young Brown often worked the circuit as a "fore man," or contact man, who went ahead on the circuit drumming up sponsors and organizing the effort. Brown refined a speech, "The Garibaldi Story," to warm up audiences for the upcoming Chautauqua, later using that discourse during his early political career. Over a twenty-year span Chautauqua filled a vital educational need for Madison and the surrounding area.[80]

If educational opportunities improved somewhat in the first two decades of the twentieth century, so also might one see limited progress in other areas. Transportation, so necessary for business and agriculture, advanced as Madison County left behind the isolation of the nineteenth century. Rail services had provided the only adequate means of travel at the turn-of-the-century. Railway workers like the men at the Louisville and Atlantic shops in Richmond, section hands, and "track-walkers," (men who preceded the trains looking for damaged rails) added to the workforce of the county. In 1899 the suggestion of an electric interurban railroad from Lexington to Richmond at first appeared to be a boon for Richmond business. Eventually Madison Countians realized that artery would preempt their own business interests in favor of the larger Lexington community. They breathed a sigh of relief when the plans fell through for such a venture.[81]

The greatest change in transportation came with the growing popularity of the automobile, and the number of autos increased slowly. About the time of World War 1 prosperity coincided with technical improvements in automobiles. In 1914 a Ford Touring Car (Model T) sold for under $500, a sum that more and more families could afford. However, most people who lived in rural areas continued to depend on horse-and-mule-drawn conveyances for several more decades.[82]

Those who lived on Madison County farms saw little change in their lives in the first two decades. Most alarming was the growth of tenant farming because of the increased acreage devoted to tobacco production. Whereas, in 1900 the county raised slightly over 1,600 acres of tobacco, twenty years later the land under tobacco cultivation had grown to over 7,200 acres. In the same time span the number of farms increased by over 800, while the total acreage in farmland declined by over 10,000 acres. Moreover, the acreage size of farms in the county declined from ninety-seven to seventy-two acres, with the smaller farms under fifty acres nearly doubling in number. Correspondingly, the number of tenant farms had doubled, now equaling nearly 36 percent of Madison County farms. The trend toward smaller farms indicated the growth of tenant farming. Over 85 percent of the tenant farmers were white.[83]

Madison County farmers continued to raise corn, wheat, hemp, and cattle. Sheep production dropped precipitously, as the predations of dogs became a serious problem for most farmers. Corn went into feeding livestock and providing meal for families. Some farmers who sold quantities of corn suspected that it went into the production of grain spirits of the illegal variety. Moonshining, always the pastime of some Madison Countians, continued to be a serious business for quite a few citizens in the southern end of the county.[84]

For an increasing number of farm families the culture of tobacco set the pattern of their lives. From the burning of plant beds in late winter to sowing the beds with tiny seeds in early spring, weeding, "setting" out the plants, "chopping out," worming, suckering, topping, cutting and "housing" in late summer, thence to "stripping" the layers from the stalk and tying into "hands" when the corn came in "case," the cultivation of tobacco predetermined the lives of entire families. The end of the cycle came with the sale of the crop at a warehouse, usually in Richmond. Often farmers had to wait until the weather was cold enough to freeze the roads or, better yet, cover them with packed snow, so that their mule-drawn "slide," or wooden sled, could more easily haul the crop to market.[85]

A confiscated still on display at the Federal Building in Richmond, ca. 1910. Courtesy David Greene.

The dependence on a single crop for most of the family income often created serious problems for the farm owner and tenant alike. The price paid by the large tobacco companies, dominated by the American Tobacco Company, fluctuated enough to raise the hopes of farmers one year and then dash them the next. While Madison County did not witness the violence and barnburning that took place in the infamous "Black Patch" war in western Kentucky during the first decade of the century, local farmers supported the idea of "pooling" their crops. Unfortunately, the efforts of such organizations as the Kentucky Tobacco Growers Association and the Burley Tobacco Society had little impact on stabilizing prices. Madison County farmers, like most of their cohorts throughout the nation, found it difficult to form a united front for action, and the threat of a "cut out" of the 1911 crop failed to gain enough public support.[86]

World War 1 temporarily broke the cycle of poor prices for farm commodities. Almost everything that could be raised on the farm, including cattle, hogs, hemp, and tobacco found ready markets at abnormally high prices. With tobacco selling for averages above forty cents per pound, many farmers bought more land and machinery, expecting the prosperity to last indefinitely. One observer noticed tobacco barns "going up all over the county" as farmers responded to increased prices. Some of the better land in the county sold for $400 per acre. More farmers bought powered machinery or a truck to make their production more efficient. Correspondingly, the number of horses and mules in the county dropped by over 20 percent in the decade from 1910 to 1920.[87]

The Madison County business community depended entirely on the health of the farm. The commercial ties of the county came under increasing influence of Louisville at the turn-of-the-century. On the annual "Louisville Day" representatives of that city would visit Richmond and other nearby towns drumming up trade against their rivals in Cincinnati. About 1905 businessmen formed the Commercial Club, a forerunner of the Chamber of Commerce, with the slogan: "Let our motto be, A Better Richmond."[88]

Madison County could not isolate itself from financial crises that struck the nation, and the Panic of 1907 struck hard at many merchants. The oldest continuous business in the county, the Valley View ferry established in 1785, could survive just about any calamity, but newer concerns like the Central Kentucky Cigar Manufacturing Company in Richmond, which offered for sale the La Superba at twenty-five cents or the Hustler for a nickel, did not survive the financial crisis.[89]

At the end of the second decade of this century, business could not have appeared better. At Court Day hogs and cattle sold for the highest prices ever, with the latter bringing eleven cents per pound. Oil wells were being drilled, promising a bonanza any day. Richmond successfully fought off an attempt to have the Federal District Court removed. In faraway Detroit Henry Ford paid a minimum wage of seven dollars a

Court day in downtown Richmond, ca. 1905. Courtesy David Greene.

day. Prospects for continued prosperity indeed looked rosy as 1920 rolled around.[90]

The conflagration in Europe that precipitated this spurt of economic growth in the late teens, did not go unnoticed by Madison Countians in its early stages. The local papers even began publishing pictures of the war's devastation and provided blow-by-blow accounts of the major battles on the western front. Before the American declaration of war in April, 1917, Madison County's sons were already scattered across the country in training camps. They had little idea of how the war would irrevocably change their lives.[91]

Like most Americans, Madison Countians wholeheartedly followed the patriotic lead of President Woodrow Wilson and, like him, they believed the war to be a crusade for democracy. The first death of the war from the county, that of Jesse Dykes, and the beginning of rationing of food and fuel did not dampen their enthusiasm. Never before had Americans been so organized and regimented. Victory Boys and Victory Girls marched and worked at odd jobs to help out in the war crisis.[92]

''WAR IS OVER,'' declared the bold headlines of the *Richmond Daily Register,* under the new editor Shelton Saufley, on November 11, 1918. Thousands of people from all over the county gathered around the courthouse for a victory celebration. One hardware store on Main

Street sold out of pistol cartridges as revelers fired into the air, shooting down some of the telephone lines. On First Street a blacksmith placed black powder between two anvils, stood back, and then ignited the powder, creating a thunderous explosion while throwing one of the anvils into the air.[93]

The momentary prosperity and the tumultuous celebration of victory at the end of World War 1 belied deep problems in Madison County, difficulties that had carried over from the nineteenth century. Disjointed material progress affected all Madison Countians in one way or another. With the automobile beginning to have its day, owners clamored for better roads. The returning soldier found he could now purchase ready-made Camel and Chesterfield cigarettes for 18 cents a pack at the corner market and see such movies as *The Battle of Love* at Richmond's newest theatre, the Alhambra.[94]

By most other standards the quality of life of many citizens in Madison County may have actually deteriorated. Overall, the total population of the county decreased by 2.5 percent between 1910 and 1920. While some of this decline is due to out-migration, much is directly related to the poor state of health of many citizens. Old scrouges like smallpox continued to haunt the area. At one time in 1900, seventy cases were counted in the College Hill community alone. A year later public health authorities reported over 700 cases of "La Grippe," or influenza, at one time. Tuberculosis, diphtheria, and polio took a heavy toll of the county's population. Pneumonia, "the old man's friend," often struck the young as well. In 1915 county officials counted 131 deaths and only 141 births. Four years later in Richmond there occured 15 more deaths than births for that year; among the black population 32 births were offset by 50 deaths.[95]

What caused these alarming statistics? If Madison followed patterns in other states and counties, the increase of tenant farming contributed to this tragedy. The lifestyle of the sharecropper led to a higher death rate than for other segments of the population. Moreover, medical knowledge and the practice of what expertise was known continued to be limited in Madison County. The valiant efforts of the Pattie A. Clay Infirmary and dedicated doctors were offset by ignorance, alcoholism, addiction to drugs and inadequate diet. Lastly, two examples should illustrate the poor state of health services in the period from the turn-of-the-century through the era of World War 1. In 1900 the Richmond School and Infirmary of Magnetic Healing operated in that city, maintaining a branch at Newby. One wonders how many Madison Countians went to their graves after having been served by such quackery. At the end of the era a local drug store advertised the appearance of "Texas Jack," "The Snake Oil King."[96]

One last legacy of World War 1 brought home to Madison Countians the tenuous nature of life in their time. Just at the end of the war a worldwide influenza epidemic reached the area. Entire families were struck down, with only those who had had previous exposure being spared. Many public meetings were called off, and health officials. urged limiting patrons in poolrooms, movies, and churches. Business nearly came to a halt as people feared contracting and spreading the malady. Mayor L. P. Evans of Richmond served as an example to children by being inoculated with a serum before a school group. While the death rate from the flu did not approach that of other parts of the country, poor roads contributed to the deaths of two individuals in the Union City community when bad weather kept them from receiving medical attention. The board of health warned: "If you have the flu stay away from people ten days after fever disappears," or "You may cause the death of your best friend."[97]

Chapter Fourteen

PROSPERITY AND DEPRESSION, 1920-1939

In the era from 1920 through 1939 Madison Countians witnessed some of the greatest changes and most profound tragedies in the history of their county, state, and nation. Often called the Era Between the Wars or the Interwar Period, it began as the world settled into the peace that followed World War I. The Age of Wonderful Nonsense, the Jazz Age, the Roaring Twenties are all names interchangeably applied to the 1920s in America. But did these appellations describe Madison County in that decade? Moreover, did Harding "normalcy" and "keeping cool with Coolidge" have an impact on the county?

At the end of the decade events suddenly shifted. October, 1929, marked the beginning of the end of the twenties' ephemeral prosperity, when the New York Stock Exchange on Wall Street took a nose dive that contributed to the arrival of the Great Depression. So much of the history of the twenties and thirties is shrouded in present-mindedness in our memories and history books that it is difficult to separate fact from myth. A few of the old questions that come to mind include: Should Hoover be faulted for the depression? Were most Americans enjoying the prosperity of the twenties when the Great Crash came in 1929? Did Franklin D. Roosevelt end the depression? Did most Americans benefit from the New Deal?

This era ended with war already being waged across the world, in Asia where the Japanese were on a rampage and in Europe with the designing Hitler having already stormed into Poland with the willful assistance of the Soviet Union. Americans by this time had debated the foreign policy of the Roosevelt administration and were lining up in either the isolationist or internationalist camps. When the war finally reached American shores in 1941, Madison County began the most abrupt changes in its history.

Before World War II, material change, one facet of "progress," while coming at a slow pace, began to appear in most every element of Madison County life. Much like the previous period during Madison's entry into the twentieth century, a step forward in one area often coincided with backsliding somewhere else. Madison Countians became more aware of technological change and its impact on communication, transportation, agriculture, and education. Life would never be quite as it had been before World War I. Yet, for many citizens, particularly the poor, whether black or white, their lives remained much the same.

The Roaring Twenties did not exactly roar in Madison County—this being the case for most rural-oriented communities of the country in the 1920s. As always, the media image of an era encompasses the highly visible, the bizarre, the famous and the infamous individuals who crowd the popular histories. Most people in the county lived much as they had before the war, the greatest change being perhaps a slightly higher standard of living touched off by the vaunted consumer durables revolution. Madison County, like similar areas across the country, contained few flappers, gangsters, or examples of F. Scott Fitzgerald's "flaming youth." But just enough of the urban flavor of the decade crept into the lives of Madisonians to heighten their awareness of the outside world, more so than ever before in their history.[1]

Communication developments made Madison Countians more aware of their world. Two events of 1920 illustrate the continuity of Madison's nineteenth century wilderness background and the advent of technology's intrusion on the lives of many residents. Not long after a farmer near Lake Reba killed a mountain wolf on his farm, moviegoers could hear the results of the presidential election of that year broadcast "Hot Off the Wire" at the Alhambra Theatre. Other modern wonders abounded. An Army biplane on a recruiting mission landed near Richmond just after World War I, stirring among many Madison Countians the dreams of flight. Although arriving a bit belatedly in the midtwenties, bobbed hair, like most trends and styles of the twenties, finally reached Madison. At the end of the decade Madisonians had already been exposed to a night baseball game, Vitaphone and Movietone "talkies" at the New Madison Theatre on the site of the old Opera House; and Richmond had its first stop light. While Richmond did not have a Great White Way, it at least had a "White Way" when in mid-1929 the Kentucky Utilities Company turned on the electricity for a new downtown lighting system. Moreover, Southern Bell Telephone system counted over 1,100 connections in the Richmond area. Most residents of the county, however, still lighted their homes by coal oil and a Rayo or Aladdin lamp rather than kilowatts and had no telephone service.[2]

A superficial statistical review of the twenties in Madison County reveals striking contrasts with the previous decade. Richmond grew from 5,622 folk in 1920 to 6,495 in 1930, and Berea neared the 2,000 mark. Madison County increased to 27,621, or by more than 1,300 in the decade. Obviously, the urban areas of the county were growing at the expense of the rural. The black portion of the total population continued declining, as fewer than 4,500 Negroes now lived in the entire county, with the majority living in towns. While the growth of the total number of citizens is modest, being 5.1 percent, many similar counties like Bourbon continued losing residents. The greatest move was to the river counties along the Ohio. Jefferson County grew by over 24 percent and Kenton by 27 percent, depleting counties like Owen, which declined by nearly 15 percent. As coal exploitation shifted to new fields, some mountain counties, such as Letcher, grew by 45 percent; Perry ballooned by 62 percent. Without coal or the proximity of the Ohio River to feed growth, Madison reversed the appalling depopulation trend of the teens, pulling itself back into its normal pattern of a slightly increasing population. However, as will be explained later, long before 1929 or 1930, the "official" beginning of the Great Depression, a dark cloud had already descended upon the Madison County farming community.[3]

If the twenties was "the prosperity decade," the era when modern business came of age in America, then there is little doubt that Madison County reflected some of what was going on in the rest of the country. In the early twenties the nation still suffered from the results of the runaway inflation of the war period, but prices had declined some. In 1921 for twenty-five cents one could purchase two pounds of coffee or one pound of peanut butter or 2½ pounds of peaches at the Richmond Welch Company. A loaf of bread cost nine cents. Just two years later a dollar would buy twelve pounds of lima beans or five pounds of Partridge Lard or ten pounds of corn meal at Jones Grocery. Most Madison County families produced some, if not all, of their food, it not being unusual for townspeople in Richmond and Berea to raise chickens and have a milk cow as well as a large vegetable garden within a short distance of the downtown areas. Moreover, a Richmond store clerk could still live comfortably on twelve dollars a week by watching her pennies.[4]

Madison County could not help but be caught up in the initial promise of the business boom of the early twenties. Local Babbits adopted the 'boosterism" practiced by the American business community. Real estate prices cooled off from the immediate postwar highs, but property values generally held up in the early twenties. Other signs appeared good. The state constructed a new armory on North Second Street. The three Richmond banks, the single Berea bank, and the few others in the county seemed stable and prosperous. New church edifices appeared in downtown Richmond with construction of the First Presbyterian Church and the Belle H. Bennett Memorial Methodist Church. In the early twenties Richmond could boast of a new chamber of commerce, a Rotary Club, and an Exchange Club, all arms of the business community. October 12, 1921, marked the first Booster's Day, or trade day, a sure sign of the business-oriented twenties.[5]

Almost anywhere one looked before 1929, the opportunities of "endless prosperity" appeared unbounded. Everyone was optimistic. The slightest sign of getting rich quick, like the hint of oil and natural gas at College Hill, touched off more enthusiasm. But try as they might, Madison Countians could not enter the new age of industrialization. The Hume plant closed soon after World War I. In the midtwenties a cannery operating at Paint Lick, just across the creek in Garrard County, in one six-day period canned 40,000 #2 containers of tomatoes. The firm employed eighty women and contracted for 225 acres of the crop, but it faded toward the end of the decade. In the late twenties a proposed cheese factory for Richmond never got off the ground, as too few farmers signed up to produce the milk required for the venture.[6]

If Madison County failed to industrialize, it followed other business trends of the twenties. Chain stores made their appearance in Richmond in the middle of the decade with the opening of the J.C. Penney store on Main Street, the 505th in that chain. By the end of the decade Richmond had A. and P. and Kroger grocery stores, a Lerman Brothers outlet, and a Goldsmith Store, the latter managed by Edward D. Wayman, a long-time Madison County businessman and political figure.[7]

The newspapers of Madison County, particularly the *Richmond Daily Register*, reacted to the modernity of that medium in the twenties. The weekly *Citizen* in Berea continued its role as the voice of the college, and the *Richmond Pantagraph* enthusiastically lived up to its subtitle, "A Republican Newspaper." After publisher Saufley of the *Register* joined the administration of Governor William "Honest Bill from Olive Hill" Fields as state insurance commissioner, Keen Johnson bought into the enterprise and took control of editorial policy. With experience at papers in Lexington, Elizabethtown, and Lawrenceburg, Johnson "threw his energies into improving the quality of life and increasing the economic life of the community."[8]

From mid-1925 onward the imprint of Johnson on the *Register* became dominant and unmistakable. In many respects he modernized the paper, adding new features such as full Associated Press coverage, cartoons, advertising campaigns, a Hollywood gossip column, radio program listings, crossword puzzles, racy serials of love's labor lost, stock market reports, sensationalized crime reports, sports coverage, and occasional "cheesecake" pictures of bathing-suited beauties so adored by the press in the twenties. Eschewing Saufley's intermittent editorial style, Johnson wrote daily comments on a wide variety of subjects, some serious and some not. For example, his comment on the advent of the Charleston and the Hoochie-Kootchie did credit to one who would one day need diplomatic skills in the political arena. The young editor found the Charleston somewhat outlandish granting "that it may be lacking in the grace which characterizes other dances," but to condemn it would be making "mountain out of a mole-hill." Johnson also introduced modern business procedures at the daily and tried to expand circulation. A 1926 campaign added over 1,000 new names to

the rolls, with one lady winning a new Hudson automobile and another
a Chevrolet as their prizes for obtaining the most subscriptions.[9]
   The pastimes and forms of entertainment of Madison Countians in
the 1920s also followed trends of that decade. The newest form of
entertainment, the radio, became the rage after the first broadcast of
Station KDKA in Pittsburgh in 1920 and "cat's whisker" took on a new
meaning. Radio stations WLW in Cincinnati and WHAS in Louisville
became the easiest for Madison Countians to pick up on a battery-
powered Atwater Kent or Grigsby Grunow. By mid-decade the *Register*
printed a radio schedule, an indication of the growth of this field.
While no station existed in the county, as early as 1929 a local group, the
Richmond Choral Club, directed by Mrs. Robert Sory, performed on the
WHAS station. With battery power, folk outside the electrically powered
areas could also listen to the new device. People would gather around a
neighbor's set or one at a general store as they might have sat around a
fire in earlier days. One older fellow at Waco maintained that the sports
programs he listened to were somehow stored in the box and that one
day the radio would have to be sent back to the factory for replenish-
ment. But the horizons of most Madison Countians quickly expanded
when they heard that first radio program, and they added another
consumer durables item to their list of necessities to be bought in the
future.[10]
   An older form of entertainment, the moving picture, became even
more popular in the twenties with the addition of sound. In the early
twenties the Phoenix Motion Picture Company bought both Richmond
theatres, the Alhambra and the Opera House. Some live entertainment
preceded the movies, like Elder's Orchestra, but more and more the
patrons came only to see such passionate films as DeMille's *Male and
Female, Sex* with Louise Glaum, and *The Sheik*, starring the immortal
Rudolph Valentino. No longer could it be claimed that Madisonians were
being left out of the mainstream of American entertainment. With
growth of the number of automobiles and improvement of roads in the
county in the twenties, more of her residents had an opportunity to
come to "town for the picture show." The silent films provided
employment for pianists, usually local women. However, the technical
improvement of "talkies" left them as one of Madison County's first
examples of "technological unemployment" in the late twenties.[11]
   The 1920s has often been called the Golden Age of Sports, when
Red Grange, Babe Ruth, Bill Tilden, and Jack Dempsey electrified a
nation thirsting for heroes. Berea and Eastern colleges and the area's
high schools fielded representative teams in various sports, but no one
captured the imagination like local hero Earle Combs. After attending
Eastern and playing baseball there in the early twenties, Combs moved
on to the Louisville Colonels for a short spell before signing with the
New York Yankees in the middle of the decade. He played with the
famous "murderer's row" of Ruth, Lou Gehrig, and Waite Hoyt, contributed to their several world championships, and eventually landed in

the Baseball Hall of Fame. The community, caught up in the spirit of it all, seemed to organize all sorts of baseball teams. A Richmond team joined the revived Blue Grass League after World War I. A *Register* headline of the decade reading ''First Christian Smothers Baptists'' could lead one to suspect a revival of the Campbellite controversy, but actually it only denoted a 12-4 victory of the baseball team of the former over the latter. Even small communities like Poosey Ridge caught the baseball bug, playing a schedule in the early twenties. Moreover, blacks also organized teams and leagues.[12]

Earle Combs in New York Yankee uniform. EKU Archives.

Older forms of entertainment continued in an age when people sought public diversions more than ever before in the history of the country. In the early twenties the American Legion Band took over responsibilities for the weekly summertime concerts at the courthouse bandstand. Local golfers in Richmond developed their own course in the twenties, following a national pattern of growing popularity for ''pasture pool.'' The Exchange Club sponsored an annual Halloween party in downtown Richmond and organized a youth band. Fourth of July festivities at Boonesborough Bathing Beach remained an important activity for midsummer diversion. A new holiday, November 11, Armistice Day, took on increasing significance as Madisonians remembered the sacri-fices of World War I. Religious memorial services and public speeches seemed the most appropriate exercises, but beginning in 1920 battles of another nature took place between the Richmond and Berea American Legion football teams. These events brought out great crowds. On one occasion the game pushed county school teachers to the brink of revolt until Superintendent B.F. Edwards called off afternoon classes, allowing students to attend the game. In 1927 the 35th National Fox Hunters Association held its field trails just outside Richmond, swelling the local population by several hundred and filling the Richmond hotels.[13]

Like most other communities in the twenties, the pace of life, the growth of business, culture itself, became dependent on the automobile. A bit belatedly, but not too far behind the rest of the nation, Madisonians joined that revolution wrought by Henry Ford. The automobile offered Madison Countians a variety of pleasures, including a chance for escape, the thrill of speed, an easier trip to the marketplace, and perhaps even an opportunity for romance. However, the road and street conditions of the early twenties often dulled these experiences. Local governments spent a good deal of their time and the taxpayer's money trying to construct and maintain a viable street and road system. Citizens of Richmond clamored for "tarvia" to be applied to their dusty streets, and most of the primary streets were paved in the twenties. In mid-decade a three-color electric signal at Third and Main streets ushered Madisonians into a new era of transportation. Living in one of the larger counties in the state, Madison residents in the fringe areas continued to fight dust, mud, and impassable roads for a good while longer. Bridge building and maintenance created problems in most areas of the county. Four years after defeat of a special road tax in 1922 Madison Countians voted for a new fund to maintain roads and build "cross pikes," this being the first road tax approved in seventy years.[14]

An estimated 2,500 autos roamed the county by mid-decade. With gasoline costing thirty-two cents a gallon and automobile prices sky-rocketing to over $2,500 for the fancier models, owners demanded improvements. State government began to assume more control and direction of the developing system of roads. Several county roads became state-maintained thoroughfares, including the main north-south artery, the Dixie Highway. That road slowly became a reality in the twenties as more sections were paved with concrete. The Richmond Exchange Club helped the cause by constructing a "tourist camp" with public restrooms and parking area to encourage tourist usage. Some citizens, however, were always looking for a quick dollar from the motorists. For example, during the reconstruction of the Dixie Highway from Berea to Round Hill, some enterprising folk on the Scaffold Cane detour lured unsuspecting drivers into deep, hidden mudholes and then charged five to ten dollars to pull them out. Most residents were more constructive, particularly when it came to the subject of bridges in and out of the county over that old barrier the Kentucky River. After nearly a decade of litigation and negotiation, the Clay's Ferry Bridge Company sold that span to the state in 1928. Within two years the state had recouped its $205,000 outlay by charging tolls, and in late 1930 the bridge became a free mode of transportation for the first time. The road from the bridge up the long hill continued to be an arduous task for most vehicles, busses of the Canfield and Reo lines actually having to back up while scaling the hairpin curves. Faster access to Clark County also came under discussion as state highway officials began the long process of planning a "free bridge" at Boonesborough to replace the Williams Ferry.[15]

The old crank telephone also began to disappear when in 1930 Southern Bell installed a "modern" common battery system in Richmond. Of course, the city fathers granted a rate increase to that company because of the new service being offered. Other improvements came to Richmond. Construction began on the first natural gas line to that city in the late twenties. By the modern standards of transportation and communication the twenties marked an era of significant change in the area.[16]

Education also showed signs of progress in the decade. The raw statistics for the twenties indicate continuing success in the assault on illiteracy, as the overall rate for Kentucky dropped to 6.6 percent from 10.2 percent in 1920. Black illiteracy fell to 15.4 percent. Kentucky continued to play the role of the border state, with a rate of illiteracy somewhere between the states of the South and the Midwest. As many as 90 percent of the elementary age children in the commonwealth attended school, but the rate fell off to only 50 percent for those of high school age, the latter because of the glaring disparity between opportunities for high school education in urban and rural areas of the state.[17]

The public school systems of Madison County struggled forward, trying to reach more students than ever before. In the early twenties a new school law, authorizing the hiring of a truant officer, increased county school attendance. Another statute changed the old trustee system into an elected five-member school board that appointed a superintendent. However, if anyone thought these "reforms" would depoliticize Kentucky schools they were to be sadly disappointed. Instead of the prospective superintendent wooing the voters, the candidates now only had to get the support of a majority of the board. School board races continued to be hard-fought affairs in both the rural and urban districts of Madison County. Sometimes the factionalism of board meetings would erupt into something more than words, as in the case of one Berea board member striking another on the head during a meeting in the midtwenties. The accused paid a fine and continued to serve on the board. Charges of nepotism could often be heard, and factionalism led to a weakened school system.[18]

School conditions for much of the county system remained somewhat primitive throughout the twenties. One former teacher reminisced about the lack of educational opportunities that he faced as he taught school for the first time in the southeastern portion of the county. Living seven miles from the Webb School, he had to travel on horseback. His education at the Berea Normal School had not fully prepared him for the difficulties of teaching in a rural Madison County community. Armed with "two erasers, a water bucket, a dipper, and a box of chalk," and not knowing that most of the parents of his charges were involved in producing moonshine, the eighteen-year-old teacher struggled to bring enlightenment to the pupils of the one-room school. He was educated as well. The students soon made him aware of a grand country school tradition, the pie supper. The young teacher knew that many men in the area carried guns. Because these same men usually drank to excess, he feared that a pie supper would only give them an opportunity to shoot up the school. Finally, a well-meaning and well-armed local gentleman guaranteed to keep the peace if the school held a pie supper. During the entire evening this patron sat in the back of the school room with a shotgun on his lap and an open box of shells on the table before him. Everyone else checked their guns at the door, and the evening continued to be peaceful. Pies sold for as much as twenty dollars, providing the school with maps, a globe, a dictionary, and other educational necessities. While in this case the pie supper provided for needed items, it also pointed out the low level of educational funding, particularly for a poorer school district like Madison.[19]

The county system did make some progress in the twenties, with high schools being added at Million and Bobtown; but the school term only extended through six months beginning in mid-July. Occasionally, when the blackberry season coincided with the opening of school, school attendance plummeted. In the twenties black schools in the county began to catch up with those for white students. As Negro population in the county decreased, their school attendance increased, actually exceeding white attendance by mid-decade. A study of the county system in the late twenties by two Eastern professors specified the handicaps that county children faced. They averaged being 1 1/2 years behind their urban peers. The study showed that most of the county schools had poor lighting and improper heating, and some even lacked sanitary privies.[20]

The Berea school system limped right along with the county. In the late twenties the citizens of that community finally, on the third attempt, passed a bond issue after being threatened with forced consolidation with the county system by the state superintendent. However, to its credit the system extended the school term to nine months in the early part of the decade.[21]

In the city of Richmond school improvements came at a greater pace. In September, 1920, the new Madison High School opened on the refurbished old Madison Female Institute campus. Less than a year later fire destroyed the old Caldwell School on North Second. Fire struck again in 1927 in the dead of winter at the high school, the cold weather hampering efforts to save the building. With arson suspected but never proven, the city board had a new school built and in service within less than a year. The Model School of Eastern merged with the Richmond system in 1922, a relationship kept intact until 1930. The city system also increased its school term to nine months in the twenties and added a gymnasium and manual training room to the black school. Football and girls and boys basketball became exciting spectator sports during the decade.[22]

Eastern Normal School grew in the twenties, attaining an enrollment of well over one thousand by the middle of the decade and adding the fourth year of college work at about the same time. The school continued its primary role as a teachers college, being renamed Eastern Kentucky State Teachers College in 1930. Herman Lee Donovan became president of the school in 1928, replacing Coates.[23]

Chautauqua at Richmond, ca. 1920. EKU Archives.

Chautauqua continued to make its yearly rounds to Richmond in the twenties, with the Exchange Club becoming the chief sponsor. Plays such as *As You Like It*, presentations by the Oceanic Concert Company, and demonstrations like the "Wonders of Science" packed in the crowds. In the early twenties Henry Allen Laine, with the aid of white supporters, organized a Colored Chautauqua for the county, coming a few weeks after it white counterpart. The black variation included a more religious theme, usually ending on a Sunday with a union service.[24]

Politics in the twenties generally meant business as usual, with no hint of a Clarence E. Woods waiting in wings to wisk Richmond or Berea or Madison County into another era of reformism. Partisan lines remained strong in the county, with the *Register* and *Pantagraph*, respectively if not always respectfully, representing the Democratic and Republican parties. The "New Era" for Kentucky state politics began a year earlier than the national Republican trend when Edwin P. Morrow of Somerset won the governorship in 1919. As usual the vote was close in Madison County, with Morrow winning by 326 votes.[25]

In the presidential races of the twenties, Madison voted Republican all three times. Harding carried the county by 350 votes, Coolidge by slightly more; and Hoover swept the county by over 1,500 votes. Except for the last election, the Republican and Democratic districts held to normal voting patterns. In the election of the ill-fated Hoover, Berea outdid its usual Republican majority as the Iowan tallied over 80 percent of the vote of the southern Madison town.[26]

National political attitudes of the twenties found willing practitioners in Madison County. For example, former Mayor Samuel Rice of Richmond, a Democrat, echoed the immortal words of Republican President Harding when he announced for office again in 1921 with the promise: "I am for getting back to normalcy—to safe and sane conditions." Most Madisonians did not deviate from their old political habits, but the exceptions were noteworthy. Forever on the leading edge of the changing times, Laura Clay ran for the state senate in 1923. As in most everything else, she startled local residents with her aggressive campaign efforts, on one occasion ascending "Big Hill in a Flivver [a Ford] aided by Mules" to speak to a crowd at McKee. Apparently, the voters of the twenty-ninth District were not quite ready for a woman senator, and she went down to defeat by over 3,000 votes. The county in general turned a bit more conservative in the twenties, voting against a proposed road bond issue in 1924 and twice rejecting the candidacy of Alben Barkley. In the middle of the decade Republicans carried everything before them, from the fiscal court to the races in the General Assembly. The *Register* remained a diehard Democratic paper even during the tumultuous and complicated presidential election of 1928. Keen Johnson praised Alfred E. Smith as the "dynamic leader of Democracy." The young editor tried to turn the tables on the controversy surrounding Smith's Catholic faith by printing a poem, "The Catholic Boy's Lament," in which the youngster is reminded that though his blood may be shed in defense of the nation, he can never be elected president because of his faith.[27]

In that campaign in 1928, Smith's religion and his antiprohibition position sealed his doom as the nominee of the Democrats. While Prohibition may have been a legitimate issue, religion should never have been. In response to the growing political prominence of Smith and the challenge of the newer immigrants, the Ku Klux Klan revived with a vengeance in the 1920s. KKK influence spread beyond the old southern states, with Indiana, ironically, becoming the mecca of Ku Kluxism. Madison County did not escape Klan activity. In the early part of the decade an occasional crossburning gave evidence of the resurgent Klan. County Judge J.D. Goodloe initially took a strong stand against the Invisible Empire, vowing to "arrest an organizer at any time." He soon relented, and by mid-1924 the Klan moved with impunity in the county.

Women Klan members came to the area to organize a distaff auxiliary. Klan activity apparently culminated with a gigantic Klan rally just outside Richmond between Lancaster and Barnes Mill roads in mid-decade taking place the same week when the Klan issue threatened to break up the national Democratic Convention. Although Klan organizers claimed that 60,000 attended the events of June 16, 1924, the number was probably closer to 6,000, still a substantial number for any public gathering. Apparently many of the robed goblins came from outside the county. The daylight festivities began with a parade of 500 masked apparitions through the streets of the county seat. A gigantic fireworks display preceded by cross burnings, speakers, and ceremonies came in the evening. The full extent of Klan activity in Madison County affairs in the twenties can only be estimated. However, at least one prominent Madison County political figure, G. Murray Smith, often complained to state Democratic leaders about the deleterious effect of the Klan on local party affairs.[28]

If one trait of the Prosperity Decade, the Klan, existed in Madison County, others were also present, none more prominently than violence, the struggles of Negros, and the impact of prohibition. Prohibition was not the genesis for the violence of the decade, but it did contribute to the general state of lawlessness. Even a cursory glance at the newspapers of the twenties leaves the unmistakable impression of an era of wanton mayhem. Only a few examples need be mentioned here. In late June, 1923, a shootout at a "Holy Roller Church" near Red Lick left one man dead and one seriously injured. On another occasion a Madisonian was shot while riding his horse, redivivus of the old West.[29]

In most parts of Kentucky blacks generally received stiffer sentences than white offenders, but while this may have been generally true for Madison, there were exceptions, in the county's record. Moreover, Madison kept its record of never having a lynching in this century. A great number of lynchings took place in the twenties in America. Several important residents, including Johnson in a key editorial printed after a particularly brutal lynching at Whitesburg, took strong positions against this crime. The good signs in the county included an acquittal of a black male accused of killing a Pine Mountain Settlement school female teacher in a change of venue. The retrial of a black man previously sentenced to fifteen years for criminal assault on a white woman is another example of Madison's somewhat atypical racial justice record. In the latter case Circuit Judge W. Rodes Shackelford allowed the trial based on new evidence, and a jury overturned the previous conviction. On the other hand, the sentences meted out for black against black crime appeared unusually short. In one such case a Negro man shot up a black dance hall, wounding several patrons, but he received only a six-month jail term.[30]

The American record on race in the twenties was not much better than that of the previous decades. The black population of Madison County continued to decline. In 1930 the mortality rate for Negroes rose by nearly two points, to twenty-one per thousand, while the white rate fell slightly. In 1928 Madison registered one of the highest death rates for tuberculosis and pneumonia of any county in the state, with a disproportionately large share among blacks.[31]

Nevertheless, there were some encouraging signs for the plight of blacks in the twenties. Beginning in 1920, W.B. Chenault began writing a "Colored Column" for the *Richmond Daily Register*. Interest in an "old folks" home and a Negro hospital proved awareness on the part of blacks for their needs. Literary societies for the ladies and baseball and football teams for the men allowed blacks cultural and athletic outlets. Henry Allen Laine continued his efforts for educational and agricultural improvements by organizing fairs for his race across the county.[32]

Prohibition had obvious impact in Madison County. First, it closed local distilleries, which were caught holding large quantities of whiskey in storage when the Volstead Act initiated prohibition earlier than anyone expected. For example, the Warwick Distillery at Silver Creek held over 4,000 barrels of their product. Consequently, much legally made liquor eventually became part of the illegal trade. The saloons on First Street opposite the courthouse closed and were taken over by second-hand stores. By early 1921 the dockets of both the Federal District Court and the Circuit Court were filled with those accused of violating the eighteenth Amendment. Bootlegging and moonshining intensified, particularly in the Big Hill section. No matter how hard Sheriff Elmer Deatherage tried he could not curtail the "shine" activity. One enterprising area even used a "community worm" to produce their product, pooling their resources to beat the law. Near the Webb School law enforcement officials found a "modern shine plant" complete with a gas burner. The problem became so acute around Berea that President Frost of the college pleaded for more law enforcement, citing the bad impact on his youthful charges. The battle continued throughout the twenties, and if Madison followed national patterns, fewer people imbibed than in previous decades. One Madisonian, W.O. Mays, served through most of the decade as the chief prohibition administrator for Kentucky and Tennessee.[33]

Notwithstanding these problems, efforts were made in the decade to improve the quality of life of Madison residents. The governments of Madison County had great difficulty providing healthier environments for their citizens even with the technical developments of the decade. Fires continued to strike fear, causing great property damage and loss of life each year. Wintertime always proved to be an especially dangerous period, as fires roaring within a furnace, stove, or fireplace could overheat and ignite surrounding combustible material. A major fire at Main and Collins streets in Richmond wiped out several businesses in 1920. With the temperature hovering near zero on a January evening in 1924, a tremendous fire, visible in Richmond, destroyed over $200,000 worth of downtown property in Berea. Only the arrival of the Richmond Fire Department saved the entire city of Berea from an even worse disaster. The venerable Madison County Courthouse also suffered damage in mid-decade when electrical wires ignited sawdust packing between floors. Water and sewage problems continued to plague the city of Richmond during the decade, particularly during the September, 1925, drought. And Water Street lived up to its name, turning into a sizable stream during a rainstorm.[34]

The general health of Madisonians slightly improved in the twenties over the terrible statistics of the previous decade. However, a few still carried the scars of World War I, the effects of "Hun gas" causing the death of a veteran as late as 1920. Most small communities now had a doctor, who sometimes advertised his services in the local newspapers. The Pattie A. Clay Infirmary added a new wing costing over $75,000. The fiscal court of the county funded an infirmary at Union City under the direction of a "keeper" who was paid $3.75 per week for each person housed at the facility. Associated Charities of Richmond held concerts and other benefits to raise funds for aid to the poor. However, periodic outbreaks of disease still made Madison Countians painfully aware of health conditions. An occasional case of diphtheria or smallpox reminded everyone that these age-old maladies could still strike suddenly and without warning. In August, 1927, a rapid increase in the number of reported cases of infantile paralysis shocked the county. Late in that month the County Board of Health forbade anyone under the age of sixteen to leave the county. A few days later the mayor of Richmond issued an order forbidding children to go onto the streets. The health of children seemed not to have advanced much in the twenties from the previous decade. For example, a check of 600 county school children in 1925 found that 90 percent were "defective," meaning that that number had one or more ailments or deformities. About 10 percent were undernourished, being ill-fed in an era of alleged prosperity.[35]

Richmond added another health facility in the early twenties when the United States Health Service fashioned the Irvinton estate on Lancaster Avenue into the Irvine-McDowell Hospital. Willed to the Kentucky State Medical Society by Mrs. William Irvine, the facility became one of two trachoma hospitals in the country. This disease, a highly contagious infection of the eye, caused blindness among many poor families in Appalachia. The hospital opened in 1926 under the direction of Dr. Robert Sory, who continued as director until the closing of the facility twenty-five years later. In the first year of operation alone this hospital treated over one thousand cases of trachoma.[36]

If there was some room for hope of progress in Madison County, the majority of her residents, those who lived on the farms, suffered tragically in the twenties. Perhaps nothing better illustrates the specious nature of the meaning of that decade than the history of agriculture in this county in the 1920s. Long before the more or less official beginning of the depression, ca. 1930, most Madison County farm families were already feeling the full effects of bad times.

The decade began with high hopes, as tobacco, land, and livestock sold for premium prices. The demonstration of a Fordson tractor and other modern machinery on the C.F. Chenault farm in mid-1920

Irvine-McDowell house, "Irvington," in Richmond which served as a U.S. Public Health Service hospital for trachoma patients. Courtesy David Greene.

appeared to forecast the future for Madison agriculture, but most farmers continued to depend on horses and mules. Tobacco and livestock were the major cash producers. In 1926 Madison shipped more cattle to Cincinnati than any other Kentucky county. Large farm owners like B.M. Igo of Lexington Road often shipped two or more carloads of cattle at a time. However, poorer farm families supplemented their incomes by selling cream, chickens, eggs, hogs, and turkeys. In season, blackberries and walnuts kept body and soul together for many a Madison County family. Blackberries in midsummer provided work for children and, as previously mentioned, often kept them out of school for several days. Walnuts could be gathered during the day in the late fall, providing after supper work for the entire family in the shelling process. By truck and railroad these and other Madison County commodities found their way into the larger markets of the country. The prices paid for these products were rarely established within the county. Madison farmers, like their cohorts across the nation, were at the mercy of forces seemingly beyond their reach.[37]

The prosperity of World War I and the continued high prices of the 1919-20 tobacco market buoyed everyone's spirits. Some forecasters began to warn of the dangers of overproduction, and in mid-1920 many farmers started to talk again of a "cut out" of the next year's crop. Local meetings in Richmond and for the state in Lexington came to naught,

Madison County delegates voting against the "cut out." With the previous year's average of $46.22 per hundred pounds a recent memory,
Madison farmers hoped for the same. The first warnings of disaster
began to filter into the county with the opening of the bright leaf
markets in Virginia and the Carolinas. In early December, 1920, the
Owensboro markets closed because of low prices offered by the tobacco
companies. Then calamity struck the burley belt, when on December 20,
1920, "Black Monday," markets opened with bids of less than half the
previous year's average. Most warehouses closed abruptly, reopening
two weeks later on January 3, 1921, but with the same results. In
Lexington, the largest tobacco market in the nation closed after only one
hour of trading. Obviously, buyers had reverted to their old practice of
"seesawing," or alternating their purchases, and not competing with
each other. To the north in Covington authorities called out the sheriff
to quell a disturbance, and in Carlisle 1,500 unruly farmers surrounded a
warehouse after an opening sales average of only 9 cents a pound. The
Richmond market struggled to stay open, but prices fell to as little as 1/4
cent per pound. When the "pinhookers," independent buyers, began
picking up most of the crop at low prices, Madison farmers knew they
were in for a long winter.[38]

At this juncture, many Madison County tobacco farmers became
part of an experiment in farm marketing. Robert Worth Bingham, publisher of the Louisville Courier-Journal, and Aaron Sapiro, a West Coast
lawyer specializing in farm marketing organizations, pushed the formation of the Burley Tobacco Growers' Cooperative Association. Moreover, both men became national leaders in the development of co-ops in
the early twenties. The idea of pooling had been tried before, but
Bingham, Sapiro, and other farm leaders believed the time was ripe for
public acceptance of cooperative marketing.[39]

Owing to the conservative nature of Madison landowners, the
county did not immediately fall in behind these leaders. Some local
farmowners like Green Clay, T. S. Burnam, and H. B. Hanger supported
the co-op, but the Home Tobacco Warehouse refused to submit to the
pooling idea. Only the impassioned oratory of Sapiro at the Madison
County Courthouse in mid-June, 1921, swayed the audience of disgruntled farmers into pledging their crops to the cooperative.[40]

From the beginning, impediments stood in the way of the burley
cooperative. The sentiments of local warehousemen and farmers clearly
divided over the issue. The Madison Warehouse became the pool house
and the Home Tobacco Warehouse remained independent. The conflict
over the pooling concept erupted in violence when two men from Silver
Creek argued the merits of the co-op in a local pool hall. The incident
ended with one slashing the throat of the other. Much of the tobacco
sold at the nonpool warehouse came from nearby mountain counties,
where the co-op had little support. Statewide the pool did stabilize
prices, but "outsiders" profited right along with co-op members.[41]

After initial success, the cooperative faded in the midtwenties,
leaving all Madison farmers at the mercy of a capricious pricing system.

Again farmers talked of a "cut out," but tenant farmers in particular feared that loss of a year's income would wipe them out. This time Sapiro's rhetoric fell on deaf ears. By 1925 average tobacco prices had fallen to less than twenty cents per hundred pounds and rarely rose above that mark for the rest of the decade.[42]

All in all, the unstable price structure and increasing costs did not deal kindly with Madison County farmers in the twenties. The value of land and buildings declined by a third of what it had been in 1920. Disregarding low prices, Madison farmers increased their tobacco acreage to over 9,000 by 1929, contributing more to overproduction and low prices. The trend toward sharecropping continued, as the percentage of Madison farms operated by tenants climbed to over 44 percent in the twenties, a figure well ahead of the state average. Nearly 90 percent of that number were sharecroppers. The number of farms increased only slightly, the total amount of farm acres decreased somewhat, and the average farm now had only sixty-six acres. Moreover, the numbers of "full owners" declined by 250 in the decade. Blacks were leaving the countryside for the city, and the amount of land cultivated by them decreased significantly. All of these trends matched many national, regional, and state patterns. Mountain people continued to come into the county seeking better economic and educational opportunities than they found in Appalachia. Many of these people went to work cultivating Madison County farmland.[43]

The 1920s ended with most people in the county believing that good times would soon return. Surely tobacco bids would rebound along with improved prices for all other farm products. Most of these same individuals hardly noticed the news coming from New York about a stock market crisis—after all, this had all happened before on numerous occasions. So what if a few stock speculators "took a bath" and lost money!

Most people who lived through the Great Depression do not recall a specific beginning date, but they do remember that for some reason things became unglued somewhere around 1930. Life for many Madisonians was difficult enough in the twenties; however, hardly any of the residents of the county escaped without searing experiences during the depression. That single word "depression" came to identify the totality of economic collapse in the 1930s. For many people the psychological scars of that experience would be worse than the economic deprivations.

It seemed that everything that could go wrong did so in the early thirties. Even the weather turned against the people. In 1930 the usual late spring-early summer rains never came, drying up fields, streams, and reservoirs. Crops withered in the fields as a heat wave descended on Kentucky. Tobacco, corn, pasture land, and gardens suffered millions of dollars of damage. Rain in late August saved some of the tobacco crop, but Richmond continued to have a severe shortage of water through the beginning of 1931. Lake Reba dried to a trickle as the parent company of Richmond Water and Light Co. entered receivership. To alleviate the problem city workers laid lines to a lake on the Hanger estate and later used tank cars to bring water over the L. and N. line from Valley View. Plentiful supplies of water for cooking and bathing became nonexistent. An exasperated Keen Johnson continually voiced his complaints against the privately owned water company's puny efforts to supply the city with water. Finally, he desperately reported that "the city reservoir is damn near dry." In less than a year Richmond's city fathers, under the leadership of Mayor William O'Neil, purchased the water and gas plant. City ownership coupled with returning rains soon improved the water supply of Richmond.[44]

To farm folk the lack of rainfall meant not just an inconvenience but a cruel loss of income. Crops of 1930 netted less than one-half their 1929 value. The market average for tobacco dropped to less than seventeen dollars per hundred pounds. But this did not end the slide of tobacco prices. A year later the average for the 1931 crop fell under ten dollars.[45]

In late 1930 people began using that word "depression" for the first time, suspecting that their economic plight would not soon end. The poor were hit particularly hard. During the winter of 1930-31 several local organizations sponsored a community wood pile for Richmond's needy. Municipal and county governments faced increasing difficulty in collecting taxes as the economy worsened. The county road fund could not finance construction and maintenance because the state fund had faltered. Completion of the new Boonesborough Bridge in 1934 did not bring the immediate economic benefits hoped for because fewer people could afford gasoline necessary to use the facility. Property assessments dropped each year in the early depression. In order to slash its tax liabilities, the L. and N. closed its line from Frankfort to Irvine, and the old Riney-B and other tracks in the county went to the scrap heap. Editor Keen Johnson noticed an increase in "thievery," as even a hobo claimed to have been robbed near the L. and N. depot in Richmond. Local businesses felt the hard times, as more and more of their customers lacked either cash or credit. Many people were laid off and most of the remainder had wages cut substantially as the depression deepened during the last two years of the Hoover administration. A few local people lost most, if not all, of their investments on Wall Street. And even if they did get their money back, they certainly lost their confidence in the nation's financial structure. For city people the back yard garden, a few chickens, and perhaps a cow became their insurance against real hunger, the first time in their lives they had perhaps faced that danger. Rural people suffered as well, for though they could raise their own food, they often lacked money and for that reason could not afford medical attention and other requirements for a quality life.[46]

Most everything that happened in other depression-ridden communities occurred in Madison County. Redpath Chautauqua became one of the first casualties and folded its tents in 1932, never to return. Changing forms of entertainment, particularly radio and the "talkies," as well as the poor state of the economy brought on the demise of this genuine American institution. Other institutions came under severe stress. Richmond did not suffer the financial crises that racked many larger cities, but did have its own troubles when the Citizens National Bank failed to reopen after the famous bank holiday of March, 1933. Eventually depositors received about three-quarters of their deposits.[47]

City and county governments came under increasing stress in the 1930s as funds ran low. The Richmond City Council and the Madison County Fiscal Court both cut expenses when possible and lowered salaries for elected officials and wages for employees.[48]

The ruinous conditions of the era struck public education a hard blow, wiping out the improvements that had been gained over a span of two generations. With nearly four times as many youngsters to educate as the Richmond and Berea districts, the county school system struggled against nearly insuperable odds. Declining tax rolls led to a fiscal crisis in the county system. County school officials tried all sorts of economy measures, including borrowing money, lowering salaries, and cutting the school term. However, school board politics continued to weaken the system. For example, in 1930 the board appointed as superintendent the daughter of one of its members. President Donovan of Eastern charged subdistrict trustees in Madison and other counties with "racketeering" in their control of teachers' positions. Lastly, in 1933 two board members resigned when it was publicized that they had voted coal contracts for their sons.[49]

School attendance dropped precipitously in Kentucky in the thirties. Older school age children dropped out to look for work or to join government programs. Many younger children did not attend school because they lacked a pair of shoes or clothing or food for lunchtime. Once they had broken the habit of attending school, their return became ever more difficult. Whereas in 1930 attendance had been nearly 55 percent for all ages, by 1940 the figure had dropped to only 39 percent. In 1934 over 1,600 white children in the county were not enrolled at all. Negro attendance actually surpassed that of the general white population, forging far ahead of rural numbers. The high school ages dropped out in large numbers, never to receive a diploma. Sometimes as many as one-third failed the county eighth grade examination.[50]

The colleges in the county fared better than the public elementary and secondary schools. Eastern's enrollment grew steadily during the depression decade, reaching over 1,000, and several new buildings gave promise for more growth in the future. Many of the students, however, came to the school with little money and had to work either at the college or around town in order to pay their expenses. Times were hard. Many students lived on less than five dollars a week, sometimes with frightening results. It was not unusual for students to faint in the cafeteria from having gone too long without a meal. Berea College's growth continued as it fulfilled its role in Kentucky higher education. By 1936 the school owned 100 buildings on a 140-acre campus; maintained a

500-acre farm and nearly 5,600 acres of forests; and operated a water plant, telephone system, ice plant, bakery, laundry, printing shop, handicraft factory, and Boone Tavern.[51]

In some ways the depression changed another important institution, i.e., politics; but in other respects it remained the same. Nationally, the Democratic Party became the majority party. The same generally held true in Kentucky, but with some notable exceptions. Politics, Kentucky's favorite indoor and outdoor sport, continued to run at its own pace, fueled by annual elections. Gone, however, was the influence of the old bipartisan combine, the conservative cabal that had defeated such candidates as Barkley and Beckham in the twenties. With the onset of the depression nearly everyone's attention turned to economic issues, and the Republican administrations of President Hoover in Washington and Governor Flem D. Sampson in Frankfort took the blame for the declining economy. Kentucky's 1931 gubernatorial election foreshadowed the presidential ballot of the next year. The Republican tide began to recede in the 1930 races when Democrats carried Madison County for the first time in nearly a generation. A few months before the Democratic gubernatorial primary Keen Johnson led a miniboom for Judge Shackelford for governor. With the slogan, "Unshackle Kentucky with Shackelford," the campaign limped along with the support of Elmer Deatherage, Shelton Saufley, and J.J. Greenleaf. However, Shackelford could find little support outside of central Kentucky and he withdrew, throwing his support to the "Terrible Turk," Ruby Laffoon of Madisonville. In the fall election, Laffoon carried the county by a slim majority, 215 votes, the first time in a long while that a Democrat had taken the county in a governor's race.[52]

Laffoon rewarded Madison's support of his campaign as Deatherage became warden of the state prison in Frankfort and Greenleaf took a federal job with Kentuckian Urey Woodson, the alien property custodian. Johnson became more active in Democratic party affairs, becoming state secretary in 1932 without relinquishing editorship of the *Richmond Daily Register*. Johnson's political star began to rise at about the same time as Saufley's fell. Ill health and public exposure of an indictment, subsequently dismissed, stemming from his years as state insurance commissioner, blunted Saufley's desire to run for statewide public office.[53]

The presidential election of 1932 revolutionized American politics as Franklin D. Roosevelt swept the race against incumbent Herbert Hoover. The New Yorker carried Madison County by over 1,100 votes, a substantial majority for a county traditionally carried by Republican presidential candidates.[54]

The administration of Roosevelt, the New Deal, immediately began to change the lives of most Madisonians. They learned a new "three Rs"—Relief, Recovery, and Reform—as a Democratic party majority in Congress bowed to the president's every suggestion in early 1933. Moreover, the process of dismantling prohibition began with legalization of 3.2 percent beer and light wines. While Madison County gave a forty-four vote majority to the dry side, the state voted for repeal of the Eighteenth Amendment in November, 1933. Local option elections returned and in the midthirties became the most hotly contested polls in the county, with Richmond usually voting wet and Berea and the rural areas voting dry.[55]

New Deal programs had an impact on many Madison County individuals as well as funding improvements for the cities, the county, and the colleges. Early Civil Works Administration programs hired over 250 men on projects ranging from county road building to constructing sewer lines and tennis courts at Eastern. Local businesses displayed the Blue Eagle of the National Recovery Administration by mid-1933. Parades and speeches aimed at drumming up support for NRA brought out crowds estimated as large as 5,000 in Richmond. Madison County youth also joined the Civilian Conservation Corps and in mid-April, 1933, fifty-nine young men left for Fort Knox for indoctrination.[56]

Most New Deal programs provided local employment as well as conservation and construction measures. Works Progress Administration projects improved roads, built streets in Richmond and Berea, improved Lake Reba, constructed a new water tank for Richmond, and erected Hanger Stadium on the Eastern campus. However, some residents could not help but rename the WPA "We Piddle Around," or "We Poke Along." National Youth Administration funds paid for student

Keen Johnson Student Union Building on the campus of Eastern Kentucky University, ca. 1941. EKU Archives.

work at Eastern and Berea colleges and helped many students stay in school. At Lake Reba the WPA established a camp for workers who, like their cohorts elsewhere, were paid twenty-two to thirty-six dollars per month depending on their skills. In 1939 the NYA took over the camp, providing high school educational training for over 150 young men. Public Works Administration projects in the county included a men's dormitory and the Keen Johnson Building at Eastern, a classroom at the city school, a gymnasium for the black city school, and over $125,000 allotted for a new county central high school. PWA payrolls paid out over $300,000 to local workers in 1939. Moreover, beginning in 1937 the first electric service for county residents became a reality with organization of a cooperative through the Rural Electrification Administration. Not every project came through, however, as Pattie A. Clay Hospital failed to get a grant in 1938. All things considered, these projects added to the material welfare of Madison Countians in the 1930s.[57]

The money that went into the pockets of WPA, CCC, NYA, and other individuals who worked for New Deal programs was only one dimension of the efforts to reach the indigent. Direct relief programs, sometimes funded locally or by the state, helped alleviate much suffering. In one week alone in 1934 local officials distributed over a ton of butter, 1,000 pounds of beef, 11,000 pounds of flour, 2,200 pounds of smoked pork, nearly 1,000 pounds of cheese, and six cases of cod liver oil to the needy of the county. In 1937, after many Madison Countians became convinced that the depression would not soon end, local leaders formed the Telford Community Center, headquartered at the William Holloway Mansion, to coordinate relief needs.[58]

The Madison County business community struggled along with everyone else in the thirties. The organization of a formal chamber of commerce group in Richmond demonstrated their growing concern that concerted action was needed to help the community. The promise of a clothing factory for Richmond in 1930 did not materialize because of the general economic decline in that first year of the Great Depression. However, by the midthirties the Kirschbaum Manufacturing Company, located on South Third Street, began making boys' clothing and provided badly needed income for the local economy. The small plant first hired 110 women, then expanded to 170, paying wages averaging thirteen dollars a week. Competition became tougher for all local businessmen. Undaunted by the depression, the *Register* ran one of its circulation contests in early 1937, again giving away an automobile.[59]

Because the majority of Madison's citizens lived on farms, the problems of agriculture in the thirties and the efforts of New Deal farm programs remained at center stage. The Agricultural Adjustment Act of early 1933 revolutionized the relationship of the federal government to agriculture. Almost overnight reduced acreages and direct payments to farmers brightened an otherwise dismal picture. "Adjustment checks" given to farmers for cutting back their production poured badly needed cash back into the community. In 1937 the federal government distributed over $200,000 to Madison farmers. The first AAA and other New Deal farm programs only temporarily alleviated the problems of farmers in Madison. Tobacco prices fluctuated during the decade, rising in 1936-37 to an average of nearly forty dollars per 100 pounds. Significantly, the opening day average price of fifteen dollars for 1939 nearly matched that of 1932.[60]

The New Deal did contribute to changing farm patterns. The first AAA aided the farm owners at the expense of their tenants or sharecroppers, and that, coupled with mechanization, depopulated vast areas of the South. For the first time in fifty years the percentage of sharecroppers among American farmers declined in the 1930s, Madison County being no exception. The proportion of tenancy of all types in Madison declined from a high of 44.2 percent in 1930 to 40.9 percent in 1940. Blacks continued to leave farms in substantial numbers in the county, as about one-half of the "non-white operators" left the land between 1930 and 1940. The total number of farms only slightly declined in the thirties, another indication that white farm ownership and tenancy was becoming the dominant feature of Madison County agriculture. The Farm Security Administration helped only a small number of tenant farmers realize their dream of owning land. Federal land banks refinanced other Madison County farms, but some farmers inevitably lost their land. Even with New Deal acreage programs Madison tobacco farmers, like their brethren across the state, continued to produce more than the market could absorb. The statistical decline of Madison agriculture so evident in the twenties held true during the depression. Land values dropped another million dollars by 1940. However, in 1940 encouraging signs would be the substantial increase in the number of cattle and the decline of corn acreage. More marginal land was now being used for pasture and retired from tillage, a trend that aided the fight against soil erosion on the poorer soils of the county.[61]

The foregoing statistical and analytical views are properly important in describing the depression decade. However, the human dimension, the personalization of the depression experience of Madison Countians has the deepest meaning. "I don't know how we did it," one survivor of the depression recalled. "I just don't know how we did it, as I look back." "Man, it was depressing," according to one man who worked for an automobile dealership, remembering those mornings when he came to work to find cars lined up because their owners could not pay for them. A saleslady in a dress shop recollected business being so slow that "you almost had to beg someone to buy something." Barter came back in vogue. A Richmond dentist struggled to make ends meet and accepted payment in kind for his services. "It was rugged," he averred. "I never ate so many potatoes in my life." For many families it was enough to "have food on the table" at every meal. On the other hand, many Madisonians would have echoed the sentiments of a farmer who argued, "I didn't know it was a depression," the reason being that times had already been tough enough in the 1920s that conditions in the thirties did not seem any worse. Sometimes the unexpected could bring good fortune, as when a family fed a hobo who the next morning "kicked off" enough coal from a railroad car to keep them in fuel for the entire winter.[62]

Workers believed themselves fortunate if they could hold a job. The threat of being laid off frightened everyone. Wages dropped to late nineteenth century standards with seventy-five cents a day often being paid to farm laborers. Blacks suffered the most, sometimes earning as little as a quarter a day for such services as ironing clothes and cleaning homes. A steady job with a thirty dollar a month salary meant a comfortable living for a small family. Some families moved about constantly, looking for a better deal on a tenant farm, seeking cheaper rent, or staying one jump ahead of the landlord. But if labor was cheap so were prices. Food and clothing prices at the depths of the depression in the early thirties now bring back sensations of nostalgia. At Richmond markets cigarettes sold for .10 a pack, sliced bread for .04 a loaf, lettuce for .06 per head, Square Deal coffee for .19 a pound, potroast for .09 per pound, 100 pounds of potatoes for $1.85, and the list could go on and on. Clothing remained relatively inexpensive. In 1933 Penny's sold "union suits" at two for .98. Elder's had men's shoes for $1.98; United Department Stores sold men's linen suits for $1.00 or women's cotton frocks for .49. A Frigidaire refrigerator at Myers sold for less than $100. As late as 1939 Lerman's advertised work shirts for .79 and work pants for .98; coveralls and work shoes brought $1.98 each. And yet, if you did not have the money, none of these astonishingly low prices made much difference. Not having enough money to purchase a stamp to send a letter to a loved one or lacking money to go to the movie could be a shattering experience for a child during the depression years.[63]

Life went on, people survived in the best way they could. Losing a job, a house, or an appliance became a common experience of many a Madisonian during the Great Depression. Some lost their farms after years of hard work and sacrifice. Parents scrimped and saved so that their children could attend school. Children worked after school to help out with family expenses. The work ethic remained strong, and only a few took advantage of welfare programs in the New Deal years. "Make do or do without" became a standard adage for most. Reading the family histories of Madison Countians who lived through the depression, one is struck by their perseverance, their humor in the face of adversity, and their ability to make adjustments. Church attendance, if not church coffers, did well in the thirties as many people turned to religion for solace. There were compensations for all the heartache caused by the state of the economy. Most survivors of the thirties remember that family life appeared closer than in later years. Families worked and played together, oftentimes under rather cramped living conditions. They entertained themselves at or near home with card games like Rook, or they danced, played pickup ball games, attended potluck suppers, and listened to the radio. "Amos and Andy," "Jack Benny," "Burns and

Allen,'' and numerous musical shows gave people a respite from the harsh realities of the depression.[64]

A trip to Richmond or Berea became a great event for many families struggling against the onslaught of the Great Depression. Movies offered an opportunity to escape for a few hours. For as little as a dime a child could go to the Madison Theatre to see Ken Maynard in *Smoking Guns,* or visit the State Theatre for viewing Bob Steele in *A Demon for Trouble.* In this Golden Age of films the popularity of gangster movies of the early thirties gave way to the western in the latter part of the decade. The old days of vaudeville were now gone, but occasionally such live groups as ''Ezra Buzzington and his Rustic Revelers'' followed showings of a movie like *Stagecoach* starring John Wayne. While some citizens complained about the opening of movie houses on Sunday in the early part of the decade, later on most people were grateful for an opportunity to escape there even on the Lord's Day. Other forms of free or inexpensive entertainment were available throughout the decade. The Exchange Club continued to sponsor the annual downtown Halloween party in Richmond. Movie stars' lives took on possibly greater importance than ever before, it being big news when Laurel and Hardy split up in mid-decade.[65]

For the children of the depression, those who grew up during the era, the 1930s added lessons that they could not have learned in school. They remember never having much beef to eat, but subsisting on beans, pork, and cornbread. In spring, poke and dandelion greens supplemented an often monotonous diet. ''Everything was always rather gray,'' because of the use of coal for heating and cooking. ''We never knew we were poor,'' ''we lived from day to day,'' ''we trusted in the Lord,'' are all impressions of school age children who now recall the Great Depression with mixed feelings of nostalgia and resentment. But the years have softened the pain, and most now believe that they learned valuable lessons of thrift, hard work, and sacrifice that have served them well in the half-century since the Great Depression.[66]

If most people's minds were constantly on the economic troubles of the thirties, politics came a close second. The Democratic ascendancy continued throughout the decade in Madison County and the state as well, but never again would that party dominate as it had in the early thirties. In the 1936 presidential election, for example, FDR narrowly carried Madison by 225 votes after having swept the county by nearly 1,200 votes in 1932. But by far the biggest political story of the decade was the rising political star of Keen Johnson.[67]

From his position as state party secretary, Johnson built a considerable backing across the state in the early thirties. Only partially allied with the Fields-Brown faction of the party in the twenties, he kept communications open with other groups as well. He supported conservation, becoming a member of the Cumberland Falls Protective Association in that organization's bid to keep the falls out of the hands of Samuel Insull. In 1935 his interests turned to the lieutenant governor's race. At the same time, Lieutenant Governor Albert Benjamin ''Happy'' Chandler set his sights on being Kentucky's next governor, in the process turning traditional Democratic party politics inside out. Both Johnson and Chandler faced the barrier of dual primaries, recently added to the process of nominating Democratic party officials by the Rhea-Donaldson faction to keep Chandler from getting the nomination. On the first ballot Johnson had the support of all factions, while Chandler had the backing of the Johnson-Talbott and Beckham-Bingham groups. Johnson won his first primary, but Chandler did not, placing second to Rhea. In the second primaries, both Chandler and Johnson won handily. In the fall general election the Democratic ticket swept into office in a much easier contest with the Republicans. Johnson and Chandler soon reconciled their political differences, and at an early January, 1936, banquet sponsored by the Madison County Historical Society in honor of Johnson, Chandler exclaimed that "Keen and I are going to do this job."[68]

While lieutenant governor, Johnson continued editorship of the *Register*, albeit often from a distance. On the campaign trail he had written columns under the title "Peregrinations of a Candidate"; now he wrote occasional articles while "substitute Governor." Johnson did not rock the boat as lieutenant governor as Chandler had done. Instead, he bided his time and paid his political dues. When Chandler ran against Alben Barkley in the 1938 Democratic senatorial primary, Johnson fully supported the governor. Barkley won that race by a wide margin, but Chandler got his chance for the United States Senate when Senator M.M. Logan died in October, 1939. In a well-orchestrated scenario, Chandler

Keen Johnson making formal announcement of candidacy for governor of Kentucky from Richmond, May 17, 1939. EKU Archives.

resigned the governorship, Johnson stepped into that office and immediately appointed the former governor to the Senate.[69]

Upon becoming governor, Johnson gave up his editorial duties with the *Register* while retaining part-ownership. He served out the remainder of Chandler's original term, girding himself for a run at the governorship in 1939. In the August primary of that year he defeated John Y. Brown, Sr., by over 34,000 votes across the state and about 2,500 in Madison County. Along the way he survived the collapse of a platform during a rally in Shelbyville in which several others received serious injuries. With the endorsement of the *Courier-Journal* and the *Lexington Herald* Johnson won in a landslide by over 106,000 ballots against Republican candidate King Swope, carrying the county by about 1,200 votes. As he prepared to take office in his own right Madison County, Kentucky, and the nation still contended with the lingering effects of the Great Depression.[70]

If the human spirit triumphed against the economic odds thrust forward by the depression, other facets of Madison County life demonstrated little, if any, deviation from previous patterns. Crime and violence may have actually increased in the early depression, out of the sheer desperation that many individuals found about them. In mid-1932 Keen Johnson editorialized about an "epidemic of slaying," that averaged, he estimated, "a homicide a week" in the county. A daylight robbery at the Paint Lick Bank that same year put everyone on notice that they were in the mainstream of a national crime wave. Organized crime, kidnappings, gangland wars, and murders all grabbed the national headlines of the decade. In Kentucky the Stoll kidnapping in 1934 came during the trial of the Lindbergh case. Kentucky's frontier brand of justice led to the killing of General Henry Denhardt by the Garr brothers in 1937, the former having been accused of murdering the sister of the latter. A Shelbyville jury acquitted the Garr brothers in a typical reaction of the era.[71]

Madison County homicides in the thirties included some of the most unusual crimes of the decade. For the first time since 1894 a Madison jury meted out the death penalty in 1932 to a black man convicted of killing an L. and N. detective. By this date the electric chair at the state penitentiary had become the accepted method of capital punishment. Two other murders in the decade reenacted themes common in the American folklore of crime, In mid-decade occurred the mysterious murder of a woman whose identity remained unanswered for several days because of the mutilation and dismemberment of the body. After about six weeks local law enforcement officials arrested Parkie Denny, a native Ohioan, for the killing of his wife Ethel, a native of Madison County. Judged guilty of murder by a Madison jury, Denney escaped the death penalty until a Fayette County jury prescribed "death's chair" in mid-1938. Meanwhile, a more typical killing occurred in Berea. On a warm evening in August, 1937, George E. Wells, a native Kentucky mountaineer, confronted Opal Sturgill, a Berea College student, and her most recent boy friend in front of Lincoln Hall on the college campus.

THE RICHMOND DAILY REGISTER

ESTABLISHED 1862—74TH YEAR. NO. 426.   RICHMOND, MADISON COUNTY, KENTUCKY, THURSDAY, NOVEMBER 9, 1939.   PRICE FIVE CENTS

JOHNSON MARGIN HOLDS AROUND 95,000

VICTORY IS CONCEDED BY JUDGE SWOPE

Republican Nominee Wires Congratulations and Best Wishes to Governor; Democratic Sweep is General

TAKE LEGISLATURE

LOUISVILLE, Ky., Nov. 9 (AP) —Former Circuit Judge King Swope, Republican candidate for governor trailing Governor Keen Johnson, Democrat, by more than 95,000 votes, today conceded Johnson's election to a full four-year term.

The Lexington jurist sent the following telegram to the governor at the Frankfort executive mansion:

"Congratulations and best wishes."

Johnson swept along with him Democratic candidates for the eight other state-wide offices and Democratic majorities in both houses of the general assembly.

With 3,849 of Kentucky's 4,341 precincts tabulated the Richmond newspaper editor and publisher had 390,592 votes to Swope's 294,-789. At one time in the count Johnson's majority climbed to nearly 97,000 but late returns from Republican areas in the eastern Kentucky mountains cut into the Democratic majority.

In the senate the Democrats are assured of 28 of the total 38 votes when the general assembly meets January 8. The Democratic majority in the house, on the basis of incomplete returns, will be 70 out of the 100 members.

WIN R. R. COMMISSIONERS

Democrats also will have all three members of the state railroad commission, the incomplete returns indicate. Robert Webb of Mayfield, a Democrat, was unopposed and Democrats Frank L. McCarthy and Harry Gaynor were leading their opponents in the Second and Third districts respectively.

The Democrats with safe leads for the statewide offices were Lieut. Gov. Rodes K. Myers, Bowling Green; Secretary of State George Glenn Hatcher, Ashland; Attorney General Hubert Meredith, Greenville; Auditor D. A. Logan, Brownsville; State Treasurer Ernest Shannon, Louisa; Clerk of the Court of Appeals Charles K. O'Connell, Louisville; Superintendent of Public Instruction John Brooker, Cynthiana and Commissioner of Agriculture William May, Prestonsburg.

Meredith and O'Connell are incumbents. The attorney general succeeded Beverly Vincent when the latter won a seat in the United States house of representatives after his election to the state office in 1935 and O'Connell succeeded (CONTINUED ON PAGE 2)

MAGISTRATES VOTE $600 FOR ARMORY

U. S. Will Build Armory Here if City and County Provide Lot for New Structure

COURT IS INFORMED

Madison fiscal court today voted unanimously to contribute $600 toward the purchase of a lot in the city of Richmond upon which will be constructed a National Guard Armory.

George Hembree, representing the National Guard unit here, told the court that the U. S. Armory Commission would build an armory here at a minimum cost of $25,000 if the city and county would furnish the site on which the proposed building is to be erected.

Mr. Hembree declared that a suitable lot could be obtained for $1,200. The county's contribution is contingent upon the city council at its next meeting contributing an equal amount.

Members of the court stated that the county budget did not provide for such an appropriation but expressed an anxiety to obtain the building for Richmond and declared that the money would be raised from a contingent fund and from the general fund, if necessary.

SUIT DISCUSSED

During the three-hour morning session which concluded the regular monthly meeting, the fiscal body discussed the suit of the City of Richmond against the Madison Fiscal Court in which the city is attempting to obtain a declaratory judgment against the county to have the county provide hospitalization for the indigent persons living within the city.

The magistrates stated that they have been informed that Mayor William O'Neil had ceased to keep hospital permits to indigent city patients, and the members stated that the city has refused to take any part in the care of the city charity while awaiting a judgment of the suit now on file in the circuit court.

JOINT OBLIGATION

County Judge Vernon Leer and County Attorney O. W. Hisle stated that the Kentucky statutes provide that the indigents living within the city are the wards of both the city and the county and must be provided for by the city and county jointly.

The fiscal court entered on the minute books that the county is willing to do its part and co-operate with the city to work out a solution to the problem while waiting on a court decision on the suit.

BROTHERS ARRESTED

Ernest and Marcus Combs Charged With Possessing Unlicensed Still

RELEASED ON BOND

Two Madison county brothers were at liberty on $300 bond each on charges of possessing two unlicensed whisky stills, resulting from a raid made by federal authorities at their home on the Berea-Cartersville road on October 25.

Ernest Combs, 29, and his brother, Marcus, 27, were arrested late Wednesday by Constable Bryan Kelley and U. S. Deputy Marshal Neal Guilfoile and arraigned early today before U. S. Commissioner S. H. Thorpe. Marcus pleaded guilty to the charge and was held to await the action of the federal grand jury here and released on bond. Ernest was released on bond pending a hearing before the commissioner Friday. He pleaded not guilty.

Constable Kelley said he and federal officers raided the home on the night of October 25 and destroyed two 14-gallon capacity copper stills. Three and one-half gallons of illegal liquor, 65 gallons of mash and four 50-gallon fermenters were confiscated at the raid, he said.

The brothers were arrested late Wednesday while stripping tobacco at the home, Kelley said.

Miss Cage to Speak at Eastern Friday

Miss Lucy Gage, professor of elementary education at Peabody College, Nashville, will speak at the Eastern Teachers College assembly hour Friday morning at 9:50.

Miss Gage, a pioneer in kindergarten and nursery work and one of the founders of the Childhood

After a brief argument between the three individuals the clash of the eternal triangle of love ended in carnage. Wells drew a pistol and fired three shots, one fatally striking Opal in the heart. Passersby, startled by the gunshots, rushed to the scene but were unable to help the victim. Wells struck the other man and then bolted down the street and disappeared into the gathering darkness. With "feeling running high" in the community around Berea, posses searched for several days for the young murderer but could find no trace. Eventually they gave up the effort. Wells probably returned to the fastnesses of the Kentucky mountains, where in various places residents claimed to have seen a furtive figure thought to be Wells hiding under houses and in sundry locations. One story even described the young fugitive as being dressed in women's clothes. Whether the stories were true or not, they soon merged with folklore, legend, and oral tradition, becoming another of the mountain tales. In this case life imitated art as the tragedy approximated parts of ballads about a young man who kills a girl, including "Pretty Polly," "Tom Dooley," and "Poor Pearl" Bryan.[72]

The overall health of Madison's citizens may also have declined in the thirties because of the stresses of the depression. Without money, many people put off visiting a doctor or dentist until problems became acute. The formation of a Madison County health unit finally became a reality in the early thirties after facing the tortuous path of county politics. Record keeping became more systematic. Pattie A. Clay Hospital continued to serve surrounding counties as well as Madison residents. The trachoma hospital stepped up its efforts as the depression deepened. Dr. Sory found that "trachoma and poverty go in one continuous cycle," and he proposed that both problems had to be attacked to rid Appalachia of this disease.[73]

The Madison health record of the thirties reflected national and state trends. Periodic outbreaks of diphtheria and polio struck down school age children. Tuberculosis reached almost epidemic proportions in mid-decade. Editor Johnson blamed it on the scope of the depression. In 1934, twenty-one Madisonians died of that malady. The next year a study of one county school revealed that all the children and the teacher had inactive cases of TB. A survey of all students in the county system in April, 1933, indicated that 3,798 out of 4,980 had health related problems. Of that number "218 underweight indigent children" received special attention, being given a pint of milk daily and a pint of cod liver oil monthly. Other diseases took their toll. For example, in 1936 health authorities alarmingly reported over 150 cases of venereal disease among the men at Camp Lake Reba. The vital statistics relating to health appear even more frightening. Blacks were particularly hard hit. In 1937 with three times the infant mortality rate of the white population, thirty-six black children were born while sixty-six blacks died. On the other hand, the 465 white births were balanced with 248 deaths. In mid-decade the black death rate of 18.6 per 1,000 far exceeded the white figure of 10.5[74]

Notwithstanding these dire statistics or the threat of violence about them, Madison Countians kept up their spirits and hopes for the future. Nor did they forget the past. In early September, 1934, 4,000 Kentuckians celebrated the bicentennial of Daniel Boone's birth at Boonesborough. Governor Ruby Laffoon gave the main address. Local history buffs led by Green Clay stepped up their efforts to have Boonesborough declared a national monument. The Pioneer National Monument Association coordinated its efforts to purchase such sites by selling 1934 specially minted half-dollars. However, these efforts failed, in part, because of depression conditions. The biggest event in years, however, came in mid-October, 1937, with the Madison County Sesqui-Centennial Celebration. The three-day event included a pageant, "Progress of the Years," repeated each evening at the newly completed Hanger Stadium. A cast of several hundred residents portrayed scenes from the county's history from "Episode I, The Dawn of Creation," complete with a "Creation Ballet," to scenes of pioneering, slavery days, the Battle of Richmond, and in conclusion, the "Grand Finale" entitled " The Wheel of Life." Delegations from as far away as Louisville visited the festivities, which combined boosterism for the county with celebration of its historic past.[75]

But even the bravado of such lavish spectacles could not wish away the Great Depression. Madison Countains struggled on against the unrelenting depression. They finally realized that the poor economic conditions would be with them for a long time to come. Hot, dry summers in mid-decade bedeviled farmers and brought a halt to plans for the 1936 county fair. In a complete turnabout mother nature brought disaster of another kind in early 1937, when flood waters descended the rivers of the Ohio Valley. The greatest flood in anyone's memory struck Valley View, Boonesborough and other points along the Kentucky River. Lake Reba overflowed its banks, and public health authorities rushed to protect the water supply from contamination. Nearly every place in the state on a river bank faced disaster. Louisville suffered nearly irreparable damage as water engulfed most of the central part of that city. During this interlude Richmond, like several other central Kentucky towns, served as temporary home for several thousand refugees from the flood waters.[76]

Through 1937 conditions in the county did not seem to improve, although the pro-FDR *Register* might exclaim to the contrary in its defense of the New Deal. The bottom fell out of the tobacco market again, just like the early depression years. Moreover, poverty still stalked the county. As late as 1938 a study indicated that over one hundred children in Richmond could not attend school because they lacked shoes. An editorial campaign by the *Register* and the efforts of the Richmond Chamber of Commerce soon brought in enough money to buy shoes for these children. However, the picture was not entirely cloudy. The city of Richmond finally opened its new water filtration plant. "It is a real joy to have clear, pure water that leaves no muddy deposit in the wash basin," declared a *Register* editorial. The black school in Richmond began to graduate more of its students. County school attendance increased in the latter part of the thirties, residents voted a new school tax, and the new central high school opened in September, 1939.[77]

In the late thirties it became increasingly difficult for Madison Countians to escape a feeling of dé jà vu, that some how the world seemed to be moving in the same way it had just before the outbreak of World War I. But life went on. Most of people's attention was taken up by events nearer to home. The opening of a new school or business after the heartbreaks of the decade revived a spirit of optimism. However, the news from Europe made people increasingly uneasy. The same week that the Madison High School Purples, under the direction of Coach Ralph Carlisle, defeated the Henry Clay Blue Devils in the boys' regional basketball tournament, the German army dissolved the last vestige of Czechoslovakian independence. A few Madisonians traveled to the 1939 New York World's Fair, visiting the "world of tomorrow," at which the president of RCA announced that television sets would soon be ready to market at about $175 per model. For most people of the county their life still revolved around local events like Court Day, at which in 1939 a genuine Indian chief sold "corn salve" on Water Street. Europe and Asia were thousands of miles and a world away from Madison County, and who could be overly concerned about the machinations of Hitler or Japanese warlords when economic depression appeared to be the greatest problem in Madison County?[78]

Chapter Fifteen
WORLD WAR AND A WIDER WORLD, 1940-1959

The years from 1940 to 1959 presented Madison Countians with the challenge of change on a scale never before witnessed in the country. World War II catapulted the United States into a position of world leadership, and, for better or worse, the old isolated regionalism and the isolationalist mood of the country were never to return. Madison County sacrificed its young men and its wealth in the quest to win the war. Moreover, construction of a munitions facility irrevocably altered the economic and social structure of the community. Migrants from nearby mountain counties flocked in to take jobs. Business boomed as money flowed into the local economy for the first time in years.

Like most Americans, Madison Countians shared in the wartime and postwar prosperity. New industries came to the county, the local colleges grew in enrollment, and highways and bridges opened the county to more complete access with the surrounding area. The extension of electricity and telephone services to most every area of the county ended once and for all the old, isolated lifestyle that had insulated much of Madison County from progress. Moreover, the advent of television in the early fifties instantaneously connected Madison County households with the wider world. The pace of life quickened. Many people began to wonder if the gains outweighed the losses. Was the material gain worth the effort?

If most Madison Countians accepted their new roles as citizens of the world and as consumers in a mass society, they also recognized that the new life had a darker side. The end of World War II offered no respite from fear of another war. Unthinkable weapons like the atomic and hydrogen bombs and the onset of the Cold War left them little time for complete relaxation. The outbreak of the Korean War only a few short years after the end of World War II reinforced the new role of the United States in the world. In microcosm the history of Madison County from 1940 to 1959 exemplified many of the important changes taking place in the county at-large during that era.

The census of 1940 documented some of the tragedies of the depression decade. Because of a declining birth rate and out-migration, the population of the county increased by only 3.3 percent. Unemployment still hovered around 10 percent. The majority of Madisonians remained on farms, a sign of their perseverance in the face of the worst agricultural disaster in the history of the nation. The number of farms decreased only slightly by a total of 127 and the rural population decreased by just 266 people. Richmond and Berea both grew in numbers. The number of blacks in the county continued to decline as they increasingly moved off to better economic opportunities. As late as 1941 many Madison County farm families depended on picking blackberries to supplement their income, making Madison the leading blackberry county in the state.[1]

Madison County's adopted son, Governor Keen Johnson, and President Franklin D. Roosevelt contended with the continued problems of the Great Depression. Johnson proved to be a "saving, thrifty, frugal governor," who made every effort to keep state expenditures under control. After the exit of the flamboyant Chandler to Washington, the editor-publisher of the *Register* was somewhat more predictable and less colorful. While most people respected Johnson, he never became a "man of the people." More importantly, he never cultivated that hail-fellow-well-met personality so revered by Kentucky politicians and their clientele.[2]

Although a tightfisted governor in times that required it, Johnson was able to throw some aid in the direction of Madison County. The county got its full share and more of state support for roads and bridges. Construction began on the new Clay's Ferry Bridge before he left office, a much improved link with Fayette County on U.S. 25. Actually the bridge was downstream at a site originally known as Cleveland's Landing, at one time a substantial shipping port in the nineteenth century. Building of the span was delayed because of the coming of the war and the loss of priority for the massive amounts of structural steel and concrete needed. Toward the end of the war the work pace increased. Over 250 feet above the Kentucky River and built on a dangerous geological fault line, the new bridge became one of the highest in the nation when completed in mid-1946. The next year Governor Simeon Willis rededicated the bridge to the war dead of Madison and Fayette counties. The Boonesborough Bridge became toll-free just at the end of the war, giving Madison Countians their first free access to Clark County.[3]

As the depression crisis lessened in intensity, Madison County Republicans reasserted themselves, particularly in their old strongholds of Berea and Brassfield. While FDR carried the county in his third presidential race in 1940, he did so by fewer than 700 votes. The efforts of his New Deal agencies in the county wound down in the early forties, in part because of the improving economic conditions of the early war years. However, even before the prosperity of the war obviated the need for such organs as WPA, CCC, and NYA, many Madisonians had already rebelled against these programs. Political rifts on the fiscal court and wrangling between city and county governments weakened the entire community's efforts to obtain federal funds. Fiscal court factionalism resulted in quarrels over road building and appointments of a road engineer and a certifying agent for WPA and CCC personnel. City and county officials clashed over the question of responsibility for indigent city residents, a dispute that erupted in several other Kentucky communities.[4]

Notwithstanding the normally turbid nature of politics in Madison County, increasingly the attention of everyone turned toward the ominous events taking place in Europe and Asia. American isolationism eroded with the outbreak of World War II in Europe on September 1, 1939, when Germany invaded Poland with the tacit consent of the Soviet Union. Roosevelt delivered a fireside chat over the radio the same day that Great Britain and France declared war on Germany. The president promised to expend "every effort" to stay out of the war. Within weeks, Congress repealed the embargo act and enacted a cash-and-carry proviso, a measure that, in effect, ended neutrality by permitting Great Britain and France to purchase war material as long as they transported the same in their own ships. After Nazi forces swept over Poland in five weeks, Hitler appeared for a time to have sated his appetite for conquest. The world settled into an uneasy calm. Unfortunately, the "phony war" of the winter of 1939-40 ended with lightning-fast German invasions of Denmark and Norway. A month later Nazi armies, flushed with victory, swept across Belgium, Holland, and Luxembourg in a matter of days. Although British and French forces fought heroically, only the evacuation of the remnants of those armies from Dunkerque saved them from an even worse disaster. Indeed, it appeared that Great Britain might soon fall to Hitler's juggernaut. Managing Editor James A. Miller, Jr. of the *Register* echoed the sentiments of many an American when he declared that "Civilization is at its greatest crisis since Golgotha."[5]

By mid-1940 more and more Madisonians began to wonder how much longer the United States could remain out of the war. They went about their daily lives, working, playing, and still worrying about the aftermath of the worst depression in the nation's history. Maybe, just maybe, the country could avoid another war like World War I. After all, with large expanses of ocean on both sides of the United States, how could any nation be foolish enough to pick on us? And, there was always something else to be concerned about rather than dwelling on the war in Europe and Asia. A sensationalized murder case like that of Marion Miley at the Lexington Country Club kept the press buzzing for months. Moreover, a little comic relief sometimes surfaced right here in Madison

County. For example, people chuckled for years about the time that two deputies picked up a gentleman in the county accused of stealing chickens, a not uncommon crime during those depression years. When the vehicle in which they were all riding became entrapped in a mudhole, the lawmen got out to push. The culprit in their custody obligingly offered to help and then drove off down the road, leaving the peace officers with more than mud on their faces. However, this Madison County desperado did show some consideration, as he parked the car only one mile down the road before hotfooting it across the fields.[6]

Of course, events in Europe increasingly intruded on everyone's life. Roosevelt asked for more money for defense, and by late 1940 the peacetime draft started calling young Madison men into the armed forces. War edged a bit closer as women in the local Red Cross chapter collected clothing to be sent to war-torn Europe and the Richmond National Guard company spent time on maneuvers in Wisconsin.[7]

German bombing raids on Great Britain and the valiant efforts of British civilians convinced many Americans that something must be done to help the allied side. After FDR's victory in 1940, he opted for lend-lease assistance after hearing the pleadings of Prime Minister Winston Churchill for more direct aid. In early March, 1941, Congress passed the measure. As the United States steadily moved toward war, or at least an anti-Nazi policy, Madison County became more directly influenced by the defense build-up at home. By midsummer, 1941, Madisonians began talking about the possibility that the federal government might build an installation in the southern edge of the county. At first the word from Washington indicated that the site would be used as a training base for a United States Army armored division. The Richmond Chamber of Commerce immediately jumped at the chance to add jobs to the payroll of the county. Chamber leaders stressed that a recent survey found that over one thousand residents had left in the previous year to seek war industry jobs in other parts of the country.[8]

Senator Chandler and Congressman A. J. May worked hard for a federal project as members of the military affairs committees in each house of Congress. Within weeks the announcement came from Governor Johnson that a site had been chosen in the county for an ammunition storage depot. An Army Signal Corps facility at Avon in Fayette County would be built first. Nearly 15,000 acres of land would be needed for the Madison site. Initially, most Madisonians, particularly businessmen, welcomed the idea as they thought of increased sales after the business drought of the depression years. If the country was going to rearm, why should Madison County not get a "slice of the defense turkey," the *Register* asked? Few people at the time realized all the ramifications of this decision by the War Department. However, as condemnation proceedings began to take over the vast area of land needed for the base, some of the best farmland in the county, over one hundred farmers in the region signed a petition protesting the taking of their property.[9]

The first week of December, 1941, came with the depot on nearly everyone's mind. The pros and cons of the proposal became a topic of hot debate at local barber shops and beauty parlors, but there was no sense of urgency. The real war still seemed far away when the first full weekend of December began. Things did not look so bad. After all, the new Burley Tobacco Growers Cooperative Association was in place and the tobacco market in Richmond was averaging over twenty-nine dollars per 100 pounds, higher than in years. The local schools had just finished their football seasons, with the new Central County High School fielding a team for the first time. Basketball fans of the new Central High School were still smarting from a defeat at the hands of Burgin, 45-37, on Friday night. Kingston had defeated nearby rival Berea in a close one, 24-22. Madison Model High School was getting ready to present its Christmas play, *Petit Noel*, while *Damien the Leper* would soon begin at Eastern. Some people were anticipating seeing their old favorites Bud Abbott and Lou Costello playing in *Hold That Ghost* at Madison Theatre beginning on Sunday. Madison County weather was not too bad, but it was reported to be thirty-one degress below zero on the Russian front near Moscow. The next draft call was predicted not to be a heavy one for the county. There had already been 173 young Madison Countians, white and black, inducted into the service.[10]

***Richmond Register,* December 8, 1941.**

For those old enough to remember, the date December 7, 1941, stands out forever in their memories. It is a scar etched there by that "day which will live in infamy," in the inimitable words of FDR, when the Japanese attacked Pearl Harbor, a naval base in Hawaii. Some Madison Countians were in their usual places in church that Sunday, some were resting from the week's labors, and a few were possibly sleeping off the effects of the previous night's festivities. Some were already serving in far-flung army and naval bases. But no one could escape the shocking news that came just after noon that the Japanese had bombed an American base. The subconscious denial that America could ever again be involved in a world war was now swept away. The next day President Roosevelt asked Congress for a declaration of war. Editor Miller that afternoon declared: "Where last week we were Democrats and Republicans, interventionists and isolationists, today we are one— Americans all—determined and powerful. Let the aggressors beware." Christmas day, 1941, took on new significance for most Madison Countians. They read of the loss of Wake Island and the beginning of the Japanese onslaught at Lingayen Gulf in the Philippines. They realized that a long war was only beginning. The most radical changes in the history of the county were about to begin.[11]

The new year 1942 brought new challenges. Draft calls skyrocketed as the armed forces expanded. Many residents and migrants became involved in getting the Blue Grass Ordnance Depot into operation as plans moved ahead at breakneck speed. The acquisition of land continued to be a problem. Owners of larger farms in the depot area, the nearly 15,000 acres bounded by U.S. 52 on the north, Speedwell Pike on the east, U.S. 25 on the west, and Kingston Pike on the south, complained that smaller farmers got more per acre than they did. Eventually, court proceedings were needed to take the last farms within the confines of the depot. Bitterness over this action continued well past the war years, eventually impacting the political ambitions of former Governor Keen Johnson. Families were uprooted, small communities along Muddy Creek and Viney Fork were bulldozed away, and only old memories remained of the heritage of the area. Several black farmers, including Henry Allen Laine, lost their land, continuing the decline of black farmers in the county. Even old cemeteries were removed. Over 900 white graves were moved and reinterred at a new cemetery off U.S. 25; 769 "Colored" dead also were taken to a new resting place on Speedwell Pike.[12]

By early April, 1942, construction work began on the storage facility. Military personnel, contractors, and construction workers descended on the area. The building of over 150 miles of roads, forty-five miles of railroad lines, hundreds of "igloos" for ammunition, and other buildings came within months. The work force at one time numbered nearly 6,500 civilian workers. The flow of migrants out of the nearby mountain counties increased with the construction of the post as they found a chance for a good-paying job close by home. Richmond became a miniboom town, as rooms for workers came at a premium and restaurants stayed open around the clock. By October, 1942, the first carloads of ammunition arrived for processing, and without much ceremony the depot went into service. Construction workers stayed on for several more months putting the finishing touches on what would become the third largest facility of its type in the United States Army's system.[13]

The work force handling the munitions and other supplies grew steadily in the first months of operation, reaching a high of 3,800 in 1943. Women and blacks had an opportunity for work in the county that had not been available in previous years. Workers starting at the bottom earned fifty-nine cents an hour, a good and steady wage for the many who had suffered through the bad times of the depression. Carpentry foremen working on the igloos earned about ninety dollars a week, an excellent salary for the early war years. For the first time in years many people had steady jobs. Many married couples took jobs at the depot. In October, 1943, a subsidiary of the Firestone Tire and Rubber Company took over operation of the depot on a "cost plus fixed fee basis" and maintained that role until after the end of the war. At one time during that period the base served as the principal army storage facility for bearings used on all types of vehicles.[14]

During the war years the depot paid more than $17 million in wages, much of which entered the Madison County economy. Businessmen reported better sales than even during the flush times of the 1920s. Madison County would never be quite the same again. While the depot undoubtedly added to business volume and the general economic welfare of Madison County's citizens, it may also have had a negative impact. Some observers noticed an increase in the consumption of alcohol. On one occasion a spot check of workers entering the facility turned up "several gunny sacks" full of half-pints of whiskey. Traffic backed up "all the way to Richmond" as guards searched automobiles. Moreover, Madison County witnessed its first real labor strife in March, 1944, when Firestone fired fifty truck drivers after they refused to help load and unload their vehicles. A study of a similar site in Utah, Tooele Army Depot, suggested that numerous social problems resulted from rapid societal change caused by the influx of migrants and money. Divorce, crime, and juvenile problems increased at an alarming rate in that area. Although no similar study has been done of Madison County, many older natives of the community complained about the depot as a harbinger of unwanted change. In a lighter vein, some guards at Post Number 10 near the scene of the heinous crime committed by Parkie Denny in 1937 claimed to have heard frightening and unearthy sounds emanating from there on several nights. After initial word of this visitation reached the public, the depot returned to its usual calm. Neither ghosts, strikes, or other distractions kept the workers of the depot from carrying out its mission.[15]

The war came closer to home when the casualty lists began to mount, the first being a former Eastern student wounded during the attack on Pearl Harbor. Those remaining on the home front did not have to wait long for the war to directly touch their lives in other ways.[16]

Wartime regulations, though sometimes evaded through the black market, impressed upon Madison Countians the need to sacrifice to help the "boys" at the war front. Actually, wartime shortages were more of an inconvenience than a sacrifice. While it might be difficult for the ladies to obtain nylon stockings, there was always leg make-up available. Men might complain about short supplies of manufactured cigarettes, but they usually could be found with a little ingenuity. If people could not find something to spend their money on because of controls or shortages, they could always pay off old debts or save for future expenditures. Everyone's expectations rose. Just as much as Americans hoped for a safer world at the end of the war they also wanted the continuation of wartime prosperity.[17]

In large cities and small towns rented rooms went at a premium. Retail store owners complained about Office of Price Administration controls and about shortages. Consumers, on the other hand, felt the pinch of an inflationary spiral of prices. War controls never really solved any of these problems, but Americans generally ate better and lived better than ever before in their lives. An "A" ration card became a permanent fixture on the window of automobiles. Even with shortages of fuel and tires, Americans traveled more than in the previous decade. And if they could not travel, there was always the movies. That industry boomed during the war. Although construction priorities were designed to limit much business expansion, the number of supermarkets in the nation more than tripled during the war years, taking a larger share of the food business that had at one time been dominated by the "mom and pop" grocery store.[18]

Only a month after Pearl Harbor the OPA established several quota systems. For example, OPA limited Madison's ration of tires to sixty and tubes to fifty for a one-month period. As General MacArthur's heroic defenders of Corregidor began making their last stand in late January, 1942, other restrictions came down from Washington, including one on sugar. "Hoarding" became an ominous word in America in the early forties, one almost as opprobrious as "Nazi." Eventually, sugar, shoes, tin cans, coffee, meat, cheese, and a few other commodities came under controls. Like people everywhere, Madison Countians made adjustments. Those on the farm supplied the city folk with enough food so that there were never anything more than spot shortages at any one time. Most of the time people ate better than ever before. Many people raised their own "Victory Gardens" and contributed the food to their own tables. Midwar food prices for many items were not much more than during the depression years. In early January, 1943, prices at Kroger's included ten pounds of potatoes for .21, twenty-four pounds of flour for $1.03, two loaves of bread for .19, sugar for .06 a pound with #10 Ration Coupons, and a pound of Spotlight coffee for only .21. As the war dragged on, tin for canning came in short supply and rationing began in March, 1943. Nevertheless, several canneries were built in the county, including new ones at Kingston and Central High School in mid-1944. Rationing programs became more pervasive and complicated in late 1943. Sales of shoes became regulated from time to time. There were never enough tires and tubes to go around, and gasoline rationing limited travel. Sometimes the shelves of businesses looked rather bleak after they had sold out of their wares. Bakeries closed after they had used up their monthly quota of sugar. For a few months in 1943-44 canned goods in stores were rationed. Such documents as the "Official Table of Consumer Point Values for Meat, Fats, Fish, and Cheese" established a complicated system of controls. Well into the last months of the war people were urged to save fats and oils for the war effort. Moreover, they received extra ration points for their efforts. Most Madison Countians cooperated, with a little grumbling, in a system of the most extreme regimentation. For the most part, the system worked to the benefit of home and foreign front alike. Actually there was little hoarding, and the infamous black market for such products as beef and tobacco only slightly slowed the war effort.[19]

The home front also kept up its end of the battle in other ways. Washington mobilized the minds as well as the bodies of all Americans through such agencies as the Office of War Information. Madison Countians were urged to work hard, and bond drives were usually oversubscribed. They paid the highest federal taxes in history, including the special 5 percent "Victory Tax." In 1943 the IRS began requiring the withholding of federal tax from paychecks. The federal budget of $9 billion in 1939 rose to over $100 billion by 1945. Madisonians paid their part of this great increase in revenue and received their share of the impact of this money on the local economy. They contributed more than money. Red Cross volunteers rolled bandages. Madison Countians cooperated with the War Production Board's scrap metal drives by donating yard fences, and the courthouse bandstand and iron fountain. They turned in large quantities of iron, steel, copper, brass, aluminum, and rubber. Scarcity of labor in 1943 brought a decision to have county school students attend classes on Saturdays so that they could finish the school term earlier and therby be available for working on farms in the summer and fall. There were individual acts of kindness as well. Mrs. Robert Bush of Doylesville, for example, averaged writing about two hundred letters a month to servicemen scattered across the world. As happens in all periods of time, the war brought out the best as well as the worst in people.[20]

All facets of Madison County life came under extreme stress in the war years. Farmers in the entire nation prospered. As in most agricultural counties, deferments given to young draft eligible farmers caused some controversy. In early 1943 Governor Johnson appointed Eastern President W. F. O'Donnell chairman of a new draft board after just such a conflict. Madison farmers had difficulty obtaining farm machinery, tools, and other equipment, but they did what was expected of them—i.e., they produced an abundance of commodities for the war effort.[21]

The old standbys of Madison County agriculture, tobacco and cattle, rapidly improved in price in 1942 and continued to pour millions of dollars into the economy at war's end. The last prewar crop year, 1941, had been the best in decades, with local tobacco doubling in price from the 1940 crop year. The setting in place of the federally backed cooperative program in 1940 had already added a sense of security to that market before the war began. Cigarettes, with their substantial burley content, increased in volume in the early forties. Sending tobacco products to the soldiers at the front became an obsession of farmers and government official alike. In the first days after Pearl Harbor the price of tobacco shot up in local markets. By late 1942 the local price had soared to an average of over forty dollars per 100 weight and stabilized near that level for the remainder of the war. Acreages devoted to tobacco culture increased yields. Whereas in 1940 tobacco acreage had dropped to less than 7,000 acres in the county, the land in production had increased to over 9,000 acres by war's end. More importantly, yields per acre also went up because of heavier use of fertilizer. Visions of continued prosperity came to most every Madison farmer.[22]

The number of farms increased slightly in the war years, a sign that agriculture was again a profitable venture. It might be added as a postscript that this would be the last period in which this would occur. After 1945 the number of farms steadily declined in all agricultural censuses. In wartime the average value of land and buildings per acre increased by about 50 percent. Other areas of Madison agriculture also demonstrated the impact of the war economy.[23]

Livestock production in the county improved. Beef cattle became much more profitable as the war intensified, and farmers responded by increasing their herds. Even milk cattle production increased as farmers began depending more on local markets. Sheep and lamb numbers fell off as the ravages of dogs continued to cause problems. Corn production remained rather strong throughout these years after falling off heavily in the depression years. A few Madison farmers began experimenting with cultivation of soybeans in 1943. Legal cultivation of hemp came back to the county again, under federal license, and several Madison farmers raised the crop for seed, which sold for as much as $12.60 per bushel.[24]

In other ways Madison County agriculture demonstrated progress. From 1940 to 1945 the number of farm tractors and trucks nearly doubled, an indication of the growing mechanization of Madison farms. More farms reported electricity and telephones, a sure sign of prosperity. Farmers paid out more money for feed, labor, fertilizer, and other essentials. Much of that circulated back into the local economy. All in all, local farmers had little to complain about during the war.[25]

The educational institutions of Madison County also made their adjustments to the war. Kentucky education had suffered serious setbacks as a result of the economic instability of the Great Depression years. Though the Madison County Board of Education and the fiscal court raised the school tax rate in the late thirties, it remained one of the lowest in the state. Madison County continued to produce one of the highest school dropout rates in the nation, a pattern that existed throughout the South in general and Kentucky in particular. Of course, bickering over school board races also grabbed the public's attention when other political avenues calmed.[26]

Higher education in the county had to make even more abrupt adjustments than did the public schools. In April, 1941, President Herman L. Donovan resigned his position at Eastern to become president of the University of Kentucky. Three days later the board of the Richmond school appointed William F. O'Donnell, the city school superintendent, as Eastern's new president. In the last two years of Donovan's tenure, a new student union facility, the Keen Johnson Student Union Building, opened along with several dormitories. Unable to believe that the campus could grow much larger, Donovan predicted that the Johnson Building (1940) would end the school's construction program for the forseeable future. There would be no building during the war years, as the school's enrollment dropped to less than a quarter of its enrollment of 1940. In 1943 a Women's Army Auxiliary Corps training school came to the Eastern campus. The school took over the old music building and turned out 1,700 clerical trainees in the single year that the program operated in Richmond. At nearby Berea College, Francis Hutchins succeeded his father, William J., as president in 1939. Another son, Robert Hutchins, headed the University of Chicago. Berea also made its contributions to the war effort. A Navy V-12 program brought hundreds of young men to the pastoral southern Madison community, imparting a bit of "color and vitality to a lonesome campus." For the first time social dancing, and not the traditional mountain variety, became the popular form of entertainment. The Hutchins administration also bowed to another modern habit, the smoking of tobacco, and for the first time allowed students to smoke cigarettes on campus. Government training programs at Eastern and Berea kept schools of their type functioning in the war years, at a time when only the larger colleges and universities could keep up their enrollments. The infusion of a new type of student into the Berea community helped speed the pace of change there, modernizing the otherwise sleepy little college town.[27]

While Americans may have cooperated more during World War II than ever before in their history, they still could disagree enough to make politics as interesting as ever. Beneath the thin veneer of bipartisanship needed for the war effort lay the issues on which political parties thrive. Kentucky and the nation began turning more toward the Grand Old Party in the congressional races of 1942. The next year Republican Simeon S. Willis defeated Democrat Lyter Donaldson for governor of the Commonwealth. Madison County gave the victor a 5,000 vote majority, a clear sign of a turn away from the Democratic dominance that had existed since the beginning of the depression. In the 1944 presidential race, FDR bucked the nationwide swing toward Republicanism by carrying the campaign against New York Governor Thomas E. Dewey. Roosevelt carried Madison County by his smallest margin in the four races, 300 votes.[28]

Women's Auxiliary Army Corp on the campus of Eastern Kentucky State Teachers College during World War II. EKU Archives.

Local option continued to be one of the most hotly contested political-social questions during the war. In a 1937 ballot drys apparently won a countywide majority of 199 votes. Berea and surrounding precincts voted nearly seven to one for local option, while in Richmond the wets carried that city by over 1,000 votes. Sixteen liquor and beer dealers in the county contested the outcome, claiming the vote to be invalid because the election had not been properly advertised. Madison Circuit Judge W. J. Baxter upheld the decision of the people in the election. Early the next year the Kentucky Court of Appeals reversed Judge Baxter's decision, agreeing with the plaintiff that the election had not been properly advertised. County Judge Vernon Leer, also serving as county alcoholic beverage administrator, refused to grant liquor licenses outside of Richmond city limits. The next round in this continuing battle between the wets and the drys came in a local option election in 1943. In the June ballot of that year the prodry group, the Citizens League for Civic Righteousness, got out the vote, soundly defeating their opponents, 4,706 to 2,741. Several weeks later Kentucky's highest court upheld the decision, and liquor sales again became outlawed in Madison County.[29]

Of course, the men in combat and the other Madisonians serving across the world were part of a larger drama. Their experiences of loneliness, fear, boredom, heartbreak, and occasional heroism only they could completely understand. The casualties of the war increased as the battles dragged on, particularly after the Allied invasion of Normandy in June, 1944. Families honored their members in the armed forces with a blue star in the window. More and more of those were replaced with gold stars, a symbol of a death in service to the United States. From 1944 to the end of the war the names of those killed, wounded, and missing mounted. Often a young soldier had only recently joined the service. For example, a Madisonian died in France in 1944 one year to the day after having been inducted. One prisoner of war in Germany later recounted having been fairly well treated by his Nazi captors during his six months of imprisonment, but he had suffered nonetheless from bitterly cold weather and lack of food. Toward the end of the war Madisonians began hearing about the atrocities of the Bataan Death March of 1942 and the near successful attempt of Germany to wipe out the Jewish people of Europe. Most Madison County families were touched by the war. Those that did not have war casualties suffered through the uncertainty of not knowing the fate of loved-ones for weeks and months. But World War II could have its lighter side. Sometimes Madisonians would meet far from home, as happened to five young soldiers in the Philippines in April, 1945. There were always the jokes about the ubiquitous Kilroy, whose name turned up everywhere from China to Europe. One local aircrew member went carrying a rabbit's foot for good luck one better by taking a complete live hare, named Beanie, on each flight over the Gilbert Islands in the Pacific. He could not be convinced that the fuzzy talisman did not work because his plane received only one scar from enemy shells in several weeks of combat.[30]

The racial segregation that had marked the history of Madison County and much of the nation for so long did not change much during the war. Blacks, like their white counterparts, enlisted and were drafted into the armed forces, which continued to be rigidly segregated. At least one local Negro received his commission as a pilot just as the war ended. Lynching in the country steadily declined in the late thirties, 1940 being the first year in memory in which one of these crimes did not occur in the South. Just before the war the University of Kentucky refused entry to a black male wishing to study engineering. In compliance with the dictates of the Day Law, all schools in Madison County, of course, remained completely segregated.[31]

Madison Countians never lacked for excitement and diversion during the war. The local rumormill kept churning away with stories, fact and fiction, about the Hanger family. Several divorces, including one settled for several hundred thousand dollars, kept that family's name in the paper for years. The violent death of Elizabeth Hanger and subsequent problems of the family made them a topic of conversation.[32]

In the early forties Madison County received a liberal dose of culture encouraged by the Cooperative Concert Association, which sponsored serious music presentations. Most people, however, preferred movies and radio. The movie industry boomed during the war by producing films both for entertainment and propaganda. With two commercial movie houses in Richmond, one in Berea, and nightly showings of films in Brock Auditorium on the Eastern campus, the Golden Age of Hollywood continued in the war years. Titles such as *Casablanca, The Sullivans, Wing and a Prayer, The Master Race, Thirty Seconds Over Tokyo, Yankee Doodle Dandy*, and *Hitler's Children* kept folks on the home front well aware of what was going on in the wider world. But there was also time for pure entertainment and escapism. Bob Hope could be seen wending his way on the *Road to Morocco* with Bing Crosby and Dorothy Lamour. *Double Indemnity, Going My Way, A Tree Grows in Brooklyn, The Horn Blows at Midnight*, and many others added another, brighter dimension to the ofttimes dreary war years. Many people danced to the music of Glenn Miller and other swing era musicians, and melodies like "I'll Be Seeing You" and "Sentimental Journey" became especially meaningful to young couples separated by the war.[33]

In the last months of the war, mid-1945, events came in a rush as the Axis forces retreated homeward. With the landing in Normandy in early June, 1944, and the American return to the Philippines in the Pacific, the end of the war became a reality to Madison Countians. The man who had led them through it all, depression and war, for over twelve years, did not live to see the end. Franklin D. Roosevelt died in early April, 1945. Not a few people noticed that in the last months of his life, the president had slowed in speech and had lost that old jocularity. With the exception of some professional Roosevelt-haters, the vast majority of Americans mourned his loss as if it were the death of a family member. Editor Vera W. Gillespie of the *Richmond Daily Register* eloquently voiced the thoughts of most Madisonians, declaring that "Franklin D. Roosevelt gave hope and courage to those people all over the world, who although trampled by the Axis regime, loved freedom and peace. He was leading his nation in a fight to win for them a better way of living . . . . Now that he is gone, we must not forget the things he stood for and thought worth fighting for."[34]

Less than one month later Germany surrendered, and Americans began hearing more reports of atrocities perpetrated by Nazis in their infamous concentration camps. Although most Madisonians were elated when the war in Europe ended on V-E Day, in the back of their minds some began to worry that other victories would bring an end to prosperity. What would happen if the army depot cut back employment? On the other hand, people talked about how wonderful it would be for wartime controls to be removed. Through the summer of 1945 sugar and meat were in short supply even as Allied armies mopped up in scattered actions across the world. World War II ended almost as abruptly as it began. About three months after V-E Day, President Harry S. Truman issued the orders to drop atomic bombs on two Japanese cities, Hiroshima and Nagasaki. Very few people understood the portents of these tremendous explosions. Most Americans were glad just to have the war in the Pacific over with, because a study of the projected invasion of the Japanese home islands estimated that United States casualties in the war would have doubled. For the first time Madisonians read about in the press and viewed in newsreels like "Movietone" and "Pathe News" the awful destruction of two cities half a world away. The celebrations that came with the surrender of Japan were not as boisterous as those at the conclusion of World War I. Noisy but law-abiding crowds of several hundred gathered in downtown Richmond and in Berea on that sultry mid-August evening in 1945 as word came that the Japanese emperor had accepted surrender terms. Churches held special services of thanksgiving. The next day Eastern and Berea colleges called off classes and many businesses closed as Madison Countians celebrated the first day of peace that they had known in over 3 1/2 years. A good number of people thought mostly of the fifty-four Madison County men who died in service to their country, thirty-two of whom died in action against Axis forces.[35]

The immediate postwar period placed new challenges before Madison Countians quite unlike those of the war years. The mechanisms of prosperity were in place. Unlike the Great Depression years, now the question was how to control growth and inflation. Fine tuning of the economy became the paramount issue. Yet, many Madisonians worried about the return of bad times, and that nagging suspicion that another depression was just around the corner lingered in the back of everyone's mind. And there was always the world situation to worry about. America's role in World War II had thrust upon her new responsibilities. Now that Nazi totalitarianism and Japanese militarism had been disposed of, the Soviet Union loomed as the dominant force throughout much of Europe and Asia, placing new international challenges before the United States. Madison County would never be isolated again. Whether the threat of war or cultural, economic, and political change, nothing would ever be the same again.

When the war ended, Madison Countians, like most other Americans, became restive about the rationing programs. They longed for a quick return to prewar days, but remembered that some of those times had been rather bleak. Servicemen and their families began counting "points," an accumulation based on time in service, combat experience, and other considerations. Of course, they all wanted to get back home before Christmas. It did not take long for Americans to react to peacetime conditions. Strikes spread across the nation as union workers scrambled to catch up with the ravages of wartime inflation. Consumers took the continued shortages with less and less patriotic stoicism once the fighting ended. Short coal supplies in late 1945 promised to make the coming winter a cold one for many Americans. When word began circulating that controls over radios, tires, meat, and nylon stockings would soon cease, everyone's interest peaked. The reconversion to a peacetime economy had immediate consequences in Madison County. The V-12 program at Berea College and the training at Eastern came to an end. Lieutenant Colonel Humbert Nelli, in command of the army depot, announced that the depot would now serve as a "Popping Plant," recovering brass from obsolete shells, and as a depository in the "putting to bed" of ammunition from dozens of army camps. As most people had feared, the depot began laying off employees in late 1945. By 1948 the numbers had been cut to only a fourth of the peak employment figures of 1943. The economy of the county suffered a corresponding decline as the federal payroll began to dry up.[36]

Madisonians made adjustments to the new times. Farmers immediately began to feel the effects of producing without total federal control. For the first time in several years the tobacco market averaged under forty dollars per 100 pounds. However, cattle and hog prices rose to all-time highs, keeping overall farm income at a rewarding level. Of course, consumers had to pay for this continued prosperity of Madison farmers. Prices paid for food began to move upward. Just before the first peacetime Christmas in four years, potatoes sold for $2.75 per 100 pounds at Thornbury's Market, Kroger sold two loaves of bread for .19, and a pound of ground beef cost .25 and pork roast .41 per pound at the A. and P. While automobiles were almost impossible to buy until 1947, for forty-five cents you could purchase a Greyhound bus ticket to Lexington. For less than fifteen dollars you could take a trip to Miami, Florida, on the bus. However, Madisonians did not soon forget the war or war-torn Europe in their rush to consume at the highest levels in their history. They continued to buy war bonds at a record pace and collected clothing in a "Victory Clothing Drive" during that first postwar winter.[37]

The G.I. Bill of Rights cushioned some of the impact of converting to peacetime by providing veterans with money for education, housing, and other uses. Students flocked back to Eastern and Berea colleages, creating housing shortages by fall semester, 1946. "Vets' Village" sprouted surplus base housing on the hill behind Hanger Stadium in Richmond. While the war may have delayed growth, Eastern's enrollment increased each year in the late forties, necessitating construction of new buildings. As a sign of its new role in Kentucky education, offering nonteaching degrees for the first time, the Richmond school became Eastern Kentucky State College in 1948. However, the school continued to stress teacher education well into the 1950s. Sports became more important at Eastern in the postwar years. It was big news in 1947 when long-time football coach Rome Rankin resigned to move on to the University of Maine. Basketball took on greater emphasis after a fine Eastern team defeated the University of North Carolina at Chapel Hill by over twenty points in 1950.[38]

Berea College made much the same adjustments and followed the same growth patterns as Eastern and other small colleges in the United States. Students rushed back to the campus when the war ended. Thirty-five of the V-12 veterans from the Berea program came back to finish their degrees at the campus, being given special status because of their income levels. As on most campuses across the nation, married housing had to be provided for returning servicemen and their families. Those "white flags flapping in the wind" were the diapers of the postwar baby boom generation. Being older and more experienced than the typical prewar college student, veterans added a new dimension to most American college campuses.[39]

The economy of Madison County in the late forties adjusted to the realities of American life in the postwar era. Agriculture dominated the local economy. However, with better roads and the new Clay's Ferry Bridge—dedicated to the war dead in 1947—more and more Madison Countians sought work in Fayette County. Burley markets fluctuated. When lower prices became the rule, the USDA drastically cut tobacco allotments in 1947. At the conclusion of the next growing season prices returned to higher levels, rising to nearly fifty dollars per 100 pounds average. The new world responsibilities assumed by the United States at the conclusion of World War II meant that consumers could not always have their way. While they might applaud the example set by President Truman when on one "Meatless Tuesday" he ate cheese souffle for lunch and broiled salmon for dinner, most Americans wanted a complete end to controls and self-imposed sacrifices. Madison Countians also noticed that prices always appeared to be ever lurching upward. Although a Coke still sold for a nickel almost everyplace, coffee had already hit forty cents a pound and pork chops fifty-nine cents a pound in 1948. Moreover, as Madisonians thrilled to the latest exploits of their movie idols and were charmed by such movies as *The Best Years of Our Lives*, they began to hear more about the wonders of television. When would they be able to enjoy this form of entertainment? Automobile factories began to catch up with demand as the major manufacturers shifted back to peacetime production. All of the standard makes were available to Madisonians, including the Kaiser-Frazer cars at W. W. Jesse Motors, which advertised that "There never was a ride like this!" Madison Countians were also taking to the air, buying and flying Piper Cubs and other aircraft. Some of their flights became so annoying that the city council of Richmond passed an ordinance prohibiting flying below 1,000 feet over that city. In early 1947 local boosters applauded the best news yet for postwar Richmond. The Westinghouse Corporation announced plans to build a lamp plant just north of Richmond, promising to employ upwards of 800 workers. In less than a year the facility opened and began producing a variety of miniature bulbs.[40]

Politics of the immediate postwar era continued trends that became apparent during World War II. Madison County political life revolved around two key issues: getting elected and voting on local option. Politics allowed Madison Countians to enjoy one of their favorite activities. With annual elections the rule, one campaign or another was always in progress. The nationwide swing away from Democratic domination became clearly a part of Madison County politics in 1945. The race for county judge in that year pitted Democratic incumbent Vernon Leer, who had served a total of fourteen years, against Republican J. L. Matherly. The challenger unseated Leer but could not carry with him a majority of the fiscal court or control of other county offices. In the 1946 races Republican John Sherman Cooper of Somerset won election to the United States Senate by defeating John Y. Brown, a perennial Democratic party office seeker. Madison went for Cooper by 512 votes, demonstrating a continuation of the Republican resurgence in the county. Although Virgil Chapman carried the congressional district, his Republican opponent W. D. Rogers narrowly took Madison County by 11 votes. The Eightieth Congress swept a Republican majority into Congress in 1946 for the first time since the late twenties. The next year gubernatorial candidate Earle C. Clements bucked the Republican surge by defeating his opponent Eldon S. Dummit by about 700 votes in the county and by a substantial majority across the state. In the last presidential election of the forties, President Harry S. Truman pulled one of the biggest upsets in American political history. Republicans at all levels from precinct captain to candidate Thomas E. Dewey overconfidently misjudged Truman and the American electorate and suffered the consequences in the 1948 presidential election. For the first time in the county's history, the black community began to break with the party of "Father Abraham." Although Dewey carried old Republican strongholds like Berea by a two to one margin, that vote could not offset the restructuring in Madison voting patterns. Truman carried the county by 725 votes, a poll indicative of his general appeal. The Democratic party's rebound continued in the 1949 local races. Democrat R. O. Moberly swamped incumbent County Judge Matherly by over 1,600 votes as the GOP candidates lost every county race. Resignation of longterm Richmond Mayor William O'Neill, who served from 1921 to 1933 and from 1937 to 1948, opened up that position for electioneering. In normally Democratic Richmond Grant Robinson, Jr. took the primary and then the mayoral race unopposed.[41]

In the late forties Madisonians continued their debate over the relative merits of legal alcohol sales. A local option election in September, 1946, continued the countywide prohibition, with a 2,400 vote majority for the drys. As usual, the county and Berea voted dry and the city of Richmond went into the wet column. Two years later a new state statute changed the nature of local option elections, allowing a city to vote itself wet while the county remained dry. That year in a special election Richmond voted for legal sales of alcohol by a 446-vote majority. After a lawsuit filed in Madison Circuit Court by drys failed to overturn the vote in the county seat, Richmond began legal sales of alcohol for the first time since 1943.[42]

Former Governor Keen Johnson left Frankfort after the inauguration of Simeon Willis in 1943, never again to hold elected public office. During the latter part of the war he served as a public relations assistant to the president of the Reynolds Metals Company, while keeping his interest in the *Richmond Daily Register.* He occasionally wrote editorials, always over his initials K.J., and continued his Democratic party partisanship. In 1946 he accepted a position as undersecretary in the Department of Labor, which took him out of the state and kept him from much activity in state politics. Another Madisonian, John D. Goodloe, a native of White's Station and a graduate of the Harvard Law School, took an appointment as chairman of the Reconstruction Finance Corporation during the Truman administration.[43]

In the late forties Madison Countians witnessed continued change in their lives, although not on the scale that they had during World War II.

Whereas Kentucky's population increased by only 3.5 percent from 1940 to 1950, in Madison County the number of inhabitants grew by 9.2 percent to over 31,000. For the entire decade an urban trend radically changed the nature of Madison County society. The urban population of the county increased by 86 percent to nearly 14,000. Rural inhabitants at midcentury represented 56 percent of the total county population, a number that would continue to decline in later decades. Richmond became the state's tenth largest city, as its population grew from 7,335 in 1940 to 10,268 ten years later, an increase of nearly 40 percent. Berea's inhabitants grew by nearly 55 percent to 3,372. The black population of the county continued to decline. By 1950, 2,749 Negroes lived in the county, representing less than 9 percent of the total population. Sixty percent of the county's blacks lived in Richmond, continuing another trend, that of black's leaving rural areas.[44]

The shift of Madison population from rural to urban areas created special problems for Berea and Richmond. Moreover, the suburbanization trend in America also influenced growth patterns in Madison County. Subdivisions began to dot the landscape near the more settled areas of Madison's towns. Richmond added downtown parking meters in July, 1946, after local merchants and shoppers complained about the lack of adequate parking space. This issue became important enough to warrant one of Keen Johnson's infrequent editorials, in this case in favor of the measure. In the first year the city fathers added more than $21,000 to city revenues from the use of meters. Water, sewage treatment, and zoning problems plagued Richmond's residents, and annexation of new subdivisions became a topic of daily discussion in the late forties. Residents of Berea became a bit more concerned about the future of their town and the domination of the college over all city utilities.[45]

Although rural population decreased significantly in the forties, those who remained on the farms lived better than ever before in the history of Madison agriculture. For the first time since the Civil War era, the number of tenant farmers declined in the county to just over 35 percent from a high of 44 percent in 1930. Consolidation of Madison farms mirrored state and national trends. Madison County ranked seventh in the state in the value of agricultural products sold in 1950, as over $6 million in commodities flowed into the economy. The adjustment in tobacco allotments in 1947 temporarily solved the problems of overproduction of burley, and market prices increased appreciably to a fifty dollar per 100 pounds average. The number of farms in the county grew slightly in the war years, but after 1945 it declined by 624 to just over 3,000 farm units. Total acreage under cultivation and for pasturage remained about the same in 1950, while the size of the average farm increased to eighty-four acres. Value of land and buildings on Madison farms increased by over 30 percent from 1945 to the end of the decade. Other signs of agricultural prosperity became evident in the late forties. The number of tractors and trucks in the countryside more than doubled in the five years after the war, indicating the continued mechanization of Madison County farms. Moreover, modern conveniences began reaching more farm families. While the number of telephone customers increased by only 14 percent in rural areas, the number of farms with electricity nearly doubled from 1945 to 1950. Most of the latter customers were served by rural electric cooperative lines.[46]

The quality of life of Madison Countians, in general, continued to improve in the 1940s. The health of Madisonians specifically improved over that of the Great Depression era because of more money to pay for better health and dental care, but the threat of polio epidemics continued to frighten children and adults alike. People began to have periodic x-ray examinations for tuberculosis, a dreaded disease that often weakened its victims without causing death. The number of cases of this disease began to drop significantly in the late forties and early fifties. As in most stages of Madison history in the twentieth century, improvements came slowly. Although there were exceptions, a study of the health of children in the remaining one-room schools in the county, carried out by a group of Madison Country women and approved by the Kentucky State Medical Association, discovered that life had not substantially improved for these children. Mrs. Shelby Carr reported, "We found conditions deplorable: children using the old bucket and dipper, insufficient food and little or no warm clothing." Her group raised more than $12,000 to pay for hot lunches, vitamins, clothing, and corrective medical and dental services. Although the report cited evidence of improvement, Mrs. Carr and other public-spirited citizens recognized that much work lay ahead to improve the lives of these children.[47]

Education, another measure of the quality of life, also demonstrated some change for the better during the 1940s. Schools remained segregated, teacher's salaries remained ashamedly low (averaging less than $1,100/year), and students were denied the opportunities that their peers were afforded in other school districts, particularly in Louisville and larger urban districts. On the positive side the percentage of Kentucky school children attending school improved over the deplorable figures of the Great Depression years back to the levels of the 1920s. However, Madison County enrollment and attendance statistics lagged behind those of the state overall. Only 52 percent of sixteen to seventeen year-olds in the county were enrolled in school in 1950, a sign of a serious dropout problem. For blacks the numbers were just as discouraging. Only about 10 percent of the total black population had attended four years of high school. The addition of a county bookmobile in 1949 did offer some hope for the improvement of educational opportunities in the coming decade.[48]

At the conclusion of the 1940s, most Madison Countians had settled back into the old comfortable living patterns of the prewar days. Economic growth offered hope for prosperous times ahead. Madison continued to receive its share of migrants from the nearby mountain counties, even as Madisonians continued to move away from the county. Some of the growth of Fayette County began to spill over into Madison. Racial conditions remained much the same as they had been before the war. Blacks and whites lived with rigid barriers between them. As the decade ended, Madison Countians could still enjoy the pleasures of smalltown and rural living. The county fair, the annual Halloween street party in Richmond, Mountain Day at Berea College, athletic events of the schools and colleges, and school and church functions continued to draw large participation levels in the forties. However, the times were changing. Like some other Americans, a few Madisonians were caught up in the flying saucer craze of the late forties, and they began to debate the merits of jet power versus that of rockets. In late 1949 there was a more down-to-earth problem: mustard gas. Several convoys of trucks transported that scourge of World War I trenches from the army depot to Colorado to be destroyed. As this remnant of the old warfare was being removed from the county, word came that the Soviet Union had successfully detonated their own version of the atomic bomb. Moreover, that same year the Chinese Communists consolidated their control over that old nation. Other events of the Cold War and the continuation of a peacetime draft continually reminded Madisonians that they were living in a far different world—a wider world—than had existed in 1940.[49]

Just as Americans thought that war was finally behind them, word reached Madison County of another conflict in faraway Asia, this time the result of Communist aggression in Korea. On June 25, 1950, the Cold War heated up to a fever pitch. President Truman announced a "police action" of American troops in support of South Korea. After only five years of relative peace, Americans were again confronted with many of the same problems they had faced during World War 11. Madisonians went off to war, again shedding their blood on foreign soil. This war did not last as long as World War 11, nor were the casualities as many as in the former war. Nonetheless, Madison Countians understood more than ever the position of world leadership that had been thrust upon the United States.[50]

The Korean War heated up the economy of the early fifties. Madison County generally continued to grow in that decade. In the opening year of the decade Richmond became a third-class city, qualifying because of its rapid increase in population in the 1940s. The state police moved into their new headquarters on Lexington Road in Richmond. An A. M. radio station, WVLK, began broadcasting in early summer from the Glyndon Hotel. After that station moved to Lexington, WEKY took to the air in 1953. The entertainment industry radically changed in the fifties, and Madison County demonstrated one of the trends when a drive-in theatre opened at Lake Carlisle near Terrill. For the first time that summer of 1950, Richmond used "fast time," daylight saving time, touching off an annual battle between city and county residents. The Madison County farming community protested that their cows refused to adjust to the attempt to change the cycles of the sun, and they continued their preference for "slow time."[51]

A new medium, television, began to have an impact in Madison County in the early fifties. Sometimes the signal was a little weak and the picture rolled as large trucks clattered by your home, but it was worth the minor inconvenience to Madisonians lucky enough to have a TV. In the afternoons children watched "Kukla, Fran, and Ollie," "Captain Video and His Video Rangers," and "Howdy-Dowdy" with his sidekicks Buffalo Bob and Clarabell the Clown. At night the adults could see "Show of Shows," "Ozzie and Harriet," and "Uncle Miltie," as well as dramas on the "U. S. Steel Hour," "Death Valley Days," and "Alfred Hitchcock." Like millions of Americans, Madison viewers followed the progress of the pregnancy of Lucy Arnaz on television as much as that of their next door neighbor. However, the news of the world, often tragic and frightening, came right into the living rooms of an increasing number of Madison County families. Even when the Korean War ended with an armistice in 1953, the nightly viewing of the troubles of the world offered no respite for local folk. Moreover, changes and trends in American society almost immediately impacted Madison County because of television. "Keeping up with the Joneses," now meant keeping up with families in New York, Chicago, and Los Angeles, not just across the street. Television in many ways replaced the family hearth, around which family members in earlier times had gathered for warmth and communication. Critics claim, however, that television eventually drove families apart as it became a "vast wasteland." Whatever the merits or demerits of TV, Madison Countians of all ages and income levels were affected by "the tube."[52]

The changing of some Richmond landmarks illustrated the nature of progress in the fifties. In 1951 the Irwine-McDowell Trachoma Hospital closed after a quarter century of service. Improvements in public health services in Appalachia lessened the need for such a facility, as the number of cases of that malady decreased in the postwar years. After many years of public service, the property reverted back to the city and work began on converting the home and grounds into a park. Joe's Delicatessen closed after fifty years of providing quick meals for downtown workers and shoppers. In the middle of the decade Zaring's Mill came down to make way for a modern Kroger's facility, the parking lot of which was built over the old town stream that bisected Richmond along Water and Main streets.[53]

Change manifested itself in other ways. Segregated public housing for blacks and whites in Richmond helped low-income Madisonians to afford decent living space. New South Central Bell Telephone Company lines to Kirksville returned service to that area of the county in 1952 for the first time in two years after the folding of the old Kirksville Telephone Company. Discussion began of laying a pipeline to the Kentucky River to bring water to increasingly thirsty Richmond and its burgeoning suburbs. Dr. Russell I. Todd, a dentist, suggested that the local water supply be fluoridated to improve the dental health of its users. The Richmond Kiwanis Club and other service organizations gave their endorsement. In the late fifties Richmond began annexing subdivisions, beginning with Greenway and Rosedale. The county increased in population as local industries and colleges expanded in the fifties. While the workforce at the army depot fluctuated with every turn of the Cold

War, other local industries steadily grew in the decade. Eastern Kentucky State College doubled in enrollment in less than ten years, rising to nearly 2,500 full-time students in the late fifties. For the first time the numbers at Eastern increased far beyond those of the campus of Berea. Although Westinghouse workers went on a brief strike in August, 1952, employment levels and labor relations there remained strong in the fifties. By the latter part of the decade the plant was pumping $1.5 million into the local economy, expanding with a new addition, and employing over 450 workers. Berea began to industrialize with the addition of the Berea Rubber Company. Employees of that firm voted against joining a union in 1953. After several years of effort, the Junior Chamber of Commerce sponsored a swimming pool that opened in Richmond in August, 1959. However, a few years later the facility closed and the property was sold.[54]

Nineteen-hundred-and-fifty-five appeared to be a banner year in Madison history. On the first day of the year, Eastern's football team, directed by Head Coach Glen Presnell, played in the Tangerine Bowl game narrowly losing to Omaha Univeristy 7-6. In March the county school board voted to consolidate all of the remaining high schools in the system into Madison Central High School, using several sources of money for expanding that facility. With the administration of the first polio inoculation in early May, Madison Countians began to hope for the end of that scourge, one that had haunted young and old alike every summer for generations. In late June, Berea College began production of Paul Green's award-winning play, *Wilderness Road*, a drama about antebellum and Civil War days in the Kentucky mountains as part of its centennial celebration. To top it all off, prices did not seem so bad in 1955. For example, on New Year's Day, 1956, at the Glyndon, you could still purchase a fried chicken dinner for $1.25 or a t-bone steak with all the trimmings for $2.50.[55]

Of course, one constant throughout the fifties was Madison County's love of politics. As usual, Republicans and Democrats competed on nearly even terms in most every election. The old voting patterns remianed much the same. Democrats normally carried Richmond, and their Republican counterparts usually took the vote of Berea and the county precincts. In the senatorial race of 1950 Earle C. Clements carried the county by 273 votes on his way to winning a return to the United States Senate. The next year Lawrence Wetherby carried Madison by only 6 votes in defeating Eugene Siler, his republican opponent for governor. Berea politics heated up in the early fifties when a new Citizens party entered the political arena in that southern Madison town in 1951. The Eisenhower phenomenon also struck Madison County in the fifties. In Ike's first run for the presidency in 1952, he carried the county by only 15 votes, while John Sherman Cooper ran ahead of the national ticket by defeating Tom Underwood by 330 votes. Four years later, Eisenhower narrowly lost the city of Richmond but carried the entire county by 300 votes, a sign of his general acceptability to the citizens of the county. Governors' races in 1955 and 1959 were also competitive. In one of the most hotly contested Democratic primaries in years, Bert T. Combs, an eastern Kentucky judge, won the county by 50 votes. However, former governor Albert Benjamin "Happy" Chandler took the state and went on to sweep this county and the rest of the Commonwealth in the November general election against Republican Edwin R. Denny. Just at the end of the decade Combs had his way, defeating Harry Lee Waterfield in the Democratic primary after teaming with former opponent Wilson Wyatt. In the 1959 gubernatorial election Combs easily defeated a former representative, Republican John Robsion.[56]

Some of the biggest local political news of the fifties involved controversy. In 1951 turmoil in the Richmond city government resulted in one councilman's resignation and the reorganization of the old utility commission into the Public Works Board. Prosecution of a former Berea tax collector charged with embezzlement in the early part of the decade ended in acquittal. A former county clerk who served in the forties and early fifties was forced into paying nearly $72,000 in excess fees not accounted for on the county's books.[57]

Another constant of Madison life—crime and violence—appeared not to change at all in the fifties. Moonshining continued to be a problem in the Red Lick area of the county, and Richmond became a haven for bootleggers desiring a place to fill up their cars with beer and half-pints of liquor for a run to a dry area. Two violent murders highlighted the continued mayhem in the county. In one instance a Madison County tenant farmer killed a creditor and then placed the body in the trunk of his car, driving around for several days not knowing what to do. He finally surrendered and, after explaining that he had only acted in self-defense, received a life sentence. In a more bizarre and complicated incident, Willie Acres killed James Orville Hymer, claiming that the latter had raped his wife. In less than six weeks a Madison County jury sentenced Acres to life imprisonment. At this point famous Kentucky trial lawyer John Y. Brown, Sr. took up the case and worked to get the defendant a new trial. In June, 1953, the Kentucky Court of Appeals granted this request. Brown defended his client by arguing that the young man had only reacted as would most other husbands under the circumstances. This "unwritten law" defense rested on the old American ideal of folk justice in which the individual has rights above the law. That was enough to convince the jury that Acres had been acting in defense of his wife's virtue, and they acquitted him.[58]

At the end of the fifties—one of the most sustained eras of general prosperity in American history—Madison County more closely reflected typical American tendencies of growth, development, and change than ever before in the history of the county. This is better demonstrated by the changes taking place in education than in any other part of life. Two major themes stand out for the role of education in Madison County in the 1950s. An effort to upgrade the opportunities of children in the county school system attacked the old inequity of education for rural children. For example, a 1951 *Courier-Journal Magazine* story graphically described the difficulties of bringing books to the more isolated regions of the county. Two one-room schools, Beech Grove and Log Cabin, could only be reached "over an almost impassable road." And yet, a bookmobile, paid for by philanthropy and supplied by the state, traveled over dirt and gravel roads to those schools, bringing reading material to students who otherwise would not have had the advantage of obtaining such materials. The conditions described could have been in just about any Appalachian county at the time. The students struggled against obstacles over which they had little control. Moreover, their peers in Richmond and other city schools had far more educational opportunities. The consolidation of Madison County schools, the slow improvement of teachers' salaries, and the development of the Minumum Foundation Program administered by the Kentucky Department of Education slowly improved such conditions. The dropout rate of Madison County sixteen to seventeen year-olds improved over that of 1950, but still less than two-thirds were enrolled in school. Integration of the city school system became the second major theme of Madison County education in the fifties. Four years prior to the 1954 landmark case *Brown v. Board of Education,* Berea College desegregated after the Kentucky General Assembly changed the Day Law, the 1904 statute that had outlawed integrated classes in private schools. Because most of the black children in the county lived in Richmond, the integration of schools after the Supreme Court decision more heavily affected that city's schools than those in Berea or county systems. In 1956 Madison High School integrated, "with no violence," but with a good deal of apprehension in the minds of both blacks and whites. Madison High School became one of the first fully integrated high schools in the state under the leadership of Superintendent A. L. Lassiter. At Sturgis and in Clay County violence threatened to break out over the integration of schools. Only the timely enforcement of the law by Governor Chandler averted the trauma of areas to the south. Madisonians were now in the mainstream of major social and cultural changes.[59]

At the end of the fifties, material progress appeared more evenly distributed than ever before in the history of the county. Madison County's growth continued apace. While the Kentucky population increased by only 3.2 percent in the fifties, Madison grew by 7.4 percent. Madison County ranked as the twelfth most urbanized county in the state, with almost half of the population living in urban areas. The growth of Richmond and Berea mirrored this development. Richmond, through annexation and industrialization, increased by 18.5 percent to over 12,000. Her sister city in the southern part of the county, Berea, reached over 4,300 in population. Although the county had an umemployment rate of 3.5 percent, 41 percent of the population made under $3,000 per year, the lowest income level of any Kentucky urban area of over 10,000. Blacks continued to take the lowest-paying jobs in the county, with over one-half of the women employed as "private house-hold workers," or servants in other words. White collar workers represented the largest single group of employees (1,800) reflecting the importance of the public schools and the Eastern and Berea faculties.[60]

Some of the most dynamic changes in the county in the fifties occurred in agriculture. While many farmers railed against the Soil Bank program initiated by Secretary of Agriculture Ezra Taft Benson, overall Madison County farmers did better than during the war years. At the conclusion of the decade tobacco averaged over sixty-seven dolloars per 100 pounds on the Richmond markets. Acreage had been cut about one-third since World War II. As the acreage decreased price increased, keeping production and demand in near equilibrium. Farm consolidation continued as the number of farm tenants declined in the county. Tenancy dropped from 35 percent to 28.6 percent from mid-decade to 1959. In those same years the average size of a Madison County farm increased from 82.8 acres to slightly over 112. The value of livestock more than doubled in that same time span. Less farmland went into cultivation and more into pasture. The total number of farms decreased by over 500. More farmers than ever before reported living on hard surface or gravel roads, making it much easier to get their products to market and their children to school. In the fifties the numbers of tractors tripled and farm trucks increased by about 50 percent. Most significantly of all, land and buildings doubled in value, a strong indication of the health of agriculture in the county.[61]

As the "fabulous fifties" concluded, Madisonians could look back at two decades of tragedy, growth, and real material progress. The coming decades would offer more of the same.

Chapter Sixteen

RUSHING TOWARD A NEW CENTURY, 1960-1985

Most of the trends that molded Madison County history in the 1940s and 1950s accelerated after 1959. Unprecedented population growth, economic development, and cultural change have marked the most recent era of the county's history.

In a few short years Eastern Kentucky State College tripled in enrollment, industry became the largest employer in the county, and agriculture lost its old economic dominance. Unlike the self-satisfied, isolated life of most Madisonians of the early twentieth century, no one in the county has been able to avoid the role of citizen in a world more complicated than their ancestors could ever have imagined. Madison Countians could escape neither the tumult of the "Sizzling Sixties" nor the frightening realities of the Cold War. More than ever before, the lives of Madison Countians reflected nearly every major development in the nation's political, social, economic, and cultural history.

Astounding population growth came in the post-1959 era, mirroring the irrevocable changes taking place in the county. In the sixties population increased by 27.6 percent to a total of nearly 43,000, giving the county a ranking of thirteenth in the state. Richmond grew by a rate of 38.6 percent to almost 17,000, much of which was directly attributable to the rapid growth of Eastern Kentucky University. Berea's expansion was even greater because of its industrial development. The southern Madison County city grew by over 60 percent during the decade, numbering nearly 7,000 by 1970. In that same year United States Census figures announced that over 55 percent of Madison Countians now lived in urban areas. Both Berea and Richmond continued to

annex subdivisions. No longer could Madisonians ignore urban problems, as urban sprawl crept into their community.[1]

In the next decade—the seventies—the county increased to over
53,000 at a slightly reduced rate of about 25 percent. Berea's growth
rate slowed somewhat as the city grew to over 8,000 by 1980. Richmond's growth rate also decreased while its population increased to
nearly 22,000. In less than a half-century the population of the county
had nearly doubled. Moreover, the earlier depopulation trend for blacks
reversed after 1960. They now represented about 6 percent of the total
county population, with most living in Richmond.[2]

What were the causes for such growth? Undoubtedly, population
increased because of improved health for the average Madisonian. After
the early sixties, polio became a thing of the past as the Salk vaccine
came into use. In 1966 the county dedicated a new $100,000 public
health facility on Boggs Lane, the Madison County Health Department.
Hospital resources in the county also began to improve. By the late
fifties, Richmond had outgrown the old Pattie A. Clay Hospital, dedicated in 1927, and two smaller hospitals. In the early sixties numerous
local citizens cooperated in planning for the future. The group acquired
land from Eastern Kentucky University on the Eastern By-pass, and
construction started in 1968. In 1970 a $3.6 million, 105-bed facility
was completed. A $1 million federal grant coupled with the efforts of
the Pattie A. Clay Hospital Auxiliary and the many benefactors throughout the years had now provided a first-class regional health program. A
decade later a $4.2 million expansion and renovation program added
more services and provided for more beds. In the mideighties the facility
added sophisticated equipment to serve its patients. Berea College
donated its hospital to the citizens of that community in 1967. In 1969 a
skilled nursing ward was added. After raising over $1 million locally,
Bereans dedicated a $4 million dollar wing in December, 1983. The
building of nursing homes and apartments for the elderly and handi-
capped, such as the 101-unit Madison Towers, and redevelopment of the
northeast sector of Richmond added immeasurably to the quality of life
in Madison County in the seventies and eighties. Public health vital
statistics gave hope for the future, as death rates for all Madisonians
declined. Between 1940 and 1982 deaths because of pneumonia, tuberculosis, and accidents decreased, while mortality for heart disease and
cancer rose. In the sixties and early seventies the black death rate nearly
doubled that of whites in the county, but by 1982 the death rates for
both races were nearly equal. Apparently, public health efforts were
finally making more adequate health maintenance services available to
Negroes.[3]

Transportation improvements made the county more attractive and
accessible to industry and migrants. Fewer Madison Countians now left
for greener pastures elsewhere and the county became somewhat of a
bedroom community for Fayette County. In 1961 work began on Interstate 75 in Madison County. Two years later I-75 opened from Rich-

mond to Athens in Fayette County, with construction of another twin bridge over the Kentucky River. By late 1966 the four-lane, limited access road ran the entire length of the county from the Kentucky River southward by Richmond and Berea into Rockcastle County near Boone Gap. The Eastern By-pass was constructed to coincide with the development of I-75. Over the years this road had been extended first to Lancaster Avenue, then to U.S. 25, and lastly to U.S. 52. As a result of the by-pass, University Plaza Shopping Center opened in 1964, and the Richmond Plaza Shopping Center came in 1969. As highway travel improved in the county, rail service lost favor, as it did across the country. In March, 1968, an era ended when the L. and N. Railroad stopped its passenger service to Richmond. Madison Countians continued their love of and dependence on the automobile into the mideighties. Even the Arab oil embargo of 1973 and the subsequent trebling of gasoline prices did not slow the usage of autos. For most every young Madison Countian, obtaining a driver's license at the age of sixteen remained a rite of passage into adulthood.[4]

As the health of Madisonians improved and their access to the outside world became more rapid and complete, these only prepared the way for the economic transformation of the county. This change came in two rather distinct forms: the growth of Eastern and the coming of new industries.

After Robert R. Martin became president of Eastern Kentucky State College in 1960, the Richmond school grew rapidly throughout the sixties and early seventies. Classroom buildings and dormitories seemed to rise overnight. The school was renamed Eastern Kentucky University in 1966, and by the midseventies over 13,000 students matriculated there. Eastern's growth during the Martin years (1960-76) was part of a general growth pattern for such regional schools across the nation. All took advantage of federal and state grant programs and revenue bonds to build facilities and start new programs. Moreover, the baby boom generation fed more college age students into the system than ever before. Although Eastern continued to turn out more teachers than any other Kentucky college, most of its students majored in fields as diverse as nursing, real estate, accounting, law enforcement, and history.[5]

As Eastern's influence over the Richmond community increased, that of Berea College on the town of Berea lessened. The college began to give up some of its control over the town's functions, including the fire department and hospital, in the sixties. Into the mideighties the college's ownership of utilities remained a point of contention between the school and the town, particularly for tax purposes. Moreover, the industrialization of Berea and the immediate area, began to erode the dominance of the college over nearly every facet of life in that community. A good bit of competition between college and noncollege citizens continues to shape the southern Madison County city. Berea College once provided the primary employment for the population of the town. Now that has been replaced by a growing industrial base. As a matter of fact, by the early eighties Berea had more industrial jobs than Richmond, a city three times the size of Berea. The requirement to pay the minimum wage forced the college to give up some of its industries. Production of *Wilderness Road* also closed, after a brief revival, because of economic conditions and light crowds caused by other tourist competition.[6]

With the rapid growth of Eastern in the sixties, the staff of that school, combined with those of the public schools and Berea College, made education the largest single growth industry and the biggest employer in the county. Moreover, the younger population density of Richmond prompted development of many businesses catering to such age groups. J. C. Powell, the successor of Martin as president of Eastern, once humorously remarked that "Richmond is the only community I know where the taverns operate on the semester system." Of course, problems aplenty came with the growth of Eastern. Most businessmen wanted the trade of the students, but some townspeople complained about the traffic and other problems associated with such a large student population in a rather small city. A "town and gown" division, like the one that had existed in Berea for years, became evident to many people in the community. For example, in July, 1968, a mostly college crowd packed a meeting of the County Democratic Party Convention and seized control of the county delegation. Most county elected officials and old party workers chose not to attend the meeting. The insurgents may have carried the day for their candidate, Senator Eugene McCarthy, but they soon lost control after the defeat of Hubert Humphrey in the 1968 presidential election.[7]

Industrial development in the county depended on several variables. A plentiful labor force, low taxes, and abundant land brought new industries into the county. (Although Kentucky is not a right-to-work state—having such a law tends to discourage unionization in the southeastern states—most factories have begun operation in Madison County as nonunion facilities.) After completion of a water line to the Kentucky River from Richmond, industrial and housing growth was assured in the central part of the county. Some spillover of industry from Fayette County came in the wake of the building of an IBM plant there in 1964. As industry came to Madison, however, the local economy became more closely tied to an often capricious national economy. Strikes, unionization, and changing technologies affected the county as much as in the more traditional industrial zones of America.[8]

The plight of the Westinghouse facility illustrated many of the problems of industrial growth. In 1966 a seven-week strike caused some economic distress in the county. Periodic layoffs and short work weeks became more threatening in the late seventies. In the early eighties Westinghouse gave up its small bulb production and sold the Richmond facility to the North American Phillips Company. The employees agreed to a 20 percent wage reduction in order to attempt to keep the plant open. Phillips promised to update the production equipment and retrain workers in more advanced manufacturing methods. The problems

Aerial view of Berea, ca. 1970s. Berea College Office of Public Relations.

Main Street downtown Richmond, ca. 1970. EKU Archives.

related to industrial development are also illustrated by Richmond's experiences with the H. K. Porter Company. In 1963 the city of Richmond sold $2 million in bonds to pay for construction of the brake lining plant. After its opening on the Eastern By-pass, numerous complaints were made about the factory's emissions. Some people worried about the possibility of asbestos fibers in the air. After a strike by employees closed the plant in August, 1975, the company decided to leave the city. A new occupant, Exide Power Systems, a maker of industrial storage batteries, opened there two years later. Other Richmond industries such as the Begley Company, Okonite Company (1968), Richmond Tool and Stamping (1969), Ajax Magnethermic Corporation (1972), Sherwin-Williams Company (1974), and Rand McNally and Company (1982) have added to growth. Financial institutions of the county have grown to keep pace with industrial development. The State Bank and Trust Company of Richmond continued as the county's largest bank Madison National Bank, First Federal Savings and Loan Association of Richmond, and Richmond Bank also contributed to the financial growth of the county. The latter bank came into business as part of Lexington financier and Madison County native Garvice Kincaid's Kentucky Group Banks. In 1969 Kincaid purchased Berea Bank and Trust Company, which had been closed by the Federal Deposit Insurance Corporation, and reopened the institution under the name of Peoples Bank and Trust Company. In 1973 Kincaid's acquisitions in the county included the Kirksville Bank, from which he organized the Bank of Richmond, and the Waco Deposit Bank. Ten years later the Richmond Bank and Waco Deposit Bank merged under new ownership after Kincaid's death. The Berea National Bank (1906) and a branch of First Federal Savings and Loan Association operated in that southern Madison city. By the end of 1984 the assets of all Madison County's financial institutions approached one-half billion dollars.[9]

Business expansion continued in other areas as well. Industrial growth in Berea became the major cause for the growth of that town in the sixties and seventies. Until World War II, the economic life of the community depended entirely on the college. In 1951, the Parker Seal Company, a plant making rubber o-rings, began to change the economic base of the area. The Berea city government and chamber of commerce aggressively pursued industry. Berea College industries, dating back to 1859, and Churchill Weavers, founded in 1922, were joined by Dresser Industries (1961), Gibson Greeting Card Company (1967), Goodyear Aerospace (1972), and Hyster Company (1973). The latter company announced a multimillion dollar expansion in 1985. Moreover, two of the most venerable Kentucky businesses, Bybee Pottery and the Valley View ferry, which celebrated its bicentennial in 1985, continued their operations in the mideighties.[10]

By the midseventies nonfarm income exceeded agricultural output in Madison County. Yet much of the character of the county still exuded that of a farming community, and agricultural interests kept control of the county government. Although the number of farmers and farm families declined steadily in the immediate postwar years, in the seventies and early eighties the farm population stabilized. In the mideighties the actual number of farms increased slightly for the first time since the Great Depression. Moreover, the *1978 Census of Agriculture* indicated that only about 15 percent of farms in the county were being cultivated by tenants, a substantial change from the over 40 percent figure of the depression years. The average farm size hovered around the 140 acre mark. Madison County farmers continued to depend almost entirely on tobacco and cattle production. Many of the smaller farms are marginally productive, with annual sales of less than $20,000. In 1980 over 77 percent of Madison farms produced less than that figure. As is true for the entire agricultural nation, the largest farms produced the most, reaped the biggest profits, and stood the best chance of surviving into the next century. Many of the owners of the small farms worked in the businesses, factories, and schools in the county, farming on the side and producing burley crops and a few cattle. Altogether, the farms of Madison County continued their dependence on tobacco as the one crop that annually brought in the most cash. In the early eighties all farmers began to worry more about the loss of their tobacco cooperative program and price support system, which for nearly a half-century had regulated production and guaranteed prices. Antismoking and anti-big government advocates in Congress continually sniped at the necessity for such a plan. Older Madison farmers shuddered at the thought of returning to the old marketing practices of the early 1930s, and they feared a loss of their tobacco crop as a steady source of income.[11]

The growth of Eastern Kentucky University, the development of a stronger industrial base, an expanded and improved transportation system, and the continued strength of Madison agriculture gave the county more economic diversity than in previous decades. However, much as in the remainder of the nation, runaway inflation, the energy crisis, and high interest rates cooled expansion in the late seventies.

After 1959 the political history of Madison County continued in its usually colorful, often turbulent path. Madisonians acted and reacted to

the momentous political developments of their day. In the sixties the
political system of the nation came under increasing strain as social
change and war rent the country. Political coalitions and alliances broke
and reformed.

In the Democratic senatorial primary of 1960, Keen Johnson made
his political comeback against old rival John Y. Brown, Sr. For the
second time he defeated Brown, in this race by 36,000 votes, winning
the honor of facing popular incumbent Republican Senator John Sherman Cooper. To some extent Johnson became a sacrificial lamb. Without the support of "Happy" Chandler or the *Courier-Journal*, Johnson
went down to a resounding defeat. Cooper won by nearly 200,000
votes, carrying Madison County by 1,900. Johnson even lost his own
home precinct. His long-time absence from state politics and lack of
contact with Madisonians for several years perhaps explains his poor
showing. It is doubtful, however, if any Democrat could have defeated
Cooper in 1960. That general election also included the presidential race
in which Richard Nixon carried the county by nearly 1,100 votes over
John F. Kennedy on his way to winning the state of Kentucky.[12]

Kennedy won the 1960 presidential race in one of the closest
campaigns in American history. Early in his term, Vice-President Lyndon
B. Johnson came to Richmond to speak at the June, 1961, graduation
ceremonies at Eastern. While in Richmond the vice-president helped
break ground for the new Alumni Coliseum. Being a consummate politician, he paid an obligatory visit to Miss Emma Watts, the mistress of
Elmwood, an estate situated just across Lancaster Avenue from the
Eastern campus. More important was the subject and tone of Johnson's
speech. Most of his talk concerned foreign policy. "In the last analysis,
we will be judged by the world, not by our creed but by our deeds," he
concluded, "Let us make sure that they are deeds of honor, of valor, and
of progress." These words presaged not only the later development of
the war in Southeast Asia, but the attempt to create the Great Society as
well.[13]

Much like the unforgettable occurrences at Pearl Harbor over two
decades before, most everyone old enough to remember the assassina-
tion of President Kennedy has that horrible moment forever etched in
memory. They will recall forever where they were and what they were
doing when they first heard of the tragedy. The day after the assassina-
tion Editor Shelton Saufley of the *Register* eloquently spoke the thoughts
of many Madisonians:

> Mr. Kennedy was a positive president. He was dedicated to
> fulfillment of his duty as he saw it. He tried to make govern-
> ment responsive to the needs of the people as he understood
> them. He was a scholarly, cultured gentleman of magnetic
> personal charm. He was a statesman of superior attainments
> who will be recorded in history as a great president.[14]

At the local level, Madison County politics continued to be competitive. In the 1961 general election, Chester Luxon took the mayor's race

Kentucky Governor Bert Combs, Vice President Lyndon B. Johnson, and Eastern Kentucky State College President Robert R. Martin leaving Eastern's Blanton House, June 6, 1961. EKU Archives.

with only token opposition after defeating incumbent Mayor Ed Wayman in the primary by 153 votes. Richmond voters also turned down a proposal for a city manager form of government. Republican Charles H. Coy pulled an upset, by 121 votes, when he defeated four-time County Judge R. O. Moberly. The way was prepared for that unseating of Moberly by a schism in the county Democratic party brought on by the intervention of the Combs administration in a local race. The resulting infighting weakened the efforts of Moberly to be reelected, As usual, Democrats carried the majority of the county offices, but Republicans won three of eight fiscal court seats.[15]

Riding the coattails of Governor Bert T. Combs, Edward "Ned" Breathitt carried the state and Madison County rather easily in the 1963 gubernatorial election against Republican Louie B. Nunn. Four years later, however, Nunn took Madison and the state from his Democratic opponent, Henry Ward.[16]

In 1964, Lyndon Johnson won by a landslide, becoming president in his own right. He won by over 2,600 votes in Madison County, even carrying the old Republican stronghold of Berea. After the Texan's victory, his administration's Great Society programs and waging of the war in Vietnam turned the poll bittersweet. Madison County reflected much of the turmoil spreading across the nation. Integration came slowly in the county in the sixties. Desegregation lawsuits began to integrate the Richmond and county school systems in the early sixties. Two local Negro women, Mrs. Talbert Miller and Mrs. Beatrice Huguely, followed the dictates of their own consciences and the instructions of Dr. Martin Luther King, Jr., when they staged their own sit-in of a drug store lunch counter in early 1962. The author of this chapter that same year had service denied at a Richmond restaurant while escorting the Harrodsburg High School football team because several members of the squad were Negroes. Fortunately, another restaurant allowed the hungry people an opportunity to eat.[17]

Examples of the lawlessness often associated with the sixties came in the 1966 mini-riots staged by some disgruntled Eastern male students. Authorities blamed the whole affair on "spring fever"; however, some damage was done to the campus. Apparently the students had no greater objective than causing some physical harm to the school. A much more serious incident came two years later as the 1968 presidential election neared. In early September of that traumatic year in American politics, the National States Rights party staged a white supremacist rally just outside Berea on U.S. 25. Racial epithets amplified by loudspeakers reached the nearby Berea black community. Just as the meeting ended several carloads of blacks opened fire on the crowd. In the ensuing gun battle one white and one black died of wounds. State and local police units quickly descended on the scene and arrested eight whites and six blacks on murder charges. Circuit Judge James S. Chenault presided over the cases and received some death threats. The whole episode ended inconclusively, as the charges were reduced and none of those arrested served long prison terms. A 1968 Madison County grand jury report criticized local law enforcement agencies for not anticipating possible trouble and for lack of security at the rally.[18]

The Republican trend so evident in the 1967 gubernatorial race continued in the presidential campaign of 1968. In one of the bitterest races in American political history Richard Nixon carried the county, state, and nation. In Madison he polled 5,325 votes to 3,884 for Hubert Humphrey and 2,558 for George Wallace. As in most elections, Democratic candidate Humphrey carried the city of Richmond, but by only 200 votes. Continuing the Republican trend, Marlow Cook defeated Catherine Peden in the United States Senate race by about 600 votes. Four years later Nixon again took the county. The taint of Watergate, however, caught up with Republican nominee Gerald Ford in 1976. In that election Jimmy Carter won the county by nearly 1,000 votes on his way to carrying Kentucky and the nation. The political pendulum swung the other way in 1980, primarily because of the Iranian hostage crisis and a declining economy. Former Governor Ronald Reagan won hand-ily. In 1984, owning to the weak candidacy of Walter Mondale and the general public acceptance of Reaganomics, the Californian carried the county by the largest margin in history, 4,664 votes.[19]

Local politics continued to be just as exciting and as exasperating as ever in the post-1959 era. Much of the excitement came from the battle in Richmond between factions led by Virgil McWhorter and Wallace Maffett. When a new Richmond Post Office on Water Street opened in 1963, the city government began considering acquisition of the old post office-federal building for conversion into a new city hall. This too became a political football tied up in intercity politics. In early 1969 the McWhorter administration bought the old post office and later pur-chased the adjacent Richmond Motor Company. After Maffett won the mayor's race later that year by sixty-five votes, plans proceeded for renovating the post office into a city hall and the garage into a combina-tion police and fire station. In the meantime the city of Richmond sued McWhorter and recovered judgment in the Madison Circuit Court for $3,600 with interest and costs for the $150 per month expense account unsupported by expense vouchers paid to McWhorter in violation of state law while he was mayor from 1967-70. In 1971 the McWhorter faction came back into power with a majority on the city commission. The conflict continued. McWhorter's faction used their majority to force the resignation of City Manager Henry Dunn and to replace the original plaque at the city hall with a larger one, touting their role in buying the facility. The Madison County Newsweek, operated and ed-ited by Jim and Betty Cox, took a strong stand for the end of control of the McWhorter faction in city affairs. In the 1973 races Maffett easily defeated McWhorter for mayor and the anti-McWhorter slate of commis-sion candidates swept into office.[20]

For whatever reasons, a few Richmond and Madison County politi-cal figures appeared to have had more than their share of scandal in the post-1959 era. One city official, in particular, having difficulty staying out of court, pleaded guilty to a "charge of attempting to commit an offense" in a vote-buying scheme but was forced to pay only a small fine.[21]

The biggest news of the early eighties in Madison political history exploded into headlines when several members of the city government and another citizen were charged with soliciting bribes in connection with a city commission vote on extending bar hours. Editor Bill Robin-son of the Richmond Register made his paper the first news agency to cover the story. After months of court proceedings and speculation by the public, two other accused officials pleaded guilty to reduced charges. The mayor was found not guilty and a city commissioner was found guilty in a second jury trial after the first had ended in a hung jury in Madison Circuit Court. The former city manager was found not guilty on a lesser charge in a trial in Madison District Court.[22]

Notwithstanding, Richmond made progress in several areas in the seventies and eighties. The city qualified several times for the coveted

All-Kentucky City award. After the city added a payroll tax to its revenues, more money became available for services. In 1985 Richmond completed a $16.6 million expansion and renovation of its Tates Creek and Dreaming Creek sewage treatment plants. The city also approved a $6.5 million dollar bond issue for water projects. Plans called for completion of a second transmission line from the Kentucky River to Richmond and a large storage facility and a new water line loop on the west side of Interstate 75. The city also contributed to the construction of an airport. A proposed second interchange for Berea on Kentucky 595 will provide direct access from I-75 to the Madison Airport. In 1983 renovation of the old National Guard Armory into the Richmond Recreation and Tourism Building offered the community a multi-purpose recreation center. That same year a new National Guard Armory was completed on Irvine Road. After years of trying to develop an industrial park, the city of Richmond created an industrial authority in 1984 known as the Richmond Industrial Corporation. Part of a recently annexed plot on the north side of the I-75-U.S. 25 interchange has been developed into an industrial park, with the Plexus Corporation as the first occupant.[23]

Bereans did not experience the political turmoil of their central Madison neighbor, although the Berea Independent School District suffered some embarrassing and questionable budget deficits in the early eighties. The city became much more self-assertive in the sixties, building a new city hall and adding a payroll tax. Long-time Mayor C. C. Hensley led the city government until his death in late 1980. Dr. Clifford Kerby became only the third mayor in the history of the town that same year. Berea also won the All-Kentucky City award, keeping pace with its sister city to the north. Bereans, like their Richmond counterparts, continue to "feel a bit short-changed" by the county government, which they believe gives only scant services for the taxes paid by urban residents.[24]

Madison County officials reacted slowly to most every problem to come before them in the post-1959 era. Land use, planning, landfills, a county library, dangerous bridges, garbage collection, a dog pound, and an aging jail comprised only a short list of problems that bedeviled the fiscal court and citizens of the county. Most people of the county wanted and got low taxes and correspondingly few services. They finally received fire protection in 1973 with the purchase of two county fire trucks and establishment of a county fire department and station. Some semblance of building codes began in the midseventies, but no comprehensive planning or land use policies have been developed for the county. A county library tax went down to a "resounding defeat" in the election of 1981 when a 4 percent tax increase was placed on the ballot. Most farm precincts voted no, while the more affluent precincts of Richmond and Berea supported the measure. The building of an airport was supported by the Richmond and Berea city governments and the Madison Fiscal Court with 90 percent matching funds provided through the Federal Aviation Administration. Howard L. Colyer, president of the airport board, labored for a dozen years before finally seeing the $1 million, 4,000 foot runway, with radio controlled lighting on a 188 acre site, opened in November, 1979. The Madison Fiscal Court and the cities of Richmond and Berea also cooperated in developing a badly needed countywide ambulance service in 1976.[25]

One of the most important and basic changes in the history of Kentucky government came with the removal of judicial powers from the county judge's office. In the midseventies a United States Sixth Circuit Court of Appeals decision highlighted the problem of having nonlawyer county judges making legal decisions. In a case involving Madison County Judge Robert Turley, the court ruled that the rights of a juvenile had been violated when he was jailed without being allowed to call his parents. After passage of a constitutional amendment, a redesigned judicial system placed civil and criminal cases in the hands of professionals trained in the law. Most Madisonians were glad for the limiting of the duties of the old county judgeship by the new judge executive system.[26]

Tragedy struck often enough in the post-1959 era for most Madisonians to ponder the age-old question of why such suffering occurred. The national struggle over the Vietnam War in the late sixties and early seventies could not help but split Madisonians into "hawks" and "doves." Many did not know which side to support. Fifteen Madison Countians were killed or reported missing in the conflict. Neither Berea College nor Eastern Kentucky University suffered the disruptions or violence of schools in other areas of the country. However, over a thousand Eastern students peacefully demonstrated and marched through Richmond after the tragic Kent State shootings in May, 1970. A not-so-peaceful sit-in at the Berea College president's office resulted in some damage to that office. In late 1972 an airplane carrying ten Madison High School football supporters crashed in a lonely Todd County field, killing all passengers and the pilot. Madisonians became painfully aware of how even the weather could appear to conspire against them when a tornado struck on April 3, 1974. On a day in which several storm centers hit the South and Midwest, a twister slashed its way across the county from Cottonburg in the west, through Newby, Baldwin, to Tates Creek, to White Hall School, and across I-75 on to the Hackett Pike-Union City area. Seven people died in the county and seventy-one throughout Kentucky that day, one which Governor Wendell Ford called "probably the most tragic day in the history of Kentucky." For several days much of the county struggled with limited electric service. In this time of trouble, many Madisonians proved their mettle, volunteering to help clean up debris and damage wrought by the storm. Flooding has continually plagued the sections of the county lying along the Kentucky River. In the spring of 1984 one of the worst floods in the history of the county struck, bringing significant loss of property.[27]

Since 1959 the history of the relationship between the Blue Grass Army Depot—the name was changed in 1962 from Blue Grass Ordnance Depot and was later merged with Avon in Fayette County—and the citizenry of Madison County has often been strained. Some old-timers still resent the taking of so much prime farmland during World War II. As the payroll of the depot first declined after World War II and fluctuated during the cooling and heating of the Cold War, some Madisonians questioned the real need for the facility. Throughout most of the sixties and seventies employment hovered around 600. As industrialization came to the county, some believed the depot an impediment to further growth. Yet other Madisonians have fought to keep the facility open.[28]

In the seventies and eighties the depot became embroiled in controversy. The mention of an army plan in the midseventies to close down the depot brought forth a concerted local effort to keep the facility open. The Chambers of Commerce, city officials and private citizens from Berea, Richmond, and the county petitioned the army to reconsider. They all claimed that closing the depot would cause much local economic distress. Congressman John Breckinridge used his influence to lead the filing of a lawsuit, and eventually an injunction halted the army's plans.[29]

It was not long, however, until some Madisonians began to have more second thoughts about the depot. Since 1963 the skies of southern Madison County have ofttimes been filled with graceful B-52 bombers. The Strategic Air Command maintains a small base at the depot for testing the accuracy of the training flights. Since the first flights some people around Berea have complained about the noise generated by the big jets. After completion of the county airport, several near-misses between the low-flying bombers and much smaller aircraft have been reported in southern Madison County. Local pilots and airport officials have argued that the bombers should change their course so as to miss the airport area or that some warning should be given of flight times, but nothing had been done to alter the possibility of a crash by late 1985.[30]

Eastern Kentucky University head football coach Roy Kidd along with players celebrating Eastern's 30-7 victory over Lehigh University in the Division 1-AA national championship at Orlando, Florida, December 15, 1979. EKU Office of Public Information.

On the ground the realtionship became even more uneasy. In 1979 the controversy moved into a new phase when forty-five residents in the Peytontown area near the depot were hospitalized after inhaling fumes from a cloud of noxious gas that escaped the confines of the depot. Canisters containing chemicals were burned that night in unusually large quantities. State police closed a section of Interstate 75 to traffic because of low visibility caused by the cloud. It was not long until a local doctor, Dr. William Grise, began to question the long-term effects on the environment of burning PCP (pentachlorophenol) laden materials. For years the depot had allowed wood treated with PCP, a preservative, to be carried off by employees for building purposes. More importantly, some people charged that abnormally high cancer rates had been noticed among workers and residents of the area near the depot. The army did finally admit that too many canisters had been burned the night that the large cloud developed, and the post commander at that time retired. Several years later a state health official gave the depot a clean bill of health. His study found that employees there did not have a higher cancer rate than residents of any other county in Kentucky.[31]

The most recent phase of the history of Madison's relationship with the depot has not been resolved. In October, 1982, army officials began to worry about the leaking of the nearly 70,000 nerve gas rockets stored in twenty-nine igloos on the site. Area residents became more concerned when army officials admitted that some of the canisters showed signs of deterioration and that a few had leaked and had been encased in protective material. The army's overall solution to the problem, constructing a multimillion dollar plant for incinerating the nerve gas rockets at the depot, touched off renewed controversy. After several public meetings, a contingent of Madison Countians traveled to Tooele, Utah, to visit an operating disposal facility. Their views were mixed. While most agreed that the plant appeared to be safely operated by the army, they still expressed fears about building such a facility in Madison County. Mayor Bill Strong of Richmond, for example, pointed out that very few people lived near the base in Utah, while his city was only a few miles from the Blue Grass Army Depot. On the other hand, he also believed the disposal plant "would be a real shot in the arm for our economy." Army officials argued that it would be more dangerous to move the rockets from Madison County to another base for destruction. As of late 1985 the problem had not been solved and tens of thousands of nerve gas weapons remained in their bunkers in central Madison County.[32]

Other problems confounded Madisonians as they faced the important issues of the late twentieth century. Madison made progress in several areas, but the pace of change was slowed by fiscal conservatism. The lack of a county library in a community with two colleges continued to be a problem in the eighties. Perhaps because some people used the Eastern and Berea libraries they did not see the need to tax themselves to provide the service for everyone. There is hope for the future of a library, however, as the Exchange Club and the Madison County Anthenaeum labored to fund a library in the late eighties.[33]

˙ Much progress has been made in education in Madison County in the twentieth century. There remains much work to be done to prepare young Madisonians adequately for the coming new century. The advent of the Minimum Foundation Program in the early sixites coupled with the Great Society educational programs to bring a spurt of development. However, Kentucky still lags behind the rest of the nation in public elementary and secondary programs. Much of this problem relates to the average Kentuckian's disdain for raising taxes to fund public education properly. In the mideighties even Eastern Kentucky University and other public higher education facilities struggled to fulfill their missions because of dwindling public dollars. Both Eastern and Berea College began new eras in 1984 with new presidents—Dr. Hanly Funderburk and Dr. John Stephenson.

Similar to many Kentucky counties, Madison graduated too few young people from its public high schools. For example, in 1970 only slightly over three-quarters of the sixteen-to-seventeen-year-olds were enrolled in school in the county. Only 38 percent of the males and 43 percent of the females who lived in the county had completed a high school education. Not enough graduates entered college. Over 45 percent of the Madison Central High School graduates entered an institution of higher learning, but even that figure was well below the national average. Other issues often intruded on the educational process. One such issue, Bible distribution during school hours, became heated in the early eighties as fundamentalist religious groups from outside the county pushed their case. Bill Robinson, editor of the *Richmond Register*, won a 1981 Kentucky Press Association award for an editorial in which he forcibly argued for separation of church and state and against the distribution. The battle ended with the county school board not allowing the use of school property and time for such religious functions. In the mideighties numerous state and national committees and commissions studied the problems of public education. Only time will tell whether their efforts and those of Madisonians bring about change.[34]

Against sometimes insuperable odds Madison's schools, teachers, and students fought to compete with the rest of the state and nation. The Madison County system, the county's largest with over 6,000 students, operates seven elementary schools, two middle schools and one high school. In 1985 plans were unveiled to build another high school to relieve overcrowding of Madison Central High School. Richmond Independent School District has an enrollment of over 800 students. The system encompasses two elementary schools and one high school, Madison High School. Berea Independent School District, Model Laboratory School, and St. Mark's Catholic School serve correspondingly fewer students. Several of the schools in the eighties added computer programming courses and other technical subjects.[35]

The quality of life of all the people of Madison County also rested on issues other than education in the mideighties. A study of Kentucky's future growth indicated that by the year 2000 Madison County would have a population of over 72,000, a rate of change of 36 percent. Yet,

Aerial view of the Eastern Kentucky University campus, 1980. EKU Office of Public Information.

Aerial view of the Berea College campus, ca. 1970s. Berea College Office of Public Relations.

the county still lacked a comprehensive land use and zoning plan in the mideighties. In 1978 the fiscal court backed down from a proposed land use study when conservative elements, backed by John Birch Society members from outside the county, raised a storm of protest against the measure. One wonders how long the quality of life of the county can survive such population pressures without comprehensive planning and zoning regulations. Madisonians will find out, as they approach the beginning of a new century, that their property values are affected by uncontrolled development. Moreover, landfills for the disposal of the refuse of their abundant lifestyle continue to confound local officials of the county and city of Richmond, as does the fear of loss of the water supply pumped from the Kentucky River to Richmond and surrounding subdivisions and water districts.[36]

While per capita income increased in the sixties and seventies, the figures for Madison County remained over $1,000 lower than state average and $2,400 less than that of the nation. There remained more poverty than many local boosters would like to have admitted in the generally affluent society of the mideighties. In 1970 more than a third of the black families in Richmond lived below the poverty level and even more lacked "some or all plumbing facilities" in their homes. The valiant efforts of Telford Community Center, Open Concern, and other local agencies aided the poor. Several projects in Richmond were aimed at rehabilitating or replacing substandard housing. The Four Mile Avenue Community Redevelopment Project began in 1983 to change the face of that northeastern section of Richmond. Rebuilding homes, replacing water lines, installing sidewalks, resurfacing streets, and the conversion of the Old Telford Center into apartments were parts of the plan. The $3.6 million project was scheduled to be completed in 1985. Madison Towers, a ten-story apartment complex for the elderly and handicapped was completed in 1984. These projects along with those on Irvine, North Madison, and Hill streets have changed the old inner city areas of Richmond, improving the quality of life for many of the citizens of that community. However, the success of these efforts also demonstrates the need for more such projects. Too many Madisonians, black and white, still struggle, living below the poverty level in the mideighties. The United Community Fund of Madison County, Inc., formed in 1977, also aided the needy. In addition, Richmond city parks at Irvine McDowell, Lake Reba, and Million added to the quality of life of everyone in the community.[37]

Madison Countians could not help but be concerned about the problems of crime in the post-1959 era. Alcohol-related arrests always seemed on the increase. In 1983, for example, Madison County ranked third in the state in arrests for public drunkenness. Crimes against property increased as the relative affluence of Madisonians increased. Farmers even began branding their cattle to protect their herds from modern day rustlers. Crime could be as humorous as the case of the drunken Clay Countian who stole a Greyhound bus and drove off down I-75 on a December afternoon in 1965 or as distressing as the gangland style bombing of a Richmond merchant's shop in the summer of 1983. If moonshining of alcohol was no longer as serious a problem, now marijuana crops dotted the landscape. While all indications were that the most violent of crimes, murder, was not as prevalent as earlier in the century, such capital crimes remained particularly disquieting. Drug-related killings in the late seventies and the execution style murder of a convenience store clerk in 1981 left people with the knowledge that they still lived in a sometimes violent world. If some had no respect for human life, it was not surprising that in September, 1984, over thirty people were arrested for staging and witnessing a barbaric legacy of Kentucky's frontier history: a dogfight. Nonetheless, the Madison Circuit Court system demonstrated an ability to adjust to changing times. Judge James S. Chenault joined in 1970 in a Model Court Project which introduced a number of innovations. Telephone answering devices for juries in session, filming of trials, and video taping are only a few of the experiments that have proved successful.[38]

As one of the oldest counties in the Commonwealth of Kentucky, Madison's heritage and concern for it have remained one of the strongest inclinations of many citizens. The Madison County Historical Society remained active in the post-1959 era. The group holds several meetings a year, publishes an occasional journal (*Kentucky Pioneer*), and works for historic preservation. In 1974 the society completed renovation of the old city hall, now used by the Richmond Chamber of Commerce. The historical society, under the presidency of James J. Shannon, Jr., acquired Mt. Pleasant in 1977 as a gift from Betsy Toy Hall. Moreover, the society commissioned oil paintings of Cassius M. Clay and General Green Clay for inclusion in the White Hall restoration. Many other museum items at White Hall were donated by society members. The capstone of historical sites in Madison County has been the development of Fort Boonesborough State Park. In 1972 the state acquired seventy-six acres to be added to land already making the foundation of the park. A $1.6 million project raised a replica fort above the flood plain site of the original pioneer settlement. The structure consists of thirty-two buildings based on Richard Henderson's 1775 drawing and encompasses an area of 203 by 301 feet. Specially treated pine logs from the forests of central Alabama were used for the construction of the fort. The recontruction draws thousands of tourists each year to the county.[39]

In other ways Madison Countians demonstrated their continued interest in history. The ante-bellum courthouse received a major renovation in the midsixties. Irvinton became the center of a city park and was placed on the National Registry of Historic Places, along with the University Building on the Eastern campus, Lincoln Hall on the Berea campus, and the Cane Springs Primitive Baptist Church near College Hill. The county also has one of the largest Civil War roundtables in the state. With construction of Fort Boonesborough several groups have formed, including the Clark County and Madison County Fort Boonesborough Bicentennial Commission. In July, 1975 over 10,000 people were entertained by Pat Boone and his family at the park. Reenactments

Dedication ceremonies for Fort Boonesborough State Park, August 30, 1974. EKU Archives.

of a frontier wedding and legislature added to the authenticity of the bicentennial celebration. The Society of Boonesborough also formed in 1975 as a hereditary organization of descendants of Fort Boonesborough pioneers. Several historical markers have been dedicated by this group at the fort. Other hereditary organizations in the county include the Boonesborough Chapter, Daughters of the American Revolution; Jemimah Boone Chapter, Daughters of the American Revolution; Berea-Laurel Ridge Chapter, Daughters of the American Revolution; James Madison Chapter, Sons of the American Revolution; and John Miller Chapter, Children of the American Revolution. Moreover, the publication of this county history is a testament to the historical awareness of many Madisonians.[40]

Epilogue

The French have an old adage: "The more things change, the more they remain the same." Some of the ironic twists and turns of Madison County history from the beginning to the mideighties would lead one to suspect that they are correct. Recent alterations in the lives of Madisonians because of the energy crisis offer some illustrations. Not a few residents are again stoking wood stoves because of high utility costs. In the early part of the century, Madison ne'er-do-wells wrecklessly raced about the countryside on horseback or in carriages. Four generations later some still do the same, except that they have exchanged horseflesh for horsepower. Rarely is it possible today to stroll along a quiet country lane for long without the solitude being broken by the blast of a high-powered vehicle or the ear-shattering noise of a stereo. Other examples of continuity abound. The old moonshiner has given way to the marijuana grower. Nearly everyone has been affected by changing technology and cultural values. The great-grandmothers of modern Madison women baked their complexion over a hot stove and worked in the broiling sun. Some lived to sing the praises of the modern gas or electric range. Now their descendants leave the luxury of an air-conditioned kitchen to lie in the sun, wrinkling their skin prematurely. The wonders of technology never ceasing, some businesses now operate indoor tanning salons.

However, there are more serious concerns as Madisonians face the end of the twentieth century. Since the beginning of World War II, evolving technological change, growing industrialization, and the challenging wider world have all placed unprecedented pressures on Madisonians. Notwithstanding the continued inequities of Madison County society in the mideighties, the average resident is healthier, better educated, better housed, and better fed than at any time in this century. But spiritually, psychologically, and emotionally are they better off than their ancestors? Was their material gain worth the effort? Do they feel more secure and at ease with the world than Madisonians at the turn-of-the-century? Have values of family, religion, and community changed and, if so, are those for better or worse?

No historian should be presumptuous enough to attempt an answer to these questions for each individual in the county. But one thing is sure: the circumscribed world of the early twentieth century will never return. There is no turning back. All Madisonians have to decide whether their lives have demonstrably improved over those of their ancestors. That decision will be based on their own values systems, which have probably changed from the time when Madisonians lived in a far different world.

Perhaps the greatest change of all has been our perception of a sense of place. Particularly those Madison Countians who consider themselves to be southerners or eastern Kentuckians feel the greatest stress on their sensibilities of place and community. Air-conditioning, tract housing, television, chain stores, and modern architecture can destroy localism and homogenize us all into folk little different from other Americans. As an old distinctive landmark is torn down, a modern building is con-tructed—one usually indistinguishable from other such structures along the nation's interstate highway system. The final assault on sense of place may be the advent of the shopping mall, which one scholar recently called the "cathedral of air-conditioned culture." Only time will tell if the Madison way of life can fend off that challenge. But, in the end, the sense of community may rely less on the physical aspects of buildings than on the thoughts and feelings of the people who live, work, and play here. In the final analysis, whether or not Madison County keeps a sense of distinctiveness, of difference about it, depends on the people. It is their decision, as it always has been.[41]

Notes

*Abbreviations: FCHQ for *Filson Club History Quarterly*; *Register* for *Register of the Kentucky Historical Society*

CHAPTER 1

[1]William D. Funkhouser, *Archaeological Survey of Kentucky* (Lexington, 1932), 259-63; Bennett H. Young, *The Pre-Historic Men of Kentucky* (Louisville, 1918), 19-20, 29-31.

[2]Young, *Pre-Historic Men*, 75-84; William D. Funkhouser and William S. Webb, *Ancient Life in Kentucky* (Frankfort, 1928), 77; Funkhouser, *Archaeological Survey*, 263.

[3]Funkhouser, *Ancient Life*, 179-80, 181-205; Young, *Pre-Historic Men*, 75-84.

[4]Funkhouser, *Archaeological Survey*, 259-263; Funkhouser, *Ancient Life*, 77-121; Young, *Pre-Historic Men*, 19-20, 29-31, 38-41, 48-55, 75-84.

[5]Young, *Prehistoric Men*, 38-41; Funkhouser, *Archaeological Survey*, 259-63.

[6]William Chenault, "The Early History of Madison County," *Register*, XXX (April, 1932), 120-21; Thomas L. Connelly, "Gateway to Kentucky: The Wilderness Road, 1748-1792," *Register*, LIX (April, 1961), 115-18; Willard Rouse Jillson, "Squire Bone, 1774-1815," *FCHQ*, XVI (July, 1942), 141, 146-48; Draper MSS, Boone Papers. C, III, 59; Draper MSS, C, IV, 6; and 2CC25; Robert L. Kincaid, *The Wilderness Road* (New York, 1947), 102-03.

Chenault, "Early History," 120-21.

[8]Madison Court Order Book C, 620-28. See earlier Court Order Books A and B as well as County Survey Books.

[9]Green Clay Chronicles, 31; Court Order Books A, B, and C.

[10]Chenault, "Early History," 120-21; Draper MSS, C, IV, 6; Connelly, "Gateway to Kentucky," 115-18.

[11]Neal O. Hammon, "Early Roads into Kentucky," *Register*, LXVIII (April, 1970), 93-131; Connelly, "Gateway to Kentucky," 110, 118-23; Draper MSS, Series C, IV, 6; Draper MSS, 17CC, 166-67; Draper MSS, Boone Papers, C, III, 59; Neal O. Hammon, "First Trip to Boonesborough," *FCHQ*, LXV (July, 1971), 249, 251-58; Madison Court Order Book A, 118-36, Court Order Book D, 23, depositions; Chenault, "Early History," 122.

[12]Draper MSS, lCC, 21-102; Chenault, "Early History," 123-24. The Draper MSS includes Colonel Richard Henderson's journal.

[13]Draper MSS, lCC, 202-06.

[14]Ibid.

[15]Chenault, "Early History," 125-26; Hammon, "First Trip," 261.

[16] Alexander Bate, "Colonel Richard Callaway, 1722-1780," *FCHQ*, XXIX (January, 1955), 169-76; and Charles Bryan, Jr., "Richard Callaway: Kentucky Pioneer," *FCHQ*, IX (June, 1935), 42-43.

[17]Chenault, "Early History," 127; W.S. Lester, *The Transylvania Colony* (1935), 163-70, based on Draper MSS. See note 18.

[18]Chenault, "Early History," 127; Draper MSS, 6S, 78-79; 11CC, 14-16; 17CC, 171-75; 12CC, 64-78, 97-110; 6S, 79.

[19]French Tipton Papers, 6: entry 4; Chenault, "Early History," 127-28.

[20]Chenault, "Early History," 128-32; Bate, "Callaway," 169-76; Draper MSS, 4CC, 29-30; Tipton, #9, 14 includes a court deposition of 1801.

[21] Chenault, "Early History," 128-32; Bate, "Callaway," 169-76; Draper MSS, 4CC, 29-30.

[22]Draper MSS, 5B, 26, 548, 26-27, 57, MSS 11C, 64; Chenault, "Early History," 130-32; Samuel M. Wilson, "Daniel Boone, 1734-1934," *FCHQ*, VIII (October, 1934), 192-93.

[23]Draper MSS, 5B, 58; 11C, 62; 16C,7.

[24]Draper MSS, 12CC, 74; 11CC, 12; 19C, 79; 22C, 5; 5B, 94, 582-94.

[25]Thomas D. Clark, *Frontier America* (New York, 1959), 20; Draper MSS, 11C, 27, 57, 76; 12CC, 200; 11CC, 13-14; 6C, 143; Bryan, "Callaway," 45-49; Wilson, "Daniel Boone," 192-93; Bate, "Colonel Callaway," 175-76.

[26]See note 25.

[27]Neal O. Hammon, "Land Acquisition on the Kentucky Frontier," *Register*, LXXVIII (Autumn, 1980), 306-08, 309-10.

[28]James Rood Robertson, (Louisville, 1914), *Petition of the Early Inhabitants of Kentucky*, #9; W.H. Miller, *History and Genealogies* (Richmond, 1907), 19-21; Bryan, "Callaway," 45-49; Bate, "Callaway," 175-76; Chenault, "Early History," 133-36; William W. Hennings, ed., *Statutes at Large: Collection of all-Laws of Virginia* (Richmond, 1819-23), X, 134.

[29]Chenault, "Early History," 133-35; Bryan, "Callaway," 45-49; Bate, "Callaway," 175-76; Miller, *History and Genealogies*, 19-21; Hennings, *Statutes*, X, 134.

[30]Draper MSS, 1CC, 206-07; 29CC, 50.

[31]Miller, *History and Genealogies*, 21; Bryan, "Callaway," 47-49; Bate, "Callaway," 176-77; Robertson, *Petition*, #9 and #10.

[32]Chenault, "Early History," 133, 138-39.

[33]Virginia Land Commission "Certificate Book," copy, *Register*, XXI (1923), 300-10; Chenault, "Early History," 128, 144; Court Order Book D, 17-18, depositions; Tipton Papers, #1,48 on the early frontier stations.

[34]Tipton Papers, 1: 103-04; Draper MSS 13 C44-45; MSS 24C73, MSS 13C50; MSS24C73, MSS 24C92, MSS 13C54, MSS 18C51, MSS 13C40, MSS 18S236; Colonel W.H. Caperton's sketch appeared in *Giel's Miscellany* on March 22, 1845 (sixty-three years later).

[35]Collins, *History of Kentucky*, 634-35 includes Colonel Caperton's sketch from *Giel's Miscellany*, March 22, 1845; see Bessie Taul Conkright, "Estill's Defeat," *Register*, XXII (September, 1924), 311-22; Tipton Papers, #1, 103-04; Draper MSS as cited in footnote 30. Also see J. Winston Coleman, *Slavery Times in Kentucky* (Chapel Hill, 1940), 6-8; Virginia Land Commission "Certificate Book," copy, *Register*, XXI (January, 1923), 300-10; Chenault, "Early History," 128, 144; and Court Order Book D, 17-18 depositions.

[36]Court Order Book D, 17-18, depositions; Green Clay Chronicles, 28-30; Chenault, "Early History," 143; J. R. Robertson, *Petitions of Early Inhabitants of Kentucky*, #30.

[37]Tipton Papers, 6: 176; Miller, *History and Genealogy*, 51; Chenault, "Early History," 144-46.

[38]Green Clay Chronicles, 4; Chenault, "Early History," 135, 145-47.

[39]Draper MSS, ICC, 161-67; Calendar, *Virginia State Papers*, I, 305-07; Madison County Court Order Books, A. See Madison Circuit Court Records for litigation details.

[40]Court Order Books, A, B, C.

[41]Ibid., Book B, 242-408; Chenault, "Early History," 119-61; Jonathan T. Dorris "Early History in Madison County Circuit Court Records," *Register*, XLIII (July, 1945), 240; Five volumes of cases in Madison Circuit Court Records; Miller, *History and Genealogy*, 199.

[42]Hennings, *Statutes*, XII, 85, 107, 118.

[43]Journal of the House of Delegates of the Commonwealth of Virginia, 1785 (Richmond, 1828), 21, 46-75, 89-90, 94-96, 110, 115, 130.

[44]Madison Court Order Book A, 1-3.

[45]Court Order Book A, 3-5, 9-13, and remaining order books up to 1849.

[46]Court Order Book A, 5, 12.

[47]Court Order Book A, 6.

[48]Court Order Book A, 8-10, 14-16.

[49]Draper MSS, 9CC, 73; Calendar, *Virginia State Papers*, IV, 652; Order Book A, 11.

[50]Green Clay Chronicles, 35-37, 40, 42-46.

[51]Court Order Book A, 22-25, 40-42; Clay Chronicles, 39.

[52]Clay Chronicles, 39-41.

[53]Court Order Books; Robert M. Ireland, *The County Courts in Antebellum Kentucky* (Lexington, 1972) is a masterly examination of Court power.

[54]Court Order Books A-E.

[55]Ireland, *The County Courts*, 12 13; State Tax Records in the Kentucky Historical Society, 255-59.

[56]Court Order Books, A-B. Of the early sheriffs only John Pittman had a low profile. All the others played an active political role in the life of the community.

[57]Court Order Book A, 1-142.

[58]Ibid.; Alma Lackey Wilse, "Kennedy Family," *Register*, XLV (April, 1947), 129-58; especially see 131-41.

[59]Court Order Book A, 1-18, 52, 78-80, 132, 149, 154, 237; also see 13, 23, 140, 143, 249; Book C, 20, 80, 94, 413.

[60]Court Order Book A, 1-17, 23, 25, 52, 78-80, 132; Book C, 9, 80, 94, 164-65, 420, 582.

[61]Court Order Book A, 2, 17, 57, 65, 78, 140, 178, 181; Book C, 535-37, 739, 774; Book D, 123, 521-27.

[62]Court Order Book C, 164-69, 537, 556, 658, 699; Book D, 170; Book B, 265, 269, 271.

[63]Court Order Book A, 18-83; David Smiley, *Lion of White Hall* (Madison, Wisc. 1962), 6; Order Book B, 11, 78-79, 125, 197, 354, 498.

[64]Court Order Book A, 31, 36-37, 45, 107.

[65]Ibid., 27, 45, 49, 60, 91.

[66]Ibid., 27, 77-80.

[67]Ibid., 97, 100-02, 124, 129, 139.

[68] William Littell, and Jacob Swigert, *Digest of Statute Laws of Kentucky, 1792-1822*, III, 567; Court Order Book A, 103-04, 177, 334. According to David Greene, a local authority on the pioneer period.

[69]Court Order Book A, 356, 461; Book B, 26; William Miller, unpublished MSS, Townsend Room, E. K. U., #16.

[70]Jonathan T. Dorris, *Glimpses of Historic Madison County* (Nashville, 1955), 27-28; *Old Cane Springs*, footnotes, 159; David C. Greene, "Diary of John Halley," *Kentucky Pioneer* (1983), 6-9.

[71]Lists, "Virginia Justices of the Peace," *Register*, XXV (January, 1927), 55-62; Chenault, "Early History," 154-55.

[72]Journal of the House of Delegates of the Commonwealth of Virginia.

[73]George L. Willis, "History of Kentucky Constitutions and Constitutional Conventions," *Register*, XXIX (January, 1931), 63-67.

CHAPTER 2

[1]Madison County Court Order Books A, B, C.

[2]Court Order Book A, 31.

[3]Court Order Book A, 144, 353; Order Book C, 267.

[4]Green Clay Chronicles, 142-44

[5]Court Order Book A, 459; Order Book B, 59, 168, 177, 179.

[6]Court Order Book B, 234, 257, 269, 312, 320, 341.

[7]Court Order Book B, 493-95, 497-99; Book C, 753; Tipton Papers, 6: 45.

[8]Tipton Papers, 6: 45, 176.

[9]Court Order Book D, 386, 414-55, 489, 499.

[10]*Richmond Republican*, June 6, November 28, 1823; Court Order Book C, 347; Book F, 50, 59; Book H, 6, 145, 264, 279.

[11]United States Census, 1850, Madison County.

[12]Court Order Book A, 49, 103, 394-413, Book B, 332.

[13]Court Order Book B, 161-62, 164, 169.

[14]Court Order Books, A, B, C; Book B, 369, Tipton Papers, 4: 68-69.

[15]Virginia Legislative Acts; Court Order Book A, 73, 139, 175. Tipton Papers, 6: 319.

[16]Court Order Book A, 311, 343, 356.

[17]Court Order Book B, 3-4.

[18]Ibid., 24, 143, 178.

[19]Ibid., 420.

[20]Executive Papers of Governor James Garrard, February 12, 1798; Court Order Book B, 626-31; Book C, 10; Book B, 601.

[21]Court Order Book C, 15-16, 42, 81-100.

[22]Court Order Books B and C are filled with examples of Clay's economic activities; Book C, 139, 195 is especially informative.

[23]Court Order Book C, 420, 424, 447, 456, 469, 476, 484.

[24]Ibid., 489, 507, 510, 531-32, 571-73, 577, 607, 652, 658.

[25]Court Order Book C, 652, 658, 726, 728, 749, 809, 844; Book D, 101, 143, 176, 227, 271-79, 289, 365-75.
[26]Court Order Book D, 477-78, 492; Book E, 15-17, 94, 185, 296-300, 373.
[27]Court Order Book F, 46, 298, 333, 454; Book G, 152.
[28]James F. Hopkins, *A History of the Hemp Industry in Kentucky* (Lexington, 1951), 117; Littell, Legislative Acts, III, 532-34, IV, 74; *Luminary*, September 11, 1813; Brown Lee Yates, "Pioneer Sketches," *Climax*, 1891, in Tipton Papers, #5, 93. U. S. Census, 1850, Madison County.
[29]Tipton Papers, 1: 39; #4, 319; #6, 21, 144.
[30]Tipton Papers, 1: 40, 53; #5, 11, 93; #6, 117; Brown Lee Yates, "Early Days in Richmond," *Climax*, 1891, no month.
[31]Tipton Papers, 1: 40, 53; #5, 11;*Richmond Republican*, December 3, December 17, December 25, 1822; October 23, 1822-24; and U. S. Census, Madison County, 1850.
[32]Madison County Tax Lists, 1788; Court Order Book A, 27, 45, 465.
[33]Court Order Book B, 327, 328, 384; Book C, 366; Books A-D.
[34]Robert R. Burnam, *History of Masonry in Madison County, Kentucky* (Louisville, 1914), 16-17; *Luminary*, September 11, 1813; *Richmond Republican*, October 22, October 29, November 5, November 12, December 22, 1822; January 8, February 19, March 26, April 9, April 16, 1823.
[35]*Richmond Republican*, October-November, 1823; March-May, 1824.
[36]*Richmond Republican*, May, 1824; Septmber 24 through October 8, 1824.
[37]Court Order Book E, 447; Book H, 154; Russell H. Todd, *This Is Boone Country*, (Louisville, 1968); Cassius Clay, *Memoirs*.
[38]Court Order Book A, 82, 149; Book B, 47, 163.
[39]Court Order Book B, 204, 231, 330, 602; Tipton Papers, #1, 107.
[40]Court Order Book A, 33, 528; Book B, 136, 140-57, 170, 220, 310, 402, 411.
[41]Court Order Book C, 288, 300, 345-46.
[42]Court Order Book D, 538.
[43]Court Order Book C, 368-409.
[44]Court Order Book B, 553-70; Book C, 240-41, 260, 291, 294, 300, 514.
[45]Court Order Book C, 531-31, 833; Book D, 62, 399, 448-49; Tipton Papers, #10, 400.
[46]Court Order Book E, 176; Book D, 448-49; Book C, 531-32, 833; Book D, 62, 399; Tipton Papers, #10: 400.
[47]Court Order Book E, 366; also Books D and F.
[48]Court Order Book D, 202-03; Book E, 215, 235-41, 401, 579; Book F, 30; Book G, 148.
[49]Court Order Book F, 185-86, 211, 267.
[50]Ibid., 267-68, 380, 394.
[51]Ibid., 360, 391, 394, 419, 457-59.
[52]Court Order Book F, 400; Book G, 148, 172, 320, 360, 369.
[53]Court Order Books F and G, especially G, 206, 283-85; Book H, 95.
[54]Court Order Book G, 54, 57, 127-29, 254, 283-85.
[55]Chenault, "Early History," *Register*, 148.
[56]*Stewart's Kentucky Herald*, September 22, 1795; Tipton Papers, 1: 32.
[57]Court Order Books C and D; Green Clay Chronicles, 62-63.
[58]Clay Chronicles, 62-63.
[59]Clay Chronicles, 226-29.
[60]*Richmond Republican*, 1822-1824; *Farmer's Chronicle*, December 26, 1835.
[61]*Richmond Republican*, 1822-1825. See November 26, 1822; February 26, April 23, October 24, 1823; February 20, 1824.
[62]*Richmond Republican*, October 22, November 5, 1822; January 8, February 19, October 31, 1823.
[63]*Richmond Republican*, April 23, April 30, May 23, August 1, October 24, 1823.
[64]*Richmond Republican*, November 5, 1822; April 23, May 2, June 6, October 24, 1823.
[65]*Richmond Republican*, April, 1823-October, 1824. See ads.
[66]*Richmond Republican*, 1822-1824.

[67]*Richmond Republican*, 1822-1824; Court Order Books D, E, and F. See D, 417, 432-34.

[68]*Farmer's Chronicle*, December 26, 1835; August 3, 1839; *Richmond Republican*, April 9, 1824; Mary Kate Deatherage, "Madison County Bibliography," M. A. Thesis, Eastern Ky. State Teachers College, 1944, 1835 events.

[69]Court Order Book E, 150; Book G, 210; Book H, 88-91.

[70]Tipton Papers, #1, 208-10, #1, 38; Bate, "Callaway," *FCHQ* (January, 1955), 169-76; J. R. Robertson, *Petitions of the Early Inhabitants of Kentucky*, 107, #7; D. Boone to Colonel Henderson letter, April 1, 1775, Draper MSS, 17CC, 166-67.

[71]United States Censuses, 1790, 1800, 1850, Madison County.

[72]Court Order Books B, C, D, E. Book C, 417, 440, 734; Book D, 6, 129.

[73]Court Order Book C, 795-96; Book D, 187; Book E, 86; Book G, 197.

[74]Court Order Book E, 86; Book G, 210-40, 295-96; Book H, 150.

[75]Court Order Book E, 145, 314, 331; Book G, 100, 126, 152. Books D and E have sporadic emancipations.

[76]Court Order Book F, 241, 259, 254; Book G, 102.

[77]Court Order Books D, E, F, G. Tipton Papers, 10: 55.

[78]Tate's Creek Church Records; Silver Creek Record Book, Cane Springs Record Book.

[79]Chenault, "Early History," 71-73; *Farmer's Chronicle*, 1835-1839; J. Winston Coleman, *Slavery Times in Kentucky* (Chapel Hill, 1940) 316; *Richmond Republican*, August 29, 1823, carried the new Town Ordinance.

[80]Tate's Creek Church Records, 1847.

[81]*Richmond Republican*, December 17, 1822; April 23, August 8, August 15, 1823; August 20, 1824, and scattered references in 1822-1824.

[82]Court Order Books A, B, C, especially Book B, 326-27, 571; Madison County Tax List in Governor's Executive Journal, Kentucky State Papers, June 24, 1792; Madison Court Order Books and Tax Lists, 1796-1824.

[83]Tipton Papers, 1: 32; *Kentucky Herald*, October 11, 1796; *Richmond Republican*, 1822-1824.

[84]Court Order Books, Indenture Sales, A-E; *Richmond Republican*,1822-1824. Also see the Lexington newspapers.

[85]Court Order Books B-H; 1792 Tax List; 1795 Tax List.

[86]Katherine Phelps Caperton, "Early Homes of Madison County, Kentucky," monograph, 1930 (EKU, Kentucky Room), 2-5.

[87]Ibid., 2-9, 22.

[88]Ibid., 18, 22-23.

[89]Ibid., 36-37.

[90]Ibid., 10, 16, 45. Dr. Russell Todd, *This Is Boone Country*, includes excellent pictures of the early homes.

[91]United States Census, 1850, Madison County.

CHAPTER 3

[1]Governor's Executive Journal, Kentucky State Papers, June 24, 1792; April 5, 1793; May 23, 1794; June 9, 1794; March 2, 1795.

[2]Madison County Court Order Book B, 125, 197, 290-95, 306, 320, 323, 370, 405, 543, 550, 553. Books B and C are helpful.

[3]Green Clay Chronicles, 38-41; Court Order Book B, 243.

[4]Court Order Book B, 249, 308, 439.

[5]Ibid., 275, 290-95, 492-93.

[6]Ibid., 493-98.

[7]Ibid., 500-12; Green Clay Chronicles, 66.

[8]Court Order Book B, 517-22.

[9]Ibid., 518-24, 534, 552, 634.

[10]Madison Court Tax List, 1792, 1794; Governor's Executive Journal, Kentucky State Papers, 1792.

[11]Chenault, "Early History," *Register*, 157; H. E. Everman, *Governor James Garrard* (n.p., 1981), 19-20; Thomas Speed, *The Political Club, Danville, Kentucky, 1786-1790* (Louisville, 1894), 38, 45, 115, 158, 166; John Mason Brown, *Political Beginnings of Kentucky* (Louisville, 1834), 107-10.

[12]*Kentucky Gazette*, July-August, 1792.

[13]Ibid., November-December, 1796; Everman, *Garrard*, 36.

[14]*Kentucky Gazette*, May 10, 1797; Executive Papers, Box 2, Jacket 8, Election Returns, 1797; Box 2, Jacket 9, 1798, Election Returns; Journal of the Kentucky House, November 1797, 14-15, 20; January, 1798, 49; Journal of the Kentucky Senate, January, 1798, 24-44.

[15]*Frankfort Palladium*, August 14, 1798. See *Palladium*, November-December, 1798, and House Journal, 1798, 17-30.

[16]Coward,*Kentucky in the New Republic* (Lexington, 1979), 131; Breckenridge Notes, MSS, Journal of Convention, July 23, August 1, 1799.

[17]Breckenridge Notes, August 1, July 29-30, 3-8, 37-38, as cited in Coward, 132-55.

[18]U. S. Census, Madison County, 1790 and 1800.

[19]Court Order Book C, 28, 196-98, 776-78; Book E, 51-53; Book G, 58-60.

[20]Court Order Book C, 309-10, 327.

[21]Ibid., 345, 366.

[22]Ibid., 22, 73-75, 268, 322, 479-80.

[23]Ibid., 565, 574, 623, 646.

[24]Ibid., 519, 582-84, 667.

[25]Ibid., 747, 751-53, 801-02, 853-55; Book D, 2, 6, 15, 26, 76-80.

[26]*Lexington Reporter*, July 15, 1809, reported Richmond patriotism. Deatherage Thesis, 1812; J. Wallace Hammack, Jr., *Kentucky and the Second American Revolution* (Lexington, 1976), 59-60; Draper MSS, 12CC, 97-110.

[27]*The Luminary*, Spetember 11, 1813; Hammack, *Second American Revolution*, 64, 75.

[28] G. Glenn Clift, "Notes on Kentucky Veterans," *Register*, LI (January, 1953), 39, 140; Deatherage thesis, 1815; Court Order Book D, 30.

[29]Court Order Book D, 189-93, 194-95.

[30]Ibid., 102, 385, 393, 520-21; Book E, 89.

[31]Court Order Book C, 810, 831; Book D, 178, 197, 394.

[32]Court Order Book C, 535-37, 615, 831; Book D, 357; Book E, 461-63.

[33]Court Order Book D, 381-93, 465.

[34]Ibid., 296-98.

[35]Ibid., 298.

[36]Ibid., 310-12, 356, 374.

[37]Court Order Book E, 110-11, 121, 210.

[38]Ibid., 118-19, 168-69, 182, 285.

[39]Detherage Thesis, 1817-1820; *Richmond Republican*, October 22, October 29, November-December, 1822; see December 17, 1822. Arndt M. Stickles, *The Critical Court Struggle in Kentucky, 1819-1829* (Bloomington, 1929), 9-13.

[40]Frank F. Mathias, "The Turbulent Years of Kentucky Politics, 1820-1850," Ph.D. dissertation, chapter two, especially 54-58, 75.

[41]Thomas D. Clark, *History of Kentucky* (Lexington, 1960), 139-140.

[42]*Richmond Republican*, November 14, November 21, 1823; February 12, 1824; Mathias, "Turbulent Years," 54-58; *Kentucky Reporter*, November 17, November 24, 1823.

[43]*Richmond Republican*, November 14, November 21, 1823; February 12, 1824.

[44]Ibid., July-August, 1823.

[45]Ibid., August 8, 1823. Significantly the top five were future Whigs, whereas Black and Kerley were Jacksonians.

[46]Ibid., April-August, 1824.

[47]Ibid., August 6, September 3, 1824; Mathias, "Turbulent Years," 54-58.

[48]Mathias, "Turbulent Years," 54-58. *Richmond Republican*, July 16, 1824 is an example, although the newspaper frequently printed their views on all issues.

[49]Court Order Book E, including 351, 425. See the *Richmond Republican*, 1822-1824.

[50]Dr. James H. Bennett, Minutes of Meetings of Richmond Philosophical Society, 1820-1825. Joint Collection, University of Missouri Historical MSS Collection, State Historical Society of Missouri MSS used with permission, see 1-6, particularly.

[51]Bennett, Minutes . . . Richmond Philisophical Society, 1-6.

[52]Bennett, Minutes . . . Richmond Philosophical Society, December, 1820-February, 1821.

[53]Ibid., December 12, 1820-February 13, 1821.

[54]Ibid.

[55]Court Order Book E, 331, 399-400, 415; Court Will Book D, 461-67.

[56]Richmond Republican, August, 1823-1824;Lexington Intelligencer, August, November, 1834-1839; Louisville Daily Courier, 1844-1846; Frankfort Commentator, 1828-1832; Frankfort Commonwealth, 1843-1850.

[57]Frankfort Commentator,1828-1832; Argus of Western America, 1830; Jaspar B. Shannon and Ruth McQuown, Presidential Politics in Kentucky, 1824-1948 (Lexington, 1950); see tables. A. D. Kirwan, John Jordan Crittenden,(Lexington, 1962), 84-85.

[58]Court Order Book E, 381, 388, 425, 461-63; Book F, 279; Book G, 67, 92.

[59]See House and Senate Journals; see Frankfort Commentator, Frankfort Commonwealth, Argus of Western American, and Lexington Intelligencer, 1820-1840.

[60]See House and Senate Journals; James W. Gordon, "Lawyers in Politics: Mid-Nineteenth Century Kentucky As A Case Study," Ph.D Dissertation, 122-23, 418.

[61]Richmond Republican, August 1, August 8, 1823; July 30, August 6, 1824.

[62]Lexington Intelligencer, August 8, August 12, 1834; August 7, August 11, 1837; August 15, 1838; August 9, 1839.

[63]Kentucky House Journal (1845-1846), 32, 43, 67, 148, 183, 194, 199, 316, 330, 358; Kentucky Senate Journal (1845-1846), 38, 102, 122, 141, 152, 166, 105, 118, 132.

[64]Court Order Books E, F, G.

[65]Ibid.

[66]Court Order Book G; Deatherage Thesis, 1832, 1833, 1836.

CHAPTER 4

[1]Squire Boone, the first Baptist preacher in Kentucky, performed the marriage of Samuel Henderson and Elizabeth Callaway at Boonesborough on August 7, 1776. Frank Masters,History of Baptists in Kentucky (Louisville, 1953), 5.

[2]Madison County Court Record Book A, 15.

[3]Ibid., 122, 139.

[4]Ibid., 266, 376; Renewals in Book B, 277, 429.

[5]Court Order Book B, 119.

[6]Ibid., 300, 304, 356, 443, 616.

[7]See chapter references in Masters,Baptists in Kentucky and John H. Spencer,A History of Kentucky Baptists (Cincinnati, 1886).

[8]Masters,Baptists in Kentucky, 40-48, 51, 56, 63-66; Spencer, Kentucky Baptists, I, 96-101, as well as scattered references and chapters on each group.

[9]See note 8.

[10]Tipton Papers, Book Z, 384-412; Masters, Baptists in Kentucky, 40-48, 51-56, 63-68, 74; H. E. Everman, Governor James Garrard (Paris, 1981), 7-10, 80-81.

[11]Masters, Baptists in Kentucky, scattered, but especially 56, 74; Spencer, Kentucky Baptists, I, scattered; Tipton Papers, Book Z, 384-412.

[12]Masters, Baptists in Kentucky, 51, 55-58, 63-68, 74, 89; Spencer, Kentucky Baptists, I, 133-34, 342-43, 464-65; Deatherage Thesis, 1786-1803.

[13]See note 12. Tipton Papers, 4: Book Z, 384-412.

[14]Tate's Creek Church Record Book, 232.

[15]Cane Springs Record Book, 1803.

[16]Tipton Papers, Book Z, 290.

[17]Ibid., 384-407.

[18]Tate's Creek Record Book, 1832.

[19]Deatherage Thesis, 1813-1821; Tipton, Book Z, 384-407. The Salem Church was actually in Estill County, while Baptist historians fail to mention a Round Top congregation which may have existed at this time.

[20]Deatherage Thesis, 1830; Tipton, #1, 224-29.

[21]Tipton Papers, Book Z, 4: 408-10; #10, 74-77; #1, 224, 229.

[22]Deatherage Thesis, 1828-38.

[23]Court Order Book A, 15; Deatherage Thesis, 1786. Some histories report a Haw Ogden as an early Methodist minister, but he never sought a license from the Madison Court.

[24]Deatherage Thesis, 1786-1790.

[25]Tipton Papers, Book Z, 306-07.

[26]Deatherage Thesis, 1799.

[27]Cane Springs Record Book, 1824.

[28]Deatherage Thesis, 1836.

[29]Tipton Papers, Book Z, 244, notes the debate.

[30]Deatherage Thesis, 1790.

[31]Tipton Papers, Book Z, 384. See the Lancaster Woman's Club, Patches of Garrard County (Danville, 1974), 346-52, for a fuller discussion of the Paint Lick Presbyterian Church. The original log church was located on the present Paint Lick Cemetary which was used in the 1790s. One of the oldest tombstones is that of John Provine, 1751-1792. He was a Revolutionary War Veteran.

[32]Tipton Papers, 1: 241-42, 248.

[33]Tipton Papers, Book Z, 384.

[34]Tate's Creek Record Book, 1837.

[35]Cane Springs Record Book, 1828.

[36]Ibid., 1813; Silver Creek Records.

[37]Tate's Creek Record Book, 1818.

[38]Ibid., 1826; Tipton, Book Z, #4, 379.

[39]Tate's Creek Record Book, 1826; Cane Springs Record Book, 1807; Tipton Papers, Book Z, 4: 379.

[40]Tate's Creek Record Book, 1816-1818.

[41]Tipton Papers, Book Z, 4: 290.

[42]Cane Springs Minutes, 1812, 1820.

[43]Tate's Creek Record Book, 1816-1818.

[44]Cane Springs Records, 1823, 1816.

[45]Tate's Creek Record Book, 1804-1816.

[46]Cane Springs Records, 1804, 1813.

[47]Ibid., 1808, 1821; Tate's Creek Record Book, 1819.

[48]Tipton Papers, Book Z, 4: 306-07.

[49]Ibid., 379; Cane Springs, 1812; Tate's Creek Baptist, 1816.

[50]Court Order Book A, 68, 189, 303-04, 465, 495, 529; Book B, 327-28, 384.

[51]Court Order Book A, 262.

[52]Ibid., 495; Book C, 242, 302, 311-12, 366.

[53]Court Order Book B, 438; Book C, 273; Book A, 186.

[54]Court Order Book A, 243; Book B, 216; Book F, 75, as examples.

[55]Court Order Books A-C; include C, 272, and Book E, 458, for unusual crafts. See Book C, 660s, 688.

[56]Court Order Book A, 222; Book B, 119; Book C, 125, 203, 210, 223, 605, 660s, 688, 734.

[57]Court Order Book E, 305, 310, 351, 363, 427-48.

[58]Court Order Book E, 438, 456, 487; Book F, 50, 114, 184-85, 268, 359, 395, 442, 458, 460, 461.

[59]Court Order Book H, 95. See Order Books A through H. Book B, 186, is an example.

[60]Court Order Book B, 155, 179, 186-87, 236; Book C, 443; Book E, 311; Book F, 264.

[61]See The Register, XXVI (1824) for lists. The Richmond Republican, 1822-1824, can be used in the EKU Archives. All newspapers but the Madison Banner were weeklies.

[62]Tipton Papers, #10:430; William Littell, Statute Law of Kentucky (Frankfort, 1809-1819), 244-245, III, 37, 525.

[63]Little, Statute, III, 525; V, 133; Robert E. Little, "Education in Madison County, Kentucky," M. A. Thesis, 49-51.

[64]Madison County Deed Book N, 181-83; Littell, Statute, V, 526; Little, "Education in Madison County," 53.

[65]Little, "Education in Madison County," 8.

[66]*Richmond Republican*, December 17, 1822; January-April, 1823; especially see March 19, March 26, April 1, 1823.

[67]*Richmond Republican*, April 30, 1823; Court Order Book E, 281.

[68]*Richmond Republican*, June 6, 1823, November 14, 1823; Little, "Education in Madison County," 13, 16, 19; *Richmond Republican*, March 19, 1824.

[69]*Richmond Republican*, August 15, August 29, 1823; January 16, January 23, June 25, 1824.

[70]Little, "Education in Madison County," 10; Court Order Book G, July 2, 1838. See the indexes to Court Order Books for 1840s.

[71]Court Order Book H, 41, 75, especially.

[72]Little, "Education in Madison County," 59-61; *Farmer's Chronicle*, August 3, 1839.

[73]Tipton Papers, 10: 430; *United States Census*, 1850, Madison County.

[74]Kentucky Historical Society, *Register*, LVIII (1956), 126; Order Book I, 402-05. An original copy of Dr. Thomas W. Ruble's *The American Medical Guide* (Richmond, Kentucky, 1810) belongs to Dr. Stanley Todd, who graciously permitted its perusal by the author. The 200-page book includes an excellent index and is most informative. See Tipton Papers #1, 14-15.

[75]*The Luminary*, September 11, 1813; Burnam, *History of Masonry*, 12-14.

[76]Burnam, *History of Masonry*, 16-17. The *Richmond Republican* carried all announcements of Masonic meetings 1822-1825.

[77]*Richmond Republican*, April 23, October 10, October 17, 1823; Tipton, #1, 85-86; "Lady of Madison" letter to *Richmond Republican*, May 23, 1823.

[78]*Richmond Republican*, June-July, 1823-1824. See July 18, July 25, 1823.

[79]Ibid., February 27, March 12, 1824.

[80]Ibid., July 9, July 23, August 27, 1824.

[81]Ibid., July, 1823-October, 1824; Tipton Papers, 1: 176, #10, 80.

[82]Court Order Book G, 139; Tipton Papers, 10: 279.

[83]Tipton Papers, 10: 262. For a detailed account see David Greene's "The 1840 Celebration at Boonesborough," Madison County Historical Society, I, #3 (October, 1969), 18-20.

[84]Tipton Papers, #10, 312; Court Order Book D, 197.

[85]Court Order Book G, 203.

[86]Court Order Book I, 258-83, 317.

[87]Tipton Papers, 1: 26.

[88]David L. Smiley, *Lion of White Hall: The Life of Cassius M. Clay* (Madison, 1962), 138-42; *Observer and Reporter*, July 11, 1849; Clay, *Memoirs*, I, 185-187.

CHAPTER 5

[1]Court Order Book H, 49, 93-96, 170, 220; Book I, 192-95.

[2]Court Order Book H, 241; Book I, 22, 28, 39, 105.

[3]Court Order Book H, 329.

[4]Ibid., 380.

[5]Court Order Book I, 31; Book H, 149, 150, 168, 172, 217, 221-25, 288-89, 373.

[6]Court Order Book H, 385; Book I, 44, 106-07.

[7]Ibid., 149-50, 154, 332; Book I, 412,

[8]Court Order Book H, 74, 99, 105, 185-87, 220, 264; Book I, 117, 136.

[9]Court Order Book H, 154, 172, 225, 265, 289, 425, 438; Book I, 38, 44, 110, 117, 149, 150, 328.

[10]*Frankfort Commentator, Frankfort Commonwealth, Louisville Daily Courier, Lexington Intelligencer*; House and Senate Journals, 1830s-1840s. Also see the *Lexington Observer and Reporter*, August 9, 1848, and the *Argus of Western America*, August 11, 1830.

[11]Curtis F. Burnam, "Reminiscence," #7, 1895, Burnam Scrapbook, unidentified newspaper clipping, EKU, Townsend Room.

[12]Tipton Papers, 6: 186-88; Deatherage Thesis, 1840, 1844; Court Order Book H, 85.

[13]Jasper B. Shannon and Ruth McQuown, *Presidential Politics in Kentucky*, 1824-1948 (Lexington, 1950), tables; Mathias dissertation, Turbulent Years, 75.

[14] *Frankfort Commentator, Frankfort Commonwealth, Louisville Daily Courier, Lexington Intelligencer;* House and Senate Journals, 1830s-1840s.

[15]Court Order Book I, 12.

[16]Ibid., 4-5, 12, 71.

[17]Court Order Book H, 398, 425; Book I, 1, 5, 31, 149-50.

[18]Court Order Book I, 117, 121, 136, 200, 211.

[19] *Saturday Morning Chronicle,* October 17, 1846 as reprinted in the *Richmond Daily Register,* September 2, 1921; Curtis F. Burnam, "Reminiscence," #3, 1895, Burnam Scrapbook.

[20]Curtis F. Burnam, "Reminiscence," #5, 1895, Burnam Scrapbook.

[21]Curtis F. Burnam, "Reminiscence" #4. Also see *Saturday Morning Chronicle,* October 17, 1846, and *Farmer's Chronicle,* 1839.

[22]Court Order Book I, 188; Clay, *Memoirs,* I, 80-81; Coleman, *Slavery Times in Kentucky,* 305-06.

[23]C. Clay to B. Clay, letter, January 6, 1844 reprinted in the *FCHQ,* XXXI; *The True American,* August 15 through October 7, 1845. The newspapers are on file at the EKU Library.

[24] J. T. Dorris, *Old Cane Springs* and Madison Campbell, *Autobiography of Elder Madison Campbell* (Richmond, 1895). An original copy of the Campbell memoir, the property of Mrs. Marie Beamon, was graciously loaned to the author. A copy is now located in the EKU Archives.

[25]Campbell, *Autobiography,* 7-12.

[26]Ibid., 12.

[27]Ibid., 6-7; Lucia F. Burnam, *What I Remember, 1854-1937* (Richmond, 1934), 9-10.

[28]Campbell, *Autobiography,* 7-19.

[29] Tate's Creek Baptist Record Book; Cane Springs Baptist Record Book.

[30]Campbell, *Autobiography,* 32-33.

[31]Tate's Creek Baptist Record Book; Cane Springs Baptist Record Book; Campbell, *Autobiography,* 42-43; The Minute Book of the Methodist Conference of Madison County, Kentucky, 1811-1844 (copy in EKU Townsend Room), 85-88, 96-97.

[32]Frank M. Masters, *A History of Baptists in Kentucky* (Louisville, 1953), 68; The Minute Book of the Methodist Conference, 85-88, 95-105, 113.

[33]Katherine Phelps Caperton, *A History of the First Christian Church* (Richmond, 1920), 1-8.

[34]"A Bicentennial History," pamphlet, gathered by Margaret Jennings, Mabel Christian, and Mrs. J. L. Whitlock (in the possession of Mrs. Marvin B. Vice, who graciously loaned it to the author).

[35]"Kirksville: A Short Sketch" by Edwin Brown. Addenda by Nettie Pond brought up to 1910. (Copy donated to EKU Archives by Mrs. Marvin B. Vice). See U. S. Census, 1870. Dr. James T. Coy, a native and extensive researcher of Kirksville area history has noted the geographical influence in the naming of Centerville.

[36]Court Order Book H, 283, 322, 344; Mathias Dissertation, 318, includes a copy of letter of Almeron Dowd, August 23, 1845.

[37]Court Order Book I, 188; Mathias Dissertation, 313; Lucia Burnam, *What I Remember,* 9-10.

[38]Ibid., 11; Kentucky House Journal, 1845-1846, 67.

[39]United States Census, 1850; Court Order Books H and I; Campbell, *Autobiography,* 24.

[40]Court Order Book I, 328, 402.

[41] Deatherage Thesis, 1845; Chenault, "Early History"; Tipton Papers, #4, 293-95 includes a list of Mexican War soldiers; Lowell H. Harrison, "The Anti-slavery Career of Cassius M. Clay," *Register,* LIX (October, 1961), 309-10.

[42]Smiley, *Lion of White Hall,* 112-29; Cassius M. Clay, IV, *Letters from the Correspondence of Brutus J. Clay, 1808-1878* (Paris, 1958), 131-43, especially see C. M. Clay to Brutus Clay, Camp near Lavaca on the Gulf of Mexico, Texas, October 12, 1846; Camargo, Mexico, December 13, 1846; and Mexico, June 18, 1847.

[43]Tipton Papers, Books Z, 4: 293-95.

[44]Todd, *This Is Boone Country,* 35, 37, 41.

⁴⁵Ibid., 36.

⁴⁶Curtis F. Burnam, "Reminiscence," #8, Scrapbook.

⁴⁷Kentucky Acts, 1838, 274-83; *Frankfort Commonwealth*, February 21, 1838; Kentucky House Journal, 1848, 33, 37, 74, 628, 746.

⁴⁸Court Order Books H and I.

⁴⁹Court Order Book I, 190, 235, 282-83.

⁵⁰Court Order Book I, 282-83, 308, 314.

⁵¹Ibid., 402-05; Dorris, *Glimpses of Madison County*, 39; Green Clay Chronicles, 73; Court Order Book I, 190.

⁵²Deatherage Thesis, 1849.

⁵³J. T. Dorris, "Major Squire Turner: Lawyer, Statesman, and Economist," *FCHQ*, XXIV (April, 1949), 33-50; Calvin Jarrett, "Cassius Marcellus Clay: A Popular Portrait," *Register*, LXIV (October, 1966), 285-89; Lowell H. Harrison, "The Anti-Slavery Career of Cassius M. Clay," *Register*, LIX (October, 1961), 309-10; Coleman, *Slavery Times in Kentucky*, 316-17; Court Order Books H and I.

⁵⁴James P. Gregory, Jr., "The Question of Slavery in the Kentucky Constitutional Convention of 1849," *FCHQ*, XXIII (April, 1949), 89-99.

⁵⁵See 1849 Constitution.

⁵⁶Kentucky House Journal, 1850-1851, 358.

⁵⁷*Frankfort Commonwealth*, August 13, 1850.

CHAPTER 6

¹Fee to George Whipple, November 1, 1853, in American Missionary Association Correspondence (on Fisk University microfilm in Hutchins Library, Berea College), item no. 43193. All subsequent references abbreviated as AMA, followed by an item number. Fisk to Whipple, January 5, 1853, AMA, 43146. John G. Fee, *Berea: Its History and Work* (published in *Berea Evangelist*, January 1, 1885-June 10, 1886), TS, 2; this work is located in the Berea College Archives, hereafter abbreviated as BCA. Cassius M. Clay, *The Life of Cassius Marcellus Clay: Memoirs, Writings, and Speeches* (1886; rpt. New York, 1969), I, 570, 571. The second volume never appeared; therefore, the volume reference is omitted from all subsequent notes.

²Clay, *Memoirs*, 570, 571; Fee to Whipple, August 26, 1853, AMA, 43175. *American Missionary* (1853), 70 (typewritten copy in BCA); this collection of excerpts contains most of the articles about or by John G. Fee in the *American Missionary*—I have used this version only in numbers before 1857, when I could not consult actual volumes of the magazine (Hutchins Library, Special Collections, has the original *American Missionary* beginning from 1857). In subsequent references the copy will be identified as typescript (TS). Fee to Whipple, June 18, 1853, AMA, 43171.

³Fee to Whipple, May 12, 1854, AMA, 43238; Fee, *Berea*, 2, 3; John G. Fee, *An Autobiography*(Chicago, 1891), 91.

⁴Besides giving Fee land, Clay also contributed $200 to the building of his house. Clay recorded this payment in his Diary, March 29,1855. Clay, *Memoirs*, 571.

⁵Fee to Clay June 22, 1854, BCA; Fee to Whipple August 1, 1854, AMA, 43255.

⁶Fee,*Berea*, 6.

⁷Clay to Arthur Tappan, October 24, 1852, AMA, 43141; Fisk to Whipple, January 5, 1853, AMA, 43146; Clay, *Memoirs*, 570, 571. Cassius Clay's popularity in the Glade and its immediate vicinity is amply attested by the number of local children who were named after him and his kin during this period—for example: Cassius M. Rawlings, Green Clay Renfro, Cassius Clay Stapp (nephew of William), Cassius Clay West, Clay S. Todd, Cassius Cornelison, Cassius M. Clay Cummins, and Cassius Clay Moody.

⁸Clay, *Memoirs*, 245.

⁹Fee, *Berea*, 1; John Wesley quoted by Fee in *The Sinfulness of Slaveholding*, (New York, 1851), 10.

¹⁰"Speech of Cassius Clay at Frankfort, Ky., from the Capitol Steps, 10 Jan 1860," pamphlet, 3, in BCA.

¹¹In May, 1853, Wiley Fisk reported eleven members of Glade Church—Fisk to Whipple, May 30, 1853, AMA, 43167; Fee to Whipple, May 3, 1853, AMA, 43164; Andrew Hill, Deposition, June 5, 1916, Founders and Founding, Fee, BCA. Apparently the Glade

Track (which was rumored to be "haunted") was on the Ridge; Galatha Merrit Rawlings, granddaughter-in-law of John Hamilton Rawlings, recalled that the course consisted of "two small ditches absolutely straight, and parallel and about eight or ten feet apart, beginning at the little draw in Center Street opposite Short and ending where Forest intersects Center." This area was still called the Race Track for fifteen years after Fee had named Berea. Galatha Rawlings, "Once Famous Race Course," *Berea Citizen*, January 19, 1928; Galatha Rawlings, "Reminiscences of Berea," *Berea Citizen*, May 10, 1928.

[12]Union Church Minute Book,MS, BCA—hereafter abbreviated as UCMB;Madison County Tax Book, 1855, Kentucky Historical Society; Hiram K. Richardson, *Memoirs of Berea* (Berea, 1940), 13. The small-scale slaveholders in the Glade District and nearby seldom owned more than ten slaves. In 1860, for example, Jesse Denham owned nine, Jeremiah Rucker four, Fergusson Moore seven, Mossiah Moore two, Madison Todd, on the other hand, owned seventeen (although he had only two in 1850). William M. Ballard owned one slave in 1850, one in 1854, and three in 1860. William Stapp and John Hamilton Rawlings had been slaveholders, but had sold all their slaves long before John G. Fee moved to Madison county—probably as part of their commitment to Cassius Clay. *Madison County Slave Censuses, 1850, 1860*; Madison County Tax Book, 1854.

[13]*Kentucky Statesman*, November 29, 1859, in Lexington Public Library. By the end of 1850 slave dealers were as prevalent in Lexington as mule traders. More than two dozen dealers regularly advertised in Lexington newspapers. The slave population of Kentucky in 1850 was 210,981 out of a total population of 982,405. By 1850 only eight counties (including Jefferson and Fayette) had more slaves than Madison County: out of a total of 15,727 people Madison County had 5,393 slaves, more than one-third of the population in bondage. J. Winston Coleman, Jr., "Lexington's Slave Dealers and Their Southern Trade," *Filson Club History Quarterly*, XII (January, 1938), 16; J. Winston Coleman, Jr., *Slavery Times in Kentucky* (Chapel Hill, 1940), 315. Lewis Collins & Richard H. Collins, *History of Kentucky* (1874; rpt. Berea, 1976), II, 260, 261.

[14]Fee to Whipple, January 9, 1851, AMA, 43093; Fee to Whipple, March, 1851, AMA, 43098.

[15]Fee to Whipple, February 25, 1850, AMA, 43030.

[16]Fisk to Whipple, January 5, 1853, AMA, 43146.

[17]Fee to Tappan, July 28, 1851, AMA, 43102; Clay to A. Tappan October 24, 1852, AMA, 43141.

[18]Fee to Whipple, May 3, 1853, AMA, 43164.

[19]Fisk to Whipple, May 21, 1855, AMA, 43320; Fisk to Whipple, October 13, 1853, AMA, 43184.

[20]Fee to Whipple, August 16, 1853, AMA, 43175.

[21]The Glade Church, built of logs hewn by James Mitchell, was established as early as 1825 or 1826, with T. S. Bronston as first preacher. French Tipton Papers I, 423, in Townsend Room, Crabbe Library, EKU.

[22]*Minutes of Scaffold Cane-Silver Baptist Church 1802-59* (typescript of original minute book in possession of Clyde Linville, Mt. Vernon, Ky.), 72, 73; Fisk to Whipple, September 1, 1853, AMA, 43178.

[23]Georgia Ann (Todd) Kinnard obit., *Berea Citizen*, October 28, 1926.

[24]*Burnam vs. Burnam*, Madison County Circuit Court Records; Civil Court Judgments, Box 39, Bundle 78, in Kentucky Archives, Frankfort.

[25]Fee, *Berea*, 4, 5. It is quite likely that Fee moved his church and center of operations up to the ridge at the point when his relationship with Wiley Fisk and those who favored Fisk was at its lowest point. Fee and Fisk were supposed to share the ministry of Glade Church and others; but Fisk's supporters certainly included slaveholders, and Fee was appalled when he returned to Madison County and found how the church had backslidden under Fisk's careless ministry. Fee spoke of Fisk as the "Apollos" of Berea—one, that is, who was the occasion of factionalism. So Fee found "the place for the church and co-operation with working friends" (italics my own) was on the ridge.

[26]Lowell H. Harrison, *The Antislavery Movement in Kentucky* (Lexington, 1978), chap. 1; *Kentucky Messenger*, December 23, 1859, in Exile File, BCA; Sidney E. Ahlstrom, *A Religious History of the American People* (Garden City, N. Y., 1975), II, "Churches," Chapter 42; Harrison, *Antislavery Movement*, 15; Fee, *Autobiography*, 60. For eyewitness

accounts (one from the perspective of a wealthy white man, the other from slave's) of segregated worship in central Kentucky at this time, see Louis Ruchames, *The Abolitionists: A Collection of Their Writings* (New York, 1963), 177; George P. Rawick, *The American Slave: A Composite Autobiograhy* (1941; rpt. Westport, Conn., 1972), XVIII, 180 ("Kentucky Slave Narratives," 3).

[27]Fee, *Autobiography*, 60, 61.

[28]Fee, "Biographical Sketch," 8, in BCA; UCMB; *American Missionary*, II (February, 1858), 42, 43. Matilda Bently, the subject of this description was about fifty years old in 1858—living with the child of her former mistress. *American Missionary*, II (May, 1858), 114, 115.

[29]Madison County Court Order Book I (1849-50), 418, 443, 446, 450, 451, 453, 454; Court Order Book K (1850-1855), 163, 239, 240, 272, 276.

[30]Court Order Book K, 242, 287, 289, 290; Book L (1855-1859), 124, 125.

[31]Court Order Book L, 353; Book M (1859-64), 565.

[32]John Cabell Chenault & Jonathan T. Dorris, *Old Cane Springs: A Story of the War Between the States in Madison County, Kentucky* (Louisville, 1936). v, 85; Jonathan T. Dorris & Maud Weaver Dorris, *Glimpses of Historic Madison County, Kentucky* (Nashville, 1955), 159, 160.

[33]Elizabeth Rogers, *A Personal History of Berea College*, [1910?] 25, MS. in BCA; Lucia F. Burnam, *What I Remember*, 13, 14, TS in Townsend Room, Crabbe Library, EKU.

[34]*Burnam vs. Burnam*.

[35]Alma Lackey Wilson, "Kennedy Family," *Genealogies of Kentucky Families* (Baltimore, 1981), I, 606, 630; Coleman, *Slavery Times*, 318: Garrard County Wills: BookM (1848-52), 266.

[36]*Burnam vs. Burnam*.

[37]Harrison, *Antislavery Movement*, 6.

[38]Unfortunately, active cruelty was not unknown; treatment of slaves in Madison County was, apparently, not notable for being humane. One of the most appalling accounts of slavery, *Narratives of the Sufferings of Lewis and Milton Clarke*, written in 1846, details first-hand experiences of slave suffering. Lewis and Milton Clarke were born and reared in Madison County, Kentucky.

[39]Clay, *Memoirs*, 573; Fee to Tappan, May 2, 1853, AMA, 43155; Fee to Clay, August 17, 1849, BCA.

[40]Fee to Tappan May 2, 1853, AMA, 43155; David L. Smiley, "Cassius M. Clay and John G. Fee: A Study in Southern Anti-Slavery Thought," *The Journal of Negro History*, XLII (July, 1957), 208; Clay, *Memoirs*, 576; Fee, *Autobiography*, 46.

[41]Asa E. Martin, *The Anti-Slavery Movement in Kentucky Prior to 1850* (Louisville, 1918; rpt. New York, 1970), 130, 131, 137; Wallace B. Turner, "Abolitionism in Kentucky," *Register*, LXIX (October, 1971), 321; Clay, *Memoirs*, 576.

[42]Fee, *Autobiography*, 55.

[43]Fee, *Berea*, 7, 8.

[44]Ibid., 9.

[45]H. Edward Richardson, *Cassius Marcellus Clay*(Lexington, 1976), 76; Victor B. Howard, "Cassius M. Clay and the Origins of the Republican Party." *Filson Club History Quarterly*, XLV (January, 1971), 59; Jane H. Pease & William H. Pease, *Bound With Them in Chains* (Westport, Conn., 1972), 84; Martin, *Antislavery Movement*, 123. According to John A. R. Rogers' *Birth of Berea College: A Story of Providence*, Otis Waters wrote that Clay's famous ultimatum was delivered in Mount Vernon, in Rockcastle County. John A. R. Rogers, *Birth* (1904; rpt. Berea, 1933), 41.

[46]Fee, *Berea*, 9; Harrison, *AntislaveryMovement*, 73.

[47]*American Missionary* (July 7, 1855), TS, 78.

[48]Howard, "Clay and the Republican Party," 60, 61; Harrison, *Antislavery Movement*, 73; *CincinnatiDaily Gazette*, July 23, 1855, quoted in Howard; Clay, *Memoirs*, 61. Cassius Clay seems to have respected John G. Fee's courage, even though it was so different from his own. William E. Lincoln recalls Clay saying, "Fee has more courage than any of us; we go into danger with our pistols—knives & friend-helpers; he goes alone with no one; trusting in God." William E. Lincoln, "Memoirs" (Letter to President Frost October 18, 1909), 28, in BCA.

[49]Fee, *Berea*, 10.

[50]John G. Fee to editor, July 4, 1856, *Newport Kentucky Weekly*, August 25, 1856, clipping in Clay-Fee correspondence, BCA.

[51]Ibid.

[52]Fee, *Berea*, 11.

[53]James S. Davis to Simeon Jocelyn, July 29, 1856, AMA, 43392; Davis to Jocelyn, August 1, 1856, AMA, 43394.

[54]Both Clay and Fee published installments of their argument in newspapers from 1856 to 1860; clippings of these letters are in correspondence between Fee and Clay in Founders and Founding Series; Fee, BCA.

[55]Clay to Davis, October 5, 1857, BCA.

[56]Fee to Jocelyn, July 15, 1857, AMA, 43485; *American Missionary* (1857), TS, 211, 212; Fee to Clay, July 28, 1857, BCA; Fee to Jocelyn, July 29, 1857, AMA, 43492.

[57]Fee to Clay, August 27, 1857, BCA; Fee to Clay, August 3, 1857, BCA.

[58]Fee to Jocelyn, August, 1857, AMA, 43503; Fee to Jocelyn September 10, 1857, AMA, 43511.

[59]Fee to Jocelyn, March 27, 1858, AMA, 43596.

[60]Fee to Jocelyn, September 10, 1857, AMA, 43512. Clay claimed that Fee "was reinforced by adventurers using force . . . " Fee had been "at first a non-resident." Clay wrote, "but, further along, allowed his friends to use force." Clay does not point out that the same men who armed themselves to protect Fee were accustomed to bearing weapons to defend Cassius Clay. Clay, *Memoirs*, 77.

[61]Fee to Tappan, December 17, 1857, AMA, 43535.

CHAPTER 7

[1]Robert S. Fletcher, *A History of Oberlin College* (Oberlin, 1943), I, 208.

[2]Fee to Whipple, June 25, 1852, AMA, 43130; Fee to Jocelyn, October 24, 1854, AMA, 43280. Fee to Jocelyn, August, 1857, AMA, 43503.

[3]Petition to AMA, May, 1854, AMA, 43245. A complete list of the signers of this abolitionist petition may be found in the MS. of *The Day of Small Things*, chapter five, in BCA.

[4]Fee to Whipple, May 12, 1854, AMA, 43239; West to Whipple, September 1, 1853, AMA, 43177; Fee to Jocelyn, August, 1857, AMA, 43506. Also see *American Missionary*, September 5, 1853, 99.

[5]Parker's Slave Report, June, 1859, AMA, 43766.

[6]Fee to Jocelyn, June 16, 1855, AMA, 106919; Fee to Jocelyn, June 21, 1855, AMA, 106932.

[7]Fee to Jocelyn, September 26, 1855, AMA, 107078.

[8]Candee to Frost, December 8, 1901, BCA.

[9]Ibid.

[10]Fee, *Berea*, 6; Fee to Jocelyn, January 4, 1856, AMA, 43358; Waters to Jocelyn, November 25, 1856, AMA, 43410; Candee to Frost, 1901, in BCA; Fee to Jocelyn November 9, 1855, AMA, 43343.

[11]Fee to Gerrit Smith, January 4, 1856, Syracuse U. Library, quoted in Mabee, 410.

[12]*American Missionary*, IX, December, 1855), TS, 13, 14.

[13]*American Missionary*, XI (1857), 7.

[14]Fee to Jocelyn, Whipple, Tappan & Goodell, April 4, 1857, AMA, 43458.

[15]*American Missionary*, May, 1857, TS, 117; Fee to Jocelyn, August 14, 1857, AMA, 43498.

[16]Fee to Jocelyn August 14, 1857, AMA, 43498.

[17]Fee, *Berea*, 24, 25.

[18]Fee to Tappan, December 17, 1857, AMA, 43535.

[19]Fee to Jocelyn, February 8, 1858, AMA, 43572.

[20]Fee to Jocelyn, February 9, 1858, AMA, 43581.

[21]Waters to Jocelyn, July 24, 1858, AMA, 108461.

[22]Harriet Beecher Stowe, in *Liberator*, quoted in *American Missionary*, II November, 1858), 269-70.

[23]Fee to Jocelyn, December 4, 1858, AMA, 43685.

[24]Ibid.

[25]Fee to Jocelyn, April 8, 1859, AMA, 43749.

[26]Elizabeth Rogers, *Personal History*, 8.

[27]Ibid.

[28]Ibid, 9; Elizabeth Rogers to Frost, April 23, 1901, BCA.

[29]Elizabeth Rogers, *Personal History*, 10, 11.

[30]Leaflet advertising Berea School dated August 19, 1858, AMA, 43396.

[31]Term dates from Rogers' *Journal*; Rogers to Frost, December 11, 1901.

[32]Elizabeth Rogers, *Personal History*, 13.

[33]Ibid.

[34]Ibid., 14.

[35]Ibid., 58, 58n.

[36]All pre-Civil War students to attend Berea are listed with biographical information in Appendix 4 of *The Day of Small Things*, MS. in BCA.

[37]Elizabeth Rogers, *Personal History*, 11.

[38]*Madison County Slave Census, 1860.*

[39]Marie Gay Foster, *Denham Family Tree*, TS, in Kentucky Historical Society; Nell Watson Sherman, *The Maupin Family* (Morton, Ill., 1962); Ruby G. Heard Maupin, *History of the Maupin Family* (1969), in Kentucky Historical Society; see Marie Gay Foster, *My Father's People: The Dejarnats* (priv. printed), in KHS; chapter 3 on "The Harris Family," W. H. Miller, *History and Genealogies of the Families of Miller, Woods, Harris . . .* (Lexington, 1907).

[40]Elizabeth Rogers, *Personal History*, 11.

[41]John A. R. Rogers' Account Book, 1857-1868, in BCA.

[42]Elizabeth Rogers, *Personal History*," 16.

[43]Other families of the community supported Fee's work in various ways (and later boasted of their early loyalty—as did the Thompsons and the Rawlings). John B. Kirby (born December, 1830), son of Jesse Kirby and Martha Burnam and grandson of John Burnam, Sr., was one of the oldest residents of Madison county, when he died in 1914. His obituary notice states that he was always a friend of Berea College (and of Fee and Fairchild) and "during its early days stood true to the cause." He was a surety for a Berea College mortgage, May 31, 1867. John B. Kirby obit. *Berea Citizen*, August 13, 1914; Rogers, *Birth*, 99; Rogers' Account Book, 1857-1868,in BCA; *Madison County Deed Book 16*, 39.

When Martha Reed Cornelison died in 1900 she was called "one of Berea's ante-Bellum friends." A daughter of Anderson Woods Reed and Charlotte Embry, Mrs. Cornelison was related to some of the most prominent slaveholders in the county, as was her husband Albert C. Cornelison. The couple had owned slaves themselves in 1850, but probably Albert Cornelison was the man (always identified simply as Mr. Cornelison) who worked occasionally as a colporteur for Fee in 1857 and 1858 and the "influential friend of the movement" who went to Richmond and secured the services of two prominent lawyers after Robert Jones was whipped. Albert and Martha Cornelison named one of their sons Cassius C. Cornelison, and their daughter Martha was probably one of Berea's pre-Civil War students. Martha (Reed) Cornelison obit., *Berea Citizen*, July 11, 1900; Fee to Jocelyn, September 10, 1857, AMA, 43511; Fee to Jocelyn, January 19, 1858, AMA, 43565; Fee to Jocelyn, April 26, 1858, AMA, 43565.

[44]Richardson, *Memoirs*, 24; Rogers toFrost, October 10, 1904, BCA; Madison County Deed BookW, 393; Estill County Deed Book D,260; Curtis F. Burnam,"Family Record," MS. in TownsendRoom, Crabbe Library, EKU.

[45]UCMB; Madison County Tax Book, 1854, 4, Kentucky Historical Society; Lincoln, 11, 12.

[46]Thompson Burnam obit.,*Berea Citizen*, July 26, 1923.

[47]Fee to Whipple, November 23, 1854, AMA, 43287.

[48]Smiley, *Lion of Whitehall*, 139, 140; "Burnam Family," no. 6 in Family History Series, Townsend Room, EKU. In his will Curtis F. Burnam bequeathed to one of his sons "the historic cane" presented to him by Cassius Clay. Madison County Will Book 3, 132-33.

[49]Curtis F. Burnam obit., *Berea Citizen*, March 25, 1909; "In Memoriam: Curtis Field Burnam" (privately printed, no date).

[50]Collins, *History of Kentucky*, I, 97, 353; *Proceedings of the Convention Establishing Provisional Government of Kentucky* [1861] (Augusta, Ga., 1863), 1.

[51]Rogers, *Journal.*

[52]Rogers, *Birth*, 58, 59.

[53]Rogers, *Birth*, 59; Elizabeth Rogers, *Personal History*, 17.

[54]Elizabeth Rogers, *Personal History*, 17, 18.

[55]Fee, *Berea*, 28; Rogers, *PersonalHistory*, 18.

[56]Fee to Clay, July 12, 1858, BCA; Fee, *Berea*, 28. What is now the Berea College campus was (in 1858) literally in "the Bresh," as the region was locally named. "The 'Bresh' was so thick that if a person stood six feet from the road he would be invisible to a passerby on the . . . highway, and except for a few paths it was impossible for a man to make his way through the woods without clearing his way with an ax." Rogers, *Birth*, 51, 52.

[57]Fee to Clay, July 12, 1858, BCA.

[58]*American Missionary*, II (September, 1858), 232-33.

[59]Rogers, *Personal History*, 18.

[60]Fee, *Berea*, 29.

CHAPTER 8

[1]A complete account of Berea's prewar colonists appears in chapter 14 in my MS. *The Day of Small Things* in BCA.

[2]*Encyclopedia of American History*, 220, 225.

[3]See entry on Beecher in DAB or, for a full-scale account, Milton Rugoff, *The Beechers: An American Family in the Nineteenth Century* (New York, 1981); Ahlstrom, II, 195.

[4]*American Missionary*, III (December, 1859), 275-77.

[5]Fee was not alone in vindicating John Brown. Many of his fellow abolitionists did so, including William Lloyd Garrison, Henry Wright, Samuel J. May, Edmund Quincey, Lydia Child, Charles Burleigh, John Greenleaf Whittier, and, among Fee's personal friends, William Goodell and Lewis Tappan. Another friend of Fee's, Gerrit Smith, had, of course, helped to finance John Brown's raid. Lawrence J. Friedman, *Gregarious Saints* (Cambridge, 1982), 212.

[6]*American Missionary*, IV (February, 1860), 37-38; Fee's notes for sermon in Beecher's Church, MS, BCA.

[7]*Louisville Courier*, November 17, 1859, quoted in *Kentucky Statesman*, November 18, 1859, Lexington Public Library.

[8]Ibid.

[9]News story from *Kentucky Messenger* (Richmond), quoted by James S. Davis in *Conogregational Herald*, VII (January 19, 1860), 1, TS in BCA.

[10]Boughton to Jocelyn, April 2, 1860, AMA, 109471.

[11]Matilda Fee to Jocelyn, November 29, 1859, AMA, 43817.

s[12]*Richmond Democrat*, quotedin *Kentucky Statesmen*, November 29, 1859, Lexington Public Library.

[13]The twenty-eight members of the initial Vigilance Committee were: "Solon Harris, Wm. T. Terrill, Samuel Bennett, Arch. Kavanaugh, Geo. Parkes, R. J. White, Claibourn White, Jno. C. Terrill, Sam. Campbell, G. W. Maupin, Col. R. J. Munday, Ed. W. Turner, Col. Wm. Harris, Jas. E. Baker, Nathan Moran, J. P. Estill, C. A. Hawkins, J. R. Gilbert, Wm. M. Miller, Col. John Kinnard, W. J. Walker, Charles Oldham, J. W. Parkes, C. R. Estill, C. Field, Jr." *Kentucky Statesman*, December 9, 1859, Lexington Public Library.

[14]*Kentucky Statesman*, December 9, 1859, Lexington Public Library.

[15]Collins, *History of Kentucky*, I, 81; Elizabeth Rogers, *Personal History*, 28; Damon to Jocelyn, December 9, 1859, AMA, 109191.

[16]Elizabeth Rogers, *Personal History*, 27.

[17]Davis to Jocelyn, December, 11, 1859, AMA, 43822.

[18] *American Missionary*, IV (February, 1860), 37; Circular No. 2, December 27, 1859, AMA, 43827; Kendrick to Jocelyn, December 13, 1859, AMA, 43823.3827.

[19] *Kentucky Statesman*, December 27,1859, Lexington Public Library.

[20] *American Missionary*, IV (February, 1860), 40.

[21] Collins, *History of Kentucky*, I, 83.

[22] Curtis F. Burnam to James S. Rollins, February 14, 1860, Burnam-Rollins Microfilm, Collection Number: 82A19 (EKU Archives), from the joint collection, U. of Missouri, Western Historical Manuscript Collection—Columbia, State Historical Society of Missouri Manuscripts. All Burnam to Rollins Letters are from the same source.

[23] *Kentucky Messenger*, December 23, 1859, clippings in Exile File, BCA.

[24] Ibid.; *Kentucky Statesman*, December 27, 1859, Lexington Public Library.

[25] *Kentucky Statesman*, December 20, 1859, Lexington Public Library; HRBC 1904, 17.

[26] Elizabeth Rogers, *Personal History*, 28.

[27] Elizabeth Rogers, "Full Forty Years," (1896), 20.

[28] Rogers, *Birth*, 74.

[29] *American Missionary*, IV (February, 1860), 38-41; Rogers, *Birth*, 75.

[30] Elizabeth Rogers, "Full Forty Years," 20, 21.

[31] Ibid., 21; Rogers, *Birth*, 75; Rogers to Jocelyn, December 28, 1859, AMA, 43828; Rogers to Frost, twenty-page letter concerning the Berea exodus, (c. September, 1893).

[32] *American Missionary*, IV (February, 1860), 41.

[33] Fee to Jocelyn, December 24, 1859, AMA, 109220; Fee to Tappan, December 29, 1859, AMA, 109236.

[34] Elizabeth Rogers, *Personal History*, 29, 30.

[35] Rogers to Jocelyn, December 28, 1859, AMA, 43828; Coleman, *Slavery Times*, 322.

[36] A complete list of exiles from Berea appears in the MS. *The Day of Small Things* in BCA.

[37] Rogers, *Birth*, 79, 80.

[38] Elizabeth Rogers, "Full Forty Years," 23.

[39] Elizabeth Rogers, *Personal History*, 30; Rogers, *Birth*, 81.

[40] Fee to Tappan, December 29, 1859, AMA, 109236.

[41] Elizabeth Rogers, *Personal History*, 30, 31.

[42] Rogers, *Birth*, 81.

[43] Fee, *Autobiography*, 119; Court Order Book K, 53.

[44] Fee, *Autobiography*, 117.

[45] *Madison County Slave Census of 1860*.

[46] Miller, *History and Genealogies*; Collins, *History of Kentucky*, II, 493; French Tipton, "The Richmond Bar," in *The Lawyers and Lawmakers of Kentucky*, ed. H. Levin (Chicago, 1897), 520-22; James W. Caperton obit., *Berea Citizen*, April 22, 1909.

[47] See chapters in Miller, *History and Genealogies* on various families named.

[48] Ibid.

[49] *American Missionary*, IV (February, 1860), 40. A number of Berea students before the Civil War shared this heritage. Ann Eliza and Mary Best were Harris descendants—their mother Nancy (Harris) Best being a cousin of the committee members who bore that surname. The Maupins who attended Berea were descended from the Maupins of Albemarle Country, just as committee members were.

[50] Candee to Clay, December 26, 1859, BCA.

[51] *American Missionary*, IV (February, 1860), 43; Clay's "Appeal to the People of Madison County," from *Louisville Journal*, April 4, 1860, quoted in Clay, *Memoirs*, 241-47; "Speech of Cassius M. Clay at Frankfort, Ky., from the Capitol Steps, January 10, 1860," pamphlet, reprinted for *Cincinnati Gazette*, 1-3: in BCA.

[52] Ibid.

[53] Fee to Clay, February 28, 1860, BCA.

[54] Fee to Tappan, February 15, 1860, AMA, 109362.

CHAPTER 9

[1] Fee to Jocelyn, January 9, 1860, AMA, 109268.

[2] *American Missionary*, IV (June, 1860), 134-36; Hanson to Jocelyn, March 13, 1860, AMA, 43855; Fee to Jocelyn, February 29, 1860, AMA, 109393A.

[3]AMA, 43855.

[4]Ibid.

[5]*Kentucky Statesman*, April 13, 1860, Lexington Public Library; *American Missionary* IV (June, 1860), 135.

[6]*Kentucky Statesman*, April 13, 1860, Lexington Public Library; Clay, *Memoirs*, 244; *Kentucky Statesman*, April 6, 1860, Lexington Public Library.

[7]*American Missionary* IV (June, 1860), 135, 136; Mallett to Jocelyn, April 13, 1860, AMA, 109503; Mont Hanson to Ernest G. Dodge, August 18, 1903, BCA.

[8]*Kentucky Statesman*, April 13, 1860, Lexington Public Library; *American Missionary*, IV (June, 1860), 134-36.

[9]Hanson's Account in *American Missionary*, IV (June, 1860), 134-37.

[10]Mont Hanson to Dodge, August 19, 1903, BCA; clipping from *Cincinnati Commercial* with Mallett to Jocelyn, April 13, 1860, AMA, 109503.

[11]Clipping, AMA, 109503.

[12]*American Missionary*, IV (June, 1860), 136.

[13]For a complete account of all the stories of the battle of Hanson's return see my MS. *The Day of Small Things*, chapter 16, in BCA.

[14]Clay, *Memoirs*, 250.

[15]*Kentucky Statesman*, April 6, 1860, Lexington Public Library.

[16]*Kentucky Whig*, undated clipping in Exile File, BCA.

[17]Clay to *Louisville Journal*, March 29, 1860, in *National Anti-Slavery Standard*, April 14, 1860, clipping in Exile File, BCA.

[18]Clay to *New York Tribune*, in *KentuckyStatesman*, April 13, 1860, Lexington Public Library.

[19]Clay to *Louisville Journal*, March 13, 1860, in *National Anti-Slavery Standard*, April 14, 1860, clipping in Exile File, BCA.

[20]Green Clay, *Cassius Clay: Militant Statesman, Moses of Emancipation 1810-1903*, TS, 118, 119, in Dorris Collection, Crabbe Library, EKU. Reporting this incident, Hanson gives the less grandiose figure of "8 to 10 friends who spent some two or three days at C. M. Clay's armed & much excitement." Of course, Hanson may have been giving the number of his own friends who were members of Clay's guard, not the total number. Hanson to Tappan, July 3, 1860, AMA, 109660.

[21]*American Missionary*, IV (June, 1860), 137.

[22]Ibid.

[23]Committee's report, April 3, 1860, in *Kentucky Statesman*, April 10, 1860, Lexington Public Library.

[24]Clay, "Speech at Republican State Convention of Kentucky," clipping from *Cincinnati Daily Gazette*, April 28, 1860, Cassius M. Clay Papers, Filson Club.

[25]*The World We Live In*, April 14, 1860, clipping in Exile File, BCA.

[26]*Chicago Press & Tribune*, reprinted in *The World We Live In*, April 14, 1860, clipping in BCA.

[27]"Resolution of the Radical Abolitionist Convention" in *Douglass Monthly*, October, 1860, quoted in Pease & Pease, *Bound*, 85.

[28]Candee to Clay, April 25, 1860, BCA.

[29]Between the first exile (December, 1859) and the fourth (April, 1860), two other Kentucky exiles occurred: Fee, Hanson and many others from Bracken County, James S. Davis from Lewis County.

[30]*Kentucky Statesman*, April 10, 1860 in Lexington Public Library; Renfro and Wright to Fee, April 20, 1860, BCA.

[31]Mallett to Jocelyn, April 6, 1860, AMA, 109486.

The exiles from Madison County in April, 1860, included the following citizens and their families: Willis Green Haley, Franklin Bland, Widow Jerusha Preston, Jesse Preston, Reuben Preston, James Walters, George Adams, Wesley Dobbs, Joel Todd, Benjamin Kirby, Joseph Williams, John Williams, Silas Williams, Widow Martha Williams, and Shadrach Roberts—some sixty people in all. A complete account of each of these families appears in my MS. *The Day of Small Things*, chapter 17, in the Berea College Archives.

[32]Clay's list of exiles, 1860, MS, BCA. In a biography of her father, Mary B. Clay mentions having in her possession names of ninety-four persons who were driven from

Kentucky by the Madison County mob; no doubt she is referring to the list her father compiled in 1860. The accuracy of Clay's list is attested by its agreement in every instance with facts that can be ascertained through other resources. Mary B. Clay, "Biography of Cassius M. Clay: Written by His Daughter," *Filson Club History Quarterly*, XLVI (July, 1972), 269.

[33]Kendrick to Jocelyn, April 6, 1860, AMA, 109485; Mallett to Jocelyn, April 6, 1860, AMA, 109486.

[34]Fee to Jocelyn, April 9, 1860, AMA, 109496; Fee to Jocelyn, April 17, 1860, AMA, 109506; Hanson to Rogers, May 25, 1860, AMA, 109582.

[35]Fee to Jocelyn, May 24, 1860, AMA, 109578. Three children may have died because of the exposure and hardship of the exile: John G. Fee's son Tappan, John F. Boughton's daughter, and the child of James Walters.

[36]Benjamin and Nancy Kirby to John G. Fee and John G. Hanson, July 13, 1860, AMA, 43876.

[37]Burnam to Rollins, June 4, 1860, in EKU Archives.

[38]Burnam to Rollins, October 18, 1860, in EKU Archives.

[39]*Encyclopedia of American History*, 228; Dorris, *Glimpses*, 144.

[40]French Tipton Papers I, 220, 221.

[41]Burnam to Rollins, February 10, 1861, in EKU Archives.

[42]French Tipton Papers I: 395; Shackelford to William Nelson, May 19, 1861, William Nelson Papers in the Filson Club, quoted in Lowell Harrison, *The Civil War in Kentucky* (Lexington, 1975), 10.

[43]Burnam to Rollins, April 22, 1861, in EKU Archives.

[44]*Encyclopedia of American History*, 231; Clark, *A History of Kentucky*, 479, 481. Captain Thomas Speed, *The Union Cause in Kentucky, 1860-1865* (New York, 1907), 142, 160; Collins, *History of Kentucky*, I, 9; Ross A. Webb, *Kentucky in the Reconstuction Era* (Lexington, 1979), 9; *Proceedings of the Convention Establishing Provisional Government of Kentucky* [1861] (Augusta, Ga., 1863), 20,21; *Military History of Kentucky* (Frankfort, 1939), 161,198; Copeland, "Where Were the Kentucky Unionists and Secessionists?" *Register*, LXXI (October, 1973), 357, 358.

[45]*Military History of Kentucky*, 154, 155, 161; Collins, *History of Kentucky*, I, 342; "Testimony of Witnesses in the Case of Killing Durrett White," [1861], TS, in Townsend Room, Crabbe Library, EKU.

[46]Lucia F. Burnam, *What I Remember*, 7, 8, 19,20; French Tipton Papers, 1: 210C, 8: 119; Miller, *History and Genealogies*, 370, 371; Broaddus Family Record, 21, in Townsend Room.

[47]Lucia F. Burnam, *What I Remember*, 14.

[48]Collins, *History of Kentucky*, I, 95.

[49]Ibid., 96.

[50]Chenault & Dorris, *Old Cane Springs*, 64,66-68, 87.

[51]Miller, *History and Genealogies*, 370, 371; Chenault & Dorris, *Old Cane Springs*, 67.

[52]"Testimony . . . Durrett White." Menelaos, a village which ceased to exist soon after the Civil War, was a post office from July, 1850, to September, 1861; it was on the postal route from Kingston by Menelaos, Silver Creek, and Scaffold Cane to Mt. Vernon. By 1867 Berea had preempted Menelaos, which apparently lay north and east of Berea at that time. ("Report on Berea Post Office, 9 September 1937," typewritten note in my possession).

[53]"Testimony . . . Durrett White."

[54]Fee to Jocelyn, December 4, 1861, AMA, 43918; Fee to Jocelyn, December 21, 1861, AMA, 43919; Collins, *History of Kentucky*, II, 96; Harrison, *The Civil War in Kentucky*, 19; Fee to Jocelyn, May 6, 1862, AMA, 110746-110747; Fee to Jocelyn, May 10, 1862, AMA, 110756; Collins, *History of Kentucky*, II, 102.

CHAPTER 10

[1]Lucia F. Burnam, *What I Remember*, 15-18; *War of the Rebellion*, 770.

[2]Ibid., 18.

[3]Hambleton Tapp, "Battle of Richmond 1862" (address to the Madison County Historical Society, July 5, 1960), in *Kentucky Pioneer*, I (October, 1968), 10; Joseph Wheeler,

"Bragg's Invasion of Kentucky," *Battles and Leaders of the Civil War* (New York, 1884), III, Pt. 1, 4; Thomas Lawrence Connelly, *Army of the Heartland: The Army of Tennessee, 1861-1862* (Baton Rouge, 1967), 194, 195. Even Morgan's enemies believed that Kentucky would become a Confederate state under his influence. J. T. Boyle reported (July 12, 1862) that all the rebels in the state would join Morgan, "if there [was] not a demonstration of force and power" from Union cavalry. Abraham Lincoln himself issued a military order concerning Morgan's inroads in the state (to Major General Halleck, Corinth, Miss., July 13, 1862): "They are having a stampede in Kentucky. Please look to it." *War of the Rebellion*, 733, 738.

⁴Wheeler, "Bragg's Invasion," III, Pt. 1, 4.

⁵Tapp, "Battle of Richmond," 11.

⁶*Military History of Kentucky*, 201; *The War of the Rebellion: A Compilation of the Official Records of the Union and Confederate Armies*, Series 1, Vol. XVI, Part 1—Reports (Washington, 1886), 884-86.

⁷Collins, *History of Kentucky* I, 110; E. Merton Coulter, *Civil War and Readjustment* (Chapel Hill, N.C., 1926), 157, 158.

⁸*War of the Rebellion*, 886,887.

⁹Fee, *Berea*, 41; Rogers, *Birth*, 85.

¹⁰Fee, *Berea*, 41; *War of the Rebellion*, 911; Frank Moore, ed., *The Rebellion Record: A Diary of American Events* (1861-63; rpt. New York, 1977), V, 407, 408.

¹¹Tapp, "Battle of Richmond," 12; *Rebellion Record*, 408; *War of the Rebellion*, 907, 908.

¹²*Rebellion Record*, 408; *War of the Rebellion*, 918; Tapp, "Battle of Richmond," 12.

¹³*War of the Rebellion*, 911, 913, 919, 926, 944.

¹⁴*War of the Rebellion*, 911, 912, 914, 915, 918, 919, 925, 926, 928; *Rebellion Record*, 410.

¹⁵*War of the Rebellion*, 931, 935, 944.

¹⁶Ibid., 931, 932, 934; Fee, *Berea*, 41. John G. Fee was not alone as a civilian spectator at the Battle of Richmond. One Union soldier reported that "a large number of civilians had come out to see the fight and were collected on hills in [the] rear. Some of them were killed . . . " (*Rebellion Record*, 418). After the battle was over many citizens examined the battlefield. John Rogers recorded in his journal that he held only a brief Sabbath meeting on August 31 because "most of the people" had gone to the battlefield.

¹⁷*Rebellion Record*, 408; *War of the Rebellion*, 920; Wheeler, "Bragg's Invasion," III, Pt. 1, 4, 5.

¹⁸*Rebellion Record*, 408; *War of the Rebellion*, 919, 920, 924. Green Clay, William Holloway and John Miller, three prominent Richmond citizens, volunteered their services as aides-de-camp to Charles Cruft and acted in that capacity all day on August 30. "Their bearing on the field," Cruft reported, "was gallant in the extreme and their coolness under fire admirable." John Miller was mortally wounded during the battle in the Richmond cemetery. *War of the Rebellion*, 923.

¹⁹*Rebellion Record*, 408; *War of the Rebellion*, 934; Wheeler, "Bragg's Invasion," III, Pt. 1, 5.

²⁰Tapp, "Battle of Richmond," 14; *Rebellion Record*, 408; *War of the Rebellion*, 934.

²¹*War of the Rebellion*, 940.

²²*Rebellion Record*, 409; *War of the Rebellion*, 920; Wheeler, "Bragg's Invasion," III, Pt. 1, 5.

²³*Rebellion Record*, 420.

²⁴Ibid., 409.

²⁵*War of the Rebellion*, 921; Dorris, *Glimpses of Historic Madison County*, 146; *Rebellion Record*, 409,410.

²⁶*War of the Rebellion*, 921.

²⁷*War of the Rebellion*, 914, 921, 931, 935, 941, 951; Tipton Papers, 6:29; *Rebellion Record*, 409, 410; *Army of the Heartland*, 216.

²⁸Tapp, "Battle of Richmond," 16, 17; *War of the Rebellion*, 909; *Rebellion Record*, 421. General William Nelson was shot by General Jefferson C. Davis at the Galt House in Louisville, Kentucky, almost a month to the day after the Battle of Richmond, September 29, 1862. He was killed almost instantly. *Rebellion Record*, 87.

[29]*War of the Rebellion*, 925, 926.

[30]Ibid., 917, 938, 939; Tipton Papers, 9:211; *Rebellion Record*, 410, 422; Tapp, "Battle of Richmond," 15, 16.

[31]*War of the Rebellion*, 931.

[32]*Rebellion Record*, 416.

[33]Lucia F. Burnam, *What I Remember*, 24, 25.

[34]Fee to Jocelyn, September 16, 1862, AMA, 110925.

[35]A. C. Quisenberry, "The Battle of Richmond, Kentucky, September, 1862," 11, 13, xeroxed pamphlet in Townsend Room, Crabbe Library, EKU; Colonel J. Stoddard Johnston, "Kentucky," *Confederate Military History*, ed. Clement A. Evans (The Blue & Gray Press), IX, 125-26; Clark, *History of Kentucky*, 458.

[36]*Rebellion Record*, 419.

[37]Mark Mayo Boatner, III, *The Civil War Dictionary* (New York, 1959), 698; Tipton Papers, 6:29; Chenault & Dorris, *Old Cane Springs*, 109.

[38]*War of the Rebellion*, 907.

[39]Court Order Book M (1859-1864), 427.

[40]Dorris, *Glimpses*, 147, 150, 151, 154; Chenault & Dorris, *Old Cane Springs*, 109; Tapp, "Battle of Richmond," 17.

[41]Lucia F. Burnam, *What I Remember*, 28.

[42]Tipton Papers [newspaper clipping], 1:180.

[43]Rogers to Jocelyn, October 22, 1862, AMA, 110978; Rogers to Jocelyn, February 17, 1863, AMA, 111179; *American Missionary*, VII (January, 1863), 15; *American Missionary*, VII (February, 1863), 37.

[44]Johnston, *Confederate Military History*, 145; Collins, *History of Kentucky*, II, 115, 116.

[45]Fee to Jocelyn, September 16, 1862, AMA, 110924; Burnam to Rollins, October 1, 1862 (from Galt House in Louisville), in EKU Archives.

[46]Mary B. Clay, "Biography of Cassius M. Clay: Written by His Daughter," *Filson Club History Quarterly*, XLVI (July, 1972), 286; *Military History of Kentucky*, 185.

[47]*In Memoriam*, 16; Curtis F. Burnam, "Reminiscences no. 4" (May 3, 1906), clipping from the *Climax*, in Curtis F. Burnam's scrapbook, Townsend Room, Crabbe Library, EKU.

[48]*War of the Rebellion*, 933; Bruce Catton, *Terrible Swift Sword* (New York, 1963), 389-90; Edison H. Thomas, *John Hunt Morgan and His Raiders* (Lexington, 1975), 53; Richard G. Stone, *Kentucky Fighting Men, 1861-1945* (Lexington, 1982), 24; *Rebellion Record*, 423; Basil W. Duke, *A History of Morgan's Cavalry* (Bloomington, Indiana, 1960), 232; *War of the Rebellion*, 933.

[49]*Rebellion Record*, 422.

[50]Chenault & Dorris, *Old Cane Springs*, 106-09; also see pp. 198-200; Duke, *History of Morgan's Raiders*, 327; *War of the Rebellion*, 932.

[51]Duke, *History of Morgan's Raiders*, 237, 238.

[52]Miller, *History and Genealogies*, 320, 443, 525.

[53]Chenault & Dorris, *Old Cane Springs*, 199; Duke, *History of Morgan's Raiders*, 235.

[54]Chenault & Dorris, *Old Cane Springs*, 231-40; Duke, *History of Morgan's Raiders*, 307.

[55]Chenault & Dorris, *Old Cane Springs*, 232-34; Miller, *History and Genealogies*, 206, 299, 314-15, 440, 451; Duke, *History of Morgan's Raiders*, 314, 315, 421, 422.

[56]Chenault & Dorris, *Old Cane Springs*, 237-42; Miller, *History and Genealogies* 451, 493, 496, 623.

[57]Chenault & Dorris, *Old Cane Springs*, 236; Miller, *History and Genealogies*, 491-93.

[58]Collins, *History of Kentucky*, I, 120; William Elsey Connelley & E. M. Coulter, *History of Kentucky* (Chicago, 1922), II, 892, 893.

[59]Lucia F. Burnam, *What I Remember*, 18, 19.

[60]Ibid.

[61]Collins, *History of Kentucky*, I, 127; Webb, *Kentucky in Reconstruction*, 8; Chenault & Dorris, *Old Cane Springs*, 121-23.

[62]Court Order Book M, 471, 472, 517, 518, 560, 563, 565, 584; Book N, 7.

[63]Fee to AMA, December 23, 1863, AMA, 111444. Sometime between January 13 and March 12, General Ulysses S. Grant came through Madison county, staying the night at Merrit Jones' house at Big Hill. Tipton Papers 6:67.

[64]Letter from Fee dated February 15, 1864, in *American Missionary*, VIII (April, 1864), 94.

[65]Fee to Jocelyn, March 29, 1864, AMA, 43990; Fee to Jocelyn, April 28, 1864, AMA, 43995; Fee, *Autobiography*, 173.

[66]Fee to Jocelyn, May 11, 1864, AMA, 43996; Fee to Jocelyn June 1, 1864, AMA, 43999.

[67]Collins, *History of Kentucky*, I, 134, 138.

[68]Fee to Jocelyn, June 4, 1864, AMA, 44000; Fee to Jocelyn, June 6, 1864, AMA, 44002; Coleman, "Lexington Slave," 22; Clark, *History of Kentucky*, 468-69. For a complete account of Fee's Camp Nelson experiences see chapters 20, 21 in MS. of *The Day of Small Things*; Webb, *Kentucky in Reconstruction*, 8; Miller, *History and Genealogies*, 130.

[69]Collins, *History of Kentucky*, I, 153.

[70]Webb, *Reconstruction in Kentucky*, 16; Court Order Book N, 18, 19, 105, 135.

[71]Rogers to Whipple & Strieby, April 18, 1865, AMA, 112381.

CHAPTER 11

[1]Elizabeth Rogers, "Full Forty Years," 30; Samuel Hanson's account of early Berea, xerox in BCA of TS in Kentucky Historical Society (original in possession of J. H. Metcalf, Paris, Ky.); Rogers, *Birth*, 93, 94.

[2]Fee to Whiting, January 6, 1866, AMA, 44290; Rogers, *Birth*, 89; Fee, *Berea*, 51; Fee, "The Induction of Colored Pupils into Berea College," August 2, 1900, MS, BCA; Ellen Wheeler to Frost, March 26, 1912, BCA. Green Clay and Cabell Chenault had taught their slaves reading, writing, and arithmetic. Jonathan T. Dorris & Maud Weaver Dorris, *Glimpses of Historic Madison County, Kentucky* (Nashville, 1955), 91.

[3]Ira V. Brown, "Lyman Abbott and Freedmen's Aid 1865-1869," *The Journal of Southern History*, XV, 34.

[4]Fee to Whipple, March 6, 1866, AMA, 44318; Wheeler to Whipple, November 22, 1866, AMA, 44376; Report of W. W. Wheeler to Berea Board of Trustees, March 31, 1866, BCA.

[5]Ellen Wheeler to Frost, March 26, 1912, BCA.

[6]UCMB.

[7]His children—Laura, Stephen, Bonapart, Miles, Caroline, and Dovie—are named in a list of his heirs (dated April 17, 1872) in Madison County Deed Book 20, 541. The Dudleys then resided on a 3 1/8 acre plot on Brushy Fork of Silver Creek which Oliver Dudley had bought from John G. Hanson.

[8]*American Missionary*, XV (May, 1871), 113; Edward Henry Fairchild, *Berea College, Kentucky: An Interesting History* (Cincinnati, 1883), 74.

[9]Fee to Whiting, April 11, 1866, AMA, 44330; Fee to Whiting, May 2, 1866, AMA, 44335; Rogers to Whiting, May 8, 1866, AMA, 44337; Berea Literary Institute Leaflet, May 30, 1866, AMA, 44340; Wheeler to Whipple, November 22, 1866, AMA, 44376.

[10]*Berea Alumnus*, IV (June, 1934), 19; *Report of the Adjutant General of the State of Kentucky*(Frankfort, 1867), II, 157.

[11]Burleigh to Edwin Fee, December, 1924, BCA; Angus Augustus Burleigh, *John G. Fee: Founder of Berea College*, undated pamphlet, 10, 11; Angus Burleigh Student File, BCA; Angus Burleigh article, *Berea Citizen*, September 25, 1930; Wheeler to Whipple, November 22, 1866, AMA, 44376.

[12]Rogers, *Birth*, 94, 96, 97.

[13]Elizabeth Rogers, "Full Forty Years," 32.

[14]Rogers, *Birth*, 99.

[15]Fee to Whipple, August 7, 1866, AMA, 44349.

[16]AMA, 44349; Reverend Charles Avery of Pittsburgh, Pennsylvania, made a bequest of $150,000 to the American Missionary Association in 1858—"as a perpetual fund for promoting the education and elevation of the colored people of the United States of America and the British provinces of Canada." *American Missionary*, II (March, 1858), 58.

[17]Fee to Strieby, (no date) AMA, 44357-44361.

[18]Richardson, *Memoirs*, 13, 28; Rogers' account book, 1857-1868. In his old age Candee recalled the following Jackson county families who were "radical abolitionists": Nichols, Robinson, Faubus, Drew, Griffin, Stephens, Morris, Saunders, Reese, Blanton, Harrison, Cox, Fowler, Logston, Lainhart, Murphy, Williams, Jones. Eight of these families had children who attended Berea by 1870. George Candee, "Reminiscences," *Berea Citizen*, October 16, 1913.

[19]Rogers' account book, 1858-1868; Burdette Bible (xeroxed copy of family record) in Burdette File: KHS; Hiram K. Richardson obit., *Berea Citizen*, July 22, 1948; Ryan Richardson obit., *Berea Citizen*, June 16, 1949; Richardson, *Memoirs*, 11, 25, 28.

[20]William H. Robe obit., *Berea Citizen*, May 18, 1905; Nelson W. Evans & Emmons B. Stiver, *A History of Adams County, Ohio* (West Union, Ohio, 1900), 849.

[21]Sampson Gentry Civil War Pension File, SC479-383, National Archives; Richardson, *Memoirs*, 15.

[22]C. C. Vaughn to AMA, February 16, 1869, AMA, 44582; Philip C. Kimball, "Freedom's Harvest: Freedmen's Schools in Kentucky after the Civil War," *Filson Club History Quarterly*, LIV (July, 1980), 282; *American Missionary*, XIV (May, 1870), 127; Howard School Reports, February, March, April, 1867, AMA, 44425, 44435, 44447, 44458. Apparently, the Freedmen's School in Richmond closed after three months; it is not mentioned in the reports after April 1867.

[23]Madison County Will Book 3, 171, 436.

[24]*American Missionary*, XV (September, 1871), 202; *American Missionary*, XII (August, 1868), 172. In 1860 Madison County had a population of 6,118 slaves, 980 of whom were mulattoes (16 percent). The Slave Census listed 881 slaveholders—357 of whom owned sets of slaves including at least one mulatto (but sometimes as many as ten): about 40 percent of slave sets were "mixed" (so that partly white slaves were very widespread without being particularly numerous). But of 110 elite slaveholders in Madison County (those owning 15 slaves or more), 70 owned at least one mulatto (most owned many more, of course; one of the exile committee, Robert Rodes Stone, for example, owned 16 mulattoes, out of a total of 28 slaves). The large-scale slaveholders, the wealthy and prosperous, were much more apt to have mulattoes among their slaves then were their poorer neighbors. Whether or not the half-white slaves of aristrocratic masters were also their children is, of course, another (and usually unanswerable) question.

Many slaveholders in Madison County owned only a few slaves, in some cases only one. On the 1850 and 1860 censuses it is clear that a great many sets of slaves could not have contained any married people living together: a single slave of one household might have a mate at another. Many households owned sets of slaves consisting of, say, two women and one little boy, or one old woman and a teenage girl—only large-scale slaveholders owned enough slaves that "normal" marital relations might be established by most people within the set. A surprising number of slaves in Madison County probably had to find sexual partners away from home. One of the great problems of freedom was the apparent necessity of "normalizing" the family relationships which slavery had imposed on its victims.

[25]Jack Burnam obit., *Berea Citizen*, January 31, 1907; Madison County Deed Book 35, 191.

[26]*Madison County Ministers' Returns*, 24, 25.

[27]Tipton Papers, 3:32 (newspaper clipping).

[28]Lucia F. Burnam, *What I Remember*, 10-12; *Madison County Slave Census 1860*; Dorris, *Glimpses*, 167.

[29]Court Order Book N, 267, 356, 411; Book O, 98, 234.

[30]*Madison County Ministers' Returns (1866-1882)*, 26, 27; *Minutes of the Trustees of Berea College*, July 2, 1872, I, 81; "Historic Black Memphians," a pamphlet for the exhibit of that name by the Memphis Pink Palace Museum Foundation, in BCA; Julia Hooks Gordon, "Family Memories of Julia A. Britton Hooks," MS (dated February 28, 1980) in possession of Selma Lewis of Memphis; Ernest Dodge to Frost, April 11, 1925, BCA.

[31]*American Missionary*, X (1866), 18; Howard, *Black Liberation*, 94; Fee, *Autobiography*, 182-183; Madison County Deed Book 22, 85, 145; Madison County Deed Book 19, 554; Madison County Deed Book 21, 175; Madison County Deed Book 24, 279; Madison

County Deed Book 16, 176, 193; Madison County Deed Book 18, 487, and Book 17, 237; *Map of Madison County, Kentucky* (D. G. Berry & Co., 1876), in the Townsend Room, Crabbe Library, EKU; map of Berea (c. 1880), badly worn, but still quite legible, in Special Collections, Hutchins Library, Berea College.

[32]Fee to Strieby, November 30, 1866, AMA, 44378.

[33]Rogers, *Birth*, 114; *American Missionary*, X (November, 1865), 247.

[34]Fairchild, *Interesting History*, 74, 75, 115; H. R. Chittenden to secretary of AMA, May 22, 1871, AMA, 44802.

[35]Candee to E. H. Dodge, August 10, 1903, BCA.

[36]Rogers, *Birth*, 115; James M. McPherson, *The Abolitionist Legacy* (Princeton, 1975), 174 (Affidavit by W. W. Wheeler in James Monroe Papers in Oberlin College Library).

[37]Elizabeth Rogers, "Full Forty Years," 31; Raphael Rogers to Frost March 11, 1904, BCA.

[38]Teacher's Reports (Rogers, Berea, March, 1868), Alvord, "Sixth Report," quoted in Philip C. Kimball, "Freedom's Harvest: Freedmen's Schools in Kentucky After the Civil War," *Filson Club History Quarterly*, LIV (July, 1980), 278; Alvord, "Report," (January 1, 1869), 43-49, quoted in Henry Lee Swint, *The Northern Teacher* (New York, 1967); Alvord, "Report," (January 1, 1869), 3-4, quoted in Swint, 130.

[39]Howard, *Black Liberation*, 105.

[40]Tipton Papers, 1:414.

[41]*American Missionary*, XV (January, 1871), 2.

[42]Rogers, *Birth*, 128, 130.

[43]*Minutes of Berea Temperance Society*; Court Order Book N, 329.

[44]Tipton Papers, 1:176.

[45]For example, E. H. Fairchild, selling a lot in Berea to Arthur Hanson (October 6, 1877), specified that no liquor should ever be made or sold there, else the property would revert to the seller or his heirs. Other examples, earlier and later, are not uncommon. Madison County Deed Book 23, 376.

[46]*American Missionary* XII (March, 1868), 55-57.

[47]*American Missionary*, XIII (August, 1869), 172. On the basis of Runkle's report the Freedman's Bureau gave the college $18,000 for the building of Howard Hall. Individual donors were frequently impressed with what they saw or heard of early Berea.

[48]Tipton Papers, 8:49.

[49]Tipton Papers, 8:40; Webb, *Kentucky in Reconstruction*, 24; George Candee, "Reminiscences," *Berea Citizen*, August 28, 1913.

[50]Tipton Papers, 1:22.

[51]Clay, *Memoirs*, 532, 533, 535, 536; *Kentucky Register*, August 7, 1874; July 30, 1875.

[52]Tipton Papers, 3:32 (*New York Herald*, December 16, 1878).

[53]The John Burnam who was killed September 20, 1877, was the son of John Burnam, Sr., one of Berea College's first trustees. In a later incident, April 21, 1878, James Burnam, nephew of the murdered John, was shot and killed by W. H. Moody at Bobtown near Kingston. (Tipton Papers, 3:32.)

[54]Burnam to Rollins, November 21, 1878, in EKU Archives.

CHAPTER 12

[1]Dorris, *Glimpses*, 66; John L. Andriot, ed., *Population Abstract of the United States* (McLean, Va., 1980), 310, 316; Joseph C. Kennedy, *Population of the United States in 1860*, I (Washington, 1864), 176-77; *Compendium of the Eleventh Census, 1890, Part I: Population* (Washington, 1892), 549.

[2]*Madison County Census, 1860* (Returns for Western Subdivision No. 2); *Compendium of the Eleventh Census, 1890*, 488; J. D. DeBow, *Statistical View of the United States: A Compendium of the Seventh Census [1850]* (Washington, 1854), 240-47.

[3]Tipton Papers, 10: 136, 138, 143.

[4]Berea City Council Minute Book 1, 1, 46.

[5]Ibid., 1, 2, 101, 144, 145.

[6]Tipton Papers, 10: 99, 102, 115, 117, 122, 126, 140, 143; Court Order Book K (1850-1855), 86, 198, 199, 213, 231, 232, 257, 429, 432; Book L (1855-1859), 287.

[7]Tipton Papers, 10: 404, 404a, 125, 145; Collins, *History of Kentucky*, I, 69; C. E. Woods to J. T. Dorris, August 30, 1936. Wallace Family Papers, EKU Archives.

[8]Tipton Papers, 10: 99, 123, 151; Berea Council Minutes Book 1, 142; Court Order Book M (1859-64), 564.

[9]DeBow, *Statistical View*, 240-47; *Census Reports, Volume V: Twelfth Census of the United States Taken in the Year 1900: AGRICULTURE*, Part 1 (Washington, 1902), 86, 87.

[10]DeBow, *Statistical View*, 240-47; Kennedy, 1860, Vol. II (Agriculture), 64, 65; *Compendium of the Tenth Census* (June 1, 1880), Part I (Washington, 1883), 776-77; *Agriculture 1900*, 645; Tipton Papers, 1: 22; Collins, *History of Kentucky*, II, 269.

[11]Kennedy, *1860*, II, 62-65; Francis A. Walker, *The Statistics of the Wealth and Industry of the United States [1870]* (Washington, 1872), 162-65, 352.

[12]*Agriculture 1900*, 86, 87, 279, 360.

[13]Fred Engle, "Madison's Heritage: Madison's Oldest Industry is Pottery," xeroxed clippings from *Richmond Register* in Townsend Room, Crabbe Library, EKU.

[14]Tipton Papers, 10:118, 138.

[15]Dorris, *Glimpses*, 55-58; Tipton Papers, 10: 99, 100; Court Order Book K, 400; Book N (1864-69), 289.

[16]Tipton Papers, 10: 97, 98, 101, 103, 104, 114, 118, 123, 141; Court Order Book I (1849-50), 444; Book K, 108; Book L, 250, 259, 403, 431; Book M, 91, 193, 299; Book N, 16, 468; Book O (1869-73), 98.

[17]Tipton Papers, 10: 112, 122, 126, 143, 144, 146, 148, 152; Dorris, *Glimpses*, 61; Berea Council Minutes Book 1, 92, 94; *Richmond Climax*, August 9, 1899 and September 6. I am indebted to Robert Grise for details concerning Richmond's electric company.

[18]Engle, "Madison's Heritage: Madison's National Bank," clippings from *Richmond Register* in Townsend Room, Crabbe Library. EKU; Tipton Papers, 10: 106, 114, 141, 149; "State Bank and Trust Company: 1875-1975," xerox provided by James J. Shannon, Jr. of Richmond.

[19]Dorris, *Glimpses*, 72, 73, 75.

[20]Tipton Papers, 5: 3; 10: 138, 104, 105; Dorris, *Glimpses*, 303.

[21]Kennedy, 1860, Vol. 4 (Religion), 398-400; *Report on the Statistics of Churches in the United States at the Eleventh Census (1890)* (Washington, 1894), 64, 162, 173, 203, 239, 283, 383, 348, 511, 546, 585, 638, 685, 712.

[22]Dorris, *Glimpses*, 112-14; Tipton Papers, 10: 133.

[23]Dorris, *Glimpses*, 115; Tipton Papers, 1: 426; 10: 116.

[24]Dorris, *Glimpses*, 116, 119, 120; Tipton Papers, 10: 98, 99, 105, 118.

[25]Dorris, *Glimpses*, 121, 122.

[26]Ibid., 84, 85.

[27]Ibid., 86.

[28]Ibid., 86, 87.

[29]Ibid., 88, 89, 91.

[30]Tipton Papers, 10: 126, 144.

[31]Dorris, *Glimpses*, 105, 106.

[32]Sarah Fee's Will in Bracken County Will Book O, 251.

[33]Burnam to Rollins, April 18, 1873, in EKU Archives.

[34]Jonathan T. Dorris, "Central University, Richmond, Kentucky," *Register*, XXXII (April, 1934), 107, 116, 117, 120-23.

[35]Tipton Papers, 6: 114; Dorris, *Glimpses*, 106, 107.

[36]Dorris, *Glimpses*, 107; *Richmond Climax*, January 25, 1899, 1.

[37]Tipton Papers, 1: 118; 10: 109, 115, 116, 117, 123, 127, 140, 142, 152; Court Order Book S (1880-82), 170, 171.

[38]Tipton Papers, 10: 115-18.

[39]Ibid., 123, 130, 138, 140, 143.

[40]Ibid., 116, 123, 126, 127, 135.

[41]Ibid., 124, 149.

[42]Dorris, *Glimpses*, 177.

[43]Chenault & Dorris, *Old Cane Springs*, 166, 237; Miller, *History and Genealogies*, 98, 298, 343, 344, 444, 493, 525, 537-39.

[44]C. E. Woods to Colonel Callahan, September 21, 1937, Wallace Family Papers in EKU Archives. Clarence E. Woods, mayor of Richmond, was apparently no admirer of James B. McCreary, whom he described as "a whole Oligarchy in one person." He also cites with satisfaction one John Rhea, who said, "McCreary is all high heels, hair dye and hypocrisy." (Woods to Dorris August 30, 1936, Wallace Family Papers in EKU Archives.)
[45]Tipton Papers, 3: 107.
[46]Census of Population, 1900, Kentucky, Vol. 52, Microfilm, Reel #152 (Washington, 1934), [Richmond], 1-48.
[47]Ibid., [Berea] 155-63.
[48]James B. McCreary to Lucia F. Burnam, March 24, 1909, quoted in In Memoriam, 48.
[49]Madison County Deed Book W, 393; Madison County Tax List 1854, 8, in KHS; Curtis F. Burnam, "Family History," in Townsend Room; Curtis F. Burnam obit., Berea Citizen, March 25, 1909.
[50]In Memoriam, 6, 8, 11, 14, 24.
[51]Ibid., 11, 12, 15; Hambleton Tapp, "Robert J. Breckenridge and the Year 1849," Filson Club History Quarterly, XII (July, 1938), 138, 142; Curtis F. Burnam, "Memorandum of my Political Career," in C. F. Burnam's scrapbook in Townsend Room, Crabbe Library, EKU; Burnam to Rollins, August 9, 1855, in EKU Archives.
[52]In Memoriam, 16.
[53]Chenault & Dorris, Old Cane Springs, 111, 199, 211.
[54]In Memoriam, 17; Burnam's scrapbook.
[55]Burnam's scrapbook.
[56]Tipton Papers, 1: 230; In Memoriam, 29;
[57]In Memoriam, 22; Tipton Papers, 5: 1; 6: 8; Chenault & Dorris, Old Cane Springs, 205.
[58]Tipton Papers, 3: 57; 4: 374; Dorris, "Central University," 102, 120-23; Dorris, Glimpses, 105; Fred A. Engle, Jr., "Central University of Richmond, Kentucky," Register, LXVI (July, 1968), 292; Kentucky Register, August 7, 1874.
[59]Berea College Trustees' Minutes, I, 285-88; II, 19, 46; Thompson Burnam obit., Berea Citizen, July 26, 1933; In Memoriam, 29. A. Rollins Burnam's services to Berea College in the Day Law defense are documented in the Trustees' Minutes (II, 46; III, 106); the Burnam connection with EKU is commemorated in Burnam Hall, named after this same man. A. Rollins Burnam followed in his father's footsteps, practicing law with Curtis F. until his (Rollins') appointment as collector of internal revenue in the 1890s. In 1896 he was elected to the Court of Appeals of Kentucky by the Republicans, serving for eight years, the last two as chief justice. He was a member of the state senate in 1907. Frequently representing his party in both state and national conventions (like his father), he also (like his father) served his home county in many local capacities: for example, director and president of the Madison National Bank and then of the Southern National Bank, both of Richmond. Dorris, Glimpses, 170.
[60]In Memoriam, 31, 34, 35, 37, 131; Samuel F. Miller (1816-1890), "regarded as the greatest son of Madison County," a native of Richmond, left Madison County when the constitution of 1849 made slavery stronger in the state than it had ever been before. Miller's bitter opposition to slavery led to his decision to move to the free state of Iowa, where he helped organize the Republican party. In 1862 Lincoln appointed Miller associate justice of the United States Supreme Court, and he served in that capacity until his death. Dorris, Glimpses, 177, 178.
[61]Cassius M. Clay, "Oration at Berea College on the Annexation of Alaska," October 16, 1895, in Dorris Collection, Townsend Room, Crabbe Library, EKU.
[62]John G. Fee, "A Word to the Convocation," undated MS., BCA; Fee's Titus letter, June 12, 1900, xerox in BCA (original in possession of Titus family).
[63]In Memoriam, 21; Berea College Trustees' Minutes, II, 45.
[64]"C. F. Burnam and Berea College," MS., in Townsend Room, Crabbe Library, EKU.
[65]Robert N. Grise, "Madison's Heritage: Early Automobile Days," xeroxed clipping from Richmond Register in Townsend Room.

CHAPTER 13

[1]Steven A. Channing, *Kentucky: A Bicentennial History* (New York, 1977), 157, 163. Officially, a century should begin in the uneven year, in this case 1901, but the public normally thinks of the even year as the beginning.

[2] *Tenth Census of the United States, 1880, Population*, 62, 393; *Census Reports, 1900, Population*, I, Part I, 181, 541; *Kentucky Register*, October 27, 1916.

[3]R. L. Marionneaux, *Geography of Madison County, Ky.* (Richmond, 1982), 5.

[4]Interview with R. L. Marionneaux, October 27, 1983, Oral History Collection, University Archives, Eastern Kentucky University [all interviews unless otherwise noted are from this collection]; Interview with James S. Chenault, January 31, 1984.

[5]*Tenth Census*, 56, 116, 155, 278-80.

[6]Ibid.

[7]Channing, *Kentucky*, 142, 158-59; *Census Reports, 1900*, 86-87, 554; Personal interview with Mr. and Mrs. Alvin D. Miller, November 29, 1982.

[8]Russell I. Todd, *This is Boone Country* (Louisville, 1968), 93-94.

[9]Mary Kate Deatherage, "Madison County Chronology and Bibliography" (M.A. thesis, Eastern Kentucky State Teachers College, 1944), 70.

[10]Deatherage, "Madison County," 69-71; Green Clay, "Madison County Chronicles." Eastern Kentucky University Library, 116.

[11]Todd, *Boone Country*, 72-74; *Madison County Newsweek*, April 17, 1974.

[12]*Madison County Newsweek*, January 14, 1971.

[13]*Madison County Newsweek*, January 14, 1971, July 3, 1974.

[14]Chenault Interview; Supplement to the *Richmond Climax*, May 24, 1905; *Madison County Newsweek*, July 2, 1970.

[15]*Richmond Register*, August 30, 1983.

[16]*Richmond Climax*, January 18, 1899, October 17, 1900, January 30, 1901, January 28, 1903, May 11, 1904; Supplement to the *Richmond Climax*, May 24, 1905.

[17]Supplement to the *Richmond Climax*, May 24, 1905; *Madison County Newsweek*, November 15, 1975.

[18]*Richmond Climax*, January 9, 1901; *Madison County Newsweek*, July 27, 1974.

[19]*Richmond Climax*, August 1 and 25, 1900, July 23, 1902; Interview with Virginia Skinner Turner, May 3, 1984.

[20]*Richmond Climax*, May 23, October 10, 1900; July 26, 1911.

[21]*Richmond Climax*, May 30, 1900, February 27, July 30, 1901; *Madison County Newsweek*, November 15, 1975; *Courier-Journal*, May 6, 1984.

[22]*Richmond Climax*, October 3, 1900; January 16, 1901; November 5, 1902; September 9, 1903; April 20, 1904; November 20, 1907; April 24, 1912.

[23]*Richmond Climax*, August 7, 1901; Todd, *Boone Country*, 81; Dorris and Dorris, *Glimpses*, 111-12.

[24]*Richmond Register*, March 7, 1983.

[25]*Richmond Climax*, March 21, 1900; *Richmond Pantagraph*, July 27, 1917; *Annals of the First Presbyterian Church, Richmond, Kentucky, 1827-1927*, 26-27.

[26]Supplement to the *Richmond Climax*, May 24, 1905.

[27]*Richmond Climax*, November 1, 1905; Interview with H. E. Richardson, October 25, 1983; Interview with William G. Adams and Woodard Adams, October 21, 1983.

[28]*Richmond Climax*, August 8, 1900; March 6, 1901; May 21, 1902; March 9, 1904.

[29]Elizabeth S. Peck and Emily Ann Smith, *Berea's First 125 Years, 1855-1980* (Lexington, 1982), 172-78; Interview with Clifford Kerby, February 13, 1984; *Berea Citizen*, June 24, 1909.

[30]Channing, *Kentucky*, 153-54.

[31]*Richmond Climax*, July 1 and 8, 1896; *Semi-Weekly Pantagraph*, December 20, 1898.

[32]*Richmond Climax*, November 4, 1896, January 13, 1897; Channing, *Kentucky*, 162-63.

[33]*Richmond Climax*, June 21, August 9, September 12, October 4, 18, 1899.

[34]*Richmond Climax*, November 15, December 6, 1899.

[35]*Richmond Climax*, January 31, February 14, 21, 1900.

[36]*Semi-Weekly Register*, February, 1900; *Richmond Climax*, May 30, August 15, 1900.

[37]*Lexington Morning Herald*, September 2, 1900; *Courier-Journal*, September 2, 1900; *Richmond Climax*, September 5, 1900.

[38]Channing, *Kentucky*, 153-54.

[39]*Richmond Climax*, November 7, 1900.

[40]For the Progressive Era see Arthur S. Link, *American Epoch, I* (New York, 1963) and Dewey W. Grantham, *Southern Progressivism* (Knoxville, 1983). For Kentucky see William E. Ellis, "Robert Worth Bingham and Louisville Progressivism, 1905-1910," *The Filson Club History Quarterly*, LIV (April, 1980), 169-95.

[41]*Richmond Climax*, June 12, July 16, 1902.

[42]*Charter, By Laws, and Ordinances of Richmond, Kentucky* (Richmond, 1901), 33-35, 40-64.

[43]*Richmond Climax*, April 3 and 17, May 29, November 6, 1901; August 17, 1904; January 4, 1911.

[44]*Richmond Climax*, January 3, 1900; March 6, August 28, 1901; April 1, 1903; September 13, 1905.

[45]*Richmond Climax*, December 28, 1904; May 3, November 15, 1905.

[46]*Richmond Climax*, November 29, 1905.

[47]*Richmond Climax*, January 31, February 7, March 14, 1906.

[48]*Richmond Climax*, March 23, 1904, August 23, 1905.

[49]*Courier-Journal*, March 13, May 15, 1907; *Richmond Climax*, August 25, September 8, 1909.

[50]*Richmond Climax*, January 10, 1906.

[51]*Richmond Climax*, January 31, 1906; November 20, 1907; July 7, 21, 1909; January 12, 1910.

[52]*Richmond Climax*, November 10, 1909.

[53]Channing, *Kentucky*, 175.

[54]*Courier-Journal*, June 19, 1906; *Richmond Daily Register*, June 1, 1946; Clay, "Madison County Chronicles," 142.

[55]*Richmond Climax*, February 28, 1900, September 13, 1905, February 2, 1910.

[56]*Richmond Climax*, June 12, November 13, 1901; July 29, 1903; March 20, April 20, 1909.

[57]*Richmond Climax*, May 11, 1910, November 8, 1911, January 21, 1912; Thomas D. Clark, *Kentucky: Land of Contrast* (New York, 1968), 154; Harry M. Caudill, *Theirs Be the Power: The Moguls of Eastern Kentucky* (Urbana, 1983), 79; Nicholas Burckel, "From Beckham to McCreary: The Progressive Record of Kentucky Governors," *Register of the Kentucky Historical Society*, LXXVI (October, 1978), 285-306; Interview with Russell I. Todd, February 21, 1984; Clarence E. Woods to J. T. Dorris, August 30, 1936, W. W. Wallace Papers, University Archives, Eastern Kentucky University; John Wilson Townsend, *"In Kentucky" and Its Author "Jim" Mulligan* (Lexington, 1935), 9.

[58]"Biographical Sketch," Lilly Family Collection, University Archives, Eastern Kentucky University, 11-IV; *Kentucky Register*, October 27, 1916; *Richmond Climax*, January 10, March 21, 1900, January 19, 1910; *Richmond Daily Register*, June 6, 1919; *Madison County Newsweek*, September 27, 1972; Channing, *Kentucky*, 156.

[59]*Richmond Climax*, May 9, October 17, 1900; May 20, 1903; January 20, July 27, November 16, 1904; March 8, 1905.

[60]Elizabeth Peck and Emily Ann Smith, *Berea's First 125 Years* (Lexington, 1982), 42-54.

[61]Ibid.

[62]*Richmond Climax*, May 27, 1903, February 10, 17, 24, March 16, 1904; Peck, *Berea's First*, 54-57; Supreme Court of United States, October Term, November 9, 1908.

[63]*Climax-Madisonian*, January 20, 1915; *Fourteenth Census of the United States, 1920, Population*, II, 32, 88, 1065, 1242, 1342.

[64]*Richmond Climax*, April 4, May 9, July 4, 1900.

[65]Dorris and Dorris, *Glimpses*, 162; *Richmond Daily Register*, January 10, July 10, 1920, May 17, 1921, November 20, 1923, September 17, 1924.

[66]Henry Allen Laine, *Foot Prints* (Richmond, 1914), 11, 30.

[67]Channing, *Kentucky*, 155-56.

[68]*Richmond Climax*, June 4, 1902, May 11, 1904, June 16, July 7, 1909; Ruth Allene Hammons, "History of the Richmond City Schools," (M.A. thesis, Eastern Kentucky State Teachers College, 1949), 21-28.

[69]Robert E. Little, "History of Education in Madison County Kentucky (M. A. thesis, University of Kentucky, 1933), 301-02, 336-39; *Richmond Climax*, October 6, 1909, February 9, 1910, April 19, 1911, May 22, 1912, May 27, 1914.

[70]Todd, *Boone Country*, 83; Little, "History of Education," 355, 368-70; *Richmond Climax*, May 30, 1900; *Richmond Climax*, January 7, 1902, September 22, 1909; *Madisonian*, June 9, 1914.

[71]Little, "History of Education," 345-54, 373-79; *Richmond Climax*, August 8, 1900, August 19, 1905, August 25, 1909.

[72]*Richmond Climax*, January 4, 1911; "Madison County School Improvement League," pamphlet, Laura Clay Papers, University of Kentucky Library.

[73]*Richmond Climax*, October 4, 18, 1911; Todd Interview; Interview with Smith Park, November 15, 1983; Interview with Nannie S. Lackey, October 7, 1983.

[74]Peck, *Berea's First*, 82-139; Dorris and Dorris, *Glimpses*, 103-06.

[75]*Courier-Journal*, April 7, 11, 21, and 24, May 14, 1901.

[76]*Courier Journal*, June 6 and 19, August 24, 1901.

[77]*Courier-Journal*, June 30, 1906.

[78]*Richmond Climax*, April 25, 1906, June 23, 1909, April 13, 1910, June 23, 1909; *Richmond Daily Register*, January 16, 1926; Dorris and Dorris, *Glimpses*, 108-10.

[79]Little, "History of Education." 384; *Courier-Journal*, June 27, 1909.

[80]*Richmond Climax*, June 5, 1912, June 3, 1914; *Climax-Madisonian*, July 14, 1915; *Richmond Daily Register*, July 3, 1919; Park Interview; Interview with John Y. Brown, Sr., November 19, 1979.

[81]*Richmond Climax*, August 9, 1899, February 27, 1901, October 1, 1902; *Climax-Madisonian*, January 20, 1915; Richardson Interview.

[82]*Richmond Climax*, February 11, 1903; *Climax-Madisonian*, October 28, 1914; *Madison County Newsweek*, May 1, 1974.

[83]"Madison County Farm Statistics, 1910-1960," Enclosure from John Wilson; *Census Reports, 1900*, V, 36, 86-87, 554; *Fourteenth Census of the United States, 1920*, II, 78-79.

[84]Park Interview; *Richmond Daily Register*, July 31, 1919; *Richmond Register*, May 5, 1984.

[85]See note 84.

[86]*Richmond Climax*, April 22, 1903; October 4, 1905; May 18, 1910; January 11, 1911.

[87]*Richmond Daily Register*, January 1 and 16, February 22, August 9, December 5, 1919; *Madison County Newsweek*, February 27, 1974.

[88]*Courier-Journal*, June 20, 1901, June 5, July 16 and 20, 1902; *Richmond Climax*, September 27, 1905.

[89]*Richmond Climax*, January 12, March 30, September 14, 1910; *Madison County Newsweek*, March 20, 1974.

[90]*Richmond Daily Register*, March 26, July 4 and 8, 1919.

[91]*Richmond Climax*, August 12, 1914; *Climax-Madisonian*, January 6, May 12, 1915; *Kentucky Register*, April 13, 1917.

[92]*Richmond Daily Register*, January 18, November 8, 1918, January 6, March 20, June 9, 1919.

[93]*Richmond Daily Register*, November 11, 1918; Interview with Turley Noland, October 15, 1982.

[94]*Richmond Climax*, December 10, 1913; *Climax-Madisonian*, January 27, 1915; *Richmond Daily Register*, May 20, December 27, 1919.

[95]*Richmond Climax*, January 31, 1900, April 3, 1901, January 14, 1914; *Richmond Daily Register*, March 1, 1919.

[96]*Richmond Climax*, February 14, 1900, July 26, 1905; *Richmond Daily Register*, August 30, 1919; Roebuck and Hickson, *The Southern Redneck*, 26-29.

[97]Lackey Interview; Noland Interview; Park Interview; *Richmond Daily Register,* January 1, 6, 7, 8, and 13, 1919.

CHAPTER 14

[1]For an excellent exposition of this interpretation of the 1920s see Paul A. Carter, *Another Part of the Twenties* (New York, 1977) and by the same author, *The Twenties in America* (New York, 1968).

[2]*Richmond Daily Register,* July 15, 1919; July 13, November 1, 1920; March 20, 1925; April 19, May 9, 1929; April 26, June 14, 1930.

[3]*Fifteenth Census of the United States, 1930,* I, 36, 432; *Fifteenth Census of the United States, 1930, Population,* III, Part I, 918, 926, 931, 944.

[4]Interview with Robert N. Grise, October 13, 1982; Interview with Nannie S. Lackey, October 7, 1983; *Richmond Daily Register,* July 2, 1921, June 27, 1923.

[5]*Richmond Daily Register,* January 10, July 9, 1920; September 21, 1921; October 21, 1922; March 28, 1923; October 16, 1924; January 8, 1927.

[6]*Richmond Daily Register,* April 29, 1921; August 21, 1926; July 5, 1928.

[7]*Richmond Daily Register,* August 25, 1924; October 11, 1928; February 27, 1929.

[8]*Richmond Pantagraph,* April 10, 1924; *Richmond Daily Register,* September 24, 1924; Elizabeth M. Fraas, "Keen Johnson: Newpaperman and Governor," (Ph.D. dissertation, University of Kentucky, 1983), 72-74, 82.

[9]Interview with Elizabeth M. Fraas, February 21, 1984; *Richmond Daily Register,* August 7, 1925, March 2, June 28, 1926.

[10]Interview with Woodard Adams, October 21, 1983; *Richmond Daily Register,* January 22, 1925, March 7, 1929.

[11]Adams Interview; *Richmond Daily Register,* July 2, November 22, 1920, January 22, May 14, 1921, February 14, 1922, March 20 and 22, 1929.

[12]*Richmond Daily Register,* April 16, 21, 1921; February 14, September 5, 11, 1922; October 28, 1927.

[13]Adams Interview; *Richmond Daily Register,* November 12, 1920, April 6, July 7, 1921, February 15, 1922, June 7, 1923, July 17, 1926, October 11, 31, 1927.

[14]*Richmond Daily Register,* February 7, 1919; July 7, November 25, 1920; October 4, 1922; March 7, 1924; May 3, August 6, 1926; October 1, 1929; Interview with R. C. Thomas, April 19, 1984; Interview with Turley Noland, October 15, 1982.

[15]Interview with Russell I. Todd, February 21, 1984; *Richmond Daily Register,* March 27, 1919, January 27, July 5, November 20, 1920, April 9, 1921, February 28, March 28, 1923, January 3, May 17, 18, and 19, 1924, August 31, 1925, July 10, August 2, 1926, January 7, 1927, July 23, 1928, March 14, 1929, October 8, 1930.

[16]*Richmond Daily Register,* July 2, November 17, 1928.

[17]*Fifteenth Census of the United States,* II, 1138, 1234; *Fifteenth Census of the United States, 1930, Population,* III, Part I, 912.

[18]*Richmond Daily Register,* August 2, 1920; February 19, 1921; July 2, August 21, October 25, 1926.

[19]Interview with H. E. Richardson, October 25, 1983; *Richmond Daily Register,* October 1, April 14, 1921.

[20]Little, "History of Education," 327-29; Russell Todd, *This is Boone Country* (Louisville, 1968), 83; *Richmond Daily Register,* January 17, July 7, November 1, 30, August 11, 1921, July 21, 1922, July 14, 1925, February 4, 1927.

[21]Little, "History of Education 373-77.

[22]Hammons, "History of Richmond City Schools," 33, 41; *Richmond Daily Register,* September 8, December 14, 1920, March 9, May 31, July 20, 1921, August 10, 1922, June 5, December 29, 1923, January 3, 1927.

[23]*Richmond Daily Register,* November 20, 1920; July 26, 1924; January 16, 1926, October 13, 1928.

[24]*Richmond Daily Register,* July 2, 1921; August 22, 1922; June 11, 1923; July 22, 1924; June 4, 1930.

[25]*Richmond Daily Register,* November 4, 1919.

[26]*Richmond Daily Register,* July 6, November 3, 1920; November 5, 1924; November 1928.

[27]*Richmond Daily Register,* February 10, 1921; April 10, October 18, November 7, 1923; August 28, 1924; March 16, November 4, 1925; January 4, November, 1926, November 9, 1927; October 11 and 15, 1928.

[28]*Lexington Herald,* June 17, 1924; *Richmond Daily Register,* November 10, December 17, 1923, June 12, 16 and 21, 1924, January 26, October 17, 1925; G. Murray Smith to Judge Samuel M. Wilson, September 24, October 24 and 29, 1924; Wilson Papers, University of Kentucky Library.

[29]*Richmond Daily Register,* June 29, 1923; October 13, November 21, 1925.

[30]*Richmond Daily Register,* April 19, May 24, 1921, February 22, 1924, February 25 and 28, 1925, March 5, October 28, 1926, December 3, 1927, November 16, 1928; Ellen E. Forderhase, "The Pine Mountain Murder," History Day Essay, Senior Division, 1985.

[31]*Mortality Statistics,* Part I, 1927, 2; *Bulletin of the State Board of Health of Kentucky,* XI (July, 1930), 9; *Vital Statistics Rates in the United States, 1900-1940,* 150, 153, 163.

[32]*Richmond Daily Register,* August 16, October 1, November 20, December 11, 1920; March 17, July 4, 1921; October 28, November 22, 1924; September 15, 1925; October 1, 1927.

[33]For an interpretation of prohibition see Norman H. Clark, *Deliver Us From Evil* (New York, 1976); *Richmond Register,* February 25, 1984; *Richmond Daily Register,* January 17, 1920, March 1, December 28, 1921, January 25, February 16, March 3, 1922, August 25, 1925, November 8, 1926, November 2, 1929.

[34]*Richmond Daily Register,* September 20, 1919; July 2, October 1, November 26, 1920; July 8, 1923; January 6 and 7, 1924; September 14, 1925; May 28, 1926.

[35]*Richmond Daily Register,* August 4, 9, December 1, 1920; July 6, 1922; July 24, 1925, September 10, October 29, November 5 and 24, 1925; August 17, September 17, 1926; March 1, August 20 and 23, 1927.

[36]*Richmond Daily Register,* November 29, 1920; June 16, 22, April 7, 1926; October 24, 1927; January 13, 1948.

[37]Richardson Interview; Thomas Interview; Interview with J. Lester Miller, November 16, 1983; *Richmond Daily Register,* September 8, 1920, December 17, 1923, January 17, August 24, 1927.

[38]*Richmond Daily Register,* August 4, 19, 1920, December 7, 10, 11, 1920, January 3, 4, 5, 6, 1921.

[39]William E. Ellis, "Robert Worth Bingham and the Crisis of Cooperative Marketing in the Twenties," *Agricultural History,* LVI (January, 1982), 99-116.

[40]*Richmond Daily Register,* January 7, 11, 12, 14, 21, and 22, February 26, March 25, April 1, 5, June 6, 14, 15, 23, and 27, August 9, September 7, 1921.

[41]*Richmond Daily Register,* December 15, 29, 1921; January 4, 13, 14, 18, and 28, February 13, December 7, and 8, 1922, January 23, 1923, June 6, 1923.

[42]*Richmond Daily Register,* September 19 and 20, 1924; January 14, 1925, January 19, November 9, 1926; December 21, 1928; December 13, 1929.

[43]Miller Interview; *Fifteenth Census of the United States, 1930, Agriculture,* II, Part 2, 753, 771, 783, 794, 804, 862.

[44]*Richmond Daily Register,* October 25, 1929; July 10, 25, and 31, August 1, 9, and 18, September 25, October 4, November 6, 1930; January 7, July 29, 1931.

[45]*Richmond Daily Register,* December 10, 1930, January 5 and 28, February 3 and 12, December 2, 1931, February 12, 1932; Family History of Beverly Burrus.

[46]*Richmond Daily Register,* March 13, October 10, November 9, 1930, March 24, 1931, March 25, August 5, 24, 1932, Jonathan Dorris, and Maud Dorris, *Glimpses of Historic Madison County* (Nashville, 1965), 17; Interview with Fred Engle, January 23, 1984; Grise Interview.

[47]Park Interview; *Richmond Daily Register,* October 15, 1929; June 26, 1931, March 1, 2, 3, 6 and 15, June 15, October 11, 1933, April 10, 1934, May 7, 1935.

[48]*Richmond Daily Register,* November 2, December 4, 1932, April 3, 5, 6, and 7, July 14, 1933.

[49]*Richmond Daily Register,* February 24, March 6 and 17, April 14 and 15, August 31, 1931, July 6, 1932; June 16, July 11, 1933; July 16, 1938.

[50]*Richmond Daily Register*, June 11, 1934; *Sixteenth Census of the United States, 1940, Education*, II, 185-86, 188-89, 191; Hammons, "History of Richmond City Schools," 52.

[51]*Richmond Daily Register*, September 14, 1931, February 5, 1935; Interview with James C. Burnett, October 9, 1977; Interview with Robert R. Martin, November 4-December 13, 1976; Interview with Casey and Thelma Morton, October 1, 1977; Family History of Bill E. Willoughby, Jr.; *Industrial Resources, Berea, Kentucky* (Berea, Chamber of Commerce and Kentucky Department of Commerce, 1966), Appendix A.

[52]*Richmond Daily Register*, November 5, 6, 1930, March 5, April 18, 23, November 5, 1931; Fraas, "Keen Johnson," 142-45.

[53]*Richmond Daily Register*, February 25, 1924, August 30, 1930; Fraas, "Keen Johnson," 88-91, 132, 145-66; *South Western Reporter*, 2nd Series, 568-70.

[54]*Richmond Daily Register*, April 9, July 2, November 10, 1932.

[55]*Richmond Daily Register*, October 15, 1932, April 4, 8, July 1, November 9, 11, 1933, May 19, 1937; *Courier-Journal*, May 19, June 17, July 7, August 5, 7, October 5, 6, 1937, January 15, 1938.

[56]*Richmond Daily Register*, April 14, 21, 27, July 31, August 24, September 1, 2, 6, December 5 and 23, 1933, January 27, March 21, April 2, 1934; *Lexington Herald*, December 3 and 28, 1933.

[57]*Richmond Daily Register*, September 25, 1935; October 5, 16, December 8, 1936; April 12, July 9 and 31, October 2, 1937; June 15, August 11, October 7, November 29, 1938; July 26, August 2, 26, September 8, October 13, 1939, September 12, 1940; August 26, 1941.

[58]Dorris and Dorris, *Glimpses*, 236; *Richmond Daily Register*, December 1, 1932, January 27, 1934, January 31, Feburary 1, 1936, November 17, 1937; Family History of John Powell; Family History of Valerie Ison; Family History of Douglas Jackson.

[59]*Richmond Daily Register*, June 17, 20 and 27, 1930; July 16, 1931; July 6, 1933; January 9, 1934; December 27 and 28, 1935; June 17, 1936; April 30, 1937.

[60]Powell Family History; *Richmond Daily Register*, December 6, 12, 16 and 18, 1933, January 4 and 25, June 25, November 14, December 4, 1934, January 12, March 20, 1935, February 7, December 1, 3, and 4, 1936, February 5, March 9, 1937, January 15, April 14, May 10, 1938, April 4, December 14, 1939.

[61]Julian B. Roebuck and Mark Hickson, III, *The Southern Redneck: A Phenomenological Study*, (New York, 1982), 37-39; *Richmond Daily Register*, February 13, 1935, September 1, 1937, August 18, December 27, 1938; *Census of Agriculture, Kentucky, 1940*, 22, 32, 42, 52, 62, 100; *Madison County, Kentucky-Farm Statistics, 1910-1960*; Miller Interview.

[62]Interview with Mrs. R. R. Richards; Adams Interview; Lackey Interview; Todd Interview; Family History of Pamela Jane Harris Clouse; Family History of David W. Chrisman; Family History of Norma Robinson.

[63]Robinson Family History; Family History of Jason Wiggins; *Richmond Daily Register*, July 20, 1933, January 4, 1934, April 20, 1939; *One Timer*, September 26, 1934.

[64]Family History of Carol Short; Family History of Jim Oliver; Family History of Lynn Whittaker; Family History of Tamara L. French; Family History of Melody Diane Hamilton; Family History of David Bruce Fraley; Burrus Family History; Robinson Family History; Family History of Carolyn M. Asbill.

[65]Adams Interview; *Richmond Daily Register*, September 29, October 3, 6, 10, 1930, February 16 and 17, 1931, November 1, 1933, August 8, September 14, 1934, March 12 and 18, 1935, November 1, 1938, March 6, 1939; *One Timer*, October 3, 1934.

[66]Robinson Family History; Family History of Jason Wiggins.

[67]*Richmond Daily Register*, March 28, November 4, 1936.

[68]Fraas, "Keen Johnson," 94, 176-83, 199, 204-09; *Richmond Daily Register*, September 9, 1935, January 4, 1936; *Courier-Journal* January 10, 1930.

[69]Fraas, "Keen Johnson," 216-18; *Richmond Daily Register*, July (daily column), 1935, August 7, 1937, July 7, 1938, October 31, 1939.

[70]Fraas, "Keen Johnson," 236-37, 260; *Richmond Daily Register*, November 9, 1939.

[71]*Richmond Daily Register*, July 27, August 2, 1932; September 21, 1937; February 8, 1938.

[2]*Richmond Daily Register*, May 31, November 17, 1932, September 19, 20, 24, and 27, 1936, February 9, 24, and 26, May 14 and 28, August 17 and 18, October 13, 1937, June 24, September 2, 1938; Personal Interview with Tom McHone, July 4, 1984; Telephone Interview with Ivan Tribe, July 10, 1984.For an interesting reading about American murder ballads see Olive Woolley Burt, *American Murder Ballads and Their Stories* (New York: Oxford University Press, 1958) and Anne B. Cohen, *Poor Pearl, Poor Girl!* (New York: American Folklore Society, 1973).

[3]*Richmond Daily Register*, April 14, 1930, October 28, 1938, March 14, 1939; Interview with Dr. Hugh Mahaffey, November 3, 1983.

[4]Mahaffey Interview; *Richmond Daily Register*, February 24, April 14, October 30, 1933, August 30, 1934, January 10, October 5, December 30, 1935, February 27, 1936, July 17, 1938; *Vital Statistics of the United States, 1937*, Part I, 49; *Bulletin of the State Board of Health of Kentucky*, IX (June, 1937), 5, 9.

[5]*Richmond Daily Register*, September 3, 1934, October 15, 1937; *Courier-Journal*, October 15, 1937; "Madison County Sesqui-Centennial Celebration," Official Souvenir Program, Townshend Room, Eastern Kentucky University.

[6]*Richmond Daily Register*, January 13 and 17, July 10, August 13, 1934, June 19, August 21, 1936, January 25-28 and 30, 1937.

[7]*Richmond Daily Register*, July 13, 1937; February 2, March 15, April 6, May 5 and 23, June 4, December 9, 1938; March 10, May 5, September 1, 1939.

[8]*Richmond Daily Register*, March 6 and 14, April 20, 1939.

CHAPTER 15

[1]*Richmond Daily Register*, June 21, July 19, 1941; *Sixteenth Census of the United States, 1940, Population*, I, 20, 23, 38, 51.

[2]Fraas, "Keen Johnson," 258; Interview with James C. Burnam, April 25, 1984.

[3]*Richmond Daily Register*, October 7, 1944, August 23, 1945, August 17, 1946; *Lexington Herald-Leader*, September 20, 1984.

[4]*Courier-Journal*, March 2, 1938, March 13, June 6, October 29, 1939, March 9, April 10, December 5, 1940, March 5, 1941; *Richmond Daily Register*, February 2, March 29, April 29, November 6, 1940, March 27, 1943, January 1, 1944.

[5]Unger, *These United States*, II, 818; *Richmond Daily Register*, May 30, June 11 and 17, 1940.

[6]*Richmond Daily Register*, June 14, 1940, October 13, 1941.

[7]*Richmond Daily Register*, March 26, May 16, August 9, November 15, 1940, January 7 and 9, 1941.

[8]*Richmond Daily Register*, June 30, November 3, 1941.

[9]Fraas, "Keen Johnson," 294-95; *Richmond Daily Register*, November 6, 21, and 22, December 1 and 12, 1941.

[10]*Richmond Daily Register*, December 6, 1941; *Madison County Newsweek*, September 27, 1972.

[11]*Sunday Herald-Leader*, December 6, 1981; *Richmond Daily Register*, December 8, 24, 25, and 26, 1941.

[12]Interview with G. Murray Smith, Jr., November 4, 1983; Todd Interview; Park Interview; Norris Interview; Fraas, "Keen Johnson," 294-95; "Map of Property Tracts," "Blue Grass Ordnance Cemetery Records," copies in the Townsend Collection, Eastern Kentucky University Library; Interview with Helen Laine Phelps by Todd Moberly, December 2, 1984.

[13]*Courier-Journal*, January 11, 20, 1942; *Richmond Daily Register*, September 5, 1945; Norris Interview; Interview with Richard McCarty, September 29, 1984.

[14]McCarty Interview; Interview with Robert P. Blythe; Richardson Interview; October 8, 1943, November 6, 1944; Enclosure from Public Information Officer, Avon, October 12, 1982.

[15]*Richmond Daily Register*, January 12, February 20, 1943, March 20, 1944, September 25, 1945; Thomas C. Alexander, "Utah War Industry During World War II: A Human Impact Analysis," *Utah History Quarterly*, LI (January, 1983), 72-92; Richardson Interview; Burnam Interview.

[16]*Richmond Daily Register*, December 9, 1941. His name was William Clyde Creech, an airman from Cumberland.

[17]John Morton Blum, *V Was for Victory* (New York, 1976), 92-105.

[18]Ibid.

[19]*Richmond Daily Register*, January 2, 21, and 26, February 3 and 16, December 31, 1943, March 28, April 4, July 24, September 8, October 18, 1944.

[20]Blum, *V Was for Victory*, 17, 39-45; *Courier-Journal*, November 16, 1943; *Richmond Daily Register*, January 12 and 21, April 7, 1943, January 12, November 9, 1944.

[21]*Richmond Daily Register*, February 3, 1943; *Courier-Journal*, 23, 1943; Blum, *V Was for Victory*, 140-41.

[22]*Richmond Daily Register*, January 8, 18, 25, December 10, 11, 24, 25, and 26, 1941, December 23, 1942, December 15, 1944, March 31, 1945; Enclosure from John Wilson.

[23]Wilson Enclosure.

[24]Ibid.; *Richmond Daily Register*, January 26, 1943; *Richmond Register*, February 11, 1984.

[25]Wilson Enclosure.

[26]Roebuck and Hickson, *Southern Rednecks*, 61; *Richmond Daily Register*, February 22, 1941; *Courier-Journal*, November 11, 1937, May 17, June 8, September 7, 1938, April 5, 1939, June 17, 1940, February 22, March 8, 1941.

[27]*Richmond Daily Register*, April 4, 1941, February 15, 1943; Chenault Interview; *Lexington Herald-Leader*, April 19, 1984; *Richmond Register*, August 30, 1983; Peck and Smith, *Berea's First 125 Years*, 191-92; Jerome W. Hughes, *Six Berea College Presidents: Tradition and Progress* (Berea, n.d.), 41.

[28]*Richmond Daily Register*, November 4, 1943, November 8, 1944.

[29]*Courier-Journal*, May 19, June 17, July 7, August 7, October 5 and 16, 1937, January 15, 1938, May 3, 1939, July 3, 1940, March 23, April 10, June 17 and 18, July 18, August 24, September 1, October 2, 1943.

[30]*Richmond Daily Register*, January 25-30, July 21, September 21, 1944, April 6, 21, May 2, 1945; *Richmond Register*, November 4, 1983.

[31]*Richmond Daily Register*, January 20, May 9, 1940, September 10, 1941, September 6, 1945; *Madison County School News*, May 8, 1940.

[32]*Courier-Journal*, July 26, 1944; Telephone Interview with Mary Frances Richards, September 24, 1984.

[33]*Richmond Daily Register*, February 10, 1940, January 9, 1943, February 17, August 18, 1945; Blum, *V Was for Victory*, 36, 46-47.

[34]*Richmond Daily Register*, April 13, 1945.

[35]*Richmond Daily Register*, May 7, June 1, July 23, August 7 and 15, 1945, June 27, 1946.

[36]"Enclosure from Public Information Officer"; Telephone Interview with William W. Ellis, October 4, 1984; *Richmond Daily Register*, August 22, September 25, October 15-16 and 25, November 9, 1945.

[37]*Richmond Daily Register*, December 6, 1945, January 5 and 30, February 25, July 2, 1946, May 15, 1947.

[38]*Richmond Daily Register*, September 19, 1946, April 22, 1947, January 29, 1948, December 21, 1950, January 1, 1958.

[39]Peck and Smith, *Berea's First 125 Years*, 192.

[40]*Richmond Daily Register*, July 5, 1946, February 12 and 15-19, March 26, May 3, 30, June 16, October 7, 1947, January 7-8, 1948.

[41]*Richmond Daily Register*, November 8, 1945, January 2, November 6, 1946, November 5, 1947, March 16, October 30, November 3, 1948, November 10, 1949.

[42]*Courier-Journal*, September 17, 1946, July 22, November 21, 1948; *Richmond Daily Register*, September 18, 23, and 27, 1948, January 1, 1949.

[43]Fraas, "Keen Johnson," 308-11; *Richmond Daily Register*, April 17, 1947.

[44]*United States Census of Population, 1950*, I, 17:4, 17:8; II, 17:16, 17:17, 17:26.

[45]*Richmond Daily Register*, July 27, 1946, October 23, 1947, January 6, 1948, January 1, December 31, 1949.

[46]Wilson Enclosure; *United States Census of Agriculture, 1950*, 85, 113, 138.

[47]Mahaffey Interview; Todd Interview; *Richmond Daily Register*, September 26, 1944; *Courier-Journal*, January 2, 1950.

[48]*Courier-Journal*, February 6, 1947; *Richmond Daily Register*, December 31, 1949; *United States Census of Population, 1950*, II, 17-32.

[49]Jack Temple Kirby, "The Southern Exodus, 1910-1960: A Primer for Historians," *Journal of Southern History*, XLIX (November, 1983), 596-97; *Richmond Daily Register*, July 11, October 29, 1947, November 8, 1949.

[50]Unger, *These United States*, II, 865.

[51]*Richmond Daily Register*, March 1, June 22, October 13, 1950, January 1, 1951.

[52]Unger, *These United States*, II, 851-55; Vincent Terrace, *The Complete Encyclopedia of Television Programs*, I (New York, 1976), 136, 194, 373-75, 383-84, 448; II, 44.

[53]*Richmond Daily Register*, January 1, 1951, January 1, December 31, 1955, January 1, 1957.

[54]*Richmond Daily Register*, January 1, November 6, 1952, January 1, 1953, January 1, 1954, January 1, 1957, January 1, 1958, January 1, 1959, January 1, 1960.

[55]*Richmond Daily Register*, December 31, 1955.

[56]*Richmond Daily Register*, November 7, 1950, November 7, 1951, January 1, November 5, 1952, November 9, 1955, November 7, 1956, January 1, 1960.

[57]*Richmond Daily Register*, January 1, 1951, January 1, 1953, January 1, 1959; *Courier-Journal*, January 1, 1951, January 1, 1953, June 4, 6, and 10, November 22, December 14, 20, and 23, 1958, January 1, February 4, April 8, December 2, 1959, January 1, November 24, 1960, June 23, December 6, 1962.

[58]Chenault Interview; Interview with John Y. Brown, Sr., November 19, 1979; *Richmond Daily Register*, September 4-5, 1952, April 4 and 7, December 4, 1953, January 1, 1954.

[59]*United States Census of Population, 1960*, I, Part 19, Kentucky, 242; Peck and Smith, *Berea's First 125 Years*, 194; *Courier-Journal Magazine*, October 21, 1951; *Courier-Journal*, January 9, 1953; *Richmond Daily Register*, January 1, 1957, January 1, 1958.

[60]*United States Census of Population, 1960*, I, Part 19, Kentucky, 6, 9, 10, 25, 117, 140, 142, 242.

[61]Ibid., 144, 154, 164; *United States Census of Agriculture, 1959*, 174, 194, 224; Wilson Enclosure; *Richmond Daily Register*, January 1, 1959, January 1, 1960.

CHAPTER 16

[1]*Richmond Daily Register*, December 29, 1971; *United States Census of Population, 1970*, I, Part 19, Kentucky, 7, 12, 365.

[2]*United States Census of Population, 1980, General Population Characteristics, Kentucky*, 5, 8, 10, 12.

[3]Mahaffey Interview; *Richmond Daily Register*, October 7, November 4, 1962, January 2, December 30, 1967; *Madison County Newsweek*, May 21, 1970, December 27, 1972, March 3, 1973; *Kentucky Vital Statistics, 1962*, 31-32; *Kentucky Vital Statistics, 1972*, 13; *1982 Annual Vital Statistics Report*, 112, 185.

[4]*Richmond Daily Register*, January 1, 1962, December 2, 1963, January 2, 1967, January 2, 1969.

[5]*Richmond Daily Register*, October 2, 1971; John Ed Pearce, "Focus on Kentucky: Madison County," *Courier-Journal Magazine*, February 1, 1980.

[6]Grise Interview; Kerby Interview; Pearce, "Madison County"; *Madison County Newsweek*, June 28, 1972.

[7]*Richmond Daily Register*, January 2, 1969; Pearce, "Madison County"; *1970 Census*, 440, 450; *1980 Census*, 115, 118, 196.

[8]*Richmond Daily Register*, January 1, 1965.

[9]*Madison County Newsweek*, December 27, 1973, March 16, 1974, September 13, 1975; *Richmond Daily Register*, January 1, November 30, 1964, January 1, 1965, January 2, 1967, January 2, 1969; *A Comprehensive Report on Richmond, Kentucky* (Kentucky Department of Commerce, 1980), 3-8.

[10]*Madison County Newsweek*, April 22, 1971, February 9, 1972, June 1, 1974; *Industrial Resources, Berea, 1978* (Kentucky Department of Commerce), 1-3; *Richmond Register*, April 6, 1985.

[11]*Richmond Daily Register*, January 1, 1960, January 2, 1961; *Richmond Register*, March 20, 1984; *1978 Census of Agriculture*, XV, 1; *1980 Census of Agriculture*, Enclosure from John Wilson.

[12]*Richmond Daily Register*, November 9, 1960; Fraas, "Keen Johnson," 324-32.

[13]*Richmond Daily Register*, June 1, 2, 1961, December 30, 1970.

[14]*Richmond Daily Register*, November 22, 23, 1963.

[15]*Courier-Journal*, December 9, 1961; *Richmond Daily Register*, November 8, 1961.

[16]*Richmond Daily Register*, November 6, 7, 1963, November 8, December 30, 1967.

[17]*Courier-Journal*, July 29, 1962; *Richmond Daily Register*, February 5, July 9, 10, 27, and 28, 1962, November 4-6, 1964.

[18]*Richmond Daily Register*, April 23 and 24, 1966, September 2, 1968; Chenault Interview; *Louisville Times*, October 24, December 4, 1968.

[19]*Richmond Daily Register*, November 6, 1968; *Courier-Journal*, November 3, 1976; *Richmond Register*, December 31, 1980, November 7, 1984.

[20]Chenault Interview; *Richmond Daily Register*, January 1, 1964, November 13, 1968, January 3, 4, 1970, January 4, 1972; *Madison County Newsweek*, December 31, 1970, January 5, February 9, 1972, May 16, October 21, December 12, 1973, February 23, 1974; Enclosure from James J. Shannon, Jr., April 1, 1985.

[21]*Richmond Daily Register*, June 26, 1970; *Lexington Herald*, June 25, 1970; *Madison County Newsweek*, November 12, 1970; *Louisville Times*, June 2, 4, and 21, 1969; *Courier-Journal*, June 5, November 1, 1969, June 6, 1970.

[22]*Richmond Register*, June 17, October 19, 1983; March 1, April 18, July 20, October 4, 1984; *Madison County Post/Advertiser*, March 9, 1983; *Courier-Journal*, April 18, October 5, 1984.

[23]*Richmond Daily Register*, December 31, 1971; *Richmond Register*, December 30, 1978; *Madison County Newsweek*, December 27, 1972, October 17, November 28, 1973, September 7, 1974, January 4, 1975; *Courier-Journal*, April 6, June 16, 1972, June 15, 1977, May 24, 1978.

[24]*Madison County Newsweek*, July 23, 1970, February 17, 1972; Kerby Interview; *Richmond Daily Register*, January 2, 1969; *Richmond Register*, December 31, 1980; Pearce, "Madison County"; *Courier-Journal*, November 6, 1971.

[25]Pearce, "Madison County"; Marionneaux Interview; *Richmond Register*, December 31, 1981, December 31, 1982, July 20, 1984; *Madison County Newsweek*, January 3, 1973, May 11, 1974; *Courier-Journal*, June 14, 1969, June 5, 1970.

[26]*Courier-Journal*, August 21, 1972, December 4, 1974; *Sunday Herald-Leader*, October 24, 1982.

[27]*Madison County Newsweek*, May 14, 1970, November 22, 1972, April 6, 1974; *Richmond Register*, April 3, 1984.

[28]Burnam Interview; Richardson Interview; Norris Interview; *Richmond Daily Register*, January 2, 1963; *Madison County Newsweek*, August 23, 1973; Enclosure from Public Information Officer, Avon, October 12, 1982.

[29]*Madison County Newsweek*, July 23, August 23, November 5, 1975.

[30]*Courier-Journal*, August 13, 1967; *Madison County Newsweek*, November 21, 1973.

[31]*Richmond Register*, December 31, 1979, September 26, 1984; *Courier-Journal*, August 21, October 2, December 13, 1979, January 25 and 30, 1980.

[32]*Richmond Register*, May 1, 1984; *Sunday Herald-Leader*, October 24, 1982; *Courier-Journal*, February 18, August 17 and 18, November 9, 1984.

[33]*Courier-Journal*, October 19, 1981.

[34]*1980 Census*, 440; *A Comprehensive Report on Richmond, 1980*, 22; *Richmond Register*, February 25, July 20, August 7, 1984; *Courier-Journal*, February 13, 1981.

[35]See note 34; *Richmond Register*, April 2, 1985.

[36]Marionneaux Interview; *Lexington Herald-Leader*, January 29, February 12, 1984; *Courier-Journal*, July 1, 1978, September 18, 1983.

[37]*1970 Census*, 376; Roebuck and Hickson, *Southern Rednecks*, 56; *Madison County Newsweek*, February 7, 1973; *Courier-Journal*, September 1, 1966; *A Comprehensive*

Report on Richmond, 1980, 6, 8, 33; *Richmond Daily Register*, January 2, December 1, 1967, January 2, 1969; Enclosure from WEKY radio station, from newscast November 22, 1982.

[38]Chenault Interview; *Richmond Daily Register*, January 1, 1965; *Richmond Register*, December 30, 1978, December 31, 1981, October 4, 1983, July 27, 1984; *Madison County Post/Advertiser*, May 11, June 29, 1983; *Courier-Journal*, September 19, 1984; Enclosure from James S. Chenault, April 3, 1985.

[39]Oral History Interview with James J. Shannon, Jr., January 24, 1984; *Madison County Newsweek*, April 29, October 28, 1971; July 3, 1974, January 1, 1975, January 3, 1976; *Richmond Daily Register*, January 1, 1964, December 30, 1967.

[40]*Madison County Newsweek*, December 29, 1971, October 4, 1972, January 19, 1974; *Louisville Times*, July 1, 1964, February 13, 1979; *Richmond Daily Register*, December 31, 1977; *Courier-Journal*, December 29, 1962, July 1, October 23 and 27, 1964.

[41]Raymond Arsenault, "The End of the Long Hot Summer: The Air Conditioner and Southern Culture," *Journal of Southern History*, L (November, 1984), 628.

Selected Bibliography
Part I
Primary Sources

Manuscripts
Curtis F. Burnam, Reminiscences."
Katherine Phelps Caperton, "Early Homes of Madison County."
Green Clay Chronicles.
Draper Manuscripts, Shane Papers.
Draper Manuscripts, Colonel Richard Henderson's Journal.
Draper Manuscripts, Boone Papers.
French Tipton Papers.

Documents and Records
Cane Springs Baptist Church Record Book, 1803-1832.
Censuses of the United States, 1790-1850.
Journal of the First Constitutional Convention of Kentucky.
Journal of the Kentucky House, 1810-1850.
Journal of the Kentucky Senate, 1816-1850.
Kentucky General Assembly Acts, 1810-1850.
Kentucky State Constitutions, 1792, 1799, 1849.
Madison County Circuit Court Records.
Madison County Court Order Books, 1786-1850.
Methodist Quarterly Conference, 1811-1845.
Minutes of Meetings of the Richmond Philosophical Society, 1820-1825. (By permission of the State Historical Society of Missouri. A Joint Collection of the University of Missouri and the Historical Society.)
Paint Lick Presbyterian Church Record.
Silver Creek Presbyterian Church Record Book.
Tates Creek Baptist Church Records.
Viney Fork (Muddy Creek) Baptist Church Records.

Government Publications
Hennings, William W., ed. *Statutes at Large: Collection of all Laws of Virginia*, 13 volumes. Richmond, Virginia: 1819-1823.
Littell, William. *Statute Law of Kentucky*, 5 volumes. Frankfort: 1809-1819.

Newspapers
Argus of Western America (Frankfort).
Commentator (Frankfort), 1817-1832.
Commonwealth (Frankfort), 1833-1850.
Farmer's Chronicle (Richmond), 1835.
Frankfort Palladian, 1796-1804.
Lexington Intelligencer, 1834-1839.
Louisville Daily Courier, 1844-1846.
Luminary (Richmond), 1813.
Richmond Republican, 1822-1824.

Unpublished Theses
Deatherage, Mary Kate. "Madison County Bibliography." M. A. thesis, Eastern Kentucky University, 1944.
Gordon, James W. "Lawyers in Politics: Kentucky, the 1850s." Ph. D. dissertation, University of Kentucky, 1981.
Little, Robert E. "Education in Madison County, Kentucky." M. A. thesis, University of Kentucky, 1933.
Mathias, Frank. "Turbulent Years in Kentucky Politics, 1820-1850." Ph. D. dissertation, University of Kentucky, 1966.

Memoirs
Brown, Edwin. "Kirksville: A Short Sketch." Undated. Addenda by Nettie Pond, 1910.
Burnam, Lucia, *What I Remember, 1854-1937*. Richmond, Kentucky, 1934.

Campbell, Madison. *Autobiography of Elder Madison Campbell.* Richmond, Kentucky, 1895.

Caperton, Katherine Phelps. *A History of the First Christian Church.* Richmond, Kentucky, 1930.

Jennings, Margaret; Christian, Mabel; Whitlock, Mrs. J. L. "A Bicentennial History." Kirksville Christian Church, 1949.

Letters

Clay, Cassius M., IV. *Letters from the Correspondence of Brutus J. Clay, 1808-1878.* Paris, Kentucky, 1958.

Articles

Bate, Alexander, "Colonel Richard Callaway, 1722-1780," *FCHQ*, XXIX (January, 1955), 166-76.

Bryan, Charles W. Jr., "Richard Callaway: Kentucky Pioneer," *FCHQ*, IX (June, 1935), 35-49.

Chenault, William, "The Early History of Madison County," *Register*, XXX (April, 1932), 119-61.

Clift, G. Glenn, "Notes on Kentucky Veterans of the War of 1812," *Register*, LI (January, 1953), 39-40.

Conkright, Bessie Taul, "Estill's Defeat," *Register*, XXII (September, 1924), 311-22.

Connelly, Thomas L., "Gateway to Kentucky: The Wilderness Road, 1748-1792," *Register*, LIX (April, 1961), 109-32.

Dorris, Jonathan T., "Early History in Madison County Circuit Court Records," *Register*, XLIII (April, July, October, 1945), 83-106, 239-55, 321-41.

Dorris, Jonathan T., "Major Squire Turner: Lawyer, Statesman, and Economist," *FCHQ*, XXV (Spring, 1951), 37-50.

Dorris, Jonathan T., "William Chenault, 1835-1901," *FCHQ*, XIX (April, 1945), 67-80.

Gregory, James P. Jr., "The Question of Slavery in the Kentucky Constitutional Convention of 1849," *FCHQ*, XXIII (April, 1949), 89-99.

Hammon, Neal O., "Early Roads into Kentucky," *Register*, LXVIII (April, 1970), 93-131.

Hammon, Neal O., "First Trip to Boonesborough," *FCHQ*, LXV (July, 1971), 249-58.

Hammon, Neal O., "Land Acquisition on the Kentucky Frontier," *Register*, LXXVIII (Autumn, 1980), 297-321.

Harrison, Lowell H., "The Anti-Slavery Career of Cassius M. Clay," *Register*, LIX (October, 1961), 300-310.

Willis, George L., "History of Kentucky Constitutions and Constitutional Conventions," *Register*, XXIX (January, 1931), 63-67.

Wilson, Samuel M., "Daniel Boone, 1734-1934," *FCHQ*, VIII (October, 1934), 183-97.

Secondary Sources

Books

Burnam, Robert R. *History of Masonry in Madison County, Kentucky, 1812-1913.* Louisville: Courier Journal Printing, 1914.

Chinn, George, *Kentucky: Settlement and Statehood, 1750-1800.* Frankfort: Kentucky Historical Society, 1975.

Clark, Thomas D. *Frontier America.* New York: Charles Scribner's Sons, 1959.

Clark, Thomas D. *History of Kentucky.* Lexington, Kentucky: John Bradford Press, 1960.

Coleman, J. Winston. *Slavery Times in Kentucky.* Chapel Hill: University of North Caroline Press, 1940.

Coward, Joan Wells. *Kentucky in the New Republic.* Lexington: University Press of Kentucky, 1979.

Dorris, Jonathan T. *Glimpses of Historic Madison County, Kentucky.* Nashville: Williams Printing Company, 1955.

Everman, H. E. *Governor James Garrard.* Paris: Cooper's Run Press, 1981.

Funkhouser, William D. *Archaeological Survey of Kentucky.* Lexington: University Press of Kentucky, 1932.

Ireland, Robert M. *The County Courts in Antebellum Kentucky.* Lexington: University Press of Kentucky, 1972.

Lancaster Woman's Club. *Patches of Garrard County.* Danville, Kentucky: n.p., 1974.

Masters, Frank M. *A History of Baptists in Kentucky.* Louisville: Kentucky Baptist Historical Society, 1953.
Miller, William H. *History and Genealogies.* Richmond, Kentucky: Pantagraph Press, 1907.
Robertson, James Rood. *Petition of the Early Inhabitants of Kentucky.* Louisville: Filson Club Publications, 1914.
Shannon, Jaspar B. and McQuown, Ruth. *Presidential Politics in Kentucky, 1824-1948.* Lexington: University Press of Kentucky, 1950.
Smiley, David L. *Lion of White Hall: The Life of Cassius M. Clay.* Madison: University of Wisconsin Press, 1962.
Speed, Thomas. *The Political Club, Danville, Kentucky, 1786-1790.* Louisville: Filson Club Society, 1894.
Spencer, J. H. *History of Kentucky Baptists, 1769-1885.* Cincinnati: Printed by Author, 1886.
Todd, Russell I. *This Is Boone Country.* Louisville: Gateway Press, 1968.
Watlington, Patricia. *Partisan Spirit: Kentucky Politics, 1779-1792.* New York: Atheneum Press, 1972.
Webb, William S. *Ancient Life in Kentucky.* Frankfort: Kentucky Geological Survey, 1928.
Young, Bennett H. *The Pre-Historic Men of Kentucky.* Louisville: Standard Printing Co., 1918.

Part II
Primary Sources

Letters, journals, and diaries
American Missionary Association Archives. Letters of John G. Fee, Matilda Fee, John A. R. Rogers, Otis B. Waters, George Candee, William E. Lincoln. Hutchins Library, Berea College. Microfilm.
Burnam-Rollins Correspondence. Joint Collection, University of Missouri, Western Historical Manuscript Collection—Columbia, State Historical Society of Missouri Manuscripts.
Eastern Kentucky University Archives. Microfilm.
Cassius M. Clay Papers. Dorris Collection, Crabbe Library, EKU.
Clarence E. Woods Letters. Wallace Family Papers. Eastern Kentucky University Archives.
Fee-Clay Correspondence. Berea College Archives.
John A. R. Rogers, Journal, 1850-1867. 2 vols. Berea College Archives.

Autobiographies, Memoirs and Personal Recollections
Burleigh, Angus Augustus. *John G. Fee: Founder of Berea College.* Undated pamphlet in BCA.
Burnam, Curtis Field. "Burnam Family History." Townsend Room, Crabbe Library, EKU. Manuscript.
——- ——- ——-. "Reminiscences." Curtis F. Burnam's Scrapbook. Townsend Room, Crabbe Library, EKU.
"Curtis Field Burnam and Berea College," [undated]. Townsend Room, Crabbe Library, EKU. Typescript.
Burnam, Lucia F. *What I Remember.* Townsend Room, Crabbe Library, EKU. Typescript.
Candee, George. "Reminiscences." Berea College Archives.
Clay, Cassius Marcellus. *The Life of Cassius Marcellus Clay, Memoirs, Writings and Speeches.* (1886, reprint) New York: Negro Universities Press, 1969.
Clay, Green. *Cassius Clay: Militant Statesman, Moses of Emancipation (1816-1903).* Dorris Collection, Crabbe Library, EKU. Manuscript.
Clay, Mary B. "Biography of Cassius M. Clay: Written by His Daughter." *Filson Club History Quarterly* XLVI (April, 1972), 123-46; (July, 1972), 254-87; (October, 1972), 340-64.
Duke, Basil W. *A History of Morgan's Cavalry.* Cecil Fletcher Holland, ed. Bloomington, Indiana: Indiana University Press, 1960.
Fairchild, Edward Henry. *Berea College, Kentucky: An Interesting History.* Cincinnati: Elm Street Printing, 1883.
Fee, John Gregg. *Autobiography of John G. Fee.* Chicago: National Christian Association, 1891.

——- ——- ——-. *Berea: Its History and Work*. Berea College Archives. Manuscript.
Hanson, Samuel. "Account of Early Berea." Berea College Archives. Photocopy.
In Memoriam: Curtis Field Burnam. Privately printed.
Richardson, Hiram K. *Memoirs of Berea*. Berea: Berea College Press, 1940.
Rogers, Elizabeth Embree. "Full Forty Years of Shadow and Sunshine: A Sketch of the Family Life of the J. A. R. Rogers Family." 1896. Berea College Archives. Manuscript.
——- ——- ——-. *Personal History of Berea College*. [1910?] Berea College Archives. Manuscript.
Rogers, John A. R. *Birth of Berea College: A Story of Providence*. Philadelphia: Henry T. Coates & Co., 1904.
Rogers, John Raphael. "Pioneering in Berea." *The Berea Alumnus*, I (June, 1931), no. 2.

Speeches and Orations
Burnam, Curtis F. "Oration on the Dedication of the Laying of the Corner Stone of Library Building Presented to Berea College by Andrew Carnegie June 6, 1905." Berea College, 1905.
Clay, Cassius M. "Oration by Cassius Marcellus Clay of White Hall, Kentucky at Berea College October 16, 1895 on the Annexation of Alaska." Cassius Clay Papers, Dorris Collection, Crabbe Library, EKU.
——- ——- ——-. "Speech of Cassius Clay at Frankfort, Kentucky, from the Capitol Steps, January 10, 1860." Printed by *Cincinnati Gazette*. Berea College Archives.
——- ——- ——-. *The Writings of Cassius Marcellus Clay, including Speeches and Addresses*. New York: Harper & Bros., 1848.
Fee, John Gregg. "A Word to the Convocation." Undated. Berea College Archives. Manuscript.
——- ——- ——-. Notes for the Sermon delivered in Beecher's Church. Berea College Archives. Manuscript.

Town and County Records
Berea City Council Minutes. Hutchins Library, Berea College. Microfilm.
Madison County, Birth, Death, and Marriage Records. Kentucky Historical Society. Microfilm.
Madison County Circuit Court Records. Kentucky Archives, Frankfort.
Madison County Court Order Books.
Madison County Deed Records.
Madison County Marriage Bonds.
Madison County Marriage Records.
Madison County Ministers' Returns.
Madison County Probate Records.
Madison County Tax Book, 1854. Kentucky Historical Society.

Censuses
United States Bureau of Census. *Twelfth Census of Population, 1900: Kentucky [Madison County]*. Washington: The Bureau of Census, 1978. Microfilm.
United States Census Office. *Population Schedules of the Seventh Census of the United States, 1850: Kentucky [Madison County]*. Washington: National Archives, 1963. Microfilm.
——- ——- ——-. *Population Schedules of the Seventh Census of the United States, 1850: Kentucky Slave Schedules [Madison County]*. Washington: National Archives, 1963. Microfilm.
——- ——- ——-. *Population Schedules of the Eighth Census of the United States, 1860: Kentucky [Madison County]*. Washington: National Archives, 1967. Microfilm.
——- ——- ——-. *Population Schedules of the Eighth Census of the United States, 1860: Kentucky Slave Schedules [Madison County]*. Washington: National Archives, 1967. Microfilm.
——- ——- ——-. *Population Schedules of the Ninth Census of the United States, 1870: Kentucky [Madison County]*. Washington: National Archives, 1965. Microfilm.
——- ——- ——-. *Population Schedules of the Tenth Census of the United States, 1880: Kentucky [Madison County]*. Washington: National Archives, 1965. Microfilm.

——· ——· ——-. *Schedules Enumerating Union Veterans and Widows of Union Veterans of the Civil War [1890]: Kentucky [Madison County].* Washington: National Archives, 1948. Microfilm.

Church and School Records
"Berea College Trustees 1858-1980." Board of Trustees Annual Reports/Committees. Berea College Archives.
Berea Grade Books, 1868-1893. Registrar's Vault, Lincoln Hall, Berea College. Manuscript.
Berea College Catalogs, 1866-1900. Berea College Archives.
Historical Register of the Officers and Students of Berea College From the Beginning to June 1904. Berea: Berea College, 1904.
Historical Register: Officers and Students of Berea College From the Beginning to June 1916. Berea: Berea College Press, 1916.
Minutes of Berea Temperance Society. Berea College Archives. Manuscript.
Rogers, John A. R. Account Book. Berea College Archives. Manuscript.
——· ——· ——-. "List of Berea Students 1858." *Berea Citizen,* July 24, 1902.
Record Book of Madison Female School 1857. Townsend Room, Crabbe Library, EKU. Manuscript.
Union Church Minute Book. Berea College Archives. Manuscript.

Newspapers and Periodicals
American Missionary Magazine. Berea College Archives.
Berea Citizen. Hutchins Library, Berea College. Microfilm.
Climax. Crabbe Library, EKU. Microfilm.
Kentucky Statesman. Lexington Public Library. Microfilm.
Mountain Democrat. Clippings in Berea College Archives.
Richmond Register. Crabbe Library, EKU. Microfilm.
True American. Lexington Public Library. Microfilm.

Government Records and Publications
Andriot, John L., ed. *Population Abstract of the United States.* McLean, Virginia: Andriot Associates, 1980.
Census Reports, Volume V: Twelfth Census of the United States Taken in the Year 1900: AGRICULTURE. Part 1. Washington: U.S. Census Office, 1902.
Compendium of the Eleventh Census, 1890. Part I: Population. Washington: Government Printing Office, 1892.
Compendium of the Tenth Census (June 1, 1880). Parts I and II. Washington: Government Printing Office, 1883.
DeBow, J. D. *Statistical View of the United States: A Compendium of the Seventh Census [1850].* Washington: Beverley Tucker, Senate Printer, 1854.
Dyer, Frederick H. *A Compendium of the War of the Rebellion: Compiled and Arranged from Official Records . . . ,* 2 vols. (1881 & 1901, reprint.) Dayton, Ohio: The National Historical Society, 1979.
Kennedy, Joseph C. *Population of the United States in 1860; Compiled from the Original Return of the Eighth Census.* 4 vols. Washington: Government Printing Office, 1864.
Kentucky Documents 1863-64. No. 26.
Moore, Frank, ed. *The Rebellion Record: A Diary of American Events with Documents, Narratives, Illustrative Incidents, Poetry, Etc.* Vol. 5. New York: G. P. Putnam, 1863.
Phisterer, Frederick. *Statistical Record of the Armies of the United States.* New York: Charles Scribner's Sons, 1883.
Report of the Adjutant General of the State of Kentucky. 2 vols. Frankfort: John H. Harney, 1867.
Report on Statistics of Churches in the United States at the Eleventh Census, 1890. Washington: Government Printing Office, 1894.
Report on the Manufacturers of the United States at the Tenth Census (June 1, 1880). Vol. II. Washington: Government Printing Office, 1883.
Walker, Francis A. *The Statistics of the Wealth and Industry of the United States [1870].* Washington: Government Printing Office, 1872.
The War of the Rebellion: A Compilation of the Official Records of the Union and Confederate Armies. Prepared by Lieutenant Colonel Robert N. Scott. Series I, Vol. XVI, Part I, Reports. Washington: Government Printing Office, 1886.

Archival Collections

American Missionary Association Archives: Kentucky and Ohio. Amistad Research Center, New Orleans. Microfilm in Hutchins Library, Berea College. Broaddus Family Record. Townsend Room, Crabbe Library, EKU. Typescript.
Burnam Family. Family History Series 6. Townsend Room, Crabbe Library, EKU. Typescript.
Clay Family. Family History Series 9a. Townsend Room, Crabbe Library, EKU. Typescript.
Curtis F. Burnam's Scrapbook. Townsend Room, Crabbe Library, EKU.
Founders and Founding Series. Berea College Archives.
French Tipton Papers. Townsend Room, Crabbe Library, EKU.
Presidents—Fairchild Collection. Berea College Archives.
William Chenault File. Townsend Room, Crabbe Library, EKU.

Secondary Sources

Biographical Cyclopedia of the Commonwealth of Kentucky. Chicago: John M. Grisham Co., 1896.
Biographical Encyclopedia of Kentucky of the Dead and Living of the 19th Century. Cincinnati: J. M. Armstrong & Co., 1878.
Boyd, Carl B., Jr. "Local Aid to Railroads in Central Kentucky, 1850-1891." *Register of the Kentucky Historical Society,* LXII (April, 1964), 112-33.
Catton, Bruce. *Terrible Swift Sword.* Vol. 2 of the Centennial History of the Civil War. New York: Doubleday & Co., 1963.
Cist, Henry M. *The Army of the Cumberland.* New York: Charles Scribner's Sons, 1882.
Clark, Thomas D. *A History of Kentucky.* New York: Prentice-Hall, Inc., 1937.
Coleman, J. Winston, Jr. "Lexington's Slave Dealers and Their Southern Trade." *Filson Club History Quarterly,* XII (January, 1938), 1-23.
——- ——- ——- . *Slavery Times in Kentucky.* Chapel Hill: U. of North Carolina Press, 1940.
Collins, Lewis & Richard H. *History of Kentucky.* 2 vols. (1874. reprint). Berea: Kentucky Imprints, 1976.
Connelley, William Elsey and Coulter, E. M. *History of Kentucky.* ed. Judge Charles Kerr. Vol. 2. Chicago: The American Historical Society, 1922.
Connelly, Thomas Lawrence. *Army of the Heartland: The Army of Tennessee 1861-1862.* Baton Rouge: Louisiana State University Press, 1967.
Copeland, James E. "Where Were the Kentucky Unionists and Secessionists?" *Register of the Kentucky Historical Society,* LXXI (October, 1973), 344-63.
Dictionary of National Biography.
Dorris, Jonathan Truman. "Central University, Richmond, Kentucky." *Register of the Kentucky Historical Society,* XXXII (April, 1934), 91-124.
——- ——- ——-. "Major Squire Turner: Lawyer, Statesman and Economist." *Filson Club History Quarterly,* XXV (January, 1951), 33-50.
——- ——- ——- . "William Chenault 1835-1901: One of the Founders of the Filson Club." *Filson Club History Quarterly* XIX (April, 1945), 67-85.
——- ——- ——- and John Cabell Chenault. *Old Cane Springs: A Story of the War Between the States in Madison County, Kentucky.* Louisville: The Standard Printing Co., 1936.
——- ——- ——- and Dorris, Maud Weaver. *Glimpses of Historic Madison County, Kentucky,* Nahsville: Williams Printing Co., 1955.
Engle, Fred A., Jr. "Central University of Richmond, Kentucky." *Register of the Kentucky Historical Society,* LXVI (July, 1968), 279-304.
Grise, Robert N. and Engle, Fred A. "Madison's Heritage." *Richmond Register.* Photocopied clipping collection in Townsend Room, Crabbe Library, EKU.
Harrison, Lowell H. *The Civil War in Kentucky.* Lexington: University Press of Kentucky, 1975.
Howard, Victor B. *Black Liberation in Kentucky: Emancipation and Freedom, 1862-1884.* Lexington: University Press of Kentucky, 1983.

Johnson, E. Polk. *A History of Kentucky and Kentuckians*. 3 vols. Chicago: The Lewis Publishing Co., 1912.

Johnson, Robert Underwood & Clarence Clough Buel. *Battles and Leaders of the Civil War*. Grant-Lee edition. Vol. I, Part 2, Vol. 3, Part 1. New York: The Century Co., 1884.

Johnston, Colonel J. Stoddard. "Kentucky" in *Confederate Military History*. General Clement A. Evans, ed. Vol. IX. Atlanta: Confederate Publishing Co., 1899.

Kimball, Philip Clyde. "Freedom's Harvest: Freedmen's Schools in Kentucky after the Civil War." *Filson Club History Quarterly*, LIV (July, 1980), 272-88.

McDougle, Ivan E. *Slavery in Kentucky 1792-1865*. (1918, reprint.) Westport, Conn.: Negro Universities Press, 1970.

Martin, Asa Earl. *The Antislavery Movement in Kentucky, Prior to 1850*. Louisville: Standard Printing Co., 1918.

Military History of Kentucky: Chronologically Arranged. Written by Workers of the Federal Writers Project of the Works Progress Administration for the State of Kentucky. Sponsored by the Military Department of Kentucky. Frankfort: The State Journal, 1939.

Miller, William Harris. *History and Genealogies of the Families of Miller, Woods, Harris, Wallace, Maupin, Oldham, Kavanaugh and Brown [many others]*. Lexington: Press of Transylvania Co., 1906.

Smiley, David L. "Cassius M. Clay and John G. Fee: A Study in Southern Anti-Slavery Thought." *The Journal of Negro History*, XLII (July, 1957), 201-13.

———. ———. ———. *Lion of White Hall*. Gloucester, Mass.: Peter Smith, 1969.

Speed, Thomas. *The Union Cause in Kentucky, 1860-1865*. New York: G. P. Putnam's Sons, 1907.

Swinford, Mac. "Mr. Justice Samuel Freeman Miller (1816-1873)." *Filson Club History Quarterly*, XXXIV (January, 1960), 35-41.

Tapp, Hambleton. "Battle of Richmond 1862," *Kentucky Pioneer* (publication of the Madison County Historical Society), 1 (October, 1968), 10-17.

———— ———— ————. "Robert J. Breckenridge and the Year 1849." *Filson Club History Quarterly*, XII (July, 1938).

Thomas, Edison H. *John Hunt Morgan and His Raiders*. Lexington: University Press of Kentucky, 1975.

Tipton, French. "The Richmond Bar." *The Lawyers and Lawmakers of Kentucky*. H. Levin, ed. Chicago: Lewis Publishing Co., 1897.

Webb, Ross A. *Kentucky in the Reconstruction Era*. Lexington: University Press of Kentucky, 1979.

Part III
Primary Sources

Newspapers
Richmond Climax, 1865-1891, 1899-1914.
Kentucky Register, 1864-1891.
Richmond Daily Register, 1917-1978.
Richmond Register, 1978-1985.
Madison County Newsweek, 1970-1979.
Lexington Herald, 1900-1985.
Courier-Journal, 1900-1985.

Oral History Interviews *(all located in Eastern Kentucky University Archives)*
Adams, William G. and Woodard. October 21, 1983.
Burnam, James C. April 25, 1984.
Chenault, James C. January 31, 1984.
Engle, Fred. January 23, 1984.
Fraas, Elizabeth. February 21, 1984.
Grise, Robert N. October 13, 1982.
Lackey, Nannie S. October 7, 1983.
Kerby, Clifford. February 13, 1984.
Mahaffey, Hugh. November 3, 1983.
Marionneaux, Ronald L. October 27, 1983.

Miller, J. Lester. November 16, 1982.
Noland, Turley. October 15, 1982.
Norris, Clyde. September 1, 1982.
Park, Smith. November 15, 1983.
Richardson, H. E. October 28, 1983.
Robinson, Norma. March 20, 1984.
Shannon, James J., Jr. January 24, 1984.
Singleton, J. Allan. January 26, 1984.
Smith, G. Murray, Jr. November 4. 1983.
Thomas, R. C. April 19, 1984.
Todd, Russell I. February 27. 1984.
Wilson, John. November 5, 1982.

Secondary Sources

Alexander, Thomas C. "Utah War Industry During World War II: A Human Impact Analysis." *Utah History Quarterly*, LXI (January, 1983), 72-92.
Annals of the First Presbyterian Church, Richmond, Kentucky, 1827-1927.
Arsenault, Raymond. "The End of the Long Hot Summer: The Air Conditioner and Southern Culture." *Journal of Southern History*, L (November, 1984), 597-628.
Blum, John Morton. *V Was for Victory*. New York: Harcourt, Brace, Jovanovich, 1976.
Burckel, Nicholas, "From Beckham to McCreary: The Progressive Record of Kentucky Governors." *Register of the Kentucky Historical Society*, LXXVI (October, 1978), 285-306.
Carter, Paul A. *Another Part of the Twenties*. New York: Columbia University Press, 1977.
Carter, Paul A. *The Twenties in America*. New York, Crowell, 1968.
Caudill, Harry M. *Theirs Be the Power: The Moguls of Eastern Kentucky*. Urbana: University of Illinois Press, 1983.
Channing, Steven A. *Kentucky: A Bicentennial History*. New York: Norton, 1977.
Charter, By Laws, and Ordinances of Richmond, Kentucky. Richmond, City of Richmond, 1901
Clark, Norman H. *Deliver Us From Evil*. New York: Norton, 1976.
Clark, Thomas D. *Kentucky: Land of Contrast*. New York: Harper and Row, 1968.
A Comprehensive Report on Richmond, Kentucky. Frankfort, Department of Commerce, 1980.
Deatherage, Mary Kate. "Madison County Chronology and Bibliography." Unpublished M. A. thesis, Eastern Kentucky State Teachers College, 1944.
Dorris, Jonathan Truman and Dorris, Maud Weaver, *Glimpses of Historic Madison County*, Nashville: Williams Printing Co., 1955.
Ellis, William E. "Robert Worth Bingham and the Crisis of Cooperative Marketing in the Twenties." *Agricultural History*, LVI (January, 1982), 99-116.
Fraas, Elizabeth M. "Keen Johnson: Newspaperman and Governor," Unpublished Ph.D dissertation, University of Kentucky, 1983.
Hammons, Ruth Allene. "History of the Richmond City Schools." Unpublished M. A. thesis, Eastern Kentucky State Teachers College, 1949.
Industrial Resources, Berea, Kentucky. Berea, 1966.
Kirby, Jack Temple. "The Southern Exodus, 1910-1960: A Primer for Historians." *Journal of Southern History*, XLIX (November, 1983), 585-600.
Laine, Henry Allen, *Foot Prints*. New York: Hopson Book Press, 1947.
Little, Robert E. "History of Education in Madison County Kentucky." Unpublished M. A. thesis, University of Kentucky, 1933.
Marionneaux, R. L. *Geography of Madison County, Ky*. Richmond: Eastern Kentucky University, 1982.
Peck, Elizabeth S. and Emily Ann Smith. *Berea's First 125 Years. 1855-1980*. Lexington: University Press of Kentucky, 1982.
Roebuck, Julian B. and Hickson, Mark, III. *The Southern Redneck: A Phenomenological Study*. New York: Praeger, 1982.
Todd, Russell I. *This is Boone Country*. Louisville: Gateway Press, 1968.
Townsend, John Wilson. *"In Kentucky" and Its Author "Jim" Mulligan*. Lexington: The John Bradford Club, 1935.

Appendix

Pioneers at Fort Boonesborough

This list of verified pioneers at Fort Boonesborough was compiled by H. Thomas Tudor, Registrar of the Society of Boonesborough and furnished compliments of the Society of Boonesborough by James J. Shannon, Jr., President. H. Thomas Tudor and James J. Shannon, Jr. were co-founders of the Society in 1975 at the Fort Boonesborough Bicentennial Celebration.

A large, marble monument has been placed near the newly constructed fort at Fort Boonesborough State Park with known pioneer names inscribed thereon and presented to the Commonwealth of Kentucky by the Society of Boonesborough in 1981. Membership in the Society is limited to direct descendants of pioneers at Fort Boonesborough.

Following each name listed below you will find a list of numbers which refer to sources of information for each name listed. All of the names listed below are taken from authentic records and although the list may not be complete, it is accurate. Many of the references contain additional information on the families of the pioneers which should be of interest to the descendants of these pioneers. Listed immediately following the name is the approximate date of arrival of the person at Boonesborough, when known.

Name	Sources	Name	Sources
ALLEN, John	2	BARNETT, Alex	5
ALLEN, Richard	2	BARNETT, Ambrose	2
ALLEN, Thomas (1775)	1	BARNETT, James (1781)	2, 13
(Surveyor)		BARNETT, John (1780)	2, 13
ANDERSON, Aletha	2	BARNETT, Joseph (by 1778)	1
ANDERSON, James (1775)	1, 2	BARNETT, Robert	2
ANDERSON, Jemina	2	BARTON, David	2
ANDERSON, John (1780)	2, 13	BARTON, Joab	4
ANDERSON, Mary	5	(killed)	
(marr. Capt. John Kennedy		*BARTON, Joshua (1775)	2, 4, 5
2nd Samuel Campbell)		(killed)	
ANDERSON, Nicholas	5, 8	BARTON, Samuel	2, 10
ANTHONY, John	8	BARTON, Thomas	2
ANTHONY, Joseph	2	BARTON, William	2
ARK, Uriel	2, 6	BAUGHMAN, Catherine	3
ASHBY, Daniel	4	BAUGHMAN, Jacob (1775)	2, 4
(killed)		(killed)	
BAILY, Thomas	2, 6	BAUGHMAN, John	2, 4, 6
BAKER, Isaac	2	(killed)	
BALLARD, Bland	2, 6	BAXTER, Col. Edward (1775)	1
BANTA, Abraham	2	BEDINGER, G. Michael	2, 3, 4, 6
BANTA, Henry Jr.	2	BEDINGER, George (1779)	1, 5, 13
BANTA, Henry Sr. (1780)	2, 13	BELL, Flowner	2
BANTA, John	2	BELL, Samuel	10
BARBORN, James	2	BELLENTINE, John	2
BARKER, Samuel (1775)	2, 13	BELLEW, Charles (1780)	2, 13
BARKER, William	2	BENNETT, John (1780)	13

*COCKE, Capt. William   2, 5, 7, 9 (1775)
COFFEE, Ambrose   2, 3, 4, 5 (1777)
COFFEE, Jesse   2
COKER, Jesse   2, 4, 5
(killed)
COLEFORT, John   1
COLLINS, Alex (1780)   2
COLLINS, Eligah   2, 6
COLLINS, Josiah   2, 6
COLLINS, Thomas   1
COLLINS, William   2, 6
COLLIER, Betts   2
COLMES, George   2, 7
COMBS, Joseph   2 (1775)
CONSTANT, John   1, 2, 6
COOK, David   1, 2, 6
*COOMBS, Cutberth   5
*COOMBS, Enos   5
COOMBS, William   2, 6
COONS, Jacob   1
COOPER, Ben   2
*COOPER, William   1, 2, 5,
(1775)   10, 13
COSSART, Peter   2, 5
(killed)
COSSART, Mrs. Peter   5
COULTER, James   2
CRADLEBAUGH, Maj. William   1, 2, 3,
(1775)   5, 6, 12, 13
CRAIG, John   2
CRAIG, Lewis   1, 2
CREWS, David   1, 2, 5, 10, 12, 13
CREWS, Mrs. David   5
CREWS, Eligah   1
CROOKE, John (1778)   1, 13
(Surveyor)
CROSS, John   4
(killed)
CURD, Charles   3
DANIEL, John (1781)   13
DAVIS, John   2, 3
DAVIS, Joseph (1780)   2
DAVIS, Samuel   1
DEAL, William   10
DEAN, Abram   2
DEAN, Susan   2
DEBAN or DESON, Joseph   13 (1780)
DIAL, Thomas   5
DONIPHAN, John   1
DONIPHAN, Joseph   2, 3, 4
DOSTER, James   3, 4
DOUGLAS, James   2
DRAKE, Joseph   4, 5
(killed)
DRAKE, Margaret   3, 10
DRYDEN, William   1
DUMPARD, John   2, 4, 6
(killed)

DUNN, John   4
(killed)
DUNNAWAY, Benjamin   3, 4
DURBIN, John   1
DUREE, Daniel   13 (1780)
DUREE, Henry   2, 13 (1780)
DUREE, Peter, Jr.   2
DUREE, Mrs. Peter, Jr.   2
DUREE, Peter, Sr.   2, 13 (1780)
DUREE, Mrs. Peter, Sr.   2
DUREE, Samuel   1, 2, 10
ELKIN, Robert   2
ELKIN, Mrs. Robert   5
ELLIS, James   2
ELLIS, Mary   2
*ELLISON, Joseph   2, 5, 13 (1780)
EMBRY, Talton   1, 2, 13 (1780)
EPPERSON, Richard   1, 5 (1776)
ESPEE, Robert   2 (by 1778)
ESTILL, Ben   1, 2
ESTILL, Boudee   1
*ESTILL, Capt. James   1, 2, 3, 5, 6,
(1775) (killed)   10, 12, 13
ESTILL, Sally   1
(born at fort 10-19-1782)
ESTILL, Samuel   1, 2, 3, 4, 5,
(1779)   12, 13
ESTILL, Wallace   2, 13 (1778)
EWING, Baker   2
FALL, William   1
(Surveyor)
*FARRAR, John   1, 2, 5, 7, 10 (1775)
FEAR or FAIR, Edmund   2, 3, 4, 5, 6
FIELDS, Col. Ezekiel H.   12
FINLEY, David   2
FINLEY, James   1, 2
FINNELL, John   2
FLEMING, Robert   1, 2, 10
FLENT, John   2
FLUTY, John   2, 13 (1778)
*FLOYD, Col. John   2, 5, 7
FOOT, Thomas   4
(killed)
FOWLER, Joseph   1
FOX, John   2
FRENCH, James   2, 5
GATLIFF, James   2
GATLIFF, Letitia   2
(became wife of Charles McGuire)
GATLIFF, Neal   2
GASS, James (1775)   13
(son of Capt. David Gass)
GASS, Jennie(1775)   13
(dau. of Capt. David Gass-killed
by Indians)
GASS, John (1775)   13
(son of Capt. David Gass-settled
Bourbon Co., Kentucky)

GASS, Mary (1775)   13
(dau. of Capt. David Gass—marr.
Wm. Black at the Fort in 1778)
GASS, Sarah (1775)   13
(dau. of Capt. David Gass—marr.
John Black)
GASS, Sarah (Mrs. David)   13
(wife of Capt. David Gass) (1775)
GASS, Capt. David (1775)   1, 2, 5, 6,
                                 12, 13
GATES, James (1776)   1, 10
GATLIFF, Capt. Charles   2
GENTRY, Martin   1
GENTRY, Richard   2
GEORGE, Catherine   2
GEORGE, John   2
GEORGE, Nicholas   2
GEORGE, Mrs. Nicholas   2
GEORGE, Whitson   2, 8
GIBBS, Julius   2
GILBERT, Samuel   1, 2
GIREY, Samuel   4
(killed)
GOODMAN, Ancil   4
(killed)
GOODMAN, Daniel   2, 4, 7
(killed)
GRANT, Israel   2
GRANT, Rebecca Boone   2
(wife of William Grant)
GRANT, Squire   2
GRANT, William   2
(also listed are 3 slaves—
Jim, Danberry & Jennie)
GRUBBS, Capt. Higgason   1, 2, 5, 13
(1778)
GRUBBS, Mrs. Higgason   5
GUERRANT, Peter   1
GOFF, Thomas   14 (1783)
HACKETT, Peter   2, 3, 13 (1779)
HALL, Edward   2, 8
HALL, Thomas   8
HALL, William   8
HAMILTON, Andrew   2
HAMILTON, John   2
HAMILTON, James   1
HANCOCK, George   11
HANCOCK, Stephen   1, 2, 5, 6, 10, 13
(1776)
HANCOCK, William   1, 2, 4, 5, 6, 10
(1776) (killed)
HAND, Edward   3
HANNA, Andrew   2
*HARMON, John   5, 7
HARGROVE, Thomas   2 (1777)
HARPER, John   8
HARPER, Peter   4, 8
HARVESTER, John   3
HARRIS, William   2, 13 (1780)

HARRISON, Ben   2
*HARRISON, John   5
HARROD, Edward   4, 10
HART, Chenoa   5
(marr. Col. John Smith)
HART, China   2
HART, Cumberland   2
HART, David   2, 10, 11
HART, Mrs. David   2
*HART, John   2, 5, 10
HART, Kiziah   2, 5
(marr. Lawrence Thompson)
HART, Mary   2
HART, Nathaniel, Jr.   2
HART, Col. Nathaniel (1775) 1, 2, 5, 7,
(killed by Indians   8, 10, 11, 12, 13
Aug. 1782)
HART, Mrs. Nathaniel   2, 5
HART, Simpson   2
HART, Susanna   2, 5
(marr. Isaac Shelby)
HART, Thomas   2, 11
HART, Thomas Richard Green   2
HAWISTON, John   2, 6
HAYES, James   2, 13 (1775)
HAYES, William   2, 5, 6, 10, 13 (1780)
(died 1790)
HENDERSON, John   2, 10
HENDERSON, Nathaniel   7, 11
HENDERSON, Nicholas   13 (1779)
HENDERSON, Pleasant   11
HENDERSON, Col. Richard   2, 5, 10,
                                 11, 12
HENDERSON, Samuel   1, 2, 7, 9, 11
HENDRICKS, Frances Holley   2
HENDRICKS, George   4
(killed)
*HICKS, William   2, 5, 10
HINES, Joseph   1
HINES, Dr.   12
HINES, Col. Richard   2, 4
(killed)
HITE, Isaac   2
HODGES, Jesse   1, 2, 3, 4, 5, 6
(Surveyor) (1777-1786)
HOGAN, James   2
HOGAN, Richard   2, 12
HOGE, William   10
HOGG, James   2, 7, 11
HOLDER, Capt. John   1, 2, 3, 5, 6,
(1775)   12, 13
HOLLEY, Frances   2
HOLLEY, Mrs. Frances   2
HOLLEY, John   4
HOLLEY, Mrs. John   5
HOOTEN, William   16
HORN, Elizabeth   3
HORN, Jeremiah   2, 6
HORN, Matthew   2, 13 (1778)

HOY, Elizabeth   5
(marr. John South)
HOY, Parthena   5
(marr. John DeJarnette)
HOY, William   2
HUGHES, Joseph   2, 10, 13 (1775)
HUNTER, Jake   2
HUNTER, John   2
HUNTER, Samuel   2
HOWARD, Benjamin   2
HOWARD, John   2
HOWARD, Margaret   2
INNES, Harry   5
IRVINE, Christopher, Jr.   2, 10
IRVINE, Christopher, Sr.   1, 2, 13
(1776) (killed 1786)
IRVINE, Col. William   1, 2, 12, 13
(1781)
JACKSON, John   2
JACKSON, Joseph   4
(killed)
*JENNINGS, Jonathan   2, 5, 7
JOCKARS, Charles   3
JOHNSON, Andrew   4
(killed)
JOHNSON, Betsy   2
JOHNSON, Rev. Coe or Cove   2
JOHNSON, Isaac   2
JOHNSON, Robert   2
JOHNSON, William   2, 7, 8, 11
JOHNSON, Jacob   4
(killed)
*JOHNSON, Thomas   2, 5
JONES, Catlett   2, 5
JOUETT, Matthew   7
KAVANAUGH, Charles   1
(son of William Kavanaugh)
KAVANAUGH, William   1
KELLEY, Beal   8
KELLEY, Joseph   4
(killed)
KELLY, Benjamin   4
(killed)
KELLY, John   3, 4, 8
KENNEDY, Jesse   2
KENNEDY, John, Jr.   2, 10
*KENNEDY, John, Sr.   1, 2, 5, 10, 13
(1775) (killed fall of 1780)
KENNEDY, Joseph   1, 2, 13 (1776)
KENTON, Simon   2, 5
KETCHAM, Jonathan   4
(killed)
KINCAID, John   2, 10
KINCAID, Thomas   2
KIRKHAM, Robert   2, 6
KIRKHAM, Samuel   2, 6
KINTLEY, William   2
KNOX, John   5
LACKEY, Sam   2

LADD, Col. John   2
LANHAM, Thomas   1
LEE, Charles   2
LEE, John   2, 6
LEWIS, Abraham   1
LINCOLN, George   4
(killed)
LIPSCOMB, William   2 (1780)
LIPSCOMB, Nathan   2, 13 (1780)
LITTLE, Thomas   2, 13 (1778)
LOCKHART, Charles   2, 6
LOGAN, Col. John   2, 5
LOGAN, Samuel   1
LONG, Joseph   2
LONG, Frances   2
LONG, Lawrence   1
LUTTRELL, Col. John P.   2, 5, 7, 10, 11
*LUTTRELL, Thomas   5
LYNCH, David   1, 2, 5, 13 (1779)
*LYNN, William   5
McAFEE, Robert   2, 7
McAFEE, George   2
McAFEE, William   2
McCLURE, Moses   4
(killed)
McCOLLUM, John   2, 6
McGEE, David   2, 3, 13 (1775)
McGEE, William   2, 6
McMILLAN, James Sr.   2, 12, 13 (1776)
McMILLAN, Margaret White   5, 12
McQUEEN, Thomas   1
McWHINNEY, William   4
(killed)
MADDEN, George   8
MANKINS, James   4
(killed)
MANNEN, John   2, 10
MARTIN, John   2, 3, 13 (1775)
MARTIN, William   1
MAUPIN, Jesse   2
MAYS, William   1
MERIWETHER, George   2
MERIWETHER, Nicholas   1
MILLER, David   2
MILLER, Thomas   1
MILLER, William   1, 2, 10, 13
(1775)
MIRAS, Michael   4
(killed)
MONTGOMERY, Alex   5
MONTGOMERY, John   2
MOORE, Charles   2
MOORE, John   2
MOORE, William   2, 7, 9
MORGAN, John   2
MORGAN, Ralph   1, 2, 5, 6, 13
(1779)
MORGAN, William   1, 2
MORRIS, Jesse   1

MORRIS, William	2, 6		*PORTWOOD, Page	2, 5, 7
MORRISON, Richard	10		PORTWOOD, Sam	2
MORTON, John	4		POWELL, Levin	2
(killed)			PROCTOR, James	1
MOSELY, Thomas	1		PROCTOR, John	2
MOUNCE or MOURNER, John	2, 13		PROCTOR, Joseph	1, 2, 4, 5,
(1780)			(1778)	12, 13
MYERS, Jacob (Miss)	1		PROCTOR, Capt. Nicholas	1, 2, 3, 4,
NEELEY, Alexander	4		(1778) (marr. Rachel,	6, 13
(killed)			widow of Capt. James Estill)	
NELSON, Edward	2, 3, 4		PROCTOR, Nicholas, Jr.	3
NELSON, Mrs. Edward	2		PROCTOR, Rachel	1
NELSON, John	2		PROCTOR, Reuben	1, 2, 3, 6
NELSON, Moses	3		QUISENBERRY, James	2
NEWBY, John	4		QUINN, Benjamin	2, 13 (1780)
NEWLAND, Abraham	12		QUINN, James	2
NOEL, Thomas	3, 4		QUINN, Thomas	2
*OLDHAM, Jesse	2, 5, 7, 8,		RANK, John	2
(1775)	12, 13		(a boy—father was probably there)	
OLDHAM, Tyree	1		RAY, Nicholas	2
(son of Jesse Oldham)			REED, Alexander	2
OVERSTREET, Michael	1		REED, James	1, 2
OREAR, William	2		RICE, John	2
OWENS, Thomas M.	2 (1775)		RICE, Joseph	1
OWINGS, John Carkey	2		RICE, Samuel	1, 2, 13 (1780)
OVERTON, Claugh	2		ROBERTS, Benjamin	2
PATTON, Lt. James	2		ROBINSON, David	2, 13 (1775)
PATTERSON, Richard	13 (1776)		ROBINSON, George	1
PATTERSON, William	3, 4, 10		ROBINSON, Samuel	4
*PEAKE, James	2, 5		(killed)	
PEAKE, Jesse	8		ROBINSON, William	2, 13 (1775)
PEAKE, John	1 (1781)		RODES, Col. Robert	1, 2, 12
PENIX, Joshua	3, 4		ROLLINS, Pemberton	2, 3, 5, 6, 12, 13
PENNEBACKER, Peter	2		(1775)	
PERRY, James	2, 6		ROSS, Ambrose	2
PETERSON, Richard	2		ROSS, Hugh	2, 6, 10
PEYTON, Anne Duffey	12		RIFFE, Gen. Christopher	2
PEYTON, Yelverton	1, 2, 10,		RIPPERDAM, Fred	2
(1780)	12, 13		RIPPERDAM, Mrs. Fred	2
PHELPS, Anthony	2		RUSSELL, James	1, 7 (before 1778)
PHELPS, George	2, 12, 13		SANDERS, Samuel	4
(1778)			(killed)	
PHELPS, Guy	2		SAPPINGTON, John	2, 13 (1780)
PHELPS, John	12		SEARCY, Anderson	2
PHELPS, Joshua	2, 13 (1776)		SEARCY, Asa	1
PHELPS, Josiah	1, 2, 10, 12		SEARCY, Bartlett	2, 4, 6, 12,13
(1776) (son of Thomas Phelps)			(1775) (killed)	
PHELPS, Lucy	2, 5, 12 (1775)		SEARCY, Charles	2
(sister of Josiah & George			SEARCY, Reuben	2, 3, 6
Phelps-marr. Capt. Brashears)			SEARCY, Richard, Jr.	2
PHELPS, Thomas	1, 2, 10, 12		SEARCY, Richard, Sr.	1, 2, 13
PHILLIPS, William	2		(1780)	
PITTMAN, John	1		SEARCY, Sam	2
PLEAKENSTALVER, John	2		SEARCY, William	2
PLECK, John	2, 6		SCOTT, James	2, 13 (1780)
POGUE, John	2		SEFER, Hugh	2, 13 (1775)
POGUE, William	2		SHIELDS, Hugh	2 (1780)
POGUE, Mrs. William	2		SHELBY, David	2
PORTER, Samuel	2, 5, 6		SHELBY, Isaac	2, 5, 11

SHELTON, David	2	TURNER, David	2
SHIRLEY, Charles	2	TURNER, John	1
SHIRLEY, Katie	2	TURPIN, Solomon	1
SHIRLEY, Michael	1, 2	TURPIN, William	1
SHORES, Thomas	2	TWIDDY, Capt. Thomas	1
SLAUGHTER, Col. Thomas	2, 7, 9	TWIDDY, William	4
SMITH, Enoch	2, 12	(killed)	
*SMITH, George	2, 5	UMPHREY, William	4
SMITH, John	2	(killed)	
SMITH, Maj. Wm. Bailey	2	VALLANDIGHAM, Benoni	2, 6
SNODDY, John	1, 2, 5, 13 (1775)	VASSAR, Joel	15
SNODDY, Samuel	1	WADE, Richard	2, 4, 5, 13 (1777)
SOUTH, John, Jr.	2, 3, 4, 6	WANE, Isaac	2
SOUTH, John, Sr.	1, 2, 3, 4, 5,	*WALKER, Joel	1, 2, 5, 10, 13
(1779)	6, 13	(1775)	
SOUTH, Mrs. John	5	WALKER, David V.	1
SOUTH, Samuel	2, 3, 5, 13(1778)	WALKER, Felix	2, 11
SOUTH, Thomas	2, 4, 5, 6, 13 (1778)	WALTON, Robert	2
(killed)		WARREN, Thomas	1, 2, 5, 13 (1779)
STAGGE, William	4	WARTIB, James	2, 10
(killed)		WATKINS, Capt. Charles G.	2
STAGNER, Barney	2, 5, 6	WATKINS, James	2
(killed)		WEBBER, John	2
STAPLETON, John	5	WELCH, Walter	3, 4
STARNES, Jacob	2, 3, 4, 5	WELLS, Richard	1
STARNES, Joseph	4, 6	WHITE, Ambrose	4
STEPHENSON, John	2, 6	(killed)	
STONE, Dudley	1	WHITE, Aquilla	1, 2, 5, 13 (1779)
*STONER, Michael	1, 2, 3, 5, 7	WHITE, Benjamin	4, 5, 8
(1775) (Surveyor and Hunter)	12, 13	(killed)	
STORMS, Jacob	13 (1778)	WHITE, Mrs. Benjamin	5
STRODE, Samuel	2	WHITLEDGE, Robert	2
SWEARINGEN, Berue	2	WHITTAKER, Capt. John	1
SWEARINGEN, Beroni	2	WILCOX, Billy	2
SWEARINGEN, Thomas	1, 2	WILCOX, Sally Boone	2
TABLOTT, Hale	1, 13 (1781)	WILCOXON, Daniel	2, 3, 6
TANNER, John	2	WILKERSON, Aletha Anderson	2
TATE, John	2, 10, 13 (1780)	WILKERSON, John	5
TATE, Robert	2, 10	WILKERSON, Mrs. John	5
*TATE, Samuel	2, 5, 13 (1775)	WILKERSON, Moses	2
TAYLOR, Edmund	2, 7	WILKERSON, William	2
TAYLOR, John	1, 5, 13 (1779)	WILKERSON, Wyate	1
(Baptist Preacher)		WILLIAMS, William	1, 2, 7, 13 (1775)
TAYLOR, Nancy	2	WILLIAMS, Edward	2, 8
(wife of Peter Taylor)		WILLIAMS, Jarrett	5
TAYLOR, Peter W.	1, 2, 12 (1780)	WILLIAMS, John	2, 5
TAYLOR, Richard	2, 10	*WITLEDGE, Richard	5
THOMAS, James	2	WILSON, Moses	2, 6
TERRELL, John	2	WOODS, Adam	1
TERRELL, Robert	2	WOODS, Capt. Archibald	1, 13 (1781)
THOMPSON, James	1	WOODS, John	2
THOMPSON, Lawrence	1, 2, 13 (1780)	WOODS, Samuel	2, 13 (1775)
TODD, Col. John	5	WOODSON, Samuel	2, 13 (1775)
TOMLINSON, William	2	WORTHINGTON, Capt. E.	2
TOWNSEND, Gerrett	5	WRIGHT, John	2
TOWNSEND, Joshua	1	WESTERVILLE, James	2
TOWNSEND, Oswald	1, 2, 5, 13 (1775)	WITHERS, John	2
(Surveyor)		YATES, James	2, 5, 13 (1775)
TRIBBLE, Thomas	12	YOCUM, Jesse	2

*Those names marked with an asterisk were present during the construction of the fort.

AUTHENTICATED ADDITIONS TO LIST

BOONE, Hannah	daughter of Josiah Boone, born in Fort.
BOONE, Josiah	cousin of Daniel Boone
FARRAR or FARROW	Louisville *Courier Journal*-1898 issue
HALLEY, John	Louisville *Courier Journal*-1898 issue
BUSH, Ambrose	Bush Family History
BUSH, John	Bush Family History
HARRISON, Richard	Louisville *Courier Journal*-1898 issue
HARRISON, Sam	Louisville *Courier Journal*-1898 issue
HARROD, James	Louisville *Courier Journal*-1898 issue
RIPPERDAN, Sarah	daughter of Frederick Ripperdan, born at Fort Boonesborough in 1781.
STARNES, Valentine	Louisville *Courier Journal*-1898 issue
STEPHENS or STEVENS, William	Ran ferry from Clark County side 1775-1776.
WILLIAMS, Daniel	Ranck's *History of Kentucky*

BIBLIOGRAPHY

(1)   List of Names from Court Depositions in Madison County Court House 1801-1806, 1807, 1808, 1811, 1814, made by the pioneers at Boonesborough.

(2)   "French Tipton Papers," Townsend Room, Eastern Kentucky University Library.

(3)   Petition from Fort Boonesborough in regard to Land Titles, October 14, 1779.

(4)   Petition from Boone's Fort, October 16, 1779.

(5)   "Fort Boonesborough" by Judge William Chenault, written for *Courier-Journal*, April 11, 1907.

(6)   *History of Kentucky* by Collins—a listing of Capt. John Holder's Company at Boonesborough, June 10, 1779.

(7)   *Colonel Richard Henderson's Journal* at Fort Boonesborough—1775.

(8)   Draper Papers—Kentucky Series "CC", Vol. 29, page 59—"Association of the Settlers of Boonesborough in 1779 for making a crop of corn."

(9)   "Convention of 1775 at Boonesborough"—minutes published June 6, 1840, in *Louisville News Letter*.

(10) Claims approved by Land Court Meeting at Boonesborough, Dec. 18, 1779, to January 3, 1780. "Certified Book of Virginia Land Commissions," *Register of the Kentucky Historical Society*, XVI September, 1923, 10.

(11) "Personnel of Transylvania Company" by Julia Alves Clore, *Kentucky Progress*, Summer, 1935.

(12) Monument erected by Boonesborough Chapter, Daughters of American Revolution which names some of the original settlers.

(13) Notebook prepared by Anna Turley Noland, a direct descendant of Capt. David Gass, on "Black" family and related families, pp. 37-38.

(14) Family records on "Goff" family in possession of Mrs. William D. Clark, Route 5, Winchester, Kentucky 40391, a direct descendant of Thomas Goff.

(15) Family records on "Vassar" and "Brandenburg" family in possession of Mrs. Frank Congleton, Sr., Richmond, Ky., whose husband and sons are direct descendants of Joel Vassar.

(16) Family records on "Hooten" family in possession of Alene Lipscomb Tudor, (Mrs. H. Thomas), a direct descendant of William Hooten and Catherine George, his wife, both of whom were at Fort Boonesborough.

Index

Miller, George Albert, 282
Miller, James A., Jr., 328, 331
Miller, John, 10, 11, 19, 20, 22, 35, 47, 49, 50, 89
Miller, Gen. John, 191, 194, 392n
Miller, Madison, 211
Miller, Margaret Ann, 211
Miller, Mary, 211
Miller, Moses, 203
Miller, R. W., 277, 287
Miller, Robert, 42, 65
Miller, Robert D., 200
Miller, Samuel F., 192, 252, 398n
Miller, Sarah, 211
Miller, Thomas Woods, 154, 161
Miller, Viney, 211
Miller, William, 11, 62
Miller, William Malcolm, 161, 203, 389n
Miller Family, 116, 161, 204, 206, 249
Miller's Tavern, 37
Million, Burrell, 89, 91
Million, George, 35
Million, Green B., 154, 161
Million, James, 58
Million, John, 35
Million, Robert, 27
Million, Squire, 35, 89, 154
Million District (in Madison County), 206
Million Station, 231
Million Tavern, 23
Mills, 24
Ministers: Adams, Fedregil, 69; Boone, Squire, 69; Brooks, Henry, 69; Burke, William, 73; Chenault, David, 72; Chilton, Thomas, 69; Crawford, James, 73; Findley, Samuel, 69; Harris, Christopher, 69, 72; Haw, James, 69, 72; Houston, Matthew, 69, 73; Kavanaugh, Charles, 69; Lythe, John, 69; McKay, Alexander, 69; Manier, John, 69; Pace, John, 69; Shaffer, C. T., 241; Shelton, Thomas, 69, 70; Tanner, John, 69; Thornton, Dozier, 69; Tribble, Andrew, 69-72, 82; Williamson, Thomas, 69; Woods, Peter, 69. See also Candee, George; Fee, John Gregg; Fisk, Wiley B.; Rogers, John A. R.
Missionary Baptist Church of Richmond, 240
Mississippi River, 20
Mitchel, William, 154
Mitchell, Belle, 215
Mitchell, Emanuel, 118
Moberly, Benjamin, 154
Moberly, R. O., 343, 359
Moberly, Thomas S., 238, 241
Moberly Family, 249
Moberly Mound, 2, 3
Model School, 303

Moody, Cassius Clay, 383n
Moody, George, 228
Moody, J. P., 223
Moody, W. H., 396n
Moore, Fergusson, 140, 384n
Moore, Mary Jane, 140
Moore, Mossiah, 384n
Moore Family, 109, 138, 139
Moran, James, 195
Moran, Nathan, 389n
Morehead, Gov. James, 84
Morgan's Raiders, 181-82, 196-201, 204, 206, 208, 246-47, 250-51
Morgan, Calvin, 196
Morgan, John Hunt, 181, 182, 196, 198-200, 208, 250, 392n
Moss, Jane, 115
Moss, John, 215
Mount Vernon, 123, 178, 183, 201, 386n
Mt. Zion Church, 185-86, 194, 240
Mullins, Larkin, 179
Munday, Lt. Col. Reuben J., 150, 152, 154, 156, 161, 171, 178, 181, 184, 188, 205, 208, 388n
Munday Family, 206
Nat Turner's Rebellion, 146
Neeley, Alexander, 2
Nelli, Lt. Col. Humbert, 340
Nelson, Maj. Gen. William, 184, 188-89, 191, 193, 393n
Nepotism, 16-17, 65, 91, 92, 101
New Orleans, 19, 20, 27, 29
Newby, John, 66, 88, 89, 99
Newby, Kentucky, 231
Newspaper List, 78
Newspapers, in the County: mentioned, 239; Berea Citizen, 239, 271; Berea Reporter, 239; Climax, 238, 272; Kentucky Herald, 238; Kentucky Rebel, 238; Kentucky Register, 226, 238, 272; Mountain Boomer, 154; Mountain Democrat, 154, 162, 178, 238; Pantagraph, 272; Richmond Climax, 272; Richmond Democrat, 149; Richmond Daily Register, 292, 298, 343, 361; Semiweekly Pantographic, 239
Newspapers (other): Cincinnati Gazette, 123; Daily Commonwealth, 157; Kentucky Messenger, 148, 154, 162; Kentucky Statesman, 147, 149, 173, 196; Kentucky Whig, 169; Louisville Courier, 147, 148, 169; True American, 120, 170; True South, 151
Nichols, Eli, 179

Negroes: politics, 281; Day Law, 281-82; 1920's, 306; 1930's, 323; World War II, 338; post-World War II, 345; population trends, 353; desegregation, 360

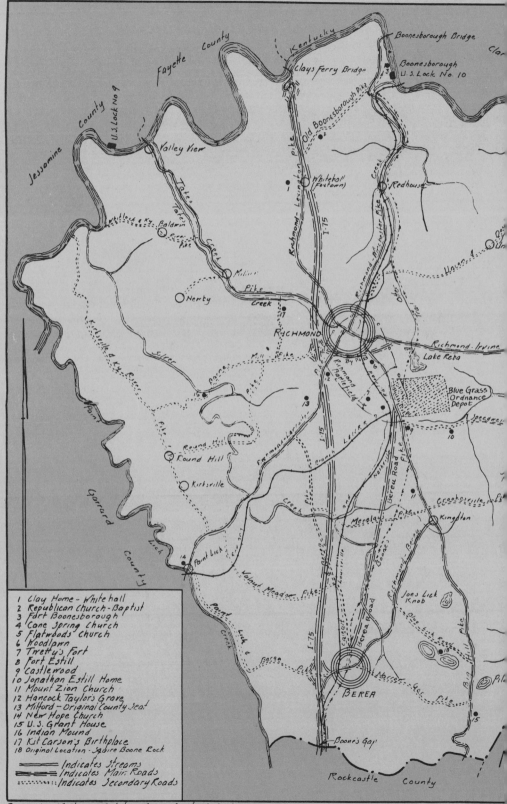

Prepared for "A Glimpse at Historic Madison County, Kentucky" - By J.T. Dorris